To Congressman James
Cleveland —

with compliments
of the author —

Charles Payne

May 4, 1971

INTERNATIONAL LAW

The Substance, Processes, Procedures
and Institutions For World Peace
With Justice

by

Charles S. Rhyne

1971

CLB Publishers, Inc.

Washington, D.C.

L.C. Card Number: 75-158819

Manufactured in the United States of America

F<small>IRST</small> E<small>DITION</small>

DEDICATED TO –

The fulfillment of the towering dreams of the giants of the law and those who follow in their footsteps with ceaseless efforts to cause those dreams to become a reality through world order with justice under the rule of law—

Anzillotti	Kunz
Bishop	Lauterpacht
Bustamante	Lycurgus
Bynkershoek	McDougal
Cassin	McNair
Castrén	Oppenheim
Cheng	Pufendorf
Cikvadze	Schwarzenberger
DeVisscher	Selden
Draco	Sørensen
Fenwick	Stone
Francois	Tanaka
Gentili	Tunkin
Grotius	Vattel
Hackworth	Verdross
Hambro	Vittoria
Jenks	Whiteman
Jessup	Wolff
Karpetz	Yokota
Kelsen	Zivs
Kiss	Zouche

——And to those, too numerous to list, whose contributions are cited throughout this Volume.

PREFACE

Man's ceaseless search for achievement has brought forth a new technologically-advanced world. That ceaseless search must now be focused on the creation of a Peaceful World through international law if an atomic holocaust is to be avoided. From the beginning of history until today, mankind's greatest dream has been a warless world, a peaceful order internationally. But never before has the achievement of this dream been so urgent. This brings one to law and its use to create world order as the peace process is largely a law process. Law is the one concept created by man which is capable of achieving and maintaining peaceful order with justice both within and among nations.

There is a conviction, based on an understanding of the sum of history, that mankind can enjoy safe and orderly progress only under the Rule of Law. While the pages of history are in large part a chronicle of wars and warriors and the weapons they used to kill, destroy and enslave, no one can dispute that the brightest chapters of history are those which record advances in utilization of law. The golden eras of man's past have always been those where the Rule of Law has prevailed, providing order, growth and progress. In every city, state, province or nation, civilization has blossomed and advanced as law has replaced force. Every new advance in civilization's progress has been accompanied by a new crest in the use of the rule of law. This fact has been true from Hammurabi to Moses to Justinian, to other great men of the law down through the ages who have made law the major factor of their day. The regressive eras of man's past have always been those where the Rule of Law has broken down bringing chronicles of fear, horror and death.

This understanding of the relationship between law, order and progress is in the public mind universally. This is true regardless of race, religion, language or form of government. It applies to international relations as well as to local or national relations. Concededly the application of the Rule of Law in the public mind to international affairs and relations is hazy and not as firmly fixed as it is to local and national affairs.

Today, new policy affecting the world community is vigorously debated in the media and elsewhere. Public opinion usually fluctuates as the debate rages but when it crystallizes, public opinion finally governs most decisions. The next step in the peace process internationally is to give permanence to the decisions by embodying them into law, into treaties or conventions. Because of the law's rapidly growing role in international affairs, it is most important that the public comprehend the principles, the content and the institutions of international law. This Book provides the history, current status and some glimpses of the future in this field of law.

Despite the public's understanding of the importance of international law, most non-lawyers conceive of this law as a difficult and mysterious subject only vaguely related to modern developments. Few lawyers admit to much of a knowledge of international law. But the legal profession must lead in educating itself and the public about international law if that law is ever to become strong enough to be accepted as a credible substitute for force as the controlling factor internationally. Given the power to destroy now possessed by mankind, the future must be based on eternal preparation for peace not on eternal preparation for war. The basic foundation for such peace preparation is the law.

This Volume is aimed at increasing the knowledge of international law and legal institutions among both laymen and lawyers. With increased knowledge should come increased acceptance, increased respect and thus increased strength for international law and its legal institutions.

Every journey begins with a first step. In a sense, this Book is one such step even though the idea of peace under law and a world ruled by law has been put forth as an ideal by the great law givers for centuries past. That the ideal has not died but lives today attests to its strength. That the time for achievement of this ideal may be at hand is a new fact created by new developments and possibilities of our day. The major new development is an ever-growing interdependence of all peoples in today's inextricably intertwined world where technology and science have shrunk time and distance, eliminated barriers such as mountains and seas, and revealed the Earth via space vehicles as a mere speck floating in a Universe of which too little is yet known.

The question before mankind is whether to continue to rely chiefly upon the age-old concept of force in conducting foreign relations, or to follow a new road to peace using the concept of

Law; whether to concentrate on law-building, or on force-building. Given the power now possessed by man the answer is clear. An unprecedented expenditure of time, manpower, and money on a vast international law-building program with an unprecedented reduction in arms must be the future program of mankind for the simple reason that this is the best way to ensure that mankind has a future. Such a development of law has come about within every civilized nation. It can be done within the entire civilized world community.

The greatest universally admired concept which all men share in common is the Rule of Law. This makes law a readily comprehensible, readily acceptable substance for a vast universal effort to create world peace.

This Volume not only compiles international law, the substance out of which the peace processes must be created, it also provides the legal profession, the judiciary and others with a compilation and description of the agencies which create international law.

When one examines the institutions and the law rules herein reviewed, one finds that many of these have come into existence in the past 25 years. Further, their growth is so rapid that a Volume such as this must be constantly up-dated and expanded. Such a program is planned.

Recent decades have witnessed—and so will the next decade—enormous changes in the nature of the world's society. This Book states the basic principles which have governed that society in the past and which must be the foundation which is increasingly relied upon as life becomes more and more internationalized. As internationalization of life has grown, so too has international law grown. While in no sense can it be said that international law is complete, yet its rapid growth into a more and more credible world legal system is clear from the vast development herein presented.

While this is a Volume with a mission, it is designed to carry out that mission by a carefully researched statement of the history and current status of international law and its agencies. In order to be technically correct and cover this subject in depth, every subject is footnoted to major authorities, books, articles and other sources where further and more detailed research can be conducted. The addresses of existing international institutions, agencies and organizations are given in the footnotes so direct contact can be made for material concerning their latest activities. To ensure credibility, some of the greatest legal experts in the world have been persuaded to review the manuscript and make suggestions for expanding the coverage of this book.

No one can review the enormous growth of international law set forth herein and the contacts and relations now being carried on among individuals in their private capacities, through multi-nation corporations, and through government representatives, without a sense of awe and elation that so much cooperative peaceful endeavor is being carried out worldwide under the Rule of Law. This Book should aid that endeavor to grow constantly so that law and its institutions will grow constantly until that great day when there will be an effective rule of law in the world community providing peaceful order with justice for all the world's peoples.

The Twentieth Century has witnessed many accomplishments heretofore considered impossible such as the splitting of the atom, a vaccine eliminating polio, men traveling in space, and men walking on the moon. We of the Twentieth Century can record no greater further accomplishment than to create that order and stability with justice internationally which is both mankind's greatest desire and mankind's greatest need. The enormous amount of law and legal institutions which exist indicate that if man but applies his capacities to the task of a world ruled by law, this great accomplishment can be achieved. It is hoped that this Book will aid in reaching that great goal.

Charles S. Rhyne

ACKNOWLEDGMENTS

In preparing this Volume, full consideration has been given to the fact that international law today must encompass the views, the experience and aspirations of the peoples of the entire world. To offset the oft-repeated claim that other volumes on this subject have been too "Western" in approach, leading legal scholars from Africa, Asia, Eastern Europe and Latin America have been requested to review the proposed text of this Volume and to make suggestions which would give full consideration to the international law views and experience of their parts of the World. These include Professor Andrew Lee, Dean and Professor of Law at Soochow University School of Law, Republic of China; Professor of Law Milan Bartos, Vice President of the Serbian Academy of Science and Art, and Rapporteur of the International Law Commission; Professor M. Cherif Bassiouni of the DePaul School of Law and Helen Claggett, Director, Latin American Division of the United States Library of Congress. William T. Mallison, Jr., Professor of Law at George Washington University National Law Center was of enormous assistance in his suggestions as to new areas of coverage and research. Lawrence Egbert performed valuable research in expanding and updating research work begun by the late great international law scholar Edgar Turlington who educated the Author in the vast field of international law as we carried out many mutual endeavors in this field. William S. Rhyne, Stuart F. Lewin, Channing Hartelius, Marc Friedman and Steven M. Selzer made major contributions by their careful research and checking of citations in the footnotes. Especially am I indebted to Terence Ogden who has worked with me on this Volume for the past year in expanding its coverage and updating prior material. The encouragement, suggestions and helpfulness of Bruno Bitker on Human Rights, Francis Browne on Intellectual Property, and Martin Domke on Arbitration are deeply appreciated. I have been privileged to have met with judges, lawyers or teachers of law from every nation. I am indebted to these law leaders of all nations, whom I have met in conferences, in offices and in homes all over the world, for their contributions which are reflected herein. So much of the contents of this volume flows directly from their knowledge, experience and wisdom. And, finally to the great lawyer and Judge, William S.

Thompson, who has travelled the world with me over the past decades, my grateful thanks for his enthusiastic help without which this Volume would never have been completed.

In expressing these words of thanks, I want to make it clear that I alone am responsible for the contents of this Book, including all editorial comment, and all fact, law, judgment or other errors.

Finally, I express my appreciation to my Administrative Assistant, Sarah P. Hendon and my Secretary, Daphne Rimmer who have typed and retyped these pages over many months of intensive effort.

Charles S. Rhyne

TABLE OF CONTENTS

CHAPTER 3

THE UNITED NATIONS AND OTHER
INTERNATIONAL ORGANIZATIONS 127

Chapter 4

Present, Past and Proposed International Courts 181

CHAPTER 5

ARBITRATION AND OTHER MEANS OF
SETTLEMENT OF INTERNATIONAL DISPUTES   265

CHAPTER 6

LAW AND INTERNATIONAL ECONOMIC DEVELOPMENT   303

CHAPTER 11

LAW FOR OUTER SPACE AND FOR SPACE COMMUNICATIONS 469

CHAPTER 12

LEGAL EDUCATION, RESEARCH AND THE DEVELOPMENT OF INTERNATIONAL LAW 489

CHAPTER 13

ENCOURAGING THE GROWTH OF INTERNATIONAL LAW: RECOGNITION
OF LAW'S POTENTIAL FOR A WORLD PEACE STRUCTURE 511

CHAPTER 14

DISARMAMENT AND ARMS CONTROL 595

ABBREVIATIONS

A. Bus. L.J.	American Business Law Journal (U.S.A.)
A.B.A.	American Bar Association (U.S.A.)
A.B.A.J.	American Bar Association Journal (U.S.A.)
AJIL	American Journal of International Law (U.S.A.)
A.J.I.L. Supp.	American Journal of International Law Supplement (U.S.A.)
Am. J. Comp. L.	American Journal of Comparative Law (U.S.A.)
Am. L. Rev.	American Law Review
Ann. Dig.	Annual Digest of Public International Law Cases (1919- ; since 1950 appears as International Law Reports; published in London)
Ann. Dr. Int'l Med.	Annales De Droit International Medical
Ann. Eur.	Annuaire Europeen, European Yearbook (Net)
Ann. Fr. Dr. Int'l	Annuaire Francais de Droit International (Fra)
Ann. Sur. S. Afr. L.	Annual Survey of S. African Law
Annuaire O. I.	Annuaire des Organizations Internationales (published in alternate years in French and English)
Ann. Uru. Der. Int'l	Anuario Uruguayo de Derecho International (Uru)
ANZUS	The Australian, New Zealand and United States Council
Arb. J.	Arbitration Journal
Arch. O. Rechts	Archiv des Offenhichen Rechts (W. Ger.)
Arch. Volk.	Archiv des Volkerrechts (W. Ger.)
ASEAN	The Association of South-East Asian Nations
ASIL	American Society of International Law
ASIL Proc.	American Society of International Law Proceedings
Athens Conf.	World Peace Through Law, the Athens Conference 1963 (1965)
Bangkok Conf.	World Peace Through Law, the Bangkok Conference, 1969 (1971)
B. Copy Soc.	Bulletin of the Copyright Society (Gr. Brit.)
Bevans	Treaties and Other International Agreements of the United States of America 1776-1949, compiled under the direction of Charles I. Bevans.
B.F.S.P.	British Foreign State Papers
BIRPI	The United International Bureaux for the Protection of Intellectual Property
Bol. Inst. Der Comp.	Boletin del Institutio de Derecho Comparado
Br. Y. B. Int'l L.	British Year Book of International Law (UK) (annually since 1920)
Calif. L. Rev.	California Law Review (U.S.A.)
Can. B. J.	Canadian Bar Journal (Can.)
Can. Y. B. Int'l L.	Canadian Yearbook of International Law (Can.) Annuaire Canadian de Droit International (Can.)

Case & Com.	Case and Comment
Case W. Res. L. Rev.	Case Western Reserve Law Review (U.S.A.)
CENTO	The Central Treaty Organization
Cheng	B. Cheng, General Principles of Law as applied by International Courts and Tribunals (London 1953)
Colum. J. Transnat'l L.	Columbia Journal of Transnational Law
Colum. L. Rev.	Columbia Law Review (U.S.A.)
Comm. Mkt. L. Rev.	Common Market Law Review (Net & UK)
Com. Int'l	Comunita Internazionale
COMSAT	Communications Satellite Corporation
COSPAR	Committee on Space Research
Cur. L. Prob.	Current Legal Problems
Current Notes	Current Notes on International Affairs
Dep't State Bull.	Department of State Bulletin
DePaul L. Rev.	DePaul Law Review Bulletin (U.S.A.)
Dir. Aereo	Diritto Aereo
Dr. Comm. & Dr. Nat'l	Droit Communautaire et Dreoit National
Duquesne U. L. Rev.	Duquesne University Law Review (U.S.A.)
E.A.S.	Executive Agreement Series, issued singly in pamphlets by the Department of State (until replaced in 1945 by the T.I.A.S.)
ECA	Economic Commission for Africa, United Nations
ECAFE	Economic Commission for Asia and the Far East, United Nations
ECE	Economic Commission for Europe, United Nations
ECLA	Economic Commission for Latin America, United Nations
ECOSOC	Economic and Social Council, United Nations
ECSC	European Coal and Steel Community
EFTA	European Free Trade Association
Egypt. Rev. Int'l L.	Egyptian Review of International Law
ELDO	European Launcher Development Organization
ESRO	European Space Research Organization
Euratom	European Atomic Energy Community
Eur. Y. B.	European Yearbook
FAO	Food and Agriculture Organization, United Nations
Far E. L. Rev.	Far Eastern Law Review (Philippines)
Foreign Relations	Foreign Relations of the United States
For. Ex. Bull.	Foreign Exchange Bulletin
Foro Int'l	Foro International
F.R.	Federal Register
GATT	General Agreement on Tariffs and Trade
Geneva Conf.	World Peace Through Law, The Geneva Conference, 1967 (1969)
Ger. Pol.	German Policy
Geo. Wash. L. Rev.	George Washington Law Review (U.S.A.)

Harv. Bus. Rev.	Harvard Business Review (U.S.A.)
Harv. Int'l L. J.	Harvard International Law Journal (U.S.A.)
Harv. L. Rev.	Harvard Law Review (U.S.A.)
How. L. J.	Howard Law Journal (U.S.A.)
H. R. Doc.	House of Representatives (United States) Document
Human Rights J.	Human Rights Journal
IAEA	International Atomic Energy Association
IAF	International Astronautical Federation
IAL	International Association of Lawyers
IBRD	International Bank for Reconstruction and Development
ICAO	International Civil Aviation Organization
ICC	International Chamber of Commerce
ICSR	Inter-American Committee for Space Research
ICSU	International Committee of Scientific Unions
ICJ	International Court of Justice
IDA	International Development Association
IFC	International Finance Corporation
IJC	International Commission of Jurists
ILAA	International Legal Aid Association
Int'l L. Mat.	International Legal Materials, American Society of International Law (U.S.A.)
IMCO	Inter-Governmental Maritime Consultative Organization
IMF	International Monetary Fund
Indian J. Int'l L.	Indian Journal of International Law (India)
Indian Y. B. Int'l Aff.	Indian Year Book of International Affairs (India)
Industr'l Prop.	Industrial Property
Inst. Dr. Int'l Ann.	Institut de Droit International, Annuaire (Swi)
INTELSAT	International Telecommunications Satellite Corporation
INTERPOL	International Criminal Police Organization
INTERUNION	Union Internationale de Financement et de Participation
Int'l Aff.	International Affairs (U.S.S.R.)
Int'l & Comp. L. Q.	International and Comparative Law Quarterly (UK)
Int'l Ass'n	International Associations
Int'l Conc.	International Conciliation
Int'l Gov't Org.	International Governmental Organization
Int'l Law.	International Lawyer
Int'l L. Mat.	International Legal Materials (U.S.A.)
Int'l Or.	International Organization (published quarterly by the World Peace Foundation since 1947)
Int'l Rel.	International Relations
Int'l Rev. Admin. Sci.	International Review of Administrative Sciences (Bel.) (also published in French edition)
Int'l Rev. R. C.	International Review of the Red Cross
IPU	Inter-Parliamentary Union

Israel L. Rev.	Israel Law Review (Israel)
ITU	International Telecommunications Union
J. Air L. & C.	Journal of Air Law and Commerce
Japan Ann. Int'l L.	Japanese Annual of International Law (Jap.)
J. Comm. Mkt. Stud.	Journal of Common Market Studies
J. Dr. Int'l	Journal de Droit International (Fra.)
J. Int'l Com. Jur.	Journal of the International Commission of Jurists (Swi) (also published in Fra., Ger., and Sp. editions, continued by the Review of the International Commission of Jurists (Swi)
J. Int'l L. & Dipl'y	Journal of International Law and Diplomacy
J. Legal Ed.	Journal of Legal Education
J. O.	Journal Official (Fra.)
J. Télé	Journal des Telecommunications
J. Trib.	Journal des Tribunaux (Bel.)
J. World L.	Journal of World Law
J. World Trade L.	Journal of World Trade Law
Ky. L. J.	Kentucky Law Journal (U.S.A.)
L. & Comp. Tech.	Law and Computer Technology (U.S.A.)
L. & Contemp. Prob.	Law and Contemporary Problems (U.S.A.)
L.N.T.S.	League of Nations Treaty Series
L'ONU	L'Organisation des Nations Unies
L. Quar. Rev.	Law Quarterly Review
L. Soc'y Gaz.	The Law Society's Gazette
I Malloy, II Malloy	Treaties, Conventions, International Acts, Protocols, and Agreements Between the United States of America and Other Powers, 1776-1909, compiled under the direction of the Committee on Foreign Relations of the United States Senate by William M. Malloy and published by the Government Printing Office.
Mcg. L. J.	McGill Law Journal (Canada)
Miller	Treaties and Other International Acts of the United States of America, edited by Hunter Miller
Minn. L. Rev.	Minnesota Law Review (U.S.A.)
Mod. L. Rev.	Modern Law Review
Mun. Att.	The Municipal Attorney (U.S.A.)
NATO	North Atlantic Treaty Organization
Neth. Int'l L. Rev.	Nederlands Tijdschrift voor Internationaal Recht (Net.)
N.D.L. Rev.	North Dakota Law Review (U.S.A.)
Nigerian B. J.	Nigerian Bar Journal (Nig.)
Nw. U. L. Rev.	Northwestern University Law Review (U.S.A.)
N.Y. Law Forum	New York Law Forum
N.Y.U.J. Int'l L. & Pol.	New York University Journal of International Law and Politics
N. Yugo. L.	New Yugoslav Law (Yug.)
N.Z. U. L. Rev.	New Zealand Law Review

OAS	Organization of American States
OAU	Organization of African States
OECD	Organization for Economic Cooperation and Development
OEEC	Organization for European Economic Cooperation
Ost. Z. of. R.	Österreichische Zeitschrift für öffentliches Recht (Aus.)
Parry	A British Digest of International Law (C. Parry *ed.*, London 1965)
P.C.I.J.	Permanent Court of International Justice
Peaslee	A. PEASLEE, INTERNATIONAL GOVERNMENTAL ORGANIZATIONS (2 ed., 1961)
Pol. Sci. Q.	Political Science Quarterly
Proces-verbaux	Permanent Court of International Justice: Advisory Committee of Jurists, *Proces-verbaux of the Proceedings of the Committee* (June 16 - July 24, 1920)
P.T.C.J.	Palent, Trademark and Copyright Journal of Research and Education U.S.A.)
Recueil des Cours	Academie de Droit International, The Hague, Recueil des Cours (Net.)
III Redmond	Volume III of Bevans, 1910-1923, compiled by C. F. Redmond
Rev. Bel. Dr. Int'l	Revue Belge de Droit International, Belgian Review of International Law, Belgisch Tijdschrift voor Internationaal Recht (Bel.)
Rev. Col. Ab. Uru.	Revista del Colegio de Abogados del Uruguay (Uru.)
Rev. Col. P.R.	Revistade Colgio de Abogados de Puerto Rico
Rev. Contemp. L.	Review of Contemporary Law
Rev. Dr. Int'l & Dr. Comp.	Revue de Droit International et de Droit Comparé (Bel.)
Rev. Egypt. Dr. Int'l	Revue Egyptienne de Droit International
Rev. Espr. Der. Int'l	Revista Espanda de Derecho International (Spa.)
Rev. Fac. Der. U. Madrid	Revista de la Facultad de Derecho de la Universidad Madrid
Rev. Fac. Dir. (U. Bahia)	Revista da Faculda de Direito (Universidade de Bahia)
Rev. Gén. A & S	Revue Géneralé de l'Air et de l'Espace (Fra.)
Rev. Gen. Dr. Int'l P.	Revue Géneralé de Droit International Publique (Fra.)
Rev. Hell. Dr. Int'l	Revue Hellénique de Droit International (Gre.)
Rev. Dr. Int'l Comp.	Revue Internationale de Droit Comparé (Fra.)
Rev. Int'l Dr. Pen.	Revue Internationale de Droit Pénal (Fra.)
Rev. Jur. Peru	Revista de Jurisprudencia Peruana (Per.)
Rev. Jur. & Pol. dO-M	Revue Juridique et Politique d'Outre-Mer
Rev. Jur. U. Int'am P.R.	Revista Juridica de la Universidad Interamericana de Puerto Rico
Rev. Tr. Dr. Eur.	Revue Trimestrielle de Droit Européen (Fra.)
Riv. Dir. Int'l	Rivista di Diritto Internazionale (Ita.)
Rut. Cam. L. J.	Rutgers Camden Law Journal (U.S.A.)
S. Ct.	Supreme Court Reporter (U.S.A.)
S. D. L. Rev.	South Dakota Law Review (U.S.A.)
SEATO	South-East Asia Treaty Organization

Sol. Q.	Solicitor Quarterly
Sørenson	Sørenson, Manual of Public International Law (M. Sørenson ed., New York 1968)
Sov. Rev.	Soviet Review (U.S.S.R)
Soviet Y. B. Int'l L.	Sovetskii Ezhegodnik Mezhdunarodnogo Prava (Soviet Year-Book of International Law) (U.S.S.R.)
St. & R.	Staat und Recht (E. Ger.)
Stat.	United States Statutes at Large (U.S.A.)
Switz. Y. B. Int'l R.	Schweizerisches Jahrbuch für Internationales Recht (Swi.)
S. W. L. J.	Southwestern Law Journal (U.S.A.)
T. I. A. S.	Treaties and Other International Acts Series, issued singly in pamphlets by the Department of State (U.S.A.)
T. Int'l R.	Tijdschrift voor Internationaal Recht
T. M. Rptr.	Trademark Reporter
IV Trenwith	Volume IV of Bevans, 1923-1937, compiled by Edward J. Trenwith
T. S.	Treaty Series, issued singly in pamphlets by the Department of State (until replaced in 1945 by the T.I.A.S.) (U.S.A.)
Tul. L. Rev.	Tulane Law Review (U.S.A.)
U.C.L.A. L. Rev.	University of California at Los Angeles Law Review (U.S.A.)
U. Det. L. J.	University of Detroit Law Journal (U.S.A.)
UN	United Nations
UNCITRAL	United Nations Commission on International Trade Law
UNCTAD	United Nations Committee on Trade and Development
UNESCO	United Nations Educational, Scientific and Cultural Organization
U.N. GAOR	United Nations General Assembly Resolutions
UNICEF	United Nations Children's Fund
UNITAR	United Nations Institute for Training and Research
U.N. R. I. A. A.	United Nations Report of International Arbitration Awards
U.N.T.S.	United Nations Treaty Series
U. Pitt. L. Rev.	University of Pittsburgh Law Review (U.S.A.)
UPU	Universal Postal Union
U.S.T.	United States Treaties and Other International Agreements (volumes published on a calendar-year basis beginning January 1, 1950)
U. St. Tom. L. Rev.	University of Santo Tomas Law Review
Va. J. Int'l L.	Virginia Journal of International Law (U.S.A.)
Va. L. Rev.	Virginia Law Review (U.S.A.)
Valp. L. Rev.	Valparaiso University Law Review (U.S.A.)
Vand. L. Rev.	Vanderbilt Law Review (U.S.A.)
Vill. L. Rev.	Villanova Law Review (U.S.A.)
WAJ	World Association of Judges
Washington Conf.	World Peace Through Law, The Washington Conference, 1965 (1967)
Wash. L. Rev.	Washington Law Review (U.S.A.)

Wash. U. L. Q.	Washington University Law Quarterly (U.S.A.)
WHO	World Health Organization, United Nations
Whiteman	Digest of International Law (M. Whiteman ed., Washington 1963)
Wis. L. Rev.	Wisconsin Law Review (U.S.A.)
W. Just.	World Justice
Wm. & Mary L. Rev.	William & Mary Law Review (U.S.A.)
WMO	World Meteorological Organization
W. Pol. Q.	Western Political Quarterly (U.S.A.)
W. P. T. L. C.	World Peace Through Law Center
W. R. L. Bklt. Ser.	World Rule of Law Booklet Series
Yale L. J.	Yale Law Journal (U.S.A.)
Y.B.A.A. & A.	Yearbook of the Association of Attenders and Alumni of the Hague Academy of International Law
Y.B. Air & Sp. L.	Yearbook of Air & Space Law
Y.B. Int'l L.	Yearbook of International Law
Y.B. World Aff.	Yearbook of World Affairs
Z. R. & Völk.	Zeitschrift für ausländisches öffentliches Recht und Völkerrecht (W. Ger.)
Z. L. & W.	Zeitschrift für Luftrecht und Weltraumrechtsfragen (W. Ger.)

CHAPTER 1

History and Sources

Section A. Introduction

§ 1-1. The Functions of International Law

International law, like any other law, is an institutional means for meeting human needs. More specifically, the task of international law is conceived as providing a juridical framework in which the individual in transnational contacts or actions may achieve his fundamental values working with other individuals, or through nation-states, international organizations and other multi-party associations or groups. Eight basic values have been described in the following terms:

(1) *Respect for the dignity of the individual*—negatively, this prohibits discrimination based upon religion, race, and all other factors which are irrelevant to individual worth; positively, this includes recognition of the general merit of all people as human beings and the particular merit of each person as an individual.

(2) *Equality before the law and the sharing of governmental power*—this includes an opportunity for fair participation in the processes of government in the international, national, and local communities.

(3) *Enlightenment and information*—this includes freedom of inquiry and opinion, which are indispensable to rational decision-making.

(4) *Psychic and physical well-being*—negatively, this requires freedom from arbitrary burdens, restrictions, and punishments; positively, it includes the opportunity to develop individual abilities.

(5) The opportunity to participate in *congenial and constructive inter-personal relationships.*

(6) *Goods and services* necessary to adequate standards of living.

(7) *Skills and "know-how"* necessary to achieve all values in a factual sense.

(8) Freedom to develop and apply *conceptions of morality and ethics*—this includes the freedom to worship God, or the freedom not to worship, depending upon individual choice.[1]

Professor Myres S. McDougal of the Yale University Law School has suggested that international law may be usefully conceived as an element in a community process.[2] Such a process may be described as *people*, with *diverse perspectives* seeking to maximize *values,* through *institutions* (including *legal institutions*), applied to resources, distributed among people.[3]

The eight values considered above may be summarized as consisting of both security and freedom. In a minimum world order system, security may be conceived as simple freedom from coercion and aggression. In an optimum world order system, security may be conceived as that involved in minimum order and in addition the freedom of each individual to achieve his values in a peaceful context without discriminations which are irrelevant to human worth and capacity. Such irrelevant considerations include racial identification, religious beliefs, sex, nationality, and national origin. The challenge and opportunity available to lawyers is to use legal institutions to build an optimum order system in which all individuals may be secure and prosperous. This may be done by using law to build economic, social and cultural bridges to world peace.

§ 1-2. Participants in International Law

The traditional approach to international law defined participants in such a way as to emphasize those rules of international law which apply only to nation-states, who, thus, were considered to be the only participants in international law with rights and duties.

The difficulty in this approach became apparent when one tried to determine how certain groups of individuals or individuals themselves could be considered "proper parties" in international disputes. The traditional explanation was that the qualifications of a "proper party" were determined by the intentions of the states who laid down the rules for a particular proceeding or transaction. Thus, although only states can ordinarily be sued or sue before an international tribunal, nothing prevents states from creating international tribunals before which individuals or other entities may

---

[1] Mallison, *The Zionist-Israel Juridical Claims To Constitute "The Jewish People" National Entity and To Confer Membership in It: Appraisal in Public International Law,* 37 GEO. WASH. L. REV. 983, 986-87 (1964).

[2] M. McDOUGAL, STUDIES IN WORLD PUBLIC ORDER 1-41 (New Haven 1960).

[3] *Id.*

bring matters directly.   This explanation, as will become more obvious later in this section, tends to place too much emphasis on the role of the nation-state in international law.   Though the writer does not mean to diminish the importance of nation-states in international law, it is, however, necessary to put that role in its proper perspective.

Growing out of considering nation-states as the proper arbitrators of who could participate in legal actions concerning international disputes, the question arose as to the status in international law of an organization created by nation-states.   Could that organization sue in its own name under the U.N. Charter?

Article 100 gives the Secretariat power to create an international civil service to carry out goals of the United Nations where the Security Council is in deadlock on a particular issue because of the Veto [Article 27(3)].   In 1948, a civil servant in an organization created by the Secretariat when the Security Council was deadlocked, was assassinated in the Middle East, and the issue before the International Court of Justice was whether the United Nations, as an international organization, could recover on behalf of its civil servant. The Court held, in an advisory opinion, that the United Nations can sue on behalf of an individual despite the fact that the Charter does not give the United Nations a separate existence, because in order to carry out the specified grants of power under the Charter, the United Nations must be an entity separate from the nations composing it.[4]   The reasoning is analogous to arguing that a certain power of the United States federal government is necessary and proper in order to carry out a power enumerated in the United States Constitution.   This decision has done much to change the status and importance of international organizations.

However, the traditional approach, even by extending the definition of the participants in international law to include those who can sue and be sued under the rules of international law, does not give a complete picture of the process of international law.   To understand this process one should consider as participants all those who affect the development of international law, not just those who can seek relief in their names under it.   By this approach, participants in our day of interdependence of nations, people, business, and world-wide communications would include not just Nation-States and international organizations, but transnational groups, private associations, multi-nation corporations, and individual persons.

---

[4] [1949] ICJ 174; 43 AJIL 589 (1949).   *See also* p. 221-22, *infra.*

The interaction of these various groups in the world community results in vast and sometimes rapid changes in international law to fulfill the needs of nations and individual persons whose trade, travel and other interests demand that orderliness which only law can provide. In ultimate, law is primarily crystallized public opinion. And those who make public opinion include nearly all of the world's peoples. Private associations such as the World Peace Through Law Center and international business organizations have a powerful impact on the development of international law in the fields of their individual concerns.

It is most difficult to evaluate the role of individuals in this picture of the rapid growth of international law. Certainly there are individuals who stand outside of their governments in international affairs as influencers of this growth. Often their status rests on morality, like Confucius, Moses, Jesus, Muhammad, and more contemporary leaders like Gandhi and the Pope. Some are important because of their dealings or leadership on a particular issue, or as head of an important international organization like the UN Secretary-General. This list is a long one and reaches far beyond the few mentioned and their numbers grow as fast transportation and communications accelerate contacts between men and nations thus of necessity requiring more and more law rules and law institutions to govern and guide these contacts.

This volume will recognize and emphasize the ever-broadening role of the world's peoples in law-making for the world.

It is clear that a new non-territorial world order is growing rapidly and that it is based not so much on states as on International Governmental Organizations, international business organizations, multination corporations, industries and individuals. This new law and new law-making process are growing in capacity and should receive increasing recognition.

§ 1-3. Application of International Law[5]

This section will briefly discuss international law as it is applied in various forums to settle or decide disputes. These forums range from the international to the municipal (i.e., "National," "domestic," "local") courts. International law is also applied every day in a non-judicial context between foreign ministries and state departments. A more extensive consideration of each method or agency is set forth in later chapters herein. This is merely an introduction to the discussion of the history and sources of international law.

---

[5] For a more detailed discussion, see Ch. 5 *infra.*

§ 1-3.1. In the International Sphere. Article 33 of the United Nations Charter provides that:

> The parties to any dispute, the continuance of which is likely to endanger the maintenance of international peace and security, shall, first of all, seek a solution by negotiation, inquiry, mediation, conciliation, arbitration, judicial settlement, resort to regional agencies or arrangements or other peaceful means of their own choice.[6]

This declaration is no more than a restatement of the five major methods to settle disputes under international law. Of them, the one most important to the day-by-day settlement of international disputes is *negotiation*. Under this method, views are exchanged, usually through diplomatic channels, and agreement comes from the mutual process of give and take. International law is an important part of this process, since should a solution be concluded, it may be based upon existing principles of international law, and furthermore, the agreement between the parties does much to help establish practices which may become part of what the parties regard as customary international law.

Inquiry is designed to facilitate the settlement of a dispute, which results from a difference of opinion as to the facts in a particular case. A neutral commission is usually appointed by the parties, but the parties still retain the right to act independently. Many of the peace treaties entered into by many states over the last 50 years have provisions to establish neutral commissions to determine facts surrounding possible breaches of the treaty. As Hackworth points out, even though the contracting parties agreed "not to declare war or begin hostilities during such investigations and before the report was submitted," they did "reserve the right to act independently on the subject matter of the dispute after the report of the Commission was submitted." [7]

Conciliation or *mediation*, like *inquiry*, is not binding on the parties to a dispute. Unlike *inquiry*, however, the agency assigned to these tasks is not only to find the facts, but also to make reports recommending a solution. This recommendation can be based on any applicable rule of international law. Most recently the Security Council and the General Assembly of the United Nations have

---

[6] For a discussion in general terms, see J. BRIERLY, LAW OF NATIONS 346-96 (5th ed. Oxford 1955); 6 G. HACKWORTH, DIGEST OF INTERNATIONAL LAW 1-147 (Washington 1940-44); 2 L. OPPENHEIM, INTERNATIONAL LAW 1-96 (Lauterpacht ed., 7th ed. London 1952).

[7] 6 HACKWORTH, *supra* note 6, at 5.

become quite important as arenas of international mediation and conciliation.

Unlike the above mentioned methods of solving international disputes, *arbitration* and *adjudication*[8] are binding on the parties in a dispute. These two processes settle international disputes by applying rules of law to the facts of the case. The only problem of either of these approaches is that no state is ever required to seek international arbitration or adjudication unless it has so committed itself by treaties and other agreements. The United Nations Charter provided for the establishment of a compulsory World Court, but all states that have accepted its jurisdiction have done so with reservations.[9]

§ 1-3.2. In Municipal (Nation-State) Courts.[10]   A widespread belief exists in many countries that municipal (i.e., national) courts should follow the rules of international law where appropriate.[11] Even where a municipal court does not follow international law, the obligation of the government of the state to adhere to its international law obligations is not reduced. This is illustrated by *Mortensen v. Peters*[12] which was decided by the Scottish Court of Justiciary (a British municipal court). In this case, the Court upheld a British statute concerning fisheries conservation as to apply it, in a way which was widely regarded as violative of international law, to foreign fishermen sailing on foreign trawlers on the high seas. The Court

---

[8]For a more detailed discussion of adjudication and the limits on the role of international courts in solving international disputes, see Ch. 4, *infra.* Arbitration is specifically discussed in Ch. 5, *infra.*

[9]*See generally* Briggs, *Reservations to the Acceptance of Compulsory Jurisdiction of the International Court of Justice,* Hague Academy of International Law, 93 RECUEIL DES COURS 225 (1958). *See also* § 4-3, p. 195, *infra.*

[10]*See generally* Bulajic̈, *Expanding Structure of International Law—the Only Alternative for Future International Relations,* in WASHINGTON CONF. 556-69; Falk, *International Law in Domestic Courts,* in *id.* at 189-203; Friedmann, *Work Paper on Some Fundamental Changes in the Structure of Contemporary International Law,* in *id.* at 528-46; Nanda, *International Law in Domestic Courts,* in *id.* at 203-14; Nuñez, *The Questions of Constitutional or Treaty Supremacy in International Law,* in *id.* at 221-23; Regala, *The Contributions of Philippine Courts in the Development of Public International Law,* in *id.* at 214-20.

[11]Lauritzen v. Larson, 345 U.S. 571, 582 (1953); the Paquette Habana, 175 U.S. 677, 44 L.Ed. 320, 20 S. Ct. 290 (1899). *See also* McCulloch v. Marineros de Honduras, 372 U.S. 10, 83 S. Ct. 671, 9 L. Ed. 2d 547 (1963) where it was pointed out that the resolution of conflicts between national and international law in a municipal court depends on that country's conception of the relationship between national and international law. The differing points of view as to this relationship are discussed in § § 1-6.6, *supra.*

[12]W. BISHOP, INTERNATIONAL LAW: CASES AND MATERIALS 78, 83 (2d ed. 1962).

had no choice but to apply the statute since it was bound by the British municipal law doctrine of the supremacy of Parliament and had no authority to question the consistency of the statute with accepted principles of international law. Thereafter, foreign governments protested the legality of the decision. The British Government agreed that the statute, as interpreted by the Court, was inconsistent with international law, and had the law of the case changed both retrospectively and prospectively. The trawler master who had been convicted and required to pay a fine had the fine remitted to him; the statute was repealed; and a fishery conservation statute which was entirely consistent with international law was enacted in its place. A central point in this situation is that the British Government as an undivided whole recognized that it was bound by international law and took steps to change the judicial decision which was inconsistent with that law.

The British Government was impelled to act as it did in order to protect British national interests.[13] The Government recognized that if it unlawfully interfered with foreign trawlers on the high seas, this would invite foreign governments to interfere with British trawlers in a similar manner. In order to protect the British interest in unimpeded high seas' fishing, it had to apply the same standards of international law to foreign fishermen that it wished to have applied to British fishermen. The only way that this result could be accomplished was to change British municipal law to make it consistent with international law. It is significant that the British recourse to international law effectively protected British national interest in maintaining an efficient high seas' fishing fleet and that there was no doctrine of British municipal law which could possibly have protected this national interest. The decision of the British Government to adhere to international law is not surprising since one of the basic purposes of international law is to protect the common interests of states upon a mutual and reciprocal basis.

§ 1-4. Sanctions

The effectiveness of international law depends on the willingness of states to abide by it. Since the decision to follow international law precepts is left to the discretion of individual states subject to their international law obligations, it would seem that international law would be, on occasion, hopelessly ineffective to control the action of states who could follow, or breach the law, depending upon whether or not it served their interests at the time. While

---

[13] *Id.* at 82.

this is possible, powerful forces nevertheless exist in the international community which might lead states to discover more often than not that it is in their best interest to follow international law. These forces can best be termed *sanctions.*

In a municipal legal system, the most powerful sanctions are compulsory reparation and punishment. While these sanctions are not as important in the international legal system since recourse to a court is often possible only if both parties agree, the sanctions of the fear of war or reprisals deters breaches of international law in much the same way. But more important internationally, however, is the positive willingness of a state to follow international law which results from the following sanctions: the effect of world opinion, the state's ultimate responsibility for its own actions or failure to act, the state's realization that it can function better if the community of nations conducts its relations according to certain generally accepted standards of performance, including mutuality and reciprocity in adherence to law. States will follow the precepts of international law because, if they do, they realize that they have a better chance of having other states also follow the same principles. Mutuality and reciprocity also give rise to a system of expectation which induces States to be willing to follow international law so that they can preserve their esteem in the world community.

The impact of systems of mass communication has brought people all over the world to realize their interdependence. Thus, world public opinion is emerging as one of the most important sanctions in international relations that states must reckon with. Acknowledge of international law and acceptance of it grows, public opinion will strengthen the effect of the "Moral Sanction" incurred by the violation of international law.

SECTION B: HISTORY

§ 1-5. Origin and Development of an International Legal System

The traditional European international law system dates from the Treaty of Westphalia of 1648, which marked the formal recognition of states as sovereign and independent political units. Even though the past system of international law is said to be technically European, it has drawn much from earlier periods of history with origins in millenia B.C., and from sources which are by no means limited to Europe.[14] The body of law made by UN-

---

[14] Comprehensive treatises on the history of the broad general principles of international law have been written by G. BUTLER & S. MACOBY, THE DEVELOPMENT OF

(Continued)

sponsored treaties, conventions, agreements and actions, especially
including the actions of its specialized agencies in rule and decision
making, is enormous; it clearly represents international law today
to be truly worldwide. Thus, the claim of European domination
in this field has faded. The sections herein on African, Asian and
Latin American international law indicate that Europe has not
really been as dominant in the international field as some writers
claim, and that the general principles of international law are
largely universally accepted. They prove that international law as
it presently exists has developed along with the development of
organized societies and is derived from the history and experiences
of all societies through all forms of relations among them.

§ 1-5.1. **The Ancient Period.** In man's earliest history, important
traces of international law are to be found in the early civilizations
he created, and if more primary material about these civilizations
had been preserved, it is highly possible that rules similar to those
found today could be shown to have existed.[15] From available

---

INTERNATIONAL LAW (London 1928); Maxey, *Development of International Law
Before Grotius,* 38 AM. L. REV. 747 (1905); Maxey, . . . *Grotius to American Independence, id.* at 815; Maxey, . . . *American Independence to 1900,* 40 AM. L. REV. 188
(1906); A. NUSSBAUM, A CONCISE HISTORY OF THE LAW OF NATIONS (New
York 1954); E. NYS, LES ORIGINES DE DROIT INTERNATIONAL (Paris 1894);
R. REDSLOB, HISTOIRE DES GRANDS PRINCIPES DU DROIT DES GENS . . . (Paris
1923); R. REDSLOB & T. WALKER, A HISTORY OF THE LAW OF NATIONS (Cambridge 1899). Valuable brief sketches of the history of international law are found in J.
BRIERLY, THE LAW OF NATIONS 1-41 (5th ed. Oxford 1954); Korff, *Introduction a
l'Histoire du Droit International,* 1 RECUEIL DES COURS 1 (1923); Korff, *Introduction
to the History of International Law,* 18 AJIL 246 (1924). *See generally* international law
texts by C. FENWICK, INTERNATIONAL LAW 3-26 (2d ed. New York 1948); W. GOULD,
AN INTRODUCTION TO INTERNATIONAL LAW 31-100 (New York 1957); A. HER-
SHEY, THE ESSENTIALS OF INTERNATIONAL PUBLIC LAW AND ORGANIZATION
31-155 (New York 1930); P. POTTER, A MANUAL DIGEST OF COMMON INTERNA-
TIONAL LAW 89-125 (New York 1932); O. SVARLIEN, AN INTRODUCTION TO
INTERNATIONAL LAW 28-40, 67-79 (New York 1955); Vinogradoff, *Historical Types
of International Law,* in BIBLIOTHECA VISSERIANA (Leiden 1923); G. WILSON & G.
TUCKER, INTERNATIONAL LAW (7th ed. Boston 1917). A few useful reference
materials on particular periods or special subjects within these periods will be appropriately cited later.

[15] B. Pramathanath, after pointing out that eminent jurists, such as F. E. Smith, Kent,
Wheaton, Oppenheim and Hall, regarded international law as the product of modern European culture, states that the object of his INTERNATIONAL LAW AND CUSTOM IN AN-
CIENT INDIA (Calcutta 1920) is "to establish the fact that the ancient Indians were well
acquainted with the rules of international law, in accordance with which they regulated
their conduct." He adds that "Mr. Martin, in his TRACES OF INTERNATIONAL LAW IN
CHINA, has pointed out the existence of international law in China before the dawn of Christianity." A.S. Hershey, in a review of S. VISWANATHA, INTERNATIONAL LAW IN ANCI-
ENT INDIA (London 1925), comments that "it is, indeed, surprising to learn what an
advanced and highly developed stage many of their ideas and customs both of international
law and diplomacy had reached. They compared very favorably (and in some respects in
advance of) with modern ideas and practices. This is particularly true of their rules of war-

(Continued)

material, we know that the few and sporadic contacts among peoples[16] possessed some characteristics of law, but these applied only to limited areas. The Egyptian Pharaohs entered into treaties with neighboring kings as early as the 14th century B.C., as did the early Hebrew kings, and many of these have been preserved on tablets and monuments. They deal with such subjects as peace, alliance, extradition, and the treatment of envoys, and their sanctions were religious, and very elaborate, including an invocation to the gods. The equivalent of modern diplomatic missions, such as sending and receiving envoys, was frequently used by the Pharaohs, but they were not, however, part of a continued practice or established custom. Ancient Chinese and Indian philosophers developed lofty precepts of universal conduct, and such schemes as the Grand Union of Chinese States, planned by Confucius (551-479 B.C.) vaguely suggest the concept of a league of independent states in the interest of order and peace. Early man also created other codes and rules of law, which seem to have been limited to the separate states of these empires, but were often violated in practice.

§ 1-5.2. **The Greek Period.** The Greeks possessed an unusual foundation for a community of interests in their common race, language, religion and customs. This was counterbalanced, however, by intense Greek loyalty to city and emphasis on the superiority of Greek culture and virtue over that of non-Greeks, who were generally regarded as "barbarians." The rudimentary system of relations

---

fare." He adds that this book "brings within our Western purview a considerable body of knowledge which should tend to broaden our horizon and make us realize that there is much that is not new under the sun or exclusively European or Occidental." Hershey, Book Review, 20 AJIL 426 (1926). Y. A. Korovin states that "it is China, India, Egypt and other ancient Eastern States which should be considered the birthplace of International Law." Korovin, *International Law,* in INSTITUTE OF STATE AND LAW 27 (ACADEMY OF SCIENCES OF THE USSR, Moscow 1961). Differences in emphasis on the importance of the rules and customs of these ancient civilizations can probably be explained by the strictness or liberality with which one interprets their resemblance to the international law rules of today.

[16] *See* All-India Seminar, Delhi University, INDIAN TRADITIONS AND THE RULE OF LAW AMONG NATIONS (Delhi 1962); Armour, *Customs of Warfare in Ancient India,* 8 TRANSACTIONS OF THE GROTIUS SOCIETY 71-138 (1923); N. CHAN, LA DOCTRINE DE DROIT INTERNATIONAL CHEZ CONFUCIUS (Paris 1940); Cheng, *International Law in Ancient China,* in 11 CHINESE SOCIAL AND POLITICAL SCIENCE REVIEW 38, 251 (1928); L. KRADER, ANTHROPOLOGY AND EARLY LAW (New York 1966); Martin, *Les Vestiges d'un Droit International dans l'Ancienne Chine,* REV. DROIT INT. 227 (1882); B. PRAMATHANATH, INTERNATIONAL LAW AND CUSTOM IN ANCIENT INDIA (Calcutta 1920); F. RUSSELL, THEORIES OF INTERNATIONAL RELATIONS 16-50 (New York 1936); W. TUNG, CHINA AND SOVIET PHASES OF INTERNATIONAL LAW (New York 1940); Verosta, *International Law in Europe and Western Asia Between 100-650 A.D.,* 113 RECUEIL DES COURS 491-615 (1964); S. VISWANATHA, INTERNATIONAL LAW IN ANCIENT INDIA (London 1925).

among independent states which the Greeks developed bears a closer relation to modern international law than that of any system prior to 1648.

Greek city states carried on an intense trade both among themselves and with the outside world, which led to the recognition of mutual obligations expressed in treaties and contracts. Their diplomatic and consular missions abroad enjoyed extensive privileges, were received with elaborate formalities, and were safeguarded by the establishment of severe penalties for those who mistreated them. Reciprocally, resident foreigners were granted some protection. Although Greeks were considered aliens in cities other than their own, they nevertheless possessed definite rights as aliens, based partly on treaties, and on the recognized rules of hospitality. The right of asylum for the persecuted seeking refuge was also recognized although not always respected, and since this right was considered to be of divine origin, temples were considered especially sacred.

The formation of the Delphic Amphictyony and the Aetolian and Achaen Leagues of the third century B.C. were early organized efforts toward international cooperation, and even offered possibilities of collective action against an aggressor. They also facilitated the development of arbitration,[17] which was a much used inter-Hellenic institution. Disputes on religious matters, boundaries, and possession of contested territories were frequently settled by arbitration. Some treaties even contained agreements to submit to arbitration disputes of a particular or even of a general character. Often a third state, rather than a single individual was named arbitrator.

One of the most striking characteristics of the Hellenic world was the large number and variety of treaties, not to be duplicated until the 19th century. Political treaties regulated peace, alliances, and commercial and financial treaties regulated such matters as imports, exports and coinage.

§ 1-5.3. **The Roman Period.** Prior to the third century B.C., Rome was a city-state like those of Greece, and as such, it recognized

---

[17] Much has been written on Greek arbitration. *See, e.g.,* C. PHILLIPSON, THE INTERNATIONAL LAW AND CUSTOM OF ANCIENT GREECE AND ROME (2 vols., London 1911); A. RAEDER, L'ARBITRAGE INTERNATIONAL CHEZ LES HELLÈNES (New York 1912); J. RALSTON, INTERNATIONAL ARBITRATION FROM ATHENS TO LOCARNO (Stanford University 1929); M. REVON, L'ARBITRAGE INTERNATIONAL— SON PASSÉ–SON PRÉSENT–SON AVENIR (Paris 1892); M. TOD, GREEK INTERNATIONAL ARBITRATION (Oxford 1913).

the independence and equality of other city-states, maintaining treaty and diplomatic relations with them. A rudimentary prototype of the organization and relations of political units similar to the new nation-states of the 17th century is discernible. Rome, like Greece, with a highly developed culture and civilization, was surrounded by "barbarians" whom it considered as objects for conquest and rule. Roman law as influenced by Cicero, was essentially the embodiment of the Greek philosophical concepts of unity and universality. The Aristotelian and Stoic concepts of natural law, considered divine and universal, which the empire embodied, went with the expansion of Roman law into Western Europe, was later applied by Christianity with the breakdown of Roman power, and has remained for hundreds of years as a symbol of law and order.

When Rome became the world's dominant power, her new obligations led her to develop a *jus gentium* (Law of Nations) which was in fact Roman civil law as applied to foreigners and to relations with the outside world. This confusing concept varies in different periods. Historically, it seems to have little to do with international relations, but, philosophically, it seems to include common legal institutions and rules found everywhere, constituting universal law. It has also been interpreted as almost indistinguishable from *jus naturale* (Natural Law), and hence to possess principles which are not only universal, but also reasonable, just and equitable. Although the *jus gentium* constituted private international law, rather than public international law, it greatly influenced the legal thought of the 16th and 17th centuries because of its authority and convenient frame of reference, and was important to the development of modern international law, as such terms as alluvion, accretion, occupation, prescription and servitude suggest.[18]

The expansion of the Empire led to greatly increased contacts with foreigners. A special office, *praetor peregrinus*, was established to handle litigation between citizens and foreigners, and between foreigners and foreigners upon Roman territory. The Romans, with their far-flung empire, greatly developed institutions of international communications and the rules to govern them. They also maintained the principle of the sanctity of international obligations and ambassadorial rights and privileges, which, like the Greeks, they solemnized through religious rituals.

Much Roman municipal law concerned war, and had implications for the future development of the international law of war. A

---

[18] *See* Nussbaum, *The Significance of Roman Law in the History of International Law,* 100 U. PA. L. REV. 682-87 (1952).

distinction was made between "just" and "unjust" wars. Force was held to be permissible only in waging "just" wars, and this distinction greatly influenced the thinking of later centuries.[19] *Fetiales,* or priests, were consulted to determine whether a given war about to be commenced was just, and these priests gave an opinion which was confirmed or set aside by the Senate. The few, acceptable causes for a just or legal war, consisted of the invasion of Roman territory, the violation of treaties, alliances, or the rights of ambassadors, and attack on an ally.

§ 1-5.4. **The Middle Period in Europe to 1648.** This period began with the Christian era, and was unified by the influences of the Roman Empire which, as the single power in the area, had left little need for international standards, and by the Christian Church, whose organization was modeled on that of the Roman Empire, and which provided a common, universal bond of spiritual humanity. The ideal was that of a world state, but neither Emperor, nor Pope could effectively compel obedience, and the authority of both was weakened by conflicts between them.

Medieval theologians contributed greatly to the development of international law by reviving the Roman doctrine of "just war." The tenets of St. Augustine were largely accepted by Thomas Acquinas who gave them added authority and a framework of analysis which greatly influenced the scholastics and other writers. The theologians, also remodeled the ancient concepts of the natural law, which they considered to be of a divine origin, and therefore superior to all human law.

The Roman system of law was replaced by the feudal system, which lasted from the ninth to the 15th centuries. It was a period of warfare, violence and anarchy. The territorial basis of sovereignty, stemming from land and its ownership, was emphasized.

The Crusades (1096-1270) united Christendom for foreign intervention and stimulated trade and the exchange of ideas. They also weakened the resources of the nobility and were thus a leading factor contributing to the decline of feudalism.

Increased trade, especially maritime commerce, resulting from the activities of the Italian cities, and the discovery of the New World and the routes to the Far East contributed greatly to international law. New, important maritime laws and codes were created,

---

[19] The distinction between "lawful" or "just" wars and those that were "unlawful" or "unjust" is especially prominent in the writings of Grotius, who stated that "justifiable causes (for war) include defense, the obtaining of that which belongs to us or is our due, and the inflicting of punishment." GROTIUS, DE JURE BELLI AC PACIS 171 (1625).

such as the old Rhodian Code during the period before the over-throw of the Roman Empire; the Amalfitan Tables in the 11th century; the Laws of Oleron for Western Europe in the 12th century; the Laws of Wisby for the Baltic states in the 13th century; the Consolato del Mare for Southern Europe in the 14th century; and the Laws of the Hanseatic League in the 16th century; the number of permanent diplomatic missions increased, and new problems raised by the discovery of the New World concerning the acquisition and distribution of land were created, in turn leading to the negotiation of important treaties and the development of rivalries among European powers.

Commercial treaties between Russia and several Germanic States, provided for the protection of persons and property, and the settlement of claims. Agreements known as "capitulations" granted Western European citizens permission to establish, and maintain settlements in Muslim countries under their own laws and administration.

Contacts among Europeans and non-Europeans were rather scanty during this period, except for certain commercial relations. In the 16th century Europeans attempted to cultivate relations with China, but without success except for the establishment of a settlement in Macao by the Portuguese. Japan was cordial to Europeans until the 17th and 18th centuries when it adopted a strict policy of seclusion.

Numerous treaties on war, and the laws governing it, were written in the 15th, 16th and 17th centuries. Some of the principal writers[20] of this period, prior to Grotius, were: Pierino Belli (1502-1575); Balthasar Ayala (1548-1584); and above all, Alberico Gentili (1552-1608), a practising lawyer whose legal approach and great legal learning experience set international law on a new course. Their contribution to international law was to remove it from the area of the quasi-religious, under which it had been considered by the Ancients, into the area of jurisprudence.

---

[20]*See* CLASSICS OF INTERNATIONAL LAW, which is edited by J. Scott and published by the Carnegie Institution of Washington. This series gives translations of the original international law treatises by Ayala, Belli, Bynkershoek, Gentili, Grotius, Legnano, Pufendorf, Rachel, Vattel, Vitoria, and others. There are also useful comments and notes with bibliographical references. These writers conceived of international law as a universal system, a view which contrasts with that of such 19th and early 20th century writers as Fauchille, Hall, Oppenheim, and Wheaton, who viewed it as a law applicable only between European States. *See also* W. JENKS, THE COMMON LAW OF MANKIND 66-74 (London 1958); Brohi, *Work Paper on Pacific Settlement of International Disputes,* in WORLD PEACE THROUGH LAW: THE GENEVA CONFERENCE 83-93 (1969) [hereinafter cited as GENEVA CONF.].

The so-called "father of international law" was Hugo Grotius (1583-1645), whose reputation and influence have been world-wide, and whose principal works have been widely translated and commented upon.   Born in Holland, Grotius was a child prodigy, entering the University of Leyden at 11, and being admitted to the practice of law at 16.   He was also a theologian, poet and historian. In 1623 and 1624, he wrote his great book, *the Law of War and Peace, De Jure Belli ac Pacis,* in which he deals with the problems of "just" war and in 1609, he proclaimed the freedom of the seas in an elaborate argument in *Mare Liberum* (Open Sea), defending the right of the Dutch to navigate the Indian Ocean which Portugal claimed as its exclusive territorial waters.   He was answered in 1635 by a distinguished Englishman, John Selden, in *Mare Clausum* (Closed Sea).

Grotius introduced into international law the theory of extra-territoriality, by which an ambassador must be considered legally outside the territory of the state to which he is accredited, and entirely exempt from its criminal jurisdiction.   Grotius also set forth a general theory of treaties, distinguishing them from contracts, emphasizing the importance of good faith in their maintenance.   He first legally analyzed the problem of neutrality, although his concept differed from that of Vattel and other writers.   The writings of Grotius have been reprinted by the Carnegie Endowment for International Peace in its *Classics of International Law.*

§ 1-5.5. **The Treaty of Westphalia to the First Hague Conference (1648-1899).**[21]   The modern state system, ushered in by the Peace of Westphalia and based on the principle of territorial sovereignty is basically West European. The burgeoning nationalism associated with this period was characterized by a conspicuous lack of unifying influences as no central power replaced the former authorities of Emperor and Pope.   Trust in a universal order of states, implied by the ascendancy of the natural law had been eroded; relations among states multiplied and gave rise to numerous important conferences, treaties and arbitrations, but without the necessary machinery to guarantee their implementation and effectiveness; and a start was made in the creation of international administrative agencies.   The American and French Revolutions articulated principles of basic liberties and democracy which epitomized Western thought and action.   The pronouncement by President of the United States, James Monroe in 1823, that the American continents

---

[21]*See* Brohi, *Basic Principles of International Law,* in ATHENS CONF. 738-55.

were no longer open to foreign colonization, not only had far-reaching political effects, but also laid the foundation for a regional system within the larger community of nations. Political, economic and social changes gave rise to imperialism, national socialism and communism, and throughout the period, positivism was followed. Emphasis was placed upon the practical application of legal principles to the point where law was seen as the legitimization of authority guaranteed by superior force.

Great law-making conferences played a more important role in this period than in any other prior period. It is significant that provisions for international cooperation were nevertheless interspersed with clauses perpetuating nationalism and imperialism. The Congress of Vienna of 1815,[22] among other things, established a modern scheme of diplomatic representation, made certain provisions about free navigation on international rivers, and denounced the slave trade. The Treaty (Declaration) of Paris of 1856 laid down important rules relating to privateering, neutral trade and blockades.[23] At the Berlin Conference in 1884, the participating powers provided, among other things, for the freedom of commerce in Africa, the freedom of navigation of certain African rivers, and prohibited the slave trade. Starting in 1889, the Pan-American conferences, the forerunner of the Organization of American States, adopted several law-making conventions.

The Jay Treaty of 1794, revived the practice of arbitration, which had fallen into disuse. The successful *Alabama Claims* arbitration at Geneva in 1872 between the United States and Great Britain and the *Bering Sea Fur Seal Fisheries* case, submitted to arbitration in 1892 by the same two countries, greatly enhanced the prestige of arbitration as an important method of the peaceful settlement of international disputes.[24]

Warfare during this period became somewhat less cruel and violent. Several attempts were made to apply the rules of humanity to the conduct of hostilities. In 1864, Lieber published "Instructions for the Government of the Armies of the United States in the Field."[25] Also in 1864, the Geneva Convention dealt with the

---

[22]*See* Strakosch, *The Place of the Congress of Vienna in the Growth of International Law and Organization,* 13 INDIAN YR. INT'L AFF. 184-206 (1964).

[23]For the text of the Declaration of Paris, see G. WILSON & G. TUCKER, *supra* note 14 at 378-79.

[24]1 J. MOORE, HISTORY AND DIGEST OF ARBITRATIONS TO WHICH THE UNITED STATES HAS BEEN A PARTY 455-761 (1906); 2 *id.,* at 495-682.

[25]For the text of this Instruction, see G. WILSON & G. TUCKER, *supra* note 14, at 349-78.

treatment of the sick and wounded in land warfare. The St. Petersburg Convention of 1868 forbade the use of certain explosive shells, and an attempt was made at Brussels, in 1874, to codify the general rules of land warfare. Furthermore, through custom, war came to be considered solely as a contest between organized armies and governments, exempting civilian non-combatants.

In this period, many great contributions were made to international legal literature. The political writings of Hobbes, Spinoza, Locke, Hegel and others; publicists such as: Samuel Pufendorf, Richard Zouche, Samuel Rachel, Cornelius van Bynkershoek, Christian Wolff, Emmerich de Vattel and Johann Jakob Moser, influenced international law.[26] Judicial decisions, collections of state papers and diplomatic notes, and treaty collections were added to general treaties and special monographs to enrich international law sources.

Three of the most important 19th century English publications on international law were those of Sir Travers Twiss, *The Law of Nations* (1861-1863); Robert Phillimore, *Commentaries upon International Law* (1854-1861); and the outstanding volume by William E. Hall, *Treatise on International Law* (1880), with a valuable eighth edition in 1924 by A.P. Higgins.

In France, the *Traite de Droit International Public* was published in 1885, by Paul Pradier-Fodere, and Henry Bonfils wrote the *Manuel de Droit International Public* which had a valuable eighth edition by Paul Fauchille (1921-1926).

In 1819, the German writer, Johann L. Kluber, published a work on the modern international law of Europe, entitled *Droit des Gens Moderne de l'Europe.* (A second and revised edition was published in 1874 by M.A. Ott.) Italian jurists who wrote on international law in this period include: Ludovico Casanova, *Lezioni di Diritto Internazionale* (1853), and Pasquale Fiore, *Trattato di Internazionale Pubblice* (1865).   Latin-American authors include the Venezuelan-Chilean jurist, Andres Bello, *Principios de Derecho de Gentes* (1832), and the Argentine jurist, Carlos Calvo, whose first edition appears in Spanish and subsequent editions are in French under the title *Le Droit International.* The well-known treatise of Friedrich de Martens was translated from the original Russian into German, *Volkerrecht* (1883-1886), and into French, *Traite de Droit International* (1883-1887). And Alphonse Rivier, a French Swiss who taught at the University of Brussels, wrote an international law treatise entitled *Principes du Droit des Gens* (1896).

---

[26] CLASSICS OF INTERNATIONAL LAW (Reprint, J. B. Scott ed. New York 1964).

Among the American writers were James Kent, *Commentaries on American Law* (1826), which included a study of international law; Henry Wheaton, *Elements of International Law* (1836); Theodore Woolsey, *Introduction to the Study of International Law* (1860); and George Davis, *Elements of International Law* (1887).

§ 1-5.6. The Hague Conferences (1899[27] and 1907[28]) to Date. The transition to the modern era of international law was ushered in by two very important law-making conferences, held at the Hague in 1899 and 1907, with the basic objective of substituting reason and law for force and war. It soon became evident, however, that prolonged discussions on the elimination of war would not be fruitful, and attention was therefore turned to efforts to regulate war, and to settle disputes principally by arbitration. The first Hague Conference, attended by 28 states, formulated three conventions concerning the pacific settlement of international disputes, the law and customs of war on land, and the principles of the 1864 Geneva Convention on maritime warfare. In addition, the Conference issued three declarations regarding prohibited weapons and methods of warfare, and created the Permanent Court of Arbitration.

The second Hague Conference, attended by 44 states, concluded 13 conventions and one declaration, mainly dealing with legal limitations upon war.[29] The Conference advocated compulsory arbitration, although none resulted, the creation of an International Prize Court, and drew up a convention for the establishment of such a Court, but this convention was never ratified. It adopted the limited concept of a Prize Court, which functioned during the First World War.

In 1908-1909, representatives of 10 leading maritime powers met at London and drafted the Declaration of London[30] which concerned the laws of naval warfare. Consisting of 71 articles, this Declaration constituted a code of rules regulating the rights of neutrals and belligerents with respect to neutral commerce. Like

---

[27] Convention for the pacific settlement of international disputes, *opened for signature* July 29, 1899, 32 Stat. 1779, T.S. No. 392.

[28] Convention for the pacific settlement of international disputes, *opened for signature* October 18, 1907, 36 Stat. 2199, T.S. No. 536.

[29] For the texts of the thirteen Hague Conventions, see G. WILSON & G. TUCKER, *supra* note 14, at 381-469. For more detailed information on the two Hague Conferences, see J. SCOTT, THE HAGUE CONFERENCES OF 1899 AND 1907 (2 vols., Baltimore 1909).

[30] For the text of the Declaration of London, see G. WILSON, HANDBOOK OF INTERNATIONAL LAW 519-30 (2d ed. St. Paul 1927).

the convention for the creation of a prize court, it also remained unratified by many nations, making it impossible to invoke during the first World War.

The efforts of the first few years of the 20th century to devise ways and means to preserve peace received a rude shock with the advent of World War I. This showed that states were no less ready than before to use force to obtain policy objectives, and that war, rather than reciprocity and mutuality, was still considered a valid and legitimate means of national policy. It also showed the impracticality of placing much faith in rules to humanize warfare, when these rules could be set aside by military necessity. And, the fundamental doctrine that treaties must be observed in good faith was ignored by Germany when, on this same plea of "military necessity," it violated the neutrality of Belgium, which had been solemnly "guaranteed" by treaty.

In January 1918, President of the United States, Woodrow Wilson, announced his Fourteen Points, which subsequently became the basis of the peace settlements and the new world order. In a speech on July 4, 1918, the President said that one of the great objectives of the war was "the consent of all nations to be governed in their conduct towards each other by the same principles of honor and of respect for the common law of civilized society that govern the individual citizens of all modern States . . ." The series of peace treaties that followed the war not only dealt with territorial and other problems created by the hostilities, but also included provisions for the reduction of armaments and the payment of reparations, and the Covenant of the League of Nations made important changes in the organization of the community of nations as well as in some of the substantive and procedural rules of international law.[31] A new principle of collective security replaced the old idea of balance of power as emphasis was placed on using sovereignty to create institutions to achieve and maintain peace, and the principle of self-determination became increasingly important. The creation of the Permanent Court of International Justice marked the culmination of years of effort to improve the judicial means of settling international disputes, and the establishment of an International Labour Organization laid a foundation for improving labor conditions throughout the world.

---

[31]For the text of the LEAGUE OF NATIONS COVENANT, see 13 AJIL SUPP. 151 (1919). For comment on the League of Nations and the prohibition of war, see Brohi, *supra* note 20.

In the decade following World War I, several efforts were made outside of the League system to reduce armaments and limit resort to war. At the Washington Conference of 1921-1922, several great naval powers attempted to limit naval armaments though with disappointing results, as the conflicting national desires of participating states made significant progress impossible. In 1924, the Geneva Protocol[32] attempted to prohibit or outlaw aggressive war, declaring it to be an international crime. The Protocol required states to submit all disputes which might give rise to hostilities to compulsory arbitration or to other peaceful means of settlement. The Protocol, an aspiration rather than a binding legal agreement, defined aggression only by declaring that an aggressor state is one which goes to war in violation of the League Covenant or the Geneva Protocol. By the Locarno treaties of 1924-1925,[33] states aimed to strengthen the peace by pledges of non-aggression, and provided for the peaceful settlement of their disputes, principally by arbitration and use of the World Court. In 1928, by the Pact of Paris,[34] often referred to as the Kellogg-Briand Pact, states renounced war "as an instrument of national policy" and agreed to settle all of their disputes by peaceful means, but the meaning of the Pact is not clear and has remained controversial.[35] (See also Chapter 14.)

It would appear, from the efforts within and outside the League system, that the decade following World War I had witnessed considerable progress in the field of international law and relations. The scope of international law had been expanded. Previously held, views of sovereignty had been weakened by the growing idea of using sovereignty to build instrumentalities and legal rules for peace through collective security. Resort to war as a right was seriously questioned, and although armaments had not been reduced, there was a growing feeling that states should not rely on their armaments for defense.

But, there were certain, definite weaknesses in the peace efforts. The United States remained outside of the League of Nations and refused to join the World Court. Enormous disabilities and reparations had been placed upon an exhausted Germany. As

---

[32] Protocol on Arbitration Clauses, *entered into force* July 28, 1924, 27 L.N.T.S. 157.

[33] 54 L.N.T.S. 289; 305.

[34] The General Treaty for the Renunciation of War, *signed* August 27, 1928, 94 L.N.T.S. 57.

[35] For the text of the Kellogg-Briand Pact, see C. FENWICK, *supra* note 14, at 684-85. For comment, see Brohi, *Peacekeeping,* in GENEVA CONF. 91-92 (Topic 1).

early as 1921, the League failed to settle the question of the surprise occupation of the Lithuanian City of Vilna by Polish troops, and in 1931, it failed to deal with the invasion of Manchuria by Japan. China was clearly entitled to League protection, but the League was unwilling or unable to provide effective sanctions against Japan. In 1933, when Bolivia and Paraguay went to war, the League passed the responsibility for action to the inter-American regional system, which proved inadequate to meet the situation. In 1935, in response to the Italian attack against Ethiopia, the League agreed on economic sanctions but, when these proved futile, the League failed to take more effective action. Thus, states came to realize that they could not rely upon the League for protection, and several accordingly withdrew. The states of the world were rapidly drifting toward another world war. This came in 1939.

The huge losses and great devastation of World War II led to a peaceful post-war period. At the same time, nations desired to avoid the past mistakes in formulating international peace-keeping machinery that had followed the first World War.

In 1941, the President of the United States and the British Prime Minister, in the Atlantic Charter, proclaimed common principles for the establishment of a future peace. Proposals for the creation of a general international organization were made by representatives of the United States, Great Britain, and Russia in Moscow in 1943, at Dumbarton Oaks in Washington in 1944, and at Yalta in early 1945. In June, 1945, the Charter of the United Nations was adopted at San Francisco, and a new world organization was born, with the hope of succeeding where the League of Nations had failed—providing the necessary machinery, and taking the necessary action to maintain order and peace through legal rules and institutions.

The period since World War II has been characterized by the cold war struggle, by unparalleled technological advance in the production of instruments of destruction, by many new international problems, by new viewpoints, and by significant changes in the structure of the international community and in the influence of newly established states.[36] In spite of this, or, perhaps, in fact, because of it, great efforts have been made by the United Nations,

---

[36]*See, e.g.,* J. SYATAUW, SOME NEWLY ESTABLISHED STATES AND THE DEVELOPMENT OF INTERNATIONAL LAW (The Hague 1961); Anand, *Role of the "New" Asian-African Countries in the Present International Legal Order,* 56 AJIL 383–406 (1962);

by a multiplicity of international organizations, and by some states and individuals, to lay a firm foundation for an enduring peace by attacking basic, fundamental problems.

§ 1-5.7. **Islamic Law.**[37] Almost unrecognizedly, through its contacts with the Western world, Islamic Law has preserved Greco-Roman legal concepts, and has made substantial contributions to international law and theory. Western scholars, such as Vitoria Ayala, and Gentili came from parts of Spain and Italy where the influence of Islamic law was great; great jurists, and theologians, like Martin Luther, studied Arabic; Western libraries carried the Arabic treaties on law; and even Grotius in his writing on the law of war recognized the humanitarian laws of what he called the "barbarians." The first codification of international law as a collection of cases and practices was made by the Muslim scholar Al-Shaybani in his *Siyyars* in the eighth century,[38] preceding similar Western works by centuries.

Islamic law cannot be viewed outside the context of its philosphy. This latter is predicated on three main tenets: Unity of God (the sovereign, and not the state or the people), unity of mankind (universality of man), and the unity of religion (continuity in progressive revelations forming a single religion, Islam, which means "peaceful submission to God"). Thus, the world is theoretically "open" to all men for their free movement and with the right to freedom of expression, thought and religion. Therefore, "just wars" were waged whenever the free propagation of Islam by peaceful means was prohibited. Where Islam could not be preached was *Dar-Al-Harb*, or land of war in contrast to *Dar-El-Islam* (land of Islam) and *Dar-El-Selm* (land of peace) where Islam existed. "Jihad" or holy war was designed to open *Dar-Al-Harb* to the freedom of propagation of Islam (not to be confused with forced conversion).

Muslim international law contributed most in the area of the law of war. It set definite rules on war booty, prisoners of war, protec-

---

[37] *See generally* M. KHADDURI, WAR AND PEACE IN THE LAW OF ISLAM (Baltimore 1955); Rechid, *L'Islam et le Droit des Gens,* 60 RECUEIL DES COURS 375-505 (1937).

It would be a misnomer to speak of Mohammedanism or Mohammedan Law. The Prophet Muhammad was never considered the originator of Islam by the bearer of its message. "Islam" means surrendering in peace to "Allah" who is the sole and central deity (God) of the universe. Thus, this section has been entitled "Islamic Law."

[38] Al-Shaybani, 749-805, whose *Siyyars* were first written in Haiderahad in 1335-36 even though he taught them during his lifetime. They were translated by M. Khadduri under the title THE ISLAMIC LAW OF NATIONS (Baltimore 1966).

tion of civilian populations, limitations of belligerent activities and reprisals, asylum, pardon, safe conduct, diplomatic immunity, negotiations and peace missions.[39]

Another area in which Muslim law has contributed is that of treaties. The Prophet made the first one, in 622, and set forth the principle that valid treaties are *pacta sunt servanda* (that treaties must be performed in good faith). Its tradition dates, however, prior to the Islamic era, and was recognized in inter-tribal relations. In 467, Meccans concluded a trade agreement through a delegation they sent to the Negus of Abbyssinia. The Muslim state established in 622 continued the effects of the trade agreement, thus recognizing a form of state succession principle.

Muslim international law is defined by Professor Hamiddullah as: "The part of the law and custom of the land and treaty obligations which a Muslim *de facto* or *de jure* state observes in its dealings with other *de facto* or *de jure* states."[40]

Still another definition of Muslim international law is:

> Muslim law is the fair regulation of the conduct of the faithful in this world and in the world hereafter. *Mutantis mutandis* Muslim international law aims at the fair regulation of the Muslim state in its foreign relations as well as the individual Muslim in his relations with the non-Muslim citizen of another non-Muslim state and any non-Muslim state. That which sanctions the individual's private conduct, and by reason of a unified source of moral precepts it prevents a duality of moral standards in national *versus* international affairs. . . . [Concluding that it is] universal inter-social public order.[41]

The formal source of Muslim international law is the *Qu'ran* and the *Sunnah* (Prophet's deeds and sayings). It is followed by its secondary sources of *Ijtihad* (legal reasoning) and *Ijma* (consensus). Because the formal source of all laws in Islam is the *Qu'ran*, Muslim international law adheres to the monistic view and resembles natural law. Its sociological significance which places the individual at its center finds its counterpart in Dugiut's views which are followed in the French lego-sociological school and by naturalists.

---

[39] T. AL-GHUNAIMI, THE MUSLIM CONCEPTION OF INTERNATIONAL LAW AND THE WESTERN APPROACH (The Hague 1968); M. KHADDURI, WAR AND PEACE IN THE LAW OF ISLAM (Baltimore 1955); Rechid, *L'Islam et le Droit des Gens,* 60 RECUEILS DES COURS 375-505 (1937).

[40] M. HAMIDULLAH, MUSLIM CONDUCT OF STATE (4th ed. Lahore 1961). *See also* MAUDUDI, ISLAMIC LAW AND CONSTITUTION (3d ed. Lahore 1967); S. RAMADAM, ISLAMIC LAW, ITS SCOPE AND EQUITY (London 1961).

[41] Bassiouni, *Islam: Concept, Law and World Habeas Corpus,* 2 RUT. CAM. L J. 160. (1970).

§ 1-5.8. **African International Law.** The African continent comprises over 11 million square miles, is populated by some 200 million people possessing varied characteristics and differences, and has a history largely determined by its size and geophysical position. The Ashanti, from Ghana, differ markedly from the Xhosa from the Cape, and many Africans are Hamites, others Semites; the Bantu (meaning people) are thought to be a combination of both. The west coast of the continent was first colonized in 1460, and ever since the 1800's whatever part of Africa was accessible to colonization was under European sway and control.

While the African continent has had no substantial impact on international law as it is known today, or even in its historical development, a history of an intra-African system of relations is recorded, as any other continent. African tribes and societies developed definite rules of conduct to govern their relations. As stated by Professor Baade:

> This is not to say that the new African states hold nothing of interest to students of comparative and international law. It is merely suggested that studies which focus on traditional and religious legal institutions are highly prone to be misleading or even mischievous—misleading because the institutions referred to are on the periphery even now and are rapidly melting away; mischievous because any emphasis on traditional or divine law necessarily poses ideological obstacles to the legal reforms which African states must undertake in order to attain modernity.

> Let us now turn to some practical examples. In the field of international law, for instance, it is submitted that little can be gained from scanning frequently obscure tribal and religious customs for evidence of 'general principles of law.' The new African states accept international law; several of them are currently before the International Court of Justice as plaintiffs against 'white' powers. They do not challenge the legal force of treaties concluded by free negotiation after independence. But they do worry about the status of pre-independence treaty obligations entered into by the colonial power; and they do object to the unilateral imposition of quite frequently disputed rules of customary international law which they did not help develop.

> Is such an attitude towards international law really to any appreciable extent the manifestation of a unique law culture? It seems much more sensible to assume that at least as regards customary international law, the new African states are merely assuming the position indicated by the present stage of their economic development and by their national ambitions. They seek to avoid, or at any rate to minimize, the constraints imposed by

an international custom which was created almost entirely by the capital exporting countries.[42]

Pre-colonial African history as recorded in the Western world contains very little about these contacts among the various tribes, and few rules comparable to those existing in European international law are said to have evolved.   Some basic characteristics, however do emerge.[43]

§ 1-5.8.1. Sovereignty of African Tribes. The concept of sovereignty has long existed on the African continent, but, unlike its Western counterpart, it was not related to territory.   Instead, it was attached to people, whose tribes were considered sovereign regardless of territorial confines, due partly to the nomadic nature of the tribes, but, more generally, to the topography of the land. This has been carried through to the contemporary trend of independent African states to place great emphasis on each state's individual sovereignty.   However, the realization that these sovereign states had their boundaries carved out by former colonial powers resulted in the Charter of African Unity declaring that, since boundaries were set by non-Africans, they are subject to change and transformation.[44]

The relationship between sovereign territory and people is evident in the jurisdictional tests applied.   The major test is still "ethnic origin," although dissatisfaction with it has recently been encountered. As stated by Professor Seidman:

> . . . Thus, the single test of ethnic origin to determine if customary law applies is no longer a sharp enough scalpel to serve well, and the exceptions devised by the courts are not altogether satisfactory.
>
> Kenya and Uganda made a first approximation at a resolution of this problem before independence. Typically, it was still phrased

---

[42] AFRICAN LAW: NEW LAW FOR NEW NATIONS 2-3 (H. Baade ed. Dobbs Ferry, N.Y. 1963).

[43] Common characteristics of African legal systems gave rise to a notion of "African Law" which has been pioneered in the United States by Professor Arthur Schiller of Columbia University. He discusses it in his introduction to AFRICA AND LAW (T. Hutchinson ed., Madison Wisc. 1968). The same notion was developed by the late Professor Kenneth S. Carlston of the University of Illinois in SOCIAL THEORY AND AFRICAN TRIBAL ORGANIZATION: THE DEVELOPMENT OF SOCIAL-LEGAL THEORY (Urbana, Ill. 1968). *See also* Allott, *Towards the Unification of Laws in Africa,* 14 INT'L & COMP. L.Q. 366 (1955).

[44] Z. CERVENKA, THE ORGANIZATION OF AFRICAN UNITY AND ITS CHARTER (New York 1969); Ouko, *East African Community,* 35 REV. INT'L SCI. AD. 47 (Paris 1969).

in racial terms. A person partly of non-African descent who did not own or occupy land in accordance with customary tenure, and who was not living in any African community in the customary way, could obtain a certificate exempting him from the jurisdiction of the native courts (and hence from the control of customary law).

Tanzania has tried to solve the problem by abandoning the ethnic test and substituting the concept of 'membership in a community.' Membership in a community may be acquired either by adoption of the way of life of the community or by community acceptance of a person as one of its members. Membership in one community may be lost by acquiring membership in another community. The adoption of membership may be general or may operate for certain acts or transactions only. Moreover, the matter will be controlled by some law other than customary law if it is apparent from the nature of the act or transaction or from the manner of life or business of the parties that they intended the matter to be so regulated.

Ghana has left the matter rather vague, presumably to permit the courts to work out detailed rules. A person is entitled to have applied in any case his 'personal law,' which is presumed to be the common law unless some system of customary law is to be applied. It has been remarked that 'if with the spread of industrialization and urbanization in Ghana, the courts tend to adopt the view that customary law ties are being severed by more and more Ghanians, there is an opening here for accelerating the demise of customary law.' Probably the Ghanian courts will not so construe the statute, although no reported cases on the subject can be found.[45]

While territory was historically not that significant in determining sovereignty which was related more to a "peoplehood" concept, it was nevertheless important. The Ashanti, Hansa and Ibo trading tribes had to buy safe-conducts for their merchants with tribute in order to permit them to pass through the territory of other tribes. In northern Nigeria, safe-conducts were given to traveling tradesmen as early as the 16th century.

§ 1-5.8.2. **Territoriality and Peaceful Coexistence in Africa.** Territoriality was in pre-colonial times marked by a principle of coexistence which reduced the impact of jealously guarded frontiers which, for all practical purposes, did not exist because of geographical considerations. Agreements were made either tacitly or expressly to observe territorial limitations, and to respect the

---

[45] Seidman, *Law and Economic Development in Independent, English-Speaking Sub-Saharan Africa*, in AFRICA AND LAW, *supra* note 43 at pp. 46-47.

migratory aspects of tribal life whenever and wherever it existed. This, in turn, directly related to the fact that contemporary African states specifically reject the notion of force in the settlement of their disputes particularly with respect to territorial or or boundary disagreements.[46] The Charter of African Unity, even though it recognizes the changing nature of boundaries, specifically rejects the use of force in their transformation.

§ 1-5.8.3. **Treaties and Agreements in Africa.** The earliest known agreements in the African continent are reported to have been made in the seventh century between Amr-Ibn-Ul-As, who led the Arabs into Egypt, defeating the Romans and the Nubians (southern Egypt and northern Sudan). Egyptians in the 11th century renewed this agreement with the Sudanese. Ashanti kings from their earliest recorded history made agreements for the safe passage of their merchant tribesmen, as have the Hausa Sultans for theirs. Ibos, who traded with what is now Guinea, Senegal, and Ghana and with European merchants and slave traders, traveled by agreement with other tribes through their territory to reach the western coast of the continent. Ashantis from Ghana traded gold for salt with Berbers and Moroccans by agreement, but trading was suspended briefly in the 11th century when Berbers, untrue to their agreement, tried to follow the Ashanti to discover the source of the gold. The initial Vortker settlers in South Africa in the 18th century made several treaties with the Bantus which the settlers consistently violated thereafter.

The principle of *pacta sunt servanda* (that treaties must be performed in good faith) was observed long before that notion had been presented by the colonial powers as a tenet of respect for treaties and agreements in European law. A distinction must be drawn between pre-colonial Africa and colonial Africa (prior to independence). In the former era, it is possible to speak of "treaties" or agreements in the understood sense of international law because the parties, tribes, were equal sovereigns. The colonial period reveals many treaties between the colonizers and the Africans who were found very receptive to "agreements" as they were accustomed to the practice and its observance. However, they were not made between equal sovereigns. Invariably they have been altered or violated by the colonial powers which had originally imposed them. They cannot, therefore, be recognized as "treaties" in the meaning of international law, even though the colonizing

---

[46] Fox, *The Settlement of Disputes by Peaceful Means and the Observance of International Law: African Attitudes,* 3 INT'L REL. 389-410 (1968).

powers continued to assert that legal consequences derived there-from when it suited their interest.

While inter-tribal trading in the pre-colonial era was limited, it was done on an individual entrepreneurial basis as sanctioned by tribal chieftains. This was true even though individuals traded for their own personal benefit. Trade agreements were made on a *quid pro quo* basis and mutuality of obligations was strongly enforced. In independent Africa, all states adhere to the principle of *pacta sunt servanda*. As stated by one author:

> With respect to treaties, we seem to be faced by a series of 'typical' cases of state succession, with, however, the distinguishing mark that the problem has not arisen until now with such pressing force and on such a large scale. It is estimated, for instance, that there are some 300-odd British treaties which might be applicable to Nigeria. By exchange of letters between the Prime Minister of the Federation of Nigeria and the United Kingdom High Commissioner on the very day of independence, the Federation assumed all rights and obligations stipulated by international agreements entered into 'on their behalf' before independence, and undertook to keep such agreements in force 'until such time as the Government of Nigeria can consider whether they require modification of renegotiation in any respect.' Nigeria was faced with three major questions in this connection: Which agreements are applicable to Nigeria? (For a country which had just reached independence and is still in the process of setting up a Foreign Office, this is no mean question.) Will the other contracting parties regard themselves to be bound as against Nigeria? How can the various agreements be denounced, and which agreements should be terminated?

> Another new African state, Tanganyika, has attempted a different solution of the treaty problem. Instead of concluding as 'inheritance agreement' with the United Kingdom, Tanganyika has filed a formal declaration with the Secretary General of the United Nations. Pursuant to this declaration, all valid bilateral treaties are kept in force on the basis of reciprocity for a trial period of two years, pending negotiations as to eventual readjustments. Multilateral treaties are to be dealt with by *ad hoc* agreements but Tanganyika undertakes to treat such agreements 'as being in force vis-a-vis other States who rely on them in their relations with Tanganyika.

> Both solutions are seemingly unexceptionable under traditional international law. Since almost all relevant agreements can be terminated unilaterally by appropriate, relatively short-term notice, the essential legal problem is the question to the extent of the other parties' obligation toward the new states. Vastly more com-

plicated is the issue of the legality of pre-independence agreements between the former colonial powers and the emerging African states on the eve of independence.

As a rule, the former colonial power will seek guarantees in three distinct fields: the continued recognition of pre-independence obligations of the colonial administration, particularly of civil service tenure and pension rights; the continued protection of minorities— not necessarily European subjects—whom the colonial powers had undertaken to protect against the dominant local ethnic or religious groups; and finally, the continued preferential treatment of the former colonial power and its nationals, especially in matters of trade, investment and the like.

While such guarantees, or some of them, could be incorporated into the independence constitutions enacted by the colonial power, such constitutional protection had already proved to be insufficient. For once independence was attained, the former dependency could— as the Union of South Africa eventually did—repeal or amend its constitution. Even the abolition of an 'unamendable' constitutional provision by revolutionary action would not be a violation of international law, as international law does not guarantee the constitutional form of sovereign states.[47]

§ 1-5.8.4. Modern African International Law.

An independent Africa and African personality began with the end of World War II.[48] This came about at the several international conferences—Bandung (Afro-Asian Conference), 1955; Accra, 1958; Addis Ababa, 1960; Casablanca, 1960; Belgrade (nonaligned nations), 1960—which, even though including other nonaligned countries, introduced African states to the world community as an important and emerging regional personality in international relations.[49] The most important expression of this personality occurred at the Summit Conference of Independent African States at Addis Ababa in 1963, where the 30 participant states were members of the United Nations.

The foundation of African international law is predicated on the awareness of Africans that they are part of a continent composed of homogeneous as well as heterogeneous groups and linked not only by race and color, but also by history and future expectations, as contained in the concept "Africa for the Africans." Essentially, this concept embodies the principle of African inde-

---

[47] *Supra* note 42, at 3-4.

[48] Baker, *Africa Since World War II*, 23 AUSTRALIAN OUTLOOK 158 (1969); Kay, *Impact of African States on United Nations*, 23 INT'L ORG. 20 (1969). For a different position, see Dugand, *Foreign Affairs and Public International Law*, 1967 ANN. SUR. S. AFR. L. 37 (1968).

[49] See Schiller, *supra* note 43.

pendence nationally, regionally, continentally, and internationally.[50] However, it also encompasses the principle of nonintervention in domestic and regional affairs and is predicated on the recognition that every African state is entitled to its freedom from foreign political, or economic domination and colonization. Because of the need to maintain strong economic ties between Africa and former colonizers, this principle, which is akin to the early doctrinal stages of defining national sovereignty, has been emphasized.[51] The observance of territorial boundaries, and respect for the diverse national interests among African nations have been continued to the present notwithstanding the difficulties encountered by individual nations in transforming tribal societies into national societies. The principle of *pacta sunt servanda* is qualified by that of *rebus sic stantibus*, which in African affairs may lead to the belief that the observance of treaty obligations depends on rapidly changing conditions. This, however, is not necessarily the case, and a distinction must be drawn between types of agreements. For political and economic agreements between African nations and their former colonial rulers, the future is less certain. It is difficult to foresee whether or not they will be adhered to considering the fact that the colonial history of Africa is still fresh in the memory of its people, who consequently fear further exploitation.[52]

§ 1-5.9. **Asian Principles of International Law.** While historically Asia occupied an important role in international affairs, as stated herein in referring to Confucius (551-479 B.C.) in § 1.5.1., the advent of the former Asian colonial states to full statehood since the end of World War II, and their participation in the United Nations has created a particular orientation of these states to the general body of customary international law, that, in certain respects differs from general, customary international law.[53] It is important

---

[50] This could be seen from a study of African rivers and waterways connecting nations and running through the continent. Yakemtchouk, *Le Regime International des Voies d'eaux Africaines,* 2 REV. BEL. DR. INT'L 480 (1969).

[51] *See* Seidman, *supra* note 45; Okigbo, *Independence and the Problem of Economic Growth in Economic Transition in Africa* 323 (Herkovitz & Harwitz eds. 1964); Green, *Multi-Purpose Economic Institutions in Africa,* 1 J. MODERN AFRICAN STUDIES 163 (1963).

[52] Seidman, *supra* note 45.

[53] For a different point of view on this subject, see W. FRIEDMANN, THE CHANGING STRUCTURE OF INTERNATIONAL LAW 317-23 (New York 1964) wherein the author states that the attitude of the newly-independent state is not "markedly different" from general, customary international law. *See also* C. FENWICK, INTERNATIONAL LAW 770 (New York 1965) where the author states that most new states have accepted much of international law "without difficulty," but the major differences concern the "good faith of treaties," and "representative democracy."

to note in this context, that, upon their arrival to national sovereignty, the main interests of these states lie in the protection of their national sovereignty and identity from the claims of the larger, more highly-industrialized states.[54] Further, these states present a challenge to present concepts of international law— "the challenge of accommodating customary international law to the new perceptions, attitudes and values of the emerging states."[55]

Corollary to the importance attached to the principle of national sovereignty is an equal importance attached to the principle of equality of states.[56] While seeming to appear as a reversion to greater nationalism, the practices of Asian states regarding these principles has to be differentiated.[57]

According to Professor Fatouros of the Indiana University School of Law:

> While such stress on state sovereignty is rightly to be considered a manifestation of nationalism, an important qualification is necessary in the case of the new states: their brand of nationalism differs in significant ways from the nineteenth-century European nationalism to which the term usually refers. Whereas in nineteenth-century Europe, nationalism as the expression of a feeling of national unity came first and the desire, struggle for, and attainment of political independence followed, in the new states of Africa and Asia, nationalism as an operative force was born during and through the struggle against the colonial power. It thus has retained the substantial social and economic features that colored the anti-colonialist resentment at the origin of the struggle.
>
> The historical background also affects in another way the attitude of the new states: the anticolonialist past of their leaders largely determines the manner in which they present their state's case to foreign powers or before international assembles. The colonial situation has bred deep-rooted attitudes of hostility and aggressiveness which were expressed but not exhausted in the anticolonialist struggle (violent or not) that preceded independence. Even in mere terms of style, anticolonialist oratory is emotional, impassioned, and aggressive. These characteristics continue to dominate, in varying degrees, the external attitudes and manners of the officials of the new states.[58]

---

[54] S. SINHA, NEW NATIONS AND THE LAW OF NATIONS 138 (The Netherlands 1967).

[55] *Id.* at 142.

[56] Fatouros, *Global Perspective,* in I THE FUTURE OF THE INTERNATIONAL LEGAL ORDER 340 (R. Falk & C. Black eds., Princeton 1969).

[57] *Id.*

[58] *Id.* at 352-53.

The extent to which the new states have influenced and changed international law is debated. While it is true, that these states have for the most part accepted the main body of international law, it is also certain that they have abetted significant change. Professor Fatouros contends that the eager participation of the new states in international relations and the U.N. has resulted in a changed body of international law concerning especially, colonialism and international development.[59]

> It has become quite clear by now that the legal status of colonial conquest and occupation has changed: colonialism, as such, the occupation and exploitation of "backward" territories by Western powers on the ground that the "natives" are unable to govern themselves and to establish an independent state, is not legal any more, under international law—at least as far as present of future action is concerned. The legal status of the fruits of past actions is by no means as clear. Although the illegality of past colonial conquest and the corresponding invalidity of present situations based on it was the main legal proposition advanced by India to justify its occupation of Goa and the other Portuguese enclaves, this position has not been supported frequently or consistently by the new states, apart from rhetorical statements of dubious effect.[60]

Concerning the second principle which has emerged into the general body of international law since the advent of the new states, development which is primarily economic, and which must be understood in the relation of the changed economic structures of the developed nations, and the rest of the underdeveloped world. Realization of this change must take into account that the industrially and technologically advanced Western Nations have now, for the most part, moved into what may be termed the "welfare state," whereas the emerging states are at a prior stage of economic development.[61] Given this understanding of the present economic structures, the second principle of international law, development, has largely taken on the aspects of international economic assistance.[62] According to Professor Fatouros:

> Much remains to be learned as to the exact relationships established by means of the multitude of formal instruments whereby capital, commodities, and technical assistance are provided. The lack of mutuality, however, (at least in purely economic

---

[59] *Id.* at 364.

[60] *Id.* at 366.

[61] *Id.* at 367.

[62] *Id.*

terms) is usually clear enough—indeed its actual extent is often exaggerated—and it implies a recognition of the need for a change in the existing allocation of resources, apart from any immediate partial, or attempted, *quid pro quo*. In this sense, it is highly desirable that economic assistance be further disentangled from the allegations of charity, indirect exploitation, or generosity that have tended to obscure its character.[63]

In addition to this basic reorientation of international law based on the emergence of new states, other attitudes are equally important. These concern the practices of new states concerning state succession to treaties, state responsibility, treatment of aliens, diplomatic immunities, law of the sea, extradition, and immunity of state trading organizations in national courts.[64]

New states, upon achieving independence generally follow the rule of customary international law that a "new state is bound to accept the international rights and obligations entered into by its predecessor."[65] However, in applying this principle, Latin-American and Asian states distinguish between two types of treaties: (1) those that created burdens "inconsistent with national interests"[66] and (2) those that enable them to "participate in the international community."[67] While new states fulfill the rights and obligations inhering in the second type of treaty, they are most reluctant to consider themselves bound by the first, and will generally seek their revision. This emphasizes their further belief that "all states have the right to participate in the formulation of treaties."[68]

The Asian states are critical of the general, customary international legal principle of state responsibility.[69] They believe that such a principle was established against their basic interests as sovereign states; that it is outmoded since it is basically a European principle and international law is concerned with people other than Europeans; that aliens should not receive better, or worse treatment than the nationals of the state; that the admission of aliens should be at the complete discretion of the receiving state alone; and that the receiving state is permitted absolute discretion in prohibiting or restricting the participation of aliens in professions and other forms of gainful employment.[70]

---

[63] *Id.*

[64] As enumerated in SINHA, *supra* note 54.

[65] *Id.* at 77.

[66] *Id.*

[67] *Id.*

[68] *Id.* at 83.

[69] *Id.* at 92.

[70] *Id.* at 92-97.

Concerning diplomatic recognition and immunities, the Asian states consider that mutual consent and reciprocity are the reasons for exchanging missions; that diplomatic immunity is absolute, but that embassy property belongs to the sending state according to the receiving state's rules of ownership and possession, and is not to be considered part of the sending state's sovereign territory,[71] and that state trading organizations having their own separate entities under municipal law should not be immune from suit in national courts.[72] Regarding the principle of extradition, the Asian states have followed the practice of considering it a moral obligation based on the "principle of solidarity and cooperation among nations."[73]

Perhaps the greatest divergence of the practice of new states in their approach to international law is in their treatment and views on the Laws of the Sea. They feel that the traditional three-mile limit should not be invariably applicable, but that it should vary ". . . according to the economic, political, geographical, biological, technical, political and defense needs of the state concerned."[74] In their opinion, this does not represent an encroachment on the rights of other states, but ". . . the inevitable consequence of the growing dependence of their peoples on the resources of the sea for food,"[75] and to safeguard their security, commercial, fiscal, and political interests.[76] Concerning the continental shelf, the new states tend to apply a wide interpretation to "natural resources to include 'bottom-fish' and other species at the sea bottom for food;"[77] as well as mineral resources and other living resources.[78]

§ 1-5.10. **Latin-American Principles of International Law.** Latin-American states assert that they have developed in their relations with one another, certain practices and principles, which, in effect, constitute a unique body of international legal principles. The evolution of these principles has occurred since their emergence into sovereign states, and they, in many respects are similar to claims presented by some other states as outlined in the previous section. The principles of state sovereignty and equality, responsi-

---

[71] *Id.* at 105-08.
[72] *Id.* at 131.
[73] *Id.*
[74] *Id.* at 114.
[75] *Id.*
[76] *Id.*
[77] *Id.* at 120.
[78] *Id.*

bility, and laws of the sea adhered to by the Latin-American states demonstrate their identity and basic orientation with the claims of Latin-American states, to those of the newly-independent, and developing nations. On numerous occasions, especially in matters before the United Nations General Assembly, is this similarity most apparent.

Aside from claims which emanate from their status as less highly developed economically, unique principles of international law have emerged. These, found in the treaties and conventions among these states, and in their resolutions and declarations concern the ten following areas: (1) mutual respect for sovereignty, (2) equality of states, (3) non-intervention, (4) international law as the standard of conduct, (5) observance of treaties, (6) repudiation of the use of force, (7) pacific settlement of international disputes, (8) mutual defense, (9) economic, social and cultural cooperation, and (10) recognition of the fundamental rights of man.[79]

Respect for the sovereignty of other states has been reflected in the several conventions entered into by the American states. For example, beginning with the Montevideo Convention on the Rights and Duties of States[80] of 1933, respect for state sovereignty was made a solemn obligation. According to Article 3:

> The political existence of the state is independent of recognition by the other states. Even before recognition the state has the right to defend its integrity and independence, to provide for its conservation and prosperity, and consequently to organize itself as it sees fit, to legislate upon its interests, administer its services, and to define the jurisdiction and competence of its courts.
>
> The exercise of these rights has no other limitations than the exercise of the rights of other states according to international law.[81]

This article was subsequently incorporated into the Charter of the Organization of American States, and the duty of states to respect the sovereignty of other states continues to be an important obligation.

The principle of state equality has been particularly important to the Latin-American states. Located geographically close to the United States, which has exerted an important influence in Latin

---

[79] C. FENWICK, THE ORGANIZATION OF AMERICAN STATES: THE INTER-AMERICAN REGIONAL SYSTEM 135-46 (Washington 1963).

[80] *See generally* INTERNATIONAL CONFERENCES OF AMERICAN STATES, 1889-1928, First Supplement 1933-1940 at 122 (Washington 1940) [hereinafter cited as INT'L CONF'S].

[81] *Id.* at 121.

America, Latin America has at times resented this influence, and felt called upon to assert the principle of state equality to protect its social, economic and political interests from the domination of the United States. According to Article 4 of the 1933 Montevideo Convention, the following principle is asserted:

> States are juridically equal, enjoy the same rights and have equal capacity in their exercise. The rights of each one do not depend upon the power which it possesses to assure its exercise, but upon the simple fact of its existence as a person under international law.[82]

This principle of legal equality was incorporated into other conventions among the Latin-American states,[83] and is presently visible in the system of majority voting in the Organization of American States.[84]

Corollary to the importance attached to the principles of sovereignty and equality, is that attached to the principle of nonintervention. The great insistence of states on this principle can best be understood in the light of past United States intervention in the affairs of Latin-American states, and the U.S. policy of police power that was enunciated by U.S. President Theodore Roosevelt in 1904.[85]

The strong feelings of the Latin-American nations resulted in the following declaration of principles at the 1936 Bueno Aires Inter-American Conference for the Maintenance of Peace:

> . . . That the following principles are accepted by the American community of Nations:
>
> (*a*) Proscription of territorial conquest and that in consequence, no acquisition made through violence shall be recognized;
>
> (*b*) Intervention by one State in the internal or external affairs of another State is condemned;
>
> (*c*) Forcible collection of pecuniary debts is illegal; and
>
> (*d*) Any difference or dispute between the American nations, whatever its nature or origin, shall be settled by the methods of conciliation, or unrestricted arbitration, or through operations of international justice.[86]

---

[82] *Id.* at 122.

[83] These included the 1936 Buenos Aires Convention, the 1945 Act at Mexico City and the Pact of Bogotá.

[84] C. FENWICK, *supra* note 79, at 136.

[85] *Id.* at 137.

[86] 6 HACKWORTH, DIGEST OF INTERNATIONAL LAW 16 (Washington 1943).

The principle that relations among states should be guided by international law has also been upheld by the Latin-American states.[87] This principle was incorporated into an Inter-American Treaty in 1938 to the effect that "[r]elations between states should be governed by the precepts of international law."[88] In addition, the American states meeting in 1939 in Panama declared the following:

> 1. That they affirm their faith in the principles of Christian civilization, and their confidence that, in the light of these principles, the influence of international law will be strengthened among nations;
>
> 2. That they condemn attempts to place international relations and the conduct of warfare outside the realm of morality;
>
> . . .
>
> 5. That they undertake to protest against any warlike act which does not conform to international law and the dictates of justice.[89]

Latin-American states emphasize the principle of *pacta sunt servanda*, that treaties be observed in good faith. The principle of *pacta sunt servanda* was incorporated into the 1938 Lima Declaration of American Principles to the effect that "(5) Respect for and the faithful observance of treaties constitute the indispensable rule for the development of peaceful relations between states, and treaties can only be revised by agreement of the contracting parties."[90]

Consistent with the respect for state sovereignty, equality and non-intervention is the repudiation of force, which was adopted by the Latin-American states as early as 1890.[91] And, according to Articles 20 and 21 of the revised Charter of the Organization of American States, the use of force is absolutely prohibited in the following terms:

> Article 20. The Territory of a State is inviolable; it may not be the object, even temporarily, of military occupation or of other measures of force taken by another State, directly or indirectly, on any grounds whatsoever. No territorial acquisitions or special advantages obtained either by force or by other means of coersion shall be recognized.
>
> Article 21. The American States bind themselves in their international relations not to have recourse to the use of force, except

---

[87] C. FENWICK, *supra* note 79 at 140.

[88] INT'L CONF'S, *supra* note 80, at 309, as quoted in *id.* at 141.

[89] INT'L CONF'S, *supra* note 80, at 332, as quoted *id.*

[90] INT'L CONF'S, *supra* note 80, at 309, as quoted in FENWICK, *supra* note 79, at 142.

[91] C. FENWICK, *supra* note 79, at 143.

in the case of self-defense in accordance with existing treaties or in fulfillment thereof.[92]

Furthermore, according to Article 19, the use of indirect force is likewise prohibited:

> No State may use or encourage the use of coercive measures of an economic or political character in order to force the sovereign will of another State and obtain from it advantages of any kind.[93]

The Pacific Settlement of International Disputes is a further principle enunciated early by Latin-American states. At the Panama Congress of 1826, Simon Bolivar proposed the creation of a council that would decide disputes among the states that could lead to armed hostilities.[94] According to Article 16 of the Treaty of Perpetual Union, adopted at the Panama Congress, the states pledged the following principle of pacific settlement:

> The contracting parties solemnly obligate and bind themselves to amicably compromise between themselves all differences now existing or which may arise in future, and in case no settlement can be reached, between the disagreeing powers the question shall be taken for settlement to the judgment of the assembly, whose decision shall not be obligatory, however, unless said powers shall have expressly agreed that it shall be.[95]

This peaceful settlement of international disputes received further support in the Plan of Arbitration adopted in Washington in 1890.[96] Although signed by 11 American states, the plan was never entered into force, because ratifications were not exchanged within one year as required by the treaty.[97] Article 10 of the plan provided that arbitration was compulsory in certain listed situations, and optional in others.[98] In 1902, a number of states signed a Treaty on Compulsory Arbitration,[99] which was later ratified by six nations, and which, in addition to compulsory arbitration of certain disputes, provided for recourse to mediation and commissions of inquiry.[100] In addition to other 20th century treaties and conventions,[101] this principle was also laid down in the Treaty of Reciprocal

---

[92] *Id.* at 144.

[93] *Id.*

[94] For a discussion of this proposal, see *id.* at 14-19.

[95] INT'L CONF'S, *supra* note 80, at xxiv, as quoted in *id., supra* note 79, at 171.

[96] INT'L CONF'S, *supra* note 80, at 40.

[97] C. FENWICK, *supra* note 79, at 172.

[98] *Id.*

[99] INT'L CONF'S, *supra* note 80, at 100

[100] C. FENWICK, *supra* note 79, at 173.

[101] *See* HACKWORTH, *supra* note 86, at 1-147.

Assistance of 1947,[102] in the Charter of the O.A.S.,[103] and in the 1948 Pact of Bogota,[104] which made arbitration compulsory for both judicial and non-judicial disputes.

The principle of mutual defense or collective security was also adopted by Latin-American states at the 1826 Congress of Panama, and in the intervening period has become more specific.[105] In 1936, at the Buenos Aires Conference for the Maintenance of Peace, the Latin-American states adopted the following language in Article 1 of the Convention for the Maintenance, Preservation and Reestablishment of Peace:

> In the event that the peace of the American Republics is menaced, and in order to coordinate efforts to prevent war, any of the Governments of the American Republics signatory to the Treaty of Non-Aggression and Conciliation of 1933, or to both, whether or not a member of other peace organizations, shall consult with the other Governments of the American Republics, which in such event, shall consult together for the purpose of finding and adopting methods of peaceful cooperation.[106]

Collective security was also adopted by the Latin-American states in the 1938 Declaration of Lima,[107] the 1939 Declaration of Panama,[108] and the 1940 Havana Declaration of Collective Security.[109] The Havana Declaration stated:

> That any attempt [attack] on the part of a non-American State against the integrity or inviolability of the territory, the sovereignty or the political independence of an American State shall be considered as an act of aggression against the States which sign this declaration.[110]
>
> . . .
>
> In case acts of aggression are committed or should there be reason to believe that an act of aggression is being prepared by a non-American nation against the integrity of inviolability of the territory, the sovereignty or the political independence of an American nation, the nations signatory to the present declaration

---

[102] *Opened for signature* September 2, 1947, 62 Stat. 1681, T.I.A.S. 1838, 21 U.N.T.S. 77.

[103] *Opened for signature* April 30, 1948, 2 U.S.T. 2394, T.I.A.S. 2361, 119 U.N.T.S. 3.

[104] *See* INT'L CONF'S, 1942-54, *supra* note 80, at 200 for text.

[105] C. FENWICK, *supra* note 79, at 218-20.

[106] INT'L CONF'S 1933-40, *supra* note 80, at 188, as quoted *id.,* at 222.

[107] *See* Fenwick, *The Monroe Doctrine and the Declaration of Lima,* 33 AJIL 257 (1939).

[108] INT'L CONF'S, *supra* note 80, at 326.

[109] *Id.,* 1933-40, at 343.

[110] *Id.* at 360, as quoted in C. FENWICK, *supra* note 79, at 225.

will consult among themselves in order to agree upon the measures it may be advisable to take.[111]

The principle of mutual defense, or collective security was further adopted by the American states in the 1945 Act of Chapultepec,[112] and the 1947 Treaty of Reciprocal Assistance.[113]

Cooperation in economic, social and cultural matters is also adhered to by the Latin-American states.[114] First suggested at the first Inter-American Conference in 1889-1890, concrete steps were taken with the adoption of the 1945 *Economic Charter of the Americas Economic Standards,* of the OAS Charter, the Economic Agreement of Bogotá, and the Charter of Punta del Este.[115] Social and cultural understanding among the American states have been formulated in the OAS Charter *Social Standards,* and Cultural Standards[116] which made the Latin-American states leaders in placing respect for fundamental human rights in the body of conventional international law.[117]

The doctrine of political asylum is adhered to by the Latin American States. In the 1928 Havana Convention on Asylum,[118] it was provided that:

1. Asylum may not be granted except in urgent cases and for the period of time strictly indispensable for the person who has sought asylum to ensure in some other way his safety.

2. Immediately upon granting asylum, the diplomatic agent . . . shall report the fact to the Minister for Foreign Relations of the State of the person who has secured asylum, or to the local administrative authority, if the act occurred outside the capital.

3. The government of the State may require that the refugee be sent out of the national territory within the shortest time possible; and the diplomatic agent of the country who has granted asylum may in turn require the guaranties necessary for the departure of the refugee with due regard to the inviolability of his person from the country.

4. Refugees shall not be landed in any point of the national territory nor in any place too near thereto.

---

[111] *Id.* at 361, as quoted in *id.,* at 226.

[112] INT'L CONF'S, 1942-1954, *supra* note 80, at 51.

[113] *Opened for signature* September 2, 1947, 62 Stat. 1681, T.I.A.S. 1838, 21 U.N.T.S. 77.

[114] C. FENWICK, *supra* note 79, at 145-46, 357-508.

[115] *Id.*

[116] *Id.*

[117] *Id.,* at 430-74.

[118] 132 L.N.T.S. 323 (1932-33).

5. While enjoying asylum, refugees shall not be allowed to perform acts contrary to the public peace.

6. States are under no obligation to defray expenses incurred by one granting asylum.[119]

In 1933, the Montevideo Conference of the American States, drafted a new convention on political asylum,[120] which provided that asylum would not be granted to persons accused of common crimes who had been prosecuted or sentenced, or to deserters from military service. The Convention also provided that political asylum is based on humanitarian considerations, not on reciprocity among States.

The Calvo Clause, adhered to by many Latin American states, is also important in international law. Incorporated into contracts between Central and Latin American Republics and aliens, it basically provided that disputes arising under the contract would be settled by recourse to local courts and remedies, and not by the intervention of the alien's government. According to Hackworth, the Calvo Clause is based on these two propositions: ". . . (1) that sovereign states, being free and independent, enjoy the right on a basis of equality, to freedom from 'interference of any sort by other states; (2) that aliens are not entitled to rights and privileges not accorded to nationals, and that therefore they may seek such redress for grievances only before the local authorities."[121]

According to Calvo:

> It is certain that aliens who establish themselves in a country have the same right to protection as nationals, but they cannot lay claim to a protection more extended. If they suffer any wrong, they ought to count on the government of the country prosecuting the delinquents, and they ought not claim any indemnity from the state to which the authors of the violence belong.[122]

§ 1-5.11. **Progress in International Law to the 1970's.** This section explores some of the weaknesses of traditional international law as it existed at the beginning of the 20th century, summarizes the progress subsequently made to solve them and indicates the general direction which may be followed in the future so that the

---

[119] *Id.*, as quoted in 2 HACKWORTH, DIGEST OF INTERNATIONAL LAW 647 (1941).

[120] SEVENTH INTERNATIONAL CONFERENCE OF THE AMERICAN STATES 168, 174 (1934).

[121] 5 HACKWORTH, DIGEST OF INTERNATIONAL LAW 635 (1941).

[122] 1 CALVO, LE DROIT INTERNATIONALE THEORIQUE ET PRATIQUE 350 (5th ed. 1896), as quoted in 5 HACKWORTH, DIGEST OF INTERNATIONAL LAW 635 (1941).

rule of law can be established throughout the considerably enlarged world community.

When the representatives of states met at the Hague in 1899 and in 1907, war was the recognized means of settling disputes. The legality of violence was perhaps the most fundamental weakness of the existing international law system. As a result of the Covenant of the League of Nations, the Pact of Paris, the Charter of the United Nations,[123] and other agreements, wars of aggression have been outlawed. The International Military Tribunal at Nuremberg declared that a war of aggression, or a war in violation of treaties is illegal in international law, and that those who plan and wage such wars commit an international crime. This decision, followed by the Tokyo Tribunal and other courts in the subsequent trials of war criminals, was approved by the United Nations, and has been codified by the International Law Commission.[124]

At the turn of the 20th century, no court existed to solve international disputes. And, it was only after World War I that a truly Permanent Court of International Justice was created, but, in World War II, it went out of existence along with the League of Nations. The Permanent Court of Arbitration, created at the first Hague Conference was not a real court, but rather a Secretariat which provided a panel of jurists from which arbitrators could be chosen. While the result was that more skilled arbitrators were available, the tribunals still remained strictly *ad hoc* in nature, without an international agreement enabling them to function on a permanent basis.

In 1945, a new International Court of Justice[125] was created as an integral part of the United Nations, but not as an autonomous entity, as was the prior World Court autonomous to the League.[126] Thus, the 127 states which are now members of the UN are automatically members of the Court. Submission of cases to the Court is basically voluntary, but the so-called Optional Clause grants compulsory jurisdiction to the Court for those states which

---

[123] For the text of the Charter of the United Nations, see FENWICK, *supra* note 14, at 688-709.

[124] R. WOETZEL, THE NUREMBERG TRIALS IN INTERNATIONAL LAW (London 1962); Woetzel, *Toward a Convention on Crimes Against Humanity,* in GENEVA CONF. 103-06.

[125] For the text of the Statute of the International Court of Justice, see C. FENWICK, *supra* note 14, at 710-21.

[126] It was this very autonomy of the first Permanent Court of International Justice vis-à-vis the League of Nations which allowed the United States to consider membership, a consideration which, by 1934, was abandoned.

sign it. Forty-five states have signed this Optional Clause but, for the most part, with disappointing limiting reservations. The development of the compulsory jurisdiction of the Court is an important task for the future. Compliance with the Court's judgment, excepting that in the *Corfu Channel* Case, has been admirable, and the quality and experience of the judges leaves little to be desired. However, the future will have to grapple with the question of how states can be induced to submit more of their cases to the Court for final decision, especially those involving important questions; with the problem of how to distinguish legal issues appropriate for adjudication from purely political questions; with the development and use of more regional courts or special chambers of the international Court; and with other means of strengthening respect for the Court and its authority.

One weakness of international law frequently pointed out is that international law is not "true" law since no international law-making body has created it. Before the 20th century, this weakness was compensated only partly by occasional, though important, law-making conferences and multilateral treaties. In the 20th century, especially since World War II, the enormous increase in the number of international organizations and agencies has resulted in new and widely-accepted rules of law in many fields, greatly supplementing the slow growth of international customary and conventional law.

Before the creation of the League of Nations, and the subsequent establishment of the United Nations, no international organization was continuously available to resolve international crises. These two organizations have moved toward filling this need, and have been harshly tested by crises which would otherwise have easily led to war. To be sure, the League of Nations seemed to be rather impotent in the Manchurian Affair of 1931, but this was the first time in history when aggression by a great power had been condemned by the community of nations. In the Ethiopian Affair of 1935-1936, the League of Nations again failed to restrain hostilities, although for the first time in history, an international body applied economic sanctions in an attempt to avoid war.

The UN has, in large part, learned from and avoided the failings of the League in providing for collective security. Korea was the first important test and marked an early stage in the development of collective security. Although a very large contribution to the forces used in Korea was made by one power, the United States, these forces were collected from many states and were under United Nations command. In the Suez case, two great powers,

France and England, for the first time in history, deferred to the judgment of an international body which condemned their resort to arms, and a United Nations international force was established to maintain peace after the withdrawal of foreign troops from the occupied areas. A representative United Nations emergency force has also played a useful role in the complicated Congo situation. But, the development of a United Nations peace or police force, adequate to meet any international crisis that can reasonably be anticipated, remains for the future.

Traditional international law aimed at governing relations among states as sovereign political units. Rights of individuals were protected, if at all, only by states. Diplomatic and consular agents have aided greatly in the protection of citizens abroad. However, claims by foreign citizens or states have had to be presented to arbitration tribunals, international courts, or mixed claims commissions by states. In the 20th century, the status of the individual[127] and the protection of his human rights have greatly improved with the community of nations taking an ever-increasing interest and role. It is a basic objective of the United Nations to protect the fundamental human rights of individuals, as evidenced by its Universal Declaration of Human Rights.[128] The economic and social rights of peoples throughout the world have received additional current information.[129] It remains for the future to develop adequate means by which these as well as other individual rights can be protected and enforced.

One of the principal weaknesses of international law is the absence or ineffectiveness of punitive sanctions. Without coercive authority the declarations, resolutions, and even the "legally" binding decisions of international bodies are observed only when states so choose. Although these rules are observed in the great majority of cases, the seriousness of their non-observance has now become a matter of survival. The advantages of compliance with international rules and principles are indeed very great, and increase as the cooperative efforts of states increase. For example, the paramount interest of states in air safety and in certain basic health requirements has impelled compliance with standards imposed by the international community. On the other hand, other important fields, such as preserving the earth's resources, and controlling over-

---

[127] W. GORMLEY, THE PROCEDURAL STATUS OF THE INDIVIDUAL BEFORE INTERNATIONAL AND SUPRANATIONAL TRIBUNALS (The Hague 1966).

[128] *See* Chapter 8 in this text on *Human Rights, infra.*

[129] *See Human Rights,* in GENEVA CONF. 398-442.

population and arbitrary violence, all of which are elemental factors in man's survival, have not yet become subjects of sufficient international cooperative efforts. The recent accelerating interest in international cooperative efforts on the environment, recovery of seabed resources and weather control indicate an ever-increasing reliance upon international community action to solve problems beyond the reach of any one nation.

Perhaps the greatest weakness of international law is its failure to devise adequate means to control force and violence. States have been reluctant to give this power to the United Nations or to regional organizations. As a consequence, peace continues to depend on the precariousness of what states consider to be their self-interest in complying with international law rules and principles. Strong nationalism, now in vogue, especially among the newly emerging states, and alleged demands of security by powerful states, at times, allure nations to act arbitrarily rather than cooperatively. However, world opinion is looking with increasing disfavor on the unbridled use of force by states in attempts to obtain their alleged "interests," and states cannot long ignore world opinion. It is, in fact, the crystallizing of world opinion in favor of its international law rules and legal institutions that offers the greatest promise for a lasting world peace.

SECTION C: SOURCES

§ 1-6. Sources of International Law

Article 38 of the Statute of the International Court of Justice, sets out the sources of international law upon which that Court may rely in arriving at its decisions:

> 1. The Court, whose function is to decide in accordance with international law such disputes as are submitted to it, shall apply:
>> a. international conventions, whether general or particular, establishing rules expressly recognized by the contesting states;
>> b. international custom, as evidence of a general practice accepted as law;
>> c. the general principles of law recognized by civilized nations;
>> d. subject to the provisions of Article 59, judicial decisions and the teachings of most highly qualified publicists of the various nations, as subsidiary means for the determination of rules of law.

2. This provision shall not prejudice the power of the Court to decide a case *ex aequo et bono* (in justice and fairness, according to equity and conscience) if the parties agree thereto.[130]

Article 59 of the Statute further provides that "The decision of the Court has no binding force except between the parties and in respect of that particular case."[131] Thus, in any particular case, there are six main sources of international law; custom, treaties and conventions, writings of authorities, judicial decisions, general principles of international law, and equity.

Both the Permanent Court of International Justice and the International Court of Justice have issued reports of judgments, advisory opinions, and orders; the first covering the period 1923-1939, and the second, 1947 to date. Arguments and memorials are found in a separate series. The United Nations has also issued the reports of international arbitral awards for the period from 1932 to 1939. The International Military Tribunal at Nuremberg published an edited stenographic report of the proceedings at that trial and the documents submitted in evidence, 1947-1949, in 42 volumes, with index.

In recent years international law and organization have expanded in an unprecedented manner.[132] A vast body of law and legal

---

[130] I.C.J. STAT. art. 38.

[131] *Id.* art. 59.

[132] J. AMERICANO, THE NEW FOUNDATION OF INTERNATIONAL LAW (New York 1947); J. BRIERLY, THE OUTLOOK FOR INTERNATIONAL LAW (Oxford 1944); J. Castanada, *The Underdeveloped Nations and the Development of International Law,* 5 INT'L ORG. 33-49 (1961); Friedmann, *Work Paper on Some Fundamental Changes in the Structure of Contemporary International Law,* WORLD PEACE THROUGH LAW: THE WASHINGTON CONFERENCE 528-48 (1967) [hereinafter cited as WASHINGTON CONF.]; FRIEDMANN, THE CHANGING STRUCTURE OF INTERNATIONAL LAW (London 1964); Friedmann, *Half a Century of International Law,* 50 VA. L.REV. 1333 (1964); L. GARCIA ARIAS, ESTUDIOS DE HISTORIA Y DOCTRINA DEL DERECHO INTERNACIONAL (Madrid 1964); C. JENKS, THE COMMON LAW OF MANKIND (New York 1963); R. JENNINGS, THE PROGRESS OF INTERNATIONAL LAW (New York 1960); Jessup, *The Use of International Law,* THE THOMAS M. COOLEY LECTURES (Univ. of Mich. 1959); J. KUNZ, THE CHANGING LAW OF NATIONS (Ohio State Univ. 1968). O. LISSITZYN, INTERNATIONAL LAW, TODAY AND TOMORROW (New York 1965); McDougal & Reisman, *The Changing Structure of International Law . . .,* 65 COLUM. L.REV. 810 (1965); A. McNAIR, THE EXPANSION OF INTERNATIONAL LAW (Jerusalem 1962); McWhinney, *Changing International Law Method and Objectives in the Era of the Soviet-Western Détente,* 59 AJIL 1 (1965); McWhinney, *The "New" Countries and the "New" International Law . . .,* 60 AJIL 1 (1966); Muskhat, *Les Caracteres Généraux du Droit International Contemporain,* 69 REV. GEN. DR. INT'L PUB. 39-75 (1965); M. NAWAZ, AN INQUIRY INTO THE HISTORICAL DEVELOPMENT OF CERTAIN CARDINAL PRINCIPLES OF INTERNATIONAL LAW (Leyden 1966); Oppenheimer, *El Derecho Internacional en el Renacimiento,* 2 REV. JUR. U. INT'AM. P.R. 33-

(Continued)

institutions has grown up through the efforts of the United Nations, the International Court of Justice, the International Law Commission, the UN Specialized Agencies, and many regional organizations. Many new, developing states in Africa and Asia, representing different social, religious, and cultural traditions and having interests and objectives differing from those of more industrialized Western States, have become members of the United Nations and are now participating actively and significantly in the world community. All of these are significant factors in the formulation of UN decisions, and in the expansion of the activities and role of international organizations in such fields as health, communications, atomic energy, labor, education, and international trade and investment. Most of these fields formerly belonged to domestic law, or simply did not exist, and when they became an area of international concern, international organizations formulated rules and norms of conduct usually in treaties which have today become part of expanding international law. Such treaties inevitably derive their substantive law from private law systems, and from the general principles of law recognized by the community of nations. International law is expanding rapidly to meet the demands of an interdependent world community.

§ 1-6.1. **Custom.** Custom is a rule of conduct resting on general approval, and developed out of habitual practice technically called *usage.* As an illustration of evolution of custom out of usage, consider the following. Between several nations some particular course of conduct arises out of necessity or convenience. Its observance by several nations is purely discretionary; other practices could just as well be followed. As time goes on, adherence to the usage is repeated and it becomes stronger as more nations observe it. Occasionally it is violated, but these occur less frequently until finally, the usage commands a general consensus among nations. At this point, it is no longer considered usage, but has become custom. It is now a rule of conduct resting on general approval. However, two difficulties remain with respect to using custom as a source of international law: proving exactly what the custom is, and determining exactly at what stage custom can be said to have

---

48 (1965); Pellicer de Brody, *¿Un Nuevo Derecho Internacional?* 30 FORD INT'L 128 (1967); B. ROLING, INTERNATIONAL LAW IN AN EXPANDED WORLD (Amsterdam 1960); G. SCHWARZENBERGER, THE FRONTIERS OF INTERNATIONAL LAW (London 1962); J. SYATAUW, SOME NEWLY ESTABLISHED ASIAN STATES AND THE DEVELOPMENT OF INTERNATIONAL LAW (The Hague 1961); W. TUNG, INTERNATIONAL LAW IN AN ORGANIZING WORLD (New York 1968); Q. WRIGHT, CONTEMPORARY INTERNATIONAL LAW: A BALANCE SHEET (New York 1955).

become authoritative. While now codified in Conventions, The Law of the Sea and Law of Diplomatic Immunity are examples of customary law of worldwide acceptance.

The reliance on custom as a source of international law was well illustrated in *The Pacquet e Habana* Case[133] which came before the United States Supreme Court in 1900. The Court ruled that the United States Government was liable for the capture of Cuban fishing boats sailing under the Spanish flag, basing its decision on the customary law rule that coastal fishing vessels and their crews are exempt as prizes of war. This rule was codified by Hague Convention XI of 1907.

Two problems arise in borderline cases concerning custom as international law: one, the difficulty of proving what the custom is; and two, the difficulty of determining exactly at what stage custom can be said to have become authoritative.

§ 1-6.2. **Treaties and Conventions.** The second source of international law, treaties and conventions, does not present these problems, since they are normally written and expressly agreed to by the parties to the proceedings. By acting as a modification of customary law as it affects the signatories, the treaties or conventions are the binding law with respect to those parties. If the treaty or convention were generally accepted by other nations, it could itself become custom. But the major problem still remains: a treaty or convention is only binding on those who adhere to it; and it can not be enforced against those who do not become a party or who only become a limited party to it. This is sometimes referred to as the "rule of unanimity."

> The general body of states ... . has no machinery . . . which allow(s) a majority of outvote a dissenting minority and to pass measures into international law which will then become binding on all whether they have agreed or not.[134]

Brierly goes on to stress, however, that the "rule of unanimity":

> does not mean that the minority has a veto power over the majority, but only that it has a right to keep itself out of a convention if it wishes. The distinction is important, because many international reforms can produce good results even though not every state accepts them. Of course, the adhesion of a particular state or states may be sometimes so important that a change is not worth making which it or they do not accept.[135]

[133] 175 U.S. 677, 44 L. Ed. 320, 20 S. Ct. 290 (1899).

[134] J. BRIERLY, THE OUTLOOK FOR INTERNATIONAL LAW 99 (Oxford 1944).

[135] *Id.*

Since treaties constitute one of the most important sources of international law to date, treaty collections have a very great value. Many states publish their own treaty series. A private listing of treaty collections was prepared by D.P. Myers in 1922, entitled "Manual of Collections of Treaties and Collections Relating to Treaties." The *United Nations Treaty Series* contains the texts of all treaties which have been registered with the Secretariat. Since 1946, 626 volumes have appeared, and there are indexes for 550 of these. The *League of Nations Treaty Series*, 1921-1946, contained 205 volumes and indexes. The Council of Europe's *European Treaty Series,* with volumes from 1949 to date, contains the texts of postwar European treaties. The Carnegie Endowment for International Peace published a collection of the texts of multi-partite international agreements, known as *International Legislation.* It was compiled by Judge Manley O. Hudson, with accompanying notes, in nine volumes, 1931-1950. G.F. von Martens compiled a collection of earlier treaties, 1791-1943, in 145 volumes. A valuable current publication by Amos J. Peaslee, entitled *International Governmental Organizations, Constitutional Documents* (2 vols. 1961), gives treaty texts as well as organizational documents of many intergovernmental organizations.

§ 1-6.3. **Writings of Authorities.**   Often cited as a source of international customary law, these scholarly writings of authorities set forth "rules" of international law, although they are not binding unless the parties to a dispute agree to be bound by them. These writings are also used to reinforce judicial decisions, since they clarify the status of customary law. Many such sources are cited throughout this volume.

International law journals contain valuable source materials, including articles, notes and comments, judicial decisions involving international law questions, book reviews and notices, and official documents. However, only a few international law journals were published prior to the 20th century.[136] During this century almost two dozen more international law journals and reviews have

---

[136]REVUE DE DROIT INTERNATIONAL ET DE LÉGISLATION COMPARÉE (1869-); the English JOURNAL OF COMPARATIVE LEGISLATION AND INTERNATIONAL LAW (1896-1951); the French JOURNAL DU DROIT INTERNATIONAL (Clunet, in French only until 1945; since then in French and English) (1874-   ); REVUE GÉNÉRALE DE DROIT INTERNATIONAL PUBLIC (1894-   ); the German ARCHIV DES OFFENTLICHEN RECHTS (1886-   ); and Niemeyer's ZEITSCHRIFT FÜR INTERNATIONALES RECHT (1891-   ); the Italian REVISTA DELL' INSTITUTO GIURIDICO INTERNAZIONALE (1897-   ).

appeared.[137] Since World War II, several valuable yearbooks and annuals have been made available.[138] These publications not only add to the basic information and analysis in the field, but evidence an increasing interest in and need for more analysis and better information services.

[137] The Argentine REVISTA ARGENTINA DE DERECHO INTERNACIONAL (1920-1922, 1938-   ); the AMERICAN JOURNAL OF INTERNATIONAL LAW (1907-   ); the AUSTRIAN ZEITSCHRIFT FÜR ÖFFENTLICHES RECHT (1919-1942); continued as the OSTERREICHISCHES ZEITSCHRIFT FÜR ÖFFENT-RECHT (1946-   ); the COLUMBIA UNIVERSITY JOURNAL OF TRANSNATIONAL LAW (formerly the INTERNATIONAL LAW BULLETIN) (1961-   ); the CORNELL INTERNATIONAL LAW JOURNAL (1968-   ); the Cuban REVISTA DE DERECHO INTERNACIONAL (1922-   ); the Dutch TIJDSCHRIFT VOOR INTERNATIONAL RECHT (contains many articles in English) (1953-   ); the ENGLISH INTERNATIONAL AND COMPARATIVE LAW QUARTERLY, which absorbed the Grotius Society publications (1952-   ); the French REVUE GÉNÉRALE DE DROIT INTERNATIONAL (1927-   ); the REVUE INTERNATIONALE FRANCAISE DU DROIT DES GENS (1935-1940, 1947-   ); the German ZEITSCHRIFT FÜR AUSLANDISCHES ÖFFENTLICHES RECHT UND VÖLKERRECHT (1929-1942, 1950-   ), the Greek REVUE HELLÉNIQUE DE DROIT INTERNATIONAL (1948-   ); the HARVARD INTERNATIONAL LAW JOURNAL (formerly BULLETIN OF THE HARVARD INTERNATIONAL LAW CLUB and later the HARVARD INTERNATIONAL LAW CLUB JOURNAL) (1959-   ); the Indian JOURNAL OF INTERNATIONAL LAW (1960-   ); the Italian REVISTA DI DIRITTO INTERNAZIONALE (1906-1943, 1953-   ); the Korean JOURNAL OF INTERNATIONAL LAW (1956-   ); the Lebanese REVUE DE DROIT INTERNATIONAL POUR LE MOYEN-ORIENT (1951-   ); NEW YORK UNIVERSITY JOURNAL OF INTERNATIONAL LAW AND POLITICS (1968-   ); the Norwegian TIDESSKRIFT FOR INTERNATIONAL RET (1930-   ); the Peruvian REVISTA PERUANA DE DERECHO INTERNACIONAL (1941-   ); the SOUTHERN AFRICAN COMPARATIVE AND INTERNATIONAL LAW JOURNAL (1968-   ); The Spanish REVISTA ESPAÑOLA DE DERECHO INTERNACIONAL (1941-   ); the Swiss REVUE DE DROIT INTERNATIONAL, DE SCIENCES DIPLOMATIQUES ET POLITIQUES (1923-   ); and DIE FRIDENS-WARTE (1934-   ); the TEXAS INTERNATIONAL LAW FORUM (1965-   ); the United Arab Republic's REVUE EGYPTIENNE DE DROIT INTERNATIONAL (1945-   ); the VIRGINIA JOURNAL OF INTERNATIONAL LAW (formerly the JOURNAL OF THE JOHN BASSETT MOORE SOCIETY) (1961-   ). For a further listing of International law periodicals, see W. GOULD, supra note 14, at 743-44. See also list of abbreviations, p.   , supra.

[138] THE UNITED NATIONS YEAR BOOK (1946-   ); THE YEARBOOK OF THE INTERNATIONAL COURT OF JUSTICE (1946-   ); the EUROPEAN YEARBOOK (1955-   ); the INTER-AMERICAN JURIDICAL YEAR BOOK (1948-   ); the ANNUAIRE DE L'INSTITUT DE DROIT INTERNATIONAL (1875-   ); the BRITISH YEAR BOOK OF INTERNATIONAL LAW (1921-   ); the Czech YEARBOOK OF INTERNATIONAL LAW (Hlidka Mexinárodniko Práva) (1942-   ); the ANNUAIRE FRANCAIS DE DROIT INTERNATIONAL (1955-   ); the German YAHRBUCH FÜR INTERNATIONALES UND AUSLANDISCHES ÖFFENTLICHES RECHT (some articles appear in English and French) (1948-   ); the Guatemalan REVISTO DE LA ASOCIACIÓN DE DERECHO INTERNACIONAL (published annually) (1954-   ); the JAPANESE YEARBOOK OF INTERNATIONAL LAW (1957-   ); the JEWISH YEARBOOK OF INTERNATIONAL LAW (1948-   ); the Spanish ANUARIO DE LA ASOCIACIÓN FRANCISCO DE VITORIA (1927-   ), and the ANUARIO HISPAUO-LUZO-AMERICANO DEL DERECHO INTERNACIONAL (1964-   ); the Soviet YEAR BOOK OF INTERNATIONAL LAW (1958-   ); the ANNUAIRE DE L'ASSOCIATION YUGO-SLAVE DE DROIT INTERNATIONAL (1931-   ). See also March, Book Review, 11 INT'L & COMP. L.Q. 1255-56 (1962).

International Law Digests contain an immense store of information on the many subjects which they cover. They also show the changing emphasis on international law concepts and the expansion of the international law fields. In the United States the following Digests have been published: J.L. Cadwalader, *Digest of the Public Opinions of the Attorneys-General, and of the Leading Decisions of the Federal Courts, with Reference to International Law, Treaties and Kindred Subjects* (1877); F. Wharton, *A Digest of the International Law of the United States* (3 Vols. 1940-1944); M.M. Whiteman, *Digest of International Law* (in process of publication, 11 volumes issued to date). In England: *A British Digest of International Law* (Parry, ed., in process of publication, 5 volumes issued to date). In 1962, a five volume French *Repertoire de la Pratique Francaise en Matiere de Droit International Public* (A.C. Kiss, ed.) was published.

Other useful sources include: the *Proceedings of the American Society of International Law*, The Hague *Recueil des Cours de l'Academie de Droit International*, the *Transactions of the Grotius Society*, and the International Bar Association. The volumes containing the lectures and research papers of experts in international law and committee reports of the World Peace Through Law Conferences in Athens (1963), Washington (1965), Geneva (1967), and Bangkok (1969) where the world's leading international law experts have compiled the status of the law on most of the currently important subjects as of the dates these conferences were held are another important source. Articles and reports of the International Law Association, the Institut de Droit International, and the Union International des Avocats are of much value. Since 1920, the Hague Academy of International Law has published in French in its *Recueil* the lectures of outstanding specialists in international law from many countries. In 1915, the Grotius Society was founded to promote the study of public and private international law in Great Britain; the papers read before the Society are published annually. The International Law Association and the Institut de Droit International were both founded in Belgium in 1873 to develop and codify international law. The International Law Association was known until 1895 as the "Association for the Reform and Codification of the Law of Nations."[139]

Prior to World War I, no large research programs in the field of international law were undertaken by groups of scholars. From

---

[139] *See* Scott, *The Institute of International Law*, 21 AJIL 716-36 (1927); Watts, *Forty Years of the Grotius Society*, 42 GROTIUS SOCIETY TRANSACTIONS 193 (1957).

1929-1939, the so-called Research in International Law, sponsored by Harvard University, consisted of drafts prepared by committees of distinguished international lawyers on more than a dozen subjects in the field.[140] These publications are valuable contributions to the substantive field and offer to the searchers of source material many useful bibliographical references. Since World War II, public and private research organizations have been studying many special problems such as disarmament and the strengthening of the United Nations.

§ 1-6.4. **Judicial Decisions.** In common law nations, judicial decisions and precedents usually merit greater weight than authoritative writings, but in civil law nations, where municipal law is not based primarily on precedents, this attitude is not shared. The result of mixing these two different judicial traditions in international law adds further to its complexity. It also enriches its intellectual content.

Article 38 of the Statute of the International Court of Justice lists judicial decisions dealing with questions of international law as a "subsidiary means for the determination of rules of law." Judge J. B. Moore in his dissenting opinion in the *Lotus* Case[141] discussed this article of the Statute:

> These directions merely conform to the well-settled rule that international tribunals, whether permanent or temporary, sitting in judgment between independent States, are not to treat the judgments of the courts of one State on questions of international law as binding on other States, but, while giving to such judgments the weight due to judicial expressions of the view taken in the particular country, are to follow them as authority only so far as they may be found to be in harmony with international law, the law common to all countries.[142]

Thus, precedents are not regarded as binding authority in international law, although court decisions help to form international custom by showing what particular courts, either municipal (*i.e.*, the courts of nation-states) or international, have accepted as inter-

---

[140] In 1929, on Nationality, Responsibility of States for Injuries to Aliens, and Territorial Waters; in 1932, on Diplomatic Privileges and Immunities, Legal Position and Function of Consuls, Competence of Courts in Regard to Foreign States, Piracy, and Piracy Laws of Various Countries; in 1935, on Extradition, Jurisdiction with Respect to Crime and the Law of Treaties; and in 1939, on Judicial Assistance, the Rights and Duties of Neutral States in Naval and Aerial War, and the Rights and Duties of States in Case of Aggression.

[141] [1927] P.C.I.J., ser. A, No. 10, at 65; 2 M. HUDSON, WORLD COURT REPORTS 71 (Washington 1935).

[142] [1927] P.C.I.J. ser. A, No. 10, at 74.

national law.[143]   Furthermore, courts will receive with respect the decisions of other courts, even domestic ones insofar as they are based on a law common to all countries.   Receiving with respect, however, is not the same as receiving as authority.   Previous court decisions are not binding on later courts, and the principle of *stare decisis* cannot be said to operate generally in international law.

§ 1-6.5. **Equity.** Principles of equity have, upon occasion, been applied in deciding international legal disputes.[144] A problem often arises, however, as to whether in international law, equity is distinct from law.[145] The provision in Article 38 of the Statute of the International Court of Justice (1945) to decide a "cause *ex aequo et bono* (according to justice and fairness) if the parties agree thereto,[146] sets up a statutory, equitable standard which, although never used by the International Court of Justice in deciding a case, has been occasionally used by other international tribunals to decide cases.[147] Furthermore, the difference between equity and decisions made *ex aequo et bono* is not clear in the present state of international law.   And, therefore, an international court using either the sources of international law laid down in Article 38 of the Statute of the International Court of Justice, or the general principles of international law to decide cases, cannot easily determine the exact rule equity should play in its decisions.   Even with these limitations, equity is still a possible source of international law.   It is misleading to make a very sharp distinction between law and equity since the principles of each are designed to achieve justice.

§ 1-6.6. **General Principles of International Law.**[148] The existence and importance of general principles of international law to the main

---

[143]For examples of the attention paid by courts to prior international decisions, see I. G. SCHWARZENBERGER, INTERNATIONAL LAW 10-13, 463-64 (2d ed. 1949).

[144]Cases include: Germany v. Portugal, 8 RECUEIL DES DECISIONS DES TRIBUNAUX ARBITRAUX MIXTES 409, 413; Cayuga Indians (Great Britain v. United States), NIELSEN REP. 203, 307 (1926); NIELSEN REP. 273-86, 305-06 opposes decision in case; also discusses "equity" in international law and in international arbitration.

[145]For a discussion of the problem, see Judge Hudson's decision in P.C.I.J. Ser. A/B, No. 70 at 73, 76-78 (1937); 4 M. HUDSON, WORLD COURT REPORTS 231-33 (1943).

[146]For a general discussion of the meaning of *ex aequo et bona,* see M. HABICHT, POWER OF THE INTERNATIONAL JUDGE TO GIVE A DECISION "EX AEQUO ET BONO" (London 1935); H. LAUTERPACHT, FUNCTION OF LAW IN THE INTERNATIONAL COMMUNITY 313-28 (Oxford 1933).

[147]The Chaco Conflict (Bolivia v. Paraguay), 3 U.N.R.I.A.A. 1817 (1938), 33 AJIL 180 (1939); Case of James Pugh, 3 U.N.R.I.A.A. 143 (1933); Guatemala-Honduras Boundary Arbitration, 2 U.N.R.I.A.A. 1307; ANNUAL DIGEST, case 46 (1933-34).

[148]*See also* Agarwala, *General Principles of International Law,* in ATHENS CONF. 735-38; Brohi, *Basic Principles of International Law,* in *id.* at 738-55; Brown, *The Ultimate*

(Continued)

body of international law have been much discussed. These discussions have been especially crucial considering the diversity of municipal (that is, the law of Nation-States) juridical systems. T. E. Holland wrote that:

> The law of Nations is but Private law 'writ large.' It is an application to political communities of those legal ideas which were originally applied to the relations of individuals. Its leading distinctions are therefore naturally those with which Private law has long ago rendered us familiar. In International, as in Private law, we are concerned with the 'Persons' for whose sake rights are recognized; with the rights thus recognized; and with the 'Protection' by which those rights are made effective. We have a 'law of Persons'; a 'Substantive law', which sets forth and explains the rights of those persons; and an 'Adjective Law', which describes the Procedure by which redress is to be obtained when those rights are violated.[149]

Completely accepting this approach to international law would present many problems. Can any private municipal law appropriately be applied in solving international problems? Or conversely should international law be applied freely in municipal courts?

There are three traditional schools of thought on the relationship of international to municipal law. This volume does not intend to resolve their differences but only to make the reader aware of the problems inherent in each.

A positivist's approach would be that international law is nothing more than positive, moral obligations. According to this position, international law is really not law at all, but moral obligations which attach themselves to an international situation when the parties find them appropriate. The dualists, on the other hand, would argue that an international law exists, but that it is completely separate from municipal law, since the arena of each is separate, making it difficult to explain the relationship between

---

Authority of the General Principles of Law, in *id.* at 756-57; Castrén, *The Fundamental Principles of International Law,* in *id.* at 757-59; Cheng, *General Principles of Law as a Subject for International Codification,* 3 CURRENT LEG. PROB. 35 (1951); CHENG, GENERAL PRINCIPLES OF LAW AS APPLIED BY INTERNATIONAL COURTS AND TRIBUNALS (1953); Cohen, *Basic Principles of International Law,* in ATHENS CONF. 759-71; Despotopoulos, *Co-existence as a Principle of International Law,* in *id.* at 771-72; Kopelmanas, 43 REV. GÉN. DR. INT'L PUB. 285 (1936); McNair, *The General Principles of Law Recognized by Civilized Nations,* in 33 BR. Y.B. INT'L L. 1 (1957); Schlesinger, *Research on the General Principles of Law Recognized by Civilized Nations,* 51 AJIL 734 (1957); Verdross, ANNUAIRE DE L'INSTITUT DE DROIT INTERNATIONAL 283 (1932); Verdross, *Hague Academy of International Law,* 52 RECUEIL DES COURS 191 (1935).

[149] T. HOLLAND, STUDIES IN INTERNATIONAL LAW 152 (1898).

the two systems.   The dualist's answer is to assert that when municipal law incorporates a principle of international law, that principle itself becomes municipal law.   This answer is not very satisfactory, however, since all it does is no more than keep the labels straight.   Furthermore, a case like *the Paquette Habana*[150] which applies a general principle of law common to both legal systems would seem to negate the value of making the classifications required by the dualist's approach.   The monists, on the other hand, would contend that international and municipal law are part of one complete system with international law acting as the basic foundation of all national systems.   This, however, results in a problem common to most Aristotelian philosophical systems, in that it is impossible to draw a line between the general and the particulars, between the general system of international law and the particular systems of municipal law.   In this case, the international legal system would break down when faced with a problem where international concern and national interest conflict.

A fourth approach has been suggested by Professor McDougal[151] who considers international law as an "interrelated power process." He would contend that where international and municipal are identical, it is because the values are identical, and where they differ, it is because the values and interests of the participants in each differ.[152]

In summary, it can be said that although Holland's approach might be overly simplified, international courts can still abstract and apply other principles from municipal law that are common to international law as well.

§ 1-6.6.1 The General Principles of Law Recognized by Nations.[153]

---

[150] 175 U.S. 677, 44 L. Ed. 320, 20 S. Ct. 290 (1899). *See also* McCulloch v. Marineros de Honduras, 372 U.S. 10, 83 S. Ct. 671, 9 L. Ed. 2d 547 (1963).

[151] McDougal, *International Law, Power and Policy,* 82 RECUEIL DES COURS 137, 167 (1953).

[152] *Id.*

[153] *See generally* Bourquin, *Régles Générales du Droit de la Paix,* 35 RECUEIL DES COURS 67-80 (1931); B. CHENG, GENERAL PRINCIPLES OF LAW AS APPLIED BY INTERNATIONAL COURTS AND TRIBUNALS (London 1953); P. GRAPIN, VALEUR INTERNATIONALE DES PRINCIPES GENERAUX DU DROIT: CONTRIBUTION À L'ETUDE DE L'ARTICLE 38, ALINÉA 3, DU STATUT DE LA COUR PERMANENTE DE JUSTICE INTERNATIONALE (Paris 1934); M. HABICHT, POST-WAR TREATIES FOR THE PACIFIC SETTLEMENT OF INTERNATIONAL DISPUTES (Cambridge 1931); C. JENKS, THE COMMON LAW OF MANKIND (New York 1958); A. LARSON, WHY NATIONS DISAGREE (Louisiana 1961); H. LAUTERPACHT, PRIVATE LAW SOURCES AND ANALOGIES OF INTERNATIONAL LAW (London 1927); H. LAUTERPACHT,

(Continued)

The three principal sources of law relied upon by international

THE FUNCTION OF LAW IN THE INTERNATIONAL COMMUNITY (Oxford 1933); H. LAUTERPACHT, THE DEVELOPMENT OF LAW BY THE INTERNATIONAL COURT (London 1958); Mann, *Reflections on a Commercial Law of Nations,* 33 BR.Y.B.INT'L L. 20-50 (1957); McNair, *The General Principles of Law Recognized by Civilized Nations, id.* at 1-19; Permanent Court of International Justice: Advisory Committee of Jurists, PROCÉS-VERBAUX OF THE PROCEEDINGS OF THE COMMITTEE (June 16-July 24, 1920) [hereinafter cited as PROCÉS-VERBAUX]; Ripert, *Les Régles de Droit Civil Applicables aux Rapports Internationaux,* 44 RECUEIL DES COURS 569-663 (1933); Verdross, *Les Principe Géneraux de Droit dans la Jurisprudence Interdationale,* 52 RECUEIL DES COURS 191-251 (1935).

Other useful references are: Abdel-Wahab, *Reflections on the General Principles of Law,* L'EGYPTE CONTEMPORAINE 30 (1963); Agarwala, *General Principles of Law Recognized by Civilized Nations,* in WASH. CONF. 547-55; E. ALACALÁ CARRERA, LOS PRINCIPIOS GENERALES DE DERECHO COMO FUENTE DE DERECHO INTERNATIONALE (Mexico 1948); Pallieri, *I Principi Generali del Diritto Riconosciuti dalle Nazioni Civili' nell'art,* in 38 DELLO STATUTO DELLA CORTE PERMANENTE DE GIUSTIZIA INTERNAZIONALE (Torino 1931); D. BALLEREAU, LA COUTOME DANS LA JURISPRUDENCE INTERNATIONALE (Paris 1941); Cheng, *The Meaning and Scope of Art. 38(1)(c) of the Statute of the International Court of Justice,* 38 GROTIUS SOCIETY TRANSACTIONS FOR THE YEAR 1952, at 125, 128 (1953); Corbett, *The Search for General Principles of Law,* 47 VA.L.REV. 811-26 (1961); G. FINCH, THE SOURCES OF MODERN INTERNATIONAL LAW (Washington 1937); Friedmann, *The Uses of "General Principles" in the Development of International Law,* 57 AJIL 279-99 (1963); Friedmann, *One Half a Century of International Law,* 50 VA. L. REV. 1333-58 (1964); L. FULLER, ANATOMY OF THE LAW (New York 1968); F. GARCÍA-AMADOR, INTRODUCCIÓN AL ESTUDIO DEL DERECHO CONTEMPORANEO 48-50 (Madrid 1959); E. HAMBRO, THE CASE LAW OF THE INTERNATIONAL COURT (Leydon 1952); Hazard, *Legal Research on "Peaceful Coexistence,"* 51 AJIL 63-71 (1957); M. HUDSON, THE PERMANENT COURT OF INTERNATIONAL JUSTICE (New York 1943); Institut de Droit International, *Les Principes Géneraux de Droit comme Source du Droit des Gens,* 37 INST. DR. INT'L ANN. (Rapport de M. Verdross at 283-98, Observations de MM. Le Fur, Nippold, Joster, Brierly, Borchard, Salvioli, Fedezzi, de la Barra, et de la Briére at 298-319, Rapport final de M. Verdross at 320-28); Jalet, *The Quest for the General Principles of Law Recognized by Civilized Nations,* 10 U.C.L.A. L. REV. 1041-86 (1963); P. JESSUP, TRANSNATIONAL LAW (New York 1956); M. KAPLAN & N. KATZENBACH, SOURCES OF INTERNATIONAL LAW (New York 1961); Lorenz, *General Principles of Law: Their Elaboration in the Court of Justice of the European Communities,* 13 AM. J. COMP. L. 1-29 (1964); McNair, *The General Principles of Law Recognized by Civilized Nations,* 33 BR. Y.B. INT'L L. 1-19 (1957); Moreno, *General Principles of International Law,* in ATHENS CONF. 773-79 (1965); Newman, *The Principles of Equity as a Source of Law,* 1 ISRAEL L. REV. 616-31 (1966); N. SCERNI, I PRINCIPI GENERALI DI DIRITTO RICONOSCIUTI DALLE NAZIONI CIVILI NELLA GIURISPRUDENZA DELLA CORTE PERMANENTE DE GIUSTIZIA INTERNAZIONALE (Padua 1932); Schlesinger, *Research on the General Principles of Law Recognized by Civilized Nations,* 51 AJIL 734-53 (1957); Schlesinger, *The General Principles of Contract Law - Report on a Study of the Common Core of Legal Systems,* in ATHENS CONF. 779-99 (1965); G. SCHWARZENBERGER, INTERNATIONAL LAW IN NATIONAL COURTS (New York 1932); Scott, *The Project of a Permanent Court of International Justice,* in THE ENDOWMENT (Washington 1926); A. STUYT, THE GENERAL PRINCIPLES OF LAW AS APPLIED BY INTERNATIONAL TRIBUNALS (The Hague 1946); de Visscher, *Contribution à l'Étude des Sources de Droit International,* 3 RECUEIL EÉNY 389-99 (Paris 1936); Wolff, *Les Principes Géneraux du Droit Applicables dan les Rapports Internationaux,* 36 RECUEIL DES COURS 479-550 (1931).

Many additional references are found in the footnotes and bibliographies contained in many of the above sources, in particular in the books by Bin Cheng and Wilfred Jenks.

courts are treaties,[154] customs and the general principles of law recognized by nations. Judicial decisions and the teachings of highly qualified publicists constitute a fourth source and are binding only between the parties in respect to a particular case; they are used as an auxiliary means of determining the rules of law. Courts also decide cases *ex aequo et bono* (in justice and fairness according to equity and conscience) if the parties agree. These sources, already a part of international law,[155] were codified in Article 38 of the Statute of the Permanent Court of International Justice, and later, with minor changes, became Article 38 of the Statute of the International Court of Justice.

§ 1-6.6.2 Article 38 of the Statute of the International Court of Justice.[156] In order to provide the necessary requirements of organi-

[154] In the early development of international law, and in fact until the twentieth century, its principal rules were supplied by custom. These rules had their origin in the practice of a single state or of a small number of states. Examples are the laws of the sea and the laws relating to diplomacy. Custom, as a source of law, however, had the unfortunate defect of being uncertain in nature and slow in growth. Without adequate international judicial machinery to determine when custom hardened into law, states were at a loss to know how many acts it took to create a custom which should be observed as law. The small number of sufficiently similar cases to constitute a precedent and the considerable period of time which often lapsed between these cases resulted in the failure of international law to keep up with the rapid new developments in international relations which it aimed to govern. The basic documents which should have supplied the evidence of custom were inaccessible, and the writers on international law, although supplying certain evidences of custom, often stated what they thought the law should be rather than what it actually was.

Later in the development of international law and particularly since the beginning of the nineteenth century, treaties have become an important source of international law. However, both bilateral and multilateral treaties have important weaknesses. Bilateral treaties regulate certain special relations between two states rather than create binding law for the community of nations. And multilateral treaties, though often referred to as *law-making treaties,* have until recently been relatively few in number and hence inevitably have failed to fulfill the needs of a rapidly growing international society.

Since the creation of the United Nations, the number of multilateral treaties has greatly increased. *See* World Peace Through Law Center Pamphlet Series, MULTILATERAL TREATIES, CONVENTIONS, PROTOCOLS AND AGREEMENTS OF THE UNITED NATIONS AND THE SPECIALIZED AGENCIES No. 7 (Geneva 1967). *See also* the Library of the Peace Palace at the Hague, *Current Problems of the Law of Treaties,* BIBLIOGRAPHY 83-87 (1965).

[155] According to the Positivist School, treaties and custom are the only sources to which the courts have recourse. For the view of the Positivist School, see Bourquin, *Règles Générales du Droit de la Paix,* 35 RECUEIL DES COURS 67-80 (1931), who also presents the views of Anzilotti Triepel, Delsen and Verdross.

[156] Article 38 of the Statute of the International Court of Justice provides:
1. The Court, whose function is to decide in accordance with international law such disputes as are submitted to it, shall apply:
(a) international conventions, whether general or particular, establishing rules expressly recognized by the contesting states;
(b) international custom, as evidence of a general practice accepted as law;

(Continued)

zation, jurisdiction and procedure for the Permanent Court of International Justice, the Council of the League of Nations, in February 1920, appointed an Advisory Committee of ten distinguished jurists to prepare plans for such a court. This Committee drafted a proposed statute which was later approved, with some changes, by the League Council. The discussions of the members of the Committee throw considerable light on the views that led to the formulation of Article 38 of the Statute, which sets out the law to be applied by the Court.[157] De Lapradelle (France) liked the short wording ". . .the Court shall judge in accordance with law, justice, and equity, . . ." holding that the duty to define law ". . . must be left to the judges."[158] A proposal submitted to the Committee by Five Neutral Powers directed the Court to apply the rule of law which it thought should be applied in default of an existing rule; but Hagerup (Norway) felt that ". . . perhaps [this proposal] goes too far, . . ."[159] and the Committee, fearing a grant of legislative power to the Court, turned down the proposal. Root (United States) originally felt that, as a practical matter ". . . in order to induce States to accept the establishment of compulsory jurisdiction, the limits of this jurisdiction must be clearly defined."[160] He felt that judges should apply only recognized rules. He believed that a great power would never agree to have its disputes settled by the application of a rule which it had not approved and especially a rule which it had specifically opposed.[161] Loder (Netherlands) said that rules had been mentioned ". . . which were, however, not yet of the nature of positive law, but it was precisely the Court's duty to develop law, to 'ripen' customs and principles universally recognized, and to crystallize them into positive rules; in a word, to establish an international jurisprudence." He, therefore, ". . . did not think that Root's fears were well-founded."[162] Phillimore (England) felt that the Court should apply the laws in force ". . . from whatever source they may be derived."[163] He referred to the case of the *California Pious Funds*

(c) the general principles of law recognized by civilized nations;

(d) subject to the provisions of Article 59, judicial decisions and the teachings of the most qualified publicists of the various nations, as subsidiary means for determination of rules of law.

2. This provision shall not prejudice the power of the Court to decide a case *ex aequo et bono,* if the parties agree thereto.

[157]PROCÈS-VERBAUX 247, 270, 287, 293, 306, 307-320, 345, 584, 620, 729-730.

[158]*Id.* at 295.

[159]*Id.* at 296, 319.

[160]*Id.* at 293.

[161]*Id.*

[162]*Id.*

[163]*Id.* at 295.

in which sentence had been rendered "... in accordance with a principle of common law; *res judicata* ... a principle which had the same character of law as any written law. Generally speaking, all the principles of common law are applicable to international affairs. They are in fact part of international law."[164] Fernandes (Brazil) said it was obvious that, if the judges are limited to the use of treaties and custom, "... the possibility of administering justice in many cases which involve legal relations between the States concerned ... is taken away from them. ... The many sides of daily life which constantly present cases unprovided for by legislation, often bring such cases before National Courts. ... What is true and legitimate in national affairs, for reasons founded in logic ... cannot be false and illegal in international affairs, where, moreover, legislation is lacking and customary law is being formed very slowly, so that the practical necessity of recognizing the application of such principles is much greater."[165]

The members of the Advisory Committee were eager to avoid the danger of having to declare a *non liquet* (lack of power) for lack of a positive rule. Hagerup pointed out that "... there might be cases in which no rule of conventional or general law was applicable. A rule must be established to meet this eventuality, to avoid the possibility of the Court declaring itself incompetent (*non liquet*) through lack of applicable rules. ..." He thought that judges of the Permanent Court should "... give judgment according to rules of law, ..." and that "... the English principle of judge-made law should be adopted: before refusing to admit a claim because no positive law exists, the judge must seek to find analogies, precedents, etc. ..."[166] Loder queried, "Did the Committee think it would be possible to create a Court which might at a given moment refuse to pronounce judgment because no applicable rule existed?"[167] De Lapradelle asserted, "[i]t is not possible to admit a declaration of *non liquet* by an international Court; denial of justice must be excluded from the International Court just as from National Courts."[168] He thought it was essential to find out in which cases no universally recognized rules existed.[169] Descamps (Belgium) stated[170] that if both a conventional rule and custom were lacking "... the judge

---

164*Id.* at 316.

165*Id.* at 345-46.

166*Id.* at 296, 317.

167*Id.* at 311.

168*Id.* at 312-313.

169*Id.*

170*Id.* at 318, 323.

must then apply general principles of law"—he must not pronounce a *non liquet.*[171]

Inclusion of "general principles of law recognized by civilized nations" as part of the law to be applied by the International Court provoked considerable discussion by publicists, and elicited widely divergent views. Cheng (China) points out that "The greatest conflict of views concerns the part played in international law by these 'general principles.' While some writers regard them merely as a means for assisting the interpretation and application of international treaty and customary law, and others consider them as no more than a subsidiary source of international law, some modern authors look upon 'general principles' as the embodiment of the highest principles—the 'superconstitution'—of international law."[172]

Article 38 of the Statute of the International Court raises interesting questions on which both members of the Advisory Committee and publicists have expressed views. Should the various sources of law listed in this Article be examined successively or may they be examined in the order of their usefulness? Is the absence of conventional and customary law the only reason for using "general principles"? Must a general principle "recognized by civilized nations" have the approval of all nations?

In the Advisory Committee of Jurists, Descamps said that "[t]he various sources of law should be examined successively."[173] Ricci-Busatti (Italy), on the contrary, thought that ". . . the judge should consider the various sources of the law simultaneously in relation to one another." To require that the sources of law be examined successively ". . . might also suggest the idea that the judge was not authorized to draw upon a certain source, for instance point 3, before having applied conventions and customs mentioned respec-

---

[171]Publicists have also pointed out the importance of avoiding a *non liquet* by recourse to general principles of law. *See, e.g.,* Ripert, *Les Règles du Droit Civil Applicables aux Rapport Internationaux,* 44 RECUEIL DES COURS 574 (1933), states that the Permanent Court of International Justice cannot pronounce a *non liquet* or refuse to judge on the pretext that it can find no applicable law. By an application or an adaptation of the general principles of law to the facts of the case, the judge develops new legal rules. It is in this sense that jurisprudence can be considered as a creative source of law, a source which is particularly important when legislation is insufficient or out-of-date.

See also Briggs, *Confidence, Apprehension and the International Court of Justice,* ASIL PROC. 25-38 (1960); Stone, *Non liquet and the Function of Law in the International Community,* 35 BR.Y.B. INT'L L. 124-62 (1939).

[172]Bin Cheng cites in this connection Le Fur, Scerni, von der Heydte, Verdross, Lauterpacht, Balladore-Pallieri, Cavaglieri, Strupp, Morelli, Scelle, Härle, de Visscher, and others.

[173]PROCÉS-VERBAUX 306, 318.

tively in points 1 and 2. That would be a misinterpretation of the Committee's intentions."[174] Cheng points out that the words "in the order following" (*en ordre successif*) were deleted during the discussions in the Committees of the League of Nations' First Assembly, thus eliminating any requirement in order of choice.[175] He adds: "The order in which these component parts of international law are enumerated is not, however, intended to represent a juridical heirarchy, but merely to indicate the order in which they would normally present themselves to the mind of an international judge when called upon to decide a dispute in accordance with international law. There is nothing to prevent these three categories of rules or principles of international law from being simultaneously present in the mind of the judge."[176] Verdross points out that a court decision is often based on a convention or custom, on the one hand, and on general principles on the other.[177]

General principles of law are often applied, not only in the absence of conventional and customary law, but also to clarify and interpret that law when it is obscure, ambiguous, or controversial. Lauterpacht points out that, normally, recourse by the Court to general principles has constituted ". . . no more than interpretation of existing conventional and customary law by reference to common sense and the canons of good faith."[178]

Article 38 of the Statute of the International Court does not require that a legal principle, in order to be considered a "general principle of law recognized by civilized nations," must exist in the legal systems of all nations. If it were otherwise, many principles which are undoubtedly general but not universal would have to be rejected. It would be unreasonable to expect a legal system of a developing state to contain many legal principles which are found in more mature and sophisticated legal systems. It would be equally unreasonable to expect a court to reject well-established general principles of law in a case between an "advanced" state whose domestic law contained such principles and an "underdeveloped" state whose law did not contain them. Although the

---

174 *Id.* at 332, 337.

175 B. CHENG, GENERAL PRINCIPLES OF LAW AS APPLIED BY INTERNATIONAL COURTS AND TRIBUNALS (London 1953) [hereafter cited as CHENG].

176 *Id.*

177 Verdross, *Les Principes Généraux du Droit dans la Jurisprudence Internationale*, 52 RECUEIL DES COURS 227 (1935).

178 H. LAUTERPACHT, THE DEVELOPMENT OF INTERNATIONAL LAW BY THE COURTS 166 (London 1958).

general principles referred to in Article 38 of the Court Statute are principles of domestic law, this does not mean that domestic laws, as such, should necessarily be applied to international disputes, but rather that the analysis of these domestic laws should lead to the discovery of general principles recognized by civilized nations.[179]

Article 38 classifies sources of international law as primary and secondary. They are predicated on the notion of *pacta sunt servanda* and *consensus*. This division of formal sources, Professor Al-Ghunaimi holds, corresponds to the Islamic division of *Adilla quat'ya* (definite or certain proof or source) and *adilla istihadiya* (reasoned source or proof). The first derives from the *Qur'an* and the *Sunnah;* the second from the determining agencies of man, be it juridical entities or individual scholars. Treaties cannot be the formal source of Muslim international law because the *Sharia* is said to be "the law of God." Treaties that conform to *Sharia* law are sources of obligations which are *pacta sunt servanda*. Secondary sources of international law (judicial decisions, teachings of publicists) are comparable to *Adilla iytihadiya* and constitute one of Islam's legal sources.[180]

§ 1-6.6.3 **Application of General Principles of Law by International Tribunals and by Treaties.**[181] References to the general principles of law have, of course, been couched in different verbal expressions, such as "principles of jurisprudence accepted by the law of all countries, . . . a universally recognized principle, . . . general principles of the common law of modern nations, . . . principles of law generally accepted by all nations, . . . rules in conformity with the leading systems of modern law, . . . the well-known rule that no one can be judge in his own suit."[182] Cheng's study reveals four main categories of principles, which, he notes, include examples of such principles cited by members of the Advisory Committee of Jurists which drafted Article 38 of the Permanent Court of Justice Statute.[183] These categories are: (1) the principle of "self preservation," (2) the principle of "good faith," which

---

[179]Ripert, *supra* note 171 at 581-82.

[180]M. AL-GHUNAIMI, THE MUSLIM CONCEPTION OF INTERNATIONAL LAW AND THE WESTERN APPROACH 108-09 (The Hague 1968).

[181]A comprehensive listing of these cases and treaties is found in CHENG at xvii-xlvi, where the cases are listed both alphabetically and according to courts and tribunals; the multipartite treaties are listed chronologically, and the bipartite treaties are listed alphabetically by countries. Official and secondary sources of the cases of various courts and tribunals, and of treaties, are found in CHENG at xlii-li.

[182]Cheng, *supra* note 175, at 26.

[183]*Id.*

requires a standard of honest and fair dealing; (3) the legal concept of "responsibility," and (4) certain general principles of law in judicial proceedings.[184] The functions performed by these general principles of law are stated by Cheng as follows:

First, they constitute the source of various rules of law, which are merely the expression of these principles. Second, they form the guiding principles of the juridical order according to which the interpretation and application of the rules of law are orientated. Thirdly, they apply directly to the facts of the case wherever there is no formulated rule governing the matter. In a system like international law, where precisely formulated rules are few, the third function of general principles of law acquires special significance and has contributed greatly towards defining the legal relations between States.[185]

Lauterpacht points out that the International Court has refrained from referring to "the general principles of law recognized by nations" *eo nomine:*

Thus in the *Chorzow Factory* case it used the following language: 'The Court observes that it is a principle of international law, and even a general conception of law, that any breach of an engagement involves an obligation to make reparation.' . . . In the Order concerning provisional measures in the case of the *Electricity Company of Sofia and Bulgaria,* it invoked "the principle universally accepted by international tribunals . . . to the effect that the parties to a case must abstain from any measure capable of exercising a prejudicial effect in regard to the execution of the decision to be given." In the Judgment concerning *Certain German Interests in Polish Upper Silesia* the Court stated that nothing, either in the Statute or the rules which govern the Court's activities or in the general principles of law, prevents it from considering certain aspects of a preliminary objection before proceeding with the examination of the case on the merits. In the *Corful Channel* case the Court invoked certain "general and well-recognized principles" including "elementary considerations of humanity, even more exacting in peace than in war" as substantiating the obligation of Albania to give notification of the existence of a minefield in Albanian territorial waters. . . . In the Advisory Opinion in the *Jaworzina* case the Court invoked the "tradition principle: *ejus est interpretare legem cujus condere"*—a principle which "must be respected by all"—in support of the interpretation given by the Conference of Ambassadors in the matter of the disputed boundary. In the *Advisory Opinion on the Effect of Awards of the*

---

[184]*Id.* at 390.
[185]*Id.*

United Nations Administrative Tribunal they relied on the "well-established and generally recognized principle of law" according to which "a judgment rendered by a judicial body in *res judicata* and has binding force between the parties to the dispute." In the case concerning the *Interpretation of the Greco-Turkish Agreement* the Court rejected as "contrary to an accepted principle of law" the contention that it is possible to accord to individual members of a corporate body the right of independent outside action in matters affecting the organization.

A State is estopped from relying on it[s] own non-fulfillment of an international obligation. . . . [This was shown] in the way in which the Court on a number of occasions was prepared to recognize the operation of the principal of estoppel—which, although it referred to it as a principle known in "Anglo-Saxon law," it considered apparently to be a general principle of law. Thus in the *Serbian Loans* case it examined in detail whether as the result of a clear and unequivocal representation of one party to the dispute, on which the other party was entitled to rely and actually relied, the latter's position had undergone a substantial change. It is possible, having regard to the language used by the Court, that it applied the same principle in the case of *Eastern Greenland.* . . . In the case of the *Société commerciale de Belgique* the Court stated that as the Greek Government expressly recognized the arbitral awards in question as possessing the force of *res judicata* it could not "without contradicting itself" contest the relevant submission of the Belgian Government. . . . [The principle of estoppel was also recognized in the advisory opinion on the International Status of South-West Africa, and again in the advisory opinion concerning the Competence of the International Labour Organization.] [186]

It has also been contended that the domain of law in international relations will be restricted if it flows only from treaties and customs, but will be greatly extended if use is made of the general principles of law.[187] Lauterpacht then points out, citing cases, that modern *ad hoc* arbitration tribunals have not hesitated to have recourse to general principles, and the Permanent Court of Arbitration has followed this practice, both before and after the creation of the Permanent Court of International Justice.[188]

Since the adoption of Article 38 of the Statute of the Permanent Court of International Justice, many treaties have included articles which provide that the court shall apply "the general principles of law recognized by civilized nations." In Article 2, paragraph 2, of

---

[186] LAUTERPACHT, *supra* note 178 at 166-67.
[187] *Id.*
[188] *Id.*

the Treaty of Conciliation and Arbitration between Finland and Norway (signed February 3, 1962; ratifications exchanged March 15, 1927) there is a specific reference to Article 38 of the Permanent Court Statute. In most treaties, however, the law to be applied is spelled out without reference to Article 38 but follows its wording identically or substantially.[189]

The great increase in the number, variety and importance of current international problems which should be settled by the rule of law rather than by force has created an urgent assignment for lawyers to attempt to enrich, diversify and develop the current body of law to meet these expanding needs. In what fields, then, and how can the general principles of law, developed by analysis and analogy from domestic law, be applied to the new problems of our rapidly changing world? The examples of general principles which follow suggest the potential expansion of our present legal facilities to meet urgent, current and future needs. Further, necessary research will undoubtedly discover and expound many other useful general principles of law, and their application to current problems.[190]

§ 1-6.6.4. The General Principles of Law. The following principles are recognized by civilized nations: (1) that the sovereign is subject to the law; (2) that the right of self-defense is limited in certain ways; (3) that states must abide by treaties; (4) that harm to one's neighbor is unlawful; (5) that disputes are to be settled by third parties; (6) that acquired rights are to be protected; (7) that consultation must be made before taking any action that affects the interests of others.

(1) An examination of the world's principal legal systems shows that *the sovereign of a state is not above the law.* This has been declared by writers on Jewish, Hindu, Islamic and Chinese law, among others. Islamic Law places sovereignty in God and not in men or political institutions which carry out the law of God on

---

[189] For the text of several of these treaties negotiated in the 1920's, *see* HABICHT, *supra* note 153 at 23, 150, 208, and 240 for Article 5 of the treaties between Germany and Switzerland, Sweden, Finland, and Estonia; *id.* at 433, 458 for Article 4 of treaties between Germany and the Netherlands and Germany and Denmark; *id.* at 383 for Article 19 of a treaty between Czechoslovakia and Norway; and *id.* at 502 for Article 19 of a treaty between Poland and Yugoslavia.

See also CHENG for numerous other more recent references; UN SECRETARIAT, SYSTEMATIC SURVEY OF TREATIES FOR THE PACIFIC SETTLEMENT OF INTERNATIONAL DISPUTES, 1928-1948, at 116-22 (New York 1949).

[190] *See* H. LAUTERPACHT, THE FUNCTION OF LAW IN THE INTERNATIONAL COMMUNITY 115 (Oxford 1933), where arbitral and judicial cases, which fill gaps *by the application of general principles of law and the principles of private law* are cited.

earth. Thus, political leaders and decision makers are the subjects of limited authority. This principle is part of both common law and civil law. It is supported by the writings of legal scholars, by the decisions of the International Court, and by provisions in the constitutions of various countries, including those of France, the Federal Republic of Germany, Japan and the Netherlands.

(2) *The principle which limits the right of self-defense* is well defined in domestic law. It requires a reasonable apprehension of danger, a proportionate use of force to meet that danger, and a determination by a third-party tribunal. Almost all legal systems contain these requirements. In the international field, many efforts have been made through the years to limit the right of self-defense. This was one of the implied purposes of the Kellogg-Briand Pact. By the decisions of the Nuremberg and Tokyo War Crimes Tribunals, it became a general principle of law. The trial by the International Military Tribunal at Nuremberg fulfilled the requirement of a third-party tribunal. The other requirements regarding the limitations on the right of self-defense were met by the Court's decision that Germany's "preventive" aggressions constituted an unreasonable apprehension of danger and that Germany's war activities were a disproportionate use of force to meet this alleged danger.

(3) *The obligation to abide by agreements* is one of the most elementary and universally accepted general principles of law. It lies at the foundation of every developed legal system. To disavow it would be tantamount to advocating chaos and anarchy. However, the emphatic approval of this broad basic principle does not solve the entire treaty question. A treaty, like a contract in domestic law, may be made in good faith, with no question by the parties of adherence to its terms—in normal circumstances. But, there are special circumstances, such as impossibility of performance through no fault of a given party, as by the outbreak of war or the negligence or deliberate adverse act of the other party. The rather vague and controversial international law doctrine of *rebus sic stantibus* (things remaining the same) is inadequate. Change in conditions is not in itself sufficient to require change in treaty agreements or the release of a party from treaty obligations. Additional principles are needed to supplement this basic principle of *pacta sunt servanda*. These, it is believed, can be derived from an analysis of the domestic law rules and principles of contract for termination of obligation.

(4) *The principle that unjustified harm* (as distinguished from prohibited acts) *done to a neighbor is a legal wrong* is a general principle of law with immense possibilities of application in the

future.   Historically, an enumeration of prohibited acts has been the common approach both in domestic and international law. However, this has often proved its weakness.   In the international field, examples are found in attempts to list prohibited acts of aggression and in the listing in bilateral extradition treaties of certain, but only a limited number of, specified crimes for which extradition may be requested.   The approach in the current domestic law of torts is a better approach to "harm done."   It makes use of general principles and reasonable tests.   The alarming increase in the sources of damage through atomic missiles alone suggests an imperative need for the development and use of this valuable general principle of unlawful harm.

(5)   It is a very important general principle of law that *controversies between parties to a dispute should be settled by third party adjudication.*   In theory, to argue for determination of such disputes by one of the parties becomes a *reductio ad absurdum.* Can it be assumed for a moment that either party would ever have the judicial independence to decide the case in favor of his opponent, regardless of how just and persuasive the opponent's case might be?   The very fact that there is a controversy is evidence of conflicting views, which each party maintains insistently. It is difficult enough for a trained court of highly skilled professional judges possessing unquestioned integrity to be truly impartial in highly explosive, controversial cases.   Fortunately, in the international field this objective has been largely attained by the International Court of Justice, as a result of the quality of its judges. The difficulty here is not with the principle of third-party adjudication or with its technical operation, but rather the reluctance of states to accept the compulsory jurisdiction of the Court without restrictive reservations and the unwillingness of states to submit to the Court voluntarily many of what they consider to be their most important disputes.

(6)   *The principle of the protection of acquired rights* is well-known to the legal systems of Western states.   Governments are allowed to take private property for the public good, with just compensation to the private owner.   This has been an invaluable principle by which public rights of way have been procured to facilitate the development of communications and thus enhance the growth of commerce and industry.   In the international field the application of this principle is essential to the future of international investment.   An important defect is the lack of a developed body of legal principles to govern the conditions and consequences

of the expropriation of private rights. The Permanent Court of International Justice has recognized the right to expropriate private property for the "public good," provided adequate compensation is paid. However, not all expropriation cases reach the International Court. Yet, the practice of nationalization and expropriation has spread to areas where the habit of due process is not well-developed and questions of "general welfare" and compensation have not reached the stage of precise standards or rules. In short, much remains to be done in this field; and its problems should be attacked promptly and vigorously in order to facilitate the growth of the rule of law in the economic, commercial and financial fields.

(7) *The principle of consultation on matters which affect the interests of others* may be found in varying degrees in different legal systems. It is particularly developed in Chinese, Japanese, and Hebraic law and has been useful practice in many fields. In the fields of currency and tariffs, however, consultation has become a matter of legal obligation. A prerequisite to changes in commercial relations required by the General Agreement on Trade and Tariffs (GATT) is consultation by the signatories. The principle also has been usefully applied to the Indus River Basin controversy between Pakistan and India.

(8) *The principle of freedom of religion, thought and expression* to many seems to be a human right, but in Islamic law it is axiomatic as a "general principle" because it is the duty of the state and the Muslims to spread the word of Islam; and, therefore, such freedom of expression, thought, and religion is so fundamental that whenever it was prohibited, the Muslim nation went to war or *Tihad*, which was then deemed justifiable.

§ 1-6.6.5. **Fields in Which "General Principles" Can Be Usefully Applied.** In the future development of a world-wide law structure, the expansion of the application of the general principles of law in various fields of international activity is clearly indicated. By way of example, their application in three important fields will be discussed very briefly: (1) the field of international investments; (2) the regulation of outer space; and (3) contract law.

(1) When a corporation or an individual in an advanced state wishes to invest capital and skill in another advanced state there should be little difficulty in determining the law to be applied. The law of either state or parts of the law of each will probably be suitable. Frequently, however, a corporation of a capital-exporting country makes contracts with a capital-importing country for long-term development and utilization of natural resources

which involve not only contractual rights but the privilege of exercising discretion in the area of the underdeveloped country that is being developed. Such a contract often specifies the law to be applied in interpreting and enforcing the contract. However, the fact that there may be a wide discrepancy between the stages of development of the legal systems of the two countries may make it wise not to provide in the contract that the law of either will govern, but rather that some other law will govern. If the general principles of law recognized by civilized nations are more often utilized and interpreted, and as a consequence become better understood, they might more frequently be chosen by the contracting parties as the governing law in such circumstances with jurisdiction vested in appropriate international tribunals. The general principles of law often constitute the most suitable system of law for the regulation of these contracts, and an "inexhaustible reservoir" of legal principles for application by international tribunals.[191] The UN is now drafting a set of principles applicable in international trade transactions.

(2) The problems of space offer a unique challenge to lawyers to develop principles of law to meet many new and complicated situations. The basis of this law for many years to come will be largely international treaties and the general principles of law derived from analogies in both domestic and international law. Much technical information resulting from the flights of space vehicles and satellites, as well as from human observation during manned space flights, is already available. Willingness to enter into reliable agreements to insure control of missiles and satellites has been indicated by some states. A United Nations resolution has urged a joint study of an inspection system which would aid in controlling the use of space for peaceful purposes only. The creation of an international space agency has been proposed. Plans to prohibit the use of outer space for military purposes have also been suggested,[192] and the legal literature on space questions has grown at

---

[191]See also M. CHRETIEN, À LA RECHERCHE DE DROIT INTERNATIONAL FISCAL COMMUN (Paris 1955); T. FOX, SOME EFFECT ON INTERNATIONAL LAW OF THE GOVERNMENTALIZATION OF PRIVATE ENTERPRISE (Chicago 1944); S. FRIEDMAN, EXPROPRIATION IN INTERNATIONAL LAW (London 1953); G. KNIGHT, TREATMENT OF CORPORATIONS IN INTERNATIONAL LAW (Washington 1938); McNair, supra note 153 at 1-19; K. AL-SHAWI, THE ROLE OF THE CORPORATE ENTITY IN INTERNATIONAL LAW (Michigan 1957).

[192]C. JENKS, THE COMMON LAW OF MANKIND 382-407 (London 1958).

an unprecedented rate in keeping with the dynamic nature of developments in this field.[193]

What, then, are some of the more important legal problems that scientific development in outer space has raised, and how can the use of the "general principles of law recognized by civilized nations" be extended to this new and vastly significant field? An immediate problem is to establish the law which will determine with the utmost clarity jurisdiction in outer space. Suggestions for the solution of this problem, in this case, do not come from the "general principles of law" but from two basic principles of international law: the principle of state sovereignty over the air space above its territory, and the principle of the freedom of the seas. The latter is recommended, because it is more practical in its application and is a more firmly established principle. Perhaps custom has already established the rule of law that space, like the open seas, is "free." Another problem of vital importance is the determination of the authority to control activities in outer space. Certainly, no one could doubt the extreme importance of control, in view of the immense strategic, scientific, and economic possibilities of the development of outer space. Here, a general principle could be developed on the basis of the existing principle of collective security, and this principle could be put into operation by the United Nations. The establishment of an international organization or agency, analogous to the International Atomic Energy Agency, for the development of the many rules and regulations that will be needed in this field could prove useful. Various codes will also undoubtedly be required to provide standards of safety, efficiency, and many other things; lawyers drafting these codes will find much to draw upon in existing sea and aviation codes. To deal with the numerous problems of space which will doubtless present themselves in the near future, it will also be important to formulate general principles of law from domestic concepts of nuisance, trespass, negligence, personal status, rights of property contracts and crime.

(3) In the field of contracts, the Law School of Cornell University has carried out a major research project in which the most

---

[193] *See* 4 N.Y. LAW FORUM 257 (Space Law Issue 1958); A. HALEY & W. HEINRICH, COLLOQUIUM ON THE LAW OF OUTER SPACE (The Hague 1958); J. HOGAN, A GUIDE TO THE STUDY OF SPACE LAW (1958); Lissitzyn, *The American Position on Outer Space and Antarctica*, 53 AJIL 126-32 (1959); A. McNAIR, THE LAW OF THE AIR (London 1953); Takano, *Legal Status of Outer Space*, 4 JAPAN ANN. INT'L L. 43-49 (1960); XITH INTERNATIONAL ASTRONAUTICAL CONGRESS, PROCEEDINGS: SECOND COLLOQUIUM ON LAW OF OUTER SPACE, 1959 (Stockholm 1959); PROCEEDINGS, THIRD COLLOQUIUM ON LAW OF OUTER SPACE, 1960 (Stockholm 1960).

important areas of contract law were explored in order to determine the extent to which there is common ground or a common core among the world's legal systems. A Report on this project, by Professor R. B. Schlesinger[194] presented at the Athens World Conference on World Peace Through Law in 1963, pointed out the importance of such a study and described the methods used in common core research. The first step was the selection of a team of legal scholars, brought up in different legal systems, each of whom was familiar with both the theory and practice of the law of his country. The first task of this team was to select the legal field in which the probability of the existence of common principles was greatest. The Report describes the procedure by which the findings of areas of agreement and disagreement were reached. In the years since the Athens Conference of 1963 the arduous task of research, conferring, drafting, editing, and revising has resulted in the publication of two monumental volumes entitled *Formation of Contracts: A Study of the Common Core of Legal Systems*, which might well serve as the prototype for studies in other fields contributing to the extent of recognition of general principles as an important source of international law.[195]

At the Washington World Conference on World Peace Through Law in 1965, Dr. C. B. Agarwala presented a paper listing 122 principles of law which the author believed are recognized throughout the world.[196] Some of them, he said, have been recognized by international courts of justice or by arbitration tribunals; others have been commented upon by authors. The principles listed fall under the following categories: law in general, law of persons, law of property, law of contracts, law of torts, evidence, criminal law, criminal procedure, constitutional and administrative law, private international law, and the rules of interpretation of statutes and instruments. The author pointed out that he had supporting authorities which led him to accept all of the listed principles as "general principles of law recognized by civilized nations."[197]

---

[194] Schlesinger, *supra* note 153 at 779-88.

[195] *See also* Levinson, *Comparative Law and the Computer: A Review of* THE FORMATION OF CONTRACTS: A STUDY OF THE COMMON CORE OF LEGAL SYSTEMS, 1 L. & COMP. TECH. No. 9, at 12 (1968).

[196] Agarawala, *General Principles of Law Recognized by Civilized Nations,* in WASHINGTON CONF. 547-55 (1967).

[197] For a discussion of the *principles of International law* as distinguished from *the general principles of law recognized by civilized nations* listed in Art. 38 of the I.C.J. STATUTE as a source of international law, see ATHENS CONF. 735-91 (1965).

The Athens World Conference presented, and the Washington World Conference reaffirmed, the following ten principles for a "World Rule of Law":

(1) All states and persons must accept the rule of law in the world community. In international matters, individuals, juridical persons, states and international organizations must all be subject to international law, deriving rights and incurring obligations thereinunder.

(2) The rule of law in international affairs is based upon the principle of equality before the law.

(3) International law and legal institutions must be based upon fundamental concepts of fairness, justice, and human dignity.

(4) International law and legal institutions must be capable of expansion, development or change to meet the needs of a changing world composed of nations whose interdependence is ever on the increase and to permit progress in political, social, and economic justice for all peoples.

(5) All obligations under international law must be fulfilled and all rights thereunder must be exercised in good faith.

(6) A fundamental principle of the international rule of law is that of the right of self-determination of the peoples of the world, as proclaimed in the Charter of the United Nations.

(7) Each individual is entitled to effective legal protection of fundamental and inalienable human rights without distinction as to race, religion, or belief.

(8) Those who are subject to international law must resolve their international disputes by adjudication, arbitration, or other peaceful procedures.

(9) International obligations, including decisions of international tribunals, must be enforced by appropriate international community action.

(10) The United Nations organization is the world's best hope for international peace under the rule of law and must be supported and strengthened by all possible means, and to this end we reaffirm our support of the principles of the Charter of the United Nations.[198]

---

[198]*Id.* at 796.

CHAPTER 2

Basic Concepts of International Law

SECTION A: INTRODUCTION

§ 2-1. Introduction[1]

The state in international law is an entity organized for public ends possessing sovereignty, or a high degree of political authority. The doctrine of sovereignty was fundamentally a 19th century concept, but is today untenable in its extreme form since it does not reflect the current needs of international relations. The United Nations Charter and other provisions of international law comprise limitations upon national freedom of action which are adopted for the common interests of the community of states in an interdependent world.

In addition to sovereign states with full international status in international law, various "legal persons" with qualified status in

---

[1] *See generally* W. BISHOP, INTERNATIONAL LAW: CASES AND MATERIALS 283-342 (2d ed. Boston 1962); J. BRIERLY, THE LAW OF NATIONS 56-63 (Oxford 1928); J. BRIGGS, THE LAW OF NATIONS: CASES, DOCUMENTS AND NOTES 65-111 (New York 1938); C. FENWICK, INTERNATIONAL LAW 155-65 (4th ed. New York 1965); C. FENWICK, CASES ON INTERNATIONAL LAW 67-80 (2d ed. Chicago 1951); 1 C. HYDE, INTERNATIONAL LAW CHIEFLY AS INTERPRETED AND APPLIED BY THE UNITED STATES 41-146, 148-58 (2d ed. Boston 1945); 2 A. KISS, RÉPERTOIRE DE LA PRATIQUE FRANÇAISE EN MATIÈRE DE DROIT INTERNATIONAL PUBLIC 447-622 (Paris 1966); 4 *id.* at 3-31; M. KOROWICZ, INTRODUCTION TO INTERNATIONAL LAW 1-324 (The Hague 1959); Krabbe, *L'Idée Moderne de l'Etat,* 13 RECUEIL DES COURS 514-83 (1926); H. LAUTERPACHT, RECOGNITION IN INTERNATIONAL LAW (Cambridge 1947); Lowenstein, *Sovereignty and International Co-operation,* 48 AJIL 222-44 (1954); McNemar, *Intervention and the Developing States— Regional Meeting,* 63 AJIL 306-11 (1969); H. LAUTERPACHT, OPPENHEIM'S INTERNATIONAL LAW, 117-56, 170-258 (8th ed. London 1954); L. ORFIELD & E. RE, CASES AND MATERIALS ON INTERNATIONAL LAW 138-72, 215, 231 (rev. ed. New York 1965); Politis, *Le Problème des Limitations de la Souveraineté et la These des Abus des Droits,* 6 RECUEIL DES COURS 5-121 (1925); Potter, *L'Intervention en Droit International Moderne,* 32 RECUEIL DES COURS 611-90 (1930); Restatement (second) of the Law §§ 94-114 (1965) [hereinafter cited as RESTATEMENT]; J. SALONGA & P. YAP, PUBLIC INTERNATIONAL LAW 61-63 (Manila 1958); G. SCHWARZENBERGER, A MANUAL OF PUBLIC INTERNATIONAL LAW 53-73, 78-81 (5th ed. New York 1967); Waldock, *The Subjects of International Law and the Problem of Recognition,* 106 RECUEIL DES COURS 138-72 (1962); 1 DIGEST OF INTERNATIONAL LAW 221-996 (M. Whiteman ed. Washington 1963) [hereinafter cited as WHITEMAN]; 2 *id.* at 1-240, 467-753; Williams, *La Doctrine de la Reconnaissance en Droit International et ses Développements Recents,* 44 RECUEIL DES COURS 203-314 (1933); G. WILSON & G. TUCKER, INTERNATIONAL LAW 47-54 (7th ed. Boston 1917).

international law also exist. Among these are: members of confederations, federations, federal states, members of unions, neutralized states, mandated territories, trust territories, protectorates, suzerainties, the Holy See, and corporations organized for public purposes. Their dominant charactertistics is that their relations with other states are limited.

The state attains full status in international law only when its existence has been generally recognized by other states. Recognition, primarily a political act, commonly performed by the chief executive of a state, may be either express or implied, resulting from the acknowledgement by a state that another state has satisfied the conditions of statehood, or from the concerted action of several states. The act constituting recognition may be formal, as by declaration, proclamation, or treaty, or it may be informal, as by any act indicating acknowledgement of international rights and obligations; and it is definitive, granting rights and establishing corresponding duties.

§ 2-2. General Rights and Duties of States[2]

The most basic right of a state is its right to exist, from which are derived many other rights: independence, equality, jurisdiction, and intercourse, each with corresponding duties. These rights and duties described and analyzed in international law textbooks, digests, legal journals, and numerous monographs; asserted by heads of state and other public officials; proclaimed in international conferences; made the subject matter of numerous laws and international conventions; and discussed in the decisions and *obiter dicta* of national and international courts, constitute a large part of the subject matter of international law.

---

[2] *See generally* Alfaro, *The Rights and Duties of States,* 97 RECUEIL DES COURS 95-202 (1959); Berezowski, *Les Sujets Non Souverains du Droit International,* 65 RECUEIL DES COURS 5-85 (1938); I. BROWNLIE, PRINCIPLES OF PUBLIC INTERNATIONAL LAW 52-97 (Oxford 1966); C. FENWICK, *supra* note 1, at 125-47; C. FENWICK, CASES, *supra* note 1, at 50-67, Gidel, *Droits et Devoirs des Nations, La Théorie Classique des Droits Fondamentaux des Etats,* 10 RECUEIL DES COURS 541-99 (1925); A. HERSHEY, THE ESSENTIALS OF PUBLIC INTERNATIONAL LAW AND ORGANIZATION 157-200 (rev. ed. New York 1930); Parry, *The Function of Law in the International Community,* in MANUAL OF PUBLIC INTERNATIONAL LAW 36-43 (M. Sørensen ed. 1968) [hereinafter cited as SØRENSEN]; Phillimore, *Droits et Devoirs Fondamentaux des Etats,* 1 RECUEIL DES COURS 29-71 (1923); RESTATEMENT §§ 94-114; J. SALONGA & P. YAP, *supra* note 1, at 66-78, G. SCHWARZENBERGER, *supra* note 1, at 53-74; 5 WHITEMAN, 1-1175; G. WILSON & G. TUCKER, *supra* note 1, at 57-62.

§ 2-3. Independence[3]

A state's right to independence, in theory, is absolute for it is sometimes termed "external manifestation of sovereignty." In practice, however, states place limitations on their complete freedom of action by treaties, contracts, municipal laws, and are limited in their complete freedom by customary international law and the general legal principles adhered to by most nations. Their right of independence, however, is not violated because these limitations are determined by the states themselves rather than by an external control. In entering into treaties and conventions, states use their sovereignty to obtain benefits for their people. An example would be air service through the ICAO conventions, postal service through the postal conventions and hundreds of other treaties or conventions. A state can denounce or withdraw from a convention and reclaim all the sovereignty it employed to obtain the service the convention provided.

The right of independence presupposes the obligation of nonintervention. In spite of this, states have historically practiced intervention for various purposes, such as: self-preservation, the prevention of illegal or oppressive acts by other states, the implementation of treaty provisions, the preservation of the balance of power, and the recovery of debts. For example, the doctrine of the balance of power aimed to preserve the independence of European states, and the Monroe Doctrine aimed to protect American states from violations of their independence by European intervention. At present, however, it is generally recognized that the right of independence excludes state intervention except, perhaps on a strict interpretation of the principle of self-preservation.

---

[3] *See generally* J. BRIERLY, *supra* note 1, at 30-33, 63-65; Fawcett, *Intervention in International Law, a Study of Some Recent Cases,* 103 RECUEIL DES COURS 347-421 (1961); A. HERSHEY, *supra* note 2, at 234-35; 1 C. HYDE, *supra* note 1, at 254-87; 2 A. KISS, *supra* note 1, at 38-48, 69-112 (1966); 1 OPPENHEIM, *supra* note 1, at 285-97, 304-20; Rousseau, *L'Independance de l'Etat dans l'Ordre International,* 73 RECUEIL DES COURS 171-253 (1948); J. SALONGA & P. YAP, *supra* note 1, at 65-66, 110-15; Stowell, *La Theorie et la Pratique de l'Intervention,* 40 RECUEIL DES COURS 91-151 (1932); A. THOMAS & A. J. THOMAS, NON-INTERVENTION (Dallas 1956); G. WILSON & G. TUCKER, *supra* note 1, at 81-95.

§ 2-4. Equality[4]

States are recognized as members of the international community on terms of legal equality with other members only when they are independent, that is free from external political control and possessing the right to determine state action in international affairs. This equality is recognized regardless of size, population, political importance, governmental organization or change in the form of government.

This right, widely recognized by legal scholars, courts, treaties, charters, and declarations, has been described as "a true theory only if it means that the rights of one state, whatever they may be, are as much entitled to the protection of law as the rights of any other, that is to say, if it merely denies that the weakness of a state is any excuse in law for disregarding its legal rights."[5] In the case of the *Antelope*, tried in 1825, the Court declared that "No principle of general law is more universally recognized, than the perfect equality of nations. Russia and Geneva have equal rights."[6] According to Article 4 of the Convention on the Rights and Duties of States of 1933, "States are juridically equal, enjoy the same rights, and have equal capacity in their exercise. The rights of one do not depend upon the power which it possesses to assure its (their) exercise, but upon the simple fact of its existence as a person under international law."[7] Article 6 of the Charter of the Organization of American States of 1948 declared that "States are juridically equal, enjoy equal rights and equal capacity to exercise these rights, and have equal duties."[8] The UN Charter supports the principle of the "sovereign equality" of

---

[4] *See generally* Anand, *Sovereign Equality of State in International Law,* 8 INTERNA-TIONAL STUDIES 213-41, 386-421 (1967); Boutros-Ghali, *Le Principe d'Egalité des Etats et les Organizations Internationales,* 100 RECUEIL DES COURS 9-73 (1960); J. BRIERLY, *supra* note 1, at 30, 65-67; I. BROWNLIE, *supra* note 2, at 250-60; E. DICK-INSON, EQUALITY OF STATES IN INTERNATIONAL LAW (Cambridge, Mass. 1920); C. FENWICK, *supra* note 1, at 260-61; C. FENWICK, CASES, *supra* note 1, at 84-87; A. HERSHEY, *supra* note 2, at 245-47; 1 C. HYDE, *supra* note 1, at 27-28, 2 A. KISS, *supra* note 1, at 48-50 (1966); P. KOOIJMANS, THE DOCTRINE OF THE LEGAL EQUALITY OF STATES (The Hague 1964); M. KOROWICZ, *supra* note 1, at 226-73; Mugera, *Subjects of International Law,* in SØRENSEN 247, 253-55; L. OPPENHEIM, *supra* note 1, at 262-81; J. SALONGA & P. YAP, *supra* note 1, at 115-18; G. SCHWARZ-ENBERGER, *supra* note 1, at 64, 153, 279, 281; Scott, *Le Principe de l'Egalité Juridique dans les Rapports Internationaux,* 42 RECUEIL DES COURS 473-630 (1932); G. WILSON & G. TUCKER, *supra* note 1, at 97-101.

[5] J. BRIERLY, *supra* note 1, at 66.

[6] 10 Wheaton 66; *see* FENWICK, CASES, *supra* note 1, at 86.

[7] *Done* December 26, 1933; 49 Stat. 3097; TS 881; 4 Trentworth 4807; 165 LNTS 19. C. FENWICK, CASES, *supra* note 1, at 86-87.

[8] *Id.* at 86.

its members in Articles 2(1) and 78. The Declaration of the Rights and Duties of States affirms the right to equality (in law) of every state,[9] and the Draft Convention on Friendly Relations Among States would make the respect of the national sovereignty of other states an affirmative duty.[10]

Corollary to a state's right of independence and equality is its immunity from suit in foreign courts by foreign nationals. While not exactly a right inherent in the fact of statehood, it is a political privilege granted by those foreign states in which suit is brought against the state. The principle of sovereign immunity is usually interjected in a lawsuit by the state being sued as a defense to the action since it attacks the jurisdiction of the municipal court to hear the case. A state, defendant in a foreign lawsuit, was not only able to plead sovereign immunity as a defense, but at the same time, could, in some states, counterclaim in the same action without waiving its immunity.

In most states, this immunity from suit remains an absolute privilege. But, since the end of World War II, several nations particularly West European countries and the United States, have distinguished between a state's activities of a purely commercial nature, for which immunity would not be interjected, and those acts necessarily incidental to its sovereign power for which immunity would automatically attach.[11] This distinction is particularly appli-

---

[9] 49 Stat. 3097; TS 881; 4 Trentworth 4807; 165 LNTS.

[10] *See* Report of the Special Committee on Principles of International Law Concerning Friendly Relations and Cooperation Among States, U.N. Doc. A/5746 (1964). *See also infra* p. 102, n. 72.

[11] *See* Banco Nacional de Cuba v. Sabbatino, 376 U.S. 398 (1964). The result in this case was changed by U.S. Statute in the passage of the Foreign Assistance Act of 1964, Public Law 88-633, October 7, 1964, 78 Stat. 1009 at 1013, Part III, ch. 1, Sec. 301, as amended by Foreign Assistance Act of 1965, P.L. 89-171, 79 Stat. 653, which deleted (3), which provided:

> (2) Notwithstanding any other provision of law, no court in the United States shall decline on the ground of the federal act of state doctrine to make a determination on the merits giving effect to the principles of international law in a case in which a claim of title or other right to property is asserted by any party including a foreign state (or a party claiming through such state) based upon (or traced through) a confiscation or other taking after January 1, 1959, by an act of that state in violation of the principles of international law, including the principles of compensation and the other standards set out in this subsection: *Provided,* That this sub-paragraph shall not be applicable (1) in any case in which an act of a foreign state is not contrary to international law or with respect to a claim of title or other right acquired pursuant to an irrevocable letter of credit of not more than 180 days duration issued in good faith prior to the time of the confiscation

(Continued)

cable to state-owned, or operated commercial enterprises, state trading organizations with separate legal entities under municipal law, whose contractual duties, rights, and obligations may give rise to lawsuits for breaches. And in certain cases, courts in these countries have ruled that in the absence of a specific waiver of immunity or political acts by the domestic sovereign to confer such immunity, the counterclaim of a state in a foreign lawsuit operates as a waiver of immunity.

While this principle of sovereign immunity has often resulted in individual hardships, particularly in those cases involving the nationalization of foreign property by a sovereign and, since in many cases it may be difficult to apply the distinction between a sovereign's official, state or public acts, and its commercial, private acts, Schwarzenberger has pointed out that existing principles of international responsibility, law and tribunals have grown to cover such exigencies.[12]

§ 2-5. The Protection of Foreign Property Abroad

Prior to the 1950's, foreign property abroad was protected solely by bilateral treaties and other agreements between nations, and these, in addition to diplomatic practices and arbitral awards, constituted the main source of international law concerning such protection. In the absence of such treaties and agreements, customary international law provided that private property, subject to the laws of the country in which it is located, could be expropriated by the host country only in the public interest, without unjustifiable discrimination, and on payment of full, or adequate, prompt and effective compensation.[13] However, because this principle was seriously violated on several occasions, and because of the increase in private capital exports, as distinguished from governmental loans and foreign aid programs, considerable concern was raised over illegal expropriations without compensation, and it was felt that further protective measures were warranted.

---

or other taking, or (2) in any case with respect to which the President determines that application of the act of state doctrine is required in that particular case by the foreign policy interests of the United States and a suggestion to this effect is filed on his behalf in that case with the court, or (3) in any case in which the proceedings are commended after January 1, 1966.

[12] G. SCHWARZENBERGER, *supra* note 1, at 102-5.

[13] G. SCHWARZENBERGER, FOREIGN INVESTMENTS AND INTERNATIONAL LAW (New York 1969); PRIVATE INVESTORS ABROAD: PROBLEMS AND SOLUTIONS IN INTERNATIONAL BUSINESS IN 1969 (V. Cameron ed. New York 1969).

One measure of protection was provided by national legislation by those nations interested in importing capital in order to further their economic growth and development. Such legislation included tax concessions, customs and import duty concessions, insurance programs and other guarantees. Bilateral treaties, however, between capital exporting and importing states continued to play the most important role in capital exportation.

Five international conventions after World War II were drafted to protect foreign property and investments abroad: the 1948 Havana Charter on Trade and Employment,[14] the Abs-Shawcross Draft Convention on Investments Abroad;[15] the Draft Convention on the Protection of Foreign Property;[16] the Convention for the Settlement of Investment Disputes between States and Nationals of Other States;[17] and the European Convention on Establishment of Companies.[18]

The Havana Charter on Trade and Employment,[19] signed in 1948, but which did not enter into force since Article 102 was not fulfilled, would have obligated signatories not to take "unreasonable or unjustifiable" measures that would injure the rights and interests of nationals of other states. Disputes were to be settled by organs of the organization and arbitration and resort to the International Court of Justice were not envisioned.

The Abs-Shawcross Draft Convention on Investments Abroad,[20] signed in 1959, attempted to ensure greater protection. It aimed to protect "all property, rights and interests, whether held directly or indirectly," (Article IX, or national investments). In defining lawful expropriation of national property, the Convention provided that:

> No party shall take any measures against nationals of another Party to deprive them directly or indirectly of their property except under due process of law and provided that such measures are not discriminatory or contrary to undertakings given by that Party and are accompanied by the payment of just and effective compensation. Adequate provision shall have been made at or prior to the time of deprivation for the prompt determination and payment of such compensation, which shall represent the

---

[14] Havana Charter for an International Trade Organization. *See* United Nations Conference on Trade and Employment, Final Act and Related Documents, E/Conf. 2/78 (1948).

[15] See 9 J. PUB. L. 116 (1960) for text and commentary on this subject.

[16] *See* COMMAND PAPERS 1257 (1960) for text.

[17] *Done* March 18, 1965. *See* WPTLC Pamphlet Series No. 2 for text.

[18] *See* 19 E.T.S. 1 (1965).

[19] G. SCHWARZENBERGER, *supra* note 13; PRIVATE . . ., *supra* note 13.

[20] J. PUBL. L., *supra* note 15.

genuine value of the property affected, be made in transferable form and be paid without undue delay.[21]

The Convention also provided that questions and disputes between the Parties involving the interpretation or application of the Convention would be referred to the International Court of Justice. Further provisions adopted by the Convention incorporating the requirements of due process of law, non-discrimination, the indirect expropriation of property, arbitration procedures to settle disputes, or to compensate the victims of illegal deprivations of property, were in the opinion of Schwarzenberger, so vague as to make the Convention meaningless for most practical purposes.[22]

The Draft Convention on the Protection of Foreign Property,[23] signed in 1962 and 1967, under the auspices of the Organization for European Economic Cooperation, provides that:

> Each Party shall at all times ensure fair and equitable treatment to the property of the nationals of the other Parties. It shall accord within its territory the most constant protection and security to such property and shall not in any way impair the management, maintenance, use, enjoyment or disposal thereof by unreasonable or discriminatory measures. The fact that certain nationals of any State are accorded treatment more favourable than that provided for in this Convention shall not be regarded as discriminatory against nationals of a Party by reason only of the fact that such treatment is not accorded to the latter.
>
> The provisions of this Convention shall not affect the right of any Party to allow or prohibit the acquisition of property or the investment of capital within its territory by nationals of another Party.[24]

Further, the Convention protects foreign property from indirect deprivation; incorporates the requirement of due process of law; and for the settlement of disputes by an arbitral tribunal. Resort to the International Court of Justice to resolve disputes involving the interpretation and application of the Convention, however, is not provided.

The Convention on the Settlement of Investment Disputes[25] between States and Nationals of Other States was signed in 1965. (Below, § 5-3.4.) Its primary purpose was to provide a mechanism whereby states could settle such disputes through conciliation and

---

[21] *Id.*

[22] G. SCHWARZENBERGER, *supra* note 1 at 187.

[23] COMMAND PAPERS, *supra* note 16.

[24] *Id.* art. 1.

[25] *Done* March 18, 1965. *See* WPTLC Pamphlet Series No. 2 for text.

arbitral tribunals and facilities, and through resort to the International Court of Justice.

The European Convention on Establishment of Companies,[26] open for signature on January 20, 1966, and prepared by the Council of Europe, offers protection to transnational companies and their subsidiaries in countries, members of the Council who have signed the Convention. The Convention provides for full equality of treatment to a company from a member Nation in these areas: taxation, the enjoyment and exercise of personal and property rights, and expropriation decrees. Personnel of such companies are to enjoy freedom of entry, residence and movement within the Party's territory. Such companies are also entitled to the full protection of the law and courts; to legal assistance and representation; and to full access to courts and administrative tribunals and authorities. Disputes involving either the interpretation or the application of the Convention are to be submitted to the International Court of Justice, unless the parties make other arrangements.

Section B: Nationality

§ 2-6. Jurisdiction over Nationals[27]

It is a well-established rule of international law that every state determines for itself who are its nationals. States however cannot

---

[26] 19 E.T.S. 1 (1965).

[27] *See generally* W. BISHOP, *supra* note 1, at 470-77; J. BRIGGS, *supra* note 1, at 144-69; I. BROWNLIE, *supra* note 2, at 302-52; de Castro, *La Nationalité, La Double Nationalité et la Super-nationalité*, 102 RECUEIL DES COURS 521-634 (1961); C. FENWICK, *supra* note 1, at 301-09; C. FENWICK, CASES, *supra* note 1, at 162-204; R. FLOURNOY & M. HUDSON, A COLLECTION OF NATIONALITY LAWS OF VARIOUS COUNTRIES, AS CONTAINED IN CONSTITUTIONS, STATUTES AND TREATIES (New York 1929); A. HERSHEY, *supra* note 2, at 347-64; 2 C. HYDE, *supra* note 1, at 1004-187; International Law Commission, *Draft Convention on the Elimination of Future Statelessness*, 48 AJIL SUPP. 62-66 (1959); *International Law Commission Drafts on Statelessness*, ASIL PROC. 155-86 (1956); Isay, *De la Nationalité*, 5 RECUEIL DES COURS 429-70 (1924); P. JESSUP, A MODERN LAW OF NATIONS 68-93 (New York 1948); 2 A. KISS, *supra* note 1, at 233-72 (1966); Oda, *The Individual in International Law*, in SØRENSEN, *supra* note 2, at 470-81; L. OPPENHEIM, *supra* note 1, at 642-75; L. ORFIELD & E. RE, *supra* note 1, at 458-538, 575-85; PARRY, *supra* note 2, at 3-300; RESTATEMENT, § § 26, 30; J. SALONGA & P. YAP, *supra* note 1, at 203-12; G. SCHWARZENBERGER, *supra* note 1, at 141-44; P. WEIS, NATIONALITY AND STATELESSNESS IN INTERNATIONAL LAW (London 1956); 8 WHITEMAN, *supra* note 1, at 1-193; G. WILSON & G. TUCKER, *supra* note 1, at 133-38.

See also J. BRIERLY, *supra* note 1, at 136-49; J. BRIGGS, *supra* note 1, at 525-80; I. BROWNLIE, *supra* note 2, at 419-44; C. FENWICK, *supra* note 1, at 318-26; C. FENWICK, CASES, *supra* note 1, at 205-81; Guha Roy, *Is The Law of Responsibility of*

(Continued)

extend their protection to anyone they would label a national without some limitation by international law.[28]   It has been the subject of treaty negotiation, as by the Convention on Conflicts of Nationality Laws,[29] signed at The Hague in 1930, the 1961 Convention on the Elimination or Reduction of Stateless,[30] from the 1954 Draft Convention on the Elimination or Reduction of Statelessness,[31] the Model Rules concerning Dual Nationality,[32] drafted by the Asian-African Legal Consultative Committee in 1965 and the 1963 European Convention on Reduction of Cases of Multiple Nationality and Military Obligations in Cases of Multiple Nationality.[33]

A national is an individual who owes allegiance to a certain state and has a claim to the protection of that state.   When a national owes allegiance to only one state, no problem exists.   When two states claim the allegiance of a national on different grounds, problems arise.   Nationality has been determined primarily according to the following principle of *jus soli* by which birth upon the soil confers nationality, the principle of *jus sanguinis* by which the nationality of the parents becomes the nationality of their children, and the rules of naturalization.   The United States, the United Kingdom, and some Latin American states generally follow the principle of *jus soli*, but a combination of the two systems is found in the laws of many other states.   At times, it is especially important for a state to determine who are its nationals (as in the case of military obligations).   In some cases, a child, upon reaching majority,

---

States for Injuries to Aliens a Part of Universal International Law? 55 AJIL 863-91 (1961); *Harvard Draft Convention on the International Responsibility of the State for Injury to Aliens,* ASIL PROC. 102-20 (1960); Healy, *La Constitution Juridique de l'Etranger Spécialement aux Etats-Unis,* 27 RECUEIL DES COURS 401-96 (1929); Oda, *The Individual in International Law, in* SØRENSEN, *supra* note 2, at 469, 481-90; L. OPPENHEIM, *supra* note 1, at 675-76, 678-95; L. ORFIELD & E. RE, *supra* note 1, at 586-92; 6 PARRY, *supra* note 2, at 3-434; RESTATEMENT, § § 164-78; Sohn & Baxter, *Responsibility of States for Injury to the Economic Interests of Aliens,* 52 AJIL 545-84 (1961); Verdross, *Les Règles Internationales Concernant le Traitement des Etrangers,* 37 RECUEIL DES COURS 327-412 (1931); 8 WHITEMAN, *supra* note 1, at 348-1291; G. WILSON & G. TUCKER, *supra* note 1, at 138-41.

[28] Nottebohm Case [1955] I.C.J. 4.

[29] Convention on Certain Questions Relating to the Conflict of Nationality Laws, *done* April 12, 1930, 179 L.N.T.S. 89. *See* 24 AJIL SUPP. 193 (1930) for text.

[30] *Done* Aug. 30, 1961, 9 U.N. GAOR Supp. 21, at 49, U.N. Doc. A/2890 (1961). *See* 48 AJIL SUPP. 62-66 (1954) for text.

[31] *Id.*

[32] *Model Articles Embodying Principles Relating to Elimination or Reduction of Dual or Multiple Nationality,* REPORT OF THE SIXTH SESSION HELD AT CAIRO 24 FEBRUARY - 6 MARCH 1964 at 33-36 (1964).

[33] *See* 59 AJIL 722-24 (1965) for text.

may choose his nationality, and state laws fix the conditions upon which naturalization is granted. Treaties have been negotiated to clarify conflicting or ambiguous rules. Some states have maintained that nationals did not have the right to renounce their allegiance, whereas others have authorized expatriation. The nationality of a woman as independent of her husband is now reflected in international conventions, although some legislation has made her nationality that of her husband. In order to limit the number of cases of multiple nationality, efforts have been made to give the individual who possesses multiple nationality the right to choose his nationality. The nationality of persons residing in a territory which has been transferred by one state to another is generally determined by treaty. Efforts have been made to reduce the hardships resulting from statelessness.[34]

SECTION C: DIPLOMACY

§ 2-7. Intercourse Between States

States carry on their relations with other states under international law by diplomatic and consular representatives and through conferences which may lead to bilateral or multilateral agreements. Meetings of heads of state to consider or decide matters of concern to their nations are more and more a common occurrence in recent years of fast air transportation.

§ 2-7.1. Diplomatic Representatives.[35] In ancient times, relations between states were relatively few; state representatives were

---

[34] Convention on the Elimination or Reduction of Statelessness, *done* Aug. 30, 1961, 9 U.N. GAOR Supp. 21, at 49, U.N. Doc. A/2890 (1961).

[35] *See generally* W. BISHOP, *supra* note 1, at 592-99; J. BRIGGS, *supra* note 1, at 373-91; Deák, *Organs of States in their External Relations . . .,* in SØRENSEN, *supra* note 2, at 381, 394-409; A. FELLER & M. HUDSON, A COLLECTION OF THE DIPLOMATIC AND CONSULAR LAWS AND REGULATIONS OF VARIOUS COUNTRIES (Washington 1933); C. FENWICK, *supra* note 1, at 552-85; C. FENWICK, CASES, *supra* note 1, at 643-65; Guiliano, *Les Relations et Immunités Diplomatiques,* 100 RECUEIL DES COURS 81-202 (1960); Harris, *Diplomatic Privileges and Immunities: A New Regime Is Soon To Be Adopted by the United States,* 62 AJIL 88-113 (1968); Harvard Research in International Law, *Draft Convention on Diplomatic Privileges and Immunities,* 26 AJIL 19-187 (1932); C. HYDE, *supra* note 1, at 1211-1310; *International Law Commission Draft Articles Concerning Intercourse and Immunities,* 52 AJIL 180-204 (1958); Karley, *Some Aspects of the Vienna Conference on Diplomatic Intercourse and Immunities,* 56 AJIL 89-129 (1962); 3 A. KISS, *supra* note 1, at 277-358 (1965); L. OPPENHEIM, *supra* note 1, at 772-828; L. ORFIELD & E. RE, *supra* note 1, at 658-78; PARRY, *supra* note 2, at 525-996; RESTATEMENT, § § 73-81; J. SALONGA & P. YAP, *supra* note 1, at 213-27; S. SCHWARZENBERGER, *supra* note 1, at 99-102, 469-72; Stuart, *Le Droit et la Pratique Diplomatiques et Consulaires,* 48 RECUEIL DES COURS 463-570 (1934); G. WILSON & G. TUCKER, *supra* note 1, at 159-80; Young, *Development of the Law of Diplomatic Relations,* 40 BRIT. Y.B. INT'L L. 140-82 (1964).

sent to other states only on special missions. By the Middle Ages, diplomacy had developed "as an art" among the Italian city states, but, for years, an ambassador was viewed with suspicion. His person, as well as his personal effects, were often in serious danger. The negotiations leading to the Treaty of Westphalia (1648) established the basis for the modern practice of establishing permanent missions abroad to maintain closer relations among states. In the next two centuries, disputes among the European allies after Napoleon's defeat at the Congress of Vienna of 1815, largely over questions of precedence, led to the Congress of Aix-la-Chapelle of 1818 to establish grades of foreign representatives and orders of precedence among diplomats. Present diplomatic procedure is enumerated in the Vienna Convention on Diplomatic Relations[36] of April 18, 1961, effective on April 24, 1964, to which optional protocols concerning the compulsory settlement of disputes and the acquisition of nationality were attached. This Convention largely clarified established rules, but, in some cases, reflected recent trends, such as the provision in Article 11 granting the receiving states the right to determine "the reasonable and normal" size of a mission.

Diplomatic agents are representatives of sovereign states sent by one head of state to another. Domestic law determines who shall be the head of state and the organization of the government dealing with foreign affairs. A state must be consulted with regard to the appointment of a foreign representative and may refuse to receive him if he is considered *persona non grata*, and may do so without giving reasons, although reasons are normally given. The appointment of a diplomat should be refused only for very good reasons based on the conviction of the receiving state that the particular individual cannot perform his functions effectively for political, social, religious, or other reasons. The receiving state may at any time, and without giving reasons, notify the sending state that any member of the mission is *persona non grata*, in which case the sending state will either recall the person or terminate his functions. The sending state may accredit the head of a mission to more than one state, unless any of the receiving states expressly object.

A diplomatic representative is given various official papers for use in his foreign mission. A letter of credence identifies him, states the general purpose of his mission and requests for him full faith on the part of the receiving state. Instructions further identify his mission and give him guidance in its performance. If he is

---

[36] *See* 55 AJIL 1064-82 (1961) for text.

called upon to perform functions outside of his instructions he may be given letters patent, granting him, for example, full powers (*pleins pouvoirs*) for negotiating a treaty. He also receives a special passport and various other papers.

Diplomatic ceremonials, which were quite complex and very formal in the early period, aimed to give weight to the diplomat and clothe his mission with dignity. In modern times, this ceremony has been greatly simplified, but it is still important to observe rules of precedence, places of honor granted in the seating of diplomats at ceremonies and conferences, and established prerogatives and courtesies.

In addition to maintaining responsibility for the internal business of the mission, the diplomat conducts negotiations with the state to which he is a representative, aids and protects his fellow citizens and the interests of the sending state in a variety of ways, seeks to promote friendly relations between his state and the receiving state, and reports to his government on a wide range of subjects. To assure the effective performance of these functions, he has been granted certain privileges and immunities, which have been codified in the Vienna Convention on Diplomatic Relations of 1961. The receiving state is bound to respect the inviolability of all classes of diplomatic agents, of the diplomatic suite, and of the mission's premises and its archives. The diplomatic agent enjoys a broad exemption from civil and criminal jurisdiction, although the sending state may waive this immunity. Exemption from customs duties is often granted as an act of international courtesy. The diplomat has the right of innocent passage while travelling through third states. He is granted a broad exemption from taxes. He also enjoys freedom of communication and of religious worship. A sending state, at the request of a third state and with the consent of the receiving state, may undertake the protection of a third state and of its nationals. The diplomatic mission may be terminated by the recall or dismissal of the diplomat. The ceremony of departure is similar to the ceremony of arrival.

§ 2-7.2. **Consular Representatives.**[37] A history of Consular Representation shows that the establishment of the office of consul pre-

---

[37] *See generally* W. BISHOP, *supra* note 1, at 599-601; J. BRIGGS, *supra* note 1, at 391-406, Deák, *Organs of States in Their External Relations . . .*, in SØRENSEN, *supra* note 2, at 386, 414-24; A. FELLER & M. HUDSON, *supra* note 35; C. FENWICK, *supra* note 1, at 690-705; 2 HYDE, *supra* note 1, at 1311-67; 3 A. KISS, *supra* note 1, at 359-417 (1965); L. LEE, VIENNA CONVENTION ON CONSULAR RELATIONS (Durham, North Carolina, 1966); L. OPPENHEIM, *supra* note 1, at 829-45; PARRY, *supra* note 2, at 1-679; RESTATEMENT § 81; J. SALONGA & P. YAP, *supra* note 1, at 232-40; G. SCHWARZ-

(Continued)

ceded that of permanent embassies and that, in the early period, the consul performed functions later assigned to the diplomat. Capitulation treaties, in effect until recently, gave consuls civil and criminal jurisdiction over nationals travelling in countries in which they were in force (e.g., the Ottoman Empire). With the practice of sending permanent diplomatic agents, the functions of consuls decreased, but later as commerce grew, their duties increased.

Heads of consular posts now fall into four classes: consuls generals, consuls, vice-consuls, and consular agents. They may be chosen from among citizens of the sending state, or, in some cases, from nationals of another state. Some states, however, will not receive their own nationals as consuls.

The document by which a consul is recognized and which grants him certain privileges is known as an *exequatur*, usually issued by the head of the sending state. The receiving state may refuse to accept an *exequatur* or, at any time, may declare that any member of the consular staff is *persona non grata*, without giving reasons. In this case, the sending state will either recall the person concerned or terminate his functions. A consul's functions are determined by his *exequatur*, by treaty, and, since 1963, by the Convention of Consular Relations[38] adopted at a conference in Vienna, which lists thirteen categories of functions. These functions primarily concern commercial and maritime interests, but the consul also aids the citizens of his state in a variety of ways. The date of the *exequatur* determines precedence as between heads of consular posts.

In a state in which the sending state is not represented by a diplomatic mission, a consular officer may be authorized to perform diplomatic acts with the consent of the receiving state. He may perform consular functions in another state with the consent of the states concerned. He may also exercise consular functions on behalf of a third state unless the receiving state objects. As in the case of the diplomatic agent, the receiving state has the right to determine "the reasonable and normal" size of the consular staff.

Consular premises are inviolable, with certain limitations, and enjoy broad exemption from taxation. Consular documents and archives are inviolable at all times. Freedom of movement and travel within the receiving state are allowed, within reasonable

---

ENBERGER, *supra* note 1, at 85-86, 102; I. STEWART, CONSULAR PRIVILEGES AND IMMUNITIES (New York 1926); E. STOWELL, CONSULAR CASES AND OPINIONS Washington 1909); G. WILSON & G. TUCKER, *supra* note 1, at 159-89.

[38] 596 U.N.T.S. 261. *See* 57 AJIL 995-1022 (1963) for text.

limitations. Freedom of communication for all official purposes is granted, including the right of a consular officer to visit a national of his country held in prison or in custody. Consuls have broad immunity from the jurisdiction of the receiving state, including exemption from liability to arrest or detention. They also enjoy some exceptions from customs duties.

Until recently the consular service was generally separate from the diplomatic service. Several states now have a unified service of several grades, making it possible to transfer a foreign service officer readily from one service to another.

§ 2-7.3. **Draft Convention on Special Missions.**[39] Adopted by the United Nations General Assembly on December 8, 1969, this Convention has as its major purpose, as stated in its Preamble, to "contribute to the development of friendly relations among nations," and "to ensure the efficient performance of the functions of special missions as missions representing the State . . ."[40]

Among other things, the Convention provides for the composition of the Special Mission; appointment and notifications required; exemption of the Special Mission from taxation; the inviolability of the premises, the archives and documents of the Special Mission; freedom of movement for the Special Mission vis-à-vis national security; freedom of communication; the personal inviolability of members of the Special Mission, and of their private accommodations; immunity from jurisdiction, exemption from social security legislation, dues and taxes, personal service, customs duties and inspection, which applies as well to the administrative, technical and private staffs of the Mission from the time of entering the territory of the receiving state until the end of the purpose of the Special Mission. The sending state, however, is empowered to waive such immunity should it so desire. Article 44 provides that if a member of the Special Mission should die, the deceased's movable property shall be freely taken out of the country. Members of Special Missions are obligated to respect the laws and regulations of the receiving state; are bound not to interfere in the internal affairs of the receiving state, and not to engage in any professional or commercial activity for profit while in the territory of the receiving state.

---

[39] G.A. Res. 2530, 24 GAOR Supp. 30, U.N. Doc. A/7630 (1968). For text see 9 INT'L L. MAT. 127-51 (1970).

[40] 9 I.L.M. 129 (1970).

§ 2-7.4. Declaration on Principles of International Law Concerning Friendly Relations and Co-operation Among States.[41] Adopted in May 1970, by the Special Committee on Principles of International Law Concerning Friendly Relations and Co-operation among States, this Declaration demonstrated the conviction of the Committee that friendly relations and cooperation among nations was one of the fundamental purposes of the United Nations. In its report, the Committee noted that "the great political, economic, and social changes and scientific progress which have taken place in the world since the adoption of the Charter of the United Nations give increased importance to these principles and to the need for their more effective application in the conduct of States wherever carried on."[42] The Committee felt that observance of the following principles of international law is necessary to the implementation of the purposes of the UN Charter:

(a) The principle that States shall refrain in their international relations from the threat or use of force against the territorial integrity of political independence of any State, or in any manner inconsistent with the purposes of the United Nations;

(b) The principle that States shall settle their international disputes by peaceful means in such a manner that international peace and security and justice are not endangered;

(c) The duty not to intervene in matters within the domestic jurisdiction of any State, in accordance with the Charter;

(d) The duty of States to co-operate with one another in accordance with the Charter;

(e) The principle of equal rights and self-determination of peoples;

(f) The principle of sovereign equality of States;

(g) The principle that States shall fulfil in good faith the obligations assumed by them in accordance with the Charter;

so as to secure their more effective application within the international community which would promote the realization of the purposes of the United Nations.[43]

The Athens World Conference on World Peace Through Law (1963), which created the World Peace Through Law Center, adopted a Statement of General Principles of International Law Adhered to by Civilized Nations which is similar in principles and context. This statement was the product of extensive dis-

---

[41] *See* 7 *UN Monthly Chronicle* 62-68 (1970) for text.

[42] *Id.* at 63.

[43] *Id.* at 63-64.

cussions among the world's greatest experts on international law during four continental conferences held in San Juan, Costa Rica; Tokyo, Japan; Logos, Nigeria; and Rome, Italy; and at the Athens Conference. It is printed in the Proceedings of that Conference. (See *supra* § 1-6.6.5, p. 73)

According to the U.N. Special Committee's Report, states are obligated not to threaten or to use force in their international relations, "to refrain from propaganda for wars of aggression, . . . to refrain from any forcible action which deprives peoples . . . of equal rights and self-determination of their right to self-determination and freedom and independence, . . . to refrain from organizing or encouraging the organization of irregular forces or armed bands, including mercenaries, for incursion into the territory of another State, . . . to refrain from organizing, instigating, assisting or participating in acts of civil strife or terrorist acts in another state or acquiescing in organized activities within its territory directed towards the commission of such acts," and "to pursue in good faith negotiations for the early conclusion of a universal treaty on general and complete disarmament under effective international control."[44]   Concerning the duty of non-intervention, the Report states that:

> No State or group of States has the right to intervene, directly or indirectly, in the internal or external affairs of any other State. Consequently, armed intervention and all other forms of interference or attempted threats against the personality of the State or against its political, economic and cultural elements, are in violation of international law;
>
> No State may use or encourage the use of economic, political or any other type of measures to coerce another State in order to obtain from it the subordination of the exercise of its sovereign rights and to secure from it advantages of any kind. Also, no State shall organize, assist, foment, finance, incite, or tolerate subversive, terrorist or armed activities directed towards the violent overthrow of the regime of another State . . .[45]

Concerning the duty of states to cooperate with each other, the Report states that such cooperation should be present in maintaining international peace and security, in promoting "universal respect" for "human rights and fundamental freedoms for all, and in the elimination of all forms of racial discrimination and all forms of religious intolerance."[46]   States are also bound to cooperate in the economic, social, cultural, educational and scientific and technologi-

---

[44] *Id.* at 64-65.

[45] *Id.* at 65.

[46] *Id.* at 66.

cal fields.[47]   According to the Report, the basis for the principles of equal rights and self-determination of peoples, and of the sovereign equality of states, is the right of all peoples and nations "freely to determine, without external interference, their political status and to pursue their economic, social and cultural development,"[48] and the corresponding duty of all states to do no act, nor to encourage in any way, the commission of any act that would detract from, or interfere with that right.

§ 2-7.5. **International Conferences.**[49]   Conferences through the years have served as a primary means of formulating, clarifying, and implementing important rules and principles for international action. They have established the consensus necessary for the adoption of treaties and other international instruments.

The rapid development of the conference method in the conduct of international intercourse has been one of the striking developments of recent years.   Conferences have largely replaced bipartite negotiation in the regulation of matters of interest to more than two states.   The number of such conferences increases from year to year, and the scope of the subject matter includes an ever-increasing list of subjects.

The first important international conference in the modern era was held at Westphalia in 1648.   It ended the Thirty Years' War and ushered in the modern state system.   This conference and other conferences of the 17th and 18th century, held among

---

[47] *Id.*

[48] *Id.*

[49] *See generally* Baldwin, *The International Congresses and Conferences of the Last Century,* 1 AJIL 565-78 (1907); F. DUNN, THE PRACTICE AND PROCEDURE OF INTERNATIONAL CONFERENCES (Baltimore 1929); K. EUBANK, SUMMIT CONFERENCES 1919-1960 (Norman, Oklahoma 1966); G. HAENSCH, DIE TECKNIK INTERNATONALES KONFERENZEN (Munich 1952); N. HILL, THE PUBLIC INTERNATIONAL CONFERENCE (Baltimore 1929); H. KINDLER, ORGANIZING THE TECHNICAL CONFERENCE (New York 1960); 3 A. KISS, *supra* note 1, at 431-48 (1965); M. MOULTON, A STRUCTURAL VIEW OF THE CONFERENCE AS ORGAN OF INTERNATIONAL CO-OPERATION (Highland Park, New Jersey 1930); L. OPPENHEIM, *supra* note 1, at 869-87; V. PASTUHOV, A GUIDE TO THE PRACTICE OF INTERNATIONAL CONFERENCES (Washington 1945); PAN AMERICAN UNION, CONGRESSES AND CONFERENCES SERIES (Washington 1943); E. SATOW, INTERNATIONAL CONGRESSES (London 1920); UNESCO, THE TECHNIQUE OF INTERNATIONAL CONFERENCES, A PROGRESS REPORT ON RESEARCH PROBLEMS AND METHODS (Paris 1951); UNION OF INTERNATIONAL ASSOCIATION, 1 BIBLIOGRAPHICAL CURRENT LIST OF PAPERS, REPORTS, AND PROCEEDINGS OF INTERNATIONAL MEETINGS (Brussels 1961); UNION OF INTERNATIONAL ASSOCIATION, LES CONGRÈS INTERNATIONAUX DE 1661 À 1899, LISTE COMPLÈTE (Brussels 1960); UNION OF INTERNATIONAL ASSOCIATION, INTERNATIONAL CONGRESS ORGANIZATION: THEORY AND PRACTICE (Brussels 1961); UNITED STATES LIBRARY OF CONGRESS, WORLD LIST OF FUTURE INTERNATIONAL MEETINGS (Washington 1959-   ).

rulers, concerned matters of interest to them, such as territorial possession and domestic problems, rather than subjects of interest to the people of their states. Matters of etiquette, ceremony, and precedence took weeks or even months to settle. The conferences were of an *ad hoc* nature and had no formulated rules of procedure or advance preparation of agenda.

The 19th century and early 20th century conferences have often been called law-making conferences. The Congress of Vienna of 1815 formulated a classification of diplomatic agents, supported the principle of free navigation on certain international rivers, provided for the neutralization of Switzerland, and condemned the slave trade. The first conference of the Latin-American Republics was called by Simon Bolivar in 1826 for the purpose of establishing a system of American states that would develop through diplomatic conferences. This objective was later realized with the creation of the Pan American Union which made the conference a principal means of its operation. The Hague Conferences of 1899 and 1907 created a Permanent Court of Arbitration and laid the foundation for the establishment of the Permanent Court of International Justice.[50]   Several important conferences in this period dealt with the laws of war.[51] Important non-political conferences in this period established organs for international co-operation in specific areas, such as the General Telegraphic Convention[52] which was followed by the Universal Postal Union of 1878, a product of the Paris Conference of 1865;[53] the Union for the Protection of Industrial Property, which was the result of a conference in 1883;[54] and the Convention for the Protection of Literary and Artistic Works, which was signed at the Berne Conference of 1886.[55]

---

[50] G. SCHWARZENBERGER, *supra* note 1, at 241, 247.

[51] The Paris Congress of 1856 on maritime rules of warfare; the Geneva Conferences of 1864 and 1868 for the amelioration of the condition of wounded soldiers; the Conference of St. Petersburg of 1868 regulating the use of explosive bullets; the Conference of Brussels of 1874 on rules of military warfare; the Hague Conferences of 1899 and 1907 dealing primarily with rules of warfare; and the London Naval Conference of 1908-1909.

[52] International Telegraphic Convention, *done* at St. Petersburg, July 22, 1875. *See* 7 AJIL SUPP. 276-78 (1913) for text.

[53] Constitution and Convention of the Universal Postal Union, *done* July 10, 1964, 16 U.S.T. 1291; TIAS 5881.

[54] *See* 38 Stat. 579 (1845) for text.

[55] *Opened for signature* September 9, 1886. French text—*Actes de la 3e Conférence Internationale pour la Protection des Oeuvres litteraires et artistiques réune à Berne du - 9 Septembre*, 1 LE DROIT D'AUTEUR 4 (Berne 1888). English text in the *Second Schedule to the Order in Council of the United Kingdom*, June 24, 1912, issued under the Copyright Act, 1911 (1 and 2 *George* 5, c. 46). Cmnd. Paper No. 5167 (Switzerland, 1887).

Since World War I, both the number and importance of conferences have increased enormously. The Paris Peace Conference of 1919 established the League of Nations which in turn called numerous conferences to resolve international problems. A 1945 conference in San Francisco established the United Nations Organization, which, together with its organs and specialized agencies, has held subsequent conferences on a host of subjects.[56]

The organization of international bodies (e.g., the Assembly of the League of Nations and the General Assembly of the United Nations) is similar to those of the ordinary peace-time conferences. The Conferences have dominant organs, a committee system and rules of procedure which deal with such matters as the selection of officers, the method of voting, language and agenda. The problems of organization and procedure of international conferences include publicity, equality of representation and of voting, the unanimity or majority principle of consent and the language problem.

International conferences held by non-governmental organizations have also played an important role in developing friendly and effective international relations between states and in advancing the rule of law internationally.[57] Like governmental international conferences they have dealt with almost every subject of international interest.

SECTION D: INTERNATIONAL AGREEMENTS

§ 2-8. International Agreements[58]

The various names by which international agreements are called include: treaty, convention, statute, protocol, pact, compromise,

---

[56] *See generally* Chapter 3, *supra.*

[57] *See, e.g.,* the World Conferences of the World Peace Through Law Center discussed throughout this volume.

[58] *See generally* American Law Institute, *supra* note 1, at 359-496; Berlia, *Contribution to the Interpretation of Treaties,* 114 RECUEIL DES COURS 287-331 (1965); W. BISHOP, *supra* note 1, at 86-208; J. BRIERLY, *supra* note 1, at 45-47, 165-75; J. BRIGGS, *supra* note 1, at 406-86; C. FENWICK, *supra* note 1, at 94-96, 514-53; M. HABICHT, POST-WAR TREATIES FOR THE PACIFIC SETTLEMENT OF INTERNATIONAL DISPUTES (Cambridge, Mass. 1931); Harvard Research in International Law, *Draft Convention on the Law of Treaties,* 29 AJIL SUPP. 653-1226 (1935); 2 C. HYDE, *supra* note 1, at 1369-1558; Waldock, *(Fourth) Report on the Law of Treaties* [1965], in 2 Y.B. INT'L L. COMM'N 3-107, U.N. Doc. A/CN.4/177 (1965); Jessup, *The U.N. Convention on the Law of Treaties,* in COLUMBIA LAW REVIEW ESSAYS ON INTERNATIONAL LAW 197-234 (New York 1965); 1 A. KISS, *supra* note 1, at 131-589 (1962); Kunz, *The Meaning and the Range of the Norm Pacta Sunt Servanda,* 39 AJIL 180-97 (1945); L.N.T.S. (Geneva 1920-1944); A. McNAIR, THE LAW OF TREATIES: BRITISH PRACTICE AND OPINIONS (Oxford 1938); W. MALLOY, TREATIES, CONVENTIONS, INTERNATIONAL ACTS, PROTOCOLS AND AGREEMENTS BETWEEN THE UNITED STATES OF
(Continued)

covenant, charter, a *modus vivendi* (feasible arrangement) and an exchange of notes. Historically, treaties were considered to be no more than simple contracts between states with respective rights and duties. But, today, treaties are also considered to be a primary source of international law and deal with subjects covering the whole range of international relations. They have been variously classified as bilateral and multilateral, simple and conditional, executed and executory, as well as according to their objectives (e.g., treaties of peace, commerce or extradition). They have been concluded not only between states, but also between states and international organizations, between states and individuals, between international organizations and individuals, and, finally, between international organizations themselves. Treaties between sovereign states are generally concluded by representatives possessing "full powers." States usually give their consent to be bound by the treaty through ratification, although consent may be given by other means. The constitutional requirements for ratification vary widely in different states.

A state may formulate reservations to a treaty and states have often done so. Although reservations have at times weakened instruments, as in the case of reservations to the compulsory jurisdiction of the International Court of Justice, they have, nevertheless, served as a means of obtaining consent by a state to be bound by many treaty provisions when other provisions of the same convention are unacceptable. Reservations must be submitted in writing and may be withdrawn at any time.

A treaty enters into force upon ratification or upon the date on which the parties agree. It often provides that it will become effective upon the exchange of ratifications, or, in the case of multilateral treaties, upon ratification by a certain number of states.

AMERICA AND THE OTHER POWERS, 1776-1937 (Washington 1910-1938); D. MILLER, TREATIES AND OTHER INTERNATIONAL ACTS OF THE UNITED STATES OF AMERICA, 1776-1863 (Washington 1931-1942); D. MYERS, MANUAL OF COLLECTIONS OF TREATIES AND OF COLLECTIONS RELATING TO TREATIES (Cambridge, Mass. 1922); L. ORFIELD & E. RE, *supra* note 1, at 29-110; Parry, *The Law of Treaties,* in SØRENSEN, *supra* note 2, at 1, 175-245, R. ROXBURGH, INTERNATIONAL CONVENTIONS AND THIRD STATES (London 1917); J. SALONGA & P. YAP, *supra* note 1, at 240-64; J. SCHNEIDER, TREATY-MAKING POWER OF INTERNATIONAL ORGANIZATIONS (Geneva 1959); G. SCHWARZENBERGER, *supra* note 1, at 147-80; J. SCOTT, TREATIES FOR THE ADVANCEMENT OF PEACE (New York 1920); B. SINHA, UNILATERAL DENUNCIATION OF TREATY BECAUSE OF PRIOR VIOLATIONS OF OBLIGATIONS BY THE OTHER PARTY (The Hague 1966); U.N. MULTILATERAL TREATIES, LIST OF RATIFICATIONS, ACCESSIONS, ETC. AS OF 31 DECEMBER 1968 (New York 1969); UNITAR, WIDER ACCEPTANCE OF MULTILATERAL TREATIES (New York 1969); U.N.T.S. (New York 1945-); DEP'T OF STATE, OFFICE OF THE LEGAL ADVISER, TREATIES IN FORCE: A LIST OF TREATIES AND OTHER AGREEMENTS OF THE UNITED STATES IN FORCE ON JAN. 1, 1969 (Washington 1969).

Treaties are generally to be interpreted according to their plain meaning, which the Permanent Court of International Justice frequently invoked but did not always follow it. The "plain meaning rule" apparently is based upon the assumption that there can be only one accurate interpretation of a particular text and that the interpretation involved in plain meaning is "clear" or "natural" or "the ordinary meaning." In the *Interpretation of the 1919 Convention Concerning Employment of Women During the Night,*[59] the Permanent Court of International Justice gave lip service to the plain meaning rule, but nevertheless carefully examined the negotiating history of the particular convention as well as of other related conventions. Probably one of the most significant criticisms of the plain meaning rule is that those interpreters who claim to use it actually provide some kind of a context to give the most accurate meaning to the words of a text. This point has been made by Judge Anzilotti in his famous dissent in the *1919 Convention* Case: "But I do not see how it is possible to say that an article of a convention is clear until the subject and aim of the convention have been ascertained, for the article only assumes its true import in this convention and in relation thereto."[60]

One of the most significant insights of contemporary semantics is that word symbols devoid of context have, at best, but little meaning. The same word symbols, located in the relevant context of conditions, can be interpreted in a manner which accords them a reasonably meaningful and objective content. Lord McNair has referred to a deceased man's "will of conspicuous brevity," the "depositive portion of which consisted only of the words 'all for mother'." As an abstract matter, it is difficult to find a word more "clear" or less "ambiguous" than "mother," because a man can have only one. The evidence adduced from the context of conditions, however, tended to show that the deceased's wife was always referred to as "mother" within the family. In addition, nothing suggested that the deceased's mother was alive at the time he made his will. In summary, the word "mother" may be regarded as clear and unambiguous in some abstract sense, but may require extrinsic evidence to identify the particular person described as "mother" in the will questioned.[61]

The Harvard Research in International Law Draft Convention on Treaties states the well-established "general purpose" approach to treaty interpretation:

---

[59] P.C.I.J. [1932] Ser. A/B No. 50, as discussed in A. McNAIR, *supra* note 58.

[60] *Id.*

[61] *Id.*

(a) A treaty is to be interpreted in the light of the general purpose which it is intended to serve. The historical background of the treaty, *travaux preparatoires*, the circumstances of the parties at the time the treaty was entered into, the change in these circumstances sought to be effected, the subsequent conduct of the parties in applying the provisions of the treaty, and the conditions prevailing at the time interpretation is being made, are to be considered in connection with the general purpose which the treaty is intended to serve. (b) When the text of a treaty is embodied in versions in different languages, and when it is not stipulated that the version in one of the languages shall prevail, the treaty is to be interpreted with a view to giving to corresponding provisions in the different versions a common meaning which will effect the general purpose which the treaty is intended to serve.[62]

On the other hand, the PCIJ in the *Lotus* Case[63] held that this preparatory work of the treaty is not to be used in interpreting it when the meaning is clear.

§ 2-8.1. *Pacta Sunt Servanda.* The established rule concerning the binding effect of international agreements is *pacta sunt servanda,* which is interpreted as meaning that agreements will be observed in good faith. Since international agreements are usually entered into in order to deal with a future state of affairs, it is apparent that an agreement should not be interpreted as inapplicable simply because future events do not correspond fully with the expectations of one or more of the parties. If such changes of conditions invalidate treaties, reasonable exepctations concerning their effectiveness would be frustrated and the entire structure of treaty law would be brought into question. *Pacta sunt servanda,* therefore, represents the normal rule which is applied almost invariably.

§ 2-8.2. *Rebus Sic Stantibus.* The doctrine *rebus sic stantibus,* which means, in effect, that treaties will be observed only while things thus stand, deals with the unusual situation of very drastic changes of circumstances which are so extreme that it would violate the intentions of the parties to the agreement, at the time it was entered into, if it were still enforced in the new situation. Since this doctrine is designed to deal only with a very unusual situation, it is understandable that judges, foreign ministries, and text writers have been very careful to invoke and apply it only in the most unusual circumstances.

One of the very rare situations in which the doctrine of *rebus sic stantibus* was invoked to terminate a treaty is set forth in the

[62] 29 AJIL SUPP. 653, 937 (1935).

[63] The S.S. Lotus [1927] P.C.I.J. Ser. A, No. 10, at 22-3.

Opinion of Acting Attorney General Biddle of the United States in Respect to the International Load Line Convention.[64] This Convention was designed to prevent competition in merchant shipping by overloading merchant vessels in a way which would jeopardize life and property at sea. Acting Attorney General Biddle stated that, in view of the drastic change of conditions involved in the Second World War in 1941 when merchant ships were essential to the Allied war effort, the Load Line Convention was not applicable to the wartime situation in which merchant vessels were being used for the transport of men and material without regard to the competitive factors which existed in peacetime. In addition, the greatest possible utilization of merchant shipping was necessary to achieve proper military objectives and this, on occasion, involved overloading merchant vessels in a manner which would not be deemed proper in peacetime. Acting Attorney General Biddle's conclusion that the particular change of circumstances was so drastic that the Load Line Convention was not applicable to the wartime situation, has not been substantially criticized. In summary, the actual wartime circumstances were not within the intention of the parties in writing the Convention.

§ 2-8.3. **The Vienna Convention on the Law of Treaties.**[65] The culmination of 20 years' work, this treaty was adopted in 1969 by the United Nations as a codification of the law of treaties. As of January 1, 1970, the Convention had been signed by 36 countries. The Convention deals with the following subjects: Conclusion and entry into force of treaties (Part II), Observance, application and interpretation of treaties (Part III), Amendment and modification of treaties (Part IV), Invalidity, termination and suspension of the operation of treaties (Part V), and Depositories, notifications, corrections and registration of treaties (Part VII). In its Preamble, the Convention expresses its belief that "the codification and progressive development of the law of treaties achieved in the present convention will promote the purposes of the United Nations set forth in the Charter, namely the maintenance of international peace and security, the development of friendly relations and the achievement of cooperation among nations. . ."

The Convention codifies many principles of customary international law related to treaties. For example, in Article 26, the

---

[64] 4 OP'S ATT'Y GEN. 119 (1941).

[65] *See* Conference Document A/Conf. 39/27 May 23, 1969; 8 INT'L L. MAT. 679-727 (1969).

principle of *pacta sunt servanda,* one of the most fundamental principles of international law, is reiterated: "Every treaty in force is binding on the parties to it and must be performed by them in good faith."[66] According to the Convention, treaties should also be interpreted in good faith in accordance with the ordinary meaning of the words to be construed and in light of its purposes (Art. 31). In Article 18, the Convention obliges states not to defeat the object and purpose of the treaty prior to its entry into force and Article 19 prohibits reservations to a treaty not permitted by the treaty.

Article 53 of the Convention also codifies the customary international law principle of *jus cogens:*

> A treaty is void if, at the time of its conclusion, it conflicts with a peremptory norm of general international law. For the purpose of the present convention, a peremptory norm of general international law is a norm accepted and recognized by the international community of states as a whole as a norm from which no derogation is permitted and which can be modified only by a subsequent norm of general international law having the same character.[67]

A treaty may be terminated for various reasons. Article 43 provides that, "The invalidity, termination or denunciation of a treaty . . . shall not in any way impair the duty of any state to fulfill any obligation embodied in the treaty to which it would be subject under international law independently of the treaty;"[68] and Article 44 provides that States may not denounce or terminate only certain parts or provisions of a treaty.

The Convention also provides that treaties may be rendered invalid. Bases for invalidity are: error (Article 48), fraud (Article 49), corruption or coercion of a representative of a State (Article 50 and 51), coercion of a state by the threat or use of force (Article 52), or by showing that the treaty conflicts with a peremptory norm of general international law (Article 53). A treaty may be terminated by consent of the parties, by conclusion of a later treaty, regarding the same subject incompatible with the first (Article 59), by its breach (Article 60), by supervening impossibility of performance (Article 61), by a fundamental change of circumstances "not foreseen by the parties" if the effect of the change is radically to transform the extent of obligations still to be performed under the treaty (Article 62), and by the emer-

---

[66] *Id.* at 1.

[67] *Id.* at 25.

[68] *Id.* at 21.

gency of a new peremptory norm of general international law conflicting with the treaty (Article 64). According to Article 63, "The severance of diplomatic or consular relations between parties to a treaty does not affect the legal relations established between them by the treaty except in so far as the existence of diplomatic or consular relations is indispensable for the application of a treaty."[69]

In general, however, the fact that a state's consent to be bound by a treaty was granted in violation of internal law, or the fact that a state representative exceeded his delegated powers, or that there was an error relating to the wording of a treaty provision, does not justify invalidation of the treaty. According to Article 34, however, a treaty cannot create either obligations or rights for a third state without its consent.

The termination of a treaty, of course, releases parties from the obligation of performance. According to the doctrine of *rebus sic stantibus*, (while things thus stand), a treaty may be voided by a basic change in circumstances. Article 62 of the Vienna Convention states that a fundamental change in the circumstances existing at the time the treaty was concluded, and which was not foreseen by the parties, may be invoked as grounds for terminating that treaty if these circumstances constituted an essential basis of consent and the change radically affects the state's obligations.[70]

When treaties have entered into force, they should be promptly transmitted to the United Nations for registration and publication. This is a very important requirement, since international agreements create duties and obligations that should be widely and readily known. Although many states have treaty compilations, these are often not available in other states, and in some cases are available only in a few centers of the states themselves. Other states not only lack treaty series but lack indexes to the official journals or gazettes in which treaty texts are published.

Among the leading general treaty compilations are: G.F. de Martens, *Recueil des Traites* (Gottingen, 1817-   ); the *British Foreign and State Papers* (London, 1841-   ); the *Deutsches Handels-Archiv* (Berlin, 1856-   ); and the *League of Nations Treaty Series,* 204 vols. (Geneva, 1920-44). The Treaty Affairs Staff of the Office of the Legal Advisor of the United States Department of State has published a volume entitled *Treaties in Force: A List of Treaties and Other International Agreements of the United*

---

[69] *Id.* at 31.

[70] *Id.*

States in Force on January 1, 1969. As of July 1, 1969, 4,954 treaties were in force between the United States and other countries. The most valuable and comprehensive post-World War II treaty compilation is the *United Nations Treaty Series,* which now contains 626 volumes. The United Nations Offices in New York City and the United Nations Information Office in Washington keep current records of treaty ratifications. (See § 1-6.2 above).

The increase in both the number of states in the international community and in the complexity of the subject matter of international relations has made the acceptance of multilateral treaties more and more difficult. Alternately, the United Nations has used resolutions and declarations to advance international purposes, since these instruments do not require ratification. The United Nations has also created international organizations to achieve goals of multilateral treaties. It has emphasized the importance of wider acceptance of multilateral treaties and has made a study of the impediments to their acceptance and of the measures that might be taken to overcome these impediments.[71]

SECTION E: JURISDICTION AND THE INDIVIDUAL

§ 2-9. Jurisdiction

The jurisdictional competence of a state is the legal authority it possesses consistent with the limitations of international law which have been developed to protect the common interests of the community of states. The jurisdiction of a state typically includes authority over its land area, over bodies of water within and adjoining its land area, over the airspace above it and over persons within its domain.

§ 2-9.1. Territorial Jurisdiction.[72]

States have acquired jurisdiction over land by discovery, occupation, conquest, cession, prescription and accretion. In the early period, discovery of previously

---

[71] UNITAR, WIDER ACCEPTANCE OF MULTILATERAL TREATIES (New York 1969).

[72] *See generally* Bastid, *Les Problèmes Territoriaux dans la Jurisprudence de la Cour Internationale de Justice,* 107 RECUEIL DES COURS 365-495 (1962); W. BISHOP, *supra* note 1, at 443-71; J. BRIERLY, *supra* note 1, at 91-102; J. BRIGGS, *supra* note 1, at 170-83; I. BROWNLIE, *supra* note 2, at 96-166, 261-73; C. FENWICK, *supra* note 1, at 402-35; J. BRIGGS, CASES, *supra* note 1, at 466-505; A. HERSHEY, *supra* note 2, at 276-94; 1 C. HYDE, *supra* note 1, at 319-58, 386-90; Mann, *The Doctrine of Jurisdiction in International Law,* 111 RECUEIL DES COURS 5-162 (1964); L. OPPENHEIM, *supra* note 1, at 451-60, 543-81; L. ORFIELD & E. RE, *supra* note 1, at 335-84; RESTATEMENT, § 10; J. SALONGA & P. YAP, *supra* note 1, at 145-49; G. SCHWARZENBERGER, *supra* note 1, at 461-63; 2 WHITEMAN 1028-1231; G. WILSON & G. TUCKER, *supra* note 1, at 107-12.

unknown land was considered adequate to grant title. Somewhat later, discovery had to be coupled with occupation in order to grant title, although occupation of coastal areas gave a *prima facie* title to unexplored interior areas. Conquest, followed by subjugation and control for many years gave title to land, but since the Covenant of the League of Nations and the Kellogg-Briand Pact, this is no longer considered valid. Title to land may pass by cession, for example, in the transfer of title by a treaty of peace as in the case of the cession of the Alsace-Lorraine by Germany to France after World War I or the lease of the Panama Canal area to the United States; by prescription, or long-continued possession, as for example, in the acquisition by the Netherlands of title to the Island of Palmas by continued exercise of sovereignty over the island for many years, even though the land was thought to be ceded to the United States by Spain (the United States had a legal claim through cession but the Netherlands had a better claim through the open exercise of sovereignty); and by accretion, as for example, in the imperceptible addition of mud islands (alluvium) in the mouth of a river.

§ 2-9.2. **Maritime and Fluvial Jurisdiction.**[73] States have jurisdiction over rivers, enclosed waters, the territorial sea and vessels within these territorial waters. A state has exclusive jurisdiction over rivers lying entirely within its land area. When a river forms the boundary between two states, the jurisdiction of each state extends to the middle of the principal channel or *thalweg*, unless otherwise established by treaty. In some cases, treaties have clarified the exact location of the *thalweg* by establishing fixed points in order to avoid ambiguity of interpretation. When the *thalweg* changes its course by alluvium, or the slow erosion of its banks, the boundary between two states and the corresponding jurisdiction of each state changes accordingly. When, however, a river makes a sudden change in its course by what is

---

[73] *See generally* W. BISHOP, *supra* note 1, at 388-92, 535-36, 539-41, 543-45; L. BOUCHEZ, THE REGIME OF BAYS IN INTERNATIONAL LAW (Leyden 1964); J. BRIERLY, *supra* note 1, at 105-07, 121-26; J. BRIGGS, *supra* note 1, at 196-209, 335, 339, 357-61; C. FENWICK, *supra* note 1, at 451-52, 455-57; C. FENWICK, CASES, *supra* note 1, at 506-28; A. HERSHEY, *supra* note 2, at 295-320; C. HYDE, *supra* note 1, at 482-89, 519-85; 4 A. KISS, *supra* note 1, at 3-25, 35-39, 153-73; J. OBIETA, THE INTERNATIONAL STATUS OF THE SUEZ CANAL (The Hague 1963); L. OPPENHEIM, *supra* note 1, at 463-88, 505-16; L. ORFIELD & E. RE, *supra* note 1, at 425-26; A BRITISH DIGEST OF INTERNATIONAL LAW 3-367 (C. Parry ed., London 1965) [hereinafter cited as PARRY]; RESTATEMENT, § § 12-14; Sahovic & Bishop, *Internal Waters*, in SØRENSEN, *supra* note 2, at 311, 332-35; J. SALONGA & P. YAP, *supra* note 1, at 140-42; G. SCHWARZENBERGER, *supra* note 1, at 487-93; G. WILSON & G. TUCKER, *supra* note 1, at 117-21; WPTLC, *Special Report on Maritime Law*, in WORLD PEACE THROUGH LAW: BANGKOK CONFERENCE (1969) (to be published) [hereinafter cited as BANGKOK CONF.].

known as avulsion, the old boundary line and former jurisdiction are retained. When a river flows through or into two or more states, each state has jurisdiction for certain purposes, such as administrative regulations and tolls. Opinion is divided on the question of whether a state can exclude a co-riparian. Treaties have often regulated the navigation by other states of the rivers of a state having exclusive jurisdiction. Current practice favors innocent passage. Some important rivers, such as the Rhine, the Congo and the Amazon, have been internationalized by treaties.

The broad rule governing enclosed waters within a state, such as lakes, bays, gulfs, estuaries, straits and canals, grants jurisdiction to that state. Very large lakes have at times been regarded as "high seas" and have therefore not been subject to the exclusive jurisdiction of the states in which they are located. Bays, the mouth of which did not exceed six miles, have historically been considered as within the jurisdiction of the states enclosing them, since an entry could not be made without violating the rule of the three-mile limit. However, some bays wider than six miles at the entrance have been claimed by states on both sides of the entrance on the basis of a prescriptive right. In recent years, the distance of 10 miles at entrance has received growing support, and in 1956, the International Law Commission proposed the acceptance of 15 miles. The question of jurisdiction over bays, gulfs, estuaries, straits and canals, and the rights of navigation should be examined in each individual case since different rules govern different bodies of water. In general, efforts have been made to grant innocent passage to all vessels in time of peace, but even this has encountered difficulties (e.g., in the troubled and important case of the Suez Canal and in the controversy over the Gulf of Aqaba).

§ 2-9.3. Jurisdiction over Territorial Waters.[74] The assertion of a high degree of jurisdiction over territorial waters, subject to the

---

[74] L. ALEXANDER, THE LAW OF THE SEA: OFFSHORE BOUNDARIES AND ZONES (Columbus 1967); P. ANNINOS, THE CONTINENTAL SHELF AND PUBLIC INTERNATIONAL LAW (The Hague 1953); W. BISHOP, *supra* note 1, at 481-517; J. BRIERLY, *supra* note 1, at 102-13; J. BRIGGS, *supra* note 1, at 196-97; I. BROWNLIE, *supra* note 2, at 167-201; Butler, *The Legal Regime of Russian Territorial Waters,* 62 AJIL 51-77 (1968); Cheng, *Communist China and the Law of the Sea,* 63 AJIL 53-60, 62-65 (1907); H. DJALAL, THE LIMIT OF TERRITORIAL WATERS IN INTERNATIONAL LAW (Ann Arbor 1962); C. FENWICK, *supra* note 1, at 442-45; C. FENWICK, CASES, *supra* note 1, at 528-37; *Geneva Convention on the Territorial Sea and Contiguous Zone, 1958,* text in 52 AJIL 834-42 (1958); Goldie, *Sedentary Fisheries and Art. 2(4) of the Convention on the Continental Shelf, a Plea for a Separate Regime,* 63 AJIL 86-97 (1969); Harvard Research in International Law, *The Law of Territorial Waters,* Second Draft (Cambridge, Mass. 1929); A. HERSHEY, *supra* note 2, at 295-97; 1 C. HYDE, *supra*

(Continued)

right of innocent passage, has for years been a generally recognized rule of international law. It was based upon a state's need for control over that area for purposes of self-preservation. Bynkershoek, writing in 1702 in *De Dominio Maris Dissertatio (The Dissertation on the Sovereignty of the Sea)*, enunciated the principle that the jurisdiction of a state extends to "where the power of men's weapons ends,"[75] which at that time was a marine league or about three miles. The three-mile limit was later recognized by several leading maritime powers, but other powers claimed up to 12 miles. A few states have made claims up to 200 miles. Twentieth century conferences have attempted to reconcile the different claims but without success. At the 1960 Geneva Conference on the Law of the Sea, the United States, the United Kingdom and Canada proposed that the territorial waters be extended to six miles, but this proposal failed by one vote to receive the two-thirds majority needed for adoption. It is generally recognized that the coastal state must permit innocent passage through the territorial waters but may take steps to prevent passage which is not innocent.

By treaties, states have extended their jurisdiction over territorial waters for special purposes. In the period from 1919 to 1933, for example, between the adoption and repeal of the Eighteenth Amendment to the United States Constitution which prohibited the manufacture and sale of intoxicating liquors, the United States was authorized by treaty with Great Britain to search and seize British vessels which violated or attempted to violate the U.S. liquor laws within a prescribed distance from the land. Later, the United States declared a "customs area" which gave customs officers the right to bring into port vessels "hovering" outside but adjacent to "customs waters."

By the doctrine of "hot pursuit" a state may pursue a ship which has committed an offense within its territorial waters and escaped to the high seas. The pursuit must start within the territorial waters

---

note 1, at 451-76, 515-19, 777-97; *International Law Commission Draft on the Regime of the Territorial Sea*, ASIL PROC. 116-36 (1956); P. JESSUP, THE LAW OF TERRITORIAL WATERS AND MARITIME JURISDICTION (New York 1927); 4 A. KISS, *supra* note 1, at 95-126 (1962); W. MASTERSON, JURISDICTION IN MARGINAL SEAS (New York 1929); L. OPPENHEIM, *supra* note 1, at 463-504; RESTATEMENT, §§ 14-15, 21-23; Sahovic & Bishop, *Territorial Sea*, in SØRENSEN, *supra* note 2, at 336-42; J. SALONGA & P. YAP, *supra* note 1, at 134-39; G. SCHWARZENBERGER, *supra* note 1, at 126-33; 4 WHITEMAN 1-498, 740-932; 6 *id.* at 278-726; G. WILSON & G. TUCKER, *supra* note 1, at 121-22; Young, *Offshore Claims and Problems in the North Sea*, 59 AJIL 505-22 (1965); Young, *Sedentary Fisheries and the Continental Shelf*, 55 AJIL 359-73 (1961).

[75] Bynkershoek, *De Dominio Maris*, in CLASSICS OF INTERNATIONAL LAW 44 (J. Scott ed. R. Magoffin trans. 1923).

or the contiguous zone. It must take place immediately and be continuous. The pursuing ship must not enter the territorial waters of another state. It must not use excessive force to obtain the return of the ship to one of its ports. The basis of the doctrine is the need of a state to exercise effective territorial jurisdiction, which would be frustrated if pursuit were not permitted.

States have also claimed the right to exploit the natural resources of the continental shelf. It is maintained that the grant of this right is "reasonable and just" as well as advantageous to the adjacent state. Questions concerning the right to this claim and the extent of the area under state control have been vigorously debated. A Convention on the Continental Shelf,[76] adopted at Geneva in 1958, gave jurisdiction to the contiguous area over the seabed and subsoil under the territorial waters "to a depth of 200 meters, or beyond that limit to an extent to which exploitation is possible." The grant of this jurisdiction does not affect the rules governing jurisdiction over the superjacent waters.

Recently, many nations, including the United States, have proposed that the ocean depth beyond 200 meters (660 feet) be internationalized, and placed under the jurisdiction and control of an international agency which would regulate the exploitation of the seabed beyond 200 meters. The profits, or royalties, from such exploitation would be specifically earmarked for economic aid to developing nations. The United Nations Seabed Committee is presently engaged in outlining the nature, duties and functions of such an international agency, and the World Peace Through Law Center has proposed a draft Treaty Governing the Exploration and Use of the Ocean Bed, also setting the 200 meter mark.[77]

Many special claims have been made to extend maritime jurisdiction beyond the three-mile limit for special purposes. These claims have generally been regulated by treaties, and special problems arising from the interpretation of these treaties have at times been settled by other treaties or arbitration. The Canadian fisheries and the disputed question of seal-fishing in the Bering Sea are important examples. The 1958 United Nations Conference on the Law of the Sea adopted a Convention on Fishing and Conservation of the Living Resources of the High Seas,[78] which emphasized the need for the cooperation of states to avoid overexploiting the living resources of the sea and gave states a special status in the seas adjacent to their coasts.

---

[76] 15 U.S.T. 471; TIAS 5578; 499 U.N.T.S. 311. *See* 52 AJIL 858-62 (1958) for text.

[77] BELGRADE CONF., to be published in 1971.

[78] *Done* April 29, 1958, 559 U.N.T.S. 285. *See* 52 AJIL 851-58 (1958) for text.

§ 2-9.4. Jurisdiction over Vessels Within Territorial Waters.[79]

States have some jurisdiction over both public and private vessels within their own waters. For many years it was held, by the fiction of extraterritoriality, that a merchant ship was "part of the territory of the country whose flag it flies," but this fiction has been rejected by modern authorities and by court decisions. Claims to jurisdiction over foreign vessels, when within the waters of a given state, have varied. According to United States practice, private merchant ships are subject to the jurisdiction of the United States only when they disturb the "public peace;" acts involving the "internal order of the vessel" are under the jurisdiction of the state whose flag the ship flies. France, on the other hand, assumes jurisdiction only when a certain act adversely affects a person other than those belonging to the ship. A British law provides that all acts committed within the marine league are subject to British jurisdiction. The case of *Regina v. Anderson*,[80] decided by the Court of Criminal Appeal of Great Britain in 1868, points out that an individual may be subject to the state of which he is a citizen, the state in whose port the offense was committed, and the state which flies the flag of the vessel on which the act was committed. The United States Supreme Court, in the case of *Schooner Exchange v. McFadden* (1812),[81] found a clear distinction between the treatment of merchant vessels and that of government-owned vessels, the latter being exempt from local jurisdiction. However, foreign government vessels, operated for commercial purposes, are treated in the same manner as private merchant vessels. Foreign vessels which enter a port under stress of weather or other necessity are not subject to the jurisdiction of the local state. In the famous "law of the flag" case of *National Maritime Union and McCulloch v. Sociedad Nacional de Marineros de Honduras,* 372 U.S. 937, 83 Sup. Ct. 877, 9 L.ed. 2d 767 (1963), the Supreme Court of the United States upheld the 4000-year-old rule of international law that the law of the flag governs in matters relating to seamen on board a ship.

---

[79] *See generally,* W. BISHOP, *supra* note 1, at 481-517, 521-25, 528-29; J. BRIGGS, *supra* note 1, at 241-47, 318-23; H. CROCKER, THE EXTENT OF THE MARGINAL SEA (Washington 1919); C. FENWICK, *supra* note 1, at 376-79; C. FENWICK, CASES, *supra* note 1, at 342-59; 4 A. KISS, *supra* note 1, at 39-78 (1962); L. ORFIELD & E. RE, *supra* note 1, at 600-20; J. SALONGA & P. YAP, *supra* note 1, at 152-56; G. SCHWARZENBERGER, *supra* note 1, at 103-04; G. WILSON & G. TUCKER, *supra* note 1, at 125-29.

[80] 11 Cox's Criminal Cases 198. *See* J. BRIGGS, *supra* note 1, at 318-20.

[81] 7 Cranch 116. *See* J. BRIGGS, *supra* note 1, at 241-45.

§ 2-9.5. Fishing Rights and Privileges.[82]

The right to fish on the high seas is not subject to the jurisdiction of any state and is limited only by the obligation of each state to recognize the similar right of other states. The right to fish within the three-mile limit is within the exclusive jurisdiction of the contiguous state. Fishing within limits normally claimed by states as within their jurisdiction has at times been authorized, as in the case of the Canadian fisheries. Controversial claims have been made with regard to the right to fish in certain waters, as in the case of seal-fishing in the Bering Sea; these claims were settled by arbitration. Some states have established special fishery zones by treaty, as was done by the European Fisheries Convention of March 9, 1964.[83]

§ 2-9.6. The High Seas.[84]

In ancient times the high seas, sometimes called the "open sea," were considered free and open to the use and navigation of all peoples. In the late Middle Ages, however, European maritime states laid claim to large areas of ocean spaces: for example, Portugal claimed the Indian Ocean and the southern part of the Atlantic Ocean, and Spain the Pacific Ocean and the Gulf of Mexico, leading to a notable early 17th century controversy. Hugo Grotius in his *Mare Liberum* maintained that the sea could

---

[82] *See generally* Dean, *The Geneva Conference on the Law of the Sea, VI, Fisheries and Conservation,* 52 RECUEIL DES COURS 625-27 (1958); C. FENWICK, *supra* note 1, at 453, 501-03; C. FENWICK, CASES, *supra* note 1, at 583-89; *Geneva Convention on Fishing and Conservation of the Living Resources of the High Seas,* 52 AJIL 851-58 (1958); PARRY, *supra* note 2, at 413-618; S. RIESENFELD, PROTECTION OF COASTAL FISHERIES UNDER INTERNATIONAL LAW (Washington 1942); Sahovic & Bishop, *Contiguous Zone,* in SØRENSEN, *supra* note 2, at 340; G. SCHWARZENBERGER, *supra* note 1, at 510-11; 4 WHITEMAN 932-1240; G. WILSON & G. TUCKER, *supra* note 1, at 122-25; *WPTLC Fisheries Law,* in BANGKOK CONF.

[83] *See* 58 AJIL 1070-81 (1964) for text.

[84] *See generally* Allen, *The Freedom of the Sea,* 60 AJIL 814-16 (1966); I. BROWNLIE, *supra* note 2, at 207-23; C. COLOMBOS, THE INTERNATIONAL LAW OF THE SEA (4th ed. London 1959); C. FENWICK, *supra* note 1, at 496-503; F. GARCIA-AMADOR, THE EXPLOITATION AND CONSERVATION OF THE RESOURCES OF THE SEA (Leyden 1959); *Geneva Convention on Fishing and Conservation of the Living Resources of the High Seas, supra* note 17; *Geneva Convention on the High Seas,* 52 AJIL 842-51 (1958); A. HERSHEY, *supra* note 2, at 307, 321-28; 1 C. HYDE, *supra* note 1, at 751-63; *International Law Commission Draft on Regime of the High Seas,* ASIL PROC. 136-54 (1956); 4 A. KISS, *supra* note 1, at 127-53 (1962); McDougal, Burke & Vlasio, *The Maintenance of Public Order at Sea and the Nationality of Ships,* 54 AJIL 25-116 (1960); M. McDOUGAL & W. BURKE, THE PUBLIC ORDER OF THE OCEANS (New Haven 1962); L. OPPENHEIM, *supra* note 1, at 582-608, 628-35; L. ORFIELD & E. RE, *supra* note 1, at 640-53; F. PIGGOT, THE FREEDOM OF THE SEAS (Oxford 1919); P. POTTER, THE FREEDOM OF THE SEAS, LAW, AND POLITICS (New York 1924); RESTATEMENT, § 22; Sahovic & Bishop, *High Seas,* in SØRENSEN, *supra* note 2, at 311, 346-51; G. SCHWARZENBERGER, *supra* note 1, at 133-35; G. WEISSBERG, RECENT DEVELOPMENTS IN THE LAW OF THE SEA AND THE JAPANESE-KOREAN FISHERY DISPUTE (The Hague 1966); 4 WHITEMAN 499-739; Young, *The Legal Regime of the Deep Sea Floor,* 62 AJIL 88-113 (1968).

not be appropriated.[85]   To this, John Selden in his *Mare Clausum*
replied that England had actually appropriated portions of the
sea.[86]   Since the early 19th century, however, the freedom of the
open sea has been universally recognized, subject of course to
appropriate safety regulations and to some special arrangements
made by treaties or resulting from custom.   The recent proposals
for recovery of seabed riches under jurisdiction of the UN or a
special international agency does not conflict with freedom of the
sea principles.   The Convention which codifies the Law of the Sea
recognizes this principle of freedom of the open seas.[87]

§ 2-9.7. **Piracy.** Professors Lauterpacht and Oppenheim suggest
the following contemporary definition of piracy:

> [E]very unauthorized act of violence against persons or goods
> committed on the open sea either by a private vessel against another
> vessel or by the mutinous crew or passengers against their own
> vessel.[88]

It should be noted that warships do not come normally within
the definition of piracy.   If a warship commits lawless acts of
violence, the normal remedy would be diplomatic protest to the
national state for redress.   Since early maritime history, pirates
have been regarded as the common enemy of all mankind.   It is
widely accepted that any state may act as the executive enforcement arm of the community of nations by seizing suspected pirates
and trying them for their alleged crimes.   Traditionally, the death
penalty was meted out to pirates, but under the laws of many
states, the death penalty has been abolished for this crime, and
lesser punishments are now imposed.

§ 2-9.8. **Environment and Pollution.** Much attention has recently
been paid to the problem of pollution of the environment.   Technological advances, manufacturing enterprises, and automobiles with
internal combustion engines have in many parts of the world created
urgent pollution problems.   In many cities of the world, clean and
safe air has been replaced by noxious pollutants and waste material
often constituting a grave danger to peoples' health.   Furthermore,
the pollution of the sea, and of beaches and resort areas caused by
the discharge of oil into the oceans has destroyed fish and other

---

[85] H. GROTIUS, MARE LIBERUM, ch. 5 (1633), translated with a revision of the Latin
text by R. Magoffin (New York 1916).

[86] 1 J. SELDEN, MARE CLAUSUM, ch. 22 (1635).

[87] Convention on the Territorial Sea and Contiguous Zones, *done* April 29, 1958, 15
U.S.T. 1606; TIAS 5639; 516 U.N.T.S. 205.

[88] 1 Lauterpacht, *Oppenheim's International Law* 609 (1962).

wildlife. Increasingly, national leaders are calling for stricter measures to prevent such environmental pollution, and several nations have ratified treaties to help cope with this problem.

The Intergovernmental Maritime Consultative Organization has sponsored recent amendments to the 1954 International Convention for the Prevention of Pollution of the Sea by Oil,[89] and two further Conventions: the International Convention relating to Intervention on High Seas in Cases of Oil Pollution Casualties,[90] and the International Convention of Civil Liability for Oil Pollution Damage.[91]

According to these Conventions, the discharge of oil from a ship, not a tanker, in excess of 60 litres per mile, with an oil content greater than 100 parts per one million parts of the mixture is prohibited unless the ship is proceeding en route, and unless the discharge is made as far as practicable from land. For tankers, it is made a crime to discharge oil less than 50 miles from shore that is greater than 60 litres per mile, and of a quantity greater than 1/15.000 of the total cargo-carrying capacity of the ship, except when the tanker is proceeding en route. State naval vessels are exempted.

Individual states are given the right to intervene on the high seas in cases of oil pollution damage under certain conditions. There must be a casualty, or related circumstances, leading the state to expect harmful pollution damage either to its coastline, or to related interests. The activities of the State must be "proportionate to the damage actual or threatened," according to [Article 5(1)] of the second Convention, and "such measures shall not go beyond what is reasonably necessary" to prevent pollution damage, and "as soon as that end has been achieved, they shall not unnecessarily interfere with the rights and interests of the flag states, and of any persons, physical or corporate, concerned." [Article 5(2)]. In order to determine what steps will be necessary, it is proper to consider the "extent and probability of imminent damage, . . . the likelihood of those measures being effective, . . . and the extent of the damage which may be caused by such measures, . . ." [Article 5(3)].

According to the third Convention, ships' owners are civilly liable for oil pollution damage caused by the escaping oil of their vessel. Liability, however, is limited to 2,000 French francs per ship's tonnage, and not to exceed 210 million French francs. If the owner

---

[89]*Done* May 12, 1954, 12 U.S.T. 2989; TIAS 4900; 3270 U.N.T.S. 3. 1962 Amendments: 17 U.S.T. 1523; TIAS 6109.

[90]*See* 9 INT'L L. MAT. at 25-44 (1970).

[91]*Id.* at 45-67.

can prove that the damage resulted from "an act of war, hostilities, civil war, insurrection or a natural phemenon of an exceptional, inevitable and irresistable character," or resulted from the actions or ommissions of a third party "with intent to cause damage," or was "wholly caused by the negligence or other wrongful act of any Government of other authority responsible for the maintenance of lights or other navigational aids in the exercise of that function," [Article III (2)], then he is not liable.

The International Commission for the Protection of the Rhine Against Pollution,[92] established in 1963 by France, Luxembourg, the Netherlands, Switzerland and West Germany, is concerned with the pollution of the 820 mile river accentuated by a tremendous population growth, over 30 million, and increased industrialization along its banks. Concern was greatest when millions of fish were killed in June, 1969. To date, funds expended by governments and private industries in purifying and sewage-treatment plants amount to nearly 2 billion dollars. The work of the Commission, with offices in West Germany, largely consists of conducting regular examinations of the river's pollution level, holding meetings with governmental officials, and anticipating pollution emergencies. At present, the Commission is preparing a study of pollution in the Rhine over the year 1969.

The World Peace Through Law Center has proposed a Draft Convention on Environmental Cooperation Among Nations for consideration at its 1971 World Conference on World Peace Through Law, in Belgrade, Yugoslavia.[93] The proposed Convention defines waste and pollution of the air, the sea, including territorial and contiguous zones and the seabed, inland waters, outer space, and the Arctic and Antarctic Regions by the disposal of nuclear substances, oil, chemicals and other noxious substances. It sets forth the fundamental right of individuals to a clean and safe air, soil and water, and unspoiled nature, and the corresponding duty of States to guarantee that right by national and international pollution control measures, by obliging States to prevent pollution or its threat. The Draft Convention envisages the creation of an International Anti-Pollution Board, the regulation of international trade, and civil liability to reduce the hazard of pollution. Professor Carl A. Fleischer of Sweden is the chief draftsman of this Convention. Professor J.W. Samuels of Canada has drafted, for the Center, a proposed Weather Control Convention which is now receiving active worldwide study by experts in that field.

---

[92] 1963 TRACTTATENBLAD 104 (Netherlands).
[93] BELGRADE CONF. to be published in 1972.

Since 1958, the European Community has been attempting to combat air pollution caused by the steel industry through various measures. The Community has expended a total of over $3 million for projects designed to research the nature and extent of air pollution, and ways to control it. Industry has expended an additional $900,000. The second pollution control program calls for an expenditure of $4 million, and will be concerned with the health of the people living in proximity to the steel industry.

§ 2-9.9. **Jurisdiction over the Airspace.**[94] Claims by a state to jurisdiction over the airspace above its territory have changed largely with varying state interests and with scientific developments in air travel. The older view claimed complete freedom of the airspace. A later view claimed territorial rights for the state of a lower zone of airspace but not of a higher zone, without defining precisely the limits of these zones or deciding whether innocent passage should be authorized. After World War I, the Aerial Navigation Convention,[95] signed in Paris in 1919, granted to states exclusive jurisdiction over the airspace above their territory and provided for the right of innocent passage in time of peace. In 1928, a Convention on Commercial Aviation,[96] with terms similar to those of the Paris Convention, was signed in Havana. In 1944, a Convention on International Civil Aviation,[97] adopted at a Conference in Chicago of the representatives of 54 countries, recognized the principle that countries have exclusive sovereignty over the airspace above their territory. According to the current view, passage through the airspace over the territory of a country is authorized only with the agreement of that country.

The United Nations, however, in its Resolution of Legal Principles governing the Activities of States in the Exploration and Uses of

[94] *See generally* W. BISHOP, *supra* note 1, at 369-80; J. BRIERLY, *supra* note 1, at 118-20; J. BRIGGS, *supra* note 1, at 320-26; Cooper, *Legal Problems of Upper Space,* ASIL PROC. 84-115 (1956); C. FENWICK, *supra* note 1, at 483-95; Goedhuis, *Questions of Public International Air Law,* 81 RECUEIL DES COURS 203-307 (1952); A. HERSHEY, *supra* note 2, at 340-45; 1 C. HYDE, *supra* note 1, at 585-617; Jennings, *Some Aspects of the International Law of the Air,* 75 RECUEIL DES COURS 513-90 (1949); 4 A. KISS, *supra* note 1, at 174-85 (1962); de La Pradelle, *Les Frontières de l'Air,* 86 RECUEIL DES COURS 121-202 (1954); L. OPPENHEIM, *supra* note 1, at 516-30; L. ORFIELD & E. RE, *supra* note 1, at 427-38; J. SALONGA & P. YAP, *supra* note 1, at 156; G. SCHWARZENBERGER, *supra* note 1, at 502-03; 2 WHITEMAN, 1270-84; 9 *id.,* at 309-24.

[95] Convention on the Regulation of Aerial Navigation, *done* October 13, 1919, 2 L.N.T.S. 173-209. *See* Hudson, INT. LEG. 359 (1931-1950) for text.

[96] *See* THE INTERNATIONAL CONFERENCES OF AMERICAN STATES 1889-1928, 385-93 (Washington 1931) for text.

[97] *Done* December 7, 1944, 61 Stat. 1180; TIAS 1591; 15 U.N.T.S. 295.

Outer Space,[98] and the 1967 Treaty on Principles Governing the Activities of States in the Exploration and Use of Outer Space, including the Moon and Other Celestial Bodies,[99] has limited this heretofore unlimited state jurisdiction over the airspace. Many questions still remain as to what constitutes "outer space," and all space crafts which have been launched, many still orbiting the Earth, have not been interfered with.

§ 2-9.10. **Aircraft Hijacking.** The hijacking of planes in flight has caused great concern to nations, since interference with free air transportation disrupts communications among Nations and peoples and endangers the lives of innocent passengers and crew. Most authorities agree that existing rules governing the freedom of air space from interference, namely the 1958 Geneva[100] and the 1963 Tokyo Conventions,[101] do not provide laws strong enough to prevent criminal hijacking.[102] Specifically, the Tokyo Convention[103] which became effective in December, 1969, does not make hijacking an international crime; that determination is left to the discretion of individual States. Moreover, it is not mandatory to detain an alleged hijacker either for criminal prosecution, or for extradition.

As a result, two draft conventions have been prepared to fill this void. The first, called a Convention for the Suppression of Unlawful Seizure of Aircraft, sponsored by the International Civil Aviation Organization,[104] provides, among other things, that a person on board an aircraft in flight "who unlawfully, by force or threat . . . seizes or exercises control over that aircraft, or attempts to perform any such act, . . . or is an accomplice of a person who performs or attempts to perform any such act, commits an offence" (Article 1). The Convention makes the offense of aircraft hijacking extraditable and calls on states to make the offense punishable under their domestic law, and to take the offender into custody to await criminal or extradition proceedings. Article 7 of the Convention provides

---

[98] *See* 6 INT'L L. MAT. 386-90 (1967) for text.

[99] *Done* January 27, 1967, 18 U.S.T. 2410; TIAS 6347. *See* J. FAWCETT, INTERNATIONAL LAW AND THE USES OF OUTER SPACE 86-91 (Manchester Univ. 1968) for text.

[100] Convention on the High Seas, *done* April 29, 1958, 13 U.S.T. 2312, TIAS 5200; 450 U.N.T.S. 82.

[101] The Tokyo Convention on Offenses and Certain Other Acts Committed on Board Aircraft, 2 INT'L L. MAT. 1042 (1963).

[102] *See* Sheehan, *Hijacking and World Law,* 16 WORLD FEDERALIST 14-16 (1970).

[103] 2 INT'L L. MAT. 1042 (1963).

[104] *See* 9 INT'L L. MAT. 68-80 (1970) for text and comment.

that if the Contracting State "in whose territory the alleged hijacker is found . . . does not extradite him, [is] obliged, without exception whatsoever and whether or not the offence was committed in its territory, to submit the case to its competent authorities for the purpose of prosecution. Those authorities shall take their decision in the same manner as in the case of any ordinary offence of a serious nature under the law of the State." Regarding jurisdiction, the Convention treats the offense as having been committed in the state where the aircraft was registered, in the state where the hijacked aircraft lands and the alleged offender leaves the aircraft, or where the hijacking actually occurred.

The second, called a Convention to Deter Aircraft Hijacking was proposed by the World Peace Through Law Center in 1969.[105] While basically similar to the ICAO proposed draft, the Convention, in addition, calls on States to "insure that persons on aircraft and the aircraft itself are protected from the presence of deadly or dangerous weapons, explosives, and any other object capable of injuring such persons or property or threatening the lawful operation of civil commercial aircraft" (Article 3). Furthermore, member states must restore immediate control of a hijacked aircraft to its lawful commander; automatically and instantly release the aircraft, crew and passengers; apprehend, disarm and restrain the alleged hijacker and effect his departure under guard, either in the hijacked aircraft, or by any other available means to the state to which the aircraft was destined before the hijacking; and refrain from detaining anyone on board for any reason, except for the alleged hijacker to the extent necessary to accomplish his expulsion and delivery to the originally scheduled destination of the hijacked aircraft.

§ 2-9.11. **Jurisdiction over Aliens.** A state has extensive jurisdiction over aliens within its territory. It determines who may enter the country, often forbidding entry to certain classes of undesirable persons (such as criminals, idiots and paupers), while encouraging others. A state may levy taxes on aliens. It has penal jurisdiction within its territorial limits, and for certain crimes committed outside of its limits. It may call upon aliens to assist in maintaining public order. It determines whether aliens may purchase or bequeath property.

Although aliens are granted civil rights, they are usually denied certain political rights enjoyed by citizens. Although the state may expel aliens, it should not discriminate against nationals of a partic-

---

[105] WPTL *Convention To Deter Aircraft Hijacking*, Pamphlet Series, No. 13 (1969).

ular foreign state. The reasons for the expulsion should be clear and valid and should be given to the foreign state upon request.

A nation has both a domestic and an international responsibility for preserving alien rights. A state's responsibility for injuries to aliens is limited to the requirements that it take reasonable precautions to avoid such injury or to provide adequate legal redress after the injury has taken place. Considerable difference of opinion exists whether a nation is liable for crimes committed abroad against its nationals. According to Paragraph 1 of Article 2 of the 1961 Harvard Draft Convention on the International Responsibility of States for Injuries to Economic Interests of Aliens,[106] "the treatment of aliens is to be governed by an international minimum standard." Article 1 of the 1961 Revised Draft on International Responsibility of the State for Injuries Caused in Its Territory to the Person or Property of Aliens,[107] provides that aliens are entitled to enjoy at least the human rights and fundamental freedoms recognized and defined in contemporary instruments.

The Draft Convention on the International Responsibility of States for Injuries to Aliens[108] embodies the principle that a state is responsible for an act or omission which is attributable to that state, which is wrongful under international law, and which causes injury to an alien. Such responsibility means that if a state causes such injury, it has a duty to compensate the victim, or a person claiming through him, or the state which is presenting the claim on behalf of the alien. The Convention further provides in Article 2 that a state cannot avoid international responsibility by invoking its municipal law, and that its responsibility is to be determined by international law principles as enumerated in Article 38, paragraph 1, of the Statute of the International Court of Justice.

The following acts or omissions are deemed unlawful and for which the duty of reparations arises: the arrest or detention of an alien in violation of law, or in a manner inconsistent with standards of civilized states, or if the state does not have jurisdiction, or if it breaches an international treaty or obligation; failure to inform a detained or arrested alien of the cause of such arrest or detention, or of the specific charges against him within a reasonable time after arrest or detention; failure to grant him a prompt trial or to ensure that his trial and any appellate proceedings against him are not unduly prolonged; failure to grant him access

---

[106] *See* 55 AJIL 548-84 (1961) for text.
[107] *Id.*
[108] *Id.*

to courts, tribunals and administrative authorities; failure to satisfy procedural requirements including time to prepare a defense, compulsory process of witnesses and evidence and the right to legal representation of his choice; and mistreatment during arrest or detention.

The Convention also declares that an alien's property is to be held inviolable, and any destruction or damage to it is illegal. Accordingly, it is also illegal to deprive an alien of the use or enjoyment of his property, his means of livelihood without compensation, and only if such action is urgently necessary "admitting of no alternative course of action."

The offending state is obligated to pay damages for bodily and mental harm, pain, suffering and emotional distress; for loss of earnings and of earning capacity; for reasonable medical and other expenses; for damage to his property or business; for harm to his reputation; for costs of defense, litigation and judgment. In addition, Article 40 provides that "Neither damages nor compensation shall be subjected to special taxes or capital levies within the State paying such damages or compensation."

§ 2-9.12. **Extraterritorial Jurisdiction.** Customary international law, international treaties and conventions have, in many instances, extended state jurisdiction beyond territorial boundaries.[109] While this principle of extraterritorial jurisdiction commonly consists of a state's authority to tax its nationals outside its territory, and to subject them to military service and to impose criminal penalties on them for acts committed either abroad or in areas not under the jurisdiction of any state, it also consists of the principles of universality, protected interests, and passive personality in conferring jurisdiction over acts committed by aliens outside the state's authority.

The principle of universality, as in the example of piracy on the high seas, confers upon any state which apprehends the pirate, jurisdiction to prosecute and punish him for this crime under international law. Other crimes conferring such universal state jurisdiction, according to the Bustamante Code of 1928, Article 308, consist of "trade in negroes and the slave traffic, white slavery, the destruction or injury of submarine cables, and all other offenses of a similar nature against international law committed on the high seas, in the open air, and on territory not yet organized into a state. . . ."[110] Universal jurisdiction, according to the penal laws

[109] G. SCHWARZENBERGER, *supra* note 1, at 94-95.

[110] Bustamante Code of Private International Law, *done* 1928. *See* INTERNATIONAL CONFERENCES OF THE AMERICAN STATES, 1889-1928 at 443 (Washington, D.C., 1931) for text.

of several states, as exemplified by the Austrian Penal Code of 1803, also applies to offenses committed abroad by an alien in the event he has not been extradited to the state where the crime was committed, and where the act was criminal in the state where committed, and if, according to the law of the state exercising such jurisdiction, no heavier punishment would be meted out than under the law of the state where the crime was committed.

War crimes, since the Nuremberg War Crimes Tribunals, also confer universal jurisdiction on all nations, not just on the state whose interests or nationals were affected by the criminal acts. The Geneva Conventions of 1949, particularly the Convention of the Wounded and the Sick of Armies of the Field (Article 49);[111] the Convention of the Wounded, Sick and Shipwrecked Members of Armed Forces at Sea (Article 50);[112] the Prisoners of War Convention (Article 129),[113] and the Convention relative to the Protection of Civilian Persons in Time of War (Article 146)[114] specifically permit the universal jurisdiction of all states to try and punish war criminals. In the 1964 *Eichmann* Case,[115] the Israeli Court based its jurisdiction to try the accused on the universal nature of the alleged crimes he had committed even though they were committed by an alien in another country, and before Israel became a state.

The principle of protected interests further extends a state's jurisdiction outside its territory to protect interests vital to its existence. According to this principle, states can punish acts committed outside their territory, even by aliens, and even if such acts are not punishable by the laws of the state where committed, if such acts endanger the security of the state, its money, official seals or marks. Such an inclusive or absolute jurisdiction has found agreement in international law because the state exercising such jurisdiction has particularly suffered as a result of the crime; it is the effect of the crime which confers jurisdiction on the state.

---

111 Convention for the Amelioration of the Condition of the Wounded and Sick in Armed Forces in the Field, *done* August 12, 1949, 6 U.S.T. 3114; TIAS 3362; 75 U.N.T.S. 31.

112 Convention for the Amelioration of the Condition of the Wounded, Sick, and Shipwrecked Members of Armed Forces at Sea, *done* August 12, 1949, 6 U.S.T. 3217; TIAS 3363; 75 U.N.T.S. 85.

113 Geneva Convention relative to the Treatment of Prisoners of War, *done* August 12, 1949, 6 U.S.T. 3316; TIAS 3364; 75 U.N.T.S. 135.

114 Convention Relative to the Protection of Civilian Persons in Time of War, *done* August 12, 1949, 6 U.S.T. 3516; TIAS 3365; 75 U.N.T.S. 287.

115 Baade, *Eichmann Trial: Some Legal Aspects,* 1961 DUKE L.J. 400.

According to the principle of passive personality, accepted by several states, a state has extraterritorial jurisdiction over aliens regarding crimes committed against its nationals outside its territory. In the *Lotus* Case,[116] decided by the Permanent Court of International Justice, involving the prosecution by Turkey of a French national, an officer of a French vessel which had collided with a Turkish vessel on the high seas, the Court in finding that Turkey had not violated international law, stated: "[it] does not think it necessary to consider the contention that a State cannot punish offences committed abroad by a foreigner simply by reason of the nationality of the victim."[117] While many states have strongly objected to this principle, its validity regarding the trial of war criminals has been upheld since belligerents have historically been empowered to try persons for crimes in violation of international law. And, in areas, not subject to the authority of a state, some states, notably Denmark, confer jurisdiction on the victim's state to try the person responsible for the crime.

§ 2-10. Extradition

This is the process through which one state surrenders to another state an individual accused or convicted of an offense outside the jurisdiction of the state of refuge, and within that of the requesting state which accordingly demands his surrender for trial and/or punishment.[118] The practice of extradition has existed since the ancient Chaldeans and Egyptian Pharoahs; was practiced in early Chinese civilization; and was first recorded in the Arab World when Meccans asked the Negus of Abbysinia to extradite newly converted Muslims (c. 618). Grotius, Burlemaqui and Vattel con-

---

[116] The S.S. Lotus [1927], P.C.I.J. Ser. A, No. 10, at 22-23.

[117] *Id.*

[118] *See generally* Bassiouni, *The Ideologically Motivated Offender and the "Political Offense" Exception to Extradition,* 19 DEPAUL L.REV. (1970); Bassiouni, *International Extradition,* 3-4 REV. INT'L DR. PEN. (1968); Bassiouni, *International Extradition in American Practice and World Public Order,* 36 TENN. L. REV. 1 (1969); W. BISHOP, *supra* note 1, at 190-93, 471-75; I. BRIGGS, *supra* note 1, at 305-17; Evans, *Acquisition of Custody over the Fugitive Offender—Alternatives to Extraditions: A Survey of United States Practice,* 40 BRIT. Y.B. INT'L L. 77-102 (1964); Evans, *The New Extradition Treaties of the United States,* 59 AJIL 351-62 (1965); C. FENWICK, *supra* note 1, at 389-98; C. FENWICK, CASES, *supra* note 1, at 420-56; 2 C. HYDE, *supra* note 1, at 1012-63; 2 A. KISS, *supra* note 1, at 200-23 (1966); Mercier, *L'Extradition,* 33 RECUEIL DES COURS 172-240 (1930); Oda, *The Individual in International Law,* in SØRENSEN, *supra* note 2, at 469, 518-25; L. OPPENHEIM, *supra* note 1, at 695-710; L. ORFIELD & E. RE, *supra* note 1, at 705-22; PARRY, *supra* note 2, at 443-835; Rolin, *Quelques Questions Relative à l'Extradition,* 1 RECUEIL DES COURS 181-227 (1923); J. SALONGA & P. YAP, *supra* note 1, at 191-97; Schoch, *European Extradition Cases,* 56 AJIL 221-27 (1962); G. SCHWARZENBERGER, *supra* note 1, at 497-502; 6 WHITEMAN 727-1122; G. WILSON & G. TUCKER, *supra* note 1, at 148-52.

sidered extradition part of the Law of Nations and as a duty of states.

As practiced today, no right to demand extradition exists apart from an international agreement, or bilateral treaty between two countries which enumerates the specific offenses for which extradition can be sought. On one hand, some states occasionally will extradite alleged offenders on the basis of reciprocity or comity, or will do so even unilaterally. On the other hand, however, some states, including European nations, refuse to extradite their nationals for any reason; other states, including the United States and Great Britain, extradite their nationals only in certain cases.

Extradition treaties, of which the 1794 Jay Treaty is an early example, detail the procedures followed in seeking the extradition of an individual, and the specific crimes, usually serious, for which extradition can be granted. The contemporary trend is not to list specific extraditable offenses *in restricto*, but to provide for general extradition in the case of conduct punishable in both the demanding and surrendering states. Almost all treaties exclude political offenses from the class of extraditable offenses, as does customary international law and practice. In this case, the difficulty lies in determining what exactly is a political offense.[119]

The procedures for obtaining the extradition of an individual are also contained in bilateral extradition treaties. The demand for the surrender of the fugitive is usually made by the executive officer of the state through diplomatic channels, and the demand must include both an identification of the offender and, either the charging document or, a summary of the evidence of his crime. If the offender has committed the same crime or crimes of equal gravity in several states, the demand of his native state takes precedence. If the crimes vary in gravity, it is argued that the demand of the state making the more serious charge be granted. Upon receiving a request for extradition, the state of refuge examines the documents submitted and/or the evidence of criminality offered, to determine whether extradition is justified. While Common Law countries require a *prima facie* showing of guilt before they will surrender a fugitive, almost all other legal systems, require only that the offense for which extradition is sought was committed within the jurisdiction of the demanding state. Some states, including the United States, provide the individual whose extradition is demanded with an opportunity for a judicial hearing, while in other countries, extradition is exclusively an administrative function.

---

[119] *See* 29 AJIL SUPP. 15-434 (1935) for text.

It is widely recognized that the rules of extradition should be codified in one international convention to replace the more than one thousand bilateral agreements now in force. Although several codes and conventions have been drafted, no single, worldwide multilateral convention has been adopted. In 1880, the Institute of International Law adopted a series or rules governing extradition. A League of Nations' Committee of Experts opposed a general convention because of the many differences in national laws and policies affecting it. In 1935, the Harvard Research in International Law prepared a Draft Convention on Extradition and a valuable Comment,[120] which sets forth the views of experts in this field. The tenth International Penal Law Congress, held in Rome in 1969, adopted resolutions supporting the need for a uniformity of practice in order to protect the rights of individuals internationally.

§ 2-11. The Right of Asylum[121]

Asylum formerly had a religious character relating to the ancient function of temples in protecting individuals against violence. Today, referred to as the "right of asylum," it is by no means completely assured. In fact, it is a doctrine rather than a "right," not recognized by some states as part of international law. Asylum is often used by fugitives from justice and political refugees to use the premises of diplomatic missions or the residences of the mission's members to prevent their arrest. The practice is to grant temporary protection in cases of imminent danger to the fugitive, as, for example, from mob violence. According to both customary international law and the provisions of treaties, such as the Havana Convention on Diplomatic Officers of 1928, and the Vienna Convention on Diplomatic Asylum of 1954,[122] fugitives from justice cannot be seized on the premises of a diplomatic mission, or in the residence of one of its members, but, persons who have committed ordinary crimes and deserters from military service should be surrendered by the head of the mission upon request.

---

[120] 29 AJIL SUPP. 15-434 (1931).

[121] *See generally* J. BRIGGS, *supra* note 1, at 536; Briggs, *The Colombia-Peruvian Asylum Case and Proof of Customary Law,* 45 AJIL 728-31 (1951); C. FENWICK, *supra* note 1, at 566-69; C. FENWICK, CASES, *supra* note 1, at 669-90; A. HERSHEY, *supra* note 2, at 385-86; Hudson, *Colombian-Peruvian Asylum Case,* 45 AJIL 19-26 (1951); L. OPPENHEIM, *supra* note 1, at 676-78; L. ORFIELD & E. RE, *supra* note 1, at 68; Reale, *Le Droit d'Asile,* 63 RECUEIL DES COURS 473-601 (1938); G. WILSON & G. TUCKER, *supra* note 1, at 186; Zarate, *Colombian-Peruvian Asylum Case,* 45 AJIL 19-26 (1951).

[122] *See* C. FENWICK, *supra* note 1, at 566.

§ 2-12. The Position of the Individual in International Law[123]

Historically, states have recognized that they are obligated to enforce the substantive rights and duties of individuals. Many writers, such as Schwarzenberger, maintain that only states are subjects of international law, and that individuals are the subjects of national law but the objects of international law.[124] This view is strongly supported by a comparison of the role of the state with that of the individual in international relations. States, not individuals, are members of the United Nations and of various other international organizations. Only states were parties to cases before the Permanent Court of International Justice and are parties to cases before the International Court of Justice. And, only states confer in international governmental conferences. However, in recent years, an increasing number of lawyers, including Kelsen, Verdross and Sir Hersch Lauterpacht, support the view that individuals should also be considered the subjects of international law, even if only indirect subjects.[125]

§ 2-12.1. Rights of the Individual.

The rights of the individual acting on behalf of the state may be distinguished from the rights of a private individual. Among the former are the rights of heads of states and various state representatives. In their official capacity, sovereigns and their retinues, diplomatic agents and certain other state representatives abroad are exempt from civil and criminal jurisdiction (which is an immunity) and from taxes (which is a substantive right), from some customs duties and from certain administrative

---

[123] *See generally* W. BISHOP, *supra* note 1, at 265-83; E. BORCHARD, THE DIPLOMATIC PROTECTION OF CITIZENS ABROAD, OR THE LAW OF INTERNATIONAL CLAIMS (New York 1915); Brownlie, *The Place of the Individual in International Law,* 50 VA. L. REV. 435-62 (1964); C. FENWICK, *supra* note 1, at 147-54; C. FENWICK, CASES, *supra* note 1, at 87-90, *Geneva Convention on the High Seas,* 52 AJIL 842-51 (1958); HARVARD RESEARCH IN INTERNATIONAL LAW, PIRACY; PIRACY LAWS OF VARIOUS COUNTRIES (Cambridge, Mass. 1932); A. HERSHEY, *supra* note 2, at at 157-58, 347; P. JESSUP, A MODERN LAW OF NATIONS (New York 1948); 2 A. KISS, *supra* note 1, at 623-65 (1966); M. KOROWICZ, *supra* note 1, at 325-89; C. NORGAARD, THE POSITION OF THE INDIVIDUAL IN INTERNATIONAL LAW (Copenhagen 1962); Oda, *The Position of the Individual in International Law,* in SØRENSEN, *supra* note 2, at 511-18; L. ORFIELD & E. RE, *supra* note 1, at 172-79; Parry, *Some Considerations upon the Protection of Individuals in International Law,* 90 RECUEIL DES COURS 657-726 (1956); J. SALONGA & P. YAP, *supra* note 1, at 79-82; G. SCHWARZENBERGER, *supra* note 1, at 80-81, 441-45; Sperduti, *L'Individu et le Droit International,* 90 RECUEIL DES COURS 733-849 (1956); Spiropoulos, *L'Individu et le Droit International,* 30 RECUEIL DES COURS 197-270 (1929); Von der Heydte, *L'Individu et les Tribunaux,* 107 RECUEIL DES COURS 297-357 (1962); Waldock, *The Individual in International Law,* 106 RECUEIL DES COURS 192-229 (1962).

[124] *See* G. SCHWARZENBERGER, *supra* note 1 at 80-81.

[125] *See* C. NORGAARD, *supra* note 123, at 26-77, for a discussion of the views of various writers, as well as a bibliography of monographs on the subject.

regulations. The right to enjoy these immunities, originally based on the principle of extraterritoriality, and for reasons of convenience and courtesy, is today primarily based on their representation of states, for states cannot generally be subjected to the jurisdiction of other states. The enjoyment of these rights creates an obligation to comply with the laws of the local state.

The individual acting in a private capacity has also been granted many rights, primarily through treaties concerning minorities, establishing mandates, the trusteeship system and human rights. Such rights were enforced procedurally by petition to international conferences, in some cases with authorization to address committees; and to private organizations which in turn presented them to conferences for consideration. The rapid development of non-governmental international organizations since World War II, has led to the establishment by the United Nations of categories of nongovernmental organizations, some of which may suggest items for consideration by UN organs and present views of their members orally; others are available for consultation by the Council or the Secretariat of the United Nations.

The power of an international organization or one of its committees or commissions often is limited to investigations of complaints made by individuals and to the publication of reports and recommendations on their findings. The International Labour Organization has set up a special procedure for handling complaints.[126] While such complaints must be presented by industrial associations and not by individuals, the procedure constitutes a safeguard of individual rights and reduces the number of petitions concerning trifles. The European Convention for the Protection of Human Rights and Fundamental Freedoms established a careful procedure by which individual petitions may be submitted to the Commission, and upon failure of the Commission to settle a case, to the Court of Human Rights.[127] Recently, in 1970, UNESCO permitted procedural revisions to allow consultative groups to present petitions alleging the violation of human rights.

In all of the above arrangements, the individual has the right to submit a complaint and to be informed whether or not it is receiv-

---

[126] International Labour Office, Constitution of the International Labour Organization, arts 22-34, at 17-20 (1969). *See generally* C. JENKS, THE INTERNATIONAL PROTECTION OF TRADE UNION FREEDOM, 142-61, 172-200 (New York 1957) and C. JENKS, SOCIAL JUSTICE IN THE LAW OF NATIONS, THE I.L.O. IMPACT AFTER FIFTY YEARS (London 1970).

[127] Council of Europe. European Convention of Human Rights (Council of Europe 1963).

able. If receivable, an investigation and report will be made to the complainant, to the state against which the complaint lies and to the headquarters of international organizations involved. Although the petitioner does not have the status of a party before an international court in these cases, his position is more favorable than that of an individual who is unable to enforce the rights he possesses.

§ 2-12.2. **Duties of the Individual.** The Nuremberg Trial and the UN General Assembly Resolution that affirmed its principles have enforced the principle that the individual is subject to certain duties under international law. Various individuals and international and national, public and private organizations have proposed the creation of an international criminal court that would establish beyond doubt the rights and duties of the individual in the international criminal field, and would also provide a means to decide such cases. The World Peace Through Law Center in 1971 published a book setting forth the views of experts, headed by Professor Julius Stone of Australia, entitled, TOWARD A FEASIBLE INTERNATIONAL CRIMINAL COURT. The conclusion of these experts, admittedly very controversial, is that an international court to try crimes such as aircraft hijacking is feasible.

Individuals have rarely been granted the right to plead before an international court. Article 2 of The Convention of December 20, 1907, which created the Central American Court of Justice,[128] gave the Court jurisdiction in cases which individuals of one Central American country may raise against any of the other contracting Governments, because of the violation of treaties or conventions, and other cases of an international character, no matter whether their own Government supports said claim or not. Individuals were subjects of rights and proceedings before the Mixed Arbitral Tribunals, created by the Peace Treaties after World War I, and before similar tribunals created after World War II. They are subjects both of rights and proceedings and of duties and responsibilities before the Court of the European Communities, and would have become a subject of international law had the 1909 Convention which established an International Prize Court[129] been

---

[128] General Treaty of Peace and Amity, *done* December 20, 1907. See 2 AJIL SUPP. 231 (1908) for text.

[129] A Convention on the Establishment of an International Prize Court was signed at The Hague in 1907. A conference at London endeavored to clarify the law to be applied by such a Court, and its work resulted in the signature of the Declaration of London of February 26, 1909, which purported to state in substance the generally recognized rules of international law concerning maritime warfare. Neither the Convention nor the Dec-

(Continued)

ratified.   Some proposals for establishing international tribunals have also included provisions advancing the status of the individual in international law.   The Nuremberg Trial and the U.N. General Assembly Resolution affirming its principles, in confirming the view that the individual is subject to duties under international law, establish individual accountability before the world community under international law proper, and exclude the defense of "superior orders" or "act of State" for international crimes.[130]   President of the United States, Richard M. Nixon, while serving as Vice President, urged that the jurisdiction of the International Court of Justice be extended to individuals in cases involving interpretation of treaties and conventions.

§ 2-12.3. **Individuals Responsible for International Crimes.** International criminal law, as far as it has been developed, holds individuals responsible for certain crimes. Two kinds of crimes committed by individuals have been recognized for many years prior to this century: piracy and the slave trade. Article 19 of the 1958 Geneva Convention on the High Seas[131] grants states the right to exercise criminal jurisdiction over pirate ships and the persons and property aboard, while Article 13 obliges states to prevent and punish the transport of slaves.

Individuals have been prosecuted by the state of which they are nationals for offenses against international law. After World War I, an attempt was made to try Kaiser Wilhelm II, but it was thwarted by the refusal of the Dutch Government to extradite him.   The Treaty of Versailles, in Article 228, gave the Allied Powers the right to try German offenders against the laws and customs of war, but the Germans were granted the right to try these criminals in their own courts, which resulted in only six convictions and these offenders were soon free.   At the Nuremberg War Crimes Trial after World War II, the Tribunal declared that individuals have international duties and that the official position of the defendants did not free them from the responsibility of performing these duties.   The principles of the Nuremberg Trial were endorsed by many nations individually and later by the United Nations.   The Genocide Convention is another step

---

laration was brought into force; but to some extent the Declaration was applied in the War of 1914. *See* G. WILSON & G. TUCKER, *supra* note 1, at 434-43 for text of the Convention.

[130] *See* § 9-9.7, *infra,* for a discussion of "superior orders."

[131] Convention on the High Seas, *done* April 29, 1958, 13 U.S.T. 2312; TIAS 5200; 450 U.N.T.S. 82.

to broaden individual responsibility for international crimes.[132] The United Nations has requested the International Law Commission, which drafted the Draft Code of Offenses against the Peace and Security of Mankind, to study the possibility of establishing an international Criminal Court and the use of a Criminal Chamber of the International Court of Justice, although no action has been taken to date. Some of the studies and views on this subject are reviewed in the Volume referred to *supra,* § 2-12.2, p. 123, TOWARD A FEASIBLE INTERNATIONAL CRIMINAL COURT.

§ 2-12.4. The Individual and the State in Muslim Law.[133] The social revolution of Islam was in recognition of the primacy of the individual and his subjection to "law," as moral obligations. The individual is just as much a subject of law as the state. The Prophet Muhammad, even before the establishment of the Muslim state, acted personally on behalf of the Faith and the followers and dealt with other tribes as such. Since all Muslims are said to be equal and responsible as leaders as well as followers, they can never escape their responsibilities and hence are recognized as subjects of law, be it national or international. Muslims are not only bound by laws and treaties but are obligated to execute and enforce them, and are personally accountable for violating law (including international law in Islam's monistic doctrine) and subject to punishment for it. Muslim history abounds with instances where violations of the law of war were punished swiftly. No defense of "act of state" or "superior orders" can be recognized, since every Muslim is personally and directly accountable to God and the state merely carries on earth the law of God. Thus, the principles of Nuremberg are very much attuned to Islamic law.

---

[132] Convention on the Prevention and Punishment of the Crime of Genocide, *entry into force* January 12, 1951, 78 U.N.T.S. 277.

[133] *See* Bassiouni, *Islam: Concept, Law and World Habeas Corpus,* 1 RUTGERS CAMDEN L.J. 160-201 (1969).

CHAPTER 3

The United Nations and Other International Organizations

§ 3.1. The United Nations [1]

The purposes of the United Nations, which came into existence in 1945, are set forth in Article 1 of the Charter. They are:

---

[1] *See generally* Addresses and Comments, *Constitutional Development of the United Nations,* ASIL PROC. 78-88 (1961); Addresses and Remarks, *Sanctions Under the United Nations Charter, id.,* at 153-83 (1951); Arangio-Ruiz, *Development of Peaceful Settlement and Peaceful Change in the United Nations System, id.,* at 124-32 (1965); ASIL PROC., COMMITTEE TO STUDY LEGAL PROBLEMS OF THE UNITED NATIONS (annual

(Continued)

1. To maintain international peace and security, and to that end: to take effective collective measures for the prevention and removal of threats to the peace, and for the suppression of acts of aggression or other breaches of the peace, *and to bring about by peaceful means, and in conformity with the principles of justice and international law, adjustment or settlement of international disputes or situations which might lead to a breach of the peace;*

reports, ASIL PROC. ANNUAL REVIEW OF UNITED NATIONS AFFAIRS (1954-); R. ASHER, THE UNITED NATIONS AND ECONOMIC AND SOCIAL COOPERATION (Washington 1957); R. ASHER, UNITED NATIONS AND PROMOTION OF GENERAL WELFARE (Washington 1957); Barclay, *Les Possibilites de l'O.N.U.*, REV. DR. INT'L 338-45 (1964); BELAUNDE, 20 AÑOS DE NACIONES UNIDAS (Madrid 1966); Berendsen, *The United Nations and International Law*, ASIL PROC. 118-31 (1947); UNITED NATIONS, BIBLIOGRAPHIE DE LA CHARTE DES NATIONS UNIES 44-52, 108-09 (New York 1955); Bindschedler, *The Delimitation of Powers in the United Nations*, 108 RECUEIL DES COURS 305-423 (1963); L. BLOOMFIELD, EVOLUTION OR REVOLUTION? THE UNITED NATIONS AND THE PROBLEM OF PEACEFUL TERRITORIAL CHANGE (Cambridge, Mass. 1957); Bogdanov, *Twenty Years of the United Nations and the Maintenance of Peace and Security* (in Russian), 1964-1965 SOVIET Y.B. INT'L L. 17-32 (1966); Bowett, *Collective Self-Defence Under the Charter of the United Nations*, 32 BR. Y.B. INT'L L. 130-62 (1955-6); P. CALVOCORESSI, WORLD ORDER AND THE NEW STATES: PROBLEMS OF KEEPING THE PEACE (New York 1962); Castrén, *United Nations*, in ATHENS CONF. 581-82 (1965); Chayes, *The Rule of Law—Now*, in *id.*, at 582-90; C. CHAUMONT, L'ORGANISATION DES NATIONS UNIES (paris 1966); Chaumont, *Nations Unies et Neutralité*, 89 RECUEIL DES COURS 5-59 (1954); G. CLARK & L. SOHN, WORLD PEACE THROUGH WORLD LAW (3d ed., Cambridge, Mass. 1966); B. COHEN, THE UNITED NATIONS (Cambridge, Mass. 1961); Cohen, *The United Nations in Its Twentieth Year*, 20 INT'L ORG. 185-207 (1966); Cohen, *Reflection on Law and the United Nations System*, 53 AJIL 243-54 (1960); Codas, *The United Nations*, in ATHENS CONF. 590-94; COMMISSION TO STUDY THE ORGANIZATION OF PEACE, NEW DIMENSIONS FOR THE UNITED NATIONS: THE PROBLEMS OF THE NEXT DECADE (New York 1966); D. COYLE, UNITED NATIONS AND HOW IT WORKS (New York 1961); Dupuy, *The Law Governing Relations Between International Organizations*, 100 RECUEIL DES COURS 457-589 (1960); EVERYMAN'S UNITED NATIONS (appears biennially—latest volume, 1959; for information on the alternate years, *see* L'O.N.U. POUR TOUS—latest volume, 1960); A. FELLER, UNITED NATIONS AND WORLD COMMUNITY (Boston 1952); C. FENWICK, INTERNATIONAL LAW 177-96 (New York 1948); Fitzmaurice, *The United Nations and the Rule of Law*, 38 GROTIUS SOCIETY TRANSACTIONS 135-50 (1953); L. GOODRICH, THE UNITED NATIONS (New York 1959); L. GOODRICH & E. HAMBRO, CHARTER OF THE UNITED NATIONS; COMMENTARY AND DOCUMENTS (Boston 1946); L. GOODRICH & P. SIMMONS, THE UNITED NATIONS AND THE MAINTENANCE OF INTERNATIONAL PEACE AND SECURITY (Washington 1956); Gross, *The United Nations and the Rule of Law*, 18 INT'L ORG. 537-61 (1965); Henkin, *The United Nations and Its Supporters: A Self-Examination*, 77 POL. SCI. Q. 504-36 (1963); R. HIGGINS, THE DEVELOPMENT OF INTERNATIONAL LAW THROUGH POLITICAL ORGANS OF THE UNITED NATIONS (Oxford 1963); Higgins, *The Legal Limits to the Use of Force by Sovereign States: United Nations Practice*, 37 BR. Y.B. INT'L L. 269-320 (1961); Hogg, *Peace-Keeping Costs and Charter Obligations: Implications of the International Court of Justice Decision on Certain Expenses of the United Nations*, 62 COLUM. L.REV. 1230-63 (1962); A. HOLCOMBE, STRENGTHENING THE UNITED NATIONS (New York 1957); Jessup & Taubenfeld, *The United Nations ad hoc Committee on the Peaceful Uses of Outer Space*, 53 AJIL 877-82 (1959); Kelsen, *A Collective Security and Collective Self-Defense Under the Charter of the United Nations*, 42 AJIL 783-97 (1948); H. KEL-

(Continued)

INTERNATIONAL LAW

2. To develop friendly relations among nations based on respect for the principle of equal rights and self-determination of peoples, and to take other appropriate measures to strengthen universal peace;

3. To achieve international cooperation in solving international problems of an economic, social, cultural, or humanitarian character, and in promoting and encouraging respect for human rights and

---

SEN, THE LAW OF THE UNITED NATIONS (New York 1950); KELSEN & OTHERS, THE UNITED NATIONS; TEN YEARS' LEGAL PROGRESS (The Hague 1956); (reviewed by Engle at 51 AJIL 850 (1957)); L. KOPELMANAS, L'ORGANISATION DES NATIONS UNIES (Paris 1947); S. KRYLOV, MATERIALY K ISTORII ORGANIZATSII OBYEDINENNYKH NATSII (Moscow 1949); [Materials on the History of the Organization of the United Nations]; Kunz, *The Swing of the Pendulum: From Overestimation to Underestimation*, 44 AJIL 135-41 (1950); Kunz, *The United Nations and the Rule of Law*, 46 AJIL 504-08 (1952); M. LEE, THE UNITED NATIONS AND WORLD REALITIES (Oxford 1965); Liang, *Notes on Legal Questions Concerning the United Nations*, 43 AJIL 134 (1949); Liang, *Who Are Non-Members of the United Nations?* 45 AJIL 505-26 (1951); Maccas, *Proposals for Harmonizing the Principles of National Sovereignty and That of Supra-Nationality*, in ATHENS CONF. 595-96; A. MEZERICK, CHRONOLOGY OF THE UNITED NATIONS (New York 1965); Martinez Moreno, *Balance Critico de la Obra de las Naciones Unidas en dos Decadas de su Existencia*, REV. JUR. U. INT'AM. P.R. 60-74 (1965); M. McDOUGAL & F. FELICIANO, LAW AND MINIMUM WORLD ORDER (New Haven 1961); H. NICHOLAS, THE UNITED NATIONS AS A POLITICAL INSTITUTION (Oxford 1959); Ottolenghi, *The United Nations and Regional Organizations as a Source of Law and Legal Institutions*, in ATHENS CONF. 596-99; Padelford, *Financial Crisis and the Future of the United Nations*, 3 THE STRATEGY OF WORLD ORDER 733-73 (R. Falk ed. New York 1966); Papahatzis, *Reorganization and Strengthening of the United Nations*, in ATHENS CONF. 599-605; A. PALLARES, CARTA Y ESTRUCTURA DE LAS NACIONES UNIDAS (Quito 1952); Peterin, *The Role of the United Nations in the Development of International Law*, in ATHENS CONF. 606-07; Potter, *The United Nations 1945-1949*, 43 AJIL 756-58 (1949); M. RAJAN, UNITED NATIONS AND DOMESTIC JURISDICTION (London 1961); Robinson, *Metamorphosis of the United Nations*, 94 RECUEIL DES COURS 497-589 (1958); Rosenne, *United Nations Treaty Practice*, 86 RECUEIL DES COURS 281-443 (1954); A. ROSS, CONSTITUTION OF THE UNITED NATIONS: ANALYSIS OF STRUCTURE AND FUNCTIONS (New York 1950); Saba, *Les Accords Régionaux dans la Charte de l'ONU*, 80 RECUEIL DES COURS 635-730 (1952); E. SADY, THE UNITED NATIONS AND THE DEPENDENT PEOPLES (Washington 1956); Schachter, *Legal Aspects of the United Nations Action in the Congo*, 55 AJIL 1-29 (1961); Schachter, *The Relation of Law, Politics and Action in the United Nations*, 109 RECUEIL DES COURS 169-256 (1963); Schwebel, *The United Nations and the Challenge of a Challenging International Law*, ASIL PROC. 83-99 (1963); Sisco, *The U.N.: An Area for Peaceful East-West Engagement*, 56 DEP'T STATE BULL. 458-63 (1967); L. SOHN, BASIC DOCUMENTS OF THE UNITED NATIONS (Brooklyn 1956); Sohn, *Authority of the United Nations To Establish and Maintain a Permanent United Nations Force*, 52 AJIL 229-41 (1958); L. SOHN, CASES AND OTHER MATERIALS ON WORLD LAW (Cambridge 1950); Sohn, *The Impact of the United Nations on International Law*, ASIL PROC. 104-09 (1952); Sohn, *The Role of the UN in Civil Wars, id.*, at 208-15 (1963); Sparkman, *The United Nations and the Future, id.*, at 136-46 (1955); Stavropoulos, *The United Nations and the Role of Law*, in ATHENS CONF. 611-18; J. STOESSINGER, FINANCING THE UNITED NATIONS SYSTEM (Washington 1964); Taubenfeld, *United Nations Consideration of the Status of Outer Space*, 53 AJIL 400-05 (1959); R. Taubenfeld & H. Taubenfeld, *Independent Revenue for the United Nations*, 18 INT'L ORG. 231-40 (1964); UNITED NATIONS, TEN YEARS OF UNITED NATIONS PUBLICATIONS, 1945-1955; A COMPLETE CATALOGUE (New York 1955);

(Continued)

for fundamental freedoms for all without distinction as to race, sex, language, or religion; and

4. To be a center for harmonizing the actions of nations in the attainment of these common ends. (Italics added)

The United Nations is founded on the following basic principles contained in Article 2 of the Charter:

The Organization and its Members, in pursuit of the Purposes stated in Article 1, shall act in accordance with the following Principles.

UNITED NATIONS BULLETIN, 1946-1954; UNITED NATIONS, UNITED NATIONS REVIEW (1954-   ); UNIVERSITY OF MICHIGAN LAW SCHOOL, INTERNATIONAL LAW AND THE UNITED NATIONS (Ann Arbor, Univ. of Michigan 1957); A. VANDEN-BOSCH & W. HOGAN, THE UNITED NATIONS (New York 1952); Verdross, *Idées Directrices de l'Organisation des Nations Unies*, 83 RECUEIL DES COURS 1-77 (1953); Verosta, *Application and Development of International Law by the United Nations*, in ATHENS CONF. 619-22; B. WORTLEY, THE UNITED NATIONS: THE FIRST TEN YEARS (New York 1957); R. YAKEMTCHOUK, L'O.N.U., LA SECURITÉ RÉGIONALE ET LE PROBLÈME DU REGIONALISME (Paris 1955); YEARBOOK OF THE UNITED NATIONS (latest volume, 1960).

On the United Nations Charter, see Addresses, *Problems Involved in Review of the United Nations Charter*, ASIL PROC. 191-212 (1954); N. BENTWICH & A. MARTIN, A COMMENTARY ON THE CHARTER OF THE UNITED NATIONS (London 1950); Borchard, *The Charter and the Constitution*, 39 AJIL 767-72 (1945); Brierly, *The Covenant and the Charter*, 23 BR. Y.B. INT'L L. 83-95 (1946); Chakste, *Justice and Law in the Charter of the United Nations*, 42 AJIL 590-601 (1948); G. CLARK & L. SOHN, WORLD PEACE THROUGH WORLD LAW (2d ed., Cambridge, Mass. 1960); Eagleton, *Covenant of the League of Nations and the Charter of the United Nations; Points of Difference*, in 3 THE STRATEGY OF WORLD ORDER 10-16 (R. Falk ed. New York 1966); Engel, *Procedures for the De Facto Revision of the Charter*, ASIL PROC. 108-16 (1965); J. DE ERICE Y O'SHEA, REVISIÓN DE LA CARTA DE LAS NACIONES UNIDAS (Madrid 1957); Fine, *Article 19 of the UN Charter, a Catalyst of Thought*, REV. DR. INT'L 25-36 (Sottile 1965); L. FITUNI, THE UNITED NATIONS AND THE SECURITY OF PEOPLES [Mirovaya Ekonomika I Mezhdunarodnye Otnosheniia] (Moscow 1957); Giraud, *La Révision de la Charte des Nations Unies*, 90 RECUEIL DES COURS 307-463 (1956); Gross, *The Charter of the United Nations and the Lodge Reservations*, 41 AJIL 535-55 (1947); Gross, *Progress Towards Universality of Membership in the United Nations*, 50 AJIL 791-828 (1956); INDIAN COUNCIL OF WORLD AFFAIRS (Bombay), REVISION OF THE UNITED NATIONS CHARTER: A SYMPOSIUM (Oxford 1956); Kunz, *Chapter XI of the United Nations Charter in Action*, 48 AJIL 103-10 (1954); G. MOROZOV, THE UNITED NATIONS AND SAFEGUARDING THE PEACE [Mirovaya Ekonomika I Mezhdunarodnye Otnosheniia] (Moscow 1960); G. MOROZOV, IMPROVING THE STRUCTURE OF THE UNITED NATIONS—URGENT TASK [Mirovaya Ekonomika I Mezhdunarodnye Otnosheniia] (Moscow 1961); Plimsoll, *The United Nations Charter: 1945-1962*, ASIL PROC. 162-74 (1962); Pollux, *The Interpretation of the Charter of the United Nations*, 23 BR. Y.B. INT'L L. 54-83 (1946); Potter, *The United Nations Charter: 1955*, 48 AJIL 275-76 (1954); Preuss, *L'article 2, ¶ 7, de la Charte des Nations Unies et les Affaires Relevant de la Compétence Nationale des Etats*, 74 RECUEIL DES COURS 553-658 (1949); L. PREUSS, ARTICLE 2, PARAGRAPH 7, OF THE CHARTER OF THE UNITED NATIONS AND MATTERS OF DOMESTIC JURISDICTION (Paris 1949); R. RUSSELL, A HISTORY OF THE UNITED NATIONS CHARTER . . . (Washington 1958); A. SALOMON, LE PRÉAMBULE DE LA CHARTE . . . (Geneva 1946); G. SCHWARZENBERGER, REPORT ON SOME ASPECTS OF THE PRINCIPLE OF SELF-DEFENSE

(Continued)

1. The Organization is based on the principle of the sovereign equality of all its Members.

2. All Members, in order to ensure to all of them the rights and benefits resulting from membership, shall fulfill in good faith the obligations assumed by them in accordance with the present Charter.

3. All Members shall settle their international disputes by peaceful means in such a manner that international peace and security, and justice, are not endangered.

4. All Members shall refrain in their international relations from the threat or use of force against the territorial integrity or political independence of any state, or in any manner inconsistent with the Purposes of the United Nations.

IN THE CHARTER OF THE UNITED NATIONS . . . (London 1958); United States Government Printing Office, REVIEW OF THE UNITED NATIONS CHARTER: A COLLECTION OF DOCUMENTS (Washington 1954); COMMITTEE ON FOREIGN RELATIONS, UNITED STATES SENATE, REVISION OF THE UNITED NATIONS CHARTER (Washington 1950); F. WILCOX & G. MARCY, PROPOSALS FOR CHANGES IN THE UNITED NATIONS (Washington 1955).

On the relations of individual countries and areas with the United Nations, see M. AL-H. AFIFI, THE ARABS AND THE UNITED NATIONS (London 1964); Brohi, *Five Lectures on Asia and the United Nations,* 102 RECUEIL DES COURS 122-212 (1961); G. DIB, THE ARAB BLOC IN THE UNITED NATIONS (Amsterdam 1956); J. EVANGELISTA, PORTUGAL VIS-A-VIS THE UNITED NATIONS (Lisbon 1961); S. FARAJALLAH, LE GROUPE AFRO-ASIATIQUE DANS LE CADRE DES NATIONS UNIES (Geneva 1963); L. GORDENKER, THE UNITED NATIONS AND THE PEACEFUL UNIFICATION OF KOREA (The Hague 1964); F. GROSS, THE UNITED STATES AND THE UNITED NATIONS (Oklahoma 1964); T. HOVET, AFRICA IN THE UNITED NATIONS (Illinois 1963); R. MACIVER, THE NATIONS AND THE UNITED NATIONS (New York 1959); New York University studies on the relations with the United Nations of the following countries: Australia, Belgium (in French), Canada, China, Denmark, Egypt, Federal Republic of Germany, France (in French), Greece (in French), India, Israel, Italy, Japan, Mexico, Pakistan, Soviet Union, Sweden, Switzerland (in French), Turkey, Uruguay, Yugoslavia; R. RUSSELL, THE UNITED NATIONS AND THE UNITED STATES SECURITY POLICY (Washington 1968); A. TAYLOR, INDONESIAN INDEPENDENCE AND THE UNITED NATIONS (London 1960); Wilcox, *The Atlantic Community and the United Nations,* 17 INT'L ORG. 683-708 (1963); Wohlgemuth, *The Portuguese Territories and the United Nations,* 545 INT'L CONC. 1-68 (1964).

On special crisis areas, see F. BOLAND & OTHERS, THE LEGAL ASPECTS OF THE UNITED NATIONS ACTION IN THE CONGO (New York 1962); D. BOWETT, UNITED NATIONS FORCES: A LEGAL STUDY OF UNITED NATIONS PRACTICE (London 1964); D. BROOK, PREFACE TO PEACE: THE UNITED NATIONS AND THE ARAB-ISRAEL ARMISTICE SYSTEM (Washington 1964); M. CONTEZAC, THE SUEZ CRISIS OF 1956 (American University, Washington 1961); INT'L CONC., *Issues Before the . . . General Assembly* (in each annual issue); W. JENKS, THE COMMON LAW OF MANKIND (London 1958); Karabus, *United Nations Activities in the Congo,* ASIL PROC. 30-38 (1961); A. LARSON, WHY NATIONS DISAGREE (Louisiana State University 1961); E. LEFEVER, CRISIS IN THE CONGO: A UN FORCE IN ACTION (Washington 1965); Riad, *The United Nations Action in the Congo and Its Legal Basis,* 17 EGYPT. REV. INT'L L. 1-54 (1961); F. SEYERSTED, THE UNITED NATIONS FORCES IN THE LAW OF PEACE AND WAR (Leyden 1966); J. STEGENGA, THE UNITED NATIONS FORCE IN CYPRUS (Ohio State University Press 1968); R. YALEM, THE KASHMIR DISPUTE, (American University, Washington 1956).

5. All Members shall give the United Nations every assistance in any action it takes in accordance with the present Charter, and shall refrain from giving assistance to any state against which the United Nations is taking preventive or enforcement action.

6. The Organization shall ensure that states which are not Members of the United Nations act in accordance with these Principles so far as may be necessary for the maintenance of international peace and security.

7. Nothing contained in the present Charter shall authorize the United Nations to intervene in matters which are essentially within the domestic jurisdiction of any state or shall require the Members to submit such matters to settlement under the present Charter; but the principle shall not prejudice the application of enforcement measures under Chapter VII.

The italicized parts of the Charter as quoted above state the determination of the United Nations to establish conditions under which justice and respect for the obligations arising from treaties and other sources of international law can be maintained.

§ 3-1.1. **The General Assembly.**[2]   The main deliberative organ of the United Nations meets usually once a year, and has the right to discuss and make recommendations on all matters within the

---

[2] *See* O. ASAMOAH, THE LEGAL SIGNIFICANCE OF THE DECLARATIONS OF THE GENERAL ASSEMBLY OF THE UNITED NATIONS (The Hague 1966); P. BRUGIÈRE, LES POUVOIRS DE L'ASSEMBLÉE GÉNÉRALE DES NATIONS UNIES EN MATIÈRE POLITIQUE ET DE SÉCURITÉ (Paris 1955); Chaumont, *The Respective Role of the U.N. General Assembly and the Security Council,* 12 REV. CONTEMP. L. 23-36 (1966); M. ESFANDIARY, THE ROLE OF THE GENERAL ASSEMBLY IN DEALING WITH THREATS OF PEACE (New York 1960); Falk, *On the Quasi-Legislative Competence of the General Assembly,* 60 AJIL 782-91 (1966); H. HAVILAND, THE POLITICAL ROLE OF THE GENERAL ASSEMBLY (New York 1951); *Issues Before the . . . General Assembly,* INT'L CONC. (in each annual issue); Johnson, *The Effect of Resolutions of the General Assembly of the United Nations,* 32 BR. Y.B. INT'L L. 97-123 (1955-6); Kerley, *Voting in the United Nations General Assembly,* 53 AJIL 324-41 (1959); Khan, *The President of the General Assembly of the United Nations,* 18 INT'L ORG. 231-40 (1964); Lande, *Changing Effectiveness of General Assembly Resolutions,* ASIL PROC. 162-70 (1964); Liang, *The General Assembly and the Progressive Development and Codification of International Law,* 42 AJIL 66-97 (1948); Munro, *Recent Developments in the Role of the General Assembly in the Maintenance of Peace,* ASIL PROC. 34-45 (1958); J. MUZAFFAR, THE "UNITING FOR PEACE" RESOLUTION (Washington 1957); Queneudec, *Le Président de l'Assemblée Générale des Nations Unies,* 70 REV. GEN. DR. INT'L P. 878-915 (1966); Rudzinski, *Election Procedure in the United Nations,* 53 AJIL 81-112 (1959); Skubiszewski, *The General Assembly of the United Nations and Its Power To Influence National Action,* ASIL PROC. 153-62 (1964); Sloan, *The Binding Force of a "Recommendation" of the General Assembly of the United Nations,* 25 BR. Y.B. INT'L L. 1-34 (1948); UNITED NATIONS GENERAL ASSEMBLY OFFICIAL RECORD; Vallat, *The Competence of the United Nations General Assembly,* 97 RECUEIL DES COURS 203-91 (1959); Vallat, *Voting in the General Assembly of the United Nations,* 31 BR. Y.B. INT'L L. 273-99 (1954); Yefimov, *Questions of the Legal Status of the U.N. General Assembly* (in Russian), SOVIET Y.B. INT'L L. 285-95 (1966).

scope of the United Nations Charter. All member nations are represented in the Assembly, each with one vote. Decisions on "important questions" are made by a two-thirds majority of those present and voting. Article 18(2) contains a list of "important questions" which does not purport to be exclusive. Article 18(3) provides, however, that the determination of additional categories of "important questions" shall be made by a simple majority of those present and voting in the General Assembly.

Article 35 of the Charter gives to the General Assembly jurisdiction co-extensive with the Security Council over any dispute or situation brought to its specific attention which is likely to endanger the maintenance of international peace and security. Article 12 prohibits the General Assembly from making any recommendation with regard to a dispute or situation which the Security Council is considering in accordance with the functions assigned to it by the Charter.

The "Uniting for Peace" Resolution, which the Assembly adopted in November 1950, established that if the Security Council failed to exercise its primary responsibility for the maintenance of international peace and security in any case where there appeared to be a threat to the peace, breach of the peace, or act of aggression, then the General Assembly should consider the matter immediately with a view to making appropriate recommendations to members for collective measures. These measures were to include in the case of a breach of the peace or act of aggression, the use of armed force, when necessary, to maintain or restore international peace and security. If the Assembly, as could often happen, were not in session at the time, then an emergency special session could be called within twenty-four hours of the proposed Assembly meeting. Such an emergency special session could be called if requested by the Security Council on the vote of any seven members or by a majority of the Members of the United Nations. This procedure was not used until the end of 1956, following the Suez and Hungarian crises. It was used again in 1960 in dealing with the Congo crisis.

The General Assembly has been organized in such a way that a great portion of its work is done in four types of committees: Main, Procedural, Standing and *Ad Hoc.* The Main Committees correspond to the major fields of responsibility of the General Assembly, consider agenda items referred to them by the General Assembly, and prepare draft recommendations and resolutions for submission to the General Assembly. On each of these committees all members of the United Nations have the right to be represented. At present seven main committees have been established. The Sixth Committee is the Legal Committee, which considers the legal and constitutional aspects of such matters as proposed amendments to the Charter, requests to the International Court of Justice for advisory opinions, and legal problems referred from other committees.

The Legal Committee has discussed various aspects of the problems of: Charter revision, arbitral procedure, the regime of the high seas, economic development, fisheries and their conservation and regulation, the question of defining aggression, international criminal jurisdiction, various International Law Commission reports, and many other similar matters.

§ 3-1.2. The Security Council.[3]   The organ assigned primary responsibility for maintaining peace and security is the Security Council. It consists of five permanent and 10 (increased from the six specified in the original Charter) non-permanent members. China, France, the USSR, the United Kingdom, and the United States are permanent members.   In electing the non-permanent members, the General Assembly is directed by the United Nations Charter to pay due regard to: a country's contribution to the maintenance of international peace and security, to other purposes of the United Nations, and also to equitable geographical distribution.   Each member is elected for a term of two years and, on retirement, is not eligible for immediate re-election.   Three members are chosen each year.

Any member of the United Nations which is not a member of the Security Council may participate, without vote, in any discussion in the Council if the Council considers that the interests of that member are specially affected.   Any state which is a party to a

---

[3] De Arechaga, *Le Traitement des Différends Internationaux par le Conseil de Securité,* 85 RECUEIL DES COURS 5-105 (1954); DE ARECHAGA, VOTING AND THE HANDLING OF DISPUTES IN THE SECURITY COUNCIL (New York 1950); Bowett, *The Security Council: Functions and Powers,* in 3 THE STRATEGY OF WORLD ORDER 185-205 (B. Falk ed. New York 1966); P. BRUGIÈRE, 'DROIT DE VETO': LA RÈGLE UNANIMITÉ DES MEMBRES PERMANENTS AU CONSEIL DE SECURITÉ (Paris 1952); G. DAY, LE DROIT DE VETO DANS L'ORGANISATION DES NATIONS UNIES (Paris 1952); KAHNG, LAW, POLITICS AND THE SECURITY COUNCIL (The Hague 1964); Kerley, *The Powers of Investigation of the United Nations Security Council,* 55 AJIL 892-918 (1961); M. MARCUS, VOTING PROCEDURES AND PRACTICES IN THE SECURITY COUNCIL OF THE UNITED NATIONS (Univ. of Michigan, Ann Arbor 1959); Munro, *The Present-Day Role of the Security Council in the Maintenance of Peace,* ASIL PROC. 131-36 (1955); A. SALOMON, L'O.N.U. ET LA PAIX: LE CONSEIL DE SECURITÉ ET LE RÈGLEMENT PACIFIQUE DES DIFFÉRENDS (Paris 1948); Schacter, *The Quasi-Judicial Role of the Security Council and the General Assembly,* 58 AJIL 960-65 (1964); Vallat, *The General Assembly and the Security Council of the United Nations,* 29 BR. Y.B. INT'L L. 63-105 (1952); Wortley, *The Veto and the Security Provisions of the Charter,* 23 BR. Y.B. INT'L L. 95-112 (1946).

dispute being considered by the Council must be invited to participate, without vote, in the discussions.

Each Council member has one vote. A decision by the Council
on any matter other than a question of procedure is by an affirmative vote of nine Council members, but must include the concurring
votes of *all* permanent members. On procedural questions a decision is by an affirmative vote of *any* nine members. However,
the Charter does not clearly define what are procedural matters.
Consequently, on votes to determine whether an issue is procedural,
the veto may apply.

In spite of the frequent use of the veto power the Security Council
has been able to perform many useful functions, not the least of
which is the maintenance of an organization to which can be referred
matters relating to threats to the peace. Under present conditions,
none of the great powers is willing to give up its veto over proposals
which might adversely affect interests which it considers vital.
Although continuing efforts are made to find ways to avoid its
improper use, the veto power has doubtlessly been an important
factor enabling great powers with widely divergent interests to
remain in the United Nations organization.

The powers of the Security Council may be divided into four
categories: investigation, conciliation and mediation, recommendation of procedures or methods of adjustment, and imposition and
enforcement of terms of settlement. In exercising its powers, the
Council is advised by the Charter (Article 36(3)) to consider the
general rule that legal disputes should be referred by the parties to
the International Court of Justice. Enforcement measures available
to the Council include military action, if necessary. All members
of the United Nations are pledged by the Charter to make available
to the Council, on its call, and in accordance with special agreements, the forces and facilities necessary to maintain international
peace and security.

Under the Security Council are subsidiary organs which it has
established as necessary. Among these is the Disarmament Commission which was established in 1952 to prepare proposals for the
regulation, limitation, and balanced reduction of all armed forces
and armaments, elimination of weapons of mass destruction, and
the effective control of atomic energy.

§ 3-1.3. **The Economic and Social Council.**[4]   ECOSOC studies
and makes reports and recommendations on international economic,

---

[4] ECOSOC, Official Records: Report by the Secretary-General, *Decentralization of the
Economic and Social Activities of the United Nations* (1962); EVERYMAN'S UNITED

(Continued)

social, cultural, educational, health and related matters. Studies are also made on human rights and fundamental freedoms by the Economic and Social Council. The Council is composed of 18 member states, six being elected each year by the General Assembly for a three-year term. Its work consists of preparing draft conventions on these subjects for submission to the General Assembly; calling international conferences when needed; giving information and assistance to the Security Council as required and, with the approval of the General Assembly, performing services within its scope for member states.

The Economic and Social Council is empowered to establish such commissions and committees as it deems necessary. Four regional economic commissions with subsidiary bodies dealing with specific subjects such as trade, communications and power have been thus established. Functional commissions and subcommissions, standing and *ad hoc* committees and special bodies have also been set up.

§ 3-1.4. The Trusteeship Council.[5]   The Charter of the United Nations established a Trusteeship System through a series of eight Trusteeship Agreements to administer and supervise eight African and Pacific territories placed under the trust of member nations. The Trusteeship Council, which first met on March 26, 1947, at Lake Success, New York, is composed of member countries administering trust territories: permanent members of the Security Council which are not administering trust territories; and as many members, elected for three-year terms by the General Assembly, as may be necessary to ensure equality in numbers between administering and non-administering members.

In 1947, the progenitor of the present Committee on Information from Non-Self-Governing Territories was formed to receive, examine and make recommendations concerning information on economic,

---

NATIONS 17-24 (1959); UNITED NATIONS, YEARBOOK OF THE UNITED NATIONS 615-21 (1960).

[5] Trusteeship Council, Official Records: Index to Proceedings; Rules of Procedure; Resolutions; Committee Reports; Reports of Visiting Missions; Texts of the Eight Trusteeship Agreements Approved by the General Assembly, 1946; Agreements, Approved by the General Assembly, in 1946 for the Camerouns (British, French), New Guinea, Ruanda-Urundi, Tanganyika, and Togoland (British, French); in 1947 for Nauru; and in 1950 for Somaliland. *See also* EVERYMAN'S UNITED NATIONS 26-27 (1959); J. MURRAY, THE UNITED NATIONS TRUSTEESHIP SYSTEM (Urbana, Illinois 1957); E. SADY, THE UNITED NATIONS AND DEPENDENT PEOPLES (Washington 1956); Sayre, *Legal Problems Arising from the United Nations Trusteeship System,* 42 AJIL 263-99 (1948); W. SELZER, THE TRUSTEESHIP COUNCIL OF THE UNITED NATIONS . . . (University of Pennsylvania 1959); C. TOUSSAINT, THE TRUSTEESHIP SYSTEM OF THE UNITED NATIONS (New York 1956); UNITED NATIONS, YEARBOOK OF THE UNITED NATIONS 437-542 (1960).

social and educational conditions and relevant recommendations from the General Assembly with regard to non-self governing territories. In examining the information and reports which it has received, the Committee is primarily concerned with those principles and objectives set forth in the pertinent chapters of the Charter, particularly in Articles 73 and 74. On the basis of the information it receives, the Committee makes recommendations concerning the particular territories. These activities and the development of the Committee have been held by some to be an example of the evolution of United Nations Law by the General Assembly well beyond the confines of the Charter. The authorities cited in the footnote so indicate.

§ 3-1.5. The Secretariat.[6]   The administrative functions of the United Nations are performed by the Secretariat, the agency which services the other organs and administers the programs and policies laid down by them. The head of the Secretariat is the Secretary-General, who is appointed by the General Assembly on the recommendation of the Security Council. The Charter does not specify the duration of his term, or procedures to be followed if, after the expiration of his term, a successor is not agreed upon. Past policy has been to elect the Secretary-General for a five-year term.

The Secretary-General appoints the staff of the Secretariat in accordance with regulations established by the General Assembly. The primary consideration in selection of the staff, according to the Charter, is to maintain a high standard of efficiency, competence and integrity, subject to an equitable geographical distribution. The Charter provides that the staff members are responsible only to the United Nations and will not seek or receive instructions from any government or authority outside the United Nations.

The first Secretary-General, Trygve Lie of Norway, served from February 1, 1946, to April 10, 1953. His successor, Dag Hammarskjold of Sweden, served from August 16, 1953 to September 10,

---

[6] S. BAILEY, THE SECRETARIAT OF THE UNITED NATIONS (New York 1962); Cohen, *The United Nations Secretariat—Some Constitutional and Administrative Developments,* 49 AJIL 295-320 (1955); E. GIRAUD, LA STRUCTURE ET LE FONCTIONNEMENT DU SECRETARIAT DES NATIONS UNIES (Paris 1955); Kunz, *The United Nations Secretary General on the Role of the United Nations,* 52 AJIL 300-04 (1958); Schwebel, *The International Character of the Secretariat of the United Nations,* 30 BR. Y.B. INT'L L. 71-115 (1953); SCHWEBEL, THE SECRETARY-GENERAL OF THE UNITED NATIONS: HIS POLITICAL POWERS AND PRACTICE (Harvard Univ. Press, Cambridge 1952); SECRETARIAT OF THE UNITED NATIONS, REPERTORY OF PRACTICE OF UNITED NATIONS ORGANS (New York 1955); W. WRIGGINS & E. BOCK, THE STATUS OF THE UNITED NATIONS SECRETARIAT . . . (New York 1953); UNITED NATIONS, YEARBOOK OF THE UNITED NATIONS 301, 371, 374, 558, 574-75, 728, 732 (1960).

1961, when he was killed in a plane crash in Africa. The third and present Secretary-General is U Thant of Burma.

§ 3-1.6. Specialized Agencies.[7] The "specialized agencies" are organizations established by intergovernmental agreements having particular responsibilities in economic, social, cultural, education, health and related fields. Agreements bringing agencies into relationship with the United Nations are in force with the following agencies: Food and Agricultural Organization of the United Nations; Inter-Governmental Maritime Consultative Organization; International Atomic Energy Agency; International Bank for Reconstruction and Development; International Civil Aviation Organization; International Development Association; International Finance Corporation; International Labor Organization; International Monetary Fund; International Telecommunication Union; International Trade Organization; United Nations Educational, Scientific and Cultural Organization; Universal Postal Union; World Health Organization; and World Meteorological Organization. A special agreement has also been made with the International Atomic Energy Agency. Provisions of the Charter concerning such agencies are in Chapters 9 and 10.

The Expanded Program of Technical Assistance of the United Nations is designed to help assist underdeveloped countries in the development of their industries and agriculture. It operates through arrangements made with eight of the aforementioned specialized agencies, plus the United Nations Bureau of Technical Assistance Operations. Technical aid under the program generally takes the form of: qualified technical experts in the field, fellowships or scholarships to nationals of underdeveloped countries, and organization of regional training centers and seminars. A Technical Assist-

---

[7] Adam, *Les Accords de Prêt de la Banque Internationale pour la Reconstruction et le Développement,* REV. GEN. DR. INT'L PUB. 41-72 (1951); K. AHLUWALIA, THE LEGAL STATUS, PRIVILEGES AND IMMUNITIES OF THE SPECIALIZED AGENCIES OF THE UNITED NATIONS AND CERTAIN OTHER INTERNATIONAL ORGANIZATIONS (The Hague 1964); R. BERKOV, THE WORLD HEALTH ORGANIZATION (Geneva 1960); C. FENWICK, INTERNATIONAL LAW 196-210 (New York 1948); INTERNATIONAL LABOR ORGANIZATION, YEAR BOOK (1930-   ); Lake Success, Library Services . . ., SELECTED BIBLIOGRAPHY OF THE SPECIALIZED AGENCIES RELATED TO THE UNITED NATIONS (New York 1949); 2 PEASLEE, INTERNATIONAL GOVERNMENTAL ORGANIZATIONS 923-41 (The Hague 1956); Pollaczek, *The United Nations and Specialized Agencies,* 40 AJIL 592-620 (1946); Saba, *Quasi-Legislative Activities of the Specialized Agencies of the United Nations,* 111 RECUEIL DES COURS 607-90 (1964); J. SCHENKMAN, INTERNATIONAL CIVIL AVIATION ORGANIZATION (Geneva 1955); UNITED NATIONS, TEACHING ABOUT THE UNITED NATIONS AND THE SPECIALIZED AGENCIES: A SELECTED BIBLIOGRAPHY (Paris 1959); Virally, *Le Rôle Politique du Secrétaire Général des Nations Unies,* ANN. FR. DR. INT'L 360-98 (1958); ZOLLIKOFER, LES RELATIONS PRÉVUES ENTRE LES INSTITUTIONS SPÉCIALISÉES DES NATIONS UNIES ET LA COUR INTERNATIONALE DE JUSTICE (Leyde 1955).

ance Board and a Technical Assistance Committee have the primary
responsibility for the operation of the expanded program.

§ 3-1.7. The International Law Commission.[8] By resolution in
December 1946, the General Assembly, with a view to implementing its obligations under Article 13(1)(a) of the Charter, established
a 17-member Commission to study the methods by which the General Assembly should encourage the progressive development of
international law and its eventual codification. Subsequently, the
General Assembly at a plenary meeting in November 1947, adopted
without a dissenting vote Resolution 174 (II), recommended by the
Sixth Committee, establishing an International Law Commission.
Article I of the Commission's Statute notes that the Commission
should concern itself primarily with public international law, although
it is not precluded from entering the field of private international
law.

The Commission was originally composed of 15 members "of
recognized competence" in international law, elected by the General Assembly from a list of candidates nominated by the members
for a three-year term. In 1955, the General Assembly extended the
term of members of the International Law Commission to five years;
in 1956, it increased the number of members to 21 and in 1961, to
25. The members do not serve as representatives of their govern-

---

[8] Briggs, *Official Interest in the Work of the International Law Commission,* 48 AJIL
603-12 (1954); H. BRIGGS, THE INTERNATIONAL LAW COMMISSION (Ithaca, N.Y.
1965); BULLETIN OF THE INTERNATIONAL LAW COMMISSION (1968-   ); Eagleton,
The Second Session of the International Law Commission, 45 AJIL 148-51 (1951);
Gotlieb, *The International Law Commission,* 4 CAN. Y.B. INT'L L. 64-80 (1966); Hazard,
The Sixth Committee and New Law, 57 AJIL 604-13 (1963); Higham, *The United Nations
International Law Commission: A Guide to the Documents, 1949-59,* 36 BR. Y.B. INT'L L.
384-97 (1960); Hogg, *The International Law Commission and the Law of Treaties,* ASIL
PROC. 8-14 (1965); Hoyt, *The Contribution of the International Law Commission, id.,*
at 2-8; Hudson, *Encouragement of the Development of International Law by the United
Nations,* 41 AJIL 104-06 (1947); Jennings, *Recent Developments in the International
Law Commission: Its Relation to the Sources of International Law,* 13 INT'L & COMP.
L.Q. 385-97 (1964); Jessup, *Development of International Law by the United Nations,*
39 AJIL 754-57 (1945); Lee, *The International Law Commission Re-Examined,* 59 AJIL
545-69 (1965); Liang, *The First Session of the International Law Commission; Review
of Its Work by the General Assembly,* 44 AJIL 527-43 (1950); Liang, *The Second Session
. . .,* 46 AJIL 509-26 (1952); Liang, *The Third Session . . .,* 47 AJIL 483-504, 667-81
(1953); *Report of the International Law Commission Covering Its Fourteenth Session,*
57 AJIL 190-268 (1963); Rosenne, *Relations Between Governments and the International
Law Commission,* 19 Y.B. WORLD AFF. 183-98 (1965); Rosenne, *The International
Law Commission, 1949-59,* 36 BR. Y.B. INT'L L. 104-74 (1960); Stone, *On the Vocation
of the International Law Commission,* in COLUMBIA LAW REVIEW ESSAYS ON THE
INTERNATIONAL LAW 117-54 (1965); Waldock, *International Law Commission and
the Law of Treaties,* UN MONTHLY CHRONICLE 69-76 (No. 5 1967); YEARBOOK OF
THE INTERNATIONAL LAW COMMISSION (1949-   ), in which documents are listed
by subject and by session.

ments but in their individual capacities as experts on international law. The Commission holds one session a year in Geneva lasting from eight to 11 weeks.

Since it began its work, the Commission has prepared a Draft Declaration of Rights and Duties of States; formulated the principles of international penal law recognized in the Charter and the judgment of Nuremberg Tribunal; prepared a Draft Code of Offences against the Peace and Security of Mankind; studied the question of defining aggression; expressed an opinion regarding the desirability and possibility of establishing an international judicial organ for the trial of persons charged with genocide and certain other crimes; made recommendations on the problem of reservations to multilateral conventions; prepared a Draft Convention on the Elimination or Reduction of Future Statelessness; and submitted proposals concerning the ways and means for making the evidence oɪ customary international law more readily available. These drafts have not been finalized, however. The Commission also prepared a draft on diplomatic intercourse and immunities which led to the Convention of Diplomatic Relations signed at Vienna on April 18, 1961, after a Conference held on the recommendation of the General Assembly and attended by 81 nations.[9]

The Commission's work on the regime of the high seas and the territorial sea was brought to a conclusion by the presentation of the articles concerning the law of the sea in its report covering its eighth session. This final report[10] was submitted to the Assembly at its Eleventh Session, and the Assembly in 1957, decided to convene the International Conference on the Law of the Sea. As a result of this Conference, international conventions were signed and have entered into force concerning the territorial sea and contiguous zone, the high seas, fishing and conservation of the living resources of the high seas, and the continental shelf.[11] A Second Conference on the Law of the Sea, which attempted to reach an agreement on the width of the territorial sea, ended in failure when a compromise proposal missed adoption by one vote.[12] In addition, the Commission has continued to study the law of treaties, state responsibility, and consular intercourse and immunities.

---

[9] United Nations Conference on Diplomatic Intercourse and Immunities, U.N. Doc. A/CONF. 20/14/Add. 1 (1961); *Vienna Convention on Diplomatic Relations*, 55 AJIL 1064 (1961).

[10] United Nations, *Report of the International Law Commission*, 51 AJIL 154 (1957).

[11] *Articles Concerning the Law of the Sea*, 51 AJIL 161 (1957).

[12] Second United Nations Conference on the Law of the Sea, Official Records, U.N. Doc. A/CONF. 19/8 (1960).

§ 3-2. Intergovernmental Agencies Related to the United Nations[13]

The United Nations has determined that its day-to-day efforts in encouraging cooperation among nations can best be accomplished through cooperation with agencies concerned with specific areas. Thus, the UN has entered into agreements with the International Civil Aviation Organization, the International Atomic Energy Agency, the International Labor Organization, the International Telecommunication Union, the Inter-Governmental Maritime Consultative Organization, the Universal Postal Union, the World Health Organization and the World Meteorological Organization.

This specific problem-oriented structure for international cooperation permits nations of all sizes and levels of development to enter into just those agreements which further their national goals. This, in turn, promotes greater confidence in international agreements as a road to world peace, and moves the law structure for world peace closer to the ideal noted by the Chief Justice of the United States, Earl Warren, that the:

---

[13] The following are a few of the numerous books and articles that have been written on various aspects of the general subject of international organizations: D. BOWETT, THE LAW OF INTERNATIONAL INSTITUTIONS (New York 1963); G. CANSACCHI, ISTITUZIONI DI DIRITTO INTERNAZIONALE PUBBLICO (Torino 1967); R. CHARPENTIER, INSTITUTIONS INTERNATIONALES (Paris 1966); C. COLLIARD, INSTITUTIONS INTERNATIONALES (Paris 1966); W. GANSHOF VAN DER MEERSCH, ORGANISATIONS EUROPÉENNES (Paris 1966); Hanrieder, *International Organizations and International Systems,* 10 THE JOURNAL OF CONFLICT RESOLUTION 297-313 (1966); Head, *The Contribution of the International Court of Justice to the Development of International Organizations,* ASIL PROC. 177-82 (1965); Higgins, *The Development of Law by the Political Organs of the United Nations,* ASIL PROC. 116-24 (1965); Jenks, *Some Constitutional Problems of International Organizations,* 22 BR. Y.B. INT'L L. 11-72 (1945); THE LEGAL PERSONALITY OF INTERNATIONAL ORGANIZATIONS (New York 1962); C. JENKS, THE PROPER LAW OF INTERNATIONAL ORGANIZATIONS (New York 1962); E. LUARD, THE PROCESS OF CHANGE IN INTERNATIONAL ORGANIZATIONS (London 1961); P. REUTER, INSTITUTIONS INTERNATIONALES (Paris 1967); A. ROBERTSON, THE LAW OF INTERNATIONAL INSTITUTIONS IN EUROPE (Manchester 1961); ROBERTSON, EUROPEAN INSTITUTIONS (London 1966); Speeckaert, *De la Structure et du Fonctionnement des Organisations Internationales Non-Gouvernmentales,* 18 INT'L ASS'N 264-74 (1966); E. STEIN & P. HAY, LAW AND INSTITUTIONS IN THE ATLANTIC AREA (New York 1967); UNIVERSITY OF BRUSSELS, INSTITUTIONS COMMUNAUTAIRES ET INSTITUTIONS NATIONALES DANS LE DÉVELOPPEMENT DES COMMUNAUTÉS (Brussels 1968); Vasak, *Work Paper on the Development of Law Through International Organizations,* in GENEVA CONF. 339-50.

Useful current information on international organizations will be found in the YEARBOOK OF INTERNATIONAL ORGANIZATIONS (12th ed. 1968-1969) and A. PEASE-LEE, INTERNATIONAL GOVERNMENTAL ORGANIZATIONS. The Union of International Associations in Brussels also publishes a PETIT REPERTOIRE DES ORGANISATIONS INTERNATIONALES. Most international law journals contain articles and notes on international organizations. See Chapter 6 on Specialized Economic organizations.

[s]elf-interest of people in our shrinking, interlocked, interdependent world are more and more identical regardless of the nation in which we live.[14]

§ 3-2.1 The International Atomic Energy Agency[15] was established on July 29, 1957, after approval of its statute at an international conference held under the auspices of the United Nations. A special agreement on the relation of the Agency to the United Nations was approved by both organizations in October-November 1957. The Agency reports annually to the UN Assembly and, when needed, to the Security Council. Its work is directed exclusively to peaceful applications of atomic energy, such as improving health and increasing prosperity throughout the world.

The IAEA is composed of a General Conference, a Board of Governors, and a Secretariat. The General Conference consists of all Agency members; it meets annually and more often as needed. The Board of Governors, which consists of 25 members, implements the decisions of the General Conference and carries out projects which further the purposes of the Agency. The Secretariat performs the usual functions of an administrative office. The Secretary-General is appointed for a four-year term by the Board of Governors with the approval of the General Conference.

The Agency promotes the development of nuclear power and the use of radioisotopes. It disseminates scientific information; offers technical assistance; develops technical skills; and studies and recommends action on the legal problems involved in nuclear hazards.

§ 3-2.2. The International Civil Aviation Organization.[16] ICAO was created on April 4, 1947, with headquarters in Montreal. It is composed of an Assembly, a Council, and a Secretariat. The Assembly, consisting of representatives of 116 member states, meets once every three years and more often if needed. The Council is the Organization's executive body, which implements directives and prepares the budget. The Secretariat, headed by a Secretary-General, performs customary administrative functions.

---

[14] GENEVA CONF. 41.

[15] Gorove, *Maintaining Order Through On-site Inspection: Focus on IAEA,* 18 CASE W. RES. L.REV. 1525-47 (1967); INTERNATIONAL ATOMIC ENERGY AGENCY, IAEA SERVICES AND ASSISTANCE (Vienna 1966); Rosen, *Proliferation Treaty Controls and IAEA,* 11 J. CONFLICT RES. 168-75 (1967).

[16] The Organization publishes a monthly bulletin and reports on meetings, and is located at: 1080 University Street, Montreal 3, Quebec, Canada. *See also* T. BUERGENTHAL, LAW-MAKING IN THE INTERNATIONAL CIVIL AVIATION ORGANIZATION. (Syracuse, New York 1969). The Warsaw Convention as sponsored by ICAO is considered in C. RHYNE, AVIATION ACCIDENT LAW 252-84 (1944).

The Organization seeks improvements in and standardization of international air navigation rules and publishes and disseminates information in the field. It is also available to settle disputes between member states. ICAO develops Convention on airplane hi-jacking, the Warsaw Convention on liabilities for accidental injury to passengers and others as well as other rules and regulations affecting aviation worldwide. The Airplane Hi-Jacking Convention is considered *ante* § 2-9.10.

§ 3-2.3.   **The International Labour Organization.**[17] Established with headquarters in Geneva, on April 11, 1919, with the adoption

---

[17] THE INTERNATIONAL LABOR ORGANIZATION, INTERNATIONAL LABOR REVIEW (monthly); ILO, LEGISLATIVE SERIES (bi-monthly); ILO, OFFICIAL BULLETIN (quarterly). Address: CH 1211, Geneva 22, Switzerland.

The following Conventions have been prepared and promulgated by the ILO. They include:

Hours of work (Industry, 1919), Unemployment (1919), Maternity Protection (1919), Night Work (Women, 1919), Minimum Age (Industry, 1919), Night Work of Young Persons (Industry, 1919), Minimum Age (Sea, 1920), Unemployment Indemnity (Shipwreck, 1920), Placing of Seamen (1920), Minimum Age (Agriculture, 1921), Right of Association (Agriculture, 1921), Workmen's Compensation (Agriculture, 1921), White Lead (Painting, 1921), Weekly Rest (Industry, 1921), Minimum Age (Trimmers and Stokers, 1921), Medical Examination of Young Persons (Sea, 1921), Workmen's Compensation (Accidents, 1925), Workmen's Compensation (Occupational Diseases, 1925), Equality of Treatment (Accident Compensation, 1925), Night Work (Bakeries, 1925), Inspection of Emigrants (1926), Seamen's Articles of Agreement (1926), Repatriation of Seamen (1926), Sickness Insurance (Industry, 1927), Sickness Insurance (Agriculture, 1927), Minimum Wage-Fixing Machinery (1928), Marking of Weight (Packages Transported by Vessels, 1929), Protection Against Accidents (Dockers, 1929), Forced Labour (1930), Hours of Work (Commerce and Offices, 1930), Hours of Work (Coal Mines, 1931), Protection Against Accidents (Dockers, Revised, 1932), Minimum Age (Non Industrial Employment, 1932), Fee-Charging Employment Agencies (1933), Old-Age Insurance (Industry, 1933), Old-Age Insurance (Agriculture, 1933), Invalidity Insurance (Industry, 1933), Invalidity Insurance (Agriculture, 1933), Survivors' Insurance (Industry, 1933), Survivors' Insurance (Agriculture, 1933), Night Work (Women, Revised, 1934), Workmen's Compensation (Occupational Diseases, Revised, 1934), Sheet-Glass Works (1934), Unemployment Provision (1934), Underground Work (Women, 1935), Hours of Work (Coal Mines, Revised, 1935), Forty-Hour Week (1935), Maintenance of Migrants' Pension Rights (1935), Reduction of Hours of Work (Glass-Bottle Works, 1936), Recruiting of Indigenous Workers (1936), Reduction of Hours of Work (Public Works, 1936), Holidays with Pay (1936), Officers' Competency Certificates (1936), Holidays with Pay (Sea, 1936), Shipowners' Liability (Sick and Injured Seamen, 1936), Sickness Insurance (Sea, 1936), Hours of Work and Manning (Sea, 1936), Minimum Age (Sea, Revised, 1936), Minimum Age (Industry, Revised, 1937), Minimum Age (Non-Industrial Employment, Revised, 1937), Reduction of Hours of Work (Textiles, 1937), Safety Provisions (Building, 1937), Statistics of Wages and Hours of Work (1938), Contracts of Employment (Indigenous Workers, 1939), Penal Sanctions (Indigenous Workers, 1939), Migration for

(Continued)

of its constitution as part of the Treaty of Versailles, ILO became the first specialized agency related to the United Nations, and in 1969, won the Nobel Peace Prize. The broad purpose of the Organization is to improve labor conditions and living standards while promoting economic and social justice to give stability in the interest of enduring peace.

Employment (1939), Hours of Work and Rest Periods (Road Transport, 1939), Food and Catering (Ships' Crews, 1946), Certification of Ships' Cooks (1946), Social Security (Seafarers, 1946), Seafarers' Pensions (1946), Paid Vacations (Seafarers, 1946), Medical Examination (Seafarers, 1946), Certification of Able Seamen (1946), Accommodation of Crews (1946), Wages, Hours of Work and Manning (Sea, 1946), Medical Examination of Young Persons (Industry, 1946), Medical Examination of Young Persons (Non-Industrial Occupations, 1946), Night Work of Young Persons (Non-Industrial Occupations, 1946), Final Articles Revision (1946), Labour Inspection (1947), Social Policy (Non-Metropolitan Territories, 1947), Right of Association (Non-Metropolitan Territories, 1947), Labour Inspectorates (Non-Metropolitan Territories, 1947), Contracts of Employment (Indigenous Workers, 1947), Freedom of Association and Protection of the Right to Organize (1948), Employment Service (1948), Night Work (Women, Revised, 1948), Night Work of Young Persons (Industry, Revised, 1948), Paid Vacations (Seafarers, Revised, 1949), Accommodation of Crews (Revised, 1949), Wages, Hours of Work and Manning (Sea, Revised, 1949), Labour Clauses (Public Contracts, 1949), Protection of Wages (1949), Fee-Charging Employment Agencies (Revised, 1949), Migration for Employment (Revised, 1949), Right to Organize and Collective Bargaining (1949), Minimum Wage-Fixing Machinery (Agriculture, 1951), Equal Remuneration (1951), Holidays with Pay (Agriculture, 1952), Social Security (Minimum Standards, 1952), Maternity Protection (Revised, 1952), Abolition of Penal Sanctions (Indigenous Workers, 1955), Abolition of Forced Labour (1957), Weekly Rest (Commerce and Offices, 1957), Indigenous and Tribal Populations (1957), Seafarers' Identity Documents (1958), Wages, Hours of Work and Manning (Sea, Revised, 1958), Plantations (1958), Discrimination (Employment and Occupation, 1958), Minimum Age (Fishermen, 1959), Fishermen's Articles of Agreement (1959), Medical Examination (Fishermen, 1959), Radiation Protection (1960), Final Articles Revision (1961), Social Policy (Basic Aims and Standards, 1962), Equality of Treatment (Social Security, 1962), Guarding of Machinery (1963), Hygiene (Commerce and Offices, 1964), Employment Injury Benefits (1964), Employment Policy Convention (1964), Minimum Age (Underground Work, 1965), Medical Examination of Young Persons (Underground Work, 1965), Fishermen's Competency Certificates (1966), Accommodation of Crews (Fishermen, 1966), Maximum Weight (1967), Invalidity, Old-Age and Survivors' Benefits (1967), Labour Inspection (Agriculture, 1969), Medical Care and Sickness Benefits (1969).

In addition the ILO has issued 134 recommendations on Labor. These include: Unemployment (1919), Reciprocity of Treatment (1919), Anthrax Prevention (1919), Lead Poisoning (Women and Children, 1919), Labour Inspection (Health Services, 1919), White Phosphorous (1919), Hours of Work (Fishing, 1920), Hours of Work (Inland Navigation, 1920), National Seamen's Codes (1920), Unemployment Insurance (Seamen, 1920), Unemployment (Agriculture, 1921), Maternity Protection (Agriculture, 1921), Night Work of Women (Agriculture, 1921), Night Work of Children and Young Persons (Agriculture, 1921), Vocational Education (Agriculture, 1921), Living-in Conditions (Agriculture, 1921), Social Insurance (Agriculture, 1921), Weekly Rest (Commerce,

(Continued)

The ILO has a General Conference, a Governing Body, and International Labor Office. The General Conference consists of national delegations composed of two government delegates, a delegate representing management, and a delegate representing labor. Its principal objective is the drafting of conventions embodying improved social standards. The Governing Body is composed of 48 members. Twenty-four of these members represent governments, of which 12 must come from major industrial countries; 12 represent manage-

1921), Migration Statistics (1922), Labour Inspection (1923), Utilization of Spare Time (1924), Workmen's Compensation (Minimum Scale, 1925), Workmen's Compensation (Jurisdiction, 1925), Workmen's Compensation (Occupation Diseases, 1925), Equality of Treatment (Accident Compensation, 1925), Migration (Protection of Females at Sea, 1926), Repatriation (Ship Masters and Apprentices, 1926), Labour Inspection (Seaman, 1926), Sickness Insurance (1927), Minimum Wage-Fixing Machinery (1928), Prevention of Industrial Accidents (1929), Power-driven Machinery (1929), Protection against Accidents (Dockers, 1929), Forced Labour (Indirect Compulsion, 1930), Forced Labour (Regulation, 1930), Hours of Work (Hotels, etc., 1930), Hours of Work (Theatres, etc., 1930), Hours of Work (Hospitals, etc., 1930), Protection against Accidents (Dockers, Reciprocity, 1932), Minimum Age (Non-Industrial Employment, 1932), Employment Agencies (1933), Invalidity, Old-Age and Survivors' Insurance (1932), Unemployment Provision (1935), Elimination of Recruiting (1936), Holidays with Pay (1936), Seamen's Welfare in Ports (1936), Hours of Work and Manning (Sea, 1936), Public Works (International Cooperation, 1937), Public Works (National Planning, 1937), Minimum Age (Family Undertakings, 1937), Safety Provisions (Building, 1937), Inspection (Building, 1937), Cooperation in Accident Prevention (Building, 1937), Vocational Education (Building, 1937), Vocational Training (1939), Contracts of Employment (Indigenous Workers, 1939), Labour Inspectorates (Indigenous Workers, 1939), Apprenticeship (1939), Migration for Employment (1939), Migration for Employment (Co-operation between States, 1939), Control Books (Road Transport, 1939), Night Work (Road Transport, 1939), Methods of Regulating Hours (Road Transport, 1939), Rest Periods (Private Chauffeurs, 1939), Income Security (1944), Social Security (Armed Forces, 1944), Medical Care (1944), Social Policy in Dependent Territories (1944), Employment (Transition from War to Peace, 1944), Employment Service (1944), Public Works (National Planning, 1944), Social Policy in Dependent Territories (Supplementary Provisions, 1945), Seafarers' Social Security (Agreements, 1946), Seafarers' Medical Care for Dependents (1946), Bedding, Mess Utensils and Miscellaneous Provisions Ships' Crews, 1946), Vocational Training (Seafarers, 1946), Medical Examination of Young Persons (1946), Night Work of Young Persons (Non-Industrial Occupations, 1946), Labour Inspection (1947), Labour Inspection (Mining and Transport, 1947), Employment Service (1948), Labour Clauses (Public Contracts, 1949), Protection of Wages (1949), Migration for Employment (Revised, 1949), Vocational Guidance (1949), Vocational Training (Adults, 1950), Minimum Wage-Fixing Machinery (Agriculture, 1951), Equal Remuneration (1951), Collective Agreements (1951), Voluntary Conciliation and Arbitration (1951), Holidays with Pay (Agriculture, 1952), Co-operation at the Level of the Undertaking (1952), Maternity Protection (1952), Minimum Age (Coal Mines, 1953), Protection of Workers' Health (1953), Holidays with Pay (1954), Vocational Rehabilitation (Disabled, 1955), Protection of Migrant Workers (Underdeveloped

(Continued)

ment, and 12 labor. The Governing Body supervises the activities of the International Labor Office and the committees and other bodies carrying out its activities. The International Labor Office, which houses the Secretariat, collects and disseminates information in the field and assists governments in drafting legislation when requested by them to do so and when approved by the General Conference. It also carries out technical cooperation programs, assists in the application of conventions, and issues various publications. ILO has prepared and released Conventions whose purposes are to improve the social and economic conditions of industry and labor. See Chapter 8 for a more detailed discussion.

§ 3-2.4. The International Telecommunication Union.[18]   ITU grew out of the International Telegraph Union which was founded in 1865, was reorganized in 1947 and became a specialized agency related to the United Nations. One of the great experts on ITU, Leonard H. Marks, in addressing the Athens Conference on World Peace Through Law in 1963 pointed out that ITU is the oldest of the specialized agencies.

The ITU is composed of a Plenipotentiary Conference, an Administrative Council, and a General Secretariat. The Plenipotentiary Conference which meets every five years is the supreme organ of the Union. The Administrative Council consists of 25 members elected by the Plenipotentiary Conference and meets once a year or more often if it considers this necessary or upon request of six members of the Union. It supervises ITU administrative functions between

Countries, 1955), Vocational Training (Agriculture, 1956), Welfare Facilities (1956), Weekly Rest (Commerce and Offices, 1957), Indigenous and Tribal Populations (1957), Ships' Medicine Chests (1958), Medical Advice at Sea (1958), Seafarers' Engagement (Foreign Vessels, 1958), Social Conditions and Safety (Seafarers, 1958), Wages, Hours of Work and Manning (Sea, 1958), Plantations (1958), Discrimination (Employment and Occupation, 1958), Occupational Health Services (1959), Consultation (Industrial and National Levels, 1960), Radiation Protection (1960), Workers' Housing (1961), Reduction of Hours of Work (1962), Vocational Training (1962), Guarding of Machinery (1963), Termination of Employment (1963), Hygiene (Commerce and Offices, 1964), Employment Injury Benefits (1964), Employment Policy (1964), Employment (Women with Family Responsibilities, 1965), Minimum Age (Underground Work, 1965), Conditions of Employment of Young Persons (Underground Work, 1965), Vocational Training (Fishermen, 1966), Co-operatives (Developing Countries, 1966), Maximum Weight (1967), Communications within the Undertaking (1967), Examination of Grievances (1967), Invalidity, Old-Age and Survivors' Benefits (1967), Tenants and Share-croppers (1968), Labour Inspection (Agriculture, 1969), Medical Care and Sickness Benefits (1969).

[18] The International Telecommunications Union publishes a monthly Journal. *See* Athens, Washington, Geneva and Bangkok Conf. Volumes where extensive consideration is given to ITU activities and accomplishments.

conferences, approves budgets, and coordinates its activities with those of other international organizations. The Secretariat, headed by a Secretary-General, performs the usual administrative functions.

ITU offers advice to its members, promotes international cooperation in the telecommunications field, advances the development of telegraph, telephone, and radio services, and prepares studies and collects and disseminates information in the field.

§ 3-2.5. The Inter-Governmental Maritime Consultative Organization.[19]

IMCO was created by a convention concluded in 1948 and which entered into force on March 17, 1958, when ratified by 21 states. Its headquarters are located in London.

IMCO is composed of an Assembly, a Council, a Maritime Safety Committee, and a Secretariat. The Assembly, which is composed of all the members of the Organization and which meets every two years, is the policy-making body. The Council, which is composed of 16 members, carries on Organization activities between Assembly sessions. The Maritime Safety Committee, which consists of 14 members including the 8 largest shipbuilding states, recommends the adoption of maritime safety regulations. The Secretariat is composed of a Secretary-General, a Secretary of the Maritime Safety Committee and a working staff.

The Organization provides means for the cooperation and exchange of information among states on technical shipping matters. It seeks the development of high standards of safety of life at sea. It attempts to obtain the removal of restrictive or discriminatory practices by governments or shipping concerns. ICMO studies and makes recommendations on shipping problems referred to it by international organizations. Finally, it convenes international conferences and prepares drafts of international conventions on shipping matters such as spillage of oil and other pollution problems.

§ 3-2.6. The United Nations Educational, Social and Cultural Organization [20]

UNESCO was established in 1945, and became a specialized agency of the United Nations by an agreement in 1946. Its headquarters are located in Paris, and member states have national offices.

---

[19] INTER-GOVERNMENTAL MARITIME CONSULTATIVE ORGANIZATION, BASIC DOCUMENTS (London 1962); IGMCO, CONVENTION ON THE INTER-GOVERNMENTAL MARITIME CONSULTATIVE ORGANIZATION (London 1961); Kano, *The Convention of the Maritime Safety Committee of the Inter-Governmental Maritime Consultative Organization*, 63 J. INT'L L. & DIPL'Y 1-16 (1965) (in Japanese). Address: 22 Berners Street, London W1, England.

[20] UNESCO, UNESCO CHRONICLE (monthly); UNESCO, UNESCO COURIER (monthly); and various other publications listed in an annual catalogue.

Membership is open to all members of the United Nations, other states may become members by a two-thirds vote of the General Conference. A country not responsible for the conduct of its foreign affairs may become a member if a request of the state which is responsible is approved by the General Conference.

UNESCO is composed of a General Conference, an Executive Board, and a Secretariat. The General Conference, which consists of representatives of the member states, meets every two years to approve Organization programs. The Executive Board, which is elected by the General Conference, is composed of 30 members. The Secretariat is composed of numerous bureaus and departments and has a staff of some 1600 professional personnel and an equal number of office and technical personnel. It is headed by a Director-General, a Deputy Director-General and several Assistant Directors-General.

The broad purpose of UNESCO is to contribute to peace and security by promoting cooperation among nations in the fields of education, science, and culture. This is accomplished through conferences, by various media, and in numerous programs. The Organization has agreements with several UN specialized agencies and cooperates closely with several others. It has agreements with several intergovernmental organizations and has working relations with many others. It also has three categories of relations with non-governmental organizations: Category A concerning consultative associate relations; Category B, information and consultative relations; and Category C, mutual information relations.

§ 3-2.7. **The Universal Postal Union.**[21] This Union was founded in 1874, with headquarters in Berne. Most UN members are also members of the Union. Other states may become members by a two-thirds vote of Union members. UPU became a specialized agency of the United Nations by an agreement in 1947.

The Union is composed of a Congress, an Executive Council, a Consultative Committee for Postal Studies, and an International Bureau. The Congress, which usually meets every five years, is composed of representatives of member governments. It examines and, when needed, revises various Acts developed by the Berne Treaty of 1874. It also elects the Executive Council. The Council,

---

[21] UNIVERSAL POSTAL UNION, *L'Union Postale Universelle: Sa Fondation et Son Développement, 1874-1949, Memoire* (Berne 1949); UPU, RAPPORTS SUR LES ACTIVITÉS DE L'UNION (annual reports); UPU, POSTAL UNION (monthly). Address: Schosshaldenstrasse 46, 3000 Berne 15, Switzerland.

composed of representatives of 27 member states, has general supervision of the International Bureau; serves as liaison with other agencies; and makes recommendations to the Congress. The Consultative Committee for Postal Studies carries on research and prepares recommendations on questions affecting postal services. The International Bureau, which is under Swiss Government supervision, is the permanent Secretariat of the Union, and a source of information for the postal agencies of member states. It has a Director-General, a Deputy Director-General, Assistant Directors-General and several Counsellors.

§ 3-2.8. The World Health Organization.[22]   This agency was established in 1948. Its constitution was signed on July 22, 1946, and entered into force on April 7, 1948. It became a specialized agency of the United Nations on July 10, 1948. All UN members may become members of WHO, and any other country may become a member if the WHO Assembly approves its application. In addition to its headquarters, which are located in Geneva, regional offices are located in Brazzaville, Washington, Alexandria, Copenhagen, New Delhi and Manila.

WHO is composed of a World Health Assembly, an Executive Board and a Secretariat.   The Assembly, which holds annual conferences, consists of representatives of member states and is attended by representatives of intergovernmental organizations and non-governmental organizations which have been admitted to official relations with the Organization. The Executive Board consists of 24 persons from member states. They are selected by the Assembly and serve in their personal capacity. The Secretariat is headed by a Director-General, a Deputy Director-General and five Assistant Directors-General who supervise the work of numerous divisions. The Secretariat has a staff of some 3,000 persons.

WHO aims to raise health standards by disseminating health information by conferences, seminars, training courses, research programs, scholarships and various other means, including a large number of publications.

§ 3-2.9. The World Meteorological Organization.[23]   This Organization grew out of the International Meteorological Organization

[22] WORLD HEALTH ORGANIZATION, BULLETIN OF THE WORLD HEALTH ORGANIZATION (monthly); WHO, INTERNATIONAL DIGEST OF HEALTH LEGISLATION (quarterly), WHO, CATALOGUE OF WORLD HEALTH ORGANIZATION PUBLICATIONS.

[23] World Meteorological Organization publications include conventions, regulations, technical manuals, guides and atlases, annual reports, and a quarterly bulletin. Address: 41 av Guiseppe-Motta, 1211 Geneva 20, Switzerland.

which was founded in 1878. WMO was established on April 4, 1951, and the International Meteorological Organization was merged with it at this time. On December 20, 1951, WMO became a specialized UN agency by an agreement with the United Nations. It also has working arrangements with various intergovernmental organizations.

WMO is composed of a World Meteorological Congress, an Executive Committee, six regional associations, eight technical commissions and a Secretariat. The Congress, which convenes at least once every four years and is composed of delegates from member states, determines policy matters. The Executive Committee, which meets annually, is composed of 21 Directors of National Meteorological Organizations. It disseminates information and makes recommendations in the field of meteorology. The six regional associations are composed of experts who undertake various studies and make recommendations to the Executive Committee and to the Congress. The Secretariat performs administrative services for WMO bodies, undertakes technical studies, and serves in a liaison capacity with member states and with other international organizations.

WMO has a wide range of activities including research projects, the coordination of national activities in the field, the development of recommendations for adoption by member states, and the dissemination of information in the field through conferences and publications.

§ 3-3. Regional Intergovernmental Organizations [24]

The same problem-orientation that fostered international non-economic agencies has also led to the development of regional organizations to promote cooperation among nations geographically related to solve problems common to all nations of the region. Such regional intergovernmental organizations foster reliance on lawful problem-solving and thus make all reliance on law more viable.

§ 3-3.1. The Asian and Pacific Council. [25] This agency, founded in Seoul in 1966, is composed of Australia, Japan, Korea, Malaya,

---

[24] Ottolenghi, *The United Nations and Regional Organizations as a Source of Law and Legal Institutions,* in ATHENS CONF. 596-99; Piggott, *The United Nations and Regional Political Organizations as a Source of Law Rules and Legal Institutions,* in *id.,* at 608-10.

[25] Weidemann, *The Asian and Pacific Council (ASPAC),* 5 GER. POL. 448-59 (1966). Address: Saranrom Palace, Bangkok, Thailand.

New Zealand, the Philippines, the Republic of China, South Vietnam and Thailand.

The Council holds Ministerial Meetings which determine policy. A Standing Committee of Ambassadors formulates proposals for technical cooperation, conducts the business of the Council between Ministerial Meetings, prepares, through committees, proposals for Ministerial Meetings, and carries out Council decisions.

The Council aims to provide continuous consultation in order to make possible a deeper understanding of the interest, aims and policies of each state. Council members pledge to preserve the national integrity and independence of each member.

§ 3-3.2.   **The Association of Southeast Asian Nations.**[26] This agency grew out of the Association of Southeast Asia which was formed in 1961 by Malaya, the Philippines and Thailand. As the two organizations merged in 1967, Indonesia and Singapore joined as well.

ASEAN policy is determined at Ministerial meetings. A Council prepares for these meetings, and carries out the continuing business of the Association between meetings. ASEAN has several permanent committees which work on projects in the cultural, economic and social fields.

§ 3-3.3.   **The Australian, New Zealand and United States Council.**[27] This Council was established in 1951, by a Treaty which entered into force on April 29, 1952.

The Council, composed of the Foreign Ministers of the powers signatory to the ANZUS Treaty, meets annually, or more frequently if necessary, to promote the objectives of the Treaty and to strengthen the association between the three countries. Each signatory power also nominates a military representative who is accredited to the Council.

The purpose of the Council is to promote peace in the Pacific Area through cooperation in accordance with the principles of the UN Charter. The most recent Council meetings were held in 1967, in Washington, D.C. and in 1968, in Wellington, New Zealand.

---

[26] Unpublished material loaned by courtesy of the Australian Embassy in Washington. Address: Foreign Ministry, Djakarta, Indonesia.

[27] Department of External Affairs, Australia, *Security Treaty Between Australia, New Zealand and the United States of America,* AUSTRALIA, TREATY SERIES No. 2 (1952); J. STARKE, THE ANZUS TREATY ALLIANCE (Australia 1965). Address: Department of External Affairs, Canberra, Australia.

§ 3-3.4. **The Central Treaty Organization.**[28] This organization was established in 1955, with the entry into force of the Pact of Mutual Cooperation, known as the Baghdad Pact, by which the Governments of Turkey and Iraq agreed to cooperate for their mutual security and defense. The United Kingdom, Iran and Pakistan signed the Pact later the same year. Iraq withdrew from the Organization in 1959.

The United States did not become a formal member of CENTO but accepted instead an invitation to participate in Council meetings as an observer. However, through full membership in the Organization's committees since the early years, the United States has supported and taken an active part in all Organization work.

CENTO's supreme authority is the Council, composed of the Foreign Ministers of member countries. It directs the work of the four main committees: Counter-Subversion, Economic, Liaison and Military. The Secretariat, headed by a Secretary-General, is located at Ankara, Turkey.

§ 3-3.5. **The Common Afro-Malagasy Organization.**[29] This organization was established in April 1955, as the successor to the African and Malagasy Union and the Afro-Malagasy Organization for Economic Cooperation. The Organization, at present, has the following 14 members: Cameroon, Central African Republic, Chad, Congo (Brazzaville), Congo (Kinshasa), Dahomey, Gabon, Ivory Coast, Malagasy, Niger, Rwanda, Senegal, Togo and Upper Volta.

The principal organs are the Conference of Chiefs of State and Government, the Council of Ministers and the Secretariat. The Conference of Chiefs of State, held once a year, is the supreme authority of the Organization. At the beginning of each session, its President is elected. He coordinates Organization activities during his one-year term of office. The Council of Ministers meets annually to prepare the agenda for the meeting of the Chiefs of State, makes recommendations on questions to be considered and implements Conference decisions. The Secretariat contains several departments corresponding to the activities of the Organization.

§ 3-3.6. **The Council of Europe.**[30] The Council of Europe was established on May 5, 1949. At present, it consists of 17 members:

---

[28] CENTO, THE CENTRAL TREATY ORGANIZATION (pamphlet revised annually). Address: Old Grand National Assembly Bldg., Ankara, Turkey.

[29] COMMON AFRO-MALAGASY ORGANIZATION, NATIONS NOUVELLES (quarterly). Address: BP 437, Yaoundé, Cameroon.

[30] DIRECTORATE OF INFORMATION, COUNCIL OF EUROPE (Strasbourg 1967); DIRECTORATE OF INFORMATION, COUNCIL OF EUROPE, PROCEDURE OF THE

(Continued)

Austria, Belgium, Cyprus, Denmark, France, the Federal Republic of Germany, Iceland, Ireland, Italy, Luxembourg, Malta, the Netherlands, Norway, Sweden, Switzerland, Turkey and the United Kingdom. Greece, an original member of the Council, served its notice of withdrawal in December 1969, to be effective June 12 1970. The unique feature of the Council is that the members of the Consultative Assembly speak in an individual capacity rather than as representatives of their governments; they are drawn from different political parties in the national parliaments and thus represent a cross-section of parliamentary opinion in the member states.

The Council operates through an intergovernmental organ, the Committee of Ministers, a Consultative Assembly and a Secretariat. The Committee of Ministers, representing the 18 member states, is the supreme organ of the Council. It normally meets about once a month. Its more important decisions are usually made unanimously. The only matter specifically excluded from its competence is national defense. The Committee is composed of the foreign ministers of member states or their representatives, and its decisions are often in the form of recommendations which are not binding on member governments, but are sometimes in the form of conventions which, of course, are binding when ratified. Numerous committees formulate programs of common action and draft conventions in cultural, educational, human rights, legal, social and various technical fields.

The Assembly, which normally meets three times a year, suggests, encourages, criticizes and advises, principally by debating issues of foreign policy and making recommendations to the Committee of Ministers. At present, it consists of 147 members proportioned according to member country population. National delegations generally reflect the strength of the political parties in each national parliament. To make recommendations or express opinions to the Committee of Ministers, a two-thirds vote is required. Resolutions and orders may be adopted by a simple majority.

CONSULTATIVE ASSEMBLY (Strasbourg 1965); P. DUCLOS, LA REFORME DU CONSEIL DE L'EUROPE (Paris 1958); K. LINDSAY, TOWARDS A EUROPEAN PARLIAMENT (Strasbourg 1959); A. ROBERTSON, THE COUNCIL OF EUROPE: ITS STRUCTURE, FUNCTIONS AND ACHIEVEMENTS (London 1961); ROBERTSON, EUROPEAN INSTITUTIONS: COOPERATION, INTEGRATION, UNIFICATION 33-64 (New York 1967); Sørensen, Le Conseil de l'Europe, 81 RECUEIL DES COURS 121-99 (1952); OFFICE OF PUBLIC AFFAIRS, UNITED STATES DEPARTMENT OF STATE, THE COUNCIL OF EUROPE (State Dep't Publ. No. 4492, 1954); W. GANSHOF VAN DER MEERSCH, ORGANISATIONS EUROPÉENNES 197-403 (Brussels 1966). Address: Avenue de l'Europe, Strasbourg, France.

Assembly debates have effected the solution of some problems which were potential sources of conflict. The classic example is the thorny issue of the Saar, long a source of conflict between Germany and France. The Assembly holds joint meetings with the European Parliament of the European Communities. It has played an important role in furthering contact between European parliamentarians and United States congressmen. Much of the work of the Assembly is done in its 12 general or permanent Committees which study and report on matters within their competence.

The Council has sponsored various European economic institutions and has criticized and interpreted European economic progress, with particular reference to the Common Market. In the social field, it has prepared agreements on social security and social and medical assistance, and has formulated a European Social Charter. In the field of public health several agreements have been concluded for measures of European cooperation. In the cultural field, the Council has prepared both a Convention on the Equivalence of Diplomas and a Cultural Convention. In the legal field, the Council has produced conventions on the peaceful settlement of disputes, on establishment of the European Court of Human Rights, the European Commission of Human Rights, on extradition, and has been concerned with various technical questions, such as civil status of delegates, and the legalization of documents.

As a measure of the Council's achievements, 63 European conventions and agreements have been signed, nearly 50 of which have entered into force. The Council has also had considerable influence on the unification of the law and practice of member states. Since 1966, these various activities have been put together and coordinated in a work program entitled "Man in a European Society." The program is approved each year by the Committee of Ministers and communicated to the Assembly for its views and then sent to governments and other international organizations for their information.

§ **3-3.7. The European Nuclear Energy Agency.**[31] This agency was created on February 1, 1958, to meet the growing need for new sources of electric power in Europe by pooling its members' resources in money, materials and technological manpower. Its work is directed exclusively toward the pacific utilization of nuclear

---

[31] European Nuclear Energy Agency publications include Activity Reports, forecasts of European nuclear energy production, technical publications, an annual catalogue of courses on nuclear science and technology in member countries, NUCLEAR NEWS, and the NUCLEAR LAW BULLETIN. Address: 38 bd Suchet, Paris 16[em], France.

energy. A Control Bureau has been established to insure against its use for any military purpose, and the Nuclear Energy Tribunal hears disputes arising from this control.

The Agency has 18 members and four associated countries. The members are: Australia, Belgium, Denmark, France, Germany, Greece, Iceland, Ireland, Italy, Luxembourg, the Netherlands, Norway, Portugal, Spain, Sweden, Switzerland, Turkey and the United Kingdom. The associated countries are: Canada, Finland, Japan and the United States.

The Agency has a Steering Committee composed of the heads of national atomic energy commissions and other authorities. Subcommittees, study groups and a Secretariat are located in Paris. Two of its important committees, the European-American Nuclear Data Committee and the European-American Committee on Reactor Physics, exchange information on new research data, make recommendations for future research, and arrange exchanges of scientific personnel and equipment.

The broad purpose of the Agency is to promote and coordinate joint projects for developing nuclear energy. The Agency stimulates scientific and technical cooperation, establishes common services, encourages the unification of legal rules and practices, and initiates studies on the economic aspects of nuclear energy. Three of its principal joint undertakings represent a total investment of over $100 million and employ some 600 experts and technicians.

The Agency has given legal assistance to member countries to help them draft legislation in the nuclear energy field. It has also arranged a course of study to acquaint countries with the practical problems in the field.

§ 3-3.8. **The League of Arab States.**[32]   The League of Arab States was founded on March 22, 1945 and includes: Algeria, Iraq, Jordan, Kuwait, Lebanon, Libya, Morocco, Saudi Arabia, the Sudan, Syria, Tunis, the United Arab Republic, and Yemen.

---

[32] M. ANABTAWI, ARAB UNITY IN TERMS OF LAW (The Hague 1962); ARAB INFORMATION CENTER, THE ARAB LEAGUE: ITS ORIGIN–PURPOSES, STRUCTURE AND ACTIVITIES (New York 1955); Aziz, *The Origin and Birth of the Arab League,* 11 REV. EGYPT. DR. INT'L 39-58 (1955); Boutros-Ghali, *The Arab League,* 1945-1955, 498 INT'L CONC. 387-448 (1954); EUROPA PUBLICATIONS, THE MIDDLE EAST (1962) (lists the members, gives a record of events 1945-1962, describes organizations, lists a daily and four monthly publications, and gives texts of the Pact of the Arab League and the Cultural Treaty); Khadduri, *The Arab League as a Regional Arrangement,* 40 AJIL 756-80 (1946); Saab, *The League of Arab States . . .,* 7 WORLD JUSTICE 449 (1966). Address: 18 Rue Youssef, El Quindi, Cairo, Egypt.

The Organization of the League consists of a Council, Special Committees, and a Permanent Secretariat. The Council is composed of representatives of the member states, each representative having one vote. It meets twice a year in designated Arab capitals. It is in charge of the League's international relations as well as the settlement of any differences that may arise between member states. The Secretariat is composed of a Secretary-General, three Assistant Secretaries-General, and a staff including nationals of all member states. Among its departments are the Administrative, the Cultural, the Legal, and the Political.

The Pact of the Arab League specifies six areas in which the member states pledge close cooperation:

(1) economic and financial affairs, including commercial relations, customs, currency, and questions of agriculture and industry;

(2) communications, including railways, roads, aviation, navigation, telegraphs, and posts;

(3) cultural matters;

(4) nationality, including passports, visas, execution of judgments, and extradition of criminals;

(5) social affairs; and

(6) public health.

The League has created Arab Postal and Telecommunications Unions. In recent years, it has emphasized economic affairs. It has created a Council of Arab Economic Unity, which, in turn, established an Arab Common Market. It also created an Arab Bank patterned after the World Bank.

§ 3-3.9. The Nordic Council.[33] This agency has enabled the Scandinavian countries of Denmark, Finland, Iceland, Norway, and Sweden to achieve a remarkable degree of collaboration. The Council is composed of 69 members, five from Iceland and 16 from

---

[33] S. ANDERSON, THE NORDIC COUNCIL: A STUDY OF SCANDINAVIAN REGIONALISM (New York 1966); Dolan, *The Nordic Council,* 12 W. POL. Q. 511-26 (1959); A. ETZIONI, POLITICAL UNIFICATION (New York 1965); Holly, *Legal and Legislative Co-operation in the Scandinavian States,* 49 A.B.A. J. 1089-91 (1963); Nagel, *The Nordic Council: Its Organs, Function and Juridical Nature,* ANNUAL JOURNAL OF THE AMERICAN ARBITRATION ASSOCIATION 51-67 (1956); Petren, *The Nordic Council: A Unique Factor in International Law,* NORDISK TIDSSKRIFT FOR INTERNATIONAL RET 346-62 (1959); Petren, *Les Résultats de Dix Ans de Cooperation Nordique,* EUR. Y.B. 27-43 (1965); Sørensen, *Le Conseil Nordique,* 59 REVUE GÉNÉRALE DE DROIT INTERNATIONAL PUBLIC 63-84 (1955). Danish Regional Office: Nordisk Råd, Christiansborg, Ridebane 10, 1218 Copenhagen, Denmark.

each of the other countries. The Council has been a complete social unit since 1965. As a result, nationals of one Northern Country, when staying in another, receive the same social benefits as nationals of the other. In 1950, Denmark, Norway and Sweden introduced legislation which provided that any of their nationals domiciled for 10 years in either of the other countries automatically became legally entitled to citizenship there.

The Council is a purely advisory body of parliamentarians from the participating states, chosen by their parliaments to represent the main political trends in their countries. Council sessions have resulted in the adoption of over 500 recommendations covering a very wide field. Although the Council does not have powers of decision, its recommendations have been approved by the member governments to a considerable degree. A Convention on a Joint Scandinavian Labor Market removes the requirement for Scandinavian citizens to obtain a work permit when seeking employment in another country party to the agreement. Where employment opportunities exist, they are open to all Scandinavians on equal terms.

Since 1946, machinery has been set up for continuing cooperation in the legal field. As a result, national laws, drafted after joint preparation, are often substantially the same. In certain sections of private law, complete juridical unity has been achieved. The laws relating to bills of exchange, promissory notes and checks, the conclusion and cancellation of checks, insurance, securities, patents, and similar matters are all virtually unified. Laws of citizenship have been sufficiently coordinated to make the establishment of a common Northern citizenship possible in the foreseeable future. Passports are no longer necessary for Scandinavian citizens traveling in the Northern countries, and currency and customs at the frontiers are now subject to only casual control.

In 1970, four members of the Nordic Council (Denmark, Finland, Norway, and Swedan) created Nordek, an organization envisaging the creation of a common customs union and the expansion of economic cooperation among the Scandinavian countries. Iceland, the fifth member of the Council, is expected to join the organization in the near future. Common tariffs will be established against other countries in two stages: by 1972, a 50 percent adjustment will be made, and by 1974, a full adjustment will be made with certain exceptions, such as chemical products (with 10 and 15-year limits), plastics (with a 15-year limit), and iron and steel (without a time-limit, but subject to negotiations every five years). The organization is also expected to adopt anti-dumping laws and common administrative customs' regulations.

Expanded economic cooperation will take place in the fields of agriculture, fisheries, economic policy, common legislation designed to develop a uniform industrial and energy policy, coordinated research and development, aid to developing nations, and education. To implement these proposals, three funds (General, Agricultural and Fisheries), with a total of over $425 million, and a Nordic Investment Bank are to be established.

§ 3-3.10. The North Atlantic Treaty Organization.[34] Founded on April 14, 1949, NATO serves basically as a regional defense Organization. Its members are: Belgium, Canada, Denmark, France, the Federal Republic of Germany, Greece, Great Britain, Iceland, Italy, Luxembourg, the Netherlands, Norway, Portugal, Turkey and the United States.

The principal organ of NATO is a Council, which is composed of representatives of the member governments, usually the Minister of Foreign Affairs or Defense. The Council normally meets two or three times a year. Each member government also has a representative on the Committee who is assisted by advisers. Permanent representatives meet once or twice a week. The Council is assisted in policy matters of a general nature by a Military Committee composed principally of the Chiefs of Staff of member countries. This Committee meets two or three times a year, but military representatives are continuously in session. In 1950, the Council established an integrated defense system for Western Europe under European Headquarters.

NATO members "agree that an armed attack against one or more of them in Europe or North America shall be considered an attack against them all" and that each of them will, accordingly, "assist the party or parties so attacked."[35] In addition, members agree to settle international disputes in which they may be involved by peaceful means, to seek to eliminate conflict, and to contribute to the development of peaceful international relations. Thus, NATO, originally conceived as a defense network, has facilitated cooperation among member states in more positive and more promising areas as well.

---

[34] NORTH ATLANTIC TREATY ORGANIZATION, NATO LETTER (monthly); NATO, FACTS ABOUT NATO; NATO, NATO HANDBOOK. Address: Brussels 39, Belgium.
[35] The full text of the North Atlantic Treaty will be found at 43 AJIL SUPP. 159 (1949).

§ 3-3.11. The Organization of African Unity.[36] This Organization, with headquarters in Addis Ababa, Ethiopia, was created on May 25, 1963, to serve as a rallying point of Pan-Africanism and a common front against colonial domination. The Charter of African Unity was based on the sovereign equality of member states, non-intervention in internal affairs, the peaceful settlement of disputes, and the complete emancipation of African territories from foreign control.

Four major organs were established: The Assembly of Heads of State and Government, the Council of Ministers, the General Secretariat, and the Commission of Mediation, Conciliation and Arbitration. The Assembly, the supreme organ of the OAU, meets once a year in ordinary session and can be convoked at the request of any member state, with approval of two-thirds of the OAU members. The Council of Ministers meets twice a year in ordinary session and can be convened in extraordinary session by the same procedure as that used for convoking the Assembly. The General Secretariat provides administrative services for OAU organs. The Secretary-General prepares the agendas of OAU conferences and reports on the Organization's activities at these conferences.

Obstacles confronting the OAU have been many and varied. Opinion has differed about the immediate objectives of the Organization, varying from the view that a supranational organization with broad powers should be established to gain respect in the international arena to the view that economic, technical, and cultural cooperation should be the dominant goal. Inter-state conflicts, especially boundary disputes, and problems resulting from the interests and influence of non-African states in Africa have also posed problems. Economic obstacles include the contrast between rich and poor states and the lack of industrialization in many states. Cultural, ethnic, and linquistic differences also make it difficult to achieve unity in practice. Also, it has been difficult to call together the heads of 38 states absorbed with pressing domestic problems. And, the failure of states to pay their allotted contributions has threatened the Organization's financial viability.

In its early period, the Organization operated rather smoothly and effectively, but when it faced the problem of creating harmony on an issue over which most of its members disagreed, as in the Congo and the Nigerian crises, it was powerless. Meetings of the

---

[36] Austin & Nagel, *The Organization of African Unity,* 22 THE WORLD TODAY 520-28 (1966); McKeon, *The African States and the OAU,* 42 INT'L AFF. 390 (London 1966). Address: P.O. Box 3243, Addis Ababa, Ethiopia.

Council of Ministers and of the Assembly became acrimonious and ineffective, often tabling important matters. The imperative need to realize the goals of the Organization should lead to every possible effort to make its activities practical and successful, but the obstacles and problems which the Organization faces make progress slow and difficult.

§ 3-3.12. **The Organization of American States.**[37] This agency is the successor of the Union of American Republics established at the First International Conference of American States in 1889. Its Charter was adopted in 1948, at the Ninth Inter-American Conference at Bogotá, Colombia. Its aims are to promote an order of peace and justice, strengthen collaboration among American states, and defend their independence.

The Charter of the OAS incorporated the general principles of pacific settlement of disputes which were spelled out in detail in the Pact of Bogotá concluded in 1948. This Pact was designed to bring up to date and supersede numerous previous Inter-American treaties dealing with this subject. Good offices and mediation,

[37] The Pan American Union (located at 17th Street & Constitution Avenue, N.W., Washington, D.C.) publishes: ANNUAL REPORTS OF THE SECRETARY GENERAL, ANNALS OF THE ORGANIZATION OF AMERICAN STATES (an official quarterly setting out official documentary results of conferences, texts of treaties, resolutions, reports, and notes on activities which was discontinued in 1958); BULLETIN OF THE PAN-AMERICAN UNION (1893-1948) (replaced by the ANNALS); CONGRESS AND CONFERENCE SERIES; DECLARATIONS OF THE PRESIDENTS OF AMERICA (1967); FORTHCOMING INTER-AMERICAN CONFERENCES AND MEETINGS (quarterly); OFFICIAL DOCUMENTS OF THE ORGANIZATION OF AMERICAN STATES (1948-1953); PROTOCOL OF AMENDMENT TO THE OAS CHARTER (1968); STATEMENTS OF LAW SERIES (gives analyses and summaries of the essential constitutional, legislative and regulatory provisions of all the Latin-American countries in matters relating to commerce, industry, and labor); and the TREATY SERIES.

See also Bowett, *Interrelación de Estados Americanos y las Nacionas Unidas Dentro del Marco de la Seguridad Colectiva,* 15 REVISTA DE LA FACULDAD DE DERECHO DE MEXICO 861-88 (1965); J. CAICEDO CASTILLA, THE WORK OF THE INTER-AMERICAN JURIDICAL COMMITTEE (Washington 1964); Claude, *The OAS, the UN, and the United States,* in 547 INTERNATIONAL CONCILIATION 3-67; G. CORNELL-SMITH, THE INTER-AMERICAN SYSTEM (London 1966); E. COROMINAS, MEXICO, CUBA Y LA O.E.A. (Buenos Aires 1965); C. FENWICK, THE ORGANIZATION OF AMERICAN STATES: THE INTER-AMERICAN REGIONAL SYSTEM (Washington 1963); Freeman, *The Contribution of the Inter-American Juridical Committee and the Inter-American Council of Jurists to the Codification and Development of International Law,* ASIL PROC. 14-23 (1965); Humphrey, *75th Anniversary of the Organization of American States,* 52 DEP'T STATE BULL. 726-30 (1965); INTER-AMERICAN INSTITUTE OF LEGAL STUDIES, THE INTER-AMERICAN SYSTEM: ITS DEVELOPMENT AND STRENGTHENING (Dobbs Ferry, New York 1966); Robertson, *Revision of the Charter of the Organization of American States,* INT'L & COMP. L.Q. 346-67 (1968); Salazer, *Evolution de l'Organisation des Etats Americains (O.E.A.); Projets de Reforme,* ANN. F. DR. INT'L 110-22 (1966); O. STOETZER, THE ORGANIZATION OF AMERICAN STATES (Dallas 1963); Stoetzer, *The Organization of American States: The Transition from an Unwritten to a Written Constitution,* 59 AJIL 315-20 (1965).

investigation and conciliation, judicial proceedings before the International Court of Justice, and international arbitration are all dealt with by this Pact.

The Inter-American Conference is the supreme OAS organ. Each member state is represented at this Conference, which meets, in principle, every five years. The Conference examines the state of relations among its members and considers proposals to further mutual understanding and cooperation in matters of common interest. Special Inter-American Conferences are also held from time to time to consider matters of particular importance. Meetings of Consultation of Ministers of Foreign Affairs consider urgent problems of common interest to the American states. Meetings may be called by the permanent Council in case of armed attack on the territory of an American state.

An Advisory Defense Committee assists the Meeting of Consultation. It consists of the highest military authorities of the American states, and its principal function is to give advice on problems of military cooperation for collective security. It may also be assigned technical studies or reports on special subjects.

The permanent Council is responsible for the preparation of draft recommendations for various programs and agreements with specialized organizations. It also acts as the provisional organ of consultation. The Inter-American Economic and Social Council, the Inter-American Council of Jurists and the Inter-American Cultural Council advise the permanent Council and render technical services to member governments.

The Council of Jurists, which is composed of representatives of each member state, is an advisory body on juridical matters. It is assigned the task of promoting the development and codification of public and private international law, and recommending uniform legislation. It meets when convened by the OAS Council, normally not less than once every two years. Its permanent committee is the Inter-American Juridical Committee, which prepares drafts for submission to it. The Juridical Committee meets annually for three months.

The Pan American Union is the OAS General Secretariat. It services the Inter-American Conference, the permanent Council, the Meeting of Consultation, and the specialized conferences, giving advice and assistance in the preparation of programs, providing technical aid and personnel, serving as custodian of documents and submitting reports on the activities of the OAS and its organs.

A Secretary-General is elected by the Council for a 10-year term and is charged with direction of the Pan American Union. There is also an Assistant Secretary-General. All personnel employed by the Union are pledged to act as international officials responsible only to the Union.

The OAS has several Specialized Organizations: The Pan American Institute of Geography and History, the Inter-American Children's Institute, the Pan American Health Organization, the Inter-American Institute of Agricultural Sciences, the Inter-American Commission of Women, and the Inter-American Indian Institute. These organizations have entered into agreements with parallel world organizations. Also, specialized conferences meet to deal with particular technical matters or to develop specific aspects of Inter-American cooperation. Other Inter-American institutions of note are the Inter-American Development Bank and the Inter-American Nuclear Energy Commission.

The Inter-American Peace Committee has also played an important role in implementing OAS objectives. Its duty is to keep constant vigilance to insure the peaceful settlement of disputes. It is also authorized to recommend measures conducive to the achievement of that end and has often been called upon and successfully discharged its duties.

In the last few years, the OAS, although praised by some authorities as an organization of "matchless efficiency," has shown some signs of weakness. Proposals for strengthening the Organization have been advanced by individual countries, by the Secretary-General, and by numerous specialists on Latin American affairs.

After many obstacles had been surmounted, a "Protocol of Amendment to the Charter of the Organization of American States," known as the "Protocol of Buenos Aires," was signed on on February 27, 1967, at the Third Special Inter-American Conference.[38] The principal changes provided by this Protocol concern the structure of the Organization, the pacific settlement of international disputes, and new economic and social principles.

The principal structural changes are as follows. A General Assembly is established as the supreme organ of OAS, replacing the Inter-American Conference. It will meet annually, whereas the Inter-American Conference met only every 5 years. The present single Council and its technical organs are replaced by three new

---

[38] Protocol of Amendment to the Charter of the Organization of American States, 6 INT'L L. MAT. 310 (1967).

councils: A Permanent Council, an Inter-American Economic and Social Council, and an Inter-American Council for Education, Science and Culture. The Inter-American Juridical Committee with headquarters in Rio de Janeiro, and replacing the former Inter-American Council of Jurists, has been expanded from nine to eleven members who will be elected by the General Assembly in June 1970, and will serve as an advisory body on juridical matters. The Inter-American Commission on Human Rights will become a statutory organ of the OAS. Its structure, competence, and procedure are to be determined by the Inter-American Convention on Human Rights,[39] the draft of which has not yet been ratified by the required eleven states. Only Costa Rica has ratified. The General Secretariat will serve as the central and permanent organ of the OAS, and the expression "Pan American Union" will disappear. The term of office of the Secretary-General and the Assistant Secretary-General are to be reduced from 10 to 5 years; they may not be re-elected more than once or be succeeded by a person of the same nationality.

Procedures for the pacific settlement of disputes have been emphasized over the years in Inter-American relations. The Protocol creates a new Inter-American Committee on Peaceful Settlement as a subsidiary organ of the Permanent Council. If this Committee fails to resolve a dispute, it reports to the Permanent Council, which, in turn, reports to the General Assembly if it cannot resolve the dispute. The General Assembly can make any recommendations that it deems advisable. The weakness in this procedure is the fact that a recalcitrant party may refuse to consent to action by the Committee or Council in which case the action of the Permanent Council is limited to making a report to the General Assembly.

The new economic and social principles commit member states by treaty to develop cooperative efforts in these fields and to support Latin American integration. Member states agree to dedicate every effort to achieve an impressive list of goals which aim to accelerate their economic and social development.

The Protocol provides that new members may be admitted when they indicate a willingness to ratify the Charter as amended and agree to fulfill the other obligations of membership, and when their application for admission has been approved by a two-thirds majority of the Permanent Council and the General Assembly. In 1967,

---

[39] *American Convention on Human Rights,* 9 INT'L L. MAT. 99 (1970).

Barbados and Trinidad and Tobago became members, but Canada has not yet applied for admission.

The proposal to establish a permanent inter-American peace force met with emphatic disapproval. The question of cooperative military action by the OAS in the interest of hemispheric security therefore remains unsolved. Factors which tend to explain this result include the strong antipathy of Latin American countries toward intervention and opposition to probable United States domination if such forces were required.

The revised OAS Charter became effective among the ratifying states when the Protocol of Amendment had been ratified by two-thirds of the signatories of the original Charter in February 1970.[40] For the other states the revised Charter will be effective only upon ratification. Twenty-one states, including the larger American states, have deposited instruments of ratification as of January 1970.

The Declaration of the Presidents of America, which was signed at the Meeting of American Chiefs of State at Punta del Este, Uruguay, on April 14, 1967, has been generally hailed as a truly historic document charting new courses of action of outstanding significance for the future of the American Hemisphere. Specific steps were agreed upon to establish a Latin American Common Market by the "complete development and progressive convergence" of the Latin American Free Trade Association and the Central American Common Market. Measures were proposed to increase the earnings of the Latin American countries from exports, modernize living conditions of rural populations, raise agricultural productivity and increase food production, promote educational development, foster science and technology, improve health, and eliminate unnecessary military expenditures. The Punta del Este Conference placed a refreshing emphasis on Latin American initiative and self-help rather than on outside assistance. The supreme task that lies ahead is to translate declarations and agreements into positive, practical accomplishment.

§ 3-3.13. **The South-East Asia Treaty Organization.**[41] This agency, established on September 8, 1954, includes: Australia,

---

[40] *See* note 38.

[41] SOUTH-EAST ASIAN TREATY ORGANIZATION, ANNUAL REPORTS, SEATO, SEATO Record (bi-monthly); SEATO, SEATO NEWSLETTER (monthly). Address: Rajadamnern Avenue, P.O. Box 517, Bangkok, Thailand.

France, New Zealand, Pakistan, the Philippines, Thailand, the United Kingdom, and the United States.

The structure of SEATO consists of a Council and a Secretariat, a Military Planning Office, and a Permanent Working Group. The Council, composed of the foreign ministers of the member states, establishes the broad policy of the Organization. Normally it meets annually at the capital of one of the member states. It is assisted by top military advisers who generally meet twice a year. National military advisers are assigned to SEATO headquarters to express national views on matters affecting the work of the Military Planning Office. A Secretary-General directs the Organization's civil activities which include cultural, economic, and research programs.

§ 3-3.14. **The Warsaw Treaty Organization.**[42] This Organization created on May 14, 1955, includes: Bulgaria, Czechoslovakia, East Germany, Hungary, Poland, Romania, and the USSR. Albania, an original member of the Organization, was expelled in 1962.

The Organization has a Consultative Political Commission which meets at least twice a year. A Unified Military Command, with headquarters in Moscow, is headed by a Supreme Commander and aided by top military officials of each of the member states. The supreme commander is a Soviet officer. The Secretariat is located in Moscow. The Organization is a 20-year mutual defense alliance. It holds joint military maneuvers, and its members agree that if one of them is attacked the others will come to its aid.

§ 3-3.15. **The Western European Union.**[43] This agency was established on May 6, 1955, with headquarters in London. Its members are: Belgium, France, Italy, Luxembourg, the Netherlands, the United Kingdom, and West Germany.

The Union has a Council, an Armaments Control Agency, a Standing Armaments Committee, an Assembly, and a Secretariat. The Council, the Union's supreme authority, meets at the ministerial level every three months and at the ambassadorial level about twice a month. It discusses current problems of common interest and reports to the Assembly. The Armaments Control Agency seeks to control stocks of armaments. The Standing Armaments

---

[42] Overstreet, *Eastern Europe and the Warsaw Pact,* in WASHINGTON CENTER FOR FOREIGN POLICY RESEARCH 49-78 (Washington 1965); Wolfe, *The Warsaw Pact in Evolution,* in INTERNATIONAL CONFERENCE ON WORLD POLITICS 203-36 (Baltimore 1966).

[43] The Union publishes annual reports of the Council to the Assembly and is located at 2 Eaton Place, London SW 1, England.

Committee develops cooperation between member states in the field of armaments. The Assembly, which meets twice a year in plenary session, operates through Committees of: Defense and Armaments, Political Questions, Space Questions, Administrative and Finance, and Rules of Procedure.

§ 3-3.16. **The South Pacific Commission.** This Commission, established in 1947, is presently composed of six nations: Australia, France, Nauru, New Zealand, the United Kingdom, and the United States. Western Samoa participates in the Commission, but does not vote. The Commission consists of 12 members—two from each country, one of which is a Senior Commissioner who presides over the Commission's meeting in an alphabetical arrangement. The Commission is advised by two bodies: the Research Council and the South Pacific Conference, which meet yearly, and at intervals of not more than three years, respectively. The Commission is staffed by a Secretary-General, and Executive Officers appointed for five-year terms. The main work of the Commission lies in the fields of health, economic and social development, agriculture, and education: political matters are expressly outside its activities, and its main task is to improve the living conditions of the people belonging to the South Pacific Island Group. The Commission's address is: Pentagon, Ause Vata, Noumea, New Caledonia.

§ 3-3.17. **Agency for Cultural and Technical Cooperation Among French-Speaking Nations.** This Agency, established in 1970 with headquarters in Paris, is composed of 21 nations where French is spoken wholly or in part. Its members include Belgium, Burundi, Bwanda, Cameroon, Canada, Chad, Ivory Coast, Dahomey, France, Gabon, Luxembourg, Madagascar, Mali, Mauritius, Monoco, Niger, Senegal, South Vietnam, Togo, Tunisia and Upper Volta. Expenses of the organization are to be borne largely by France (40 percent) and Canada (32.4 percent). A French-speaking group from the United States State of Louisiana is expected to become an associate member. Its address is the Secretary of State, Au Affaires Etrangeres, Administration Centrale, 20 rue Monsieur Paris VII, France.

§ 3-3.18. **The Antarctic Treaty.**[44] This Treaty, signed in 1958, is presently adhered to by 16 nations: Argentina, Australia, Belgium, Chile, Czechoslovakia, Denmark, France, Japan, the Netherlands, New Zealand, Norway, Poland, South Africa, United Kingdom,

---

[44]*Opened for signature* December 1, 1959, 12 U.S.T. 794, T.I.A.S. 4780, 402 U.N.T.S. 71.

the U.S.S.R. and United States. The Treaty, among other things, provides for the reservation of the Antarctic Continent solely for scientific purposes. International collaboration of scientific programs is fostered by the Scientific Committee on Antarctic Research (SCAR) of the International Council of Scientific Unions. The Treaty also provides that disputes between the contracting parties are to be settled by the International Court of Justice. Of interest to the pursuit of scientific research on the continent was the recent signing of the Treaty to Prevent Nuclearization of Antarctica.

§ 3-4. Other Intergovernmental Organizations

Several international inter-governmental organizations have been constituted to improve the comprehensiveness and quality of those components of the international law structure of concern to governmental entities. These organizations contribute a valuable impetus toward making the rule of law the effective implement for the maintenance of world peace in the second half of the 20th century.

§ 3-4.1. The Hague Conference on Private International Law.[45]
Established as an intergovernmental organization on July 15, 1965, it consists of 25 states, including most of the European states, Canada, Japan, and the United States.

The Conference meets in plenary session in principle every four years to study the progressive unification and harmonization of the rules of private international law. Special commissions of experts, meeting at regular intervals, formulate draft conventions, prepared in such a way as to facilitate their adoption in domestic law. Among these conventions are: matters of international judicial assistance, the recognition of foreign judgments, and the unification of the conflicting rules relating to sales, to adoptions. The Conference Session of October 1968 centered on the problems of conflict of laws arising in the field of recognition of foreign divorce decrees

---

[45] HAGUE CONFERENCE ON PRIVATE INTERNATIONAL LAW, ACTES ET DOCUMENTS; HAGUE CONFERENCE ON PRIVATE INTERNATIONAL LAW, WORKING DOCUMENTS AND BIBLIOGRAPHIES. Address: 2 C Javastnaat, The Hague, Netherlands.

and in the field of torts, and of the procedural question of taking evidence abroad. The Permanent Bureau at The Hague is headed by a Secretary-General and three Secretaries of different nationalities.

§ 3-4.2. The International Institute for the Unification of Private Law.[46]

This Institute was originally founded in 1926, and re-constituted by a multilateral agreement of April 21, 1940. Its headquarters are located in Rome. The Institute has 42 members and is linked with other international organizations by inter-governmental agreements.

The Institute has a General Assembly, a Governing Council, a Permanent Committee, and a Secretariat. The General Assembly meets every year and appoints the Governing Council of 17 members. The Permanent Committee is composed of five members. The Secretariat is headed by a Secretary-General and an Assistant Secretary-General.

One of the main activities of the Institute is the drafting of uniform laws in the field of private international law. It has prepared draft conventions such as a Convention on the Enforcement Abroad of Maintenance Obligations, concerning interfamilial support; a Uniform Law on Agency in International Relations concerning private law matters of a patrimonial character; and a Convention on a Uniform Law on the International Sale or Purchase of Goods. It also serves as a valuable source of information, with its large and and well-equipped library of specialized publications.

§ 3-4.3. The United International Bureau for the Protection of Intellectual Property.[47]

This agency is the Joint Secretariat of the International Union for the Protection of Industrial Property and

---

[46] INTERNATIONAL INSTITUTE FOR THE UNIFICATION OF PRIVATE LAW, YEARBOOK; INTERNATIONAL INSTITUTE FOR THE UNIFICATION OF PRIVATE LAW, ANNUAL REPORT; INTERNATIONAL INSTITUTE FOR THE UNIFICATION OF PRIVATE LAW, BIBLIOGRAPHICAL BULLETIN; INTERNATIONAL INSTITUTE FOR THE UNIFICATION OF PRIVATE LAW, UNIFORM LAW CASES. Address: 28 Via Panisperna, Rome, Italy.

[47] The work of this organization is also discussed in § 7-4 of this book. Address: 32 Chemin des Colombettes, Place des Nations, Case Postale 18, 1211 Geneva 20, Switzerland.

the International Union for the Protection of Literary and Artistic Works.

The International Union for the Protection of Industrial Property, "the Paris Union" (see § 7-2), was established in 1883 and now has 70 member states. Its aim is to insure and develop the international protection of industrial property and to offer legislative assistance to developing countries.

The International Union for the Protection of Literary and Artistic Works, "the Berne Union" (see § 7-3), was established in 1886. Its aim is to insure and develop the international protection of literary and artistic works. See Chapter 7 where these conventions are considered in more detail.

§ 3-5. Nongovernmental International Legal Organizations

Primary support for the development of a world law system for the peaceful settlement of disputes between nations, and for cooperation among the nations of the world on all matters of common concern must come from the lawyers of the world. It is they who will use a world law structure on a day-to-day basis.

Many organizations have been founded to facilitate contact among the lawyers of the world in the interest of improving the world structure of law. The work of these organizations is just now beginning to bear fruit and will become increasingly important in the interdependent world of the last third of the 20th century.

§ 3-5.1. The Asian-African Legal Consultative Committee.[48]
The Committee was created on November 15, 1956 through the initiative of the Indian Branch of the International Law Association. Its members are: Burma, India, Indonesia, Iraq, Japan, Pakistan, the Sudan, and the United Arab Republic. A permanent Secretariat is maintained in New Delhi, India, at: 20 Ring Road, Lajpat Nagor IV.

The Committee usually meets once a year to examine questions under consideration by the International Law Commission. It then calls to the attention of that Commission its views on these questions. It also makes recommendations on legal problems

---

[48]*See* ASIAN-AFRICAN LEGAL CONSULTATIVE COMMITTEE, SECRETARIAT, REPORT OF THE SESSION (New Delhi 1957).

referred to it by governments and communicates its views on legal problems to the United Nations and other organizations.

§ 3-5.2. **The Association of Attenders and Alumni of The Hague Academy of International Law.**[49] The Association was established in 1923 at The Hague, where its Secretariat is located. It has 450 members and 150 associate members in 64 countries.

The purpose of the Association is to maintain intellectual and fraternal relations between attenders and alumni of The Hague academy and, to this end, it organizes conferences and meetings and encourages the publication of articles by its members. At its last five conferences, in Copenhagen, Munich, Tunis, Prague and Oslo, the following subjects were discussed: The Individual in International Law, Modern Technology and International Law, Economic Development and International Law, International Arbitration, and the Notion of Mankind in International Law.

§ 3-5.3. **The Institute of International Law.**[50] The Institute was founded on September 11, 1873, in Ghent, Belgium. Its membership is limited to 60 full members and 72 associates, chosen as a result of their distinguished contributions in the field of international law. The Institute aims to promote and contribute to the maintenance of peace, in particular by the codification of international law. Its *Annuaire* is a rich international law source.

The Institute has held 53 sessions to date. Its officers are a President; First, Second, and Third Vice-Presidents; a Secretary-General; and a Treasurer. There are also various commissions which carry out its projects.

§ 3-5.4. **The Inter-American Bar Association.**[51] The Association was created on May 16, 1940, in Washington, D.C. by representatives of 20 Bar Associations from 13 American countries. Its members include 40 Bar Associations in the United States, 49 Bar Associations in Central and South America, and 1500 individual lawyers.

The Association seeks to establish and maintain good relations among the associations and national and local organizations of law-

---

[49] The Association publishes a Yearbook. Address: P.O. Box 882, Peace Palace, The Hague, Netherlands.

[50] INSTITUTE OF INTERNATIONAL LAW, ANNUAIRE (more than 50 volumes issued to date); INSTITUTE OF INT'L LAW, TABLEAU GÉNÉRAL DES RESOLUTIONS DE L'INSTITUT, 1873-1956. Address: 1 Avenue de la Grenada, Geneva, Switzerland.

[51] INTER-AMERICAN BAR ASSOCIATION, CONFERENCE PROCEEDINGS; INTER-AMERICAN BAR ASS'N, NEWSLETTER, 1730 K Street, N.W., Washington, D.C. 20006.

yers in the American countries. Other objectives include the development of international jurisprudence, particularly through the study of comparative law, and the study of uniform commercial laws of American countries.

The topics considered at its biennial meetings include: the continental shelf, international rivers, amendments to the UN Charter, the right of asylum, unification of laws of bills of exchange, promissory notes, maritime bills of lading and trademarks, arbitration of international disputes under Inter-American treaties, quota restrictions on imports, Inter-American cooperation in the control of monopolies, and treaty provisions regarding the right of aliens to engage in trades and professions.

The Association has held 16 conferences to date. The most recent was in Rio de Janeiro, Brazil, in June 1969, the theme of which was "Juridical Procedure of Latin American Integration."

§ 3-5.5   The Inter-American Bar Foundation.[52]   The Foundation was incorporated in 1957 as a companion organization of the Inter-American Bar Association to receive and disburse funds donated for the support of educational, literary, scientific and charitable projects designed to promote the study of law and improve the the administration of justice in the Western Hemisphere. In 1961, the Foundation, in cooperation with the U.S. Department of State, sponsored two workshops for the study of American jurisprudence. The first was held at the Southwestern Legal Foundation in Dallas, Texas, for a group of Colombian lawyers; the second in Curitiba, Brazil, for a group of Brazilian lawyers. In 1963, 86 lawyers and professors from 12 countries participated in a workshop on the Legal Aspects of the Latin American Free Trade Association, held in Montevideo, Uruguay. In 1965, the Foundation cooperated with the American Bar Association in sending two bilingual teams, each of three U.S. lawyers and professors, to lecture in Portuguese in Brazil and in Spanish in Argentina, Peru and Colombia. The Foundation is now engaged in a program of international legal exchanges, research projects and legal workshops.

§ 3-5.6.   The International African Law Association.[53]   The Association founded in Paris on September 29, 1959, to promote the

---

[52]The Foundation has mimeographed copies of the *Proceedings of the Montevideo Conference on Latin-American Economic Integration of 1965.* Address: 1730 K Street, N.W., Washington, D.C. 20006.

[53]INTERNATIONAL AFRICAN LAW ASSOCIATION, THE JOURNAL OF AFRICAN LAW. Address: P.O. Box 1176, Addis Ababa, Ethiopia.

study of African legal systems with emphasis on customary law in the interest of law reform. It is composed of individual members and national sections, and has a President, Vice Presidents, an English and a French Secretary-General, a Treasurer, and two Assistant Secretaries.

§ 3-5.7.   **The International Association for the Protection of Industrial Property.** The Association was founded on May 8, 1897 in Brussels to promote the protection of industrial property, improve and unify the national legislation in the field, and encourage adherence to industrial property conventions. Its present headquarters are at Muhlebachstr/Kirchweg 5, 8008 Zurich, Switzerland. It has more than 3000 members in 26 countries, including national groups, industrial organizations and individuals. The Association holds a Congress every three years. It also has a large Executive Committee, and a Bureau. Its officers are a President, a Rapporteur-General, a Secretary-General, and a Treasurer-General.

§ 3-5.8.   **The International Association of Democratic Lawyers.** The Association was established in October 1946 to facilitate the exchange of ideas among lawyers from different countries; to develop respect for democratic principles in the administration of justice, contribute to the cause of world peace, and assist dependent peoples in their struggle for independence. Its office is located in Brussels at 49 av Jupiter. Its membership consists of individuals and groups of lawyers from 58 countries, and the Association holds congresses every three years. Its Administrative Council meets annually. It has a President, 17 Vice-Presidents, a Secretary-General and 10 Secretaries.

§ 3-5.9.   **The International Association of Lawyers (Union Internationale des Avocats).**[54] The Association was founded in 1927 and is concerned with practical problems of the legal profession, the judiciary, and international order. Its principal office is located in Brussels. It maintains administrative offices in Paris and Milan. Its membership is organized on the basis both of national legal associations and individual lawyers. Forty-three national associations in 34 countries are now members. The Association has a President, a Vice-President, and three Secretaries-General (a Council and a Bureau, which serves as a secretariat). It holds a congress every two years.

---

[54]INTERNATIONAL ASSOCIATION OF LAWYERS, BULLETIN; IAL, ARBITRAGE INTERNATIONAL COMMERCIAL; IAL, LES BARREAUX DANS LE MONDE, IAL, LES JURISDICTIONS INTERNATIONALES. Address: Lucien Janson, 56 av F. D. Roosevelt, Brussels 5, Belgium.

§ 3-5.10. The International Association of Legal Science.[55] The Association was founded on July 19, 1950 in London; its present name was adopted in March 1955 to promote legal science through the study of foreign legal systems, to undertake research on various branches of the law and hold round table discussions, congresses and colloquia. Its membership is composed of national committees in 39 countries. It has a Council and an Executive Committee, composed of an Honorary President, a President, a Vice-President, five members, a Director of Scientific Research, and a Secretary-General.

§ 3-5.11. The International Association of Penal Law.[56] The Association was founded in 1924. Its purpose is to exchange ideas between states in matters of penal law, to carry forward research projects on particular problems, and to develop both substantive and adjective international penal law. The latest Congress was the tenth International Penal Law Congress held in October 1969, in Rome. The Association publishes the quarterly Revue Internationale de droit Penal with French and English articles.

Its headquarters are located in the Faculty of Law of the University of Paris. Its membership is composed of national groups and individuals in 65 countries. The Association has a General Assembly which meets every four years, an Executive Council, an Executive Committee, and a Secretariat.

§ 3-5.12. The International Association of Youth Magistrates. The Association grew out of the International Association of Juvenile Court Judges which was founded in 1928. The present name was adopted in 1958. Association headquarters are located in Brussels at 13 Rue des Quai-Bras. Its members are Juvenile Court Magistrates, national associations and individuals. Its aims are to promote protective legislation for children, stimulate research on the causes of juvenile delinquency with a view to reducing the number of juvenile delinquents, and serve in a liaison capacity between persons and organizations working in this field.

The Association has an Assembly which meets at least every two years, a Board of Directors, and a Bureau which performs administrative functions. The Board of Directors is composed of a President, a Deputy President, a Senior Vice-President, two Vice-Presidents, a General Secretary, and a Treasurer.

---

[55] The Association publishes a bulletin; it also publishes a booklet describing the association and its activities. Address: High Cliff, Eden Park, Lancaster, United Kingdom.

[56] The Association publishes a REVIEW and the proceedings of its congresses. Address: Faculté de droit, de l'Université de Paris, Paris, France.

§ 3-5.13. The International Bar Association.[57] The Association was founded on February 17, 1947, and is a federation of 58 national Bar Associations in 43 countries. It also has individual lawyers as patrons or subscribers. Its headquarters are located in London, England. The Association holds a General Meeting of delegates of member organizations every two years. A Council meets annually. Officers are: a President, a Chairman, a Secretary-General, an Assistant Secretary-General, a Treasurer, and an Assistant Treasurer.

The topics considered at its biennial meetings have included: an international code of ethics for the legal profession, international shipbuilding contracts, double taxation, administration of enemy property, international economic cooperation, international penal law, prize law, copyright law, the constitutional structure of the United Nations, protection of foreign investments, restrictive trade practices, legal aid, insurance against the risks of judicial procedure, and problems of liability and compensation in connection with the use of nuclear energy.

§ 3-5.14. The International Commission of Jurists.[58] The Commission established in July 1952, with headquarters in Geneva, is primarily concerned with promoting respect for the rule of law and the mobilization of international legal opinion in cases of flagrant violation of fundamental principles of justice. It seeks to realize this objective by publications and by regional and world conferences. It has 65 National Sections and holds a world conference every three years. The Commission's Executive Committee of five members meets three times a year. It has an Honorary President, a President, two Vice-Presidents, a Secretary-General and an Executive Secretary.

The principles of the rule of law governing Commission activities were formulated by a Congress in Delhi in 1959. In addition to promoting political and civil rights, the role of social, economic, educational and cultural conditions in the pursuit of legitimate individual aspirations in a free society was emphasized. The regional conferences in Lagos in 1961, Bangkok in 1965, and Dakar in 1967, applied these principles to the situations of newly independent countries. The Congress of Rio de Janeiro of 1962, dealt with the obligation of the Executive and of administrative agencies to observe the

---

[57]Its publications include INTERNATIONAL BAR NEWS, Conference Reports, and reports on some of the topics considered at its biennial meetings. Address: 501 Fifth Avenue, New York, New York 10017.

[58]*International Commission of Jurists,* JOURNAL (twice a year); IJC, BULLETIN (quarterly); IJC, NEWSLETTER; also various special studies and reports. Address: 2 Quai du Cheval Blanc, 1211 Teneva 24, Switzerland.

rule of law in making decisions affecting the rights of the individual. It proclaimed the responsibility of lawyers to provide leadership in the struggle against poverty, ignorance and all forms of discrimination that jeopardize the rule of law. Its activities include observer missions and recommendations based on on-the-spot inquiries.

§ 3-5.15. **The International Criminal Police Organization.**[59] INTERPOL was founded in 1923 in Vienna to promote mutual assistance between all criminal police authorities within the limits of their national laws and to establish and develop institutions likely to aid in the repression of common law crimes and offenses. Its headquarters have been located in St. Cloud, a suburb of Paris, since 1946. Its membership is made up of official police bodies in 103 countries.

INTERPOL holds an annual conference, which elects an Executive Committee composed of a President, two Vice-Presidents, and six delegates from different countries. It takes an active part in drafting international conventions to be submitted to the United Nations and other international organizations in the fields of international crime suppression, arrests, extradition, repatriation of minors, and identification of air accident victims. It maintains a criminal identification file with information on some 300,000 known international criminals and operates a central radio communications network for the speedy exchange of criminal records and information.

§ 3-5.16. **The International Federation of Women Lawyers.**[60] The Federation was created in August 1944, during the Third Conference of the Inter-American Bar Association to further the progress of jurisprudence in all its aspects. Its membership consists of affiliated organizations and individuals.

The Federation holds a conference every two years. Its Executive Committee meets twice a year. It has an Honorary President, a President, a Vice-President, a Secretary-General, a Recording Secretary, a Treasurer, an Editor, and 21 Standing Committees. Its committee work includes: comparative constitutional law, international law, legal education, the legal status of women, uniform commercial law and several other fields.

---

[59]INTERNATIONAL CRIMINAL POLICE ORGANIZATION, INTERNATIONAL POLICE REVIEW; also publishes various special reports. Address: 60 Boulevard Gouvion, Ste. Cyr, Paris 17, France.

[60]The Federation publishes a Newsletter five times a year. Address: 17 Safialishah Avenue, Tehran, Iran.

§ 3-5.17. **The International Law Association.**[61] The Association was established in Brussels on October 18, 1873, under the name "Association for the Reform and Codification of the Law of Nations" to study and develop public and private international law. to formulate proposals for the solution of conflicts of law and for unification of laws, and the maintenance of international peace. It adopted its present name in 1895. Its headquarters are located in London. Its membership is composed of both individuals and corporations. It has branches in 35 countries.

The Conference, which is the governing body, meets every two years. It has an Executive Committee which acts for the Association between meetings of the Conference. It has a President, a Chairman of the Executive Council, a Treasurer, and a Secretary-General. The wide range of subjects on which reports have been made at its biennial conferences include: collisons at sea, marine insurance, execution of foreign judgments, jurisdiction in territorial waters, rules of procedure for international arbitration, extradiction, expropriation, commercial arbitration, human rights, and the peaceful coexistence of states.

§ 3-5.18. **The International Legal Aid Association.**[62] The Association was established in July 1960, on the initiative of the International Bar Association. Membership is open to international and national Bar Associations, Law Societies, legal aid organizations, organizations and committees interested in legal aid work, and individuals. Its headquarters are in London. Its Assembly meets every two years and elects a Board of Directors. The Association has a Treasurer, and a Secretary-General.

The Association's aim is not to provide direct legal aid but to promote its introduction where it does not exist and to help to improve systems that are already working. It provides a central body to guide and supervise legal aid groups and cooperates with all international organizations interested in the administration of justice. Its International Legal Aid Directory contains details of the legal aid plans in various countries, provinces, and states, comprehensive information about the various levels of advice and legal

---

[61] The Association publishes Conference Reports and various special reports. Address: 3 Paper Buildings, Temple, London EC 4, England.

[62] INTERNATIONAL LEGAL AID ASSOCIATION, THE LEGAL AID ASSOCIATION; ILAA INTERNATIONAL LEGAL AID DIRECTORY; ILAA, HOW TO PROVIDE A SIMPLE LEGAL AID PLAN; ILAA, *Legal Aid Facilities in Central and South America;* ILAA, LEGAL AID FACILITIES IN EUROPE. Address: 113 Chancery Lane, London WC 2, England.

assistance obtainable in each country, and information concerning the necessary qualifications for applying and receiving aid.

§ 3-5.19. The International Maritime Committee.[63] The Committee was founded in Brussels in 1897, is composed of national associations in 24 countries. It has a President, a Vice-President, and a Secretary-General. Its principal objective is to develop a uniform maritime law, and to this end it has drafted numerous conventions. It also seeks to organize national groups and help to coordinate their efforts.

§ 3-5.20. The International Red Cross.[64] This Agency is composed of the International Committee of the Red Cross, the League of Red Cross Societies, and National Red Cross Societies. It holds conferences every several years. A Permanent Commission meets twice a year.

The International Committee of the Red Cross was founded in 1863 as the International Committee for Relief of Wounded Soldiers; its present name was adopted in 1880. Its headquarters are located in Geneva, and its officers are of Swiss nationality.

It promoted the Geneva Conventions of 1864, 1906, 1929, and 1949 dealing with a series of matters concerning victims of war; offers humanitarian assistance to belligerants and civilians; and aims to aid all in distress situations with available services. Presently, it is engaged in overseeing the treatment of certain civilians in prisons to apply some of the humanitarian provisions of the Geneva Conventions to conflicts of a non-international character.

The League of Red Cross Societies comprises the World Federation of National Red Cross, the Red Crescent, Red Lion and Sun Societies. Its headquarters are in Geneva. Its membership is over 194,000 individuals in 106 countries. It has a Board of Governors, an Executive Committee and various advisory committees and bureaus, and serves as the coordinating agency for international disaster relief and has carried out dozens of relief operations for victims of floods, volcano eruptions, hurricanes, cholera and various other natural disasters.

---

[63] The Committee publishes a Bulletin. Address: 33 rue Jordaenstraat, Antewerp, Belgium.

[64] The International Red Cross Committee publishes a monthly review, annual reports, and a catalogue of its publications; the League of Rec Cross Societies publishes a quarterly, annual reports, and various special reports.

§ 3-5.21.   **The Inter-Parliamentary Union.**[65]   The Union was founded on June 30, 1889, to secure the cooperation of the respective states in the firm establishment and democratic development of the work of international peace and cooperation between nations. Its headquarters have been located in Geneva since 1921, and its membership consists of 76 nations parliamentary groups.   The Union's Council, composed of two members from each national group, holds a conference every year or two in one of the affiliated parliament countries.   An Executive Committee of 10 members operates through five Standing Committees, which have considered such matters as the limitation of armaments, the codification of international law, international control of trusts and cartels, and regional economic solidarity and economic progress.   An Inter-Parliamentary Bureau, headed by a Secretary-General, serves as its Secretariat.   It also has an International Center for Parliamentary Documentation which collects information on the organization and functioning of parliaments throughout the world.

§ 3-5.22.   **The World Peace Through Law Center.**[66]   The Center was created in 1963 at the Athens World Conference on World Peace Through Law, which followed the preparatory efforts by the American Bar Association Special Committee on World Peace Through Law.   Subsequent World Conferences have been held in Washington in 1965, Geneva in 1967, and Bangkok in 1969, and a Fifth Conference is scheduled for Belgrade in 1971.   The Center's headquarters are located in Geneva.

The Center has formulated a comprehensive Global Work Program covering: Peace Keeping, Disarmament, Space law and International Communications Research and Legal Information by Computer, Industrial and Intellectual Property, Transnational Trade and Investments, Housing and Urban Development, Development of Law by International Organizations, Impact of Science and Technology on Law, Legal Aspects of Peaceful Cooperation among Nations, Human Rights, Research, Legal Education and Training.

---

[65] INTER-PARLIAMENTARY UNION, CONFERENCE PROCEEDINGS; IPU CONSTITUTIONAL AND PARLIAMENTARY INFORMATION; IPU, PARLIAMENTS: A COMPARATIVE STUDY OF THE STRUCTURE AND FUNCTIONING OF REPRESENTATIVE INSTITUTIONS IN 41 COUNTRIES. Address: 6 Rue Constantin, Geneva, Switzerland.

[66] The Center publishes: The World Jurist monthly; LAW AND COMPUTER TECHNOLOGY (a monthly journal), A World Law Directory, a volume on LAW AND JUDICIAL SYSTEMS OF NATIONS, and various research reports and topical pamphlets. The Center also has arranged three World Exhibits: *Of Law Codes and Historic Legal Documents (1965), Of Computers and the Law (1967)* and *Of Law and Economic Development (1969).* Address: 75 Rue de Lyon, 1211 Geneva 13, Switzerland.

Center membership is open to all members of the legal profession of the world. The Center's supreme body is the Plenary Session at World Conferences held every two years. Projects approved by the plenary session are implemented by an Executive Committee composed of a President; Vice President for Asia, for Europe, for the Americas, for Australasia, a Secretary-Treasurer and a Director-General. The Center has drafted Conventions on airplane hijacking, seabed minerals use, environment, and weather control. It has over 100 committees working on many subjects of international law including a special committee on each UN specialized agency and on each transactional regional agency. To carry out this extensive program, the Center has members in 131 nations.

§ 3-5.23. **The World Association of Judges.**[67] The Association was established in Geneva in 1966 as a part of the World Peace Through Law Center. Its members are High Court Judges from all areas of the world. The WAJ holds a World Assembly of Judges at each World Conference on World Peace Through Law. The WAJ brings to bear the unique role of the highest ranking judges of the world in furthering the use of law as an instrument of peaceful cooperation among nations. The offices of the WAJ are a Chairman, Vice-Chairman for Asia, for Europe, for the Americas and for Australasia, and a Secretary-General. The WAJ publishes a bi-monthly bulletin and other information on judicial administration and other subjects.

§ 3-5.24. **The Law Association for Asia and the Western Pacific (LAWASIA).** The Association established in 1966, is composed of about 1300 members (lawyers and legal associations) from 19 countries in the Asian region: Afghanistan, Australia, Ceylon, Republic of China, Fiji, Hong Kong, India, Indonesia, Iran, Japan, Korea, Malaysia, Nepal, New Zealand, Philippines, Singapore, Thailand, Republic of Vietnam and Western Samoa. It is designed to serve both regional and professional interests, holds conferences (the first was in 1968 in Kuala Lumpur; second is scheduled for January 1971 in Manila), sponsors legal research to increase the knowledge of the area's legal systems, and publishes legal texts and a journal. The Association is governed by a Council which is composed of one member from each country, with a President, three Vice-Presidents, a Treasurer, a Secretary-General and an Executive Committee. The Association is financed by grants from the Asian Foundation, the Ford Foundation and from its membership. The address of the association is: 174 Phillip Street, Sydney, Australia.

---

[67] The Association publishes a Bulletin (monthly). 75 Rue de Lyon, 1211 Geneva 13, Switzerland.

CHAPTER 4

Present, Past and Proposed International Courts

§ 4-1. Introduction

The distinction between judicial and non-judicial methods of resolving disputes is not always clear. Consequently, some preliminary comment is necessary in order to distinguish the judicial institutions discussed in this Chapter from arbitral and other non-judicial institutions discussed in Chapter 5. These are essentially the differences of form and procedure found in these institutions, rather than·their differences of function and purpose which are more difficult to distinguish, and which, in practice, often overlap considerably.

181

A judicial institution, or court, is generally organized on a permanent basis under a statute defining its jurisdiction and conferring the necessary juridical powers upon it so it can function effectively. Courts are normally composed of one or more judges elected for a specified term under conditions which theoretically will permit them to exercise independent judgment under the generally accepted principles of third-party adjudication. Neither the statute nor the rules of a court are alterable by special agreement of the disputing parties.

This is generally not the case in non-judicial proceedings, which are usually conducted under a special agreement or "compromis" which constitutes the "statute" of the tribunal. In addition (and this is perhaps one of the most important distinguishing features of the judicial institution), disputants are not permitted to choose the law the court must apply. In non-judicial proceedings such as arbitration, disputants will often specify the applicable law, and otherwise delimit the jurisdiction and power of the tribunal. This, of course, is not to deprecate non-judicial methods, as they possess the virtue of flexibility not often found in courts, often making them more adaptable to the needs of the international community.

Non-judicial methods or mechanisms of resolving international disputes are normally utilized to settle individual cases or classes of cases through special bilateral or multilateral agreements between nations. They are generally non-institutionalized in that no permanent organization is created to exercise the judicial function, although temporary institutions such as tribunals, panels, commissions, or boards may be established.

This rather arbitrary classification breaks down somewhat when an attempt is made to classify arbitral tribunals, and in particular, the Permanent Court of Arbitration which is discussed in Chapter 5. Arbitral tribunals do exercise an essentially judicial function, and their proceedings are similar to those of a court. In addition, their judgments are determined and pronounced in much the same manner as those of a judicial tribunal. The distinction of arbitral tribunals from courts lies not in the function arbitral tribunals perform, as indeed they are judicial in nature and are binding on the parties, but in their structure, procedure, and the scope of their jurisdiction.

The judicial institutions discussed in this chapter, are all of recent origin, having been established in the 20th century. They should be examined in the light of two basic objectives outlined by noted authorities on international law: that an effective international judicial institution must be an impartial tribunal free from improper influences by the parties submitting to its jurisdiction; and that it must be composed of independent judges learned in the law and capable of applying the rules of law in a consistent and objective manner. Fulfillment of those two basic objectives would assure the stability of a court and inspire the confidence of all who are under its jurisdiction.

A major purpose of this book is to acquaint the legal profession and the public with the growing number of judicial agencies and other organizations that settle international disputes. That the number of these agencies is increasing augurs well for the needed increase in the use of the international judicial process as that process can make an enormous contribution to the creation and maintenance of a peaceful world community. That decisions by judges under law are preferable to decisions via death-dealing force on battlefields, no one can reasonably dispute. Existing agencies empowered to settle international disputes must become better known and more used. New agencies created for that purpose must also become better known and more used.

Besides the United Nations and its subsidiary organs, and the International Court of Justice, regional organizations play important roles in settling international disputes. Regional organizations such as the Organization of African States, the Organization of American States, the Council of Europe, the Arab League, and the North Atlantic Treaty Organization are empowered to settle international disputes arising among members.

Specialized agencies and functional institutions also contribute to this judicial process. The International Telecommunications Convention[1] provides that disputes are to be settled by either diplomacy or compulsory arbitration. The International Labour Organization Convention[2] mentions that disputes concerning the interpretation and application of the Convention, or of Conventions to be enacted by the Organization are to be settled by the International Court of Justice, and other disputes are to be settled by the organization. The Convention creating the International Atomic Energy Agency[3] provides that disputes are to be referred

---

[1] International Telecommunications Convention, *opened for signature* December 21, 1959, 12 U.S.T. 1761, T.I.A.S. 4892.

[2] International Labour Organization Convention, *done* October 9, 1946, 62 Stat. 3485, T.I.A.S. 1868, 15 U.N.T.S. 35.

[3] Statute of the International Atomic Energy Agency, *done* October 26, 1956, 8 U.S.T. 1093; T.I.A.S. 3873, 276 U.N.T.S. 3.

to the International Court of Justice for settlement, or parties must agree to negotiation or other methods. The Convention creating the International Civil Aviation Organization[4] mentions that such disputes are to be settled by the Council, but appeals from the Council's decisions can be lodged with the International Court of Justice, a special tribunal or arbitration. The Convention creating the Intergovernmental Maritime Consultative Organization[5] provides that the Organization's Assembly will settle disputes, as do the Convention creating the International Wheat Agreement,[6] the International Coffee Agreement,[7] and the International Sugar Agreement.[8] The General Agreement on Tariffs and Trade[9] provides that disputes are to be settled by diplomacy and negotiation, and if these methods fail to achieve a solution, then the Contracting Parties will recommend one. Disputes concerning UNESCO are referred to the International Court of Justice, and those involving the Universal Postal Union are settled by arbitration. The Conventions creating the World Health Organization,[10] the World Meteorological Association[11] and the Food and Agriculture Organization[12] provide that disputes are to be settled by the respective assemblies, the International Court of Justice or by other means. The Conventions creating the International Monetary Fund,[13] the International Bank for Reconstruction and Development,[14] the International Develop-

---

[4] Convention on International Civil Aviation, *done* December 7, 1944, 61 Stat. 1180, T.I.A.S. 1591, 15 U.N.T.S. 295.

[5] International Maritime Consultative Organization, *opened for signature* March 6, 1948, 9 U.S.T. 621, T.I.A.S. 4044, 289 U.N.T.S. 48.

[6] International Wheat Agreement, *done* October 15, 1961, T.I.A.S. 6537.

[7] International Coffee Agreement, *done* March 18, 1968, T.I.A.S. 6584.

[8] International Sugar Agreement, *opened for signature* January 1, 1969. See United Nations Sugar Conference, 1968, Summary of Proceedings, 23 U.N. Doc. TD/SUGAR. 7/12, 56.

[9] General Agreement on Tariffs and Trade, *done* October 30, 1947, 61 Stat. (5), (6), T.I.A.S. 1700, 55-61 U.N.T.S.

[10] Constitution of the World Health Organization, *done* July 22, 1946, 62 Stat. 2679, T.I.A.S. 1808, 14 U.N.T.S. 185.

[11] Convention of the World Meteorological Organization, *done* October 11, 1947, 1 U.S.T. 281, T.I.A.S. 2052, 77 U.N.T.S. 143.

[12] Constitution of the United Nations Food and Agriculture Organization, *opened for signature* October 16, 1945, 12 U.S.T. 980, T.I.A.S. 4803.

[13] Articles of Agreement of the International Monetary Fund, *opened for signature* December 27, 1945, 60 Stat. 1401, T.I.A.S. 1501, 2 U.N.T.S. 39.

[14] Articles of Agreement of the International Bank for Reconstruction and Development, *opened for signature* December 27, 1945, 60 Stat. 1440, T.I.A.S. 1502, 2 U.N.T.S. 134.

ment Association[15] and the International Finance Corporation[16] provide that disputes are to be settled within the organization. The International Center for the Settlement of Investment Disputes was especially created to solve such disputes. The European Nuclear Energy Agency, the Asian-African Legal Consultative Committee, the European Court of Human Rights, the Inter-American Commission of Human Rights and the Court of Justice of the European Communities also decide international disputes.

Rules regarding the introduction and reception of evidence before international tribunals generally follow the procedures practiced in civil law judicial systems. Anglo-American common law practices concerning the reception of evidence have exerted little influence, primarily because of the absence of the jury system in international tribunals. Documentary evidence is most generally used in international tribunals; the oral testimony of witnesses occurring rarely. Evidence is always admitted into the adjudicative process if it conforms with the time limits prescribed by the tribunal and objections to the reception of certain evidence must rely on specific grounds in order to be upheld by the tribunal. Consequently, national tribunals tend to consider all evidence submitted to them by the parties. Documents introduced which are portions, or extracts, should be so designated, and the names, descriptions, and addresses of all witnesses should be presented to the tribunal and the opposing party. International tribunals, in contrast with common law courts, have the power to request additional evidence. They rarely remove evidence from the record of the proceedings, and simply ignore or disregard forged or perjured testimony and documents. International tribunals follow the *best evidence* rule.[17]

§ 4-2. The Permanent Court of International Justice [18]

The first worldwide international judicial institution to be established was the Permanent Court of International Justice. The Pre-

---

[15] Articles of Agreement of the International Development Association, *done* January 26, 1960, 11 U.S.T. 2284, T.I.A.S. 4607, 439 U.N.T.S. 249.

[16] Articles of Agreement of the International Finance Corporation, *done* May 25, 1955, 7 U.S.T. 2197, T.I.A.S. 3620, 264 U.N.T.S. 117.

[17] For discussion of the Best Evidence rule, *see* C. McCORMICK, HANDBOOK OF THE LAW OF EVIDENCE 408-25 (St. Paul, Minnesota, 1954) and 4 WIGMORE, EVIDENCE §§ 1174-1282 (Boston, 1940).

[18] *See generally* ABA, *Draft of Revised Statute of the International Court of Justice,* REPORT OF STANDING COMMITTEE ON PEACE AND LAW THROUGH THE UNITED NATIONS 18-25 (1963); Bastid, *Les Problems Territoriaux dans la Jurisprudence de la Cour Internationale de Justice,* 107 RECUEIL DES COURS 360-495 (1962); M. BET, THE ATTITUDE OF THE UNITED NATIONS MEMBERS TOWARD THE USE OF

(Continued)

amble to the Covenant of the League of Nations, adopted April 28, 1919, enumerated among the means of securing its objects: "the firm establishment of the understanding of international law as the actual rule of conduct among governments, the maintenance of

ADVISORY OPINION PROCEDURE (1966); Brownlie, *The Individual Before Tribunals Exercising International Jurisdiction*, INT'L & COMP. L.Q. 701-20 (1962); Carlston, *Development and Limits of International Adjudication*, ASIL PROC. 182-86 (1965); Chaudhri, *Contributions of Judges McNair and Read to International Law through the International Court of Justice*, GROWTH OF INTERNATIONAL LAW AND PAKISTAN 64-84 (1965); Cheng, *The First Twenty Years of the International Court of Justice*, 20 Y.B. WORLD AFF. 241-56 (1966); Dimitryevic, *The Tendencies in Accepting the Jurisdiction of the International Court of Justice*, 12 N. YUGO. L. 104-14 (1961); Doeker, *Das Connally Amendment und die Obligatorische Internationale Gerichtsbarkeit*, 11 ARCH. VÖLK. 155-67 (1963); Doeker, *International Politics and the International Court of Justice*, 35 TUL. L. REV. 767-93 (1961); J. DOUMA, BIBLIOGRAPHY OF THE INTERNATIONAL COURT, INCLUDING THE PERMANENT COURT, 1918-1964 (Leyden 1966); M. DUBISSON, LA COUR INTERNATIONALE DE JUSTICE (Paris 1964); A. FACHIRI, THE PERMANENT COURT OF INTERNATIONAL JUSTICE (London 1932); Favoreu, *Récusation et Administration de la Preuve devant la Cour Internationale de Justice*, in 11 ANN. FR. DR. INT'L 233-77 (1965); Fitzmaurice, *Hersch Lauterpacht - The Scholar as Judge*, 37 BR. Y.B. INT'L L. 1-72 (1961); Fitzmaurice, 38 *id.*, at 1-84 (1963); Gormley, *The Procedural Status of the Individual before Supranational Judicial Tribunals*, 4 U. DET. L.J. 382-40, 405-46 (1964); Gross, *Limitation Upon the Judicial Function*, 58 AJIL 415-31 (1964); Gross, *Problems of International Adjudication and Compliance with International Law: Some Simple Solutions*, 59 *id.* at 48-59 (1965); Gross, *The Time Element in the Contentious Proceedings in the International Court of Justice*, 63 *id.* at 74-86 (1969); P. GUGGENHEIM, REPERTOIRE DES DÉCISIONS ET DES DOCUMENTS DE LA PROCÉDURE ECRITE ET ORALE DE LA COUR PERMANENTE DE JUSTICE INTERNATIONALE ET DE LA COUR INTERNATIONALE DE JUSTICE (Geneva 1967); Hambro, *Quelques Problèmes Touchant à la Cour Internationale de Justice*, 15 REV. HÉLL. DR. INT'L 1-9 (1962); HAMBRO, THE CASE LAW OF THE INTERNATIONAL COURT (Leyden 1963); von der Heydte, *The Individual and International Tribunals*, 107 RECUEIL DES COURS 287-358 (1962); M. HUDSON, THE PERMANENT COURT OF INTERNATIONAL JUSTICE, 1920-1942 (New York 1943); M. HUDSON, WORLD COURT REPORTS . . . (4 vols., Washington 1934-1943); C. JENKS, THE PROSPECTS OF INTERNATIONAL ADJUDICATION (London 1964); Johnson, *The Contribution of the International Court to International Law Through the South West Africa Case*, 4 NIGERIAN B.J. 46-54 (1963); M. KATZ, THE RELEVANCE OF INTERNATIONAL ADJUDICATION (Harvard University Press 1968); A. LAUTERPACHT, THE DEVELOPMENT OF INTERNATIONAL LAW BY THE PERMANENT COURT OF INTERNATIONAL JUSTICE (London 1934); Lenefsky, *Advisory Opinions as a Problem Solving Process*, 11 VILL. L. REV. 525-45 (1965); Liacouras, *The International Court of Justice and Development of Useful "Rules of Interpretation" in the Process of Treaty Interpretation*, ASIL PROC. 161-69 (1965); Division of Bibliography, Library of Congress, *List of References on the Permanent Court of International Justice*, (1923, Supp. 1926); Matine-Daftary, *La Cour Internationale de Justice*, REVUE DE DROIT INTERNATIONAL 5-11 (Sottile 1964); A. McNAIR, THE PLACE OF LAW AND TRIBUNALS IN INTERNATIONAL RELATIONS (Manchester 1957); L. OPPENHEIM, INTERNATIONAL LAW 42-88 (7th ed., London 1952); Permanent Court of International Justice: Advisory Committee of Jurists, PROCÈS-VERBAUX OF THE PROCEEDINGS OF THE COMMITTEE (June 16-July 24, 1920) (with Annexes, 1920); PERMANENT COURT OF INTERNATIONAL JUSTICE, PUBLICATIONS: SERIES A (Judgements and Orders), SERIES B (Advisory Opinions), SERIES C (Acts and Documents Relating to Judgments and Advisory Opinions), SERIES D (Acts and Documents Concerning the Organization of the Court), SERIES E (Annual Reports), and SERIES F (General Index); Pharand, *Analysis of the*

(Continued)

justice, and a scrupulous respect for all treaty obligations in the dealings of organized peoples with one another."[19]

Accordingly, Article 14 of the Covenant provided that "the Council shall formulate and submit to the members of the League for adoption, plans for the establishment of a Permanent Court of International Justice."[20] In February 1920, an Advisory Committee of Jurists was charged with the duty of preparing a draft statute for the establishment of such a court. The draft which was subsequently prepared was adopted with amendments on December 3, 1920.

The Permanent Court of International Justice was not constituted as an organ of the League of Nations as the present International Court of Justice is an organ of the United Nations. The Statute of the Permanent Court was an instrument completely independent of the Covenant of the League. Thus, the International Judicial Community constituted by the states party to the Statute was not conceived as being necessarily identified with the International Community constituted by the members of the

Opinion of the International Court of Justice on Certain Expenses of the United Nations, 1 CAN. Y.B. INT'L L. 272-97 (1963); Read, *The World Court and the Years to Come,* 2 CAN. Y.B. INT'L L. 164-71 (1964); S. ROSENNE, THE WORLD COURT: WHAT IT IS AND HOW IT WORKS (Leyden 1962); Schacter, *Enforcement of International and Judicial Arbitral Decisions,* 54 AJIL 1-24 (1960); C. SMITH, THE RELATION BETWEEN PROCEEDINGS AND PREMISES (Oslo 1962); L. SOHN, CASES ON WORLD LAW, bibliographical references at 1038-42; *Step-by-Step Acceptance of the Jurisdiction of the International Court of Justice,* ASIL PROC. 131-36 (1946); Stillmunkes, *Le "forum prorogatum" devant la Cour Permante de Justice Internationale et La Cour Internationale de Justice,* REV. GEN. DR. INT'L P. 665-86 (1964); Stone, *The International Court and World Crisis,* 536 INT'L CONC. 1-64 (1962); J. SYATAUW, DECISIONS OF THE INTERNATIONAL COURT OF JUSTICE: A DIGEST (Leyden 1962); Venkata Raman, *The Role of the International Court of Justice in the Development of International Customary Law,* ASIL PROC. 169-77 (1965); J. VERZIJL, THE JURISPRUDENCE OF THE WORLD COURT (Leyden 1964-1966); de Visscher, *La Chose Jugée devant la Cour Internationale de la Haye,* 1 REV. BEL. DR. INT'L 5 (1965); Waldock, *General Course on Public International Law,* 106 RECUEIL DES COURS 5-250 (1962); Zile, *A Soviet Contribution to International Adjudication: Professor Krylov's Jurisprudential Legacy,* 58 AJIL 359-88 (1964).

For leading articles, comments, notes and summaries of judicial decisions relating to the Court, see the many Law Journals (*e.g.,* A.J.I.L.) which are published in many nations, the Yearbooks of many nations (*e.g.,* BR. Y.B. INT'L L. ANN. DIG.) and standard international law casebooks and texts. *See also* contributions on the Permanent Court by Beckett, 39 RECUEIL DES COURS 125-69 (1932); 50 *id.* at 193-305 (1934); Bruns, 62 *id.* at 551-670 (1937); Caloyanni, 38 *id.* at 651-778 (1931); Feinberg, 59 *id.* at 591-705 (1937); Hudson, 8 *id.* at 345-511 (1925); Negulesco, 57 *id.* at 5-96 (1936); Rundstein, 43 *id.* at 113 (1933); Saivioli, 12 *id.* at 5-113 (1926); Scerni, 65 *id.* at 565-681 (1938); Strupp, 33 *id.* at 357-481 (1930); and de Visscher, 26 *id.* at 5-75 (1929).

[19]*Preamble of the Covenant of the League of Nations, 1919,* M. HUDSON, INT'L LEGISLATION 112 (1931); 13 BFSP 316; 13 A.J.I.L. Supp. 128 (1919).

[20]*Id.* art. 14.

League. Although it did not occupy a formal relationship to the League, the Court nevertheless was envisaged as part of the total complex of machinery to settle international disputes.

It is unnecessary to describe the provisions in the Statute of the Permanent Court since detailed comments on its successor, the Statute of the International Court of Justice, are found in the next section. Important substantive differences between the two Statutes, however, will be mentioned briefly. Members of the League of Nations were not *ipso facto* parties to the Statute of the Permanent Court, as members of the United Nations are parties to the Statute of the International Court of Justice. The Statute of the Permanent Court, unlike that of the International Court, contained no provisions for amendment. Thus, subsequent changes required the unanimous consent of all parties. This was accomplished over a period of several years during which a Commission of Jurists recommended changes in the Court's Statute which were ultimately approved and went into effect in 1936. The amendments increased the number of judges, abolished the position of Deputy Judge and constituted the Court as permanently in session, excepting judicial vacations.

The Permanent Court's activities extended from January 30, 1922, until the summer of 1940, when Germany invaded the Netherlands. During the subsequent hostilities, the Court's officers and judges removed themselves to Geneva, Switzerland, where they were able to maintain administrative continuity, although no judicial sessions were held. During the period of its existence, the Court held a total of 49 sessions, and resolved approximately 60 different international legal disputes. Without doubt, the Court vindicated the hopes of those responsible for its establishment and laid a firm foundation for its successor, the International Court of Justice, and its decisions were consistent with the established rules of international law and have been highly praised by legal scholars. by legal scholars.

§ 4-3. The International Court of Justice[21]

The present International Court of Justice is faced with many of the same problems that plagued the Permanent Court of Inter-

---

[21]S. Barnett, Interpretation of the United Nations Charter by the International Court of Justice (Ann Arbor, Mich. 1958); Briggs, *Confidence, Apprehension and the International Court of Justice,* ASIL Proc. 25-38 (1960); Bulajic, *World Peace and Peaceful Settlement of International Disputes,* in World Peace Through Law: The Athens Conference 157-67 (1965) [hereinafter cited as Athens Conf.]; Chagla, *Rule of Law at the International Court of Justice,* ASIL

(Continued)

national Justice, and indeed its current effectiveness is presently limited for many of the same reasons that the Permanent Court was limited.

The International Court of Justice was established by the Charter of the United Nations in accordance with principles outlined in Article 92 through 96.

> Article 92. The International Court of Justice shall be the principal judicial organ of the United Nations. It shall function in accordance with the annexed Statute, which is based upon the Statute of the Permanent Court of International Justice and forms an integral part of the present Charter.

Authorities have stated that use of the word "principal" indicates that additional United Nations judicial institutions were contemplated for the future, although no specific provisions to effectuate that end were inserted in the Charter. In contrast to the other main organs of the United Nations (the General Assembly, Security Council, Economic and Social Council, Trusteeship Council, and Secretariate), the Court operates independently under

---

PROC. 237-43 (1960); Codas, *International Court of Justice,* in ATHENS CONF., at 167-70; Fitzmaurice, *The Law and Procedure of the International Court of Justice,* BR. Y.B. INT'L L. 1-12 (1950); *id.* at 1-29 (1951); *id.* at 1-68 (1952); *id.* at 1-71 (1953); *id.* at 20-97 (1955-6); *id.* at 203-94 (1957); *id.* at 1-162 (1958); *id.* at 183-232 (1959); Gross, *Participation of Individuals in Advisory Proceedings before the International Court of Justice,* 52 AJIL 16-41 (1958); Hudson, *The Succession of the International Court of Justice to the Permanent Court of International Justice,* 51 AJIL 569-73 (1957); P. JESSUP, THE INTERNATIONAL COURT OF JUSTICE OF THE UNITED NATIONS—WITH TEXT OF STATUTE (New York 1945); Kaira, *International Court of Justice,* in ATHENS CONF., at 183-5; Kerno, *L'Organisation des Nations Unies et la Cour Internationale de Justice,* 78 RECUEIL DES COURS 511-74 (1951); P. LIACOURAS, THE INTERNATIONAL COURT OF JUSTICE (Durham, N.C. 1961); O. LISSITZYN, THE INTERNATIONAL COURT OF JUSTICE: ITS ROLE IN THE MAINTENANCE OF INTERNATIONAL PEACE AND SECURITY (New York 1951); L. OPPENHEIM, INTERNATIONAL LAW 42-88 (7th ed., London 1952); S. ROSENNE, THE INTERNATIONAL COURT OF JUSTICE: AN ESSAY IN LEGAL THEORY (Leyden 1957); S. ROSENNE, THE WORLD COURT: WHAT IT IS AND HOW IT WORKS (Leyden 1962); de Visscher, *Reflections on the Present Prospects of International Adjudication,* 50 AJIL 467-75 (1956); Tarumi, *Comment on the International Court of Justice,* in ATHENS CONF., at 192-93; Wade, *The International Court of Justice,* in *id.,* at 193-99; L. WEHLE, THE UNITED NATIONS BY-PASSES THE INTERNATIONAL COURT AS THE COUNCIL'S ADVISOR . . . (Philadelphia 1950); Wright, *The International Court of Justice and the Interpretation of Multilateral Treaties,* 41 AJIL 445-53 (1947); N. ZACARIÓS NOGAIM, LA CORTE INTERNATIONAL DE JUSTICIA Y SU ESTATUO; DESARROLLO HISTÓRICO, REFORMAS, CRÍTICA (Mexico 1948); P. ZOLLIKOFER, LES RELATIONS PRÉVUES ENTRE LES INSTITUTIONS SPÉCIALISÉES DES NATIONS UNIES ET LA COUR INTERNATIONALE DE JUSTICE (Leyde 1955).

For a comprehensive list of references on the World Court, see the BIBLIOGRAPHY OF THE COURT published annually. *See also* the Court's YEARBOOK which covers: the organization of the Court, biographies of the judges, the Court's jurisdiction, texts governing that jurisdiction, the work of the Court, a summary of the judicial activity of the Court, and the Court's finances.

its own statute. The reference in the Charter to the Statute of the Permanent Court of International Justice assured judicial continuity, thereby making available to the International Court of Justice the jurisprudence and experience of the Permanent Court of International Justice.

> Article 93. (1) All Members of the United Nations are *ipso facto* parties to the International Court of Justice.
>
> (2) A state which is not a Member of the United Nations may become a party to the Statute of the International Court of Justice on conditions to be determined in each case by the General Assembly upon the recommendation of the Security Council.

The significance of paragraph (1) of the above-quoted Article is not that each member automatically is subject to the jurisdiction of the Court, but that each state, by virtue of membership in the United Nations, has the right or option to utilize the International Court by accepting its jurisdiction either qualifiedly or unqualifiedly. Thus, paragraph (1) does not impose the Court's jurisdiction on members; it rather confers the privilege of accepting its jurisdiction.

Switzerland, Liechtenstein, and San Marino are parties to the Statute of the International Court by virtue of paragraph (2) of Article 93. They were admitted upon the proviso that the Court's Statute be accepted and that they agree to abide by any decision reached by the Court in cases to which they are a party. They further agreed to contribute to the Court's expenses.

Non-member states which are parties to the Statute are, for purposes of election of judges and other matters affecting the Court, treated on an equal basis with members of the United Nations. Even without being a party to the Statute, a state may make use of the Court if, as laid down by the Security Council, it accepts either in general or in a given case the jurisdiction of the Court and agrees to abide by its decisions. In no case may such a party be placed in a position of inequality before the Court.

> Article 94. (1) Each Member of the United Nations undertakes to comply with the decision of the International Court of Justice in any case to which it is a party.
>
> (2) If any party to a case fails to perform the obligations incumbent upon it under a judgment rendered by the Court, the other party may have recourse to the Security Council, which may, if it deems necessary, make recommendations or decide upon measures to be taken to give effect to the judgment.

Only one State, Albania, has failed to carry out a decision of the Court, in the *Corfu Channel* Case,[22] involving Albania and Great Britain. No sanctions were imposed because Great Britain did not pursue the matter in the United Nations Security Council as it was entitled to do under paragraph (2) of the above-quoted Article.

> Article 95. Nothing in the present Charter shall prevent Members of the United Nations from entrusting the solution of their differences to other tribunals by virtue of agreements already in existence or which may be concluded in the future.

Under Article 95, states may create or become parties to regional international courts or other dispute-resolving mechanisms outside the United Nations. Six European nations have done so by creating the European Court of Justice, to settle disputes between members of the European Communities. In addition 15 of the 17 members of the Council of Europe have adhered to the jurisdiction of the European Court of Human Rights, and many other nations have signed arbitration agreements which have been instrumental in resolving many international disputes.

> Article 96. (1) The General Assembly or the Security Council may request the International Court of Justice to give an advisory opinion on any legal question.
>
> (2) Other organs of the United Nations and specialized agencies, which may at any time be so authorized by the General Assembly, may also request advisory opinions of the Court on legal questions arising within the scope of their activities.

This power has been exercised on many occasions and represents an extremely important function of the Court. Unlike judgments, advisory opinions are not designed to settle particular disputes, but to give information on specific legal questions, and are, therefore, not legally binding.

The Statute of the International Court of Justice is divided into five Chapters: Organization of the Court, Competence of the Court, Procedure, Advisory Opinions and Amendment. The first Chapter, dealing with organization, contains Article 2 through 33. Its most important provisions are as follows:

> Article 2. The Court shall be composed of a body of independent judges, elected regardless of their nationality from among persons of high moral character, who possess the qualifications required in their respective countries for appointment to the highest judicial offices, or are juris-consults of recognized competence in international law.

---

[22] [1949] I.C.J. 4.

Article 3. The Court shall consist of 15 members no two of whom may be nations of the same state.

Articles 4 to 15 define the method of electing judges to the Court. Judges are to be nominated by national panels selected by states represented on the Permanent Court of Arbitration. In the case of members not so represented, judges are selected by national panels appointed for that purpose by their governments under the same conditions as those prescribed for members of the Permanent Court of Arbitration. To be elected, a candidate must receive a simple majority in both the General Assembly and Security Council, voting independently of each other. Judges are elected for nine years and may be re-elected.

On January 1, 1971, the composition of the Court was as follows:

Order of Precedence	Country	Date of Expiration of Term of Office
President		
Sir Muhammad Zafrulla Khan	Pakistan	February 5, 1973
Vice-President		
F. Ammoun	Lebanon	February 5, 1976
Judges		
Sir Gerald Fitzmaurice	United Kingdom	February 5, 1973
L. Padilla Nervo	Mexico	February 5, 1973
I. Forster	Senegal	February 5, 1973
A. Gros	France	February 5, 1973
C. Bengzon	Philippines	February 5, 1976
S. Petren	Sweden	February 5, 1976
M. Lechs	Poland	February 5, 1976
C. D. Onyeama	Nigeria	February 5, 1976
F. de Castro	Spain	February 5, 1979
H. C. Dillard	United States	February 5, 1979
L. Ignacio-Pinto	Dahomey	February 5, 1979
E. J. de Aréchaga	Uruguay	February 5, 1979
P. D. Morozov	U.S.S.R.	February 5, 1979

The following judges have served as Presidents or Vice-Presidents before the present holders:

President	Vice-President	Term of Office
J. G Guerrero	J. Basdevant	1946-1949
J. Basdevant	J. G. Guerrero	1949-1952
Sir Arnold McNair	J. G. Guerrero	1952-1955
G. H. Hackworth	A. H. Badawi	1955-1958
H. Lakestad	Sir Muhammad Zafrulla Khan	1958-1961
B. Winiarski	R. J. Alfaro	1961-1964
Sir Percy Spender	V. K. Wellington Koo	1964-1967
J. L. Bustamante y Rivero	V. M. Koretsky	1967-1970

Judges to the Court are not elected as representatives of their countries but are selected as individuals on the basis of their personal qualifications and knowledge of international law. In electing the judges, the Security Council and General Assembly must satisfy themselves that the main cultural and legal systems of the world are represented.

Articles 16 to 33 of the Statute concern administrative matters such as certain rules to which the judges must conform. These include prohibitions against engaging in any political or administrative function, or in any other occupation of a professional nature which may cause a conflict of interest problem. A judge must disqualify himself if he has previously served as advocate, agent, or representative of any party or principal involved in litigation before the Court.

The seat of the Court is established at The Hague, in the Netherlands. However, under Article 26, the Court can form special chambers of three or more judges to deal with a particular case or class of cases outside The Hague. Although the International Court has never exercised this power, it represents an important provision for future growth and expansion of its operations.

Article 29 of the Statute provides that the Court is to elect each year a Chamber of Summary Procedure, which is available for speedy business. Although this Chamber has never been used, it is also an indication of expansion potential.

Article 31 stipulates that when the Court includes upon the bench a judge of the nationality of one of the parties, any other party may choose an *ad hoc* judge to sit in the case. And, if the Court does not include one judge from each nation which is party to a dispute, any other party may appoint a judge to sit for particular case providing the appointee is chosen preferably from among those persons who have been nominated as candidates by the Permanent Court of Arbitration.

The second Chapter of the Statute, containing Articles 34 through 38, is very important as it involves the Court's competence and jurisdiction to hear and decide cases.[23] Only states may be

---

[23]*See generally* R. ANAND, COMPULSORY JURISDICTION OF THE INTERNATIONAL COURT OF JUSTICE (New York 1962); Bleicher, *ICJ Jurisdiction: Some New Considerations and a Proposed American Declaration,* 6 COLUM. J. TRANSNAT'L L. 61-90 (1967); Briggs, *Reservations to the Acceptance of Compulsory Jurisdiction of the International Court of Justice,* 93 RECUEIL DES COURS 223-367 (1958); A. FARMAN-FARMA, THE DECLARED JURISDICTION OF THE INTERNATIONAL COURT OF JUSTICE . . . (Montreux 1952); Hambro, *Some Observations on the Compulsory Juris-*

(Continued)

parties to disputes before the Court (Art. 34). The Court has jurisdiction over the following matters:

> Article 36. 1. The jurisdiction of the Court comprises all cases which the parties refer to it and all matters specially provided for in the Charter of the United Nations or in treaties and conventions in force.
>
> 2. The states parties to the present Statute may at any time declare that they recognize as compulsory *ipso facto* and without special agreement, in relation to any other state accepting the same obligation, the jurisdiction of the Court in all legal disputes concerning:
>
> > a. the interpretation of a treaty;
> >
> > b. any question of international law;
> >
> > c. the existence of any fact, which, if established, would constitute a breach of an international obligation;
> >
> > d. the nature or extent of the reparation to be made for the breach of an international obligation.
>
> 3. The declarations referred to above may be made unconditionally or on condition of reciprocity on the part of several or certain states, or for a certain time.

Paragraphs 4 through 6 of Article 36 indicate that Declarations shall be deposited with the Secretary-General of the United Nations and that previous Declarations filed by nations formerly parties to the Statute of the Permanent Court of International Justice shall be held valid for acceptance of the compulsory jurisdiction of the new International Court of Justice. The article provides that, in event of a dispute over jurisdiction, the matter shall be settled by the decision of the Court.

As stated in the Statute, the Court's jurisdiction is broad enough to cover virtually any international legal dispute that may arise among nations. In spite of that fact, the power of the Court to hear contentious cases depends upon the willingness of states to accept the compulsory jurisdiction of the Court or upon their willingness to submit a case under special agreement.

---

diction of the International Court of Justice, 25 BR. Y.B. INT'L L. 133-58 (1948); Hambro, *La Compétence de la Cour Internationale de Justice,* 76 RECUEIL DES COURS 125-215 (1950); Lawson, *The Problem of the Compulsory Jurisdiction of the World Court,* 46 AJIL 219-39 (1952); B. MAUS, LES RÉSERVES DANS LES DÉCLARATIONS D'ACCEPTATION DE LA JURIDICTION OBLIGATOIRE DE LA COUR INTERNATIONALE DE JUSTICE (Geneva 1959); I. SHIHATA, THE POWER OF THE INTERNATIONAL COURT TO DETERMINE ITS OWN JURISDICTION (The Hague 1964); J. VIDAL, LA JURIDICCIÓN OBLIGATORIA DE LA CORTE INTERNACIONAL DE JUSTICIA DE LA HAYA (Santiago 1965); Waldock, *The Decline of the Optional Clause,* 32 BR. Y.B. INT'L L. 244-88 (1955-56).

As of June 30, 1969, 45 states have filed Declarations with the Secretary-General accepting the compulsory jurisdiction of the Court. States which are now subject in varying degrees to the Court's jurisdiction by virtue of declarations made under paragraph (2) of Article 36 of the Statute are: Australia, Belgium, Cambodia, Canada, China, Colombia, Denmark, Dominican Republic, El Salvador, Finland, France, Gambia, Haiti, Honduras, India, Israel, Japan, Kenya, Liberia, Liechtenstein, Luxembourg, Malawi, Malta, Mauritius, Mexico, Netherlands, New Zealand, Nicaragua, Nigeria, Norway, Pakistan, Panama, Philippines, Portugal, Somalia, Sudan, Sweden, Switzerland, Turkey, Uganda, United Arab Republic, United Kingdom, United States, and Uruguay.

These Declarations vary from unconditional acceptances to those that are extremely qualified. The elimination of all such reservations and worldwide acceptance of the compulsory jurisdiction of the Court is a constant objective of those seeking to make it a more effective institution and to establish the international rule of law.

Nations which have not accepted the compulsory jurisdiction of the Court may become parties before the Court only through their express consent in each case or as indicated in Article 36 and 37 of the Court Statute.

The International Court of Justice, by virtue of Article 38, in deciding disputes submitted to it, is empowered to apply:

(a) international conventions, whether general or particular, establishing rules expressly recognized by the contesting states;

(b) international custom, as evidence of a general practice accepted as law;

(c) the general principles of law recognized by civilized nations;

(d) subject to the provisions of Article 59, judicial decisions and the teachings of the mostly highly qualified publicists of the various nations, as subsidiary means for the determination of rules of law.

Article 38 further states that the Court is not bound by precedent, but the judges are empowered to try cases *ex aequo et bono*, i.e., according to general principles of equity and the "conscience of the Court," if the parties agree.

The third Chapter of the Statute, dealing with the procedures of the International Court is generally set forth in Articles 39 to 64 and expanded upon in rules which the Court itself adopted in accordance with Article 30.[24] Under Article 40, contentious cases

---

[24] *See* C. DE VISSCHER, ASPECTS RÉCENTS DU DROIT PROCÉDURAL DE LA COUR INTERNATIONALE DE JUSTICE (Paris 1966).

are generally submitted to the Court by application or special agreement. A state, party to the Statute, which has filed a Declaration accepting the compulsory jurisdiction of the Court, may, by written application, submit a case to the Court against another state which has filed a similar Declaration. If no Declaration of Acceptance is filed by the parties, jurisdiction can be conferred upon the Court only by special agreement as to a particular case or class of cases. However, the parties cannot alter the terms of the Statute, the Charter of the United Nations, or the rules of the Court through special agreement. Article 41 gives the Court power to take interim measures for the protection of a party to a dispute if the facts so warrant, and Article 43 provides for written and oral proceedings.

Article 46 stipulates that hearings are to be public unless the the Court determines otherwise. Article 53 states that if one party fails to appear, the other party can submit a request for judgment in its favor. Article 54 provides that the Court's deliberations, after the case has been presented, shall be in private and remain secret. Article 55 provides that all matters will be decided by the majority vote of the judges present. Article 56 stipulates that the judgment rendered in each case state the reasons on which it is based, with any judge being entitled to render a separate opinion. Article 58 requires all opinions to be signed and published, including dissenting opinions. According to Article 59, the decision of the Court has no binding effect except on the parties and in reference to that particular case. Judgments are final and without appeal; however, in the event of a dispute as to the meaning of a judgment, the parties can request the Court to interpret it for them.

In the absence of the right of appeal, Article 61 becomes important as it provides that upon discovery of new evidence or facts of a possibly decisive nature, a party to a dispute can request a revision of the judgment, providing ignorance of the fact was not due to negligence. The application must be made within six months after discovery of the fact.

Article 62 provides that those having a legal interest in the outcome of any case can intervene. Intervenors are bound by Article 63 to the Court's construction of the treaty or convention which may be the subject of a dispute.

The fourth Chapter of the Statute comprising Articles 65 through 68 outlines the procedures under which the Court renders advisory opinions. The Court may, as mentioned above, give an opinion on any legal question submitted to it by the General Assembly,

Security Council, or other organs or specialized agencies of the United Nations. These requests are required to be submitted to the Court with a specific statement, as to what the opinion is to cover and is to include all necessary written documents and materials to assist the Court in its deliberations. Upon receipt of such a request, the Registrar of the Court gives notice to all states entitled to appear before the Court. The Registrar is also required to notify states and international organizations, considered by the Court or the President to be unlikely to be able to furnish information on the question before the Court, that the Court will be prepared to receive written statements or to hear oral statements or to hear oral statements from them.

The fifth Chapter of the Statute contains Articles 69 and 70 which outline Amendment procedures. The Statute can be amended in the same way as the United Nations Charter, that is, by the General Assembly, or by a General Conference of Members of the United Nations. However, non-member states parties to the Statute may vote. The Court itself can suggest changes in the Statute to the United Nations, a power as yet unexercised.

The rules of the International Court of Justice were adopted on May 6, 1964, and in general follow those of its predecessor, the Permanent Court of International Justice.

Article 1 describes the method of determining seniority of the judges, when their terms of office become effective, and similar administrative matters. Article 5 sets forth the Declaration which each judge must make upon accepting appointment to the Court:

> I solemnly declare that I will perform my duties and exercise my powers as judge honorably, faithfully, impartially, and conscientiously.

Article 7 provides for appointment of "assessors" who may sit with the Court and assist in their deliberations, but who may not vote. Succeeding articles define the duties of the Court's President and the procedures to follow in event of the disqualification of a judge. The duties and powers of the Registrar, who serves as the regular channel of communication to and from the Court, are also defined.

In addition, provision is made for the procedures followed if the Court decides to exercise its right to create special chambers to hear specific cases or classes of cases, pursuant to Article 26 of the Statute.

Article 32 outlines the procedures for an application to follow when submitting a case to the Court and, in like manner, the contents of an application submitted by two disputing parties upon completion of a special agreement. Such documents shall contain:

(a) The name of the party making the application

(b) The name of the party against whom the claim is made:

(c) A statement of the statutory provision upon which the Court's jurisdiction is founded.

(d) The precise nature of the claim and a succinct statement of facts and grounds upon which the claim is based.

Upon receiving an application, the Registrar forthwith sends a copy to the state against which the claim is made. The applicant then files a Memorial which is also transmitted to the respondent, who will then file a Counter-Memorial.

A party which wishes to raise a preliminary objection to the Court's jurisdiction will file within the time limit fixed for the Counter-Memorial, not a Counter-Memorial but Preliminary Objections. Proceedings on the merits are then suspended and a time limit is fixed within which the other party presents a written statement of its observations and submissions on the preliminary objections. Oral proceedings are then held on the preliminary objections and the Court gives its decision on jurisdiction in the form of a judgment. If it upholds the objection, the case proceeds no further. This was the situation in the *Interhandel* Case where the where the Court found no jurisdiction because Interhandel had failed to exhaust local remedies available to it in the United States.[25] But, if the Court overrules the objections or joins them, or some of them, to the merits, time limits are once more fixed in the written proceedings for the filing of the Counter-Memorial and the other pleadings after the termination of which hearings are held on other pleadings, after the termination of which hearings are held on the merits. The Memorial will contain a detailed statement of the facts, the applicant's interpretation of the law, and all relevant documents and evidence. The Counter-Memorial will contain the same information, only written from the viewpoint of respondent. The applicant can reply to the Counter-Memorial, and respondent can file a rejoinder, which normally will complete the written argument.

In every case (Art. 37), the President of the Court will ascertain the views of the litigants as to the procedure to be followed, taking

---

[25] [1957] I.C.J. 105.

into account their particular desires in order to set mutually convenient dates for filing the written pleadings and for the oral argument.

When proceeding by "special agreement," the procedure outlined in the rules is as follows:

(a) A copy of the agreement under which the parties are submitting the dispute, and in which a request for the Court to assume jurisdiction is made, must be filed.

(b) The parties each submit a Memorial containing a statement of facts, their interpretations of the law applicable, and all documents and evidence relevant to the claim. Each party receives a copy of the Memorial filed by the other.

(c) Counter-Memorials are prepared by each party, either admitting or denying facts, and reinterpreting the law as they see it.

(d) Following the above exchange, if necessary, each party can then submit a reply.[26]

Upon completion of the written proceedings on the date set by the Court, no new written evidence or documents can be submitted without the special permission of the Court.

The Court then sets a date for the oral hearings at which witnesses, experts, advocates, and other necessary or interested parties will appear. After all parties have been heard, the Court will render its judgment.

Article 61 of the Rules of Court provides for interim protection (used in the *Anglo-Iranian Oil Company* Case[27]), and Articles 68 and 69 provide for settlement and discontinuance. These procedures were applied in the *Barcelona Traction* Case.[28]

Cases in which the Court has found that it could not adjudicate on the merits owing to lack of jurisdiction or from some other reason, or which it has removed from its list at the request of one or both of the parties, are as follows: *Protection of French Nationals in Egypt*[29] (France v. Egypt) measures against French nationals by the Egyptian Government, subsequently desisted from: proceedings discontinued under Article 69 of the Rules of Court

---

[26] Covenant of League of Nations, 1919, 1 M. HUDSON, INT'L LEGISLATION 112; 13 BFSP 316, 13 AJIL Supp. 128 (1919).

[27] [1952] I.C.J. 93.

[28] [1964] *id.* at 6.

[29] [1950] *id.* at 107-08.

and the case removed from the list by order: *Anglo-Iranian Oil Company*[30] (United Kingdom v. Iran) nationalization of the oil industry in Iran: objection to jurisdiction upheld by a judgment; *Nottebohm*[31] (Liechtenstein v. Guatemala) claim for compensation for action against a Liechtenstein citizen contrary to international law: preliminary objection overruled in a first judgment but claim found inadmissible in a second judgment; *Monetary Gold*[32] (Italy v. France, the United Kingdom, the United States) ownership of gold removed from Rome to Germany in 1943: the Court found that it was unable to adjudicate on the rights of Italy in the absence of Albania whose interests would constitute the subject-matter of any decision on the merits; *Electricité de Beyrouth Company*[33] (France v. Lebanon) measures by the Lebanese Government against a French company: dispute subsequently settled, proceedings discontinued under Article 69 of the Rules of Court and case removed from the list by order; *Treatment in Hungary of Aircraft and Crew of United States of America*[34] (United States v. Hungary; United States v. U.S.S.R) U.S. aircraft forced to land on Hungarian territory: Court found that it had no jurisdiction and ordered both cases removed from its list; *Antarctica*[35] (United Kingdom v. Argentina; United Kingdom v. Chile) sovereignty over land and islands in the Antarctic: the Court found that neither Chile nor Argentina had accepted its jurisdiction to deal with the cases, which it ordered removed from its list; *Aerial Incident of October 7, 1952*[36] (United States v. U.S.S.R.) acts of U.S.S.R. fighters against a U.S. aircraft and its crew off Japan: the Court found that the Soviet Union had not accepted its jurisdiction to deal with the dispute and made an order removing the case from its list; *Certain Norwegian Loans*[37] (France v. Norway) payment of debts on Norwegian loans floated in France claimed at gold value of the coupons and bonds: preliminary objection to jurisdiction upheld by a judgment; *Interhandel*[38] (Switzerland v. United States) vesting by U.S. Government of shares of the General Aniline and Film Corporation which were owned by Interhandel, a

---

[30] [1952] *id.* at 93.
[31] [1955] *id.* at 4.
[32] [1954] *id.* at 19.
[33] [1954] *id.* at 107-08.
[34] [1954] *id.* at 65.
[35] [1956] *id.* at 12-14, 15-17.
[36] [1956] *id.* at 9-11.
[37] [1957] *id.* at 9.
[38] [1957] *id.* at 105.

company registered in Switzerland: preliminary objection upheld by a judgment; *Aerial Incident of July 27, 1955*[39] (Israel v. Bulgaria) destruction of an El Al Israel airliner by Bulgarian anti-aircraft guns in 1955: preliminary objection upheld by a judgment; *Aerial Incident of July 27, 1955*[40] (United States v. Bulgaria) same incident: proceedings discontinued and case removed from the Court's list by an order; *Aerial Incident of July 27, 1955*[41] (United Kingdom v. Bulgaria) same incident: proceedings discontinued and case removed from the Court's list by an order; *Aerial Incident of September 4, 1954*[42] (United States v. U.S.S.R.) acts by U.S.S.R. military aircraft over the Sea of Japan against a United States Navy aircraft: the Court found that it had not before it any acceptance by the U.S.S.R. of its jurisdiction and made an order removing the case from its list; *Barcelona Traction*[43] (Belgium v. Spain) bankruptcy in Spain of Canadian company whose share capital was claimed to belong largely to Belgian nationals: proceedings discontinued and case removed from the Court's list by an order; *Aerial Incident of November 7, 1954*[44] (United States v. U.S.S.R.) destruction of United States aircraft in Japanese territorial air space: the Court found that it had not before it any acceptance by the U.S.S.R. of its jurisdiction and made an order removing the case from its list; *Northern Cameroons*[45] (Cameroon v. United Kingdom) complaints concerning the administration of the Trust Territory of the Northern Cameroons: the Court dismissed preliminary objections but found in its judgment that the judicial function was not engaged and that it could not adjudicate upon Cameroon's claim.

§ 4-4. The Record of International Court of Justice

The following are contentious cases, in the order in which they have been reported by the Court in U.N. publication, *The International Court of Justice:*

> *Corfu Channel.* This dispute, which gave rise to three Judgments by the Court, arose out of the explosions of mines by which some British warships suffered damage while passing through the Corfu Channel in 1946, in a part of the Albanian waters which

---

[39] [1959] *id.* at 127.

[40] *Id.*

[41] *Id.*

[42] U.N., *The International Court of Justice*, E.69.I.18, 29-30 (7th ed., 1969).

[43] [1964] *id.* at 6.

[44] *Supra*, note 42, at 31.

[45] [1963] *id.* at 15-196.

had been previously swept. The ships were severely damaged and members of the crew were killed. The United Kingdom accused Albania of having laid or allowed a third party to lay the mines after mine-clearance operations had been carried out by the Allied naval authorities. Owing to the political situation at the time, the incident caused grave tension between the two States. The case was brought before the United Nations, and, in consequence of a recommendation by the Security Council, it was referred to the Court. The first of three Judgments (25 March 1948) dealt with the question of the Court's jurisdiction, which Albania had challenged.

The second and most important Judgment (9 April 1949) related to the merits of the problem. The Court found that Albania was responsible under international law for the explosions that had taken place in Albanian waters and for the damage and loss of life which had ensued. It did not accept the view that Albania had itself laid the mines. On the other hand, it held that the mines could not have been laid without the knowledge of the Albanian Government. In this connexion, the Court took into account certain circumstantial evidence which established the responsibility of the territorial Government. Albania, for its part, had submitted a counter-claim against the United Kingdom. It accused the latter of having violated Albanian sovereignty by sending warships into Albanian territorial waters and of carrying out mine-sweeping operations in Albanian waters after the explosions. The Court did not accept the first of these complaints. It upheld the generally admitted principle that States are entitled, in time of peace, to send their warships through international straits without first obtaining the leave of the coastal State. The Court found that this was a case of innocent passage. On the other hand, the mine clearance operation of 12 and 13 November 1946, having been effected against the will of the Albanian Government, the Court found that it constituted an inadmissible intervention in the affairs of Albania. In spite of the default of the Albanian Government and its dilatory attitude, the Court held that the action of the British Navy was a violation of Albanian sovereignty.

In a third and final Judgment (15 December 1949), the Court assessed the amount of reparation due by Albania to the United Kingdom. This amount had been determined as a result of an expert enquiry and Albania was ordered to pay the United Kingdom a total sum of £844,000 for the damage caused to the ships and as compensation for the deaths of members of the crews and for personal injuries suffered by them.

Fisheries. The Judgment delivered by the Court in the Fisheries Case set a term to a controversy which had been pending between the United Kingdom and Norway for a very long period. In 1935,

Norway enacted a decree by which it reserved certain fishing ground situated off the northern coast of Norway for the exclusive use of its own fishermen. The question at issue was whether this decree, which laid down a particular method for drawing the base-lines from which the width of the Norwegian territorial waters had to be calculated, was valid in international law. This case, which aroused considerable interest, especially in maritime States, gave rise to prolonged and voluminous proceedings. In its Judgment of 18 December 1951, the Court found that, contrary to the sub-missions of the United Kingdom, neither the method employed for the delimitation by the 1935 decree nor the lines themselves fixed by the said decree were contrary to international law.

Protection of French Nationals and Protected Persons in Egypt. As a consequence of certain measures adopted by the Egyptian Government against the property and persons of various French nationals and protected persons in Egypt, France instituted proceedings in which it invoked the Montreux Convention of 1935, concerning the abrogation of the capitulations in Egypt. However, the case was not proceeded with, as the Egyptian Government desisted from the measures in question. By agreement between the parties, the case was struck off the Court's List (Order of 29 March 1950).

Asylum. The granting of asylum in the Colombian Embassy at Lima on 3 January 1949, to a Peruvian national, Mr. Haya de la Torre, a political leader accused of having instigated a military rebellion, was the subject of a dispute between Peru and Colombia which the parties agreed to submit to the Court. The Pan-American Havana Convention on Asylum (1928) laid down that, subject to certain conditions, asylum could be granted in a foreign embassy to a political offender who was a national of the terri-torial State. The question in dispute was whether Colombia, as the State granting the asylum, was entitled unilaterally to "qualify" the offence committed by the refugee in a manner binding on the territorial State—that is, to decide whether it was a political offence or a common crime. Furthermore, the Court was asked to decide whether the territorial State was bound to afford the necessary guarantees to enable the refugee to leave the country in safety. In its Judgment of 20 November 1950, the Court answered both these questions in the negative, but at the same time it specified that Peru had not proved that Mr. Haya de la Torre was a common criminal. Lastly it found in favour of a counter-claim submitted by Peru that Mr. Haya de la Torre had been granted asylum in violation of the Havana Convention, as it considered that the asylum had been irregularly granted because Mr. Haya de la Torre had sought refuge in the Embassy some three months after the suppression of the military rebellion, which showed that the "urgency" prescribed by the Havana Convention as a condition for the regularity of asylum no longer existed.

On the very day on which the Court delivered this Judgment, Colombia filed a request for an interpretation. By this request, Colombia sought to obtain from the Court a reply to the question whether the Judgment implied an obligation binding the Colombian authorities to surrender the refugee, Mr. Haya de la Torre, to the Peruvian authorities. In a Judgment delivered on 27 November 1950, the court declared that the questions raised by Colombia were new questions, that they had not been presented in the preceding case, and that therefore the Court could not decide upon them by way of interpretation. The Court further pointed out that a request for interpretation could only be founded on a dispute between the parties concerning the meaning of the Judgment, which dispute could not have arisen because the request for interpretation had been submitted on the same day as the delivery of the Judgment. The Colombian request was therefore dismissed.

Haya de la Torre. This case, a sequel to the earlier proceedings, was instituted by Colombia by means of a fresh application. Immediately after the Judgment of 20 November 1950, Peru had called upon Colombia to surrender Mr. Haya de la Torre. Colombia refused to do so, maintaining that neither the applicable legal provisions nor the Court's Judgment placed it under an obligation to surrender the refugee to the Peruvian authorities. The Court confirmed this view in its Judgment of 13 June 1951. It declared that the question was a new one, and that although the Havana Convention expressly prescribed the surrender of common criminals to the local authorities, no obligation of the kind existed in regard to political offenders. While confirming that asylum had been irregularly granted and that on this ground Peru was entitled to demand its termination, the Court declared that Colombia was not bound to surrender the refugee; these two conclusions, it stated, were not contradictory because there were other ways in which the asylum could be terminated besides the surrender of the refugee.

Rights of Nationals of the United States of America in Morocco. By a decree of 30 December 1948, the French authorities in the Moroccan Protectorate imposed a system of licence control in respect of imports not involving an official allocation of currency, and limited these imports to a number of products indispensable to the Moroccan economy. The United States maintained that this measure affected its rights under treaties with Morocco and contended that, in accordance with these treaties and with the General Act of Algeciras of 1906, no Moroccan law or regulation could be applied to its nationals in Morocco without its previous consent. In its Judgment of 27 August 1952, the Court held that the import controls were contrary to the treaty between the United States and Morocco of 1836 and the General Act of Algeciras since they involved discrimination in favour of France against the United States. The Court considered the extent of the consular jurisdiction of the United States in Morocco and held that the United States was entitled to exercise such jurisdiction in the French Zone in all disputes, civil or criminal, between United States citizens or persons protected by the United States. It was also entitled to exercise such jurisdiction to the extent required by the relevant provisions of the General Act of Algeciras. The Court rejected the contention of the United States that its consular jurisdiction included cases in which only the defendant was a citizen or protégé of the United States. It also rejected the claim by the United States that the application to citizens of the United States of laws and regulations in the French Zone of Morocco required the assent of the United States Government. Such assent was required only in so far as the intervention of the consular courts of the United States was necessary for the effective enforcement of such laws or regulations as against United States citizens. The Court rejected a counter-claim by the United States that its nationals in Morocco were entitled to immunity from taxation. It also dealt with the question of the valuation of imports by the Moroccan customs authorities.

Ambatielos. In 1919, Mr. Ambatielos, a Greek ship owner, entered into a contract for the purchase of ships with the Government of the United Kingdom. Mr. Ambatielos claimed he had suffered damage through the failure of the United Kingdom Government to carry out the terms of the contract and as a result of certain Judgments given against him by the English courts in circumstances which were alleged to be contrary to international law. The Greek Government took up the case of its national and claimed that the United Kingdom was under a duty to submit the dispute to arbitration in accordance with Treaties between the United Kingdom and Greece of 1886 and 1926. The United Kingdom objected to the Court's jurisdiction. In a Judgment of 1 July 1952, the Court held that it had jurisdiction to decide whether the United Kingdom was under a duty to submit the dispute to arbitration but, on the other hand, that it had no jurisdiction to deal with the merits of the Ambatielos claim. In a further Judgment of 19 May 1953, the Court decided that the dispute was one which the United Kingdom was under a duty to submit to arbitration in accordance with the treaties of 1886 and 1926.

Anglo-Iranian Oil Company. In 1933, an agreement was concluded between the Government of Iran and the Anglo-Iranian Oil Company. In 1951, laws were passed in Iran for the nationalization of the oil industry. These laws resulted in a dispute between Iran and the Company. The United Kingdom took up the case of the latter and instituted proceedings before the Court. Iran disputed the Court's jurisdiction. In its Judgment of 22 July 1952, the Court decided that it had no jurisdiction to deal with the dispute. Its jurisdiction depended on the declarations by Iran and the United Kingdom accepting the Court's compulsory jurisdiction under the optional clause of the Statute. The Court held that the declaration by Iran, which was ratified in 1932, covered only disputes based on treaties concluded by Iran after that date, whereas the claim of the United Kingdom was directly or indirectly based on treaties concluded prior to 1932. The Court also rejected the view that the agreement of 1933 was both a concessionary contract between Iran and the Company and an international treaty between Iran and the United Kingdom, since the United Kingdom was not a party to the contract. The position was not altered by the fact that the concessionary contract was negotiated through the good offices of the Council of the League of Nations. By an order of 5 July 1951, the Court had indicated interim measures of protection, that is, provisional measures for protecting the rights alleged by either party, in proceedings already instituted, until a final Judgment is given. In its Judgment the Court declared that the order of 5 July 1951 had ceased to be operative and that the provisional measures therefore lapsed.

Minquiers and Ecrehos. The Minquiers and Ecrehos are two groups of islets situated between the British Channel Island of Jersey and the coast of France. Under a special agreement between France and the United Kingdom, the Court was asked to determine which of the parties had produced a more convincing proof of title to these groups of islets. After the conquest of England by William, Duke of Normandy, in 1066, the islands formed part of the Union between England and Normandy which lasted until 1204, when Philip Augustus of France conquered Normandy but failed to occupy the islands. The United Kingdom submitted that the islands then remained united with England and that this situation was placed on a legal basis by subsequent treaties between the two countries. France contended that the Minquiers and Ecrehos were held by France after 1204, and referred to the same medieval treaties as those relied on by the United Kingdom. In its Judgment of 17 November 1953, the Court considered that none of these Treaties stated specifically which islands were held by the King of England or by the King of France. Moreover, what was of decisive importance was not indirect presumptions based on matters in the Middle Ages, but direct evidence of possession and the actual exercise of sovereignty. After considering this evidence, the Court arrived at the conclusion that the sovereignty over the Minquiers and Ecrehos belonged to the United Kingdom.

Nottebohm. In this case Liechtenstein claimed restitution and compensation from the Government of Guatemala on the ground that the latter had acted towards Mr. Nottebohm, a citizen of Liechtenstein, in a manner contrary to international law. Guatemala objected to the Court's jurisdiction but the Court overruled this objection in a Judgment of 18 November 1953. In a second Judgment of 6 April 1955, the Court held that Liechtenstein's claim was inadmissible on grounds relating to Mr. Nottebohm's nationality. It was the bond of nationality between a State and an individual which alone conferred upon the State the right to put forward an international claim on his behalf. Mr. Nottebohm, who was then a German national, had settled in Guatemala in 1905 and continued to reside there. In October 1939—after the beginning of the Second World War—while on a visit to Europe, he obtained Liechtenstein nationality and returned to Guatemala in 1940, where he resumed his former business activities until his removal as a result of war measures in 1943. On the international plane the grant of nationality was entitled to recognition by other States only if it represented a genuine connexion between the individual and the State granting its nationality. Mr. Nottebohm's nationality, however, was not based on any real prior connexion with Liechtenstein, since he always retained his family and business connexions with Germany and had been settled in Guatemala for 34 years. Moreover, the object of his naturalization was to enable him to acquire the status of a neutral national in time of war. For these reasons, Liechtenstein was not entitled to take up his case and put forward an international claim on his behalf against Guatemala.

Monetary Gold Removed from Rome in 1943. A certain quantity of monetary gold was removed by the Germans from Rome in 1943. It was later recovered in Germany and found to belong to Albania. The 1946 agreement on reparation from Germany provided that monetary gold found in Germany should be pooled for distribution among the countries entitled to receive a share of it. The United Kingdom claimed that the gold should be delivered to it in partial satisfaction of the Court's Judgment of 1946 in the Corfu Channel case . . . Italy claimed that gold should be delivered to it in partial satisfaction for the damage which it alleged it had suffered as a result of an Albanian law of 13 January 1945. In the Washington statement of 25 April 1951, the Governments of France, the United Kingdom and the United States, to whom the implementation of the reparations agreement had been entrusted, decided that the gold should be delivered to the United Kingdom unless, within a certain time-limit, Italy or Albania applied to the Court requesting it to adjudicate on their respective rights. Albania took no action in the matter, but within the prescribed time-limit Italy made an application to the Court. Later, however, Italy raised the preliminary question as to whether the

Court had jurisdiction to adjudicate upon the validity of the Italian claim against Albania. In its Judgment of 15 June 1954, the Court decided that, in order to determine whether Italy was entitled to receive the gold, it was necessary to determine whether Albania had committed an international wrong against Italy and whether it was under an obligation to pay compensation to Italy. To go into the merits of such questions would be to decide a dispute between Italy and Albania which the Court had no jurisdiction to do without Albania's consent. For this reason the Court could also not decide the question of priority as between the claims of Italy and the United Kingdom, for this question could arise only if it was decided that, as between Italy and Albania, the gold should go to Italy.

Electricité de Beyrouth Company. This case between France and Lebanon arose out of certain measures adopted by the Lebanese Government which the Electricité de Beyrouth Company, a French limited company, regarded as contrary to undertakings entered into by that Government. These undertakings, which related to concessions of French companies and companies with French capital in Lebanon, formed part of an agreement between France and Lebanon of 1948. After the case had been brought before the Court by France on 11 August 1953, the Lebanese Government and the Electricité de Beyrouth Company entered into an agreement on 26 March 1954, for the settlement of the dispute by a repurchase of the concession. The agreement was ratified by the Lebanese Parliament on 30 June 1954. Moreover, it was agreed between the French and Lebanese Governments that as soon as a settlement was reached, France would discontinue the proceedings. On 23 July 1954, therefore, the French Government informed the Court that it was not going on with the proceedings, and on 29 July 1954, the Court made an order for the removal of the case from the List.

Treatment in Hungary of Aircraft and Crew of United States of America. On 3 March 1954, the United States of America instituted proceedings against the Hungarian People's Republic and the Union of Soviet Socialist Republics "on account of certain actions of the Hungarian Government in concert with the Government of the Union of Soviet Socialist Republics" regarding an aircraft and crew of the United States which had been forced to land on Hungarian territory. The United States relied on Article 36, paragraph 1, of the Court's Statute, which provides that the jurisdiction of the Court comprises all cases which the parties refer to it, and it stated that it submitted to the Court's jurisdiction for the purpose of the two cases and indicated that it was open to the other two Governments to do likewise. In a letter to the Court dated 30 April 1954, the Government of the Union of Soviet Socialist Republics attributed responsibility for the incident to the

United States and said that it regarded as unacceptable the proposal of the Government of the United States that the Court should examine the case. In a letter to the Court dated 14 June 1954, the Hungarian Government stated that it was unable to submit to its jurisdiction in the matter. The Court found that in the circumstances it did not have jurisdiction to deal with these cases and on 12 July 1954, it made two orders removing them from the List.

Aerial Incident of 10 March 1953. On 29 March 1955, the United States instituted proceedings against Czechoslovakia on account of "certain wrongful acts committed by MIG-type aircraft from Czechoslovakia within the United States zone of occupation in Germany on 10 March 1953." In its application to the Court, the United States Government stated that it submitted to the Court's jurisdiction for the purposes of the case and that it was open to the Czechoslovak Government to do likewise. The United States Government relied on Article 36, paragraph 1, of the Court's Statute, which provides that the Court's jurisdiction comprises all cases which the parties refer to it. In a letter to the Court, Czechoslovakia attributed responsibility for the incident to the United States and considered that there was no reason for the case to be dealt with by the Court. The Court found that Czechoslovakia had not accepted its jurisdiction to deal with the dispute and on 14 March 1956, it made an order removing the case from the List.

Antarctica. On 4 May 1955, the United Kingdom instituted proceedings before the Court against Argentina and Chile concerning disputes as to the sovereignty over certain lands and islands in the Antarctic. In its application to the Court, the United Kingdom stated that it submitted to the Court's jurisdiction for the purposes of the case, and although, as far as it was aware, Argentina and Chile had not yet accepted the Court's jurisdiction, they were legally qualified to do so. Moreover, the United Kingdom relied on Article 36, paragraph 1, of the court's Statute, which provides that the jurisdiction of the court comprises all cases which the parties refer to it. In a letter of 15 July 1955, the Government of Chile informed the Court that in its view the application of the Government of the United Kingdom was unfounded and that it was not open to the Court to exercise jurisdiction. In a note of 1 August 1955, the Government of Argentina informed the Court of its refusal to accept its jurisdiction to deal with the case. In these circumstances, the Court found that neither Chile nor Argentina had accepted its jurisdiction to deal with the cases and on 16 March 1956, it made orders removing them from the List.

Aerial Incident of 7 October 1952. On 2 June 1955 the United States instituted proceedings against the Union of Soviet Socialist

Republics on account of "certain wilful acts committed by fighter aircraft of the Soviet Government against a United States Air Force B-29 aircraft and its crew off Hokkaido, Japan, on 7 October 1952." In its application to the Court, the United States Government stated that it submitted to the Court's jurisdiction for the purposes of the case and that it was open to the Soviet Government to do likewise. The United States relied on Article 36, paragraph 1, of the Court's Statute, which provides that the jurisdiction of the Court comprises all cases which the parties refer to it. In a letter to the Court, the Soviet Union attributed responsibility for the incident to the United States and considered that there was no reason for the question to be dealt with by the Court. The Court found that the Soviet Union had not accepted its jurisdiction to deal with the dispute and on 14 March 1956, it made an order removing the case from the List.

Certain Norwegian Loans. Certain Norwegian loans had been floated in France between the years 1885 and 1909. The bonds of these loans stated the amount of the obligation in gold or in currency convertible into gold, as well as in various national currencies. From the time when Norway suspended the convertibility of its currency into gold, the loans had been serviced in Norwegian kroner. The French Government, espousing the cause of the French bondholders, filed an application requesting the Court to declare that the debt should be discharged by payment of the gold value of the coupons of the bonds on the date of payment and of the gold value of the redeemed bonds on the date of repayment. The Norwegian Government raised a number of preliminary objections to the jurisdiction of the Court and, in the Judgment it delivered on 6 July 1957, the Court found that it was without jurisdiction to adjudicate on the dispute. Indeed, the Court held that, since its jurisdiction depended upon the two unilateral declarations made by the parties, jurisdiction was conferred upon the Court only to the extent to which those declarations coincided in conferring it. The Norwegian Government was therefore entitled, by virtue of the condition of reciprocity, to invoke in its own favour the reservation contained in the French declaration which excluded from the jurisdiction of the Court differences relating to matters which were essentially within the national jurisdiction as understood by the Government of the French Republic.

Right of Passage over Indian Territory. This dispute, which gave rise to two Judgments by the Court, arose out of the following set of facts. The Portuguese possessions in India included, at some distance inland from the port of Daman, the two enclaves of Dadra and Nagar-Aveli which, in mid-1954, passed under an autonomous local administration. Portugal claimed that it had a right of passage to those enclaves and between one enclave and the other to the extent necessary for the exercise of its sovereignty and subject to the regulation and control of India; that that right derived from agreements concluded in the eighteenth century between Portugal and the Marathas, from local customs established between Portugal and the successive sovereigns of the Indian peninsula, from general international custom in regard to enclaves and from the general principles of law recognized by civilized nations; that, in July 1954, contrary to the practice previously followed, the Indian Government had prevented Portugal from exercising the right of passage claimed by it and that that situation should be redressed. The first Judgment—that of 26 November 1957— related to the jurisdiction of the Court, which was challenged by India. The Court rejected four of the preliminary objections raised by India and joined the other two to the merits. In the second Judgment—that of 12 April 1960—after rejecting the two remaining preliminary objections, the Court gave its decision on the claims of Portugal, which India maintained to be unfounded. After examining the situation of Dadra and Nagar-Aveli during the Maratha period and the practice subsequently developed in regard to those enclaves, the Court found that Portugal had in 1954 the right of passage claimed by it but that such right was limited to the passage of private persons, civil officials and goods in general and did not extend to armed forces, armed police, arms and ammunition. The Court found finally that India had not acted contrary to the obligations imposed on it by the existence of the right of passage thus found to belong to Portugal.

Application of the Convention of 1902 Governing the Guardianship of Infants. The Swedish authorities had placed an infant of Netherlands nationality residing in Sweden under the régime of protective upbringing instituted by Swedish law for the protection of children and young persons. The father of the child, jointly with the deputy-guardian appointed by a Netherlands court, appealed against the action of the Swedish authorities, but the measure of protective upbringing was maintained. The Netherlands Government claimed that the decisions which instituted and maintained the protective upbringing were not in conformity with Sweden's obligations under the Hague Convention of 1902 governing the guardianship of infants, the provisions of which were based on the principle that the national law of the infant is applicable. In its Judgment of 28 November 1958, the Court held that the 1902 Convention on guardianship did not include within its scope the matter of protection of children as understood by the Swedish law on the protection of children and young persons and that the 1902 Convention could not have given rise to obligations in a field outside the matter with which it was concerned. Accordingly the Court did not, in this case, find any failure to observe the Convention on the part of Sweden.

Interhandel. In 1942, the Government of the United States of America vested almost all of the shares of the General Aniline and Film Corporation (GAF), a company incorporated in the United States, on the ground that those shares, which were owned by Interhandel, a company registered in Bâle, belonged in reality to the I. G. Farbenindustrie of Frankfurt, or that the GAF was in one way or another controlled by that company. In an application dated 1 October 1957, the Swiss Government asked the Court to declare that the United States Government was under an obligation to restore to Interhandel the assets of that company which had been vested or, alternatively, that the dispute on the matter between Switzerland and the United States was one that was fit for submission for judicial settlement, arbitration or conciliation. Two days later, the Swiss Government asked the Court to indicate, as an interim measure of protection, that the United States should not part with these assets so long as proceedings in this dispute were pending and, in particular, should not sell the shares of the General Aniline and Film Corporation which were claimed by the Swiss Federal Government as the property of its nationals. On 24 October 1957, the Court made an order in which it noted that, in the light of the information furnished to the Court, it appeared that the sale of the shares in question could only be effected after the termination of judicial proceedings pending in the United States, in respect of which there was no indication of a speedy conclusion; that it was the stated intention of the United States Government not to take action at that time to fix a time schedule for the sale of the shares and that accordingly there was no need to indicate interim measures of protection. The United States raised preliminary objections to the jurisdiction of the Court and, in its Judgment of 21 March 1959, the Court found that the application of the Government of the Swiss Confederation was inadmissible in regard both to the principal claim and to the alternative claim for the reason that Interhandel had not exhausted the local remedies available to it in the United States courts.

Aerial Incident of 27 July 1955 (Israel v. Bulgaria). This case arose out of the destruction by Bulgarian anti-aircraft defence forces of an aircraft belonging to an Israel airline. Israel instituted proceedings before the Court by means of an application in October 1957. Bulgaria having challenged the Court's jurisdiction to deal with the claim, Israel contended that, since Bulgaria had in 1921 accepted the compulsory jurisdiction of the Permanent Court of International Justice for an unlimited period, that acceptance became applicable, when Bulgaria was admitted to the United Nations in 1955, to the jurisdiction of the present Court by virtue of Article 36, paragraph 5, of the Statute, which provides that declarations made under the Statute of the former Court, which are still in force, shall be deemed, as between the parties to the

Statute, to be acceptances applicable to the new Court for the period which they still have to run and in accordance with their terms. In its Judgment on the preliminary objections, delivered on 26 May 1959, the Court found that it was without jurisdiction on the ground that Article 36, paragraph 5, was intended to preserve only declarations in force as between States signatories of the Charter, and not subsequently to revive undertakings which had lapsed on the dissolution of the Permanent Court.

Aerial Incident of 27 July 1955 (United States of America v. Bulgaria). This case arose out of the incident which was the subject of the proceedings mentioned under [Aerial Incident of 27 July 1955 (Israel v. Bulgaria)]. The aircraft destroyed by Bulgarian anti-aircraft defence forces on 27 July 1955, was carrying several United States nationals who, like the other passengers and the members of the crew, were killed. In its application instituting proceedings, the United States Government asked the Court to find that the Bulgarian Government was liable for the damage caused through the deaths of the United States nationals and the destruction of their property on board the aircraft and to award damages and costs. Bulgaria filed preliminary objections to the Court's jurisdiction and the proceedings on the merits were therefore suspended. Before the date fixed for the hearings of the Bulgarian objections, the United States Government informed the Court that, as a result of further considerations of questions of jurisdiction raised by the statement of Bulgaria's preliminary objections and the United States observations thereon, it had decided to request the discontinuance of the proceedings. The Bulgarian Government did not oppose such discontinuance and, in an order made on 30 May 1960, the Court directed that the case should be removed from the List.

Aerial Incident of 27 July 1955 (United Kingdom v. Bulgaria). This case arose out of the same incident as that mentioned under [Aerial Incident of 27 July 1955 (Israel v. Bulgaria) and Aerial Incident of 27 July 1955 (United States of America v. Bulgaria)]. The aircraft destroyed by Bulgarian anti-aircraft defence forces on 27 July 1955, was carrying several nationals of the United Kingdom and Colonies who, like the other passengers and members of the crew, were killed. The United Kingdom Government asked the Court to declare that Bulgaria was responsible for the losses sustained by the citizens of the United Kingdom and Colonies by reason of the deaths of persons on board, as well as for the loss of personal effects and freight owned by citizens of the United Kingdom and Colonies carried on the aircraft and to award damages and costs against Bulgaria. The United Kingdom filed its Memorial within the time-limit fixed but, before the date fixed for the filing of the Bulgarian Counter-Memorial, the United Kingdom Government informed the Court of its decision to discontinue the proceedings, having regard to the decision of the Court of 26 May 1959, that it had no jurisdiction in respect of the case concerning this incident brought by Israel against Bulgaria. Bulgaria did not oppose the discontinuance of the proceedings and, on 3 August 1959, the Court made an order removing the case from the List.

Sovereignty over Certain Frontier Land. By a special agreement signed in March 1957 between the Netherlands and Belgium, the Court was asked to settle a dispute as to the sovereignty over two plots of land situated in an area north of the Belgian town of Turnhout where the frontier between the two countries presents certain unusual features, there being a number of enclaves formed by the Belgian commune of Baerle-Duc and the Netherlands commune of Baarle-Nassau. The Court was informed that this situation was of very ancient origin. From the documents produced by the parties it appeared that a Communal Minute drawn up by the authorities of these two communes between 1836 and 1841 (on which the Netherlands relied) attributed the two plots in question to Baarle-Nassau, whereas the Descriptive Minute of the frontier annexed to the Boundary Convention of 1843 which was concluded after the separation of Belgium from the Netherlands (and on which Belgium relied) attributed them to Baerle-Duc, as did also the special map annexed to the Boundary Convention. The Netherlands Government maintained that the Boundary Convention recognized the existence of the status quo as determined by the Communal Minute, under which sovereignty over the disputed plots was recognized as vested in the Netherlands, and that the provision by which the two plots were attributed to Belgium was vitiated by a mistake as was evident from a mere comparison of the terms of the Communal Minute with those of the Descriptive Minute. The Netherlands claimed further that its sovereignty over the disputed plots had been established by the exercise of various acts of sovereignty since 1843. After considering all the evidence produced, the Court concluded that the Boundary Convention did determine to which state the various plots in each commune belonged and that no case of mistake had been made out and, finally, that the acts relied upon by the Netherlands as establishing its sovereignty were largely of a routine and administrative character and were insufficient to displace Belgian sovereignty established by the Boundary Convention. In its Judgment delivered on 20 June 1959, the Court accordingly found that sovereignty over the two disputed plots belonged to Belgium.

Arbitral Award Made by the King of Spain on 23 December 1906. On 7 October 1894, Honduras and Nicaragua signed a convention for the demarcation of the limits between the two countries, one of the articles of which provided that, in certain circumstances, any points of the boundary line which were left unsettled should be submitted to the decision of the Government of Spain. In October 1904, the King of Spain was asked to determine that part of the frontier line on which the Mixed Boundary Commission appointed by the two countries had been unable to reach agreement. The King gave his arbitral award on 23 December 1906. Nicaragua contested the validity of the award and, in accordance with a resolution of the Organization of American States, the two countries agreed in July 1957 on the procedure to be followed for submitting the dispute on this matter to the International Court of Justice. In the application by which the case was brought before the Court on 1 July 1958, the Government of Honduras claimed that failure by the Government of Nicaragua to give effect to the arbitral award constituted a breach of an international obligation and asked the Court to declare that Nicaragua was under an obligation to give effect to the award. After considering all the evidence produced, the Court found that Nicaragua had in fact freely accepted the designation of the King of Spain as arbitrator, had fully participated in the arbitral proceeding, and had thereafter accepted the award. Consequently, the Court found in its Judgment delivered on 18 November 1960 that the award was binding and that Nicaragua was under an obligation to give effect to it.

Aerial Incident of 4 September 1954. On 22 August 1958, the United States of America instituted proceedings against the Union of Soviet Socialist Republics on account of "certain wilful acts committed by military aircraft of the Soviet Government on 4 September 1954, in the international air space over the Sea of Japan against a United States Navy P2-V-type aircraft, commonly known as a Neptune type and against its crew." In its application to the Court, the United States Government stated that it submitted to the Court's jurisdiction for the purposes of the case and that the Soviet Government was qualified to do likewise. The United States relied on Article 36, paragraph 1, of the Court's Statute, which provides that the jurisdiction of the Court comprises all cases which the parties refer to it. In a letter to the Court, the Soviet Union attributed responsibility for the incident to the United States and said it considered that in this case there were no questions which needed to be considered by the Court and that it saw no basis for turning this question over for examination by the Court. In the circumstances, the Court found that it had not before it any acceptance by the Government of the Union of Soviet Socialist Republics of the jurisdiction of the Court to deal with the dispute and that therefore it could take no further steps upon the application. The Court accordingly made an order on 9 December 1958, removing the case from the List.

Barcelona Traction, Light and Power Company, Limited. On 23 September 1958, the Belgian Government filed an application instituting proceedings against Spain in connexion with the adjudication in bankruptcy in Spain in 1948 of the Barcelona Traction, Light and Power Company, Limited, a joint-stock company formed in Toronto in 1911. The application stated that the share capital of this company had, for more than 25 years, belonged largely to Belgian nationals. The Belgian Government claimed that the measures, acts, decisions and omissions of the organs of the Spanish state by virtue of which the company was declared bankrupt and its property liquidated were contrary to international law and that the Spanish State was responsible for the damage that resulted therefrom and was consequently under an obligation to restore the property, rights and interests of the company as they existed prior to its adjudication in bankruptcy or, if such restitution is wholly or partly impossible, to pay to the Belgian State equivalent compensation. As an alternative, the Court was asked to declare that compensation must be paid up to the amount of the share of the capital owned by Belgian nationals together with the amount of the sums standing due to them at the date of the adjudication in bankruptcy. In May 1960, the Spanish Government filed preliminary objections to the jurisdiction of the Court and the proceedings on the merits were suspended. Before the date fixed for the filing of its observations and submissions on the objections raised by Spain, the Belgian Government informed the Court that it was not going on with the proceedings. The Spanish Government indicated that it had no objection to a discontinuance. Accordingly, the Court made an order on 10 April 1961, removing the case from the List. [See, however, Barcelona Traction, Light and Power Company, Limited for new application: 1962.]

Compagnie du Port, des Quais et des Entrepôts de Beyrouth and Société Radio-Orient. This case between France and Lebanon arose out of certain measures adopted by the Lebanese Government with regard to two French limited companies, the Compagnie du Port, des Quais et des Entrepôts de Beyrouth and the Société Radio-Orient. The French Government considered these measures to be contrary to certain undertakings embodied in an agreement concluded between France and Lebanon in 1948 relating to concessions of French companies and companies with French capital in Lebanon. France instituted proceedings against Lebanon by means of an application on 13 February 1959. Lebanon raised preliminary objections to the jurisdiction of the Court but, before a date had been fixed for the hearings on the preliminary objections, the Court was informed by the parties that satisfactory arrangements had been concluded, the situation of the Compagnie du Port, des Quais et des Entrepôts de Beyrouth having been settled for the future by a convention of 13 April 1960, between the State of Lebanon and the company, together with an exchange of letters between the President of the Council of Ministers of

Lebanon and the Ambassador of the French Republic at Beirut, and the Société Radio-Orient having been fully satisfied by a decision of the Council of Ministers of Lebanon dated 11 May 1960. The President of the Court accordingly made an order on 31 August 1960, removing the case from the List.

Aerial Incident of 7 November 1954. On 7 July 1959, the United States of America instituted proceedings against the Union of Soviet Socialist Republics on account of the destruction of 7 November 1954, of a United States Air Force B-29 aircraft in the Japanese territorial air space over Hokkaido, Japan. In its application to the Court, the United States Government stated that it submitted to the Court's jurisdiction for the purposes of the case and that the Soviet Government was qualified to do likewise. The United States relied on Article 36, paragraph 1, of the Court's Statute, which provides that the jurisdiction of the Court comprises all cases which the parties refer to it. In a letter to the Court, the Soviet Union attributed responsibility for the incident to the United States and said it considered that in this case there were no questions which needed to be solved by the Court and that it did not see any basis for the filing of this case with the Court. In these circumstances, the Court found that it had not before it any acceptance by the Government of the Union of Soviet Socialist Republics of the jurisdiction of the Court to deal with the dispute and therefore it could take no further steps upon the application. The Court accordingly made an order on 7 October 1959, removing the case from the List.

Temple of Preah Vihear. In an application instituting proceedings against Thailand filed on 6 October 1959, Cambodia complained that since 1949 Thailand had persisted in the occupation of a portion of Cambodian territory where there are the ruins of a holy monastery, the Temple of Preah Vihear, a sacred place of pilgrimage and worship for the people of Cambodia. Cambodia asked the Court to declare that territorial sovereignty over the Temple belonged to the Kingdom of Cambodia and that Thailand was under an obligation to withdraw the detachments of armed forces it had stationed since 1954 in the ruins of the Temple. On 23 May 1960, the Government of Thailand filed preliminary objections to the jurisdiction of the Court and the proceedings on the merits were suspended. On 26 May 1961, the Court delivered a Judgment in which it rejected the two preliminary objections raised by Thailand, and upheld its jurisdiction. In its Judgment on the merits rendered on 15 June 1962 the Court found that the Temple of Preah Vihear was situated on Cambodian territory. It also held that Thailand was under an obligation to withdraw any military or police force, or other guards or keepers stationed in the Temple or in its vicinity on Cambodian territory. Finally, it ruled that Thailand was under an obligation to restore any sculptures or similar objects removed by it since it occupied the Temple in 1954.

South West Africa. On 4 November 1960, Ethiopia and Liberia instituted separate proceedings against South Africa in a case concerning the continued existence of the Mandate for South West Africa and the duties and performance of South Africa, as mandatory power. The Court was requested to make declarations to the effect that South West Africa remained a Mandate, that South Africa had been in breach of and had obligations thereunder and that the Mandate, and hence the Mandatory Authority, was subject to the supervision of the United Nations. On 20 May 1961, the Court issued an order in which if found that Ethiopia and Liberia were in the same interest and joined the proceedings instituted by these two Governments. South Africa thereafter filed preliminary objections to the jurisdiction of the Court, and the proceedings on the merits were suspended. On 21 December 1962, the Court delivered a Judgment in which it rejected the four preliminary objections raised by South Africa, and upheld its jurisdiction. Judgment in the second phase was given on 18 July 1966. The Court, by the President's casting vote, the votes being equally divided (seven-seven), found that Ethiopia and Liberia could not be considered to have established any legal right or interest appertaining to them in the subject matter of their claims and accordingly decided to reject them.

Northern Cameroons. On 30 May 1961, the Republic of Cameroon instituted proceedings against the United Kingdom. It complained that the United Kingdom, by administering the Northern Cameroons as an integral part of Nigeria, had been in breach of the Trusteeship Agreement for the Territory of the Cameroons under British Administration. It also complained that in its administration of the Territory, the United Kingdom had created such conditions that the Trusteeship led to its attachment to Nigeria instead of to the Republic of Cameroon. The United Kingdom objected to the jurisdiction of the Court. The Court dismissed objections relating to the non-existence of a dispute between the parties and non-compliance with its Rules, but found that it could not adjudicate upon the merits of Cameroon's claim. No decision on the merits could have any practical effect since, as had been recognized by Cameroon, no Judgment of the Court could affect the decisions of the General Assembly terminating the Trusteeship Agreement and providing for the attachment of the territory to Nigeria, in accordance with the results of a United Nations supervised plebiscite, nor could it give the United Kingdom any possibility of satisfying the Republic of Cameroon.

Barcelona Traction, Light and Power Company, Limited (New Application: 1962). As related in [Barcelona Traction, Light and

Power Company, Limited] above, the case instituted by Belgium against Spain on 23 September 1958, was removed from the Court's List on 10 April 1961. However, negotiations failed to produce a settlement and on 19 June 1962, Belgium submitted a new application. It asked the Court to adjudge and declare that Spain is under an obligation to Belgium to make reparation for the damage caused by the conduct of its organs to the Belgian shareholders of Barcelona Traction; and that such reparation should as far as possible annul all the consequences for Belgian nationals of the acts contrary to international law committed by the organs of the Spanish State. The Court was asked to determine the compensation to be paid by Spain to Belgium by reason of all the incidental damage suffered by Belgian nationals, and to declare that in the event of annulment of the consequences of the acts complained of proving impossible, Spain shall be under an obligation to pay compensation to Belgium amounting to 88 per cent of the value of the business on 12 February 1948, increased by an amount corresponding to all the incidental damage suffered by Belgian nationals. In March 1963, the Spanish Government filed preliminary objections and the proceedings on the merits were accordingly suspended. On 24 July 1964, the Court delivered a Judgment in which it rejected the first two preliminary objections raised by Spain and joined the other two to the merits. Public hearings in this case were held on April 15, 1969. Representatives of the Belgian Government and of the Spanish Government are in process of presenting the cases of these Governments. The proceedings on the merits were accordingly resumed.

North Sea Continental Shelf (Denmark/Federal Republic of Germany) (Federal Republic of Germany/Netherlands). On 20 February 1967, the Netherlands Minister for Foreign Affairs, as agreed among the States concerned, filed with the Court two Special Agreements, submitting to the Court differences which had arisen between the Federal Republic of Germany and the Netherlands concerning the delimitation, as between the respective parties, of the continental shelf in the North Sea. The Court was asked to decide what principles and rules of international law are applicable to the delimitation as between the parties of the areas of the continental shelf in the North Sea which appertain to each of them beyond partial boundaries determined by existing conventions. The respective parties to the two Special Agreements agreed to delimit the continental shelf between their countries in pursuance of the Court's decision. In two Orders by the Judge discharging the duties of President of the Court, 21 August 1967 was fixed as the time-limit for the filing of the Memorials of the Federal Republic of Germany and 20 February 1968 for the filing of the Counter-Memorials of Denmark and the Netherlands in the two cases. On 26 April 1968 the Court made an order in which it found Denmark and the Netherlands to be in the same interest, joined the proceedings in the two cases, and in modification of the directions given in two Orders of 1 March 1968 concerning the filing of Rejoinders by Denmark and the Netherlands, fixed 30 August 1968 as the time limit for the filing of a common Rejoinder by those two states. In the meantime *ad hoc* judges had been appointed by the parties, without objection of any party. Public hearings were opened on 23 October 1968 and *ad hoc* judges were immediately selected by the parties. On 20 February 1969, the International Court of Justice delivered judgement. According to a Communique of that date, the Court rejected the contention of Denmark and the Netherlands to the effect that the delimitations in question had to be carried out in accordance with the principle of equidistance as defined in Article 6 of the 1958 Geneva Convention of the Continental Shelf, holding: that the Federal Republic of Germany, which had not ratified the Convention, was not legally bound by the provisions of Article 6; that the equidistance principle was not a necessary consequence of the general concept of continental shelf rights, and was not a rule of customary international law. The Court also rejected the contentions of the Federal Republic of Germany in so far as these sought acceptance of the principle of an apportionment of the continental shelf into just and equitable shares. It held that each Party has an original right to those areas of the continental shelf which constituted the natural prolongation of its land territory into and under the sea. It was not a question of apportioning or sharing out those areas, but of delimiting them. The Court found that the boundary lines in question were to be drawn by agreement between the Parties and in accordance with equitable principles, and it indicated certain factors to be taken into consideration for that purpose. It is now for the Parties to negotiate on the basis of such principles, as they have agreed to do.

The following Advisory Opinions are summarized in the order in which they have been reported by the Court in U.N. publication *The International Court of Justice:*

Conditions of Admission of a State to Membership in the United Nations (Article 4 of the Charter). Since the creation of the United Nations some 12 states had unsuccessfully applied for admission. Their applications were rejected by the Security Council in consequence of a veto imposed by one or other of the states which are permanent members of the Council. A proposal was then made for the admission of all the candidates at the same time. The General Assembly referred the question to the Court. In the interpretation it gave of Article 4 of the Charter, in its advisory opinion of 28 May 1948, the Court declared that the conditions laid down for the admission of states were exhaustive and that if these conditions were fulfilled by a state which was a candidate, the Security Council ought to make the recommendation which would enable the General Assembly to decide upon the admission.

Competence of the General Assembly for the Admission of a State to the United Nations. The preceding opinion given by the Court did not lead to a settlement of the problem in the Security Council. A member of the United Nations then proposed that the word "recommendation" in Article 4 of the Charter should be construed as not necessarily signifying a favourable recommendation. In other words, a State might be admitted by the General Assembly even in the absence of a recommendation, this being interpreted as an unfavourable recommendation. This would, it was suggested make it possible to escape the effects of the veto. In the advisory opinion which the Court delivered on this subject on 3 March 1950, it pointed out that the Charter laid down two conditions for the admission of new members: a "recommendation" by the Security Council and a "decision" by the General Assembly. If the latter body had power to decide without a recommendation by the Security Council, the Council would be deprived of an important function assigned to it by the Charter. The absence of a recommendation by the Security Council as the result of a veto, could not be interpreted as an "unfavourable" recommendation, since the Council itself had interpreted its own decision as meaning that no recommendation had been made.

Reparation for Injuries Suffered in the Service of the United Nations. As a consequence of the assassinationa in Palestine of Count Bernadotte, the United Nations Palestine Mediator, and other members of the United Nations Missions to Palestine, the General Assembly asked the Court whether the United Nations had the capacity to bring an international claim against the State responsible with a view to obtaining reparation for damage caused to the Organization and to the victim. If this question were answered in the affirmative, it was further asked in what manner the action taken by the United Nations could be reconciled with such rights as might be possessed by the State of which the victim was a national. In its opinion of 11 April 1949, the Court held that the Organization was intended to exercise functions and rights which could only be explained on the basis of the possession of a large measure of international personality and the capacity to operate upon the international plane. It followed that the Organization had the capacity to bring a claim and to give it the character of an international action for reparation for the damage that had been caused to it. The Court further declared that the Organization can claim reparation not only in respect of damage caused to itself, but also in respect of damage suffered by the victim or persons entitled through him. Although according to the traditional rule, diplomatic protection had to be exercised by the national State, the Organization should be regarded in international law as possessing the powers which, even if they are not expressly essential in the Charter, are conferred upon the Organization as being essential to the discharge of its functions. The Organization may require to entrust its agents with important missions in disturbed parts of the world. In such cases, it is necessary that the agents should receive suitable support and protection. The Court therefore found that the Organization has the capacity to claim appropriate reparation, including also reparation for damage suffered by the victim or by persons entitled through him. The risk of possible competition between the Organization and the victim's national state could be eliminated either by means of a general convention or by a particular agreement in any individual case.

Interpretation of Peace Treaties with Bulgaria, Hungary and Romania. This case concerned the procedure to be adopted in regard to the settlement of disputes between the States signatories of the peace treaties of 1947 (Bulgaria, Hungary, Romania, on the one hand, and the Allied states, on the other). In the first opinion (30 March 1950), the Court stated that the countries which had signed a treaty providing an arbitral procedure for the settlement of disputes relating to the interpretation or application of the treaty were under an obligation to appoint their representatives to the arbitration commissions prescribed by the treaty.

Notwithstanding the opinion given on 30 March 1950, the three States, which had declined to appoint their representatives on the arbitration commissions, failed to modify their attitude. A time-limit was given to them within which to comply with the obligation laid down in the treaties as they had been interpreted by the Court. After the expiry of the time-limit, the Court was requested to say whether the Secretary-General, who, by the terms of the treaties, was authorized to appoint the third member of the arbitration commission in the absence of agreement between the parties in respect of this appointment, could proceed to make this appointment, even if one of the parties had failed to appoint its representative. In a further advisory opinion of 18 July 1950, the Court replied that this method could not be adopted since it would result in creating a commission of two members, whereas the treaty provided for a commission of three members, reaching its decision by a majority.

International Status of South West Africa. This advisory opinion, given on 11 July 1950, at the request of the General Assembly, was concerned with the determination of the legal status of the territory, the administration of which had been placed by the League of

Nations after the First World War under the mandate of the Union of South Africa. The League had disappeared, and with it the machinery for the supervision of the mandates. Moreover, the Charter of the United Nations did not provide that the former mandated territories should automatically come under trusteeship. The Court held that the dissolution of the League of Nations and its supervisory machinery had not entailed the lapse of the mandate, and that the mandatory power was still under an obligation to give an account of its administration to the United Nations, which was legally qualified to discharge the supervisory functions formerly exercised by the League of Nations. The degree of supervision to be exercised by the General Assembly should not, however, exceed that which applied under the mandates system and should conform as far as possible to the procedure followed in this respect by the Council of the League of Nations. On the other-hand, the mandatory power was not under an obligation to place the territory under trusteeship, although it might have certain political and moral duties in this connection. Finally, it had no competence to modify the international status of South West Africa unilaterally.

Voting Procedure on Questions relating to Reports and Petitions concerning the Territory of South West Africa. In the proceding advisory opinion, the Court considered that South West Africa had the status of a territory under international mandate and that the supervisory functions of the League of Nations were to be exercised by the United Nations. The degree of such supervision was not to exceed that which applied under the mandates system. On 11 October 1954, the General Assembly adopted a special Rule F on voting procedure to be followed by the General Assembly in taking decisions on questions relating to reports and petitions concerning the territory of South West Africa. According to this rule, such decisions were to be regarded as important questions within the meaning of Article 18, paragraph 2, of the United Nations Charter and would therefore require a two-thirds majority of members of the United Nations present and voting. In its advisory opinion of 7 June 1955, the Court considered that Rule F was a correct application of its earlier advisory opinion. It related only to procedure, and procedural matters were not material to the degree of supervision exercised by the General Assembly. Rule F could not therefore be considered as instituting a greater degree of supervision than applied under the mandates system. Moreover, the General Assembly was entitled to apply its own voting procedure and Rule F was in accord with the requirement that the supervision exercised by the General Assembly should conform as far as possible to the procedure followed by the Council of the League of Nations.

Admissibility of Hearings of Petitioners by the Committee on South West Africa. In this advisory opinion, of 1 June 1956, the

Court considered that it would be in accordance with its advisory opinion of 1950 on the international status of South West Africa for the Committee on South West Africa, established by the General Assembly, to grant oral hearings to petitioners on matters relating to the Territory of South West Africa if such a course was necessary for the maintenance of effective international supervision of the mandated territory. The General Assembly, which now carried out the supervisory functions formerly exercised by the Council of the League of Nations, was legally qualified to carry out an effective and adequate supervision of the administration of the mandated territory. Under the League of Nations, the relevant legal provisions made no reference to hearings and no hearings were in fact granted. The League Council would, however, have been competent to authorize such hearings. Although the degree of supervision to be exercised by the General Assembly should not exceed that which applied under the mandates system, the grant of hearings would not involve such an excess in the degree of supervision. Under the existing circumstances, the hearing of petitioners by the Committee on South West Africa might be in the interest of the proper working of the mandates system.

Reservations to the Convention on the Prevention and Punishment of the Crime of Genocide. In November 1950, the General General Assembly asked the Court a series of questions as to the position of a State which attached reservations to its signature of the multilateral Convention on Genocide if other states, signatories of the same convention, objected to these reservations.

The Court considered, in its opinion of 28 May 1951, that even if a convention contained no article on the subject of reservations, it did not follow that they were prohibited. The character of the convention, its purpose and its provisions must be taken into account. It was the compatibility of the reservation with the purpose of the convention which must furnish the criterion of the attitude of the state making the reservation, and of the state which objected thereto. The Court did not consider that it was possible to give an absolute answer to the abstract question put to it.

As regards the effects of the reservation in relations between states, the Court considered that a State could not be bound by a reservation to which it had not consented. Every State was therefore free to decide for itself whether the state which formulated the reservation was or was not a party to the convention. The situation presented real disadvantages, but they could only be remedied by the insertion in the convention of an article on the use of reservations.

A third question referred to the effects of an objection by a State which was not yet a party to the convention, either because it had not signed it or because it had signed but not ratified it.

The Court was of the opinion that, as regards the first case, it would be inconceivable that a State which had not signed the convention should be able to exclude another state from it. In the second case, the situation was different; the objection was valid, but it would not produce an immediate legal effect; it would merely express and proclaim the attitude which a signatory state would assume when it had become a party to the convention. In all the foregoing the Court adjudicated only on the specific case referred to it, namely, the Genocide Convention.

Effect of Awards of Compensation Made by the United Nations Administrative Tribunal. The United Nations Administrative Tribunal was established by the General Assembly to hear applications alleging non-observance of contracts of employment of staff members of the Secretariat of the United Nations or of the terms of appointment of such staff members. In its advisory opinion of 13 July 1954, the Court considered that the General Assembly of the United Nations was not entitled on any grounds to refuse to give effect to an award of compensation made by the United Nations Administrative Tribunal in favour of a staff member of the United Nations whose contract of service had been terminated without his assent. The Tribunal was an independent and truly judicial body pronouncing final judgments without appeal within the limited field of its functions and not merely an advisory or subordinate organ. Its judgments were therefore binding on the United Nations Organization and thus also on the General Assembly.

Judgments of the Administrative Tribunal of ILO upon Complaints Made Against UNESCO. The Statute of the Administrative Tribunal of ILO (the jurisdiction of which had been accepted by UNESCO for the purpose of settling certain disputes which might arise between the organization and its staff members) provided that the Tribunal's judgments should be final and without appeal subject to the right of the organization to challenge them on the ground, *inter alia*, that a decision of the Tribunal confirming its jurisdiction was wrong. It further provided that in the event of such a challenge, the question of the validity of the decision should be referred to the Court for an advisory opinion, which would be binding.

UNESCO alleged that four judgments given by the Tribunal in favour of staff members were invalid on the ground that the Tribunal had wrongly decided the question of its own jurisdiction. The organization contended that the staff members, who had held fixed-term appointments and who had complained of the Director-General's refusal to renew their contracts on expiry, had no legal right to such renewal, and that consequently the Tribunal had no jurisdiction, since it was competent only to hear complaints alleging non-observance of the terms of appointment of officials and of provisions of the Staff Regulations. It accordingly requested an advisory opinion of the Court.

The Court was of the opinion that an administrative memorandum which had announced that all holders of fixed-term contracts would, subject to certain conditions, be offered renewals, might reasonably be regarded as binding on the organization and that it was sufficient, to establish the jurisdiction of the Tribunal, that the complaints should appear to have a substantial and not merely artificial connexion with the terms and provisions invoked. The Court was not concerned with the decisions of the Tribunal on the merits. On the issue of jurisdiction, it expressed the opinion that the Administrative Tribunal had been competent to hear the complaints in question.

Constitution of the Maritime Safety Committee of the Inter-Governmental Maritime Consultative Organization. The Inter-Governmental Maritime Consultative Organization comprises, among other organs, an Assembly and a Maritime Safety Committee. Under the terms of article 28(a) of the Convention for the establishment of the organization, the Committee consists of 14 members elected by the Assembly from the members of the organization having an important interest in maritime safety, "of which not less than eight shall be the largest ship-owning nations." When, on 15 January 1959, the Assembly, for the first time, proceeded to elect the members of the Committee, it elected neither Liberia nor Panama, although those two States were among the eight members of the Inter-Governmental Maritime Consultative Organization which possessed the largest registered tonnage. Subsequently, the Assembly decided to ask the Court whether the Maritime Safety Committee was constituted in accordance with the convention for the establishment of the organization. In its advisory opinion of 8 June 1960, the Court replied to this question in the negative.

Certain Expenses of the United Nations. Article 17, paragraph 2, of the Charter of the United Nations provides that "the expenses of the Organization shall be borne by the Members as apportioned by the General Assembly." On 20 December 1961, the General Assembly adopted a resolution requesting an advisory opinion on whether the expenditures authorized by it relating to United Nations operations in the Congo and to the operations of the United Nations Emergency Force in the Middle East constituted "expenses of the Organization" within the meaning of this Article and paragraph of the Charter. The Court in its advisory opinion of 20 July 1962, replied in the affirmative that these expenditures were "expenses of the United Nations." The Court pointed out that under article 17, paragraph 2, of the Charter "the expenses of the Organization" are the amounts paid out to defray the costs of carrying out the purposes of the Organization. After examining the resolutions authorizing the expenditures in question the Court concluded that they were so incurred. The Court also analyzed the principal arguments which had been advanced against the conclusion that these expenditures should be considered as "expenses of the Organization" and found these arguments to be unfounded.

§ 4-5. An Appraisal of the Work of the International Court of Justice.

There is no lack of potential business for the International Court of Justice on the side of adjudication, to say nothing of its additional function as adviser on legal questions to the General Assembly, the Security Council and other UN organs and agencies. Thus, failure to use the International Court of Justice cannot be blamed on a lack of justiciable disputes. Indeed, the number of such disputes continues to grow in direct proportion to the rapid development of international organizations and to the countless bilateral and multilateral treaties being negotiated daily. Nor can failure to utilize the Court be blamed on criticism of the past performance of either the present judges or those of the Permanent Court of International Justice. Neither Court has ever been tainted by charges of irresponsibility. In fact, the opposite is true. Jurists from every legal system have continually praised the Court's decisions, results and contributions to the progressive development of the international judicial process.

In spite of the favorable record of the International Court of Justice, critical review of the Statute and Rules of the Court has been undertaken with a view towards identifying and correcting some of the problems which have developed due to changes in the international community. The procedures of the Court should perhaps be amended to facilitate the prosecution of claims, and the jurisdiction of the Court should be expanded to cover individuals as well as states.[46]

The failure of the organs and agencies of the United Nations to make more frequent requests for advisory opinions on legal questions is attributed by some observers to a feeling on the part of the members of these organs that law has little relevance to the problems

---

[46] C. JENKS, THE COMMON LAW OF MANKIND (London 1958); A. LARSON, WHY NATIONS DISAGREE (Louisiana 1961); Potter, *Legal Aspects of the Situation in Korea*, 44 AJIL 709-13 (1950); Potter, *Principal Legal and Political Problems Involved in the Kashmir Case*, 44 AJIL 361-63 (1950); Wright, *Some Legal Aspects of the Berlin Crisis*, 55 AJIL 956-65 (1961).

The Court is presently considering a draft revision of the Rules on the basis of a report submitted to it by a Committee of five of its members. It had become evident that it was desirable to adapt the Rules adopted in 1946 to recent transformations.

involved in the maintenance of international peace and security under existing conditions. International law experts have pointed out in their writings and speeches that several factors have seriously limited the Court's growth and effectiveness.

1. *Its Inaccessibility*—It is claimed that states are reluctant to litigate before the ICJ because of the great cost of transporting counsel, witnesses, and others to The Hague.[47]

2. *Diverse Background of the Judges*—Observers have maintained that it is unrealistic to expect parties to a dispute representing one or even two legal systems to consent to adjudication by judges coming from legal, political and cultural systems which are foreign, and in some cases even hostile, to their own.[48] This objection is made even though judges from the disputing states may be serving on the Court, and other judges may have the same legal traditions.

3. *Inadequate Representation of Legal Systems and Geographic Areas*—Some states, especially in Africa and Asia, maintain that they are not well represented on the Court.[49] This condition, however, has been alleviated by the election of judges from Senegal, Nigeria, the Philippines, and Pakistan.

4. *Uncertainty of Law Applied*—Many writers have emphasized that the Court has not been used as much as it could because international law has many gaps;[50] its sources are not clearly defined and readily available; and that interpretations of some of its principles have not been uniform.[51]

5. *Jurisdiction of the ICJ*—Many states have accepted the jurisdiction of the ICJ only with reservations, because of an apparent fear that the Court may exceed what these states consider to be the Court's proper jurisdiction, for example, by interfering in their "domestic jurisdiction," notably the United States in its Connally Amendment, thereby seriously impairing the principle of compulsory jurisdiction.[52] Under the Connally Amendment the United

---

[47] Harvey, *Work Papers - Summary on Existing and Proposed International Courts,* in WASHINGTON CONF. 119-28 (1965).

[48] *Id.* at 122.

[49] *Id.* at 121.

[50] *Id. See also* Deutsch, *A Plan for Reconstruction of the International Court of Justice,* 49 A.B.A.J. 537 (1963).

[51] *Id.* at 120.

[52] *Id.*

States reserves to itself the decision in each case as to whether the case involves "domestic" or international questions.[53]

---

[53] Despite the Connally Amendment, the United States has nevertheless ratified 28 international treaties, 4 Geneva Conventions, and 21 bilateral treaties providing for the compulsory jurisdiction of the International Court of Justice over a dispute that is not settled first by other means of negotiation. These include the following:

I. Multilateral

Protocol on military obligations in certain cases of double nationality, *conlcuded* at The Hague, April 12, 1930 (50 Stat. 1317; TS 913).

Convention for limiting the manufacture and regulation of narcotic drugs, *concluded* at Geneva, July 13, 1931 (48 Stat. 1543; TS 863).

Convention on international civil aviation (ICAO), *opened for signature* at Chicago December 7, 1944 (61 Stat. 1180; TIAS 1591).

Constitution of the Food and Agriculture Organization of the United Nations (FAO), *signed* at Quebec October 16, 1945 as amended (1950) (60 Stat. 1886; TIAS 1554; 12 U.S.T. 980; TIAS 4803

Constitution of the United Nations Educational, Scientific, and Cultural Organization (UNESCO), *concluded* at London November 16, 1945 (61 Stat. 2495; TIAS 1580.

Convention on the privileges and immunities of the United Nations, *adopted* by the UN General Assembly February 13, 1946 (1 U.N.T.S. 16).

Constitution of the World Health Organization (WHO), *opened for signature* at New York July 22, 1946 (62 Stat. (3) 2679; TIAS 180).

Instrument for the amendment of the constitution of the International Labor Organization (ILO), *dated* at Montreal October 9, 1946 (62 Stat. 3485; TIAS 1868).

Convention on Road Traffic, *dated* at Geneva September 19, 1949 (3 U.S.T. 3008; TIAS 2487).

International Sanitary Regulations (WHO Regulations No. 2), *adopted* by the Fourth World Assembly at Geneva May 25, 1951 (7 U.S.T. 2255; TIAS 3625).

Treaty of Peace with Japan, *signed* at San Francisco September 8, 1951 (3 U.S.T. 3169; TIAS 2490).

Universal copyright convention, *dated* at Geneva September 6, 1952 (6 U.S.T. 2731; TIAS 3324).

Constitution of the Intergovernmental Committee for European Migration (ICEM) (6 U.S.T. 603; TIAS 3197).

Protocol amending the slavery convention of September 25, 1926 (46 Stat. 2183; TS 778), *opened for signature* at New York December 7, 1953 (7 U.S.T. 479; TIAS 3532).

Protocol limiting and regulating the cultivation of the poppy plant and the production of, and international and wholesale trade in, and use of opium, *opened for signature* at New York from June 23 to December 31, 1953 (14 U.S.T. 10; TIAS 5273).

International convention for the prevention of pollution of the sea by oil, *signed* at London May 12, 1954 (12 U.S.T. 2989; TIAS 4900).

Supplementary convention on the abolition of slavery, the slave trade, and institutions and practices similar to slavery. *Done* at Geneva September 7, 1956 (18 U.S.T. 3201; TIAS 6418).

Statute of the International Atomic Energy Agency, *done* at New York October 26, 1956 (8 U.S.T. 1093; TIAS 3875).

The Antarctic Treaty, *signed* at Washington December 1, 1959 (12 U.S.T. 794; TIAS 4780).

Constitution of the International Rice Commission as amended at Saigon November 19, 1960 (13 U.S.T. 2403; TIAS 5204).

Agreement for establishment of the Indo-Pacific Fisheries Council as *amended* at Karachi January 6-23, 1961 (13 U.S.T. 2511; TIAS 5218).

(Continued)

Perhaps the greatest barrier to full acceptance of the International Court of Justice is the erroneous assumption that it will assume non-law jurisdiction to resolve all the world's ills. The

Agreement for facilitating the international circulation of visual and auditory materials of an educational, scientific and cultural character, *done* at Lake Success July 15, 1949 (TIAS 6116, 17 U.S.T. 1578).

Convention on the settlement of investment disputes between states and nationals of other states, done at Washington March 18, 1965 (17 U.S.T. 1270; TIAS 6090).

Single convention on narcotic drugs, 1961, *done* at New York March 30, 1961 (TIAS 6298; 18 U.S.T. 1407).

Protocol relating to the status of refugees. *Done* at New York January 31, 1967 (TIAS 6577; 19 U.S.T. 6223).

Optional protocol to the Vienna convention on consular relations concerning the compulsory settlement of disputes. *Done* at Vienna April 24, 1963 (TIAS 6820; 21 U.S.T.).

Convention on offences and certain other acts committed on board aircraft. *Done* at Tokyo September 14, 1963 (20 U.S.T. 2941; TIAS 6768).

Convention of Paris for the protection of industrial property of March 20, 1883, as revised. *Done* at Stockholm July 14, 1967. U.S. instrument of ratification of Articles 13 through 30 deposited May 25, 1970. Articles 13 through 30 will enter into force for U.S. three months after date of notification by Director General of BIRPI of deposit. Articles 1-12 not in force for the United States.

II. Geneva Conventions

Geneva Convention relating to the Condition of the Wounded and Sick of the Armed Forces in the Field (6 U.S.T. 3114; TIAS 3362).

Geneva Convention relating to the Condition of the Wounded, Sick or Shipwrecked Members of the Armed Forces at Sea (6 U.S.T. 3217; TIAS 3363).

Geneva Convention relating to the Treatment of Prisoners of War (6 U.S.T. 3316; TIAS 3364).

Geneva Convention relating to the Protection of Civilian Persons in Time of War (6 U.S.T. 3516; TIAS 3365).

III. Bilateral

    A. Commercial Treaties with:

Belgium	Feb. 21, 1961	14 U.S.T. 1284; TIAS 5432
China	Nov. 4, 1946	63 Stat. (2) 1299; TIAS 1871
Denmark	Oct. 1, 1951	12 U.S.T. 908, TIAS 4797
Ethiopia	Sept. 7, 1951	4 U.S.T. 2134; TIAS 2864
France	Nov. 25, 1959	11 U.S.T. 2398, TIAS 4625
Germany, F.R.	Oct. 29, 1954	7 U.S.T. 1839; TIAS 3593
Greece	Aug. 3, 1951	5 U.S.T. (2) 1829; TIAS 3057
Iran	Aug. 15, 1955	8 U.S.T. 899; TIAS 3853
Ireland	Jan. 21, 1950	1 U.S.T. 785; TIAS 2155
Israel	Aug. 23, 1951	5 U.S.T. 550; TIAS 2948
Italy	Feb. 2, 1948	63 Stat. (2) 2255; TIAS 1965
Japan	Apr. 2, 1953	4 U.S.T. 2063; TIAS 2863
Korea	Nov. 28, 1956	8 U.S.T. 2217; TIAS 3947
Luxembourg	Feb. 23, 1962	14 U.S.T. 261; TIAS 5306
Netherlands	Mar. 27, 1956	8 U.S.T. 2043; TIAS 3942
Nicaragua	Jan. 21, 1956	9 U.S.T. 449; TIAS 4024
Pakistan	Nov. 12, 1959	12 U.S.T. 110; TIAS 4683
Togo	Feb. 8, 1966	TIAS 6193; 18 U.S.T. 1
Viet-Nam	Apr. 3, 1961	12 U.S.T. 1703, TIAS 4890

    B. Other Bilateral Agreements

Treaty with Canada relating to cooperative development of water resources of the Columbia River Basin, Jan. 17, 1961 (15 U.S.T. 1555; TIAS 5638).

Consular Convention with Korea, Jan. 8, 1963 (14 U.S.T. 1637; TIAS 5469).

great social, economic and security questions which dominate the world community and control mankind's future such as population control, technological, scientific, and other aid for under-developed nations, arms control or disarmament, are not "law questions" for the Court. The opposition in the United States to the elimination of the so-called Connally self-judging reservation prohibiting full acceptance of the Court's jurisdiction is based on this fear. This fear that enormous policy and political non-law questions will be decided by the Court is clearly erroneous. Under the Court's Statute they are beyond the Court's jurisdiction. As its decisions clearly establish, the Court has been extremely careful to confine itself to jurisdiction over law matters which are specifically spelled out in that Statute. Not once has the Court or its predecessor, been charged by any responsible critic with exceeding its jurisdiction. Some responsible critics have indeed charged the Court with timidity in the opposite direction. And, if the Court were ever to be so rash as to exceed its jurisdiction, such a decision could hardly command the application of even the rather weak enforcement procedures now in existence for the Court's decisions.

The Court should be fully accepted for what it is, i.e., a very limited agency which can decide international law disputes, a function which its record to date proves that it has done, and will do, with great competence.

Many efforts have been made to enhance the usefulness of the International Court of Justice. The UN Secretary-General has declared that he would do everything in his power to assist the Court to make its maximum contribution to the cause of world peace, and members of the Court have made suggestions for enhancing the Court's usefulness and for obtaining wider recognition of its status.

§ 4-6. Regional and Specialized Courts.[54]

The concept of regionalism in international juridical organization, briefly encouraged by the 10-year existence of the Central American Court of Justice prior to World War I, has become a significant factor in the development of peaceful means of resolving international legal disputes since the end of World War II. The experience of the highly successful European Court of Justice and of Human Rights has sparked new interest among lawyers throughout the world in the possible usefulness of such courts. Proposals have

---

[54] Munir, *Regional and Specialized Courts*, in ATHENS CONF. 219-33; Sotela, *Establishment and Use of the Regional and Specialized Courts*, in *id.* at 245-49.

been made for the creation of several regional international courts, and for specialized courts to apply and interpret certain multilateral conventions. These proposals all require careful consideration in their relations to the International Court of Justice.

It has been argued that coexistence of regional courts and a world court would risk jurisdictional conflicts, prejudice the unity and universality of international law, and tend to undermine the supremacy of the International Court of Justice. To protect against the risk of jurisdictional conflicts, proper arrangements for advance coordination of the creation of regional courts, suitable limitation of their jurisdiction by the terms of their constituent instrument, and careful definition in these instruments of their status in relation to the International Court should be enacted. The unity and universality of international law and the supremacy of the International Court could be maintained by provisions in the statutes of new regional courts providing that appeal from the regional court could be made to the International Court and that the law to be applied by the regional courts would be the same as that prescribed for the International Court of Justice.

Proponents of regional courts assert that the establishment of regional courts would obviate some of the frequent objections to the International Court of Justice. States, reluctant to take their cases to the International Court because of the expense and inconvenience involved, might litigate much more readily before a regional court. In a regional court, states would find no lack of representation of their legal systems, cultures or geographical areas. Moreover, there is no inherent conflict in the coexistence of regional courts and the International Court of Justice. Cases of dominantly regional interests and importance would be taken to the regional courts with appeal to the International Court, while cases involving states outside of the local region could be taken directly to the International Court.

As an alternative to a separate international regional court, such as the European Court of Justice, it has been suggested that chambers of the International Court of Justice might sit in areas where it would seem advantageous to have some sort of regional court. Articles 26 to 29 of the Statute of the International Court, by providing for Chambers, could be used to facilitate their possible use as regional courts. Chambers could be used for special categories of cases, for particular cases, or for summary judgment. The use of chambers of the International Court of Justice as regional courts would facilitate the consistent development of a truly universal body of law. They would serve only upon request of the parties and with their consent to its jurisdiction. To date, no case has been submitted to special chambers.

The value of specialized courts has been well illustrated by the success of the European Court of Justice which was established for the express purpose of administering three treaties of the Coal and Steel Community, the Economic Community, and the Atomic Energy Community. Regional and specialized courts would have limited jurisdiction, in contrast with the broad general jurisdiction possessed by the International Court of Justice. They could resolve disputes arising under the Agreement on Tariffs and Trade, the International Coffee Agreement, and other important multilateral conventions.

The Consensuses of the four Continental Conferences on World Peace Through Law, in 1961 and 1962, recommended four major types of judicial machinery: Regional international courts, with the right of appeal to the International Court of Justice; regional international courts, with the same broad jurisdiction as the International Court of Justice and having no right of appeal; regional chambers of the International Court of Justice, operating under the jurisdiction of that Court and with right of appeal to the full Court; and, for technical matters, specialized tribunals, established by international agreements and without the right of appeal.

The Consensus of San Jose (at the American Conference on World Peace Through Law) recommended "That a Supreme Court of Justice for the Americas be created with jurisdiction over all subjects of international law and international matters" (Art. VI), and "That to ensure uniformity on matters of international law, appeals from the Supreme Court of Justice for the Americas should be allowed to the International Court of Justice" (Art. VII).[55] The Consensus of Tokyo adopted at the similar Asian Conference recommended,

> That there be established a global system of regional chambers of the International Court of Justice from which appeals to the full court would be permissible (Art. VI),
>
> That there be established an Asian court of justice with a carefully drafted jurisdiction over matters of regional concern (Art. VII), and
>
> That efforts be made to establish a series of specialized international courts and tribunals to operate under agreement reached

---

[55] A.B.A., *Consensus of San José*, in Document, AMERICAN CONFERENCE ON WORLD PEACE THROUGH THE RULE OF LAW (1961).

between nations having a common interest in matters specifically assigned to their jurisdiction. These matters could include, among other things, trade in certain vital commodities or other items; international investment, public or private; water rights and related problems; and international economic activities, carried on through United Nations and international organizations (Art. XIII).[56]

§ 4-6.1. **The Central American Court of Justice.**[57] The first permanently constituted international judicial body to sit in judgment of disputes between nations as municipal tribunals do in individual disputes, the Central American Court of Justice was constituted by the General Treaty of Peace and Amity,[58] signed in Washington, D.C. on December 20, 1907, by the Central American Republics of Nicaragua, Costa Rica, Honduras, Guatemala and El Salvador. The Court was formally inaugurated on May 25, 1908 at its seat in Cartago, Costa Rica.

The Convention creating the Court of Justice was one of several negotiated in Washington to resolve the many disputes and controversies that had plagued the Central American Republics since the dissolution of the Federation to which they belonged during the early part of the 19th Century. The United States and Mexico invited the five nations to Washington for the purpose of negotiating conventions and protocols designed to keep the peace. A Court of Justice was proposed and accepted in principle by the partici-

---

[56] W.P.T.L.C., WORKING PAPERS OF ASIAN CONFERENCES (Tokyo Sept. 17-20, 1961).

[57] See J. ANCHISI CÁCERES, LA CORTE DE JUSTICIA CENTROAMERICANA (Guatemala 1951); Anderson, *The Peace Conference of Central America*, 2 AJIL 144-52 (1908); CORTE DE JUSTICIA CENTROAMERICANA, ANALES (San José, Costa Rica); Dennis, *Pacific Settlement and Pan American Court of Justice*, 21 AJIL 137-45 (1928); J. EYMA, LA COUR DE JUSTICE CENTROAMERICAINE (Paris 1928); C. Fenwick, LA CORTE DE JUSTICIA CENTROAMERICANA: CINCUENTENARIO DE SU CREACIÓN (Washington 1957); Ed. Comment, *The First Case Before the Central American Court of Justice*, 2 AJIL 835-42 (1908); Gomez Reinoso, *El Tribunal de Justicia Interamericana . . .*, REVISTA DE DERECHO INTERNACIONAL 119-24 (Havana 1943); Gutierrez, *La Corte de Justicia Centroamericana*, REV. COL. AB. URU. 261-402 (San José, Costa Rica 1949); Hudson, *Central American Court of Justice*, 26 AJIL 759-87 (1933); E. MARTIN, LA LABOR DEL PACIFISMO Y LA CORTE DE JUSTICIA CENTROAMERICANA . . . (San José, Costa Rica 1908); A. MORENO, LA CONFERENCIA DE WASHINGTON DE 1907 Y LA CORTE DE JUSTICIA CENTROAMERICANA (San Salvador 1957); Sanabria, *Inter-American Court of Justice*, in ATHENS CONF. 240-45; J. SCOTT, THE INTER-AMERICAN TRIBUNAL OF INTERNATIONAL JUSTICE (Washington 1937); Scott, *The Central American Peace Conference of 1907*, 2 AJIL 121-44 (1908); Scott, *The Closing of the Central American Court of Justice*, 12 AJIL 380-82 (1918); Sotela, *Inter-American Court of Justice*, in WASH. CONF. 143-54 (1967); I. Zanotti, Judicial Settlement of Inter-American Legal Disputes, 1958 (unpublished thesis in American University library, Washington, D.C.

[58] For text of Treaty, see 2 AJIL Supp. 231 (1908).

pating nations, and the details were worked out during the succeeding sessions of the Peace Conference.

The agreement contained the following provision, quoted below in part:

> Article 1. The High Contracting Parties . . . To constitute and maintain a permanent tribunal which shall be called the "Central American Court of Justice" to which they bind themselves to submit all controversies or questions which may arise among them, of whatsoever nature and no matter what their origin may be, in case the respective Departments of Foreign Affairs should not have been able to reach an understanding.

In addition to states, individuals were permitted to press claims before the Court if the claimant had exhausted the local remedies available within a state against which a claim was made, or if a "denial of justice" existed (Article 2). The Court through special agreement could also hear claims involving a state party to the Convention and a non-signatory power (Article 3).

The Central American Court was composed of five judges. Each nation selected one judge for a term of five years and was responsible for paying the salary of the judge so elected, besides paying an annual contribution to the expenses of the Court. In addition, each state elected two substitute judges to sit in event of illness or other forced absence of the regular judge. The Court was established for a 10-year period with provisions for renewal of the Convention under which it was established.

Article 18 stipulated that the Court could take such interim measures as were deemed necessary to protect a claimant. Article 21 stated that the Court must apply international law, but it did not refer to the sources of that law. The right to hear cases *ex aequo et bono* was not conferred on the Court. Decisions, including dissenting opinions, were to be written and signed by each judge (Article 29). During its 10-year existence the Court heard 10 cases, five during the first five years, and five during the second five-year period. Briefly summarized, those cases were as follows:

> *Honduras and Nicaragua v. Guatemala and El Salvador.*[59] In this case the Court took the initiative in bringing the parties before it upon information presented by Costa Rica summarizing charges by Honduras that peace was threatened by revolutionaries from Guatemala and El Salvador active in fomenting revolt in Honduras and illegally crossing the border. The Court's decision absolved the respondents.

[59] December 19, 1908, 3 AJIL 434-36, 729-36 (1909).

Diaz v. Guatemala.[60] In this case, Diaz, a national of Nicaragua, alleged false imprisonment and arrest at the hands of Guatemala officials. The Court held that it could not take jurisdiction because the plaintiff failed to exhaust local remedies available in Guatemala.

1910 Revolt in Nicaragua.[61] During the Estrada revolt in Nicaragua the Court offered to mediate, and through its President sent a draft of a proposed agreement to settle the dispute to the two factions. This was rejected by both sides and the Court of Justice took no further action.

Salvador Cerda v. Costa Rica.[62] Plaintiff, a national of Nicaragua, alleged a denial of justice in Costa Rica based upon the "equal rights of Citizens of Central America" provision in the Conventions. The Court did not take jurisdiction because plaintiff failed to exhaust his local remedies. Costa Rica did not defend the charges.

1912 Revolt in Nicaragua.[63] Essentially the same situation as in the 1910 revolt, and the Court again was unsuccessful in attempts at mediation.

Felipe Molena Larios v. Honduras.[64] Plaintiff, a national of Nicaragua, alleged illegal arrest and mistreatment by officials in Honduras. The Court did not take jurisdiction on grounds that the plaintiff failed to exhaust local remedies. Honduras did not appear to defend the charges.

Election of President Gonzales Flores of Costa Rica.[65] Five individuals from each of the Central American Republics asked the Court to overturn the election of Flores and authorize new elections under the incumbent, alleging that the previous election was fraudulently conducted.

The Court held that the claim was inadmissible because interference in the internal affairs of Costa Rica would result if it took jurisdiction.

Alijandro Bernudez y Nunez v. Costa Rica.[66] Claimant alleged mistreatment at the hands of Costa Rica officials, and that he had been subjected to illegal explusion. The Court held in a 3 to 2 decision that the claimant failed to exhaust local remedies. The dissent accepted claimant's position that since he could not re-enter Costa Rica there was no way of exhausting such remedies.

---

[60] March 6, 1909, 3 AJIL 737-47 (1909).
[61] 1 Anales de la Corte de Justicia Centroamericana 146-64 (1911).
[62] 1 Anales de la Corte de Justicia Centroamericana 199-214, 357-60 (1911).
[63] 2 Anales de la Corte de Justicia Centroamericana 129-50, 185-92 (1912).
[64] 3 Anales de la Corte de Justicia Centroamericana 26-67 (1913).
[65] 4 Anales de la Corte de Justicia Nos. 9-11, 1-119 (1914).
[66] 4 Anales de la Corte de Justicia Centroamericana Nos. 11-13, 1-12 (1914).

Costa Rica v. Nicaragua.[67] This case was undoubtedly one of the most important heard by the Court, and coupled with the succeeding case involving the same issues, eventually led to Nicaragua's unwillingness to renew the Convention establishing the Court, causing the Court's dissolution upon expiration of the 10-year term.

In the Bryan-Chamorro Treaty between the United States and Nicaragua, in exchange for $3,000,000 Nicaragua conferred on the United States the right to construct a canal across Nicaragua and to establish a naval base at the Gulf of Fonseca. Costa Rica asserted her riparian rights on the San Juan River, alleging that the canal would infringe on those rights. For that reason the Costa Rica government asked that the Treaty be held invalid. The Court decided against Nicaragua, and accepted the view of Costa Rica. The Nicaraguan judge, filing the lone dissent, alleged that the Court exceeded its power by invalidating the Treaty.

El Salvador v. Nicaragua.[68] Essentially the same situation existed in this case as in Costa Rica v. Nicaragua except the rights affected were those of El Salvador in the Gulf of Fonseca. Again the Court decided against Nicaragua. This ultimately led to Nicaragua's refusal to renew the Convention. Consequently, the Court was dissolved on March 17, 1918.[69]

The experiences of the Central American Court were of significant value to the drafters of the Statute of Permanent Court of International Justice.[70] Thus, for example, greater steps were taken towards assuring the independence of judges appointed to the later Permanent Court of International Justice because many felt that one of the weaknesses of the Central American Court was the fact that each judge served essentially as a representative of his country since he was both elected and paid by his government.

§ 4-6.2. The Court of Justice of the European Communities.[71]

This Court serves the three European Communities formed by

---

[67] September 30, 1916, 5 Anales de la Corte de Justicia Centroamericana 87-103, 122-228 (1915); 11 AJIL 181 (1917).

[68] 6 Anales de la Corte Justicia Centroamericana 96-170 (1916-1917); 1916 United States Foreign Relations 853; 11 AJIL 621 (1917).

[69] *International Judicial Machinery* in A.B.A. Documents: the Asian & Australian Conference on World Peace Through the Rule of Law 27-30 (1961). *See also* M. HUDSON, PERMANENT COURT OF INTERNATIONAL JUSTICE 52-62 (New York 1943).

[70] M. HUDSON, *id.*

[71] The Court is located at 12 Rue de la Côte d'Eich, Luxembourg. *See generally* Adler, *The E.E.C. Court of Justice,* 7 CAN. B.J. 102-27 (1964); A. ANDRÉ, BEWEISFÜHRING UND BEWEISLAST IM VERFAHREN VOR DEM GERICHTSHOF DER EUROPÄISCHEN GEMEINSCHAFTEN (Carl Reymanns 1966); G. BEBR, JUDICIAL CONTROL OF THE EUROPEAN COMMUNITIES (New York 1962); G. Bebr. *Protection of Private Interests Under the European Coal and Steel Community,* 42 VA. L.REV. 879 (1956); L. BRINK-
(Continued)

Belguim, France, Germany, Italy, Luxembourg and the Netherlands. By separate treaties those six nations have formed the European Coal and Steel Community, the European Economic Community

HORST, THE RULES OF PROCEDURE OF THE COURT OF JUSTICE OF THE EURO-PEAN COMMUNITIES (Leyden 1962); Campbell, *Three Decisions of the Court of Justice*, 59 L. SOC. GAZ. 653-56 (1962); Cohn, *Aspects of the Procedure Before the Court of Justice of the European Communities*, 1 SOL. Q. 309-19 (1962); CCH COMM. MKT. REP. (Chicago)—gives a survey of the literature on the law of the European Communities and a listing of cases before the Court of Justice of the European Communities; COUR DE JUSTICE DE LA COMMUNAUTÉ EUROPÉENE DU CHARBON ET DE L'ACIER, RECUEIL DE LA JURISPRUDENCE DE LA COUR (Luxembourg 1954-) (for summaries of cases see AJIL and ANN. DIG.); Donner, *The Court of Justice of the European Communities*, INT'L & COMP. L.Q., Supp. Pub. No. 1, at 66-75 (1961); Donner, *The European Court of Justice*, 59 L. SOC. GAZ. 444-48 (1962); Donner, *National Law and the Case Law of the Court of Justice of the European Communities*, 1 COMM. MKT. L. REV. 8-16 (1963); Donner, *Les Rapports Entre la Compétence de la Cour des Communautes Européennes et Les Tribunaux Internes*, 115 RECUEIL DES COURS 5-58 (1965); EURO-PEAN COMMUNITY COURT OF JUSTICE, BIBLIOGRAPHIE ZU EUROPÄISCHEN RECHTSPRECHUNG BETREFEND DIE ENTSCHEIDUNG ZU DEN VERTRAGEN ÜBER DIE GRUNDING DER EUROPÄISCHEN GEMEINSCHAFTEN (1965); W. FELD, THE COURT OF THE EUROPEAN COMMUNITIES: NEW DIMENSIONS IN INTERNA-TIONAL ADJUDICATION (The Hague 1965); Feld, *The Judges of the Court of Justice of the European Communities*, 9 VILL. L. REV. 37-58 (1963); Feld, *The Court of Justice of the European Communities: Emerging Political Power? An Examination of Selected Decisions of the Court's 1961-1962 Term*, 38 TUL. L. REV. 53-80 (1963); Feld, *The Significance of the Court of Justice of the European Communities*, 39 N.D. L. REV. 35-49 (1963); Feld, *The European Community Court: Its Role in the Federalizing Process*, 50 MINN. L.REV. 423-42 (1966); Gaudet. *The Court of Justice of the European Communities*, in ATHENS CONF. 203-17 (1965); Goerens, *The Benelux Court of Justice*, in *id.* at 218-19 (1965); H. GOLSONG, DAS RECHSCHUTZSYSTEM DER EUROPAISCHEN MENSCHENRECHTSKONVENTION (Carlsruhe 1958); Gormley, *The Procedural Status of the Individual Before Supranational Judicial Tribunals*, 41 U. DET. L.J. 282-340, 405-46 (1964); Gormley, *The Significant Role of French Administrative Jurisprudence as Presently Applied by the Court of the European Communities, with Emphasis on the Administrative Law Remedies Available to Private Litigants*, 8 S.D. L.REV. 32-77 (1963); Herzog, *Procedure Before the Court of Justice of the European Communities*, 41 WASH. L. REV. 438-88 (1966); Knaub, *La Procédure devant la Cour de Justice des Communautés Européennes*, 3 REV. TR. DR. EUR. 269-318 (1967); Kheitmi, *La Fonction Consultative de la Cour de Justice des Communautés Européennes*, *id.* at 553-94, 759-78; Kovar, *Le Droit des Personnes Privées à Obtenir devant la Cour des Communautés le Respect par les Etats Membres du Droit Communautaire*, 12 ANN. FR. DR. INT'L 509-43 (1966); Lagrance, *Role of the Court of Justice of the European Community*, 26 L. & CONTEMP. PROB. 400-17 (1961); Lecourt, *Note on the Comparison Between the Court of Justice of the European Communities and the International Courts*, in WASHINGTON CONF. 128-130; Lloyd, *The Court of Justice of the European Economic Community*, 16 CUR. L. PROB. 34-53 (1963); Looper, *The Jurisdiction of the Court of Justice of the European Communities To Annul Executive Action*, 36 BR. Y.B. INT'L L. 174-223 (1960); Lorenz, *General Principles of Law: Their Elaboration in the Court of Justice of the European Communities*, 13 AM. J. COMP. L. 1-29 (1964); Lorenz, *General Principles of Law: Their Elaboration in the Court of Justice of the European Community*, in THE AMERICAN JOURNAL OF LAW READER: THE EUROPEAN COMMUNITY 458-75 (H. Yntema ed., New York 1966); W. McCLURE, WORLD LEGAL ORDER 231-34 (Chapel Hill 1960); McMahon, *The Court of the European Communities*, BR. Y.B. INT'L L. 320-51 (1961); McMahon, *The Court of the European Communities*, 1 J. COMM. M. STUD.

(Continued)

(Common Market), and the European Atomic Energy Community (Euratom). The establishment of this Court on October 7, 1958, marked one of the most significant developments in the expansion of international judicial institutions in the past decade. It should be noted that the Court exists for the Communities and not to resolve all disputes which may arise between the member states. Thus, it does not attempt to perform the functions of the International Court of Justice in the latter regard. The law applied by the European Court of Justice, with certain exceptions, is the law of the treaties which created the Communities, rather than municipal for international law.

According to Article 164 of the Treaty establishing the European Economic Community,[72] the Court of Justice was established to "ensure observance of law and justice in interpretation of . . . 'the treaty'." Similar provisions are found in the Coal and Steel Community[73] and the Euratom[74] treaties. The Court, therefore, is an institution common to all three Communities.

1-21 (1962); Opsahl, *National Courts and the Community Court Under Article 177 of the E.E.C. Treaty*, in LEGAL ESSAYS: A TRIBUTE TO FREDE CASTBERG ON THE OCCASION OF HIS 70TH BIRTHDAY (Oslo 1963); V. PELLICIER, LA JURISDICCIÓN DEL TRIBUNAL DE JUSTICIA DE LA COMUNIDADES EUROPEAS (Madrid 1965); Pettiti, *The European Court of Justice*, in ATHENS CONF. 236-39; Reuter, *The Rule of Law of the European Coal and Steel Community*, 80 J. DR. INT'L 5 (1953); Riesenfeld, *The Decisions of the Court of Justice of the European Communities*, 56 AJIL 724-28 (1962); Riphagen, *The Case Law of the European Coal and Steel Court of Justice*, 2 NETH. INT'L L. REV. 384 (1955); Scheingold, *The Court of Justice of the European Communities and the Development of International Law*, ASIL PROC. 190-95 (1965); R. SOCINI, LA COMPETENZA PREGIUDIZIALE DELLA CORTE DE CIUSTIZIA DELLA COMUNITÀ EUROPEE (Milan 1967); Stein, *The Court of Justice of the European Coal and Steel Community*, 51 AJIL 821-29 (1957); Stevens, *The Principle of Linguistic Equality in Judicial Proceedings and in the Interpretation of Plurilingual Legal Instruments: The Regime Linguistic in the Court of Justice of the European Communities*, 62 NW. U. L. REV. 701-34 (1967); Thompson, *The Bosch Case*, 11 INT'L & COMP. L.Q. 721-41 (1962); A. TIZZANO, LA CORTE DI GIUSTIZIA DELLA COMUNITA EUROPEE (Naples 1967); D. VALENTINE, THE COURT OF JUSTICE OF THE EUROPEAN COMMUNITIES (London 1965); VALENTINE, THE COURT OF JUSTICE OF THE EUROPEAN COAL AND STEEL COMMUNITY (The Hague 1955); Valentine, *The First Judgments of the Court of the European Coal and Steel Community*, 20 MOD. L.REV. 596-619 (1957); Valentine, *The Jurisdiction of the Court of Justice of the European Communities to Annul Executive Action*, 36 BR. Y.B. INT'L L. 174-223 (1960); G. VERPRAET & J. LECERF, L'EUROPE JUDICIAIRE: LA COUR DE JUSTICE DES COMMUNAUTÉS EUROPÉENES AU SERVICE DE 185 MILLIONS D'EUROPÉENS (Brussels 1970); E. WALL, THE COURT OF JUSTICE OF THE EUROPEAN COMMUNITIES (London 1966); Wolf, *The Role of the Court of the European Communities in the Anti-trust Structure of the Common Market*, 3 FORDHAM L.REV. 621-38 (1962-63); I. Zanotti, *supra* note 35, at 226-44.

[72] March 25, 1957, 4 EUR. Y.B. 413 (1958).
[73] April 13, 1951, 1 EUR. Y.B. 359 (1955).
[74] March 2, 1954, 5 EUR. Y.B. 455 (1959).

The Court of Justice is composed of seven judges, appointed for six years by agreement among the governments of the member states, "from among persons of indisputable independence who fulfill the conditions required for the holding of the highest judicial office in their respective countries or who are jurists of a recognized competence."[75]

The Council of Ministers for the Communities, by unanimous vote, may increase the number of judges. The Court is assisted by two "advocates-general" who have the duty "to present publicly, with complete impartiality and independence, reasoned conclusions on cases submitted to the Court of Justice, with a view to assisting the latter in the performance of its duties." The advocates-general must possess the same qualifications as judges of the Court. Inasmuch as the judges rarely deliver a fully documented opinion from which their reasoning in a particular case can be determined, the advocates, whose detailed opinions are fully documented, serve as an important source of law and have indeed influenced the development of a distinct community law.

The Court of Justice serves each Community according to provisions contained in the applicable treaty. With respect to the European Coal and Steel Community, the jurisdiction of the Court is set forth as follows:

> *Art. 33.* The Court shall have jurisdiction over appeals by a Member State or by the Council for the annulment of decisions and recommendations of the High Authority on the grounds of lack of legal competence, major violations of procedure, violation of the Treaty or of any rule of law relating to its application, or abuse of power. However, the Court may not review the High Authority's evaluation of the situation, based on economic facts and circumstances, which led to such decisions or recommendations, except where the High Authority is alleged to have abused its powers or to have clearly misinterpreted the provisions of the Treaty or of a rule of law relating to its application . . .
>
> *Art. 42.* The Court shall exercise jurisdiction as may be provided by any clause to that effect in a public or private contract to which the Community is a party or which is undertaken on its behalf.
>
> *Art. 43.* The Court shall exercise jurisdiction in any other case provided for in an additional provision of this Treaty. It may also exercise jurisdiction in any case relating to the purposes of this Treaty, where the laws of a Member State grant it such jurisdiction.

---

[75] March 25, 1957, 4 EUR. Y.B. 413 (1958).

The Common Market treaty defines the Court's jurisdiction in the following articles:

Art. 173. The Court of Justice shall review the lawfulness of acts other than recommendations or opinions of the Council and the Commission. For this purpose, it shall be competent to give judgment on appeals by a Member State, the Council or the Commission on grounds of incompetence, of errors of substantial form, of infringement of this Treaty or of legal provisions relating to its application, or of abuse of power.

Any natural or legal person may, under the same conditions, appeal against a decision addressed to him or against a decision which, although in the form of a regulation or a decision addressed to another person, is of direct and specific concern to him.

The appeals provided for in this Article shall be lodged within a period of two months dating, as the case may be, either from the publication of the act concerned or from its notification to the appellant or, failing that, from the day on which the latter had knowledge of that act.

Art. 177. The Court of Justice shall be competent to make a preliminary decision concerning:

(a) The interpretation of this Treaty;

(b) the validity and interpretation of acts of the institutions of the Community; and

(c) the interpretation of the statutes of any bodies set up by an act of the Council, where such statutes so provide.

Where any such question is raised before a court or tribunal of one of the Member States, such court of tribunal may if it considers that its judgment depends on a preliminary decision on this question, request the Court of Justice to give a ruling thereon.

Where any such question is raised in a case pending before a domestic court or tribunal from whose decisions on appeal lies under municipal law, such court or tribunal shall refer the matter to the Court of Justice.

Art. 178. The Court of Justice shall be competent to hear cases relating to compensation for damages as provided for in Article 215, second paragraph.

Art. 179. The Court of Justice shall be competent to decide in any case between the Community and its employees, within the limits and under the conditions laid down by the relevant statute of service or conditions of employment.

Art. 180. The Court of Justice shall be competent within the limits laid down below, to hear cases concerning:

(a) The fulfillment by Member States of the obligations arising under the Statute of the European Investment Bank. The

Board of Directors of the Bank shall, in this respect, dispose of the powers conferred upon the Commission by Article 169;

(b) the conclusions of the Board of Governors of the Bank. Any Member State, the Commission or the Board of Directors of the Bank may lodge an appeal in this matter under the conditions laid down in Article 173; and

(c) the conclusions of the Board of Directors of the Bank. Appeals against such conclusions may be lodged under the conditions laid down in Article 173, provided that they may only be lodged by a Member State or by the Commission, and only on the groups of an infringement of formal procedures laid down in Article 21, paragraph 2 and paragraphs 5 and 7 inclusive of the Bank.

Art. 181. The Court of Justice shall be competent to make a decision pursuant to any arbitration clause contained in a contract concluded, under public or private law, by or on behalf of the Community.

Art. 182. The Court of Justice shall be competent to decide in any dispute between Member States in connection with the object of this Treaty, where such dispute is submitted to it under the terms of a compromise (*sic compromis*).

The provisions defining the jurisdiction of the Court in the Euratom treaty, excepting Article 180 of the above-quoted treaty, are identical to those of the European Economic Community (Articles 146 and 150-155).

The Court's jurisdiction has been likened to that of a federal supreme court in that it has power to resolve conflicts among member states concerning interpretation of the Treaty, or disputes between institutions of the Communities. It resembles the French Conseil d'Etat, or similar institutions in other civil law nations, in that one of its most important functions, and, indeed, the one it has most frequently been called upon to perform, is to review acts of administrative officials of the institutions, generally the High Authority of the Coal and Steel Community and the Commissions of the Common Market and Euratom.

The Court's civil jurisdiction arises from its right to hear cases when the Communities sue or are sued in tort, and again in cases involving contract matters (for example, its power to invalidate contracts between two corporations within member states if they violate terms of the Treaty, such as in transport rate discriminations or other business practices restricted by the Treaties).

The Court serves as an international tribunal and can apply international law in resolving conflicts over treaties to which the Communities are parties, or in cases in which a member state signs a treaty inconsistent with the obligations assumed through membership in the Communities.

The present Court officially replaces the Court of Justice which served the Coal and Steel Community. But, in fact, the new Court is a continuation of the old with a greatly expanded jurisdiction. Four of the present seven judges served on the old Court.

The original Court heard 97 appeals. From among these, 27 judgments were handed down, covering 35 appeals. Two stays of execution were granted, and 15 appeals were withdrawn. The remaining 45 cases were carried over to the new Court.

Most of the recently pending cases involved appeals by the Government of the Federal Republic of Germany and various German firms against High Authority decisions abolishing certain special transport rates in Germany which had been considered discriminatory. Other typical appeals were by the Dutch, Italian and Luxembourg Governments against the High Authority's decision to publish road transport rates.

In another case, the French Industry Association and 11 French steel firms combined to appeal the High Authority's position on the opening of the Kalenkirchen/Venlo frontier station. In this case, the plaintiffs claimed that the situation involved discrimination against them by the German State railways.

It should be noted that any judgment against a party (except member states) is enforceable as a municipal court judgment in the state of which the party is a national. Measures which can be taken against a state to enforce court decisions are set forth in the Treaty and range from fines to loss of rights under the Treaty. To date, no state has failed to abide by any decision of the Court.

The European Court of Justice is an excellent example of the ability of an international judicial institution to effectively administer the rules of law established by multilateral treaties governing matters of extreme economic, social, and political importance to the member states. The Court has a distinguished record and undoubtedly has been an important factor in the success of the European Communities. Its experience serves as a valuable and noteworthy precedent for those regional judicial institutions which may be formed in other areas of the world.

§ 4-6.3. **The European Court of Human Rights.**[76] This Court was established by the European Convention for the Protection of Human Rights and Fundamental Freedoms[77] as a court of law resort when human rights complaints could not be resolved by the European Commission of Human Rights.

The Court consists of a number of judges equal to that of the member of the Council of Europe. No two judges may be nationals of the same state (Article 38). They must either "possess the qualifications required for appointment to high judicial office or be jurisconsults of recognized competence" (Article 49), and are elected for a term of nine years (Article 41).

For the consideration of each case before it, the Court shall consist of a chamber composed of seven judges, with each party in a particular case entitled to place its judge on the Court as an *ex officio* member. The two most important provisions of the Convention govern jurisdiction and submission of cases to the Court. They are as follows:

> *Art. 45.* The jurisdiction of the Court shall extend to all cases concerning the interpretation and application of the present Con-

---

[76] The Court's address is Avenue de l'Europe, Strasbourg, France. *See generally* N. ANTONOPOULOS, LA JURISPRUDENCE DES ORGANES DE LA CONVENTION EUROPÉENNES DES DROITS DE L'HOMME (Leyden 1967); Comte, *The Application of the European Convention of Human Rights in Municipal Law,* 4 J. INT'L COM. JUR. 94-133 (1962); COUNCIL OF EUROPE, EUROPEAN COURT OF HUMAN RIGHTS, RULES OF COURT: RÈGLEMENT (Strasbourg 1965); Golsong, *The European Convention on Human Rights Before Domestic Courts,* 38 BR. Y.B. INT'L L. 445-56 (1962); Greenberg & Shalit, *New Horizons for Human Rights: The European Convention, Court, and Commission of Human Rights,* 63 COLUM. L.REV. 1384-1412 (1963); McNulty, *The Practice of the European Commission of Human Rights,* 11 HOW. L.J. 430-41 (1965); Mosler, *Organisation und Verfahren des Europäischen Gerichtshofs für Menschenrechte,* 20 Z. R. & VÖLK. 415-49 (1960); Pelloux, *La Cour Européenne des Droits de l'Homme,* 1 J. INT'L & COMP. L. 79-90 (1968); Pettiti, *On the European Court of Human Rights,* in ATHENS CONF. 233-36; Robertson, *The European Court of Human Rights,* 8 INT'L & COMP. L.Q. 396-403 (1959); Robertson, *Lawless of the Government of Ireland,* 38 BR. Y.B. INT'L L. 536-47 (1962); ROBERTSON, HUMAN RIGHTS IN EUROPE: THE EUROPEAN COMMISSION OF HUMAN RIGHTS AND THE EUROPEAN COURT OF HUMAN RIGHTS (New York 1963); Rolin, *Has the European Court of Human Rights a Future?* 11 HOW. L.J. 442-52 (1965); Schwelb, *On the Operation of the European Convention of Human Rights,* 18 INT'L ORG. 558-85 (1964); Vasak, *The European Convention of Human Rights Beyond the Frontiers of Europe,* 12 INT'L & COMP. L.Q. 1206-31 (1963); Walter, *The Present Scope of Jurisdiction of the Commission and the Court of the European Convention of Human Rights . . .,* 26 Z.R. & VÖLK. 352-70 (1966); Weil, *The Evolution of the European Convention on Human Rights,* 57 AJIL 824-27 (1963); G. WEIL, THE EUROPEAN CONVENTION ON HUMAN RIGHTS: BACKGROUND, DEVELOPMENT AND PROSPECTS (Leyden 1963); YEARBOOK OF THE EUROPEAN CONVENTION OF HUMAN RIGHTS, THE EUROPEAN COMMISSION AND EUROPEAN COURT OF HUMAN RIGHTS (The Hague 1955-).

[77] Nov. 4, 1950, E.T.S. No. 5; BR. Y.B. INT'L L. 317-41.

vention which the High Contracting Parties or the Commission shall refer to it in accordance with Article 48.

Art. 48. The following may bring a case before the Court, provided that the High Contracting Party concerned, if there is only one, or the High Contracting Parties concerned, if there is more than one, are subject to the compulsory jurisdiction of the Court or, failing that, with the consent of the High Contracting Party concerned, if there is only one, or of the High Contracting Parties concerned if there is more

(a) the Commission;

(b) a High Contracting Party whose national is alleged to be a victim;

(c) a High Contracting Party which referred the case to the Commission;

(d) a High Contracting Party against which the complaint has been lodged.

Reasons are given for the judgment of the Court, and dissenting judges are entitled to deliver a separate opinion. The judgment of the Court is executed under supervision of the Committee of Ministers.

The Court has been called upon to decide only 10 cases, since the Commission of Human Rights has been successful in resolving most cases submitted to it. The particular significance of the Court lies not in its accomplishments but in its availability when needed and in its potential as a model for the future. In informational bulletin B (70) 73 issued by the Council of Europe in November 1970, the European Court of Human Rights had heard the following cases since its creation in 1959:

The *Lawless, Wemhoff, Matznetter and Delcourt* cases finished with judgments of 1st July 1961, 27th June 1968, 10th November 1969 and 17th January 1970, finding that there had been no breach of the Convention by Ireland in the first case, by the Federal Republic of Germany in the second, by the Republic of Austria in the third and by the Kingdom of Belgium in the fourth.

The Court held that there had been a violation of the Convention in the *Stugmuller* case (judgment of 10th November 1969) and in the *Neumeister* case on one of the three issues raised in it (judgment of 27th June 1968). These cases concerned the Republic of Austria.

In its judgment of 23rd July 1968 in the case relating to certain aspects of the *laws on the use of language in education* in Belgium, the Court decided that the legislation in issue conformed to the requirements of the Convention except on one out of the six matters which it had to examine.

The *De Becker* case was struck off the Court's list on 27th March 1962 at the request of the Commission and of the Belgian Government; the Commission had earlier informed the Court that the Applicant was also agreeable to this course.

Lastly, the *"Vagrancy cases"* (De Wilde, Ooms, and Versyp) and the *Ringeisen* case are still pending before the Court.

Nine of these various cases were brought before the Court by the European Commission of Human Rights; the Government of Austria, however, being the Government concerned in the cases of *Neumeister, Stugmuller* and *Matznetter* also referred them to the Court. The *"Vagrancy cases"* have been brought before the Court by the Belgian Government.

§ 4-6.4. **The European Nuclear Energy Tribunal.**[78] The expansion of nuclear energy raises many problems, including health and safety, transport of radioactive materials, and liability in accident cases. The European Nuclear Energy Agency is concerned with these and other problems and has tried through international conventions and other means "to further the development of the production and uses of nuclear energy for peaceful purposes" through the cooperation of participating countries.

In 1960, the European Nuclear Energy Agency appointed a Tribunal to resolve disputes arising from the Agency's activities composed of seven judges of the highest integrity and competence. No more than one judge of any state may serve on it, and if a party to a dispute does not have a judge on the Tribunal, it may choose one to sit in the case. The Tribunal elects its President and appoints a Registrar. A quorum of five judges is necessary to make its proceedings valid. Decisions are by majority; the President may cast a vote only in case of tie. Sessions of the Tribunal are held in public unless the Tribunal decides otherwise. The official languages are English and French, and the proceedings are governed by the Rules of Procedure which regulate oral and written proceedings, questions of evidence, rules regulating decisions, interim measures, revisions of the decision, and other matters.

§ 4-6.5. **International War Crimes Tribunals.**[79] Due to the events of World War II within the Axis States, the United States, Great

---

[78] Address: 38 Suchet, Paris 16er, France. *See* ORGANIZATION FOR ECONOMIC COOPERATION AND DEVELOPMENT, EUROPEAN NUCLEAR ENERGY AGENCY, EUROPEAN NUCLEAR ENERGY TRIBUNAL (Paris 1957, 1963).

[79] For extensive bibliographical references, see L. SOHN, CASES AND OTHER MATERIALS ON WORLD LAW 967-74 (Brooklyn 1950).

For more current references, see R. WOETZEL, THE NUREMBERG TRIALS IN INTERNATIONAL LAW 282-306 (New York 1962).

(Continued)

Britain, France and the USSR created an *ad hoc* international tribunal to try Axis leaders. Though the merit of holding these tribunals has been questioned, it is clear that the proceedings gave the defendants due process of law, added a record of the committed, and established a precedent of tribunal punishment for crimes against humanity.

The Tribunal consisted of four judges, one of whom, selected by the others, served as President; four alternate judges also sat throughout the trial. Each country which created the Tribunal had a Chief Prosecutor, several principal assistant prosecutors, a basic staff of prosecutors who participated in the preparation and argument of cases in court against specific defendants or particular categories of crimes, a supporting executive and administrative staff, and a staff of interpreters.

Great effort was made to insure a fair trial, a difficult task for a tribunal confronted with the type of crimes committed and the intense pressures of public opinion. The trial was open to the public, although the relatively small size of the court room limited the number of persons who could attend, and newspaper reporters covered the proceedings throughout the trial. Each defendant was given an opportunity to choose his defense counsel. The evidence that convicted many of the 22 defendants mainly consisted of written orders signed by these defendants, that commanded subordinates to perform acts which were unmistakable crimes under the laws of the states involved in the trial. The fact that some of the defendants were acquitted and that others were given different penalties indicates the care with which the Tribunal weighed the evidence. The Tribunal laid down rules of procedure, including rules to protect defense counsel, which were strictly enforced, as, for example, when defense counsel protested that they had not had time to adequately prepare their defense as a result of the failure of the prosecution to supply required documents, the Tribunal granted additional time. The full record of the Trial is set forth in 44 volumes, containing a transcript of the proceedings and documents offered in evidence. An extensive literature covering the many aspects of the trial is also available.

For comments on the Trial by some of its judges, see Biddle, *The Nuremberg Trial,* 33 VA. L.REV. 679-96 (1947); Birkett, *International Legal Theory Evolved at Nuremberg,* 23 INT'L AFF. 317-25 (1947); de Vabres, *Le Procès de Nuremberg Devant les Principes Moder di Droit Pénal International,* 70 RECUEIL DES COURS 477-580 (1947); Lawrence, *The Nuremberg Trial,* 23 INT'L AFF. 151-59 (1947).

The official record of the proceedings of the Trial and the documents submitted in evidence were published in 44 volumes at Nuremberg under the title, TRIAL OF THE MAJOR WAR CRIMINALS BEFORE THE INTERNATIONAL MILITARY TRIBUNAL.

The Nuremberg Trial, the first truly international war crimes trial in history, elicited varying opinions as to its work. Proponents felt that the alternatives to having a trial were either to take no action at all, or to meet violence with violence, both of which were untenable. Critics attacked the composition of the Tribunal as a court of victors against vanquished, and maintained that the judgments were not valid because the Tribunal applied "laws" which were not laws at the time the defendants committed the alleged criminal acts. Of course, many other objections were raised both to the creation of the Tribunal and to its composition, jurisdiction, and operation, and many answers to these objections were given. Beyond doubt, however, the Trial had two important merits: it pointed out a serious gap in international judicial machinery; raised the question whether war crimes should be punished and, if so, by what means; and, produced an authoritiative record of the commission of acts which a civilized world should not condone and the verity of which could not be challenged by propaganda.

Following the creation of the Nuremberg Tribunal another international war crimes tribunal was set up in Tokyo to try alleged war crimes committed in the Far East. This Tribunal followed substantially the same procedure as that used at Nuremberg. It also made a record of its deliberations which has been published.

§ 4-7. Proposed International Courts.[80]

Numerous proposals have suggested the creation of new international judicial decisions to modify or extend the existing system of international and regional courts to settle international disputes through the law process. These proposals have called for new regional courts for the Americas, Africa, Asia and the Arab world; for new separate courts for lower-level international disputes; and

---

[80] The World Peace Through Law Center has been influential in catalyzing discussion concerning improving the system of international courts. *See* Deutsch, *A Plan for Universal Compulsory Jurisdiction for the World Court,* in ATHENS CONF. 170-83; Boggero, *Treaties Regarding International Courts: A Proposal,* in WASHINGTON CONF. 626-27; Chang, *Expansion of the Scope of the Organization, Affairs, and Authority of the International Court of Justice,* in *id.* at 655-59; Harvey, *Work Paper Summary on Existing and Proposed International Courts,* in *id.* at 119-28; National Bar Association of Peru, *A Proposal for the Settlement of International Disputes,* in *id.* at 747-48; Rosenberg, *A Step Toward World Peace Through Law Which Precludes Resort to Force,* in *id.* at 131-43; Stone, *Remarks by the Chairman,* in *id.* at 116-18; Tavolaro, *Introductory Remarks,* in *id.* at 113-116; Avramov, *Peacekeeping,* in WORLD PEACE THROUGH LAW: THE GENEVA CONFERENCE 101-02 (1969) [hereinafter cited as GENEVA CONF.]; Brohi, *Work Paper on Pacific Settlement of International Disputes,* in *id.* at 83-93; Marks, *Peacekeeping and the Settlement of International Disputes,* in *id.* at 94-98; Molloy, *Comments on Peacekeeping,* in *id.* at 106-09; Simon, *The Establishment of an Efficient International Court,* in *id.* at 485-93; Tanaka, *Some Observations on the World Court and World Law,* in *id.* at 98-101.

for new courts to hear disputes dealing with specialized subject matters.

The Charter of the United Nations expressly recognizes the legitimacy of the regional approach to solve international problems (See *supra* § 4-3). Even though creation of regional and specialized courts would certainly be feasible, the desirability of creating them would have to be weighed carefully. The greater accessibility of regional and specialized courts might encourage resort to legal settlement of international disputes since interests of primarily regional concern could best be adjudicated by courts employing norms which conform to regional diversity.

§ 4-7.1. Proposed International Court for Lower Level Disputes. A proposal for the creation of an International Court for "lower level disputes" was made in 1965 in Pamphlet No. 1 of the World Peace Through Law Center, "An Attainable International Court System" by Donald A. Wehmeyer. A Brief summary of the proposal is given below.

The present international legal system lacks a readily accessible court to deal with minor, unspectacular cases, not of sufficient importance to submit to the International Court of Justice. Many examples of such cases can be found in the legal offices of countries throughout the world, such as minor problems of air transport and transit, of patents and copyrights, of extradition, of diplomatic immunity, and of treaty interpretation. Some of these, and similar questions can be resolved at times by other means, but many of them often remain to fester and irritate when an impartial settlement by a lower international court could provide a useful means of settlement.

A proposal to create a lower level international court should appeal to legal offices in governmental ministries, and legislative offices, lawyers and their legal organizations, and legal scholars. It would ease the world-load of government officials, remove a strain from legislative officials, and attract lawyers and legal scholars who are shocked by the inadequacy of present international judicial machinery, and eager to see its improvement.

The composition of the court should at first be very simple. In the beginning a one-man court in most of the largest nations with regional courts for smaller nations might suffice, with a flexible arrangement for adding judges if the parties to a suit so desired. Many lower level domestic courts are one-man courts, and justice has been obtained in these courts.

A formula for the jurisdiction of the court is simply stated in the pamphlet as follows:

> In disputes in which a settlement would involve a monetary or property transfer type result, there would exist a presumption that recourse would be had to the tribunal at such time as one party considered that this means of settlement is appropriate, subject to non-concurrence by the other side.
>
> In the case of disputes where a non-monetary or non-property transfer result would be involved, recourse could be had to the court if the parties so desired.

Maintaining that a first step toward the creation of a lower level international court system would be the drafting of a basic treaty to be sponsored by an initial group of interested states, the pamphlet proposed a draft for such a treaty.

Treaty for Adjudication of Disputes
(Substantive Provisions)

The undersigned States, party to this Treaty

Believing that an important contribution to the cause of World Peace can be made by the development of a suitable framework for greater application of the rule of law in the international community.

Being persuaded that such a framework can be realized by creation of a simple, viable and readily available court system for settlement of international disputes in accordance with the rule of law,

Agree as follows:

Article I

There shall be established a Tribunal having special competence in disputes between parties to this Treaty as provided in Article II.

Article II

The Tribunal shall have jurisdiction as follows:

1. In disputes between parties to this Treaty in which a decision would involve a monetary or property transfer settlement, a presumption shall exist that the parties will have recourse to the Tribunal. Recourse shall be had to the Tribunal at the instance of either State, provided that the other State concerned concurs.

2. In disputes between parties to this Treaty in which a decision would involve other than a monetary or property transfer settlement, recourse may be had to the Tribunal at the instance of either party to the dispute provided that the other State concerned concurs.

Article III

1. The Tribunal shall have its permanent location in _____
_____ . It shall sit in the capital of the States party to this Treaty to hear cases. Unless the parties to the dispute agree otherwise, disputes shall be heard in the State invoking the Treaty.

2. The Tribunal shall have authority to employ such staff as may be necessary for the performance of its duties.

3. The Tribunal shall determine its own internal rules of procedure.

4. Expenses of the Tribunal shall be shared by the States party to this Treaty.

Article IV

1. The Tribunal shall consist initially of a single judge, selected by the parties to this Treaty. Additional judges may be added to the Tribunal as required by agreement of the States party to this Treaty.

2. Judges shall be persons of high moral character, who possess the qualifications required in their respective countries for appointment to the highest judicial offices, or who are jurisconsults of recognized competence in international law.

3. Cases shall normally be heard by a single judge. However, procedural arrangements may be made for the increase in this number in particular cases upon the request of a party to the dispute.

4. Judges shall receive an annual compensation of at least $25,000 which may not be decreased during the term of office. Appointments shall be for a period of fifteen years. When engaged in the business of the Tribunal, judges shall be entitled to diplomatic privileges and immunities.

5. Details pertaining to functioning of the Tribunal as well as rules of procedure before the Tribunal shall be agreed by the parties to this Treaty and shall be filed with the depository state of this Treaty as a related document. States party to the Treaty shall be informed by the depository government of such rules and agreed changes thereto.

Article V

1. The Tribunal, whose function is to decide in accordance with international law such disputes as are submitted to it, shall apply:

   a. International conventions, whether general or particular, establishing rules expressly recognized by the contesting states;

   b. international custom, as evidence of a general practice accepted as law;

c. the general principles of law recognized by civilized nations;

d. subject to the provision that a judgement of the Tribunal or any other court of competent jurisdiction shall be *res adjudicata* only as between the parties to the cause and as to the cause in which the judgement was rendered, judicial decisions and the teachings of the most highly qualified publicists of the various nations, as subsidiary means for the determination of rules of law.

Article VI

1. This Treaty is entered into pursuant to Article 95 of the Charter of the United Nations.

2. Participation in the present Treaty in no way affects the rights and responsibility of the respective parties with respect to the International Court of Justice under the Charter of the United Nations and the Statute of the Court.

Article VII

Each party to this Treaty undertakes to comply with the decision of the Tribunal in any case to which it is a party.

§ 4-7.2. Proposed North American Regional International Court. The World Peace Through Law Center in an effort to put the proposal for an International Court for Lower Level Disputes into practical operation, appointed a Special Committee for the purpose of drafting a treaty for the establishment of a North American Regional Court to settle cases between Canada, Mexico, and the United States. The Chairman of this Committee, Mr. Philip W. Amram, of the United States, submitted the following Draft Treaty for presentation to the Geneva World Conference on World Peace Through Law in July 1967.

Draft Treaty

The undersigned States, parties to this Treaty (hereinafter referred to as the "Parties"),

Seeking to enlarge the rule of law in international affairs.

Being of the opinion that this can be accomplished by the creation of a simple, effective and readily available regional international court system for the judicial adjudication of disputes between them,

Agree as follows:

Organization of the Court

(1) The official name of the Court shall be "The North American Regional International Court."

(2) The Court shall be composed of one judge, or of an uneven number of judges more than one, elected from time to time by the unanimous written vote of the Parties which shall be deposited at the seat of the Court. No judge may be a national of any of the Parties. Judges shall be of high moral character and learned in the law, and possessed of special competence in international law.

(3) Judges shall be elected for a term of   years, to run from the date of appointment. They shall receive compensation at the rate of $ per   , in United States currency; when actually employed in the work of the Court, which may not be decreased during their term.

(4) A judge shall take oath upon entering into his office that he will faithfully and impartially perform functions of his office.

(5) A judge may be removed from office during his term in office only by the unanimous vote of the parties, after a full hearing, in the event of his unwillingness or inability to perform the duties of the office, or for breach of duty.

(6) A judge may resign his office by written resignation addressed to each of the Parties, to be effective as set forth in the letter of resignation.

(7) A judge elected, as provided in Article I (2), to fill a vacancy resulting from resignation or removal of a judge shall hold office for the then remaining balance of the term of the judge who has resigned or been removed.

(8) If the Court consists of more than one judge, the members of the Court shall elect their own Chief Judge by majority vote.

(9) A judge shall be entitled to diplomatic privileges and immunities in the territory of the Parties thereto, when engaged in his official duties.

Article II

(1) The Court shall have its permanent seat at   All files and records of the Court shall be maintained at its office located at the seat. This shall not prevent the Court from sitting at such other places within the territory of the Parties as the Court may deem desirable from time to time, pursuant to Article VI(4).

(2) The office of the Court shall be open at all times, during regular business hours, for the receipt and deposit of documents relating to the business of the Court.

Administration
Article III

(1) The budget of the Court shall be fixed each year at least six months in advance by unanimous agreement of each of the Parties. Each Party shall contribute one-third of the budget.

(2) The Court shall appoint its own Registrar and all other professional and non-professional employees within the limits and at the salaries fixed in the budget. If the Court consists of more than one judge and a disagreement arises between the judges with respect to any such appointment, the decision of the Chief Judge shall govern.

(3) All salaries and compensation of judges, the Registrar and all other employees of the Court shall be exempt from all income or other taxation by the Parties and by any political sub-divisions thereof.

(4) The judge, or the Chief Judge if the Court consists of more than one judge, shall have exclusive jurisdiction over all administrative matters, including the approval of travel and other expenses of the judges and all employees, within the limits fixed in the budget.

Competence of the Court
Article IV

(1) Only the Parties may be parties in cases before the Court.

(2) The jurisdiction of the Court comprises all disputes of any character which the Parties agree to refer to it, either by provisions in treaties or international disputes to the Court. The agreement to submit the matter to the Court must be express and must refer to the Court by its official name. [See Article I(1)]. The Court shall have no jurisdiction over any dispute in the absence of such an agreement.

(3) In the event of a dispute as to whether the Court has jurisdiction, the matter shall be settled by the decision of the Court.

Law To Be Applied
Article V

(1) The Court, whose function is to decide in accordance with international law such disputes as are submitted to it, shall apply:

a. international conventions, whether general or particular, establishing rules expressly recognized by the contesting Parties;

b. international custom, as evidence of a general practice accepted as law;

c. the general principles of law recognized by civilized nations;

d. subject to the provisions of Article VII (2) judicial decisions and the teachings of the most highly qualified publicists of the various nations, as subsidiary means for the determination of rules of law.

(2) This provision shall not prejudice the power of the Court to decide a case *ex aequo et bono,* if the Parties agree thereto.

Procedure

Article VI

(1) The official language of the Court shall be English.

(2) The Court may, by rules of Court, regulate the practice and procedure in all proceedings brought before the Court, including, *inter alia*, process, service, pleadings, motions, hearings on the merits and rules of evidence.

(3) Proposed rules of Court shall become effective sixty (60) days after copies thereof have been furnished to the Parties, provided that no objection is filed thereto by any Party. If written objection is filed by any Party to any proposed rule, it shall become effective, but this shall not affect other proposed rules to which no objection is filed, the latter shall come into effect after the expiration of the sixty (60) days' period.

(4) With respect to any rule as to which a Party may have filed a written objection, the Parties and the Court shall consult with respect thereto, to effect, if possible, such amendments or modifications of the proposed rule as will result in its unanimous acceptance.

(5) In all proceedings before the Court, each Party to the proceeding shall be represented by an attorney of record, who shall be either an accredited official of the government of the Party, or a duly admitted member of the Bar of the highest court of the country of the Party. The attorneys of record shall be entitled to diplomatic privileges and immunities in the territory of the Parties when engaged in their official duties.

(6) The Court shall have power to issue subpoenas for the appearance of witnesses. The Parties, within the limits of their domestic law, agreed to effect service of such subpoenas and aid in the production of witnesses who may be within their territory. Nothing in this section shall require a Party to violate the immunity of any person from compulsory appearance as a witness, nor shall it affect any privilege with respect to testimony, which any person may have under the domestic law of the country of which he is a national or a resident.

(7) Hearings before the Court, on motions or on the merits, shall be held at the seat of the Court or, if the Court so directs, at any other place within the territories of the Parties. No Party may object to the decision of the Court on the place so selected by the Court.

(8) If the Court consists of more than one judge, motions shall be heard by a single judge or by the full bench, as the Chief Judge may direct. Hearings on the merits shall, in all cases, be before the full bench only.

(9) Hearing shall be public, unless the Court otherwise directs or unless all Parties to the proceedings otherwise request. Appropriate minutes shall be made of all hearings, either by stenographic record or by mechanical or electronic recording. Transcripts of the minutes, or any part thereof, shall be available to any Party upon request and upon payment of the cost of preparing the same.

Judgments
Article VII

(1) The judgment of the Court on any motion or on the merits shall be in writing and shall state the reasons on which it is based. If the Court consists of more than one judge, and a motion or a hearing on the merits has been heard by the full bench, the judgment shall be the decision of the majority of the judges. A concurring judge may file a concurring opinion and a dissenting judge may file a dissenting opinion.

(2) A judgment shall have no binding force except between the parties thereto and in respect of that particular case.

(3) Copies of the judgment shall be mailed forthwith by the Registrar to the attorneys of record of the parties to the case.

(4) The judgment is final and without appeal. In the event of dispute as to the meaning or scope of the judgment, the Court shall construe it upon request of any party thereto.

(5) An application for revision of a judgment may be made only when it is based upon the discovery of some fact of such a nature as to be a decisive factor, which fact was, when the judgment was given, unknown to the Court and also to the party claiming revision, always provided that such ignorance was not due to negligence.

(6) The proceedings for revision shall be opened by a judgment of the Court expressly recording the existence of the new fact, recognizing that it has such a character as to lay the case open to revision, and declaring the application admissible on this ground.

(7) The Court may require previous compliance with the terms of the judgment before it admits proceedings in revision.

(8) The application for revision must be made at the latest within six months of the discovery of the new fact.

(9) No application for revision may be made after the lapse of ten years from the date of the judgement.

(10) Each Party undertakes to comply with the judgment of the Court in any case to which it is a party.

(11) In the event of the refusal of a Party to appeal and defend an action over which the Court has jurisdiction, the Court may, if it

is satisfied of its jurisdiction and of the merits of the controversy, enter a judgment by default against the defaulting Party, which shall have the same validity as a judgment entered against a Party who has appeared and defended the action.

(12) Unless otherwise directed in the judgment, each party to the action shall bear its own costs.

General Provisions
Article VIII

(1) This Treaty is entered into pursuant to Article 95 of the Chater of the United Nations.

(2) Participation in the present Treaty in no way affects the rights and responsibilities of the respective Parties with respect to the International Court of Justice under the Charter of the United Nations and the Statute of the Court.

(3, *et seq.*) (Here include customary clauses for signature, ratification by the Parties, deposit of documents of ratification; effective date; possible accession by other States; denunciations; term of the Treaty and renewals.)[81]

§ 4-7.3. **Proposed International Criminal Court.**[82] The need for an international judicial body to try violations of criminal law has been recognized for many years. In 1925, at the Conference of the Interparliamentary Union, a recommendation to create a Criminal Chamber of the Permanent Court of International Justice was put forth. The International Law Association, at its Conference in Buenos Aires, favored the creation of a criminal court, and at a subsequent conference in Vienna submitted a draft statute of an international criminal court. The International Association of Penal Law also prepared a draft statute for such a court. In 1937, 13 states signed a convention providing for the creation of a penal court, but this convention never came into force because of World War II.

Numerous conferences since the last war have favored the creation of an international criminal court. Various aspects of the organization, jurisdiction and procedure of such a court have been discussed in the literature of the subject—for example, whether the court should be permanent or *ad hoc*, whether it should be an independent tribunal or a Chamber of the International Court of Justice,

---

[81] Amram, *Report of the Committee on Lower Level International Courts*, in GENEVA CONF. 614-18 (1967).

[82] J. STONE, AN INTERNATIONAL CRIMINAL COURT (W.P.T.L.C., Geneva 1971). Hudson, *The Proposed International Criminal Court*, 32 AJIL 549-55 *Courts of International Criminal Jurisdiction*, in WASHINGTON CONF. 792-810; Woetzel, *Toward a Contion on Crimes Against Humanity*, in GENEVA CONF. 103-06.

whether a single court should be established or lower court with appeal to a supreme court, the number of judges and the method of their selection, various questions of procedure, and the means of enforcing the court's judgments.   In spite of the emphasis by writers and by specialists at conferences and in legal journals and and the generally accepted view of the importance of its creation to the development of adequate international legal machinery, no permanent international criminal court has, to date, been established.

The World Peace Through Law Center has recently published a book by experts on the subject "Toward a Feasible International Criminal Court." Edited by Professors Robert Woetzel of Boston College, and Julius Stone of Australia, the purpose of the book is to clarify some main issues concerning the establishment of such an International Criminal Court, in conjunction with the Center's proposed plan and draft instruments for such a court.   Members of the Center's International Criminal Law Commission contributed 26 substantial chapters discussing such topics as the status of the individual in international law; individual responsibility for international crimes; petitional procedures for human rights' protection; draft statutes for an international criminal court; defenses and excuses before an international criminal court; and the composition and procedures of an International Criminal Court.

§ 4-7.4. **Proposed World Equity Tribunal.** Even the most avid proponents of international adjudication admit that the settlement of international disputes by courts has its limitations. Many disputes are not primarily legal in nature. In fact, these are often the very disputes which cause the most trouble. Thus, international quasi-judicial machinery to resolve the disputes which are not strictly legal in character should be created.   In the historical development of the common law, a similar need led to the creation of courts of equity.

Two distinguished jurists, Grenville Clark and Louis B. Sohn, in a book dealing with world peace and law propose the creation of a World Equity Tribunal.[83]   Like the International Court of Justice, this Court would become a principal organ of the United Nations.   Its purpose would be to supplement, not to replace, diplomacy, mediation, conciliation, commissions of inquiry, good offices, and other non-legal means of settlement. Suggestions for the organization of the Tribunal, its jurisdiction, the enforcement of its recommendations, and various other matters are spelled out

---

[83] G. CLARK,& L. SOHN, WORLD PEACE THROUGH LAW (Harvard University Press, 3d ed. 1966).

by the above-mentioned authors, and in view of the importance of establishing adequate peace machinery to replace violence in international relations, this proposed equity tribunal should not be overlooked.

§ 4-7.5. **Proposed International Courts of Habeas Corpus.** The aim of habeas corpus is to offer a legal remedy for wrongful imprisonment. This was an objective of the English Magna Carta, the Bill of Rights and the Fifth and Fourteenth Amendments of the United States Constitution and of the Universal Declaration of Human Rights. The aim of world habeas corpus is to eliminate the suppression of individual rights and in its place apply due process throughout the world.

At the Washington Conference on World Peace Through Law in 1965, Luis Kutner described the structure of a proposed international court system of habeas corpus.[84] The plan calls for nine circuit courts, with the right of appeal to a Supreme Court. The nine circuits would be: (1) the Communist-Orient Circuit, (2) the USSR-East Europe Circuit, (3) the Western Europe Circuit, (4) the Islam Circuit, (5) the Southern Africa Circuit, (6) the Non-Communist Orient Circuit, (7) the Austral-Oceania Circuit, (8) the Latin America Circuit, and (9) the Anglo-America Circuit. The choice of circuits is based on geographical propinquity of states and on legal, cultural, religious, and historical considerations.

Any detained person, or other person on his behalf, may invoke the court's jurisdiction. Authorities of the detaining government would have the right to intervene to defend its action against the detained person, but, in doing so must bring the detained person into court. If a state does not appear, or if it fails to bring the detained person into court, the court may proceed with the case and decide it on available evidence. At the trial, the petitioner would have to show that he had exhausted local remedies or that such action would be futile.

Enforcement of decisions would depend largley on the voluntary compliance of the state involved. Cases of a state's refusal to comply would be referred to regional organizations for action. If this proved ineffective, resort may be had to the UN Security Council and to the General Assembly. The test suggested for

---

[84] L. Kutner, *Structure of the Proposed International Court of Habeas Corpus,* in WASHINGTON CONF. 368-74; Kutner, *World Habeas Corpus, Human Rights and World Community,* 17 DEPAUL L. REV. 1 (1967), detailing his court plan; Bassiouni, *Islam: Concept, Law and World Habeas Corpus,* 2 RUT. CAM. L.J. 160 (1970), with an introduction by Mr. Justice Zaffrullah Khan.

enforcement action is that of "reasonableness." The diplomatic sanctions that might be used include the explusion of the offending state from the United Nations or the severing of communications with the offending state. Economic sanctions would also be available.

§ 4-7.6. **Proposed Inter-American Court of Justice.**[85]   The dissolution of the Central American Court of Justice, and the unsuccessful attempts to re-establish the Court have led to many new proposals for an Inter-American Court of Justice to settle disputes among the American states. These proposals have been presented at the Conferences of the American States held in the 20th century, and can be divided into three categories: (a) those suggestions stating that efforts to establish such a court should be limited to strengthening the Permanent Court of International Justice; (b) those suggestions that an Inter-American Court should be established distinct from the PCIJ and ICJ, and even without unanimous agreement and participation of all American states; and (c) those recommendations that an Inter-American Court not be established unless all American states participate and submit to its jurisdiction.[86]

Of these proposals, the one recommending the creation of a special chamber of the ICJ for the American states has met with the greatest approval. The establishment of such a chamber would reduce the costs of litigation and degree of inconvenience in prosecuting or defending a claim in the ICJ, and would provide a uniform judicial system for the Americas consonant with the ICJ and the rest of the world since it is necessary to have a single international judiciary in order to promote the universal application and administration of justice. Such an American Chamber of the ICJ would also fill the serious gap that presently exists in OAS machinery to settle disputes and would enable the OAS to reach its full potential. While the obligation to settle disputes peacefully is contained in a number of treaties dealing with investigation, mediation, conciliation and arbitration, which were brought together in the Pact of Bogota of 1948,[87] American states at the present

---

[85] *See* Zanotti, *Proposals Made for the Continuation of an Inter-American Court of Justice and the Resolutions Adopted by Inter-American Conferences, 1923-1954, supra* note 35, at 90-139; *Comparative Analysis of the Proposals Made for the Creation of an Inter-American Court of Justice, id.* at 139-64; Warren, *The Projected Inter-American Court of Justice as a Part of the Inter-American Peace Machinery* (unpublished thesis, Stanford University Library, Palo Alto, California).

[86] Zanotti, *supra* note 35, at 90-139.

[87] Charter of the Organization of American States, Bogotá, April 29, 1948, 146 AJIL Supp. 43 (1952). *See also* Rio Treaty of Reciprocal Assistance, INT. CONFERENCES 1942-1954, 178.

time are not legally obligated to submit their controversies either to arbitration or to the ICJ. Instead, they are obligated to refrain from the use of force, and to seek some peaceful means of resolving their disputes, although if no agreement as to the means of settling the dispute can be reached, the dispute remains unsettled. Only if the controversy constitutes a "threat to the peace" does the machinery of the OAS go into action, with disputing parties being obliged to cooperate. Thus, some American judicial or arbitral tribunal should be established to settle controversies before they become threats to the peace.

Perhaps a solution to the controversy of whether the Court should be distinctly "American" or a branch of the ICJ, would be to utilize both institutions, since each has its own particular usefulness in the Western Hemisphere. A chamber of the ICJ could be established to hear disputes normally within the jurisdiction of that Court, and a distinct Inter-American Court of Justice could be established to adjudicate matters covered by special agreements or conventions signed by the American states. The existence of the European Court of Justice to resolve disputes over the many technical aspects of the European Communities is an example of how such a regional court would not be inconsistent with the aims, purposes and functions of the ICJ. The European Court is discussed *supra* § 4-6.3.

§ 4-7.7. Proposed Inter-American Court of Human Rights. The Council of the OAS, at a meeting on October 2, 1968, adopted a Preliminary Draft Inter-American Convention on the Protection of Human Rights,[88] which provides for the organization, jurisdiction and procedure of an Inter-American Court of Human Rights.

The Court shall be composed of seven judges of the highest integrity and competence. Each state, party to the Convention, shall propose the names of three candidates, at least two of whom shall be of its own nationality. Judges shall be elected for a term of six years by absolute majority vote and by secret ballot. No more than one judge of any state shall serve on the Court, and five judges must be present to constitute a quorum for transacting business. When a judge is a national of a state which is a party to a case before the Court, an *ad hoc* judge shall be selected by the other members of the Court to take his place.

---

[88] *See* Council of the Organization of American States, *Draft Inter-American Convention on Protection of Human Rights,* COUNCIL SERIES OEA/SER. G/V 17-22 (Washington 1968).

The jurisdiction of the Court is limited to cases submitted by states party to the Convention on Protection of Human Rights and cases submitted by the Commission. It shall have jurisdiction in all cases involving interpretation and application of the Convention's provisions. States party to the Convention may recognize the Court's jurisdiction "unconditionally or on the condition of reciprocity or for a specified period only" by a declaration submitted to the Secretary of the Court. Failure to obtain a friendly settlement by the Inter-American Commission on Human Rights in accordance with procedures established by the Convention is a prerequisite to the submission of a case to the Court. The Court shall decide whether it has jurisdiction in any case in which its jurisdiction is challenged. It shall be competent to determine compensatory damages, which shall be executed through domestic procedures for executing judgments against the state. When requested by the OAS General Assembly, the Permanent Council or the Commission, the Court shall serve in a consultative capacity in interpreting treaty provisions for the protection of human rights. It may also advise the states parties to the Convention on the conformity of their domestic laws with treaty provisions, when requested.

The judgment of the Court shall be final and without appeal. It shall state the reasons on which it is based. A judge shall have the right to deliver a separate or dissenting opinion. The Court shall interpret a decision if requested by a party to the Convention within 60 days of notification. States party to the Convention "undertake to abide" by the Court's decisions. The Court shall draft its rules of procedure and its regulations.

The expenses of the Court shall be paid from the budget of the Organization of American States. The Court shall operate from the headquarters of the Pan American Union until its seat has been determined.

The Convention shall come into force when seven states have ratified it. States shall have the right to denounce the Convention after a five-year period from the date of its entry into force. Amendments may be proposed by states party to the Convention by the Commission, or by the Court.

Attention should be called to the noteworthy efforts of the Inter-American Council of Jurists with respect to the implementation of a resolution adopted at the Ninth International Conference of American States with regard to a proposed Inter-American Court of Human Rights. The establishment of such a court is a constant objective of many American states, and the matter has been under intensive study since the Inter-American Conference on War and Peace held in Mexico in 1945.

§ 4-7.8. Proposed Central American Court of Justice. The Charter of the Organization of Central American States.[89] provides for the creation of a Central American Court of Justice, to be composed of the Presidents of the Judiciary of the Member states. The functions of the Court, according to Article 15, are to hear legal disputes submitted to it by Member States and to comment on plans for the unification of Central American legislation, when requested to do so. The Court is to meet whenever it deems it necessary or when convoked by the Executive Council of the Organization. To date no statute for the Court has been drafted.

§ 4-7.9. Proposed European Court of Justice. At the Third Conference of the European Ministers of Justice, held in Dublin in May 1964, a report presented by the Department of Legal Affairs of the Council of Europe recommended the creation of a European Court of Justice. The Netherlands' Delegation at that Conference also submitted a report which included a recommendation to create a Regional Court of Justice of Europe. The principal objective of these recommendations was to assure uniformity of interpretation of international conventions. The Ministers adopted a Resolution which stated their conviction that one of the best ways to attain uniform interpretation of treaties would be to create a Regional Court of Justice.

§ 4-7.10. Proposed African, Arab, and Asian Regional Courts of Justice. At the Asian Conference on World Peace Through Law (Tokyo, 1961) the delegates approved a resolution "That there be established an Asian Court of Justice with a carefully drafted jurisdiction over matters of regional concern."[90]

In Lagos, Nigeria, in 1961, delegates to the African Conference on World Peace Through Law recommended the creation of a Court of Justice for African nations and a Court of Justice for Arab nations.[91] No official action in this direction has been taken by governments to date.

---

[89] *Charter of the Organization of Central American States,* December 12, 1962, INT'L L. MAT. 235 (1963).

[90] A.B.A., *Consensus of Tokyo: Asian and Australian Conference on World Peace Through Law,* Tokyo, 4 COMMITTEE ON WORLD PEACE THROUGH LAW (1961-62).

[91] A.B.A., *Consensus of Lagos: African and Middle Eastern Conference on World Peace Through Law,* 4 COMMITTEE ON WORLD PEACE THROUGH LAW (1961-62).

§ 4-7.11. Proposed World Trade Court. Many have suggested the creation of a World Trade Court to pass upon the ever growing number of disputes arising out of international trade transactions. Such a court would be available both to nations and to individuals as well as to multi-nation corporations. At the Fourth World Conference on World Peace Through Law in Bangkok, Thailand, this idea of a World Trade Court was coupled with the proposal of a World Trade Council to operate in the trade area as the Security Council does today on political matters. It was pointed out that the United Nations spends more than 90 percent of the time of its personnel, and the same percentage of its budget, on matters of trade and economic development so that a great need for such a Court and Council exists.

CHAPTER 5

Arbitration and Other Means of Settlement of International Disputes

§ 5-1. Introduction

The Charter of the United Nations enjoins the parties to a dispute likely to endanger peace to "seek a solution by negotiation, enquiry, mediation, conciliation, arbitration, judicial settlement, resort to regional agencies or arrangements, or other peaceful means of their own choice." (*Article 33*)

This Chapter will consider the methods described in the Charter which were not dealt with in the preceding Chapter on Judicial Settlement. Primary emphasis will be placed on arbitration of international disputes between states and on international commercial arbitration.

It is appropriate to note initially that an arbitral tribunal is generally *ad hoc* or temporary, often being constituted to settle one particular controversy. The parties can choose the members by agreement and often may prescribe the law and procedure to be applied by the tribunal. However, international arbitral decisions should be based, notwithstanding the informality of their procedures, on general principles of international law.

Conciliation is also used to settle international disputes, and consists basically of referring such disputes to commissions or other international bodies agreed upon by the parties to the dispute to investigate and clarify the facts, and to bring the parties to an agreement through a report containing proposals to settle the dispute. Neither this report, nor its proposals are binding.

After World War I, states adopted several treaties providing for the conciliation of international disputes, although its use has never been frequent. The Locarno Pact of 1925,[1] the General Act for the Pacific Settlement of Disputes,[2] the General Convention of Inter-American Conciliation,[3] and the Pact of Bogota[4] are examples of such treaties.

Conciliation is also contained in the United Nations Charter in those articles empowering both the General Assembly and the Security Council to maintain international peace and security. The General Assembly, according to Article 11, may discuss any questions relating to the maintenance of international peace and security and make recommendations to the States concerned, provided that the Security Council is not discussing the matter, and according to Article 14, may recommend measures to solve any dispute or situation likely to lead to a breach of the peace. According to Chapter VI of the Charter (Articles 33 to 38), the Security Council may recommend that the parties to a dispute affecting international peace and security, follow the procedures of conciliation.

In addition, the United Nations has established Commissions of Conciliation to conciliate international disputes. An example of

[1] The Locarno Pact of 1925 comprised four *Arbitration Conventions* between Germany and each of the following four nations: Belgium, France, Czechoslovakia and Poland; *opened for signature* October 16, 1925, 54 L.N.T.S. 289.

[2] General Act for the Pacific Settlement of Disputes, *opened for signature* May 5, 1928, 45 Stat. 2744, 90 L.N.T.S. 177.

[3] General Convention of Inter-American Conciliation, *opened for signature* January 5, 1929, 46 Stat. 2209, 100 L.N.T.S. 401.

[4] Charter of the Organization of American States, *opened for signature* April 30, 1948, T.I.A.S. No. 2361, 119 U.N.T.S. 3.

such a conciliation commission was the one created by the General Assembly in 1948, to assist the governments and authorities involved in the Palestine question to reach peaceful solution.

Mediation, another means of settling international disputes, occurs when a third party brings the parties to a dispute together informally to help them solve their differences. The mediator's main task is to urge a compromise of the dispute, rather than to solve its legal merits. As distinguished from "good offices," which consists only of bringing the disputants together, the mediator's role is more positive. Not only does he offer his advice, but he also attempts to conciliate the dispute by offering a possible solution, which, however, is not binding on the parties.

The mediator may be either states individually or collectively, individuals or international organizations. Examples of mediation by international organizations are: the appointment of a Mediator by the United Nations General Assembly in 1948 to effect a peaceful solution of the Palestinian situation; the creation of a Committee of Good Offices on the Indonesian Question by the UN Security Council in 1947 to resolve the dispute between the Netherlands and Indonesia; and the appointment of a Mediator by the UN Security Council in 1964 to solve the Cyprus situation.

§ 5-2. Arbitration of Disputes Between States[5]

Arbitration has a long and distinguished history far antedating the existence of international judicial settlement of international

---

[5] *See generally* Anderson, *The Relations Between International Tribunals of Arbitration and the Jurisdiction of National Courts,* ASIL PROC. 35-48 (1909); L. AUDRY, LA PRÉVISION DE LA SENTENCE ARBITRALE (Paris 1914); Aymar, *The Relations Between International Tribunals of Arbitration and the Jurisdiction of National Courts,* ASIL PROC. 52-61 (1909); A. BALASKO, CAUSES DE NULLITÉ DE LA SENTENCE ARBITRALE EN DROIT INTERNATIONAL PUBLIC (Paris 1938); T. BALCH, INTERNATIONAL COURTS OF ARBITRATION (6th ed., Philadelphia 1915); Brohi, *Work Paper on Pacific Settlement of International Disputes,* in WORLD PEACE THROUGH LAW: THE GENEVA CONFERENCE 83-93 (1969) [hereinafter cited as GENEVA CONF.]; P. CALVILLO, ESTÁ OBLIGADO MÉXICO A SOMETER A ARBITRAJE LAS EXPROPIACIONES AGRARIAS Y PETROLERAS (Mexico 1942); Caribiber, *L'aribitrage International entre Gouvernements et Particuliers,* 76 RECUEIL DES COURS 221-317 (1950); K. CARLSTON, THE PROCESS OF INTERNATIONAL ARBITRATION (New York 1946); A. CHAUDRK, THE PROSPECTS OF INTERNATIONAL ARBITRATION (Karachi 1966); A. CORSI, ARBITRATI INTERNAZIONALI; NOTE DI CRÍTICA DOTTRINALE E STORICA (Pisa 1893); H. CORY, COMPULSORY ARBITRATION OF INTERNATIONAL DISPUTES (New York 1932); F. DREYFUS, L'ARBITRAGE INTERNATIONAL (Paris 1892); J. DUMAS, LES SANCTIONS DE L'ARBITRAGE INTERNATIONAL (Paris 1905); H. LA FONTAINE, PASICRISIE INTERNATIONALE: HISTOIRE DOCUMENTAIRE DES ARBITRAGES INTERNATIONAUX (Berne 1902); H. LA FONTAINE, BIBLIOGRAPHIE DE LA PAIX ET DE L'ARBITRAGE INTERNATIONAL (Monaco 1904); Hjejle, *Importance of*

(Continued)

disputes. References to arbitration extend as far back as Thucydides in the fifth century B.C. The tradition of arbitration in the Arabian Peninsula as a means of resolving intertribal disputes was so well established that it became part of Muslim law. Aly (who was from

Mediation and Conciliation, in WORLD PEACE THROUGH LAW: THE ATHENS CONFERENCE 395-96 (1965) [hereinafter cited as ATHENS CONF.]; O. HOIJER, LA SOLUTION PACIFIQUE DES LITIGES INTERNATIONAUX . . . (Paris 1925); Hull, *Obligatory Arbitration and the Hague Conferences,* 2 AJIL 731-43 (1908); C. HYDE, LEGAL PROBLEMS CAPABLE OF SETTLEMENT BY ARBITRATION (Baltimore 1913); Ibingira, *Arbitration, Conciliation and Other Means of Resolving International Disputes,* in ATHENS CONF. at 396-400 (1965); INTER-PARLIAMENTARY UNION, L'ARBITRAGE OBLIGATOIRE EN 1913 . . . (Brussels 1914); Johnson, *The Constitution of an Arbitral Tribunal,* 30 BR. Y.B. INT'L L. 152-78 (1953); Jully, *Arbitration and Judicial Settlement - Recent Trends,* 48 AJIL 380-408 (1954); H. LAMMASCH, DIE LEHRE VON DER SCHIEDSGERICHTS-BARKEIT (Stuttgart 1914); A. DE LAPRADELLE & N. POLITIS, RECUEIL DES ARBITRAGES INTERNATIONAUX (Paris, Vol. 1, 1905; Vol. 2, 1924); Lazar, *Peaceful Settlement of International Conflicts,* ATHENS CONF. at 408-10 (1965); Makoski, *L'Organisation Actuelle de l'Arbitrage Internationale,* 36 RECUEIL DES COURS 267-384 (1931); W. MANNING, ARBITRATION TREATIES AMONG THE AMERICAN NATIONS . . . (Washington 1924); A. MÉRIGNHAC, TRAITÉ THÉORIQUE ET PRATIQUE DE L'ARBITRAGE INTERNATIONAL (Paris 1895); G. MOCH, HISTOIRE SOMMAIRE DE L'ARBITRAGE PERMANENT (Monaco 1910); J. MOORE, HISTORY AND DIGEST OF THE ARBITRATIONS TO WHICH THE UNITED STATES HAS BEEN A PARTY (6 vols., Washington 1898); Moore, *International Adjudications,* MODERN SERIES 14-41 (1929); Newcomb, *New Light on Jay's Treaty,* 28 AJIL 685-93 (1934); L. OPPENHEIM, INTERNATIONAL LAW 22-43 (7th ed., London 1952); PERMANENT COURT OF ARBITRATION, TRAITÉS GÉNÉRAUX d'ARBITRAGE COMMUNIQUÉS AU BUREAU INTERNATIONAL DE LA COUR; J. RADA, EL ARBITRAJE EN LA HISTORIA (Lima 1925); A. RAEDER, L'ARBITRAGE INTERNATIONAL CHES LES HELLÈNES (New York 1912); J. RALSTON, INTERNATIONAL ARBITRATION FROM ATHENS TO LOCARNO (Stanford Univ., 1929); DAVID DAVIER MEMORIAL INSTITUTE OF INTERNATIONAL STUDIES, REPORT OF A STUDY GROUP ON THE PEACEFUL SETTLEMENT OF INTERNATIONAL DISPUTES (London 1966); M. REVON, L'ARBITRAGE INTERNATIONAL SON PASSE - SON PRESENT - SON AVENIR (Paris 1892); Root, *The Relations Between International Tribunals of Arbitration and the Jurisdiction of National Courts,* 3 AJIL 529-37 (1909); D. SANDIFER, EVIDENCE BEFORE INTERNATIONAL TRIBUNALS (Chicago 1939); J. SCOTT, SOVEREIGN STATES AND SUITS BEFORE ARBITRAL TRIBUNALS AND COURTS OF JUSTICE (New York 1925); SHAMMA, *Arbitration, Conciliation and Other Means of Resolving International Disputes,* in ATHENS CONF. at 412-17; J. SIMPSON & H. FOX, INTERNATIONAL ARBITRATION: LAW AND PRACTICE (New York 1959); A. SNOW, LEGAL LIMITATIONS OF ARBITRAL TRIBUNALS (Philadelphia 1911); L. SOHN, CASES ON WORLD LAW (Brooklyn 1950) (*see especially* Bibliography on Arbitration at 1036-38); *The Function of International Arbitration Today,* 108 RECUEIL DES COURS 9-113 (1963); J. STONE, LEGAL CONTROLS OF INTERNATIONAL CONFLICT (Sydney 1954); A. STUYT, SURVEY OF INTERNATIONAL ARBITRATIONS, 1794-1938 (The Hague 1939); Summers, *Present Trends in the Policy of the United States on the Legal Settlement of Disputes,* 5 VA. J. INT'L L. 201-09 (1965); Summers, *International Arbitration,* in WORLD PEACE THROUGH LAW; THE WASHINGTON CONFERENCE 299-310 (1967) [hereinafter cited as WASHINGTON CONF.]; UN, REPORTS OF INTERNATIONAL ARBITRAL TRIBUNALS (New York 1949); UN SECRETARIAT, SYSTEMATIC SURVEY OF TREATIES FOR THE PACIFIC SETTLEMENT OF INTERNATIONAL DISPUTES (New York 1949); A SURVEY OF TREATY PROVISIONS FOR THE PACIFIC SETTLEMENT OF INTERNATIONAL DISPUTES 1949-1962 (New York 1966); C. DE VISSCHER, THEORIES ET REALITES EN DROIT INTERNATIONAL PUBLIC (Paris 1953); Wilson, *Reference of Disputes in Obligatory Arbitration Treaties,* 25 AJIL 469-90 (1932).

Mecca), the third caliph after the Prophet, was challenged by Moawiya (Governor of Damascus). After commencing war, they set up an arbitration tribunal of a representative of each side who arbitrated the question. The object of "Tahkim" (arbitration) was "solh" (reconciliation) by the imposition of terms set forth by the arbitrators who became, if need be, its enforcers as well. Subjection to arbitration was voluntary, except where by tradition (custom and usage) it was deemed morally mandatory. In that system, moral obligations were the same as legal obligations, and the impact of social pressures (intertribal) made the need for independent enforcement unnecessary. In the Middle Ages, the Pope became an arbitrator in various international disputes. However, it was not until the 19th century that arbitration began to play a significant role in international relations.

A pioneer effort in settling international controversies was the Jay Treaty of 1794[6] between England and the United States providing for arbitration of certain issues concerning the boundary between Canada and the United States arising after the Revolutionary War. The great purpose of this Treaty which arbitration served to perfection was to remove the controversy from the political arena. The result in reality resembled a negotiated settlement rather than a decision based on legal rights, although the tribunal was always expected to render its decision "on the basis of respect for law."

The success of the Jay arbitrations gave new impetus to the use of arbitration as a means of resolving international disputes. In the 177 years following the Jay Treaty, over 177 disputes between nations have been settled by arbitration, many of a highly controversial and political nature, as for example, boundary disputes. On another occasion, that of the *Alabama* claims arbitration[7] involving claims against a neutral arising from damages caused by warships constructed in its shipyards, an award by a neutral arbitral tribunal of $15,500,000 in damages was paid. Other prominent examples from among the many cases in which difficult political issues were resolved by this method include the Bering Sea Arbitration of 1893 and the arbitration between Great Britain and Venezuela in 1897. In these instances, settlement by arbitral tribunals of important questions with significant political implications demon-

---

6 Treaty of Amity Commerce and Navigation, 1 Malloy 590; MOORE, DIGEST OF INT'L ARBITRATION 327.

7 United States - Great Britain, Claims Arbitration, 1872, 4 Papers Relating to the Treaty of Washington 49. For text of the treaty of May 8, 1871, *see* 17 Stat. 865.

strated the feasibility of resort to legal means to resolve potentially dangerous disputes peacefully.

In summary, arbitration during the 19th century was useful as a device to remove major disputes from the arena of public passion and controversy and to settle them according to law. International arbitration proved that if disputes can be removed from the area of inflamed emotion, the resort to quiet, unpublicized legal processes can serve as an exemplary means for settling controversies between nations.

§ 5-2.1. **The Permanent Court of Arbitration.**[8] The Permanent Court of Arbitration was created at the Hague Conference of 1899 by the adoption of a Convention on the Pacific Settlement of International Disputes.[9] This Court is not a court in the traditional sense but consists of a permanent panel of jurists whose members may be selected by disputants to serve on particular arbitral tribunals. A tribunal may resolve a dispute either according to the procedure specified by the parties, or, if they fail to specify, according to procedures set out in the Hague Convention. Arbitration is not obligatory on the signatories to this Convention. The intention in creating the Court was to encourage nations to submit their

---

[8] *See generally* T. BALCH, INTERNATIONAL COURTS OF ARBITRATION (Philadelphia 1915); Borel, *Les Voies de Recours Contre les Sentences Arbitrales,* 52 RECUEIL DES COURS 5-105 (1935); Clarke, *A Permanent Tribunal of International Arbitration: Its Necessity and Value,* AJIL 342-409 (1907); Cour Permanente d'Arbitrage, *Réglement d'Arbitrage et de Conciliation pour les Conflits Internationaux entre deux Parties dont l'une seulement est un Etat,* NETH. INT'L L.REV. 339-50 (1962); W. DARBY, INTERNATIONAL ARBITRATION, INTERNATIONAL TRIBUNALS . . . (London 1900); François, *La Cour Permanente d'Arbitrage: son Origine, sa Jurisprudence, Son Avenir,* 87 RECUEIL DES COURS 460-551 (1955); François, *La Liberte des parties de choisier les arbitrer dans les Conflits entre les Etats,* INTERNATIONAL ARBITRATION; LIBER AMICORUM FOR MARTIN DOMKE 89-94 (The Hague 1967); A. HIGGINS, THE HAGUE PEACE CONFERENCES (Cambridge 1909); F. HOLLS, THE PEACE CONFERENCE AT THE HAGUE . . . (New York 1914); Hudson, *American Members of the Permanent Court of Arbitration during Forty Years,* 35 AJIL 135-40 (1941); W. HULL, THE TWO HAGUE CONFERENCES (Boston 1908); E. LEMONON, LA SECONDE CONFÉRENCE DE LA PAIX, LA HAYE (Paris, 1912); McNulty, *The Practice of the European Commission of Human Rights,* 11 HOW. L.J. 430-42 (1965); F. MONCONDUIT, LA COMMISSION EUROPÉENNES DE DROIT DE L'HOMME (Leyden 1965); Myers, *The Origin of the Hague Arbitral Courts,* 8 AJIL 769-802 (1914); M. ROBINSON, ARBITRATION AND THE HAGUE PEACE CONFERENCES, 1899 AND 1907 (Philadelphia 1936); J. SCOTT, THE HAGUE COURT REPORTS (Washington 1916); H. WEHBERG, KOMMENTAR ZU DEM HAAGER ABKOMMEN BETREFFEND DIE FRIEDLICHE ERLEDIGUNG INTERNATIONALER STREITIGKEITEN (Tubingen 1911); Lémenon, *La Contribution des Conférences de la Paix de la Haye au Progrès du Droit International,* 37 RECUEIL DES COURS 533-669 (1931); G. WILSON, THE HAGUE ARBITRATION CASES (Boston 1915).

[9] Convention on the Pacific Settlement of International Disputes, *opened for signature* July 29, 1899, 32 Stat. 1779, T.S. 392.

controversies to arbitration by providing improved arbitral procedures and qualified arbitrators.

Between 1899 and 1914, the Court decided 15 cases which had not been resolved through diplomatic channels. Perhaps the most significant of these was the *North Atlantic Coast Fisheries* Case[10] involving a dispute over the rights of United States citizens to fish off the coast of Newfoundland and to cure and dry their catch at various points on the shore. The issue had been a source of tension between Great Britain and the United States for almost a century, and attempts to solve it by treaty had proved unsuccessful. In 1908, the parties agreed to arbitrate the case under the procedures of the Permanent Court of Arbitration. The decision was accepted by both parties. Other cases decided by the Court in this period included the dispute over the maritime frontier between Norway and Sweden, a dispute between the Netherlands and Portugal over a boundary on the Island of Timor, and international disputes involving the claims of nationals, seizure of vessels and interpretation of treaties.

During this period, widespread support grew for the settlement of international disputes by the arbitral process. In response to this expression of public opinion, several nations entered into bilateral treaties agreeing to submit to arbitration any future disputes which might arise between them. Often, however, the treaty contained the reservation that matters concerning "the vital interest, independence, and national honor" of the signatory nations would not be subject to the treaty. Nevertheless, these treaties were the basis for the resolution by arbitration of many international disputes and represented an advance toward acceptance of the rule of law.

The second Hague Conference convened in 1907 in the hope that the Permanent Court of Arbitration could be developed into a truly permanent tribunal rather than a panel from which arbitrators were selected and that the member nations would ratify a general treaty of arbitration. The members of the second Conference worked out a modest list of subjects upon which they hoped nations would agree in advance to submit to compulsory arbitration. Unfortunately, the delegates had to work under the shadow of reservations such as those aforementioned and the type of national policies which had created them. As a result of these handicaps (although it did revise the 1899 Convention), the Con-

---

[10] North Atlantic Coast Fisheries Case (United States v. Great Britain), Hague Court Reports (Scott) 146 (Perm. Ct. Arb. 1910).

ference was unable to establish a permanent court with compulsory jurisdiction.

The "Court" which was established by the Hague Conventions consists of a list of arbitrators, which is circulated to all signatories. The arbitrators are nominated by the signatories, with each party entitled to nominate not more than four persons "of known competency in questions of international law, the highest moral reputation, and disposed to accept the duties of arbitrator" for a term of six years. If parties wish to have recourse to the Court for settlement of a dispute, they must select the arbitral panel which is to decide the case from this list. If they are unable to agree upon a panel, then they are each to appoint two arbitrators from the list, only one of whom can be a national or a person placed on the list by the party making the selection. These arbitrators then select an umpire to complete the tribunal. If the parties choose arbitrators outside the list of arbitrators comprising the "Court," the cases heard under this procedure are called "special arbitrations". All administrative business of the Court is handled by the Administrative Bureau in the Hague, operating under the supervision of a Permanent Council consisting of diplomatic envoys of the contracting powers.

The Permanent Court of Arbitration decided 30 cases from its establishment in 1899 until 1931, but only five since 1931, partly due to the creation of the Permanent Court of Justice in 1920 and its successor, the present International Court of Justice, and partly to the reluctance of nations to submit disputes to outside arbitration. Because of this inactivity, the Court's abolition was urged at the First Assembly of the League of Nations in 1920. Since it was thought that the Court would still play an important role in solving certain international disputes, which require the adaptability of an arbitral process, the proposal received no support. In fact, the Court continues to be available to settle disputes, and has expanded its jurisdiction to include cases between parties only one of which is a state, under new rules approved by the Administrative Bureau on March 26, 1962. The Court is also still active in nominating candidates for election as judges of the International Court of Justice. Each national group in the Court may nominate four candidates for election by the United Nations General Assembly and Security Council. In addition, the Court continues to render valuable services in the fields of conciliation and inquiry.

§ 5-2.2. **Arbitral Conventions.**[11] Treaties and conventions providing for arbitration of disputes not solvable by diplomacy have not been uncommon. One of the first such comprehensive treaties referring all disputes between two nations to arbitration was the one between Colombia and Peru in 1829, and this has been followed very widely both among Latin American nations and others as well, particularly those of Europe. In 1902, nine Latin American nations meeting in Mexico City signed a treaty on compulsory arbitration which required them to submit all controversies which diplomacy could not settle to the decision of arbitrators. Specifically covered by the treaty are disputes arising over diplomatic privileges, boundaries, rights of navigation, and the validity, construction and enforcement of treaties, as well as other controversies not affecting either the independence or national honor of one of the interested nations. The General Treaty of Inter-American Arbitration,[12] signed at Washington in 1929, binds the contracting parties "to submit to arbitration all differences of an international character" which are juridical in nature and which cannot be adjusted by diplomacy. Exceptions are allowed only for controversies within the domestic jurisdiction which "are not controlled by international law" and those affecting the interests or referring to the actions of a state not a party to the treaty.

The American Treaty on Pacific Settlement,[13] or "Pact of Bogotá" signed at Bogotá, Colombia, in 1948, contains a chapter on arbitration. This chapter contains detailed provisions for the selection of the Tribunal, permits a dissenting opinion, and provides for a review of the award by the same tribunal at the request of one of the parties if a previously unknown existing fact, which the tribunal believes will have a decisive influence on the award, is discovered. Moreover, the Pact of Bogotá provides that, if one of the parties should fail to carry out the obligations of the arbitral award, the other parties may propose a meeting of consultation of Ministers

---

[11] For discussion of particular arbitral conventions *see* P. BAKER, THE GENEVA PROTOCOL (London 1924); Brierly, *The General Act of Geneva 1928,* 11 BR.Y.B. INT'L L. 119-34 (1930); Garner, *Senate Reservations to the Inter-American Arbitration Treaty,* 26 AJIL 333-36 (1932); *The General Act, 1928,* 25 AJIL SUPP. 204-15 (1931); Myers, *Acceptance of General Treaty of Inter-American Arbitration,* 30 AJIL 57-63 (1936); Treaty of Peace between Colombia and Peru, Sept. 22, 1829, COLLECCIÓN DE TRATADOS PÚBLICOS 72 (Bogotá 1866); Wehberg, *Le Protocole de Génève,* 7 RECUEIL DES COURS 5-140 (1925); Whitton & Brewer, *Problems Raised by the General Treaty of Inter-American Arbitration,* 25 AJIL 447-69 (1931).

[12] General Treaty of Inter-American Arbitration, *opened for signature* January 5, 1969, 49 Stat. 3153, 130 L.N.T.S. 135.

[13] Charter of the Organization of American States, *opened for signature* April 30, 1948, T.I.A.S. No. 2361, 119 U.N.T.S. 3.

of Foreign Affairs to agree upon "appropriate measures" to insure the fulfillment of the arbitral award. Although 21 countries signed this Pact, only nine have ratified it, and it is in effect only among those nine nations.

Debates on the subject of arbitration and security in the Assembly of the League of Nations over the course of several years led to the adoption of the Geneva Protocol of 1924[14] on the pacific settlement of international disputes. While this never came into force, the Ninth Assembly of the League of Nations subsequently adopted the General Act of 1928[15] on the pacific settlement of international disputes, providing various alternative means for the settlement of disputes, such as conciliation by commissions constituted by the parties to the dispute, and resort to the Permanent Court of International Justice, or the Permanent Court of Arbitration. The Act further provides that if the constitutional law of a party to a dispute does not permit, or only partially permits, its judgment to become effective contrary to international law, the injured party will receive equitable compensation. Twenty-three nations were parties to the Act at the end of 1938.

In 1949, the General Assembly of the United Nations approved a proposed revision of the 1928 agreement[16] aimed at restoring its efficacy by bringing up-to-date reference in the General Act to the League of Nations and the Permanent Court of International Justice. Six nations have ratified the Revised Act.

In 1957, the representatives of the 15 governments which are members of the Council of Europe signed the European Convention on the Pacific Settlement of Disputes. A Chapter providing for arbitration as a means of settling disputes was also contained in this convention.

Judicial tribunals have sometimes been criticized because the law they apply does not reflect the interpretation of the concepts of justice of both parties, owing to an inequitable representation of legal systems on the tribunals. By placing greater emphasis on arbitration, where both sides to a dispute are equally represented, and where an impartial umpire, who has been selected without bias, completes the tribunal, such complaints lose their force.

---

[14] Protocol on Arbitration Clauses, *entered into force* July 28, 1924, 27 L.N.T.S. 157.

[15] General Act of 1928, 11 BR.Y.B. INT'L L. 119-33 (1930), 93 L.N.T.S. 343.

[16] Revised General Act for the Pacific Settlement of Disputes, *registration* September 20, 1950, T.I.A.S. 912, 71 U.N.T.S. 101.

§ 5-2.3. Arbitral Procedure.[17]   Arbitral proceedings are usually commenced through an exchange of notes between the contending governments called a *compromis*. Another means of achieving this same end is to include in a treaty a clause in general terms providing for formation of an arbitral tribunal. This is known as the clause *compromissorie*.

The importance of the *compromis* is that it specifies the issues and the law to be applied in this particular case, as well as the applicable procedure. Normally, *compromis* will provide that each of the parties before the arbitral tribunal choose one or two arbitrators by a designated means and that these arbitrators will then select one additional arbitrator, as the umpire, who acts usually in one of two ways. One method is for the arbitrators selected by the parties to go as far as they can towards reaching a decision, and to refer to the umpire only when they have reached an impasse. The other method is to have the umpire participate in the proceedings from the beginning.

The International Law Commission has adopted model rules on arbitral procedure aimed at insuring that nations which have agreed to arbitration perform in good faith.[18] These rules, intended only as guides, were considered for a time as a possible source of an international convention, but have instead been suggested as a model for inclusion in bilateral and multilateral international treaties and agreements and in special arbitral agreements. The report states that the basic idea behind these rules is "that an agreement to arbitrate involves in substance an international obligation equivalent to a treaty obligation. Having once entered into it (which they

---

[17] *See generally* A. ACCREMENT, LA PROCEDURE DANS LES ARBITRAGES INTERNATIONAUX (Arras 1905); C. BISHOP, INTERNATIONAL ARBITRAL PROCEDURE (Washington 1931); K. CARLSTON, THE PROCESS OF INTERNATIONAL ARBITRATION (New York 1946); Carlston, *Procedural Problems in International Arbitration,* 39 AJIL 426-50 (1945); K. Carlston, *Codification of International Arbitral Procedure,* 47 AJIL 285-301 (1913); King, *An Innovation in International Arbitral Tribunals, the Swiss-Allied Accord,* 46 AJIL 464-83 (1952); R. MORRIS, INTERNATIONAL ARBITRATION AND PROCEDURE (New Haven 1911); Permanent Court of Arbitration, *Rules of Arbitration and Conciliation for Settlement of Disputes Between Two Parties of Which Only One Is a State,* 57 AJIL 500-12 (1963); J. RALSTON, INTERNATIONAL ARBITRAL LAW AND PROCEDURE . . . (Boston 1910); J. RALSTON, THE LAW AND PROCEDURE OF INTERNATIONAL TRIBUNALS (Stanford Univ. 1926, Supp. 1936); Ralston, *Draft Convention on Arbitral Procedure of the International Law Commission,* 48 AJIL 296-99 (1954); J. SIMPSON & H. FOX, INTERNATIONAL ARBITRATION: LAW AND PRACTICE (New York 1959); Suratgar, *The Sapphire Arbitration Award, the Procedural Aspects: A Report and a Critique,* 3 COLUM. J. OF TRANSNAT'L L. 152-209 (1965); UNITED NATIONS SECRETARIAT, COMMENTARY ON THE DRAFT CONVENTION ON ARBITRAL PROCEDURE (New York 1955).

[18] Draft Code of Offenses Against the Peace and Security of Mankind, Report of the Int'l Law Commission, Sixth Session (U.N. Doc. A/2693, 1954).

are free not to do) the parties are legally bound to carry it out and, in consequence, to take all steps necessary to enable arbitration to take place and the disputes finally to be liquidated; and, similarly, to refrain from action, positive or negative, which would impede or frustrate that consummation . . . . Subject to the over-ruling principle of non-frustration, they can adopt what procedural or other rules they like." The model rules include sections on: the existence of a dispute and the scope of the undertaking to arbitrate; the *compromis*; constitution of the tribunal; powers of the tribunal in the process of arbitration; deliberations of the tribunal; interpretation, validity, and annulment and revision of the award, respectively.

These model rules seek to increase resort to arbitration not by creating a general obligation to submit controversies to arbitration, but by facilitating the carrying out of arbitral agreements on the assumption that states which have agreed by treaty to submit certain disputes to arbitration actually wish to do so. In view of the success of arbitration during the Nineteenth and early Twentieth century, it is to be hoped that this method will receive greater consideration in the future as a means of settlement of international disputes.

Bilateral treaties providing for arbitral settlement of international disputes may contain clauses such as the following general one:

> All differences relating to international matters in which the High Contracting Parties are concerned by virtue of a claim of right made by one against the other under treaty or otherwise, which it has not been possible to adjust by diplomacy, which have not been adjusted as a result of reference to an appropriate commission of conciliation, and which are justiciable in their nature by reason of being susceptible of decision by the application of the principles of law or equity, shall be submitted to the Permanent Court of Arbitration established at The Hague by the Convention of October 18, 1907, or to some other competent tribunal, as shall be decided in each case by special agreement, which special agreement shall provide for the organization of such tribunal if necessary, define its powers, state the question or questions at issue, and settle the terms of reference.[19]

Conclusion of more treaties with such provisions could be a noteworthy factor in furthering the development of the international rule of law.

---

[19] Documents, Asian and Australian Conference on World Peace Through Law 51 (Tokyo, 1961).

The 1907 Hague Convention[20] requires that the *compromis* signed by states wishing to use the Permanent Court of Arbitration define: the subject of the dispute, the manner of appointing arbitrators, any special powers which may eventually be given to the tribunal, where it shall meet, the languages and any special conditions the parties may agree upon.

The Convention allows the parties to determine the rules of procedure themselves, or to utilize those rules contained in the Convention, whether or not they have selected their arbitrators from the Hague list; it provides for secret proceedings, and decision by majority vote. The arbitral award is final, and any dispute as to its interpretation is to be decided by the tribunal.

The language of various *compromis* as to the law to be applied varies considerably, of course. Sometimes reference may be made to general principles of international law or to principles of equity and justice. Special legal rules may be specified as being applicable and controlling. For example, the *compromis* between Honduras and El Salvador concerning the boundary dispute between them established the principles to be invoked as governing prescriptive rights to the territory.

§ 5-3. Settlement of Disputes by Commission[21]

The mechanism of the commission has been of great value in obtaining solutions to legal questions that would otherwise have fallen prey to the vagaries of politics. The concept of a commission is related to, although distinct from, that of an arbitral tribunal. In fact, several commissions have recently been formed to lend a permanence and constancy to the making available of arbitrators, mediators, and conciliators.

§ 5-3.1. The European Commission of Human Rights.[22] The European Convention for the Protection of Human Rights, in Article

---

[20] Hague Convention (1907), *opened for signature* October 18, 1907, 36 Stat. 2199, T.S. 536.

[21] Lambadarios, *Settlement of International Disputes by Administrative Organs and Methods Within the Framework of International Economic Institutions*, in ATHENS CONF. 401-08.

[22] *See generally* EUROPEAN COMMISSION OF HUMAN RIGHTS, DOCUMENTS AND DECISIONS (The Hague, 1955); THE EUROPEAN COMMISSION AND EUROPEAN COURT OF HUMAN RIGHTS, YEARBOOK OF THE EUROPEAN CONVENTION OF HUMAN RIGHTS (The Hague 1955); McNulty & Eissen, *The European Commission of Human Rights: Procedure and Jurisprudence*, 1 J. INT'L COM. JUR. 198-223 (1958); *Rules of Procedure of the European Commission of Human Rights*, 8 ANN. EUR. 383-

(Continued)

19, provides for the creation of a European Commission of Human Rights. The Commission is to serve as an impartial, international organ to which complaints can be made in the event of failure by a state, party to the Convention, to secure the rights and freedoms defined in the Convention. Each of the High Contracting Parties is represented on the Commission by one member.

Under Article 24 of the Convention, any High Contracting Party may refer to the Commission through the Secretary-General of the Council of Europe any alleged breach of the provisions of the Convention by another High Contracting Party.

The Commission hears claims of individuals as well as those presented by states, according to the following procedures:

(1) The Commission may receive petitions addressed to the Secretary-General of the Council of Europe from any person, non-governmental organization or group of individuals claiming to be a victim of a violation by one of the High Contracting Parties of the rights set forth in the Convention, provided that the High Contracting Party against which the complaint has been lodged has declared that it recognizes the competence of the Commission to receive such petitions. Those of the High Contracting Parties who have made such a declaration undertake not to hinder in any way the effective exercise of this right.

(2) Such declarations may be made for a specific period.

(3) The declaration shall be deposited with the Secretary-General of the Council of Europe who shall transmit copies thereof to the High Contracting Parties and publish them.

(4) The Commission shall only exercise the powers provided for in this Article when at least six High Contracting Parties are bound by declarations made in accordance with the preceding paragraphs.[23]

The Commission deals with claims only after domestic remedies have been exhausted according to the generally recognized rules of international law, and only within six months from the date of the final domestic decision.

The procedure prescribed by the European Convention for the Protection of Human Rights for handling complaints of violations of human rights is as follows:

---

407 (1961); Stychmans, *La Commission Europeenne des Droits de l'homme et le Proces Equitable,* 81 J. TRIB. 533-43 (1966); Weil, *Decisions in Inadmissible Applications by the European Commission of Human Rights,* 54 AJIL 874-81 (1960).

[23] McNulty & Eisen, *The European Commission of Human Rights: Procedure and Jurisprudence,* 1 J. INT'L COM. JUR. 198-223 (1958).

(1) Complaints by individual members of the public of violation of their rights are brought first before national courts.

(2) Within six months of final judgment, any signatory State may bring the dispute before the Commission, whether or not the individuals or groups of individuals concerned are its own nationals.

(3) The Commission decides whether cases are inadmissible or outside its competence or whether to appoint a Sub-Commission to hold an investigation. The Sub-Commission will effect a friendly settlement if possible; or, if not possible, it will prepare a report containing its opinion and proposals. This report is then transmitted to the Committee of Ministers.

(4) Any States concerned, or the Commission, may refer the matter to the Court within a period of three months provided that the State or States in question have accepted the jurisdiction of the Court. Where the case is not brought before the Court, or where the States concerned have not accepted the jurisdiction of the Court, the Committee of Ministers will take a decision in light of the report, which is final, irrevocable and binding.

(5) Only States or the Commission may bring a case before the Court. In this event, the Court constitutes a Chamber of seven judges to hear the case. The Chamber will either decide the case to be inadmissible or outside the competence of the Court, or conversely, it will pass judgment, which is final, irrevocable and binding.

(6) The Secretary-General of the Council of Europe may at any time request signatory States to furnish an explanation of the manner in which its internal law assures the effective implementation of any of the provisions of this Convention.[24]

The Commission has examined several hundred complaints and has resolved them, in the great majority, by friendly negotiation.

§ 5-3.2. The Inter-American Commission of Human Rights. The Inter-American Commission of Human Rights, an autonomous body within the structure of the Organization of American States, states in its Preamble that it aims "to promote respect for human rights."[25]

The Commission is composed of seven members elected by the Council of the Organization of American States from a list of candidates presented by member states of the Organization. No more than one national of any state may serve. Commission members have a four-year term of office; they elect their president and vice-president who serve for two-year terms, and are eligible for one re-election.

---

[24] YEARBOOK OF EUROPEAN CONVENTION OF HUMAN RIGHTS, *supra* n.22.

[25] ORGANIZATION OF AMERICAN STATES, INTER-AMERICAN COMMISSION ON HUMAN RIGHTS (OEA/Ser. L/V/ 1.5).

The Commission meets once or twice a year in regular sessions for a period not to exceed eight weeks and may be convoked by its president or by a majority of its members for a special meeting. The Pan American Union in Washington is its permanent seat, but it can hold meetings in any American state upon agreement by a majority of its members and with the consent of the state concerned. In practice, its investigations have led it to hold meetings in several of these states.

The Commission aims to increase the familiarity of the peoples of America with human rights. It recommends to states measures for the protection of human rights by domestic legislation. It prepares reports of problems and activities in the human rights field and is the source of information on human rights measures adopted by American states. In the performance of its functions, it may examine the human rights situation in any American state, with the consent of the state concerned, and may request relevant information. However, it is not authorized to decide individual charges of human rights violations.

Upon receipt of charges of numerous serious human rights violations in Cuba, the Commission addressed to the Cuban Government a summary of the most important charges, pointing out the contradictions between Cuban laws and the American Declaration of the Rights and Duties of Man and recommending the adoption of laws in accordance with that Declaration. The Commission then requested the consent of the Cuban authorities to a visit by the Commission in the territory to observe first-hand the human rights situation. Since there was no reply to this request, the Commission, after taking testimony in Florida of persons who had served prison terms in Cuba, prepared a report, including specific cases of maltreatment, torture and sudden death. In view of the failure of Cuban authorities to reply, the Commission reported its findings to the Council of the Organization of American States.

Upon receipt of charges of repeated and serious human rights violations in Haiti, the Commission requested relevant information from Haitian authorities. When these authorities failed to provide adequate information, the Commission requested consent to study the situation in the country. When this and subsequent requests were rejected by the Haitian authorities, the Commission prepared a report of the Haitian human rights situation and sent copies to the member governments of the Organization.

Another important area of Commission human rights activities was in the Dominican Republic (see Chapter 8 on Human Rights).

To charges of human rights violations in Paraguay, Guatemala, Nicaragua, Ecuador and Honduras, each government replied to the Commission's requests for information; and Ecuador and Honduras invited the Commission to observe the situation in their countries.

The Commission has been active in promoting respect for human rights in many other ways. It has prepared a draft Inter-American Convention on Freedom of Expression, Information and Investigation, which has been transmitted to the member governments for their observations. It has also prepared a preliminary draft Inter-American Convention on Protection of Human Rights,[26] which the Council of the Organization adopted in its entirety in October, 1968, and transmitted to the governments for their observations. It examined and reported on the situation of political refugees in America, and made recommendations which are now under consideration. Through a General Program of Work, its members engage in the preparation of studies and reports on human rights subjects. It has increased general awareness of human rights by lectures and seminars. It has encouraged the formation of national committees of human rights and has developed a scholarship program in cooperation with the General Secretariat to encourage studies in the field.

From a tentative beginning but a few years ago, the Commission has become an active, useful, basic organ of the Organization of American States.

§ 5-3.3. The Commission of Mediation, Conciliation and Arbitration of the Organization of African Unity.[27] The Organization of African Unity (OAU)[28] was established in Addis Ababa, Ethiopia, by the independent states of Africa on May 25, 1963. By Article 3[29] of its Charter, these states affirm the principle of "peaceful settlement of disputes by negotiation, mediation, conciliation or arbitration." By Article 19[30] they "pledge to settle all disputes among themselves by peaceful means." To assure this end, they decided to create a Commission of Mediation, Conciliation and Arbitration,

---

[26] Inter-American Convention on the Protection of Human Rights, *opened for signature* June 8, 1960 (OEA/Ser. L/V/II 14 Doc. 33).

[27] Elias, *The Commission of Mediation, Conciliation and Arbitration of the Organization of African States,* 40 BR. Y.B. INT'L L. 336-54 (1966).

[28] Charter of the Organization of African Unity, *opened for signature* May 25, 1963, 2 I.L.M. 766.

[29] *Id.* Art. 3.

[30] *Id.* Art. 19.

and by Article 7[31] of the Charter they made this Commission one of the four principal OAU organs, thus emphasizing the importance which they attached to it.

The Commission was established as an autonomous body within the OAU by a Protocol drafted by a special committee approved by the Council of Ministers, and signed on July 21, 1964, by the OAU Assembly. Its seat is in Addis Ababa.

The Commission consists of 21 members, no two of whom may be nationals of the same state. Each member state of the OAU may nominate two candidates who must be persons of recognized competence. The Assembly of Heads of State and Government elects Commission members for a term of five years from a list of the nominated candidates.

A President of the Commission and two Vice-Presidents are elected by the Assembly of Heads of State and Government for a five-year term. They constitute the Bureau of the Commission. Their function is to consult with the parties to arrive at the most appropriate method of settling a dispute between them.

The administrative expenses of the Commission are borne by the OAU. Other expenses in connection with proceedings are regulated by the rules of procedure.

The jurisdiction of the Commission extends only to States. A dispute may be referred to the Commission by a single party, by parties jointly, by the Council of Ministers or by the Assembly of Heads of State and Government. If one or more parties refuse to accept the Commission's jurisdiction, the Bureau refers the question to the Council of Ministers.

The Commission adopts its own working methods and its rules of procedure. Commission members enjoy diplomatic immunities and privileges. Member states are obliged to cooperate fully with those engaged in any proceeding.

Parties may resort to mediation, conciliation, or arbitration to settle a dispute. If they choose mediation, the President of the Commission, with the consent of the parties, appoints one or more members to serve as mediators, whose function is limited to reconciling party claims. After examination of the issues in dispute he submits to the parties a written proposal, which, if accepted, becomes the basis of a protocol or arrangement.

The parties may prefer conciliation as the best method of settling their dispute. In this case, one or more parties may present a peti-

---

[31] *Id.* Art. 7.

tion to initiate conciliation proceedings. If presented by only one party, that party must indicate that it has given written notice to the other party. The petition must include a summary statement of the grounds of the dispute. The President of the Commission, upon receipt of the petition, appoints a Board of Conciliators composed of five members, three of whom, including the chairman, are appointed by the President and one by each of the parties. Only one person from a given state may serve as a member of the Board. It is the duty of the Board to clarify the issues and to bring about an acceptable agreement between the parties, if possible. During the proceedings the parties are represented by agents and may be assisted by counsel. Upon completion of the proceedings, the Board drafts a report indicating that the parties have come to an agreement or that it has been impossible to reach an agreement. The terms of the agreement and Board recommendations may be included in the report if this seems desirable. The report is sent to the parties and to the President of the Commission. It may be published only with the consent of the parties.

When arbitration is requested, the arbitral tribunal is formed as follows: each party selects one arbitrator with legal qualifications from among Commission members, and the two thus chosen select a chairman also from among Commission members. If the two arbitrators disagree in their choice of a chairman, the Bureau appoints the chairman. If the parties agree, the President of the Commission may appoint two more arbitrators, who are not necessarily members of the Commission, to serve on the tribunal. The arbitrators must all be of different nationalities. They must not be nationals of the parties or domiciled in the territory of the parties or employed by them. Persons who have served as mediators or conciliators in the same dispute are not eligible to serve on the tribunal. Acceptance of recourse to the tribunal constitutes acceptance of the award. In the *compromis* concluded by the parties, they agree to arbitrate and to accept the decision of the arbitral tribunal. It also specifies the subject matter of the dispute and indicates the place where the tribunal will be held. It may, in addition, indicate the law to be applied and certain other matters. Otherwise, the arbitrators will apply treaties between the parties, international law, the OAU Charter, and the UN Charter. The case can be decided *ex aequo et bono* only if the parties agree. Hearings are held *in camera* unless the arbitrators decide on public sessions. The award must be in writing and must give reasons for every point of the decision.

§ 5-3.4. Conciliation Commission and Arbitral Tribunals for the Settlement of Investment Disputes.[32]

A Convention on the Settlement of Investment Disputes between States and Nationals of other States,[33] concluded in Washington on March 18, 1965, entered into force on October 14, 1966. By April 1970, a total of 63 states had signed, and 54 states had ratified the Convention.

The Convention establishes an International Centre for Settlement of Investment Disputes to provide facilities for conciliation and arbitration of investment disputes between Contracting States and nationals of other Contracting States. The Centre is located at the Headquarters of the International Bank for Reconstruction and Development (World Bank) which sponsored the Convention.

The Convention is the result of very careful preparatory work. Working papers and discussions by World Bank staff members were followed by regional consultative conferences and by numerous meetings of a Legal Committee consisting of representatives of 61 member countries.

The Centre has an Administrative Council and a Secretariat. Each Contracting State has one representative on the Council, with the Chairman of the Bank serving as Council Chairman. The main functions of the Council are to elect the Secretary-General of the Centre and to adopt a budget, administrative and financial regulations and rules of procedure for arbitration and conciliation proceedings. The Council holds an annual meeting and special meetings may be convened when needed.

---

[32] *See generally* Broches, *The Convention on the Settlement of Investment Disputes: Some Observations on Jurisdiction,* 5 COLUM. J. TRANSNAT'L L. 263-80 (1966); Broches, *Applicable Law and Default Procedure,* INT'L ARB. LIBER AMICORUM MARTIN DOMKE, 12-22 (The Hague 1967); Delaume, *La Convention pour le Règlement des Différends Relatifs aux Investissements entre Etats et Ressortissants d'Autres Etats,* 93 J.DR. INT'L 26-49 (1966); Farley, *Commentary: The Convention on the Settlement of Investment Disputes between States and Nationals of Other States,* 5 Duquesne U. L.REV. 19-30 (1966); Firth, *The Law Governing Contracts in Arbitration under the World Bank Convention,* 1 N.Y.U. J. INT'L L. & POL. 253-76 (1968); Hynning, *World Bank's Plan for the Settlement of International Investment Disputes,* SYMPOSIUM ON STRUCTURES AND SAFEGUARDS 145-72 (1966); INTERNATIONAL CENTRE FOR SETTLEMENT OF INVESTMENT DISPUTES, ANNUAL REPORT (in English, French, and Spanish): Hynning, *Convention for the Settlement of Investment Disputes between States and Nationals of Other States;* Hynning, *International Centre for the Settlement of Investment Disputes . . . What It Is . . . What It Does . . . How It Works* (in English, French and Spanish) Hynning, *List of Contracting and Other Signatory States* (in English and French–Revised periodically); Rodley, *Some Aspects of the World Bank Convention on the Settlement of Investment Disputes,* 4 CAN. Y.B. INT'L L. 43-63 (1966); Roulet, *La Convention du 18 Mars 1965 pour le Règlement des Différends Relatifs aux Investissements entre Etats et Ressortissants d'Autres Etats,* 22 SWITZ. Y.B. INT'L R. 121-56 (1966); *World Bank Convention on Investment Disputes,* 21 ARB. J. 180-84 (1966).

[33] Convention on the Settlement of Investment Disputes between States and Nationàls of Other States, *entered into force* October 14, 1966, I.C.S.I.D./2 (English).

The Secretariat consists of a Secretary-General, one or more Deputy Secretaries-General and a staff. The Secretary-General is elected for a six-year term. He serves as the Centre's principal legal representative and officer. He has the power to "screen" requests for arbitration or conciliation where the dispute is "manifestly" outside the Centre's jurisdiction.

The Inaugural Meeting was held on February 2, 1967, with representatives of all Contracting States present. At this meeting, the General Counsel of the World Bank, Mr. Aron Broches, was elected Secretary-General of the Centre and provisional regulations and administrative arrangements were adopted. At its first Annual Meeting, the Council adopted definitive regulations and rules to replace the provisional instruments. It also approved administrative arrangements to be concluded between the Centre and the Permanent Court of Arbitration by which, with the approval of the latter, either institution could conduct a proceeding at the seat of the other.

The Convention provides for a Panel of Conciliators and a Panel of Arbitrators. Each Contracting State may select four persons for each Panel and the Chairman of the Council is authorized to appoint Conciliators and Arbitrators if the parties fail to do so. Panel members must be persons of moral integrity and legal competence. An effort is made to assure representation of the principal legal systems of the world.

The basis of the Centre's jurisdiction is the consent of the parties, which may be given in any of several ways but cannot be withdrawn unilaterally. The dispute submitted for resolution must be one involving rights and not merely interests. The parties must be a Contracting State and a national of another Contracting State. When the national of a State and another Contracting State have agreed to submit or have submitted to arbitration under the Convention, the State of the national cannot offer him protection or assistance.

Proceedings are instituted by a request addressed to the Secretary-General. The parties have a large measure of freedom in constituting the Conciliation Commission and the Arbitration Tribunal. They may even appoint Conciliators and Arbitrators who are not on the Panels. The Commission and the Tribunal have the power to determine their jurisdiction in any given case. The rules of procedure adopted by the Administrative Council apply unless the parties agree to apply other rules. An Arbitral Tribunal must apply the law agreed upon by the parties. If the parties do not agree upon a specific body of law to be applied, the Tribunal must apply the law of the state party to the dispute and applicable rules of international law. If a party fails to appear to present a case, the Tribunal may give an award by default. The award of the Tribunal is final and without appeal, although the tribunal may entertain a request for revision of the award, its interpretation, a supplement to it, or its annulment. The parties are obliged to comply with the award and enforce the pecuniary obligations imposed by it as though it were a final decision of a domestic court. The place of the proceedings is determined by agreement of the parties.

The International Court of Justice is granted jurisdiction over disputes between Contracting States with regard to the interpretation or application of the Convention, which are not settled by other means. However, the International Court is not granted jurisdiction to review the decision of a Conciliation Commission or an Arbitral Tribunal.

§ 5-3.5. **International Claims Commissions.** Under traditional international law, individuals could not present their claims directly against foreign states. These claims had to be presented on their behalf by the state of which the claimant was a national, but this has changed with Claims Commissions.

Mixed claims commissions substituted judicial for negotiated determination of many disputes. A commission was constituted in accordance with provisions of a convention between the state of the claimant and the state of the defendant. It was generally composed of a national of the claimant state, a national of the defendant state and a national of another country. Its jurisdiction and its power and duty to decide a case were determined by the convention which created it. It decided cases in accordance with the provisions of the convention and the principles of international law. Claims brought before mixed commissions included those between nationals of one state and those of another state, those between two states, and those between a national of one state and the government of another state.

Traditionally, claims were handled by government espousal and by international commissions. In recent years, however, the vast number of claims presented, the need for lump sum settlements, and the nature of the international climate have contributed to the development of national claims commissions. These commissions are an interesting combination of the national and international, since they derive their authority from both international agreement and municipal legislation. One authority[34] has summarized the advantages and disadvantages of national claims commissions. He contends that their most favorable aspect is that claims are removed from the diplomatic realm and obtain relatively quick settlement. A quick though inadequate settlement may prove to be more equitable and more useful to the parties than a more fully adequate settlement which is long deferred. National commission, lump sum settlement eliminates the need for state espousal of claims, with the delays and problems involved in satisfying the rule of exhausting local remedies, the involvements with national policy considerations and various procedural problems including language difficulties and different interpretations of the law.

The use of national claims commissions does present some unfavorable aspects, however. Commissions may not reflect generally accepted principles of international law, although they may reflect the principles of international law accepted by the state adjudicating the claims, thus tending to increase the fragmentation of the law of international claims at a time when great efforts are being made to achieve a world rule of law. National commission, lump sum settlements, providing only partial indemnification, conflict with the principles of just and adequate compensation, at least in the claims based on the nationalization of property. Also, numerous difficulties connected with the conclusion of lump sum agreements with foreign countries, and the expense and difficulty of obtaining evidence from abroad exist.[35]

§ 5-3.6. **Commissions of Inquiry.** The 1899 and 1907 Hague Conventions contained provisions to have disputes settled by international commissions of inquiry, and the *Dogger Bank* Case of 1904[36] is often cited as a case in which hostilities were averted through such a commission. As a result of international interest in

---

[34] R. LILLICH, INTERNATIONAL CLAIMS: THEIR ADJUDICATION BY NATIONAL COMMISSIONS (Syracuse, N.Y. 1962). (Citations of books, articles, international agreements, statutes, and miscellaneous references on this subject are at 123-33).

[35] *See generally* A. BEAUCOURT, LES COMMISSIONS INTERNATIONALES D'EN-QUÊTE . . . (Paris 1909); M. BOKANOWSKI, LES COMMISSIONS INTERNATIONALES D'ENQUÊTE . . . (Paris 1908); Ermacora, *International Enquiry Commissions in the Field of Human Rights,* 1 J. INT'L & COMP. L. 180-219 (1968); Franck & Cherkis, *The Economic Problem of Fact-Finding in International Disputes,* 18 CASE W. RES. L.REV. 1483-1524 (1967); N. HILL, INTERNATIONAL COMMISSIONS OF INQUIRY AND CONCILIATION (Worcester, Mass. 1932); E. LÉMONON, LA SÉCONDE CONFÉRENCE DE LA PAIX 73-94 (Paris, 1912); A. LEROY, LES COMMISSIONS INTERNATIONALES D'ENQUÊTES AU XXᵉ SIÉCLE (Saumur 1910); D. MYERS, THE COMMISSIONS OF INQUIRY; THE WILSON-BRYAN PEACE PLAN (Boston 1913); Wilson, *Report of the International Commission of Inquiry in the Loss of the Dutch Steamer Tubantia,* 16 AJIL 432-33 (1922).

this method of resolving disputes, international joint commissions were established, some of which are still active and successful (such as the International Joint Commission regarding boundary waters between the United States and Canada). Similar institutions have had a particularly significant role in the Western Hemisphere.

§ 5-4. Other Means of Settling International Disputes[37]

Diplomatic negotiation, the oldest of all methods, is still the most common means of resolving international disputes. Such negotiations clarify the facts, explore the validity of the arguments made by the parties, present various formulas for compromise and, more often than not, result in an effective solution.

When diplomatic negotiations are handicapped by unfriendly relations between the parties, or when diplomatic relations are suspended, a third state may offer its good offices.[38] In such a case, the third state may try to bring the parties together so that they can start negotiating directly, or it may simply act as a messenger transmitting the proposals of one party to another, or it may, in fact, operate as a mediator, for the terms "good offices" and "mediation" are sometimes used interchangeably.

Although the creation of the United Nations has tended to eclipse the Hague Conventions on pacific settlement of disputes, "good offices" still remain an effective means of settling disputes. For example, in 1958, Tunisia and France accepted the United States'

---

[36] Dogger Bank Case (Great Britain v. Russia), Hague Court Reports (Scott) 403. This case is also known as the *North Sea Incident* and as the *Hull Incident*.

[37] *See generally* A. FATTAL, LES PROCÉDURES DIPLOMATIQUES ET RÈGLEMENT DES DIFFÉRENDS INTERNATIONAUX (Beyrouth 1967); Fox, *Conciliation of International Economic Disputes: A Case Study*, in ATHENS CONF. at 388-94; O. HOIJER, LA SOLUTION PACIFIQUES DES LITIGES INTERNATIONAUX (Paris 1925); H. KELSEN, EL ARREGLO NO JUDICIAL DE LAS CONTROVERSIAS INTERNACIONALES SEGÚN LA CARTA DE LAS NACIONES UNIDAS (Cordoba, Argentina 1949); S. KERTESZ, THE QUEST OF PEACE THROUGH DIPLOMACY (New Jersey 1967); A. LALL, MODERN INTERNATIONAL NEGOTIATION: PRINCIPLES AND PRACTICE (New York 1966); Metzger, *Settlement of International Disputes by Non-Judicial Methods*, 48 AJIL 408-21 (1954); W. O'BRIEN, THE NEW NATIONS IN INTERNATIONAL LAW AND DIPLOMACY (London 1965); L. OPPENHEIM, INTERNATIONAL LAW 1-21 (7th ed., London 1952); UN SECRETARIAT, SYSTEMATIC SURVEY OF TREATIES FOR THE PACIFIC SETTLEMENT OF DISPUTES (New York 1949).

[38] *See, e.g.,* de la Barra, *La Médiation et la Conciliation Internationales*, 1 RECUEIL DES COURS 557-67 (1923); Dennett, *American "Good Offices" in Asia*, 16 AJIL 1-25 (1922); *Editorial Comments on the Turko-Italian War*, 6 AJIL 463-67, 719-22 (1912); I. EFREMOV, LA MÉDIATION ET LA CONCILIATION INTERNATIONALES (La Flèche 1925); C. FOURCHAULT, DE LA MÉDIATION (Paris 1900); E. MALIK, LA MÉDIATION ET LES BONS OFFICES (Paris 1900); J. MEYNAUD, LA MÉDIATION (Amsterdam 1961); Z. RISTIC, LA MÉDIATION (Paris 1939); J. ZAMFIRESCO, DE LA MÉDIATION (Paris 1911).

offer of "good offices," and the result was that disputes which had arisen as a consequence of the French attack on the Tunisian side of the Algerian border, were eased. As another example, it is important to recognize the role of the UN Secretary-General. His impartiality, effectiveness as an administrator and wide knowledge of international affairs have been exemplified on numerous occasions by his activities and contributions in settling disputes.

A most active role may be played by a mediator, who assists in the conduct of the negotiations and guides them toward a solution acceptable to both parties. Mediation is sometimes conducted by an eminent citizen of a third state or by one or more governments. The armistice in Palestine, for instance, was obtained through the United Nations' mediation of Count Bernadotte and Ralph Bunche. War between Bolivia and Paraguay was brought to a conclusion owing largely to the mediation of five neutral powers between 1935 and 1937.

It is difficult to give a precise definition of conciliation,[39] although it can generally be distinguished from inquiry, adjudication, arbitration and mediation. Commissions of inquiry limit their action to a settlement of facts, although this does not hold for conciliation commissions. The judge and the arbitrator rest their decisions on the law, whereas the conciliator considers other elements of adjustment in drafting his proposal for resolving a dispute. Carefully prepared rules of procedure are followed by judge and

---

[39] *See* van Asbeck, *La Tâche et l'Action d'une Commission de Conciliation,* NETH. INT'L L.REV. 1-9 (1956); P. BROWN, LA CONCILIATION INTERNATIONALE (Paris 1925); P. COT, LA CONCILIATION INTERNATIONALE (Paris 1968); Efremoff, *La Conciliation Internationale,* 18 RECUEIL DES COURS 5-147 (1927); Efremoff, LES TRAITÉS INTERNATIONAUX DE CONCILIATION (3 vols., Paris 1932); Efremoff, *Organisation de la Conciliation comme Moyen de Prévenir les Guerres,* 59 RECUEIL DES COURS 103-222 (1937); Efremoff, *Organisation Adéquate de la Conciliation Internationale,* 59 RECUEIL DES COURS 124-145 (1937); S. GAVRILOVIC, L'ORGANISA-TION DES COMMISSION DE CONCILIATION . . . (Paris 1932); S. HAMZEH, INTER-NATIONAL CONCILIATION WITH SPECIAL REFERENCE TO THE WORK OF THE UNITED NATIONS CONCILIATION COMMISSION FOR PALESTINE (The Hague 1963); P. HETTE, L'EVOLUTION DE LA CONCILIATION INTERNATIONALE (Paris 1934); D. JORDAN, SYLLABUS OF LECTURES ON INTERNATIONAL CONCILIATION BY JORDAN AND KREHBIEL (Stanford Univ. 1912); Mandelstam, *La Conciliation Internationale d'Après la Pacte de la Société des Nations,* 14 RECUEIL DES COURS 337-643 (1926); Montagne, *L'Evolution de la Conciliation Internationale,* REV. DR. INT'L 50-104 (1938); Murdock, *Arbitration and Conciliation in Pan America,* 23 AJIL 273-92 (1929); Nguyen-Quoc-Dinh, *Les Commissions de Conciliation: Sont-elles aussi des Commissions d'Enquête?* 38 REV. GÉN. DR. INT'L P. 561-674 (1967); Rostworowski, *Procédure de Conciliation,* 33 INST. DR. INT'L ANN. 835-74 (1927); Scott, *The Pan-American Confer-ence on Conciliation and Arbitration,* 23 AJIL 143-53 (1929); C. VULCAN, LA CONCIL-IATION DANS LE DROIT INTERNATIONAL ACTUEL (Paris 1932); Williams, *The Pan-American and League of Nations Treaties of Arbitration and Conciliation,* 10 BR. Y.B. INT'L L. 14-32 (1929).

arbitrator; the conciliator does not rely primarily on formal rules of procedure, although model rules are available if he chooses to follow them. The mediator possesses political authority independent from the parties; the authority of the conciliator is only that which is given to him by the parties.

In practice, treaties sometimes ignore such distinctions. For example, the General Convention of Inter-American Conciliation of 1929[40] specifies that the commission of inquiry will also have the character of a conciliation commission. The important objective, of course, is to adopt that procedure which can best achieve an effective solution of the problems involved in the dispute. The success of conciliation lies in the high quality of the conciliators, the confidence which parties place in them, and the desire of the parties to a dispute to reach an equitable solution without victory or defeat for either party.

It was originally hoped that conciliation would be an ideal means of resolving political disputes between states. Although this hope has not been realized, conciliation has nevertheless served as a useful adjunct of arbitration and other means of pacific settlement.

Conference,[41] as a means of settling disputes, may refer to a formally arranged bilateral negotiation such as that between Japan and Russia at Portsmouth in 1905, but it may also involve the presence of many states not directly involved in the dispute. It provides an opportunity for states with minor interests to participate in finding a settlement as well as for disinterested states to act as mediators, bringing the main disputants together. A conference can serve as a means both for settling political disputes and for legislating new rules for the future. In the former capacity, conference differs from mediation in that it relies on the invocation of public opinion, although opportunities for confidential negotiation, characteristic of mediation are also present. Summit conferences between heads of states are usually called to create an atmosphere

---

[40] General Treaty of Inter-American Conciliation of 1929, *opened for signature* January 5, 1969, 46 Stat. 2209, 100 L.N.T.S. 401.

[41] *See generally* F. DUNN, THE PRACTICE AND PROCEDURE OF INTERNATIONAL CONFERENCES (Baltimore 1929); R. GRUBER, INTERNATIONALE STAATENKONGRESSE UND KONFERENZEN (Berlin 1919); N. HILL, THE PUBLIC INTERNATIONAL CONFERENCE (Baltimore 1929); Liang, *What is an International Conference?* 44 AJIL 333-41 (1950); Moulton, *A Structural View of the Conference as an Organ of International Cooperation* (unpublished 1930); V. PASTUHOV, A GUIDE TO THE PRACTICE OF INTERNATIONAL CONFERENCES (Washington 1945); P. POTTER, INTRODUCTION TO THE STUDY OF INTERNATIONAL ORGANIZATION (New York 1920); E. SATOW, INTERNATIONAL CONGRESSES (London 1920); Sibert, *Quelques Aspects de l'Organisation et de la Technique des Conferences Internationales,* 48 RECUEIL DES COURS 391-454 (1934).

favorable to negotiation rather than to settle concrete disputes. They often leave specific problems for future resolution if the atmosphere has been made favorable for negotiation.

The American Republics, through congresses or conferences, either among the nations of Central and South America, or in conjunction with other countries, have taken many steps to provide for peaceful settlement of international disputes. While not all of these efforts have been wholly successful, the cumulative effect of them has advanced the cause of pacific settlement of international disputes. These advances have had, in addition to their intrinsic merit, the effect of creating important precedents and examples.

Reflecting Simón Bolivar's devotion to international union and peace, the delegates to the Panama Congress of 1826, signed the Treaty of Perpetual Union[42] which provided:

> The contracting parties solemnly obligate and bind themselves to amicably compromise between themselves all differences now existing or which may arise in future, and in case no settlement can be reached between the disagreeing powers the question shall be taken for settlement to the judgment of the assembly, whose decision shall not be obligatory, however, unless said powers shall have expressly agreed that it shall be.[43]

Numerous similar conventions and conferences were held throughout the 19th century. The 1923 Gondra Treaty[44] signed at Santiago by the American Republics, provided that all controversies between two or more parties which could not be settled by diplomatic negotiations or arbitration should be investigated by a commission composed of five members, all nationals of American States. Under the Convention, each party to a dispute appoints two members, only one of whom may be a national of the party. A fifth commissioner is then appointed, by agreement, to act as president. The Río[45] and Bogotá[46] treaties of 1947 and 1948 contain similarly detailed provisions for commissions of investigation and conciliation which, in case of dispute, must be convened by the Council of the

---

[42] INT'L CONFERENCES OF AMERICAN STATES, 1889-1928 at xxiv (Washington 1931).

[43] Treaty of Perpetual Union, art. 16, *id.* at xxiv.

[44] 1923 Treaty to Avoid or Prevent Conflicts between the American States, *opened for signature* May 3, 1923, 44 Stat. 2527, 33 L.N.T.S. 25.

[45] INTER-AM. CONFERENCE FOR THE MAINTENANCE OF CONTINENTAL PEACE, CONGRESS AND CONFERENCE SERIES, No. 53.

[46] Charter of the Organization of American States, *opened for signature* April 30, 1948, T.I.A.S. No. 2361, 119 U.N.T.S. 3.

Organization of American States at the request of either party to the dispute. Failing agreement on the appointment of the commission, it can be chosen from a permanent panel of American conciliators. Provision for consultation by Ministers of Foreign Affairs in case of serious disputes between parties to the treaty is also provided for as described in the following chapter.

The European Convention for the Peaceful Settlement of Disputes,[47] like the Pact of Bogotá, contains detailed sections providing various non-judicial alternative means for settlement of disputes arising among the signatories. Also, the North Atlantic Treaty Organization[48] provides that international disputes arising among its signatories will be settled by peaceful means so that international security and justice are not endangered. But aside from setting forth that good offices procedures "within the NATO framework" will be utilized for deciding cases not otherwise settled, NATO provides little of the elaborate procedural structure for pacific settlement such as is contained in the aforementioned treaties.

In cases not regarded as susceptible to judicial or arbitral solution, the mechanisms mentioned above can supply alternative means of settlement which provide safeguards for the parties assuring them that they will receive a fair hearing and decision from a impartial third party. The existence of such mechanisms assures disputants of the availability of peaceful solutions to international disputes, a factor, in itself, reducing tensions. Because of the knowledge that they may be forced to accept an unfavorable decision, settlement by the parties, as by compromise, is encouraged. And, the parties to a dispute are provided with a face-saving method of accepting politically difficult decisions. Therefore, to the extent that disputes not covered by obligations to undertake judicial or arbitral solution, are required by binding agreements to be decided by other methods, such as good offices or conciliation, the cause of peace may be advanced.

§ 5-5. Commercial Arbitration[49]

Arbitration is a particularly desirable method of settling disputes arising out of private international transactions. Often disputes of

---

[47] European Convention for the Peaceful Settlement of Disputes, April 29, 1957, 5 EUR. Y.B. 347

[48] North Atlantic Treaty, *opened for signature* April 4, 1949, 63 Stat. 2241, T.I.A.S. 1964, 34 U.N.T.S. 350.

[49] *See generally* P. Benjamin, *Soviet Treaty Practice on Commercial Arbitration since 1940,* 53 AJIL 882-89 (1959); Carabiber, *L'Evolution de l'Arbitrage Commercial Interna-*

this kind do not involve serious legal issues. For this reason, commercial controversy lends itself particularly readily to resolutions by arbitrators drawn from the business community or from the legal profession. Advantages of commercial arbitration proceedings are that they may be arranged to suit the convenience of the parties; that the procedure may be specified or eliminated; and, that the proceedings may be carried out in private, thereby protecting the good names of the parties. In addition, the *compromis* can specify the questions to be decided and thereby prevent a decision on narrow procedural reasons or legal technicalities. And, finally, arbitration can be less expensive than court procedure.

A typical arbitration clause is as follows:

> Any controversy or claim arising out of or relating to this contract, or the breach thereof, shall be settled by arbitration in accordance with the Rules of . . . (name agency) and judgment upon the award rendered by the Arbitrators may be entered in any court having jurisdiction thereof.[50]

The aforementioned agency rules delineate the arbitral procedure and the selection of the arbitrators. Use of such agencies has led to a change in the former standard procedure where each party

---

tional, 99 RECUEIL DES COURS 119-229 (1960); Domke, *International Commercial Arbitration: Its Present Status and Future Prospects,* in WASHINGTON CONF. at 293-99; Domke, *United Nations Conference on International Commercial Arbitration,* 53 AJIL 414-26 (1959); DOMKE, INTERNATIONAL TRADE ARBITRATION (New York 1958); Duke University, *Commercial Arbitration* (Durham 1952); Economopoulos, *International Commercial Arbitration,* in ATHENS CONF. at 385-87; Hazard, *Commercial Discrimination and International Law,* 52 AJIL 495-598 (1958); Hudson & Sohn, *Fifty Years of Arbitration in the Union of International Transport by Rail,* 37 AJIL 597-611 (1943); INTERNATIONAL CHAMBER OF COMMERCE, L'ARBITRAGE COMMERCIAL ET LA LOI DANS LES DIFFÉRENTS PAYS . . . (Bâle 1949); Langen, *International Commercial Arbitration most energetically supported the Development of Supranational Law and thus World Peace Through Law,* in WASHINGTON CONF. at 311-20; Pellieri, *L'Arbitrage Privé dans les Rapports Internationaux,* 51 RECUEIL DES COURS 291-403 (1935); H. PARKER, THE HISTORY AND DEVELOPMENT OF COMMERCIAL ARBITRATION (Jerusalem 1959); Rotenstreich, *Supervisory Functions of Courts over International Commercial Awards,* in WASHINGTON CONF. at 320-22; Rundstein, *L'Arbitrage International en Matiére Privée,* 23 RECUEIL DES COURS 331-459 (1928); P. SANDERS, INTERNATIONAL COMMERCIAL ARBITRATION (ed. of three volumes World Handbook, Paris 1956, 1960, 1967); Sultan, *The United Nations Arbitration Convention and United States Policy,* 53 AJIL 807-26 (1959); United Nations Conference on International Commercial Arbitration, *Final Act and Convention on the Recognition and Enforcement of Foreign Arbitral Awards* (New York 1958); UN ECONOMIC COMMISSION FOR ASIA AND THE FAR EAST, COMMERCIAL ARBITRATION FACILITIES (New York 1954); UN ECONOMIC COMMISSION FOR EUROPE, TABLE OF BILATERAL PROVISIONS RELATING TO THE ENFORCEMENT OF ARBITRAL AWARDS AND THE ORGANIZATION OF COMMERCIAL ARBITRATION (Geneva 1957).

[50] Standard arbitration clause of the American Arbitration Association as quoted in Pollzien, *General Remarks,* in INTERNATIONAL LICENSING AGREEMENTS 17 (G. Pollzien & G. Bronfen ed. 1965).

selects one arbitrator and these two arbitrators select a third, for a system in which the arbitrators are often all selected from a panel of professional disinterested arbitrators maintained by the agency concerned. Examples of such an agency are the Inter-American Commercial Arbitration Commission, which was established in 1934 to provide for arbitration in the Americas and the American Arbitration Association in New York, which was established in the Americas in 1926 and which maintains 31 Regional Offices in the United States.

Establishment of uniform or standard rules of procedure among the leading arbitral agencies might encourage resort to arbitration by reducing the international trader's uncertainty and simplifying the procedures, as advocated by the Third International Arbitration Congress, held in Venice, Italy in October 1969. Development of a standard arbitration clause to refer disputes arising under private international commercial agreements to arbitral agencies may be advocated for similar reasons.

Domestic statutes to insure that any international agreement to submit future disputes to arbitration is considered irrevocable, that performance of the arbitration agreement may be directed by court order, and that court review of arbitration agreements be limited in such a way that the legitimate intent of the agreement will not be frustrated, have been enacted in some countries and are a desirable stimulus to commercial arbitration.

Merchants in Europe in the 15th century could be reasonably certain of finding arbitration tribunals freely accessible anywhere, regardless of the nationality or residence of parties appearing before them, and capable of enforcing, on the spot, a decision rendered in accordance with a system of commercial laws roughly uniform throughout the continent. With the time fast approaching when the number of international transactions will approach the number of domestic ones, a similar equally effective international apparatus is again badly needed.

The most recent development in the field of private arbitration was the conclusion, under United Nations auspices, of a Convention on the Recognition and Enforcement of Foreign Arbitral Awards.[51] Signed by 25 nations in 1958, it entered into force on June 7, 1959. As of December 31, 1969, the Convention had been signed by 44 states and ratified by 39. Before delineating the scope of this convention, however, it is useful to refer briefly to the two

---

[51] Convention on the Recognition and Enforcement of Foreign Arbitral Awards, *registration* June 7, 1959, 330 U.N.T.S. 3.

earlier agreements on international arbitration: the Geneva Protocols of 1942[52] and the Geneva Convention of 1927.[53] The Protocols were concerned primarily with the validity of the agreement of the parties to submit to arbitration present or future differences arising out of a given contract or transaction. The Geneva Convention on arbitration, relating to the execution of foreign arbitral awards, reversed the provisions of the 1923 protocol which had provided that an arbitral award would be enforced only in accordance with the law of the forum. The 1927 convention provided that an arbitral award made under an agreement covered by the 1924 protocol "shall be recognized as binding and shall be enforced in accordance with the rules and procedure of the territory where the award is relied upon."[54] The party seeking to enforce the arbitral award was required to supply the original award or an authenticated copy as documentary evidence to show the finality of the award, and as evidence, where necessary, to show compliance with the preceding conditions.

The United Nations Conference on International Commercial Arbitration of 1958, which produced the aforementioned recent Convention, resulted from a proposal of the International Chamber of Commerce to the Economic and Social Council of the United Nations to conclude a convention on the enforcement of foreign arbitral awards. Forty-five states participated at the conference. The most important feature of the new convention appears to be that the parties seeking enforcement in the country of the debtor need only produce the award itself (or a certified copy of it) and the agreement to arbitrate. The burden is now on the debtor to prove that the award has not become "binding" or has been set aside or suspended. Under the United Nations Convention an agreement to arbitrate would be recognized as binding upon all adherents. At the present time, this is not the law in many countries. The Convention, therefore, gives a more precise understanding of the scope of the arbitration clause in commercial contracts. This should remove a great deal of uncertainty, and should tend to make arbitration more valuable and useful.

From the standpoint of the businessman, the best kind of justice is that which is simple, expeditious, economical and final. Arbitration provides a method of resolving conflicts which meets these

---

[52] Protocol on Arbitration Clauses, *entered into force* September 24, 1923, 27 L.N.T.S. 157.

[53] Convention for the Execution of Final Arbitral Awards, *entered into force* July 25, 1929, 92 L.N.T.S. 301.

[54] *Id.*

criteria. With the certainty that commercial arbitration is available, and that its awards are enforceable, the hinderance to international trade which arises out of fears of becoming entangled in legal disputes abroad should be eliminated. Under this Convention, the businessman will be able to understand with much greater precision the effect of any arbitration clause he might insert in a contract, and much of the insecurity evoked by the prospect of judicial litigation will be dissipated.

§ 5-5.1. The International Chamber of Commerce: Conciliation and Arbitration.[55]

The International Chamber of Commerce provides means for settling business disputes of an international character by conciliation or by arbitration. Conciliation is an optional means of settlement requiring the consent of the parties to a dispute. It is provided by a conciliation committee composed of three members who serve without remuneration. The members are appointed by the President of the ICC, who selects one member of the nationality of each of the parties concerned and a national of a third country, who serves as chairman.

Each party to a dispute is required to submit, in writing, a statement of his claims, together with all relevant supporting documents. After an exchange of these statements between the parties, a conciliation meeting is arranged at the ICC International Headquarters. At this meeting, each party, in person or by an authorized agent, makes an oral statement of his case and answers questions by the conciliators. The conciliation committee then prepares a report indicating the agreement reached, making any recommendations to the parties for settling the dispute, or simply noting failure to reach an agreement. In the large majority of cases, this conciliation procedure, which usually takes about four months, leads to a settlement of the case.

In the ICC structure, arbitration proceedings are administered by a court of arbitration, a secretariat and national committees. The Court of Arbitration does not try cases but takes administrative measures to establish and supervise the Arbitral Tribunal which does. The Court of Arbitration, which serves without renumeration, is composed of a chairman, vice-chairman, technical

---

[55] *See* Bockstiegel, *Arbitration of Disputes between States and Private Enterprises in the International Chamber of Commerce,* 59 AJIL 579-86 (1965); Cohn, *The Rules of Arbitration of the International Chamber of Commerce,* 14 INT'L & COMP. L.Q. 132-71 (1965); INTERNATIONAL CHAMBER OF COMMERCE, GUIDE TO ICC ARBITRATION (Brochure No. 1963-1); INTERNATIONAL CHAMBER OF COMMERCE, RULES OF CONCILIATION AND ARBITRATION, *entered into force* June 1, 1955 (5th ed. 1967); Logothetis, *Enforcement of Arbitration Decision,* in ATHENS CONF. at 411-12.

advisers, a Secretary-General, and members selected by the ICC national committees and generally holds a meeting once a month. Its decisions are by majority vote with the chairman casting the deciding vote. Six members constitute a quorum. The Secretariat of the Court has its seat at the headquarters of the ICC.

The Arbitral Tribunal is usually composed of an uneven number of arbitrators, typically one or three. If the parties agree on the choice of a single arbitrator, they nominate him for confirmation by the Court of Arbitration. If they fail to nominate an arbitrator, the Court appoints one. If the parties prefer a tribunal composed of three arbitrators, each party nominates one arbitrator for confirmation by the Court; the third arbitrator, who serves as chairman, is appointed by the Court. The nationality of the sole arbitrator and the nationality of the third arbitrator must be different than that of either of the parties. If a party's choice of arbitrator is challenged, the Court examines the ground of the challenge and makes a final decision.

Proceedings before the Tribunal are initiated by a Request for Arbitration, which must contain a full statement of the claimant's case, with all relevant supporting documents, and an indication of the desired number of arbitrators and any nominations for their appointment. This request is transmitted to the Secretariat of the Court, which in turn sends the request and supporting documents to the defendant. The defendant's reply is sent to the claimant, who can make a counter-claim which is transmitted to the defendant. After the defendant has replied to the request for arbitration or the claimant has made his counterclaim, the case goes to the Tribunal. Any question concerning its jurisdiction is decided by the Tribunal.

The site of the proceedings of the Tribunal is determined by the Court, unless the parties agree in advance to a named location. The Tribunal, in ascertaining the relevant facts of the case, may call witnesses or appoint experts. Unless a hearing is requested by one of the parties, the Tribunal may decide the case on the basis of the documents submitted. If a hearing is requested, the Tribunal summons the parties to appear at a given time and place. If a party fails to appear without adequate cause, the Tribunal may proceed without him. Hearings are held in private. Parties appear in person or are represented by authorized agents.

Before granting an award, the arbitrators must obtain the approval of the Court of Arbitration. The principle purpose of this requirement seems to be to assure that the form of award makes it most capable of enforcement. The award must specify the amount of the costs and indicate the party who must pay them. These decisions are final and without appeal. The Secretariat sends copies of the award to the parties, but does not publish them, presumably on the theory that the interest of the parties in privacy is more important than the jurisprudential value of the award.

Arbitration tribunals appointed by the ICC Court of Arbitration have decided approximately 2,000 cases in more than 40 years. The principle merits of this arbitration are the speed and low cost of the proceedings. Parties also consider it an advantage to be able to submit their disputes to a permanent Arbitration Center with tested rules of procedure and with highly qualified arbitrators available.

§ 5-6. *Ad Hoc* Tribunals

Professor Burton Andrews has proposed a change in international relations by the negotiation of a treaty wherein the signatories agree that in event the peace between any two or more nations of the world, whether signatories or not, is threatened, that an *ad hoc* tribunal can be set up to consist of not less than four arbitrators or judges, by either the General Assembly of the UN, the Security Council of the UN, the World Court, or by the parties themselves, or by any combination of these, with authority to invite or summon the two or more nations to appear before the tribunal to litigate the merits of the threat to the peace with a view to a proposed settlement by the tribunal from which, when it is made, any or all of the parties may seek review by the World Court.

Professor Andrews argues in support of his proposal that this would create a procedure through which the peace forces in the world, whenever there is a threat to the peace, could focus world public opinion on the trouble spot and make their influence felt by starting a process for its resolution by peaceful means. He further argues that the peace forces in the world today have no adequate vehicle to set in motion when peace is threatened.

This proposal is generally familiar to the people of the world so it can be understood and accepted. It has its prototype in the development of the early common law of England when the nobility were gradually induced to cease their private wars and to litigate their quarrels in the King's Courts. Also, India and Pakistan set up such an *ad hoc* tribunal on their border dispute over the Ran of Ketch. That tribunal, urged strongly at the Washington Conference on World Peace Through Law in 1965, since the dispute had flared up while the conference was in session, handed down a decision accepted and implemented by the parties.

§ 5-7. Some Suggested Improvements in Arbitration Machinery

A suggested alternative solution to the problems arising out of uncertainty of enforcement is that uniform arbitral laws containing provisions for enforcement of arbitration agreements be drafted for enactment by the nations of the world. This would serve to reduce complaints by governments on behalf of their nationals alleging a denial of justice on the part of the state with whom the national entered into an agreement.

The American states have been pioneers in this field. In 1933, the Seventh International Conference of American States recommended that the principles and standards of commercial arbitration be included in the legislation of American states. Failure of action in accordance with this recommendation led to the drafting of a uniform law by the Inter-American Juridical Committee.[56] This draft law was adopted by the Inter-American Council of Jurists after discussion at its 1956 meeting. It provides for recognition and enforcement of arbitration clauses and awards, and for the constitution of arbitral tribunals. In addition, it stated that awards should have the force of final judgments rendered by courts, although subject to judicial review for abuses. Similarly, the Council of Europe has considered a draft uniform law prepared by the Rome Institute for the Unification of Private International Law.

Another suggestion in the area of arbitration concerns the drafting of an arbitral convention to deal with the special situation arising when private individuals, persons or legal entities enter into contracts or other legal agreements with states or governmental agencies. A model rule proposed by the International Law Commission might be utilized to settle disputes in this type of situation. Short of this, inclusion of arbitration clauses in contracts between individuals and governments or their agencies has been strongly and widely urged.

The Iranian Consortium Agreement of 1954 provides for a Mixed Conciliation Commission to resolve disputes, and a similar arrangement for arbitration was concluded between the National Iranian Oil Company and the Italian firm, Agip Mineria. Similarly, the Turkish Petroleum Law of 1954 and the petroleum law for the former Federation of Mali contained provisions for arbitral settlements. Libya and Saudi Arabia also have included arbitration articles in agreements with private organizations.

---

[56] Final Act of the Third Meeting of the Inter-American Council of Jurists 28 (1956).

In 1958, an award by an arbitration tribunal determined certain rights and obligations of the Arabian American Oil Company and the Government of Saudi Arabia under their concession agreement. The Egyptian Government in 1957, in the dispute over the nationalization of the Suez Canal Company, felt that compensation and claims in connection with the nationalization of the Suez Canal Maritime Company should be referred to an arbitration tribunal if the parties were unable to reach an agreement. The question of compensation for shareholders was ultimately settled without resort to arbitration.[57]

The need for a comprehensive system for reporting arbitral decisions, and insuring that the grounds of the latter are published, has been suggested as being essential in the development of a law of international arbitration. This reflects the feeling that the merchant in international trade needs to know with more certainty what law will be applied in any dispute arising from a contract for arbitration into which he might enter.

Liaison and cooperation between lawyers and legal organizations with interested commercial groups can also be valuable. National and international arbitral societies and chambers of commerce have been active in the field of arbitration. Both commercial and legal organizations could benefit from greater interchange of ideas on possible solutions to problems in this area, particularly concerning questions such as how and what sort of standard clauses may be developed, rules and procedures for arbitration, and facilities for efficient conduct of arbitration.

It has been suggested that international commodity authorities established by multilateral treaties might establish arbitral boards to handle cases arising in connection with transactions to the commodity with which they are concerned.

The inclusion in bilateral treaties of clauses providing for mutual recognition of arbitral decisions is another method of increasing the use of that means of settling disputes, although naturally even more desirable are similar provisions in multilateral agreements such as the United Nations Convention. Typical of such bilateral clauses is the following:

> Contracts entered into between nationals and companies of either Party, and nationals and companies of the other Party, that provide for the settlement by arbitration of controversies, shall not be deemed unenforceable within the territories of such other Party

---

[57] Bassiouni, *The Nationalization of the Suez Canal and the Illicit Act in International Law,* 14 DE PAUL L. REV. 258-98 (1965).

merely on the grounds that the place designated for the arbitration proceedings is outside such territories or that the nationality of one or more of the arbitrators is not that of such other Party. No award duly rendered pursuant to any such contract, and final and enforceable under the laws of the place where rendered, shall be deemed invalid or denied effective means of enforcement within the territories of either Party merely on the grounds that the place where such award was rendered is outside such territories or that the nationality of one or more of the arbitrators is not that of such Party.[58]

The aim and purpose of the clause is to protect the alien and his interests on the basis of non-discrimination, rather than to attempt the reformation of the internal law. This is done by a rule precluding any alienage bar or disability with respect to the validity and enforceability of the arbitration award that is carried across international boundaries for execution. Other treaty provisions designed to meet the specific needs of particular parties can be very valuable as a means of facilitating arbitration, and merit study and encouragement.

To this end, the newly created United Nations Commission on International Trade Law which recognized the need for progressive harmonization and unification of rules governing trade relations of a private law nature involving different countries, placed international commercial arbitration as a priority on its agenda. The Third Session of that Commission, held in April 1970, in New York, dealt with the various aspects of international commercial arbitration. On the basis of detailed reports by the Secretary-General of the United Nations, and by a Special Rapporteur, trade customs and practices in using arbitration clauses will be investigated, as well as possible improvements relating to the various international conventions and draft-reform laws on arbitration agreements and the enforcement of foreign arbitral awards.

---

[58] United Nations Convention, *opened for signature* June 26, 1945, 59 Stat. 1031, 1 U.N.T.S. xvi, T.S. 993.

CHAPTER 6

Law and International Economic Development

§ 6-1. Introduction

The most practical, and most promising, application of law internationally lies in the furtherance of economic progress and cooperation among peoples and nations. In economic and trade development, new forces and new factors in the world community outdate both traditional international and domestic law in content and principle. A new social and economic order is emerging in the world from aid and trade which, of necessity, is bringing with it a new legal framework for the world community. This trend is both a reflection of, and a catalyst for, an increasing interdependence among the peoples and nations of the world.

The internationalization of technology coupled with growth in foreign trade and aid has had an enormous impact on the growth of international law, and it is in this area that international law has grown the most. Domestic markets in developing nations are increasing enormously as a part of this picture. And, the UN picture largely mirrors this, and demonstrates that law is indeed responsive to peoples' needs. The UN presently devotes 95 percent of its staff and a larger percentage of its funds to the development of emerging nations. UN law making or creation, chiefly through its special agencies, has burgeoned in this field.

The great need is for increasing acceptance of international fair labor standards in world trade and adequate international machinery to avoid injury to developed and developing nations flowing from abnormally low wages in developing nations or low prices internationally edicted by managed economies. Fair trade rules internationally are in the best interest of all the world's peoples. These will be the subject matter of more and more international law. This chapter indicates the law that exists, and the ideas, principles, agencies, and current or past subject matter of the law in this area. New subjects like environment and seabed development will undoubtedly be joined by others as the peoples of the world adjust to an ever increasing interdependence—as they seek to achieve common desires and interests.

That this aid and trade is creating a new order and unity, and this new world legal framework, is clear from the facts collected in this chapter on more than 30 international economic organizations whose documents of creation, or whose rules and agreements, are law or are becoming accepted more and more as law rules. A focus upon the vast new areas of activity known as development assistance and measures to promote transnational trade clearly describes new paths to a world legal framework providing an ever increasing world order with justice. This is true because order with justice is a basic foundation for peaceful trade.

Old proposals, old institutions, old approaches have not given the acceleration to law which is needed internationally by commercial interests whose fast transportation and communication have literally made the whole world one market. In trade and aid new ideas, plans and proposals are advanced constantly which produce new institutions creating world order under law to further the common interests of the world's peoples.

That access to finance, technology, management, and trade must be provided to all peoples and all nations of the world is a major undeniable fact. Old law as well as new law must be drafted and adapted to govern and guide the new economic and trade relations which are coming into existence among nations on a scale undreamed of in the past.

§ 6-1.1 **UN and Economic Development.** The image of the UN in the world is largely created by its action on political issues. In fact, however, more than 95 percent of its funds and most of its functions are spent in the work of aiding development and trade of developing nations. In many ways, the UN Development Program now constitutes its most important function. Here, the UN is performing an ever-growing function to create those stable conditions required for a world at peace.

Developing countries generally include those whose annual per capita national income does not exceed the equivalent of $500. Examples are India which has an average of $70 per capita yearly income, Burma with $60 and Ethiopia with $50. The developing nations include three-fourths (3/4) of all humanity, and occupy most of three continents, i.e., South America, Asia and Africa.

Of the UN's 25,000 employees in 1970 (advisers, experts, and others working directly for or in the name of the UN), 22,000 are engaged in some 90 areas of development aid. At the UN Pledging Conference for the Development Program, 111 nations pledged $182,674,000 for 1968, covering expert planning, consulting and survey costs on over 3,000 projects whose total construction costs were around $2 billion.

As examples of accomplishments, UN Development experts have discovered fabulous new natural resources in some nations. Uranium, vitrium and other minerals were discovered in Somalia; oil was found in Abu Dhabi; manganese and iron in Upper Volta; iron in Guinea and Liberia; dolomite in Togo; geothermal power in El Salvador; copper and molybedenum in Panama; copper in Argentina; lead and zinc in Tunisia and Nicaragua; and nickel in Botswana. New underground water supplies were discovered in Jordan, Lebanon and Jamaica.

The legal foundation of this new and rapidly growing field of UN activity is uncertain and rests more upon implied than express powers, and almost imperceptibly the UN has moved farther and accomplished more in the economic field than in any other. Helping nations to help themselves is not a dramatic matter. It produced no crises, no deaths, no war, no newspaper headlines and no strident radio and television statements.

Yet, the Development Program, and loans from the World Bank and similar UN agencies, have probably prevented many frictions, many crises, and probably some conflicts by eliminating some of their causes. Providing finances to upgrade life in scores of nations is a slow, often tedious effort but measured in results, if properly appreciated, this is a most significant achievement.

Travel and trade is encouraged by many multi-nation, regional and international bodies, some created by the UN with others of independent origin. These, as described in this Chapter, are bringing many new international law rules and many new international legal institutions into existence.

§ 6-1.2. **A World Trade Council: World Trade Court.** A World Trade Council to police or settle disputes or complaints in international trade, such as the Security Council in the political sphere, is greatly needed, and attached to the World Trade Council should be a World Trade Court. Arbitration is the chief dispute mechanism presently available, but it is slow, expensive, and often unsatisfactory. A permanent, always available World Trade Council, and World Trade Court would enormously help world traders. GATT's Council of Representatives performs much the same function in the sphere of complaints of contravention against GATT, which may have taken place, or which are threatened. National Courts and the European Court of Justice which functions so well for the Common Market, are the only available permanent court forums for trade disputes. What is in effect a World Investment Dispute Court, has been created by the World Bank. The speed with which the idea for this investment "Court" progressed from idea to adoption in treaty form, indicates that the same reaction could be expected for the much broader field for a much needed World Trade Court.

§ 6-1.3. **Development Funds Nation to Nation.** Important factors affecting law in the international economic development picture are funds given or loaned by developed nations to developing nations. Nation to nation developmental assistance is largely keyed to the national purposes of the grantor, or lender nations.

Financial information on levels of development loans and grants from 16 nations to developing nations are quite interesting. The figures for 1967, for example, illustrate the picture. They show $7 billion that year in such aid funds. The recipients and amount as stated in millions of dollars were compiled by the Organization for Economic Cooperation and Development as follows: Australia— 167.2, Austria—38.8, Belgium—98.8, Canada—213.0, Denmark— 28.0, France—831.1, Germany—546.8, Italy—202.8, Japan—390.6, Netherlands—113.5, Norway—15.5, Portugal—46.6, Sweden—59.9, Switzerland—3.0, United Kingdom—498.0, and United States— 3,723.0. The OECD reports that, in 1968, development funds for developing nations from public and private sources totalled over $11 billion and, that in 1969 the amount was even greater (not including grants and loans, made by Russia and other nations information on which was unavailable).

These nation to nation grants or loans cover a wide variety of purposes from arms to water systems. Their total amount far exceeds the UN's Development Program and in some respects complements it by financing projects planned originally by UN experts. Some of the funds are aimed at stimulating multi-nation corporate or other trade and investment activities of interest to the donor or lending nations.

§ 6-1.4. **The Multi-Nation Corporation.** Any realistic picture of economic development and world trade and its effect on international law must include the burgeoning growth and the tremendous impact of multi-nation corporations. By this is meant a corporation doing business in more than one nation directly or indirectly. Globalization of business and the major part played by the multi-nation corporation in that globalization, is an irreversible fact of our day. Historically, the multi-nation corporation began to appear around 1900. The number of such corporations grew slowly until the 1950's and the 1960's when they multiplied enormously in scope and number. Their impact internationally is accelerating constantly. Many corporations now do business in over 100 nations.

While sometimes regarded as solely a United States phenomenon, the facts prove the contrary. Corporations created in England, Japan, Germany, Italy, Switzerland, France and other nations are major participants in the rapidly growing multi-nation corporate field whose participants largely disregard national boundaries and look upon the world as their market and all peoples as their customers. They also look more and more to a growing world money market for their finances. Law is rapidly coming into existence to fulfill the needs of these developments and this chapter reports on that law.

One problem facing the multinational corporation concerns double taxation. Generally, if a company maintains wholly-owned subsidiaries carrying out its activities in a foreign country, and organized under the laws of a foreign country, the domestic company and the subsidiary are regarded as separate entities, and the income of each is taxed in the country of incorporation. The problem occurs when the profits of the subsidiary are distributed to the parent company. According to the tax laws of most states, these distributed profits are incorporated into the parent's income, and they are again subject to taxation. To resolve this burden, several countries have adopted means to eliminate or lessen this double taxation by permitting the parent either to deduct or credit taxes levied by foreign nations. If the rate of the foreign tax equals or exceeds the rate of the domestic tax, then the parent company pays no domestic tax on the distributed profits. But, if the foreign tax rate is less than the domestic tax rate, then the domestic tax is usually the difference between the two rates.

§ 6-1.5. International Finance: an International Stock Exchange. Ownership of great multi-nation corporations is becoming more and more worldwide and the need for an International Stock Exchange has been suggested. The multi-nation corporation has caused a vast internationalization of commercial and investment banks. These financial institutions have created complex international networks for the purposes of marketing stocks and bonds of these corporations. A corporation that can organize its productive qualities, finances, marketing and management in Tokyo or London or Berlin or New York has found it can do the same 3,000 or 6,000 miles from those cities in any of 100 or more cities or nations.

Sidney F. Rolfe, in a recent study for the International Chamber of Commerce entitled "The International Corporation," states:

> A number of students believe that the world's economy of the future will be dominated by 300 or 400 super international corporations.[1]

It is a well-known fact that multi-nation corporations have financial resources beyond those of some of the developing nations with which they do business, and the multi-nation corporation is an important factor in the economic development of developing nations. The multi-nation corporation can raise capital that may be out of reach of local business, can take greater risks and can bring capital, jobs, technology, training, education, know-how in production, marketing and other skills. "Capital" in its broadest sense, i.e., human, material, intellectual, can be mined up from the world by these multi-nation corporations and their unique capacity to assemble great resources. Such a corporation's greater efficiency can lower the cost of products and expand payrolls and local trade, all of which elevate the standard of living of peoples in developing nations. In many ways, the growth of the multi-nation corporation is in direct response to the need to close the gap between the rich and the poor. The multi-nation corporation is welcomed in developing nations because of this fact.

The things people want and try to obtain—their aspirations and desires—are basically the same and these are becoming more and more the same throughout the world. With the assistance of multination transportation, communications, and trade, people are in fact becoming more and more alike in dress, in habits and in desires. The best way to meet the ever growing massive consumer demands developing around the world is through great international business organizations.

The multi-nation corporation eliminates some political problems inherent in economic aid provided by governments to developing nations, but these corporations bring with them certain problems of their own. These relate to import and export restrictions, taxation, guarantees or measures providing protections against arbitrary discrimination, such as agreement to accept decisions of the World Bank's Investment Dispute Convention or other arbitration or dispute settlement agreements. Multi-nation corporations hesitate to send organizational and technological resources into developing nations without these and other protections.

---

[1] S. Rolfe, *The International Corporation* 15 (report, 22nd Congress of the Int'l Chamber of Commerce, Istanbul May 31, 1969).

Law and legal institutions are quite basic to the existence and operations of multi-nation corporations, and many of the organizations described in this chapter were created to meet the needs of these corporations. The whole of the law of the nations in which these corporations operate sometimes applies to them and their operations, their employees, their trademarks, copyrights, patents, their land and their property. In some instances, anti-trust laws having extra-territorial effect are said to inhibit operations of the multi-nation corporation. But these laws, and legal problems are merely illustrations of the new law rules and legal institutions which are so essential to the proper operation of the multi-nation corporation and its importance to the developing nations and the world economy.

Investments and trade contribute to stability and progress in relations among nations. They are a powerful force for international understanding, and goodwill in the field of transnational business.

That globalization of business is leading to a globalization of law is irrefutable. That this is a wonderful development for mankind is also irrefutable. New legal frameworks required for international business, and transnational corporate activities, are coming into existence out of sheer necessity. Business interests in international trade and development are providing new approaches, new subject matters, new insights and above all new supporters of law for peaceful world order. And, to deal with these and other problems facing the growth of such international business activity, the World Peace Through Law Center at its Belgrade World Conference in 1971, will create a new Section entitled: Multi-Nation Business Law.

§ 6-2. Multilateral Commodity Agreements and International Commodity Organizations.[2]

The Preamble of the Charter of the United Nations records the determination of the peoples of the signatory powers to "establish conditions under which justice and respect for the obligations arising from treaties and other sources of international law can be maintained, and to promote social progress and better standards

---

[2] For some of the international commodity agreements creating international commodity organizations and for preliminary efforts looking toward the advisability of establishing such organizations, see in particular UN Conference on Trade and Development Commodity Surveys; M. VAN MEEHAEGHE, INTERNATIONAL ECONOMIC INSTITUTIONS (London 1966); *Economic Development in General and Development Agreements,* 105 RECUEIL DES COURS 271-369 (1962).

of life." This objective is further expanded in Article 55, paragraph (a), wherein it is stated that in order to create conditions of stability and well-being essential for peace and security, "higher standards of living, full employment, and conditions of economic and social progress and development" shall be promoted by the United Nations.

There is no area in which the establishment of the international rule of law can offer a greater potential for the well-being and prosperity of all nations, than in that of trade and economic development. The security afforded by clearly-defined rules governing trade and investment, coupled with international judicial tribunals which can enforce and interpret those rules, could well be the greatest single factor promoting economic, social and political stability during this period of rapid change.

In recent years, there has been an increased emphasis on international organization for the purpose of regulating and stabilizing international commercial relations. This has been particularly true with respect to trade in certain vital commodities upon which many nations of the world depend for their economic well-being.

The Economic and Social Council of the United Nations has devoted a great deal of time and energy to the study of problems of international commodity trade, which has led to various suggestions for regulation and stabilization of trade in vital commodities.

In order to facilitate inter-governmental consultation and action on commodity problems, ECOSOC established an Interim Coordination Committee for international commodity arrangements in March 1947. Until 1958, this body consisted of a Chairman nominated by the contracting parties to the General Agreement on Tariffs and Trade (GATT), a member chosen by the Food and Agriculture Organization (FAO) concerned particularly with agricultural primary commodities, a member specializing in non-agricultural primary commodities, and a member of wide experience in the problems confronting countries undergoing development whose economies are chiefly dependent on the production and international marketing of primary commodities. The latter two members were nominated by the Secretary General.

Until 1955, the Interim Coordinating Committee prepared an annual review of international commodity problems and their relation to general economic condition. The review also contained the Committee's observations and recommendations on inter-governmental consultation and action. From 1955, the review was confined to a discussion of inter-governmental consultation and action, the task of reviewing the commodity situation having been assigned to the Commission on International Commodity Trade.

Acting on recommendations of the Interim Coordinating Committee, the Secretary-General of the United Nations convened various inter-governmental conferences on specific commodities, such as tin, sugar, and wheat, resulting in the revision of old or the creation of new agreements. In addition, an agreement on olive oil, adopted in October 1955, entered into force on June 26, 1959. Other conferences have been held or are in the process of being organized, and there has been marked progress in the regulation of commodity trade. The coordinating committee has the task of coordinating the activities of the individual commodity study groups and councils. Thus, studies on such import products as rubber, cotton, wool, tea, tin, wheat and sugar are being undertaken by inter-governmental study groups and councils and are related to the economic programs of the United Nations through the Interim Coordinating Committee.

§ 6-2.1. **The Commission on International Commodity Trade.** The Economic and Social Council established a subsidiary organ called the Commission on International Commodity Trade in 1954. This Commission consisted of 18 members, and operated: "to examine measures designed to avoid excessive fluctuations in prices and the volume of trade in primary commodities, and to keep under review the situation in world markets for such commodities." The Commission is also entrusted with certain functions previously exercised by the Interim Coordinating Committee.

According to amendments adopted in 1958, the Commission was reconstituted to study and analyze developments in intransit international commodity trade, including excessive fluctuations in the prices and volume of trade and variations in the terms of trade. The effect of such developments on both the international and domestic economic position of countries participating in international commodity trade, especially on the economic development of the less developed nations, was also subject to careful study. The Commission is authorized to bring its views and recommendations before the Economic and Social Council.

§ 6-2.2. **The International Coffee Council.**[3] Established pursuant to an Agreement which was signed by 69 states on September

---

[3] Bilder, *The International Coffee Agreement, 1962,* 63 L. & CONTEMP. PROB. 328-91 (Duke University 1963); Bilder, *The International Coffee Agreement, 1962,* 57 AJIL 888-92 (1963); UNESCO, *United Nations Coffee Agreement, 1962,* E/CONF., 4217;
(Continued)

28, 1962, this Council entered into force on December 27, 1963. Its purpose is to increase the purchasing power of coffee-exporting countries by keeping prices at fair levels and by increasing consumption throughout the world.   It also aims to achieve a reasonable balance between supply and demand by bringing about a long-term equilibrium between production and consumption.   The Council is assisted by an Executive Board composed of seven representatives of exporting states and seven representatives of importing states.   An Executive Director is in charge of administrative services.

A renegotiated International Coffee Agreement,[4] effective for a five-year period, was approved by the 66-nation International Coffee Council on February 19, 1968.   The Agreement is very comprehensive, consisting of 20 chapters, including 72 articles and containing three annexes.   The Organization continues to function through a Council and an Executive Board, with an Executive Director heading an administrative staff.   The Council is the supreme authority of the Organization, and is composed of a representative and one or more alternates from all of the member states with a Chairman and First, Second, and Third Vice Chairmen. It holds regular sessions twice a year and special sessions as it so decides.   Its objectives are set out in Article 1 of the Agreement as follows:

> 1. To achieve a reasonable balance between supply and demand on a basis which will assure adequate supplies of coffee to consumers and markets for coffee to producers at equitable prices and which will bring about long term equilibrium between production and consumption;
>
> 2. to alleviate the serious hardship caused by burdensome surpluses and excessive fluctuations in the prices of coffee which are harmful both to producers and to consumers;
>
> 3. to contribute to the development of productive resources and to the promotion and maintenance of employment and income in the Member countries, thereby helping to bring about fair wages, higher living standards, and better working conditions;
>
> 4. to assist in increasing the purchasing power of coffee-exporting countries by keeping prices at equitable levels and by increasing consumption;
>
> 5. to encourage the consumption of coffee by every possible means; and

International Coffee Agreement, 1962, 469 U.N.T.S. 169; 515 *id.* 322; WORLD COFFEE INFORMATION CENTER, INTERNATIONAL COFFEE AGREEMENT, 1968 (Washington 1969). Address: 5 Queen Street, London SW 1, England.

    [4] *Entered into force* December 30, 1968, doc. ICC-11-26 (E) Rev. 2, 28 February 1968.

6. in general, in recognition of the relationship of the trade in coffee to the economic stability of markets for industrial products, to further international cooperation in connection with world coffee problems.[5]

The Agreement also provides that the Council decide disputes and complaints concerning the interpretation or application of the Agreement. The Executive Board, which now consists of eight exporting and eight importing members, is responsible to the Council and works under its direction. The staff is responsible to the Executive Director who is appointed by the Council.

At the second plenary meeting in 1968, the Council established an Executive Committee and empowered it to create such committees necessary to implement the Agreement. Accordingly, it established the following committees: 1) steering committee; 2) economic committee I; 3) economic committee II; 4) statistical committee; 5) credentials committee; 6) working patties set up by various committees: a) administrative, b) promotion, c) legal, d) production and stocks, e) obligations of importing countries, f) new markets, g) obstacles to consumption, h) international coffee fund, i) groupings of countries, j) definitions, and k) quota flexibility.

§ 6-2.3. **The International Cotton Advisory Committee.**[6] This Council was founded in accordance with a resolution adopted by a special study group at a meeting held on September 5-9, 1939, of some of the principal cotton exporting countries. The study group was reconvened in 1945 at the conclusion of World War II, and a new Committee was appointed to prepare a report to include definite proposals for international collaboration looking toward a reduction in cotton surpluses through the regulation of exports, export prices, and production. It also sought means of expanding cotton consumption. The study group was unable to arrive at an agreed program at the time; however, a recommendation to continue the Committee itself for the purpose of studying the international problems involved was accepted. Rules and regulations of the Committee were adopted on May 28, 1952, to which many major cotton producing and consuming nations have since subscribed.

The Committee created three main organs to fulfill its objectives: (1) a Plenary Meeting of the Committee composed of repre-

---

[5] *Id.* art. 1.

[6] *See* issues of the ANNUAIRE O. I.; *International Cotton Advisory Committee,* 14 INT'L ORG. 368-69, 695-96; A. PEASLEE, 2 INTERNATIONAL GOVERNMENTAL ORGANIZATIONS 1102-15 (2d ed. 1961). Address: Room 5441, South Agriculture Bldg., Washington, D.C. 20005.

sentatives of member governments which is held at least once a year; (2) a Standing Committee composed of representatives of all member governments, which meets each month; and (3) an Executive Secretary and staff.

The functions of the Committee set forth in Article 1, Section 1, of the Rules and Regulations are:

> to observe and keep in close touch with developments in the world cotton situation; to collect and disseminate complete, authentic and timely statistics on world cotton production, trade consumption, stocks and pieces; to suggest as and when advisable to the governments represented any measures the Advisory Committee considers suitable and practicable for the furtherance of international collaboration.

Membership is open to all members of the United Nations or of the Food and Agricultural Organization having a substantial interest in the purchase and sale of cotton. The Advisory Committee functions in much the same way as a domestic trade association by collecting valuable information on cotton production and prices and by rebating information of importance to members. Undoubtedly, this agreement has been instrumental in many ways in alleviating many of the problems involved in cotton trade. The Committee, an inter-governmental organization, functions as a forum for the exchange of views but has, as yet, been unable to agree on directives toward an international agreement to solve the cotton surplus problem.

§ 6-2.4. The International Olive Oil Agreement.[7]

Signed in October 1955, the Agreement became effective on June 26, 1959. It was renegotiated in 1963, and made effective to September 30, 1969. In May 1969, the 16 countries, representing about 95 percent of the world's olive oil producers, attended a meeting of the International Olive Oil Council in Madrid to discuss revision and renewal of the 1963 Agreement.

§ 6-2.5. The International Rice Commission and the UN Food and Agriculture Organization Study Group.[8]

In November 1948, the UN Food and Agriculture Organization (FAO) sponsored the establishment of the International Rice Commission with membership open to all FAO members. Its purpose was to stabilize the

---

[7] Information obtained from U.S. Government Departments. For further information see *International Agreement on Olive Oil, 1956,* 336 UNTS 177.

[8] *See* issues of the ANNUAIRE O.I.; *International Rice Council,* 3 INT'L ORG. 339 (1949); 4 *id.* 314, 380 (1950); 1 A. PEASLEE, *supra* note 6, at 661-62. Address: FAO Far Eastern Regional Office, Bangkok, Thailand.

world rice market and to provide a means by which problems arising through trade in rice could be discussed and solved.

The basic functions of the International Rice Commission were taken over by an FAO Study Group established in 1964. Its purpose is both to examine the extent to which greater intra-regional trade, particularly among developing countries, may promote a balanced expansion in world rice exports without overburdening the importing countries' balance of payments or restricting the access of third countries, and to explore the technical feasibility and desirability of rice arrangements covering two or more regions which include developed as well as developing countires. Thirty-seven countries are members of the Commission.

§ **6-2.6. The International Rubber Study Group.**[9] The Rubber Study Group composed of 30 major rubber consuming and producing countries operating without a formal agreement between them, operates under a basic document revised in 1950 and 1961 called "Terms of Reference." The functions and duties of the group are to make such studies of the world rubber position as it sees fit in order to provide continuous, accurate information regarding the supply and demand position and its probable development.

The Committee is empowered to consider measures designed to expand the consumption of rubber and also to make recommendations and submit reports as particular problems arise. The organs are: (1) the Study Group which meets whenever the governments deem it necessary; (2) a Management Committee whose membership is determined by the Study Group and which meets at least once every six months, and (3) a Secretariat. This informal association is designed primarily to serve as a vehicle for an exchange of ideas and discussion of problems of the international rubber trade.

§ **6-2.7. The International Sugar Council.**[10] An International Agreement regarding the Regulation of Production and marketing of Sugar, concluded on May 6, 1937, was superseded by the International Sugar Agreement of October 1, 1953. A revised Agreement of December 31, 1958, expired on December 31, 1963, although some of its provisions were continued in force by Proto-

---

[9] ANNUAIRE O.I. 183-84; *International Rubber Study Group,* 4 INT'L ORG. 546 (1950) (for other references, see index to other INT'L ORG. volumes); 2 A. PEASLEE, *supra* note 6, at 1352. Address: 5-6 Lancaster Place, London WC 2, England.

[10] ANNUAIRE O.I. 177; EVERYMAN'S UNITED NATIONS 186 (New York 1959); *International Sugar Council,* 15 INT'L ORG. 348 (1961). *See id.* at 356 for bibliographies; 2 A. PEASLEE, *supra* note 6, at 1364-96. Address: Haymarket House, 28 Haymarket, London SW 1, England.

cols, the last of which expired on December 31, 1968. A new International Sugar Agreement was adopted by a UNCTAD Sugar Conference in 1968, effective on January 1, 1969, for a period of five years. Fifty-two nations are members.

The 1969 Agreement established an International Sugar Council with headquarters in London.[11] The Council has a Council of Delegates, and Executive Committee, an Executive Director, and a staff. The Council of Delegates is composed of all members of the Organization, with a Chairman and a Vice-Chairman, one chosen from among the delegates of importing members and the other from among delegates of exporting members. The Chairman and Vice-Chairman are not paid by the Organization and do not have the right to vote; their voting rights may be exercised by another member. The Council shall hold a regular session each half of the quota year; special sessions may be held when needed; and shall establish Rules of Procedure which set out formulas for distributing votes among exporting and importing members. The Executive Committee, which consists of eight exporting and eight importing members, is elected by the Council. Its functions are delegated to it by the Council. The Executive Director, who serves as chief administrative officer, is elected by the Council.

The Objectives of the Organization are:

1. to raise the level of international trade in sugar, particularly in in order to increase the export earnings of developing exporting countries;

2. to maintain a stable price for sugar which will be reasonably remunerative to producers, but which will not encourage further expansion of production in developed countries;

3. to provide adequate supplies of sugar to meet the requirements of importing countries at fair and reasonable prices;

4. to increase sugar consumption and in particular to promote measures to encourage consumption in countries where consumption *per capita* is low;

5. to bring world production and consumption of sugar into closer balance;

6. to facilitate the coordination of sugar marketing policies and the organization of the market;

7. to provide for adequate participation in, and growing access to, the markets of developed countries for sugar from the developing countries;

---

[11] UN Sugar Conference, 1968, Summary of Proceedings, TD/SUGAR 7/12 (United Nations Publication, Sales number: E. 69. II. D.6).

8. to observe closely developments in the use of any form of substitutes for sugar, including cyclamates and other artificial sweeteners; and

9. to further international cooperation in sugar questions.

The Council is financed by member contributions and publishes a monthly *Statistical Bulletin,* a monthly *Press Summary,* an annual *Pocket Sugar Year Book,* and *World Sugar Economy, Structure and Policies, Volumes I and II.*

§ **6-2.8. The International Sultana [Raisin] Agreement.**[12] At an international conference in Rome in July 1962, Australia, Greece, Iran, South Africa, Spain, Turkey, and the United States established a statistical office and a permanent secretariat in Melbourne, Australia, to provide a means of convoking future meetings to discuss their mutual raisin industry problems. In June 1963, Australia, Greece, and Turkey signed and later ratified an agreement "to implement a minimum price export stabilization programme for all markets for the 1963-64 season." In June 1964, at a meeting in Munich, the representatives of Australia, Greece and Turkey entered into a new agreement, to be effective for a two-year period, for the purpose of setting a minimum base price each year subject to the approval of the governments of the three countries. The Agreement has been subsequently renewed and committees have been formed to advise on marketing problems, on publicity and advertising, and on scientific research.

§ **6-2.9. The International Tin Council.**[13] A first International Tin Agreement was concluded on December 9, 1953, and went into effect on July 1, 1956. It created an International Tin Study Group to discuss common problems in connection with the production, consumption and trade in tin, to consider possible solutions to the problems which are unlikely to be solved by the ordinary development of world trade in tin, and to formulate and transmit recommendations to participating governments. A second International Tin Agreement created the International Tin Council.

---

[12] Australia, Greece, Iran, Turkey and the United States produce 95 per cent of the world production of sultana or dried vine fruits (raisins and currants). *See* U.S. DEPARTMENT OF AGRICULTURE, COMPETITION IN WORLD RAISIN MARKETS (Washington 1967).

[13] ANNUAL REPORT OF THE INTERNATIONAL TIN COUNCIL (since 1937); THE STATISTICAL BULLETIN (monthly since 1933); THE STATISTICAL YEARBOOK (since 1937). *See also* INTERNATIONAL TIN COUNCIL, 14 INT'L ORG. 37 (1960), 15 *id.* 384, 586 (1961); ANNUAIRE O.I. 174-75; EVERYMAN'S UN 186 (1959); *International Tin Council,* 14 INT'L ORG. 37 (1960); 15 *id.* 348 (1961); 15 *id.* 546 for bibliography. Address: 28 Haymarket, London SW 1, England.

A third Agreement, adopted on April 14, 1965, and effective for a period of five years, continued the life of the Council, revising its membership and functions. The present Council, consisting of one representative of each of the 23 member states, has a Chairman and two Vice-Chairmen, one from among the delegates of producing countries and one from among consuming country delegates. The Council appoints a Secretary and a Manager of the Buffer Stock, whose duties are determined by the Council. The Chairman, the Secretary, and the Manager must not hold, or must cease to hold, any financial interest in the tin industry or the tin trade while in office and must seek or receive instructions regarding their functions only from the Council. Council meetings are held at least four times a year at the seat of the Council in London or at such other places as determined by the Council. Since the total number of votes in the Council is 2,000, each member contributes one and two-thousandth of the budget for each vote it holds.

The Council determines the floor and ceiling prices for tin metal and the quantities of tin which may be exported from producing countries. It may authorize special exports and impose conditions which it deems necessary. Articles 10 to 13 of the Agreement provide for the establishment, management, operation and other matters concerning the buffer stock. Complaints by any member state or disputes between member states are to be settled by the Council. In this connection, the Council may be required to seek the opinion of an advisory panel consisting of two persons nominated by the producing countries, two persons nominated by the consuming countries, and a chairman selected by the four persons thus nominated or, if they fail to agree, by the Council Chairman.

§ 6-2.10. **The International Wheat Council.**[14] The Council was established by an Agreement adopted March 1, 1949 and extended in 1953, 1956, 1962 and 1967, effective until June 30, 1971. The Activities of the Council are similar to those of the International Sugar Council. An additional function of the organization not possessed by the International Sugar Council is that "guaranteed purchases" by each of the "importing" countries and "guaranteed sales" by each of the exporting countries are prescribed and "basic minimum and maximum prices" are set forth. Disputes and complaints are handled in essentially the same manner as by the International Sugar Council. The organs of the Council are: (1). the

---

[14] Information obtained from U.S. Government Departments. *See also* ANNUAIRE O.I. 176-77; EVERYMAN'S UN 186 (1959); *International Wheat Council,* 15 INT'L ORG. 739 (1961) (for other references, see index to other INT'L ORG. volumes). Address: 28 Haymarket, London SW 1, England.

Council itself with headquarters in London, composed of one delegate from each exporting and one from each importing member;
(2) an Executive Committee composed of four members elected
annually from exporting countries and eight members elected
annually from importing countries; (3) a Price Review Committee
consisting of 13 members; and (4) a Secretariat. The Council is
composed of 49 nations.

§ 6-2.11. **The International Vine and Wine Office.**[15] Established by the International Wine Office Agreement of November
29, 1924, the Office began operations in 1928. The Office collects,
studies and publishes information about wine and promotes the
interests of winegrowers. The organization takes steps to insure
the purity and authenticity of wines and attempts to suppress
fraud and unfair competition. An agreement on wine nomencla-
ture known as the Madrid Agreement to assure accurate regional
designations of wine, was also signed. Twenty-five countries are
members.

§ 6-2.12. **The International Wool Study Group.**[16] Operating
under "Terms of Reference" adopted in 1947, the Group comprises
representatives of those countries substantially interested in the
production, consumption, and trade of wool. It meets at times
and places mutually convenient to the members for the purpose of
discussing common problems in connection with wool production,
consumption and trade, on which it collects information, and publishes statistics useful to its members. It also is responsible for
considering possible solutions to problems or difficulties which are
unlikely to be resolved by the ordinary development of the world
wool trade. It does not have specific regulatory powers, although
it can formulate and transmit recommendations to the participating
governments. The Study Group has a Management Committee, and
a Technical Committee. Secretariat expenses are maintained by the
United Kingdom. Forty-three nations are members.

§ 6-2.13. **Status of Agreements on Cocoa.** Although no international cocoa agreement presently exists, considerable efforts are
currently being made to draft such an agreement. However, an

---

[15] International Vine and Wine Office publications: ANNUAIRE; ATLAS MONDIAL
DE LA VIGNE ET DU VIN; LEXIQUE DES TERMES TECHNIQUES DE LA VITICUL-
TURE ET DE L'OENOLOGIE; MONTHLY BULLETIN; ANNUAIRE O.I. 199-200; 2 A.
PEASLEE, *supra* note 6 at 1555-59. Address: 11 Rue Roguepine, Paris 8er, France.

[16] *See* issues of ANNUAIRE, O.I.; 2 A. PEASLEE, *supra* note 6, at 1560-61. Address:
Ministry of Materials, Horseguards Ave., Whitehall, London SW 1, England.

International Cocoa Trades Federation and an International Office of Cocoa and Chocolate have attempted to fill this void.

The International Cocoa Trades Federation, established in 1962, aims to promote and organize joint action by all or any of the associations formed or to be formed in any part of the world for the purpose of promoting and developing the cocoa trade. At present, five national associations are members of the Federation, which meets annually and elects a Council.

The International Office of Cocoa and Chocolate, established in 1930, in Antwerp. Belgium, is composed of national associations in 24 countries and individual manufacturers in Chile, Denmark, Egypt, Ecuador, Finland, Peru, the Philippines and Portugal. It is also composed of a General Assembly which meets every five years, an Administrative Council and Bureaus. The Office aims to conduct research on all questions concerning the cocoa and chocolate industry; inform national associations of the solutions discovered; and collect and disseminate relevant information.

§ 6-2.14. **Status of Agreements on Tea.**[17] An International Tea Agreement, negotiated in 1933, was last renewed for a five-year period in 1959, but, not being renewed again, expired on March 31, 1955. The original nine members of the Agreement: Ceylon, India, Indonesia, Kenya, Malawi, Mozambique, Pakistan, Tanzania and Uganda; India and Ceylon being the two principal producers, however, continue to maintain a statistical and information center which collects and publishes statistics on the international productions, export, import and stocks of tea.

§ 6-2.15. **The Organization of Petroleum Exporting Countries.** This Organization, known as OPEC, has 10 members: Iran, Iraq, Saudi Arabia, Kuwait, Qatar, Abu Dhabi, Libya, Alteria, Indonesia, and Venezuela. These states grant concessions which produce much of the oil produced by non-socialist states. While the concessions are granted to private companies including Standard Oil Company of New Jersey, Standard Oil Company of California, Gulf Oil Company, Texaco Oil Company, Mobil Oil Company, British Petroleum Company, Royal Dutch Shell Company and Compagnie Francaise des Petroles, the importance of this oil supply is such that high governmental officials sometimes participate in negotiations relative to price, royalties and amount of production. The legal aspects of these agreements are of great importance.

---

[17] ANNUAIRE O.I. 142; *International Tea Committee*, 5 INT'L ORG. 347 (1951).

§ 6-2.16. The Development of Agreements on Other Commodities.

Work is underway on agreements similar to those on coffee, cotton, and others just described on many other subjects. Sulphur is a good example. Canada has been selling sulphur produced as a natural gas by-product below the cost of producing sulphur in Mexico, Poland, France and other sulphur producing nations. Private and public conferences to solve this problem are being held. The network of fair trade law applicable to transnational sales of commodities is certain to grow rapidly.

§ 6-3. International Organizations Facilitating Investment, Trade and Commerce.[18]

Such organizations are essential to improve the international economic process. By setting up tariff agreements, establishing common trade unions, and making money available to less developed nations, these organizations transform some of the raw materials in the economies of Nation-States into products useful for international economic development.

Since the end of the Second World War, nations throughout the world have increasingly sought to develop a law program and an organizational structure to facilitate international investment, trade

---

[18] *See generally* Aguiar, *World Problems in Fiscal Matters,* in WORLD PEACE THROUGH LAW: THE ATHENS CONFERENCE 335-43 (1965) [hereinafter cited as ATHENS CONF.]; Bhandari, *Law Rules To Encourage International Investment,* in *id.* 261-3; Abranches, *Law Rules To Encourage International Investment,* in *id.* 271-80; Grant, *Economic Associations and International Trade,* in *id.* 353-65; Jennings, *International Investment,* in *id.* 280-84; Ladas, *Industrial Property and Economic Development,* in *id.* 366-78; Mawalla, *Law Rules To Encourage International Investment,* in *id.* 292-98; Naritomi, *Investment,* in *id.* 298-300; Naritomi, *Transnational Trade and Investment,* in WORLD PEACE THROUGH LAW: THE WASHINGTON CONFERENCE 281-82 (1967) [hereinafter cited as WASHINGTON CONF.]; Pollzien, *Law Rules To Encourage International Investment,* in ATHENS CONF. 302-09; Ray, *Economic Development,* in *id.* 309-19; Ray, *Transnational Trade and Investments. Guarantees of Foreign Investments,* in WASHINGTON CONF. 266-81; Schmitthoff, *Work Paper on Transnational Trade and Investments,* in WORLD PEACE THROUGH LAW: THE GENEVA CONFERENCE 261-76 (1969) [hereinafter cited as GENEVA CONF.]; Svec, *Transnational Trade and Investments,* in *id.* 301-6.

For articles specifically dealing with taxation of investments, see Dertilis, *Taxations of Investments in Debtor Countries: The Principles of Taxation at Domicile or at Source,* in ATHENS CONF. 267-71; Payot, *International Juridical Problems Involved in Taxation,* in *id.* 300-01; Willis, *International Legal Problems of Taxation,* in *id.* 324-28.

For articles particularly concerning private investment, see Cobos, *The International Legal Problems of Taxation, id.* 324-8.

For articles particularly concerning private investment, see Cobos, *The International Protection of Small Investment,* in WASHINGTON CONF. 660-63, Wilkins, *The Common Interest in Private International Investment,* in ATHENS CONF. 319-24.

For the treaties establishing ECSC, EEC, EFTA, GATT, OECD, and the European Convention for the Protection of Human Rights and Fundamental Freedoms, see E. STEIN & P. HAY, DOCUMENTS FOR LAW AND INSTITUTIONS IN THE ATLANTIC (New York 1967).

and commerce. Significant advances toward the creation of this organizational structure have been made at the regional level: nations with a commonality of interest and economic position have entered into agreements to lessen trade barriers, to encourage intraregional commerce and investment, and to promote technical cooperation.

The achievements of these organizations have been significant, and their accomplishments portend increased economic cooperation among nations, because the commonality of interest, which gave impetus to today's international economic organizations, is expanding. As the world continues to shrink in terms of time and distance and nations become increasingly interdependent, expanded international agreements and a strengthened international law structure will help ensure economic progress.

§ 6-3.1. Activities of the United Nations. As stated above, the United Nations has done more than any other international organization to facilitate international investment, trade, and commerce. Its activities, consuming 95 percent of its annual budget and designed primarily to help speed the economic development of the developing nations, have been varied, and have touched upon all aspects of international finance and development.

§ 6-3.1.1. The General Agreement on Tariffs and Trade[19] and

---

[19] Address: Villa Le Bocage, Palais des Nations, 1211 Geneva 10, Switzerland. For further information on GATT, see ANNUAIRE O.I. 77-9; A. BLUM FLOR, ACUERDO GENERAL SOBRE ARANCELES ADUANEROS Y COMERCIO (GATT) (1958); BUREAU OF INTERNATIONAL COMMERCE, U.S. DEPARTMENT OF COMMERCE, GENERAL AGREEMENT ON TARIFFS AND TRADE (Washington 1964); G. CURZON, MULTILATERAL COMMERCIAL DIPLOMACY: AN EXPLANATION OF THE IMPACT OF THE GENERAL AGREEMENT ON TARIFFS AND TRADE ON NATIONAL COMMERCIAL POLICIES AND TECHNIQUES (New York 1966); EVERYMAN'S UN 22, 450, 530-35 (1959); Friedman, *Relations Between the IMF and the GATT*, INT'L FINANCIAL NEWS SURVEY (1955); *General Agreement on Tariffs and Trade*, 15 INT'L ORG. 729-30 (1961) (for other references, see index to other INT'L ORG. volumes); *GATT: An Analysis and Appraisal for the General Agreement on Tariffs and Trade*, FLETCHER SCHOOL OF LAW AND DIPLOMACY, U.S. COUNCIL OF THE INTERNATIONAL CHAMBER OF COMMERCE (New York 1955); GATT: WHAT IT IS (Geneva 1967); Gerhard, *Tariffs and Trade in the Common Market*, EUROPEAN REGIONAL COMMUNITIES 193-213 (New York 1962); Goiter, *GATT After Six Years: An Appraisal*, 8 INT'L ORG. 1-19 (1954); Goodwin, *GATT and the Organization for Trade Co-operation*, Y.B. WORLD AFF. 229-55 (1956); Hollis, *Dispute Settlement Under the General Agreement on Tariffs and Trade*, in M. DOMKE, INTERNATIONAL TRADE ARBITRATION 77-85 (New York 1958); Jackson, *Puzzle of GATT*, 1 J. WORLD TRADE L. 131-61 (1967); Liebhafsky, *Ten Years of GATT*, in S. ECON. J. (Chapel Hill, N.C. 1958); M. DE MEERHAEGHE, INTERNATIONAL ECONOMIC INSTITUTIONS 157-86 (London 1966); V. MUHAMMAD, LEGAL FRAMEWORK OF WORLD TRADE (New York 1958); 1 A. PEASLEE, *supra* note 6, at 688-743; U.S. DEPARTMENT OF STATE, ANALYSIS ON GENERAL AGREEMENT

(Continued)

International Anti-Dumping Code.[20] The most common devices for controlling international trade are currency controls, tariffs, and quota restrictions on imports and exports. Their utilization by a state constitutes one of the most important aspects of its international economic policy.

The establishment of the General Agreement on Tariffs and Trade (GATT) on October 30, 1947, has been the most comprehensive undertaking by governments for the reduction of barriers to world trade. The Agreement consists of schedules of tariff commitments; a set of common rules of trade; and procedural provisions under which the parties to the Agreement sponsor negotiations, settle disputes, and administer the Agreement.

There are 76 contracting parties to GATT, with six countries participating under special agreements. The Agreement is being applied *de facto* by 10 other countries, mostly African states. Member states are responsible for over 80 percent of world trade. world trade.

As expressed in the Preamble, GATT was born out of a recognition by the contracting parties that:

> their relations in the field of economic endeavor should be conducted with a view to raising standards of living, insuring full employment and a large and steadily growing volume of real income and effective demand, developing the full use of the resources of the world and expanding the production and exchange of goods . . .

The Preamble envisages that the contracting parties will achieve these ends:

> by entering into reciprocal and mutually advantageous arrangements directed to the substantial reduction of tariffs and other barriers to trade and to the elimination of discriminatory treatment in international commerce . . .

ON TARIFFS AND TRADE (Pub. No. 2983, Washington 1947); U.S. DEPARTMENT OF STATE, GATT, AN EXPLANATION OF ITS PROVISIONS AND THE PROPOSED AMENDMENTS (Pub. No. 5813, Washington 1947); U.S. DEPARTMENT OF STATE, INTRODUCING ORGANIZATION FOR TRADE CO-OPERATION (Pub. No. 6268, Washington 1957); *Actions Taken on Strengthening Administration of GATT*, DEP'T STATE BULL. (Washington 1951); *United States Participation in the General Agreement on Tariffs and Trade*, 61 COLUM. L. REV. 505-690 (1961); White, *Achievements of GATT and Prospects for the Future*, UNITED NATIONS REV. 34-37, 68 (New York 1957).

[20] de Jong, *The Significance of Dumping in International Trade*, J. WORLD L. 162-88 (1968); U.S. SENATE COMMITTEE ON FINANCE, THE REPORT OF THE U.S. TARIFF COMMISSION ON S. CON. RES. 38, REGARDING THE INTERNATIONAL ANTI-DUMPING CODE . . . (Washington 1969).

In substance, this means that all parties to the Agreement shall receive "most-favored-nation" treatment in tariff, customs, and tax matters. The effect of the above provision is somewhat mitigated, however, by Article I, Paragraph 2, in which preferences in force exclusively between two or more of the territories listed in an attached annex, and other preferences specifically referred to, were permitted to remain in existence. With very limited exceptions, existing preferences were not to be increased and no new preferences created. Some new departures from most-favored-nation treatment have been permitted for customs unions and free trade areas under Article XXXIV and by waivers.

The reduction of tariff barriers is provided for through provisions for multilateral tariff negotiations. The tariff schedules prepared through negotiation consist of a list of the regulated products with applicable rates. A party to GATT commits itself not to increase its tariffs above the rate specified for each product listed on the appropriate schedule. The most extensive tariff negotiations, supplemented by some concessions on non-tariff barriers, were conducted at the Kennedy Round, completed on June 30, 1967.

Tariff concessions alone would be of little benefit to trade if countries were free to nullify them by use of other devices. Consequently, the governments also agreed upon a set of rules called "General Provisions of the GATT,"[21] designed to protect the value of the tariff concessions, to bring about a relaxation of non-tariff trade restrictions and controls, and to assure the greatest possible observance of the principle of non-discrimination in trade matters.

The contracting parties agree to provide special national treatment with respect to international taxation and other regulations for imported goods, and freedom of transit of goods across the territory of signatory states. Matters such as customs procedures, fees, and valuation of goods were also regulated within certain limits. Other provisions of the Agreement covered the problem of "marks of origin," publication and administration of trade regulations, general elimination of quantitative restrictions, restrictions to safeguard the balance of payments, exchange arrangements, subsidies, state trading enterprises, and related subjects.

The advantages of a multilateral approach such as GATT lie largely in overcoming a reluctance of most nations to make commitments by which foreign goods are more freely admitted to their

---

[21] General Agreement on Tariffs and Trade, *signed* October 30, 1947, 61 Stat. 56, TIAS 1700, 55 U.N.T.S. 187.

own markets. If many countries make similar commitments simultaneously, this reluctance can be more easily overcome. The alternative bilateral approach, on the other hand, results in sporadic piecemeal agreements which give much less promise of reducing barriers to trade generally and often produce a widely fluctuating international price situation.

Mechanisms, such as the Council of Representatives, created for settling disputes arising under the Agreement, generally result in their settlement through negotiation between the parties concerned or through mediation by the parties acting jointly.

In 1965, the GATT member states met in Geneva to bring into effect a new Chapter (Part IV) on trade and development under the general principles and objectives which are to govern the policies of contracting parties regarding developing countries. It specifies certain general undertakings by both developed and developing countries and provides a procedure for consultation to deal with differences arising in implementing these commitments. It also lists various forms of joint action to promote trade with, and development of, less developed contracting parties.

In 1965, the Committee on Trade and Development was established to coordinate GATT activities, especially those concerning developing countries, with the UN Conference on Trade and Development (UNCTAD), and to review the application of new Chapter provisions. As an indication of the spirit of cooperation pervading the field of international trade, a new International Trade Center has been established at Geneva, under the auspices of GATT and UNCTAD, to give trade information and trade promotion advice.

The first 12 articles of the Agreement of Implementation for Article VI of the General Agreement of Tariffs and Trade constitute the Anti-Dumping Code.

The Code defines dumping as the introduction of exports "into the commerce of another country at less than its normal value." It also defines "less than normal value" and "domestic industry." It determines the extent of injury necessary for the assessment of dumping and provides investigation and administrative procedures. It specifies anti-dumping duties and the provisional measures that can be taken when a preliminary decision has been made that there is dumping. And, it describes how anti-dumping action can be taken by a third party.

The Code recognizes "that anti-dumping practices should not constitute an unjustifiable impediment to international trade, that anti-dumping [procedures] may be applied against dumping only if such dumping causes or threatens material injury to an established industry or materially retards the establishment of an industry." It further recognizes that it is desirable "to interpret the provisions of Article VI of GATT and the elaborate rules for their application in order to provide greater uniformity and certainty in their application."

§ 6-3.1.2. The International Bank for Reconstruction and Development (World Bank).[22]

This bank commenced operations in June 1946, pursuant to an Articles of Agreement drafted at the Bretton Woods Conference in July 1944. It is a specialized agency of the United Nations, having as its main objective the economic development of its member countries for the purpose of raising the standards of living of the peoples of the world. The Bank is able to lend to member governments, governmental agencies, or private enterprises; however, if the borrower is not a government, the guarantee of the member government is required to facilitate the loan.

The original membership of 28 nations has increased to 115 countries, each of which is a stockholder of the Bank subscribing to the Bank's capital according to its economic means. The larger part of the Bank's resources, however, has been obtained by borrowing in international capital markets.

The resources of the Bank were initially directed toward European postwar reconstruction, but since 1948, it has increasingly turned toward lending for economic development. As of June 30, 1970, the Bank had made 725 loans totaling $15.5 billion

---

[22] The World Bank has sponsored the Convention on the Settlement of Investment Disputes between States and Nationals of Other States, which led to the creation of the International Centre for Settlement of Investment Disputes. *See* Chapter 5 of this volume; Broches, *Remarks by the Chairman: Settlement of Investment Disputes Between States and Nationals of Other States,* in GENEVA CONF. 258-61. Address: 1818 H Street, N.W., Washington, D.C. 20433.

For further information on the International Bank for Reconstruction and Development, see ARTICLES OF AGREEMENT; ANNUAL REPORTS (include statements on the year's activities, financial statements, a description of loans by areas, and useful statistics); LOAN REGULATIONS; SUMMARY PROCEEDINGS OF THE ANNUAL MEETINGS; ANNUAIRE O.I. 55-7; Botting, *New Concepts in Economic Assistance for Underdeveloped Countries: the Fund, the Bank and the IFC,* 14 W. POL. Q. 498-501 (1961); Broches, *International Bank for Reconstruction and Development,* in ATHENS CONF. 264-67; Broches, *Development of International Law by the International Bank for Reconstruction and Development,* ASIL PROC. 33-8 (1965); EVERYMAN'S UN 22, 30, 196, 354, 449, 450, 451, 494-98, 536-37 (1959); *International Bank . . .,* 5 INT'L ORG. 735-36 (1961) (for other references, see index to other INT'L ORG. volumes); A. VAN MEERHAEGHE, *supra* note 19, at 1221-1361; 2 A. PEASLEE, *supra* note 6, at 942-72, 1137, 1172; *World Money: Fund and Bank,* 74 ECONOMIST (October 1960).

to finance high-priority development projects in 88 countries or territories.

The main principles governing the Bank's lending operations, as stipulated by its Articles of Agreement, are as follows:

> The Bank must be satisifed, before making a loan, that the borrower would be unable to obtain finance from other sources on conditions reasonable for the borrower.

> The Bank's loans must be for high-priority productive purposes and, except in special circumstances, for specific projects of reconstruction or development.

> The Bank must pay due regard to the prospects that the borrower, and if the borrower is not a member, that the guarantor will be in a position to meet its obligations under the loan.

> The Bank must ensure that the proceeds of any loan are used only for purposes for which the loan was granted, giving attention to considerations of economy and efficiency.

> The Bank is prohibited from making "tied" loans; that is, it must not impose any conditions requiring the proceeds of its loans to be spent in any particular member country or countries.

> Only economic considerations shall be relevant to the Bank's decisions; it must not be influenced by the political character of the members concerned.

The World Bank has been a significant factor in the economic development of many of the states which have received loans. It has been financially successful: net earnings amounted to approxi-$213 million for fiscal year 1970.

§ 6-3.1.3. The International Development Association.[23]

The Articles of Agreement of this organization, an affiliate of the World Bank, came into force in January 1961. Its purposes are essentially the same as those of the World Bank, that is, to promote economic development, increase productivity, and thus raise standards of living in the less developed areas of the world included within the Association's membership. This is to be achieved particularly by providing finance to meet important development requirements on terms which are more flexible and bear less heavily on the balance of payments than conventional loans, thereby

---

[23] *See generally* I.D. Ass. Articles of Agreement, Annual Reports, and Summary Proceedings of Annual Meetings. Address: 1818 H Street, N.W., Washington, D.C. 20433. *See also* ANNUAIRE O.I. 57; *International Development Association,* 15 INT'L ORG. 737 (1961) (for other references, see index to other INT'L ORG. volumes); Metzger, *The New International Development Association,* 49 GEO. L.J. 23-44 (1960); M. VAN MEERHAEGHE, *supra* note 19, at 143-59; 2 A. PEASLEE, *supra* note 6, at 1137-57.

furthering the developmental objectives of the World Bank and supplementing its activities.

IDA makes "soft" loans bearing no interest. Credits extended to date have been for a term of 50 years with repayment in foreign exchange due to begin after a ten-year period of grace. Thereafter, one percent of the principal is repayable annually for 10 years and three percent is repayable annually for the final 30 years. A service charge of three-fourths of one percent per annum is made on the amounts withdrawn and outstanding to meet IDA's administrative costs.

The resources of the organization are principally in the form of subscriptions and contributions from member governments. By December 31, 1970, the bank had extended 237 credits totaling $2.9 billion to help finance development projects in 55 countries, leaving resources available for commitment of approximately $320 million. IDA's funds were replenished by member governments in 1968-1969 by $1.2 billion. It has been agreed upon to replenish IDA by $2.4 billion in 1971-1972.

§ 6-3.1.4. **The International Finance Corporation.**[24] The IFC came into existence on July 20, 1956, and now has 95 members. Its purpose is to further economic development by encouraging the growth of productive private enterprise in member countries, particularly in the less developed areas. A unique feature of IFC is that it operates for the sole purpose of assisting the international expansion of private enterprise.

IFC provides risk capital for productive private enterprises, in association with private investors and management. It encourages the development of local capital markets and stimulates the international flow of private capital. It makes investments in the form of share subscriptions and long term loans, carries out standby and underwriting arrangements, and provides financial and technical assistance to privately controlled development finance companies. It neither seeks nor accepts government guarantees in its operations.

---

[24] For more information on this corporation, see its Articles of Agreement, Annual Reports, General Policies Statement (12-page booklet in Arabic, French, German, Spanish), Loan Regulations, and Summary of Proceedings of Annual Meetings. Address: 1818 H Street, N.W., Washington, D.C. 20433.

See also EVERYMAN'S UN 22, 30, 196, 200, 450, 498-502 (1959); *International Finance Corporation,* 15 INT'L ORG. 737 (1961) (for other references, see index to other INT'L ORG. volumes); Nurick, *The World Bank, the International Finance Corporation and Foreign Investment,* 19 FED. B.J. 308-16 (1959); M. VAN MEERHAEGHE, *supra* note 19, at 136-143; 2 PEASLEE, *supra* note 6, at 1172-88.

The Corporation is responsible for the appraisal and supervision of all projects submitted to the World Bank Group relating to manufacturing, mining, and developmental finance, irrespective of which member of the Group is to provide the financing.

The authorized capital of IFC is $110,000,000 of which $107 million was subscribed as of September 30, 1970. The sources of IFC funds have been capital subscriptions, earnings, revolvements of funds through repayments, sales of investments, and acquisition by other of IFC's standby or underwriting commitments. It has available a line of credit from the World Bank of $200 million, out of approximately $428 million which the Corporation is authorized to borrow for relending to private enterprises. As of June 30, 1970, IFC had made a total of 210 commitments totaling $447 million. Net earnings for fiscal year 1970 were $9.1 million.

IFC has invested primarily in manufacturing, industrial and development finance companies, but is prepared to consider investments in other types of enterprises (for example, projects relating to agriculture, service industries, public utilities and tourism), provided the proposals meet the Corporation's regular investment criteria. The Corporation also will commit funds for promotional purposes when an enterprise is being created. The Corporation has set a maximum of $50,000 in promotional costs for a single project.

An enterprise which seeks to qualify for financial assistance by IFC must show that it is of economic priority to the country concerned, that the project is judged to be a sound and profitable business venture and that the presence of IFC is needed to realize the project. It normally provides financing by subscribing to shares usually in conjunction with a long-term loan. Only in exceptional circumstances will it provide loan capital without equity or an equity feature. IFC's investments in shares are usually denominated in the currency of the country in which the enterprise is located. Loans are generally expressed in terms of U.S. dollars. Exchange risks on loans are assumed by the borrower.

The normal range of final maturities of IFC loans is from seven to 12 years, although in exceptional cases IFC is prepared to extend loans with longer final maturities. Amortization is usually on the basis of semi-annual maturities and IFC customarily allows a grace period before amortization payments begin. A Commitment fee of one percent per year is charged on the undisbursed portion of a loan. IFC's investment agreements conform to the normal practices of long term investors and contain standard protective covenants.

There is no standard form application of IFC financing. Before making a detailed appraisal of an investment proposal, IFC expects certain preliminary information, similar to that required by a private investment institution. Such information includes a description of the enterprise, its legal status, its financial history, its present and proposed operations, the purpose for which financing is required and the amount sought, financial forecasts of operating results and, in the case of a manufacturing enterprise, the costs and availability of raw materials and other inputs together with a review of technical assistance or other agreements where relevant.

§ **6-3.1.5. The International Monetary Fund.**[25] A Specialized Agency of the United Nations with 115 members, the Fund is a major instrument in facilitating international trade and investment.

Its purposes, as set forth in Article 1 of the Articles of Agreement of December 27, 1945, are:

> (i) to promote international monetary cooperation through a permanent institution which provides the machinery for consultation and collaboration on international monetary problems;
>
> (ii) to facilitate the expansion and balanced growth of international trade, and to contribute thereby to the promotion and maintenance of high levels of employment and real income and to the development of the productive resources of all members as primary objectives of economic policy;

---

[25] Address: 19th & H Streets, N.W., Washington, D.C. 20431. For further information on the International Monetary Fund, see its Articles of Agreement, "Annual Reports" (describe the work of the Fund, give a review of the year, and include numerous tables and charts), Annual Report of Exchange Restrictions, Direction of International Trade (monthly), International Financial News (weekly), List of Publications, Prices in National Currencies, Summary Proceedings of Annual Meetings.

See also ANNUAIRE O.I. 59-62; EVERYMAN'S UN 22, 30, 449, 450, 451, 488-94, 536-37 (1959); H. AUFRICHT, CENTRAL BANKING LEGISLATION (presents, in English, the complete text of the Central Banking and monetary laws of 21 countries); Gold, *Interpretation by the International Monetary Fund of Its Articles of Agreement,* 16 INT'L & COMP. L.Q. 289-329 (1962); J. GOLD, THE FUND AGREEMENT IN THE COURTS (Washington 1962); Gold, *The Interpretation by the International Monetary Fund of Its Articles of Agreement,* 3 INT'L & COMP. L.Q. 256-77 (1954); Hexner, *Worldwide International Economic Institutions: A Factual Review,* 61 COLUM. L.REV. 354-74 (1961); *International Monetary Fund,* 15 INT'L ORG. 738-39 (1961) (for other references, see index to other INT'L ORG. volumes); Loftus, *The International Monetary Fund: A Selected Bibliography,* 1 IMF STAFF PAPERS 471 (1951); Loftus, 3 *id.* 171 (1953); Loftus, 4 *id.* 467 (1954); Loftus, 6 *id.* 476 (1956); M. VAN MEERHAEGHE, *supra* note 19, at 94-121; 1 PEASLEE, *supra* note 6, at 639, 705-07, 735, 837, 946, 959; 2 *id., supra* note 6, at 942, 1143, 1177, 1258-94, 1381.

(iii) to promote exchange stability, to maintain orderly exchange arrangements among members, and to avoid competitive exchange depreciation;

(iv) to assist in the establishment of a multilateral system of payments in respect of current transactions between members and in the elimination of foreign exchange restrictions which hamper the growth of world trade;

(v) to give confidence to members by making the Fund's resources available to them under adequate safeguards, thus providing them with opportunity to correct maladjustments in their balance of payments without resorting to measures destructive of national or international prosperity.

(vi) in accordance with the above, to shorten the duration and lessen the degree of disequilibrium in the international balances of payments of members.

The provisions of the agreement specify that each member shall have a quota, a portion of which is to be paid in, with the balance subject to call.

The Agreement is quite comprehensive. It includes sections covering subscriptions to the Fund, par values of currencies to stabilize exchange rate, transactions with the Fund, including those with agencies dealing with the Fund, limitations on the operations of the Fund, and conditions under which its resources can be utilized. In addition, provisions cover capital transfers, scarce currencies, and the general obligations of the members. On the whole, these obligations are intended to avoid restrictions on current payments and discriminatory currency practices and to strive toward convertibility of foreign-held balances. In addition, members are obliged to furnish necessary information and statistics to the Secretariat.

The Fund possesses full juridical personality and, in particular, the capacity to contract, to acquire and dispose of movable and immovable property and to institute legal proceedings. The organs of the Fund, according to Article 12, are: a Board of Governors, Executive Directors and a Managing Director and his staff. All powers of the Fund are vested in the Board of Governors consisting of one governor and one alternate appointed by each member in such manner as it may determine.

The Fund approved an agreement in 1962 and extended in 1965 until 1970 whereby 10 industrial members undertook to lend the Fund up to $6 billion, if this should be needed to cope with an impairment of the international monetary system. These arrangements were used to help finance the drawings made by the United Kingdom in 1964, 1965 and 1968. The amount still available as of September 1968 was $4.7 billion.

In the 1966 annual meeting of the Fund, the Board of Governors decided to have a direct exchange of views on international liquidity between the Fund Executive Directors and Deputies of the same 10 nations participating in the above General Arrangements to Borrow. Four such meetings took place before June 1967, and in September 1967, the Governors requested the Executive Directors to proceed with work relating to the establishment of a new Fund facility based on Special Drawing Rights as well as on improvements of the present rules and practices of the Fund in the light of the experience and developments of the last 20 years. The proposed Amendment to the Articles of Agreement was approved by the Governors in May 1958, and went into effect on October 1, 1968, with $9.5 billion allocated. As of January 1, 1970, $3.4 billion had been drawn; as of January 1, 1971, an additional 2.9 billion had been drawn; and it is expected that by January 1, 1972, an additional $3 billion will be drawn. From March 1947, to April 30, 1970, the Fund provided a total of $20.9 billion of foreign exchange with repayment by repurchase of $10.5 billion.

§ 6-3.1.6. The United Nations Conference on Trade and Development.[26] UNCTAD is composed of 133 member states, 123 of which are members of the United Nations and 10 of which are members of one of the Institutions of the UN or of the International Atomic Energy Agency.

The impetus to convene UNCTAD grew out of the desire of developing nations for a voice in matters of trade and economic development greater than that provided them through participation in GATT. In 1964, UNCTAD and GATT jointly established the International Trade Center, described in § 6-3.1.1. of this volume.

UNCTAD is an organ of the UN General Assembly. Membership is thus open to all members of the UN and meets its specialized agencies. The Conference meets every three years. The Trade and Development Board serves as the executive body of UNCTAD, and a Secretariat is headed by a Secretary-General appointed with the approval of the UN General Assembly.

UNCTAD's activities center primarily upon solving the following problems: how to lessen the economic vulnerability and how to

---

[26] *See* Etre, *The Birth of UNCTAD: An Important New Legal and Economic Development*, in WASHINGTON CONF. at 671-80 (1967).

stablize the export revenue of the developing countries, the great majority of which are commodity exporters; how to open the developed countries' markets to the first industrial and semi-manufactured exports of the developing countries; how to encourage and facilitate the flow of capital from the rich to the poor countries; and how to promote the regional and sub-regional cooperation and economic integration of often non-viable small national entities.

After a first Conference in Geneva, March 23-June 16, 1964, the functions of UNCTAD were defined by Resolution 1955 (XIX) of the UN General Assembly as follows:

1. to promote international trade especially with a view to accelerating economic development, particularly trade between countries at a different stage of development, between developing countries and between countries with different systems of economic and social organization;

2. to formulate principles and policies of international trade and related problems of economic development;

3. to make proposals for putting the said principles and policies into effect, and to take such other steps within its competence as may be relevant to this end;

4. to review and facilitate the co-ordination of activities of other institutions within the United Nations system in the field of international trade and related problems of economic development;

5. to initiate action where appropriate in co-operation with the competent organs of the United Nations for the negotiation and adoption of multilateral legal instruments in the field of trade;

6. to be available as a center for harmonising the trade and related development policies of governments and regional economic groupings;

7. to deal with any other matters within its competence.

A second Conference on Trade and Development was held in New Delhi from January through March 1968. The scope of the Conference was outlined in the agenda of five Committees and three Working Groups:

Committee 1: commodity problems and policies;

Committee 2: expansion and diversification of exports of manufactures and semi-manufactures of developing countries;

Committee 3: growth, development finance and aid (the synchronization of national and international policies);

Committee 4: problems of developing countries with regard to invisible factors, such as shipping;

Committee 5: trends and problems in world trade and development;

Working Group 1: world food problems: the transfer of technology;

Working Group 2: trade, expansion and economic integration among developing countries;

Working Group 3: special problems of landlocked countries.

Although many observers have expressed disappointment in the failure of the second Conference to formulate a unified response to the problem of underdevelopment, UNCTAD has achieved certain substantive results. The need for international agreement on such products as cocoa, rubber, sugar and coarse fibers was emphasized. A "generalized non-reciprocal, non-discriminatory system of tariff preferences in favor of the developing countries" was called for. A recommendation for the allocation of one per cent of the gross national product of developed countries for aid was approved. Special declarations were issued on: hunger in the world, trade expansion, and regional integration among developing countries.

§ 6-3.1.7. **The UN Economic Commission for Africa.**[27] Established by the UN Economic and Social Council on April 29, 1958, the Commission maintains headquarters in Addis Ababa, Ethiopia. It also maintains offices at Kinshasa, Congo; Lusaka, Zambia; Niamey, Niger; and Tangier, Morocco. All independent African states which are UN members are eligible for membership on the Commission and states having territorial responsibilities in African and non-self-governing territories are eligible for associate membership. As of April 1968, there were 40 members and six associate members. The Commission has a Secretariat, headed by an Executive Secretary, and includes the following divisions: Trade and Economic Cooperation, Natural Resources and Transport, Industry and Housing, Research and Statistics, Human Resources Development, ECA/FAO (The UN Food and Agriculture Organization discussed in § 6-3.1.11.) Joint Agriculture, and Administration, Conference and General Services.

The functions of the Commission are: to promote and facilitate concerted action for the economic and social development of Africa; to maintain and strengthen the economic relations of African countries and territories, both among themselves and with other countries and territories of the world; to undertake or sponsor investiga-

---

[27] *See* ECA's annual reports; *Economic Commission for Africa,* 15 INT'L ORG. 282-84 (1961); EVERYMAN'S UN 20, 32, 271-77 (1959); 2 PEASLEE, *supra* note 6, at 1771.

tions, research, and studies of economic and technological problems and developments; to collect, evaluate, and disseminate economic, technical, and statistical information; to assist in the formulation and development of coordinated policies in promoting economic and social development in the region; and to perform such advisory services as the countries and territories of the region may request. The Commission also assists the Economic and Social Council, when requested, by taking responsibility for the resolution of economic problems within the region, in particular problems of technical assistance, and cooperates with other UN organs and specialized agencies.

§ 6-3.1.8. The UN Economic Commission for Asia and the Far East.[28] Established in 1947, with headquarters in Bangkok, this Commission has 27 members including Afghanistan, Australia, Burma, Cambodia, Ceylon, Republic of China, France, India, Indonesia, Iran, the Republic of Korea, Japan, Laos, Malaysia, Mongolia, Nepal, the Netherlands, New Zealand, Pakistan, the Philippines, Singapore, Thailand, U.S.S.R., United Kingdom, United States, the Republic of Vietnam and Western Samoa. The three associate members of the Commission are Brunei, Fiji, and Hong Kong.

Sessions of the Commission are held annually, and are attended by high-ranking and interested observers. The services of the Commission have developed along lines of fact-finding, analysis and dissemination of information, followed by recommendations to governments, and assistance to governments in their economic programs. The Commission also renders advisory services to governments upon request.

The main subsidiary bodies are the committees on: Trade, Industry and Natural Resources, and Transport and Communications, which are further divided into various subcommittees. Periodic conferences are held in the fields of: economic development, planning, trade, statistics, and water resources.

Working parties and seminars, study trips and group visits, training centers, and regional research centers, have all been undertaken under ECAFE sponsorship. The annual *Economic Survey of Asia and the Far East,* supplemented by the quarterly *Economic Bulletin for Asia and the Far East,* contains systematic reviews of economic developments in each country and in the region as a whole, and is a standard reference work for all who are interested in the economies

---

[28] *See Economic Commission for Asia and the Far East,* 15 INT'L ORG. 500-01 (1961); EVERYMAN'S UN 20, 32, 226, 227, 245-60, 436; 2 PEASLEE, *supra* note 6, at 1771.

of the region. The document also serves as a background paper for the Commission's annual meeting.

§ 6-3.1.9. **The UN Economic Commission for Europe.**[29] This Commission was established by the UN Economic and Social Council on March 28, 1947, with headquarters in Geneva. There are thirty-one members of the Commission, comprising the nations of Europe and the United States. The Commission meets for a two or three week session each year.

The objectives of the Commission are to initiate and participate in measures for facilitating concerted action for the economic reconstruction of Europe, for raising the level of European economic activity, and for maintaining and strengthening the economic relations of the European countries both among themselves and with other countries in the world." To this end, the Commission records economic, technological and statistical information.

The main subsidiary bodies and committees are: Committee on Agricultural Problems, Coal Committee, Conference of European Statisticians, Committee on Electric Power, Committee on Gas, Committee on Housing, Building and Planning, Inland Transport Committee, Steel Committee, Timber Committee, Committee on the Development of Trade, and the Body of Water Resources and Water Control Problems.

The Secretariat is comprised of the Office of the Executive Secretary and the following divisions: General Economic Research, Energy, Industry, Transport, Environment and Housing, Statistical, and joint ECE/FAO Divisions on Agriculture and Timber as well as an Office of Technical Assistance.

§ 6-3.1.10. **The UN Economic Commission for Latin America.**[30] This Commission was established by the Economic and Social Council on February 25, 1948, to assist in the formulation and development of coordinated policies to promote economic development in the Latin American region. Its other functions are similar to those of the ECE and the ECAFE.

---

[29] *See Economic Commission for Europe,* 15 INT'L ORG. 284-86 (1961). EVERY-MAN'S UN 19-20, 32, 226, 227-45 (1959); 2 PEASLEE, *supra* note 6, at 1771; J. Siotis, *ECE in the Emerging European System,* INTERNATIONAL CONCILIATION 1-72 (1967).

[30] *Economic Commission for Latin America,* 15 INT'L ORG. 501-03 (1961); ECLA, A BASIC GUIDE TO THE COMMISSION AND ITS SECRETARIAT (New York 1966); EVERYMAN'S UN 20, 32, 226, 227, 260-71 (1959); 1 PEASLEE, *supra* note 6, at 132, 135, 138; 2 *id., supra* note 6, at 1573, 1588, 1771; UNECLA, A BASIC GUIDE TO THE COMMISSION AND ITS SECRETARIAT.

The 29 members of the Commission include all Latin American and Caribbean states, as well as Canada, France, the Netherlands, the United Kingdom and the United States. Its two associate associate members are British Honduras and the West Indies Associated States. The Federal Republic of Germany and Switzerland participate in a consultative capacity.

The headquarters are located in Santiago, Chile. The Commission normally meets every two years in one of the Latin American capitals. In alternate years, the Committee of the Whole usually meets in Santiago to review progress and prepare the annual report to the Economic and Social Council.

The Commission has established two permanent bodies to meet specific needs: the Central American Economic Cooperation Committee and the Trade Committee. These subsidiary bodies have in turn established working groups and special committees. They include subcommittees on: Trade, Transport, Electric Power, Statistical Coordination, Housing, Building, and Planning, and a Commission for Industrial Initiatives. The Trade Committee has set up a Working Group on the Regional Market and a Central Bank Working Group.

The Secretariat comprises an office of the Executive Secretary at Headquarters and branch offices in Bogota, Mexico City, Montevideo, Port-of-Spain, Rio de Janeiro, and Washington. The Secretariat has divisions for Economic Development and Research, Social Affairs, Trade Policy, Industrial Development, Agriculture (jointly with FAO), Statistics and Administration. There are also programs for Natural Resources and Energy, Transport, and the Latin American Economic Projections Center.

The Secretariat works very closely with the Latin American Institute for Economic and Social Planning, set up under the aegis of the Commission in 1962, with financial contributions from the United Nations Special Fund and the Inter-American Development Bank. A Joint ECLA/Institute/IBD Program for the Integration of Industrial Development was established in 1964.

§ 6-3.1.11. **The UN Food and Agriculture Organization.**[31] Established on October 16, 1945, the FAO consists of a Conference, a Council, and a Secretariat. The Conference, which meets every two years, is composed of one representative from every member state; it is the policy-making organ of FAO. The Council, which is elected

---

[31] OFFICE OF PUBLIC INFORMATION, UNITED NATIONS, BASIC FACTS ABOUT THE UNITED NATIONS 41-42.

by the Conference, consists of representatives of 27 member states; it governs between Conference sessions. The Secretariat, headed by a Director-General, performs the usual administrative functions of the Organization.

The purposes of FAO are:

> to raise levels of nutrition and standards of living; to secure improvements in the efficiency of the production and distribution of all food and agricultural products from farms, forests and fisheries; to better the conditions of country dwellers; and by these means, to contribute to an expanding world economy.

Among its many activities, the Organization combats animal disease epidemics, promotes utilization of the resources of the sea, and assists in soil erosion control and forestation. FAO has taken the leadership in the international Freedom from Hunger Campaign which aims to obtain worldwide awareness of the problems of hunger and malnutrition, and has assisted in the struggle against them. FAO's five high-priority areas of activity are: 1) the wider introduction of high-yielding crops, 2) efforts to fill the "protein gap," 3) a concerted war on waste, 4) the mobilization of human resources for rural development, and 5) attempt to increase earnings and holdings of foreign exchange in the developing world.

§ 6-3.2. **The African Development Bank.**[32] Established on September 19, 1964, the African Development Bank began operations on July 1, 1966, with 32 African countries as members. The Bank has a President and two Vice Presidents, a Board of Governors and a Board of Directors. The Board of governors, composed of one representative from each member state, is vested with all the powers of the Bank. It meets once a year or more often as required; and to date it has held four meetings; the last meeting was in August 1968, in Nairobi, Kenya. The Board of Directors, which is composed of nine members elected by the Board of Governors, conducts the general operations of the Bank and functions in continuous sessions at the principal office of the Bank in Abidjan, Ivory Coast.

The initial authorized capital stock of the Bank, consisting of 250 million units of account, is equivalent to U.S. $250 million, half to be subscriptive and half callable. As of December 31, 1969, $63 million had been paid in convertible currencies.

---

[32]Its publications include: the AGREEMENT ESTABLISHING THE AFRICAN DEVELOPMENT BANK, pamphlets on Loans and Investments, Technical Assistance, Cooperation with National Development Finance Institutions, the Use of Consultants, and Annual Reports of the Board of Governors. Address: BP No. 1387, Abidjan, Ivory Coast.

The Bank aims to contribute to the economic and social development of its members both individually and jointly. It seeks to encourage investment of public and private capital in Africa, to use its normal capital resources to make or guarantee loans and investments, and to provide technical assistance in the preparation, financing and implementation of development projects. The Bank is currently processing many loan requests from its members and is also undertaking pre-investment studies, some of which are in cooperation with the UN Development Program. It also has working relations with other UN Specialized Agencies. Other activities include the dissemination of information on business, and the work of a research institute studying economic problems of a regional nature.

§ 6-3.3   **Afro-Asian Organization for Economic Cooperation.**[33] Founded in Cairo in 1958, at an economic conference of Afro-Asian countries, its Constitution and By-Laws were adopted in 1960. The Organization is a voluntary, non-political, non-profit-making, and autonomous organization composed of 38 regular member states and eight associate member states with a Central Chamber of Commerce in 45 countries. The Organization has a President, a First and Second Vice Presidents, and a Secretary-General. Its organs are the Conference, the Council, and the Center. The Conference, which meets at least every two years, elects the Council, determines general policy, and formulates the work program. The Council, which meets at least once every year, is composed of the President, two Vice Presidents, and 12 members elected by the Conference; it has the powers and functions of the Conference, except when the Conference is in session. The Center is the executive organ; it consists of the Secretary-General and his staff and performs the general functions of a Secretariat.

§ 6-3.4.   **Arab Economic Unity Council and the Arab Common Market.**[34] The Permanent Economic Committee of the Arab League, established in 1945, was replaced in 1950, by the Economic Unity Council established by the Security Pact, to serve as the principal policy-making economic body.

The Council (inactive for several years) is composed of one representative from each member state. The Presidency is held for one

---

[33] Its publications include: the Constitution of the Organization, its By-laws and Rule of Procedure, and Reports of Council Sessions and of the Secretary-General. Address: Cairo Chamber of Commerce Bldg., Midan Ul–Falaki, P.O. Box 507, Cairo, Egypt.

[34] ASIL, 3 INTERNATIONAL LEGAL MATERIALS 1096-1101 (1964). Address: P.O. Box 507, Cairo, Egypt.

year in turn by a national of each member state. The Council is assisted by economic and administrative committees, as well as a Permanent Technical Advisory Office composed of experts and a Central Office of Statistics.

The principal aim of the Council is to secure freedom of travel, the free transfer of capital, the free exchange of goods and to promote other economic activities. The Council also coordinates economic, financial, and trade policies and drafts needed legislation.

At a session held in August 1964, a "resolution of the Arab Economic Unity Council to Establish the Arab Common Market" was adopted. Its goals are: to promote the free transit of persons and capital, to facilitate the exchange of both national and foreign commodities, and to reduce residence and employment restrictions on nationals of member states. In addition, there is a Kuwaiti Fund for financing economic development plans in Arab States with some $200 million for such purposes.

§ 6-3.5. The Asian Development Bank.[35]   On the initiative of the U.N. Economic Commission for Asia and the Far East (ECAFE), an Agreement or Charter signed in 1965, created the Asian Development Bank: the Agreement went into effect on August 22, 1966 with an initial subscription of $650 million. The principal office of the Bank is located in Manila, Philippines, and branch offices or agencies may be established elsewhere. As of December 31, 1969, the authorized capital of the Bank, composed of subscriptions from the 33 members of the Bank, totalled $978 million, the ordinary capital resources of the bank including borrowings, ordinary reserve and net income totalled $401.4 million of which $339.4 million was in convertible currencies, and the Bank had made a total of 27 loans amounting to $139.7 million.

The Bank has a Board of Governors, a Board of Directors, and officers. The Board of Governors, which consists of one Governor and one Alternate from each member state, is the policy-making body; it meets at least once annually. The Board of Directors is composed of 10 members, seven representing regional countries, and the other three representing non-regional countries, who hold office for two years. The Board of Directors exercises all powers delegated

---

[35] Its publications include: the Agreement Establishing the Bank; a pamphlet on Operational Information: THE DOORS ARE OPEN (Selected addresses by the President of the Bank, Takeshi Watanabe); Annual Reports, pamphlets on Operation Information, Uses of Consultants, and Guidelines for Procurement under Asian Development Bank Loans, and press releases on various loans, technical assistance and other matters. Address: P.O. Box 126, Makati, Rizal, Philippines.

to it by the Board of Governors. The Bank has a President, a Vice President, and a staff. The President, elected for a five-year term, is responsible for the Bank's organization and operation. The Vice-President performs the normal functions of a deputy or alternate. The staff consists of a Treasurer, A General Counsel, a Chief Information Officer, and an Internal Audit or who assist in the operation and service functions of the bank.

According to Article 2 of the Articles of Agreement, the Bank's functions are:

1. to promote investment in the ECAFE region of public and private capital for development purposes;

2. to utilize the available resources for financing development, giving priority to those regional and sub-regional as well as national projects and programs which will contribute most effectively to the harmonious economic growth of the region as a whole and having special regard to the needs of the smaller or less developed member countries in the region;

3. to meet requests from members in the region to assist them in the coordination of their development policies and plans with a view to achieving better utilization of their resources, making their economies more complementary, and promoting the orderly expansion of their foreign trade, in particular, intra-regional trade;

4. to provide technical assistance for the preparation, financing and execution of development projects and programs, including the formulation of specific project proposals;

5. to cooperate with the United Nations, its organs and subsidiary bodies including, in particular, ECAFE and with public international organizations and other international institutions, as well as national entities whether public or private, which are concerned with the investment of development funds in the region, and to interest such institutions and entities in new opportunities for investment and assistance; and

6. to undertake such other activities and provide such other services as may advance its purpose.

Article 61 of the Agreement establishing the Bank contains the following provision for arbitration:

If a disagreement should arise between the Bank and a country which has ceased to be a member, or between the Bank and any member, after adoption of a resolution to terminate the operations of the Bank such disagreement shall be submitted to arbitration by a tribunal of three arbitrators. One of the arbitrators shall be appointed by the Bank, another by the country concerned, and the third, unless the parties otherwise agree, by the President of the International Court of Justice or such otner authority as may have been prescribed by regulations adop·ed by the Board of Governors.

In addition to its many activities, the Bank has completed an agricultural survey of the Asian region to provide the basis for its future operations in this sector. It is also taking preliminary steps for undertaking a sub-regional survey of transportation.

§ 6-3.6. The Bank for International Settlements.[36] Located in Basel, Switzerland, the Bank was created by an inter-governmental convention signed at The Hague, January 20, 1930. The Swiss Confederation granted the bank a special Charter and Statutes which are annexed to the convention. It is composed of the central banks of 26 countries.

The Bank has a share capital of 500 million gold francs, of which 125 million gold francs have been paid. Approximatelv three-quarters of the shares are owned by central banks, and one quarter by others. Rights of representation and voting at General Meetings are exercised by the central banks or their nominees of the 25 European countries and the United States to which the shares were issued. The Board of Directors, which is responsible for the administration of the Bank, is composed of 13 members, eight of whom are Governors of European central banks.

The Bank has four main activities carried out mainly with central banks which must conform with the monetary policies of those banks. First, it acts as agent or trustee in connection with international settlements (e.g. as agent for the Organization for Economic Cooperation and Development, as trustee or fiscal agent for several international loans, and as depository of the European Coal and Steel Community). Second, it provides a forum where the Governors of central banks meet. Third, it is a center for monetary and economic research and information for the benefit of central banks. Fourth, it cooperates closely with the International Bank for Reconstruction and Development, the International Monetary Fund, and the European Investment Bank.

§ 6-3.7. The Benelux Economic Union.[37] Established in 1958, at The Hague, on the signature of a treaty between Belgium, the

---

[36] Data used in this section were supplied by the bank. Address: Zentrolbahnstrasse, Basel, Switzerland

[37] Benelux publishes: a Bulletin six times a year, a Quarterly Statistical Bulletin, its basic texts, and a pamphlet entitled, *What Is the Significance of Benelux? See also* W. DO-ZIER, BENELUX—A STUDY IN ECONOMIC UNION (Washington 1959). Address: 17-23 av de la Joyeuse Entrée, Brussels, Belgium.

Netherlands and Luxembourg, the Benelux Union entered into force in 1960. However, preparation for the economic integration of these countries began in 1944 with a Customs Convention signed in London.

The aims of the Union are: to develop closer economic links between the three countries by ensuring free circulation of persons, goods, capital and service; to follow a coordinated policy in the fields of economics, finance and social endeavors; and to follow a common policy regarding foreign trade. These aims are carried out by the Committee of Ministers, the Consultative Inter-Parliamentary Council, the Council of the Economic Union, the General Secretariat, the Economic and Social Advisory Council and various committees. The Committee of Ministers supervises the application of the Benelux Economic Union Treaty and ensures the pursuit of its aims. Toward these ends it makes decisions, establishes conventions, makes recommendations, and issues directives. The Consultative Inter-Parliamentary Council communicates its views on matters of concern to the Union including the cultural relations between the three countries, their cooperation in foreign policy and the standardization of their laws. The Council, composed of senior officials from the three countries, implements the decisions and recommendations of the Committee of Ministers, makes proposals for the functioning of the Union and coordinates committee activities. The General Secretariat performs administrative functions for all of the organs and committees of the Union. The Economic and Social Advisory Council formulates and submits to the Committee of Ministers opinions on problems influencing the functioning of the Union. The various committees of the Union makes recommendations to the Committee of Ministers and implement its decisions.

Activities of the Union include harmonizing internal fiscal systems, establishing a central accounts index with an interstate team of auditors and accounting system; harmonizing development plans, social welfare legislation, and telecommunications; and setting up a regional development bank and a joint college of advanced commercial studies.

§ 6-3.8. **The Central African Customs and Economic Union.**[38] Established by a treaty signed in 1964, which entered into force on January 1, 1966, the original members, of this Union were Cameroon, the Central African Republic, Chad, Congo (Brazzaville),

---

[38] BUREAU OF ECONOMIC AFFAIRS, U.S. DEPARTMENT OF STATE, MULTINATIONAL ECONOMIC ORGANIZATIONS IN AFRICA, A SUMMARY DESCRIPTION (Washington 1968). Address: BP 946, Bangui, Central African Republic.

and Gabon. However, Chad and the Central African Republic have subsequently renounced membership. Headquarters were originally located at Bangui, Central African Republic, but are now located in Brazzaville, Congo. The organization of the Union consists of a Supreme Heads of State Council, a Ministerial Economic Council, and a Secretariat. The presidency rotates among the members.

The broad original purpose of the founders of the Union was to integrate the economies of the region. Some specific Union functions are: to remove trade barriers within the region, to coordinate fiscal policies and regional industrial distribution and development, to establish common external tariffs, and to pool resources for costly development projects.

§ 6-3.9. The Central American Bank for Economic Integration.[39] Established in 1961, by the Treaty of Central American Economic Integration, the Bank is primarily designed to promote the integration of Central American economies, and to coordinate their economic policies. Its initial assets were provided by capital subscriptions from each of the five member states of $4 million. Grants and loans from other governments and international lending institutions had raised the assets of the Bank to more than $100 million, with total available resources amounting to $207.7 million (including loans).

The Treaty provides for the granting of loans to member states only when they have ratified specified multilateral treaties. In considering grants of loans the Bank supports only projects with a regional impact which are "economically sound and technically feasible." Stress is laid on "balanced economic development" to avoid disproportionate economic gains by one or more member states.

§ 6-3.10. The Central American Common Market.[40] The Central American Common Market was the result of several important treaties. The Multilateral Treaty on Central American Free Trade and Economic Development signed on June 10, 1958, established a limited list of free trade goods to be expanded over a 10-year period. The General Treaty on Central American Economic Integration, often referred to as the Treaty of Managua, was accepted by all five Central American states (Costa Rica, Guatemala, Honduras,

---

[39] Data used in this section were supplied by the Organization of American States. Address: Apartado Postal 772, Tegucigalpa, DC, Honduras.

[40] R. HANSEN, CENTRAL AMERICA: REGIONAL INTEGRATION AND ECONOMIC DEVELOPMENT 34-45 (Washington 1967); Simmonds, *The Central American Common Market,* INT'L & COMP. L.Q. 911-45 (1967).

Nicaragua, and El Salvador) by the end of 1963. It granted rights of free trade to all Central American products, except for reservations made in the Treaty. As a result, there are now only a few items on which tariff restrictions are likely to remain for some time. The principal aim of this Treaty was to create a common market within a five-year period.

The Managua Treaty created an Economic Council, an Executive Council, and a Permanent Secretariat to implement its objectives. The Economic Council, which meets in principle four times a year, is composed of Ministers of Economy of the Central American states. It is the supreme organ which handles important matters relating to economic integration. The Executive Council, which is composed of the Vice Ministers of Economy, does preliminary work on matters to be considered by the Council. The Permanent Secretariat, headed by a Secretary General, serves both of the above Councils; it also prepares background material and published reports.

The Central American Convention on the Equalization of Import Tariffs, signed in 1959, provided for access for some Central American products to a protected market.

The following have been considered major achievements of Central American integration: "the improved allocation and use of existing Central American resources through the process of trade creation, . . . the beginning of a structural change in the Central American economies" and ". . . the attraction of increasing international assistance in the field of vital infrastructure expenditures."

The Central American Common Market plans the eventual elimination of all tariffs and barriers between members and the establishment of a common external tariff for the rest of the world. So far, practically all internal barriers have been removed and agreement has been reached on 98 percent of the items in the regional customs classification; uniform tariffs now apply to 87 percent of these items and the others are to be equalized over a five-year period. Intra-regional trade has been increased from $34 million in 1960 to more than $200 million. It is expected that a common customs administration will be created in 1971, and further goals include a unified fiscal policy, a regional industrial policy and coordinated regional policies in public health, education, labor, transportation, and agriculture.

§ 6-3.11. The Council for Mutual Economic Aid.[41]

Composed of Bulgaria, Czchoslavakia, the German Democratic Republic, Hun-

---

[41] Data used in this section were supplied by the Council. Address: Petrovka 14, Moscow, U.S.S.R.

gary, Mongolia, Poland, Rumania, and the USSR, COMECON was established in 1949. Its present Statute was adopted on December 14, 1959, and entered into force on April 13, 1960. At the end of 1951, Albania, an original member, withdrew from the Council, and in 1964, Yugoslavia became an associate member. Other socialist countries have participated in the work of Council organs.

An Executive Committee, composed of a representative from each member state serves as the principal organ of the Council. Its function is to carry out the Council's goals of coordinating development efforts, raising industrialization standards, increasing productivity, and developing close economic ties between member states.

In May 1970, seven members of the Council voted to create a new bank, to be entitled the International Investment Bank, which will be operational on January 1, 1971, and which will be composed of Bulgaria, Czechslovakia, East Germany, Hungary, Mongolia, Poland and Russia. Total capital has been fixed at one billion transferable rubles, and each nation's contribution to the fund has been fixed on the basis of the ratio of its exports to total intra-CMEA trade. Each nation will have one vote, and decisions will be by majority vote.

§ 6-3.12.　**The Council for Technical Cooperation in South and Southeast Asia (the Colombo Plan).**[42]　This Council originated in the meeting of Commonwealth foreign ministers held in Colombo, Ceylon, in January 1950, to permit an exchange of views on world problems and to consider the vital needs of the countries in this area. A Consultative Committee for Cooperative Economic Development of South and Southeast Asia was established. Its work and reports led to the formal establishment of the Council. The primary purpose of the Council, according to its constitution, is to assist the economic development of South and Southeast Asia by providing technical assistance through bilateral agreements or by joint schemes where more than two states are involved.

The 24 members of the Council are: Afghanistan, Bhutan, Burma, Cambodia, Ceylon, India, Indonesia, Iran, Republic of Korea, Laos, Malaysia, Maldive Islands, Nepal, Pakistan, the Philippines, Singapore, Thailand, and the Republic of Vietnam from within South and Southeast Asia; and Australia, Canada, Japan, New Zealand, the United Kingdom, and the United States from outside the area.

---

[42] Data used in this section were supplied by the Bureau of the Colombo Plan. Address: P.O. Box 596, Colombo, Ceylon.

The Colombo Plan has the following organs: a Consultative Committee, composed of ministers and senior officials of member governments who meet annually at a national capital; a Council, which meets regularly in Colombo composed of one representative from each member government and a Bureau which provides administrative services for the Council. The Council, whose headquarters are located at Colombo, maintains working relations with the UN Development Program.

Since 1950, external assistance from the main group of donors (Australia, New Zealand, Canada, Japan, United Kingdom, and the United States) has amounted to over $25 million. Capital aid takes the form of grants and loans for national projects; commodities include food grains, fertilizers, consumer goods, machinery and equipment. During the 1967-68 period, $2.8 million was received.

This aid is used in accordance with the objectives of the Colombo Plan, especially to train Asian students in technical fields. From 1950 to December 1967, approximately 52,329 students had received technical training and 10,790 experts, and equipment valued at $342.8 million had been provided.

§ 6-3.13.   **The Economic Community of Eastern Africa.**[43] Founded in May 1966, by Terms of Association, its members are Burundi, Ethiopia, Kenya, Madagascar, Malawi, Mauritius, Rwanda, Somali Republic, Tanzania, and Zambia. Since the Economic Community may be merged into the East African Community, its organs were designated as an Interim Council of Ministers and an Interim Economic Committee. The organization is being serviced by the UN Economic Commission for Africa in Addis Ababa, Ethiopia, since permanent headquarters have not been agreed upon. The interim and proposed functions of the organization include: joint planning of industrial development, coordination of transport and agricultural projects, research cooperation, and the development of a common market.

§ 6-3.14.   **The European Communities.**[44] Since the end of World War II, six Western European countries—France, Germany, Italy, Luxembourg, Belgium and the Netherlands—have taken progres-

---

[43] Bureau of Economic Affairs, *supra* note 38, at 18. Address: P.O. Box 3081, Arusha, Republic of Tanzania.

[44] The Institutions and Joint Services of the three European Communities issue a comprehensive Catalogue of their publications. For bibliographical references on the ECSC, the EEC and Euratom, see WASHINGTON CONF. 180, 182-83, 184. Address: Quai d'Orsay, Paris, France.

sive steps toward economic integration and eventual political union. To achieve those objectives, three "Communities" have been formed, each operating under a separate Treaty but possessing certain common institutions designed to assure proper coordination of policy. The three Communities are: The European Coal and Steel Community, the European Economic Community (Common Market), and the European Atomic Energy Community (Euratom).

Two institutions are common to all three Communities: the Court of Justice of the European Communities (see § 3-6.2), and the European Assembly. While the powers of the Assembly are defined in the Treaties establishing the three Communities, the authority of the Court of Justice, however, is described in a separate protocol.

The Assembly is composed of 142 members chosen from the national assemblies of the six member states with the number from each determined according to a system of proportional representation. The Parliament meets several times each year at its headquarters in Strasbourg, France, and discusses matters such as: the budgets for the Communities, contents of reports submitted by various organs of the Communities, political problems over which disputes between members may have arisen, and numerous other matters relating to the purposes of the organizations.

§ 6-3.14.1.   **The European Coal and Steel Community.**[45]   A major step towards European economic integration was taken when the last instrument of ratification of the treaty establishing the European Coal and Steel Community was deposited in July 1952. The treaty has as its primary objectives: the pooling of coal and steel production of the six signatory nations and the elimination of all customs duties on coal and steel and all other restrictions such as quotas, exports and import licenses, discriminatory freight rates and price differentials among members. In addition, the Community seeks to regulate cartels and to impose standards of fair competition on the industries involved. All major coal and steel mergers are subject to Community approval, and cartels are authorized only if they contribute to productivity and do not hinder competition.

The Community also acts as a new social agency for Europe's coal and steel industry. Housing and health measures, as well as a system of subsidizing and retraining technologically or economically

---

[45] Treaty Establishing the European Coal and Steel Community, April 18, 1951, 1 European Y.B. 359 (1955) or H.M.S.O. 1962.

displaced workers are being instituted. Workers in the Community are free to seek work wherever possible without regard to national boundaries. In addition, the Community can regulate pricing policies, labor practices, transport rates, unfair business practices, and numerous other related matters in respect to coal and steel.

The Institutions of the Community are: the High Authority, the Assembly (or Parliament), and the Council of Ministers. The High Authority is composed of nine members elected for six-year terms (two each from France, Germany and Italy, and one from each of the Benelux nations). It constitutes the executive organ responsible for "assuring the achievement of the purposes stated in this treaty." It applies the rules and regulations created by the Treaty through "administrative rulings" which are subject to appeal to the Court of Justice of the European Communities. These rulings have the effect of law and must be obeyed by both member states and private corporations within those member states. Each "member is obliged to enforce such rulings in its municipal courts."

Article 9 of the Treaty states that "the members of the High Authority shall exercise their functions in complete independence, in the general interest of the community." In the fulfillment of their duties, members of the High Authority neither solicit nor accept instructions from any government or other organization. They must abstain from all conduct incompatible with the supranational character of their functions.

Article 18 establishes a Consultative Committee, attached to the High Authority, consisting of not fewer than 30 nor more than 51 members. It includes an equal number of coal and steel of producers, workers, consumers and dealers. The members of the Committee are appointed in their individual capacity for a period of two years and are generally available for the purpose of giving advice to the High Authority when requested.

The second institution of the Coal and Steel Community is the Assembly. Article 20 of the Treaty states that "the Assembly, consisting of representatives of the peoples of the member States of the Community, shall exercise the supervisory powers which are granted to it by this Treaty." Those powers are enumerated throughout the treaty in various sections. The Assembly meets once each year for a session which may not last beyond the end of the fiscal year.

Article 24 of the Treaty states that the Assembly shall discuss in open session the general reports submitted to it by the High Authority. If a motion of censure based on the report is introduced in the Assembly, votes may be taken thereon after a period of not less than three days following its introduction. If the motion of censure is adopted by "two-thirds of the votes cast representing a majority of the total membership," the members of the High Authority must resign in a body. The qualifying clause, "representing a majority of the total membership," requires that the two-thirds vote must include the votes of four member states of the Community.

The third institution of the Coal and Steel Community is the Council of Ministers, which consists of representatives appointed by the member states. Meetings of the Council are called by its President, at the request of a member state or of the High Authority, to consider broad questions of policy such as matters concerning the alteration of any provisions of the Treaty or modification of decisions of the High Authority. Major decisions, such as amendments, require unanimous consent of all members of the Council; others require only a majority vote.

§ 6-3.14.2 **The European Economic Community (Common Market).**[46] Following ratification of a Treaty concluded in Rome on March 25, 1957, the Common Market came into being on January 1, 1958. This organization is designed to integrate the economies of the six signatories, and to that end, provides for introducing a customs union over a 12 to 15-year transition period. During that time, tariffs and quotas are to be reduced gradually on all goods traded between members, and a common tariff towards nations outside the "six" is to be adopted. It is the latter feature of the Treaty which distinguishes it from a Free Trade Area. In addition, the Treaty governs matters such as: the development of common policies on agriculture, transport, and commerce; the establishment of a social fund for retraining workers; the creation of an investment bank; and other measures to facilitate the free movement of workers, capital and services within the Community.

---

[46] For further information see COMM. MKT. L. REV. (London 1962-); Farrell, *The Common Market: An Example of Peaceful Cooperation,* 34 YEARBOOK OF THE ASSO-CIATION OF ATTENDERS AND ALUMNI OF THE HAGUE ACADEMY OF INTERNA-TIONAL LAW 71-6; Hay, *The Contribution of the European Communities to International Law,* ASIL PROC. 195-201 (1965); INSTITUT D'ETUDES EUROPÉENNES, UNIVER-SITÉ LIBRE DE BRUXELLES, INSTITUTIONS COMMUNAUTAIRES ET INSTITUTIONS NATIONALES DANS LE DÉVELOPPEMENT DES COMMUNAUTÉE (Brussels 1968); Rivikin, *Africa and the European Economic Community,* 3 FINANCE AND DEVELOP-MENT 12-128 (1966); S. SCHEINGOLD, THE RULE OF LAW IN EUROPEAN INTEGRA-TION (New Haven 1965); W. VAN GERVEN, PRINCIPES DU DROIT DES ENTENTES DE LA COMMUNAUTÉ ECONOMIQUE EUROPÉENNE (Brussels 1966).

The administration of the Treaty is the responsibility of a nine member "Commission" which roughly corresponds to the High Authority of the Economic Coal and Steel Community, although it is not an independent executive. In addition, there is an Assembly of 142 members, an Economic and Social Committee of 101 members, and a Council of Ministers. Provisions are made for consultative bodies on specific problem areas such as transportation and monetary affair.

The Council is composed of one representative of the government of each member state. Various provisions in the Treaty outline the powers of the Council, which generally acts by a majority vote of its members. Unanimous consent, however, is required for a change in the Treaty or for other basic decisions. However, where conclusions of the Council require a qualified (i.e., two-thirds) majority, the votes of its members are weighted, with Germany, Italy and France receiving four votes, Belgium and The Netherlands receiving two, and Luxembourg receiving one.

The executive institution of the Common Market is the Commission composed of nine members, with not more than two members having the nationality of the same state, and each nation entitled to at least one member. The powers of the Commission are defined in Article 155 which states that the Commission shall:

Insure the application of the provisions of this Treaty and of the provisions enacted by the institutions of the Community in pursuance thereof;

formulate recommendations or opinions in matters which are the subject of this Treaty, where the latter expressly so provides or where the Commission considers it necessary;

under the conditions laid down in this Treaty dispose of a power of decision of its own and participate in the preparation of acts of the Council and of the Assembly; and

exercise the competence conferred on it by the Council for the implementation of the rules laid down by the latter.

The EEC has been largely responsible for the remarkable economic progress of its members. In light of the progress achieved, the member states have decided to speed up the implementation of the treaty by making additional tariff cuts by abolishing industrial quotas and by moving faster towards common policies.

§ 6-3.14.3. **The European Atomic Energy Community.** This Community came into being at the same time as the Common Market (1958). Its responsibility is to promote a common effort among the six members in the development of nuclear energy for peaceful purposes. Euratom introduced a common market for nuclear products and has undertaken an extensive study of nuclear research in the Community. It has also established four major research centers to coordinate and encourage national research. These centers are located at Ispra, Italy; Mol, Belgium; Karlsruhe, Germany; and Petten, The Netherlands.

The institutions of the Atomic Energy Community which are not common to the communities generally are: The Council, composed of one delegate from each member state, and the Commission, the executive authority of the treaty, composed of five members from different nations chosen for their general competence and impartiality. Attached to the Commission with consultative status is a Scientific and Technical Committee composed of 20 members appointed by the Council with the advice of the Commission.

To ensure the smooth running and increased activity in nuclear industry, a Common Market in nuclear materials was introduced in 1959 which eliminates internal export and import duties on nuclear products. A common tariff is applied to third countries. The Commission has set up a security control system designed to guarantee that fissile materials will not be improperly used. The basic health standards drawn up by Euratom in 1959 were the first international nuclear safety laws to be binding on governments.

§ 6-3.14.4. **Merger of the European Communities.** Prior to July 1967, each of the European Communities had its own executive organ and its own Council of Ministers. On July 1, 1967, the three Communities merged their separate administrative and policy-making organs into a single Executive and a single Council to serve all of them as a prelude to establishing a single European authority. In addition, two new organs were created: A Commission and a Council, which together with the European Assembly and the Court of Justice serve all of the communities.

The Commission assumes all the former powers of the High Authority of the ECSC and of the Commissions of the EEC and Euratom. It is presently composed of 14 members, three each from Germany, France, and Italy; two from the Netherlands and Belgium; and one from Luxembourg. The number of Commission members was reduced to nine on July 1, 1970, but there has been discussion of a possible amendment of the original treaty to maintain the number of members at 14, in order to provide sufficient manpower to deal with the possible entry of Denmark, Norway and the United Kingdom into the organization. The Commission is composed of a President, four Vice-Presidents and nine members, who act in their individual capacities and are forbidden to accept instructions from national governments. It initiates and executes the policies of the Communities, takes steps to ensure the establishment of an economic union and supervises the Common Market and the Nuclear Common Market. The Commission reports annually to the Community Parliament.

The Council is composed of a minister from each member state. It replaces the several councils of the EEC, Euratom and the ESCS, and is the final policy-making organ of the Communities. However, its decisions are based upon proposals from the Commission, and every effort is made to decide matters of special importance unanimously.

In addition to the above Community organs, several other bodies aid Community work. These include an Economic and Social Committee, a Consultative Committee, a Monetary Committee, Short-Term and Medium-Term Economic Policy Committees, a Committee of Central Bank Governors, a Budgetary Policy Committee, a Transport Committee, and a Scientific and Technical Committee.

§ 6-3.14.5. The European Investment Bank.[47] The Bank was created on March 25, 1957, by the Treaty which established the European Economic Communities (EEC). Its members are the six EEC countries: Belgium, France, Germany, Italy, Luxembourg, and the Netherlands. The Bank has a capital stock of one billion dollars.

The principle aim of the Bank is to contribute to the balanced development of the Common Market. It also operates in countries associated with the Common Market by providing non-profit loans and guaranties. Its activities include assistance to the less developed regions of the member states, the modernizations of enterprises and various other projects of interest to several member states.

§ 6-3.14.6. EEC Company Law. As part of the EEC's continuing role in promoting an integrated, harmonious economic community of European Nations, the Commission, on June 24, 1970, approved and sent to the Council, a draft statute containing a new European law on Corporations. The principal aim of the draft law is to complement national laws dealing with corporations created by different EEC members, such as mergers, holding companies, and joint subsidiaries. Under the new law, a European

---

[47] This Bank publishes an annual report. Address: 2 Place de Metz, Luxembourg.

company, a merger or formation of a holding company requiring $500,000 capital, or a joint subsidiary with $250,000, would be under the jurisdiction of the Court of Justice of the Communities, and maintained on a Community register of companies. The headquarters of the Company can be in any, or several, of the Member States, but for purposes of taxation, headquarters will be defined as the place of actual management. A European company is required to have a board of management, a supervisory board, and a general stockholders' meeting. The draft European Company Law also calls for the creation of Workers' Councils, with workers' representatives on the supervisory board, whose approval is required on all decisions dealing with hiring, firing, seniority, vocational training, industrial health and safety, creation and management of social facilities, wages working hours, and vacations.

§ 6-3.14.7. EEC Common Monetary Plan. In October 1970, the Common Market released its plan for "full economic and monetary union, possibly including a common currency by the end of the Seventies."[48] The plan, known as the Werner Report, stressed the advantages of a common monetary plan, which would require amending the Treaty of Rome which formed the EEC. One such advantage would be better economic planning among the members to fight inflation and balance of payments difficulties to achieve stable currencies. It was felt that uncoordinated measures undertaken on purely national levels would be unable to stabilize the effects of currency crises in one member's economy which, in turn, could lead to setbacks for common policies in trade, agriculture and capital movements. In 1969, the Common Market countries had accepted the coordination of medium-term and short-term economic policies, and means of supporting a Member that had balance of payments difficulties for two years.

To achieve such a monetary union, the Werner Report recommended that main decisions concerning economic policy be made at the Community level, requiring the transference of certain national powers to the Community. The Report realized the political significance of this transfer and called it a further step toward full political integration of the Community.

Common monetary union calls for "the full and permanent convertibility of currencies, the elimination of margins of fluctuation in their exchange, the permanent fixing of their relations to parity,

---

[48] European Community Information Service, Press Release, *Common Market Economic and Monetary Union Plan Released* (Washington, October 22, 1970).

and the complete freeing of all capital movements."[49] National currency tokens would be maintained but a common monetary unit was preferred.

The Werner Report also called for the creation of two new Community institutions: a Center of Decision for Economic Policy, and a Community system of central banks. Both institutions will be empowered to make binding decisions, and the Center of Decision would be politically responsible to a European parliament.

The Report further stressed the necessity for coordination of Members' budgetary policies. Before Members adopt final budgets, the Community will review them to ascertain whether they are compatible with Community objectives. Also, common tax policies will be instituted.

Underlining the seriousness of the new common monetary union, the Common Market announced in November 1970, the creation of an international loan in the new European currency, designated by the symbol ₤. Loans in this new currency will be to Community industries, and will bind the members' currencies at the official parity on the day of issue for the duration of the loan.

§ 6-3.14.8. **Association of EEC and the African and Malagasy States.** The Governments of the six members of the EEC, the Council of EEC, and the 18 associate Malagasy and African States (Burundi, Cameroon, Central African Republic, Chad, Congo-Brazzaville, Congo-Kinshasa, Dahomey, Gabon, Ivory Coast, Malagasy Republic, Mali, Mauritania, Niger, Rwanda, Denegal, Somalia, Togo and Upper Volta) signed the Convention of Association on July 1963. A new Convention was signed on July 29, 1969, but as of May 6, 1970, only France of the EEC had ratified the new Convention, while 14 of the African associates had done so.

The Association aims to promote the expansion of trade between the EEC and the associated states, to strengthen the economic equilibrium and independence of the associate states by facilitating the diversification of the economy as well as the industrialization of the associated states. In order to accomplish these aims, the Association prepares feasibility studies for projects to be financed with new aid money, helps the Africans participate in trade fairs, and pays for African training programs.

The Association is composed of a Council, an Associate Committee, a Parliamentary Conference and an Arbitration Court. The Association Council meets annually and consists of one minister

---

[49] *Id.*

from each of the associated states and each of the community members, and the members of the EEC Commission. The Associate Committee conducts the day-by-day business and consists of 24 representatives, one from each signatory country. The Parliamentary Conference meets annually and is composed of 54 members from the associated states, and 54 from the European parliament. An Arbitration Court with a president, two European and two African judges may be appointed to settle any disputes which may arise.

§ 6-3.14.9. Association of the EEC and the Partner States of the East African Community. The Association was established on July 26, 1968, on signature of an agreement by representatives of the EEC and three partner states of the East African Community. The agreement lapsed on May 31, 1969, when the Arusha Convention expired. On September 24, 1961, a new association agreement was signed between the EEC and the East African Community. France was the first state to ratify the agreement on April 14, 1970. The members of the Association are the governments of the six members of the EEC, the EEC Council, and the governments of the three countries of the East African Community (Kenya, Tanzania and Uganda). The aims of the association are to promote the expansion of trade between the EEC and the East African states, strengthen the economic equilibrium and independence of the associate states by facilitating the diversification of the economy as well as the industrialization of the associated states. The Association Council has the power to give effect to the provisions of the agreement and supervise their implementation.

§ 6-3.15. The European Free Trade Association.[50] The European Free Trade Convention, commonly called the Stockholm

---

[50] The association's publications include: THE EFTA BULLETIN, the EFTA ANNUAL REPORTS, EFTA TODAY AND TOMORROW, THE OPERATION OF A FREE TRADE AREA, THE STOCKHOLM CONVENTION, THE FINLAND-EFTA AGREEMENT, BILATERAL AGRICULTURAL AGREEMENTS, and several agricultural reports.

See generally R. BARNARD, THE COMMON MARKET—THE TRANSITION PERIOD 185-212 (1960); R. BEEVER, EUROPEAN UNITY AND THE TRADE UNION MOVEMENTS (Leyden 1960); M. CAMPS, THE EUROPEAN COMMON MARKET AND FREE TRADE AREA (Princeton 1957); M. CAMPS, THE EUROPEAN FREE TRADE ASSOCIATION—A PRELIMINARY APPRAISAL (London 1959); *European Free Trade Association,* 15 INT'L ORG. 728 (1961) (for other references, see index to other INT'L ORG. volumes); *The Six and the Seven,* FINANCIAL TIMES (London, Nov. 7, 1960); Martin, *Restrictive Trade Practices in the European Free Trade Association,* 1 INT'L & COMP. L.Q. SUPP. 89-99 (1961); F. MEYER, THE EUROPEAN FREE-TRADE ASSOCIATION (New York 1960); 1 PEASLEE, *supra* note 6, at 24, 620-42; 2 *id. supra* note 6, at 1620; UNITED KINGDOM, NEGOTIATIONS FOR A EUROPEAN FREE TRADE AREA (London 1959). Address: 32 Chemin des Colombettes, 1211 Geneva 20.

Convention, which was signed on November 20, 1959 and came into force on May 3, 1960, established the European Free Trade Association. EFTA has seven full members: Austria, Denmark, Norway, Portugal, Sweden, Switzerland, and the United Kingdom. By an Agreement of Association, concluded in Helsinki on March 27, 1961, which came into force in June 1961, Finland became an associate member.

The principal organ of the Association is the Council, which meets at the ministerial level three or four times a year and at the official level generally once a week. Every member state is represented on the Council. A Joint Council composed of representatives of all EFTA countries and Finland usually meets at the same times as the Council. The Council is assisted by: a Customs Committee, a Committee of Trade Experts, an Agricultural Review Committee, a Budget Committee, an Economic Development Committee, a Consultative Committee, and an Economic Committee. *Ad hoc* committees or working parties are created to study special problems. The Council is also served by a Secretariat with headquarters in Geneva, and the Association has an Information Office in Washington.

The objectives of the Association are stated in Article 2 of the Stockholm Convention:

> to promote in the area of the Association and in each member state a sustained expansion of economic activity, full employment, increased productivity and the rational use of resources, financial stability and continuous improvement in living standards;
>
> to secure that trade between member states takes place in conditions of fair competition;
>
> to avoid significant disparity between member states in the conditions of supply of raw materials produced within the area of the Association; and
>
> to contribute to the harmonious development and expansion of world trade and to the progressive removal of barriers to it.

The Convention contains provisions dealing with: tariff reductions, drawback, deflections of trade, elimination of the protective element in revenue duties and internal taxes, and the elimination of export duties and quantitative export restrictions.

§ 6-3.16. The Inter-American Development Bank.[51] Established by an Agreement of the members of the Organization of American

---

[51] Address: 808 Seventeenth Street, N.W., Washington, D.C. 20577. For further information, see AGREEMENT ESTABLISHING THE INTER-AMERICAN DEVELOPMENT BANK (Washington 1962); F. HERRERA, AMÉROCA LATINA: INTEGRACIÓN ECO-

(Continued)

States, the Bank came into force on December 30, 1959, with 23 members, and operations commenced in October 1968.

The Bank has a Board of Governors, a Board of Executive Directors, a President, an Executive Vice-President, and a sizeable staff composed exclusively of citizens of member states. The Board of Governors, which meets annually, consists of a Governor and his alternate from each member state. The Board of Executive Directors is in continual session in Washington. The President who presides at these meetings is elected by the Board of Governors.

The Bank contributes to the economic development of member states, by granting loans and providing technical assistance. It has given active support to Latin American economic integration through: its export financing program, development projects, preinvestment studies, training and research, and institutional aid. In 1965, the Bank established the Institute for Latin American Integration in Buenos Aires which conducts courses on the problems of individual countries, holds seminars on the legal and economic aspects of Latin American integration, conducts valuable research, and issues publications including a monthly bulletin.

The Bank is the principal source of foreign economic aid to Latin American countries. During the first 10-year period of its existence, from 1959 to 1969, the Bank has granted a total of close to $3.5 billion in loans. In turn, these loans helped to finance economic and social development projects that totalled $9.6 billion, underscoring the Bank's role in marshalling domestic capital in the Latin American States. For the decade, the bank's lending by sectors is as follows: Agriculture (24.3%); Industry and Mining (16.8%); Transportation and Communications (15.2%); Electric Power (13.9%); Water Supply and Sewage Systems (13.3%); Urban Development and Housing (9.4%); Education (4.0%); Preinvestment (1.9%); and Export Financing (1.2%). For the year ending December 31, 1970, the Bank made additional loans amounting to $644.1 million and total Bank reserves are $6 billion.

NÓMICA Y REINTEGRACIÓN POLÍTICA (Washington 1962); THE INTER-AMERICAN BANK—INSTRUMENT FOR LATIN AMERICAN DEVELOPMENT (1962); Third Meeting of the Board of Governors, Round Tables on *Europe's Role in Latin American Development and Private Enterprise and the Development of Latin America* (Buenos Aires 1962); ANNUAIRE O.I. 124-25; Cutler, *The Inter-American Bank,* 16 BUS. L. 21-36 (1960); *Inter-American Development Bank,* 15 INT'L ORG. 173, 307 (1961); 1 PEASELEE, *supra* note 6, at 824-53; Smith, *The Inter-American Development Bank,* 19 FED. B.J. 374-82 (1959).

§ 6-3.17. The International Bank for Economic Cooperation.[52] Established on January 1, 1964, this Bank is composed of: Bulgaria, Czechoslovakia, East Germany, Hungary, Mongolia, Poland, Rumania, and the USSR. The Bank functions through a Council, a Board, and a Board of Auditors. The Council is composed of three representatives from each member country. The Board has a Chairman and 7 other members. The Auditing Board has a Chairman and 4 other members. The Bank aims to promote the economic cooperation and development of the national economies of member states, to expand their cooperation with other countries, and generally to widen their commercial and other economic relations.

§ 6-3.18. The Latin American Free Trade Association.[53]   On February 18, 1960 seven Latin American republics signed the Treaty of Montevideo, designed to establish a Free-Trade Area and a Free Trade Association.   The seven signatory nations— Argentina, Brazil, Chile, Mexico, Paraguay, Peru and Uruguay— comprise 70 percent of the Latin American population.   In preparing for the Treaty, and in its implementation, the contracting parties have had the assistance of the UN Economic Commission for Latin America and of the Inter-American Economic and Social Council.

According to the Preamble of the Agreement, the Association envisages the gradual and progressive establishment of a Latin America Free Trade Area.   Since Treaty members include several signatories to the General Agreement on Tariffs and Trade, the Treaty has been written to conform to the GATT provisions covering regional customs unions and free trade areas.   The Treaty sets out goals and the proposed means of achieving them but does not contain definite commitments or concessions.   Instead, it establishes an administrative framework for negotiations leading to reciprocal progressive tariff reductions and to the eventual establishment of a Free Trade Area to foster diversification and expansion of trade and to promote closer economic integration.   The Treaty aims to achieve these goals within a period of 12 years through two series

---

[52] The data used in this section were supplied by the bank. Address: 15 Kuznetski Most, Moscow K-31.

[53] Address: Cebollati 1461, Casilla de Correo, Montevideo, Uruguay. For further information see ANNUAIRE O.I. 122-23; Latin American Free Trade Association, in 15 INT'L ORG. 206, 531 (1961); ASPECTOS LEGALES DE LA ASOCIACIÓN LATINO-AMERICANA DE LIBRE COMERCIO (Montevideo 1966); R. LAWSON, INTERNATIONAL REGIONAL ORGANIZATIONS 345-60 (New York 1962); PAN AMERICAN UNION, THE ALLIANCE OF PROGRESS AND LATIN AMERICAN DEVELOPMENT PROSPECTS: A FIVE-YEAR REVIEW, 1961-1965 (The Johns Hopkins University Press, Baltimore 1967), 2 PEASLEE, *supra* note 6, at 1573-89.

of negotiations. One series concerns national schedules, the other a common schedule. The former will specify the annual reduction of duties and charges which each contracting party gives to the others. These reductions are to average 8 percent so that over a 12-year period barriers would be completely removed. The latter will list the products on which the signatories collectively agree to eliminate duties, charges and other restrictions so far as intra-area trade is concerned and will be negotiated at three-year intervals with 25 percent of the total value of trade among the parties eliminated during each period.

The Treaty provides that efforts should be made to fix common treatment of outside capital, goods and services and to reconcile their import and export regimes. Coordination of industrialization policies is also sought. The Treaty grants temporary advantages for signatory countries with less developed economies to permit them to introduce or expand productive activities particularly the industrialization of raw materials and to support technical assistance programs to raise productivity levels in specific industrial sectors.

The agreement contains important limitations with regard to agricultural products, which constitute the bulk of the present trade within the zone. There are also escape clauses in the agreement applicable to various situations, such as the danger of "serious repercussions on specific productive activities of vital importance for the national economy," or an unfavorable balance of payments. These clauses indicate that the success of the agreement may depend largely on the good faith of the signatories. It should be noted in this connection that certain of the escape clauses require authorization of all the contracting parties before resort may be had to them beyond an emergency period of one year.

The supreme organ of the Association is the Conference. Decisions are generally by affirmative vote of two-thirds of the parties, providing there are no negative votes. The permanent organ of the Association is the Standing Executive Committee. The agreement is open to accession by other Latin American states but does not permit signatories to made reservations. Bolivia, Colombia, Ecuador, and Venezuela have adhered to the Treaty.

Under the Treaty, each signatory retains its own tariffs on imports originating outside the Free-Trade Area. However, the contracting parties commit themselves to reconcile their import and export systems; and to direct their policies to create other conditions favorable to the establishment of a Latin American Free-Trade

Area; and to undertake studies and projects for this purpose coordinating this work with that of any other international organizations in the field.

One of the advantages of having such a free trade zone is that existing industrial plants may be given an opportunity to make fuller use of installations which presently are not being utilized to capacity. To the extent that imports from within the zone can replace those from without, foreign exchange reserves will be saved which can subsequently be used to import machinery and equipment necessary for continued industrialization from outside the region. The creation of the expanded regional market should permit diversification of foreign trade and a consequent growth of manufacturing, all of which will lead to the accelerated economic development of the member states.

§ 6-3.19. **The Organization for Economic Cooperation and Development.**[54]   The OECD has evolved from the Organization for European Economic Cooperation[55] which was composed of 18 European States, with Canada and the United States participating as Associate Members. The OEEC was established to facilitate the reconstruction of the economies of Western Europe after the World War II.

As that goal was being achieved, the OEEC continued its activities, thus fulfilling the need for permanent economic cooperation between its members and North America. The governing body of the OEEC was the Council, which alone was responsible for action by the Organization in the form of binding decisions. Unless otherwise agreed, its decisions were taken by mutual agreement of the full members of the Organization.

The OEEC was instrumental in promoting the high degree of economic cooperation among the nations of Western Europe which has contributed greatly to their rapid recovery. The progressive liberalization of intra-European trade and payments and the return

---

[54] For a complete list of OECD publications, see OECD: CATALOGUE OF PUBLICATIONS (1968).

See also the OECD DRAFT CONVENTION ON THE PROTECTION OF FOREIGN INVESTMENTS (1962). Address: Chateau de la Muette, 2 rue André Pascal, Paris 16er France.

[55] For information on the former operations of this organization, see THE OEEC: HISTORY AND STRUCTURE (Paris 1956); OEEC, THE PROBLEM OF RISING PRICES (Paris 1961); ANNUAIRE O.I., at 209-11; Mallet, *History and Structure of OEEC,* 1 EUROPEAN Y.B. 62-70 (1955); *Organization for European Economic Cooperation,* 15 INT'L ORG. 744 (1961) (for other references, see index to other INT'L ORG. Volumes); 1 PEASLEE, *supra* note 6, at 68, 370, 446, 463, 496, 511, 512, 515, 583, 620, 622, 639; 2 *id. supra* note 6, at 1620-38.

to multilateral trade on a wider basis were also among its distinct accomplishments.

The European Payments Union, which ensured the transferability of European currencies among its members, made possible at the end of 1958, general convertibility of these currencies after years of bilateral regulation and control. In addition, it provided certain credit facilities and, upon its termination, was superseded by the mechanism of the European Monetary Agreement.

With the attainment of convertibility there was a spreading conviction that it would be desirable to create a broader framework for economic cooperation in which Canada and the United States would be full Members with Western Europe. The first steps toward reshaping and strengthening economic cooperation between North America and Western Europe were taken at the Western Summit meeting held in Paris in December 1959.

On the initiative of the Western Summit meeting, Ministers from the 20 countries concerned commissioned in January 1960, a report from a group of four experts on a proposed reform of the OEEC. In April, the "Four Wise Men" recommended that the OEEC be transformed into a remodelled economic organization to be known as the "Organization for Economic Co-Operation and Development" (OECD) in which Canada and the United States should take part as full members. On December 14, 1960, Ministers from the 20 Governments signed the OECD Convention in Paris under which the OEEC was reconstituted as the OECD and its legal personality was to continue in the new Organization. The Convention came into force on September 30, 1961, and its present members are: Austria, Belgium, Canada, Denmark, France, Germany, Greece, Iceland, Ireland, Italy, Japan, Luxembourg, Netherlands, Norway, Portugal, Spain, Sweden, Switzerland, Turkey, United Kingdom, and the United States.

The aims of the OECD are set forth in Article 1 of the Convention:

(a) to achieve the highest sustainable economic growth and employment and a rising standard of living in Member countries while maintaining financial stability, and thus to contribute to the development of the world economy;

(b) to contribute to sound economic expansion in Member as well as non-Member countries in the process of economic development; and

(c) to contribute to the expansion of world trade on a multilateral non-discriminatory basis in accordance with international obligations.

The Convention provides that the Members will, individually and jointly:

> promote efficient use and development of their economic resources; encourage research and vocational training; endeavor to prevent developments dangerous to their economies or those of other countries; pursue efforts to reduce or abolish obstacles to the exchange of goods, services and current payments and extend the liberalization of capital movements; and contribute to the economic development of both Member and non-Member countries in the process of economic development, in particular, by the flow of capital to those countries.

The OECD has retained much of the operating machinery of the OEEC, including the Council, composed of all the Members, which may meet in sessions of Ministers or of permanent representatives. At sessions of permanent representatives, the Secretary-General acts as the Chairman. As in the OEEC, the Council may make decisions that are binding on the members. The Council has established an Executive Committee and a sizable Secretariat, headed by a Secretary-General and two Deputy Secretaries-General and including numerous divisions. There are also Departments of Economics and Statistics, Trade and Payments, and Development. There are Directorates of Scientific Affairs, Manpower and Social Affairs, Industry and Energy, and Agriculture. The Organization includes the European Nuclear Energy Agency and a Development Center. Among its committees are those on: Economic Policy, Economic and Development Review, Payments, Trade, Invisible Transactions, Development Assistance, Technical Cooperation, Scientific and Technical Personnel, Scientific Research, Manpower and Social Affairs, Industry, Energy, Agriculture, and Fisheries.

§ 6-3.20. **Union Internationale de Financement et de Participation (Interunion).** Established in March 1969, as a credit bank to serve medium- and long-term credit needs of established international companies, the Bank also guarantees loans granted by other institutions.

The 10 banks composing Interunion are: La Campagnie Financière de l'Union Européene, La Banque de l'Union Européene Industrielle et Financière, and La Société Financière Desmarais pour l'Industrie et le Commerce, of Paris; the Marine Midland Overseas Corporation of New York; the Banque de Bruxelles and the Banque Belge pour l'Industrie, of Brussels; the Bayerische Vereinsbank, of Munich; the Royal Bank of Canada International, Ltd. of

Nassau; the Banque Commerciale de Bale, of Basel; the British-owned Hambros Investment Co., Ltd., of Zurich; and La Centrale Finanziera Generale of Milan.

Interunion is registered in France and has a subsidiary in Curacao in the Netherlands Antilles, which can pay interest tax-free and can take in deposits from any source. In addition to its own capital, the Bank has access to credit granted by the international group of banks which own it.

§ 6-3.21. The Union of Central African States.[56] Established by a Charter signed at Fort Lamy, Chad, on April 2, 1968, the Union consists of: the Central African Republic, the Republic of Chad, and the Democratic Republic of the Congo (Kinshasa).

Its economic functions include the development of a common external tariff, the free movement of goods within the Union, a common economic policy and common transport and telecommunications organizations. The organs of the Union are the Conference of Chiefs of State, the Council of Ministers and an Executive Secretariat. Its headquarters are located in Gangui, Central African Republic.

§ 6-3.22. The West African Economic Customs Union.[57] This Union was created by a Convention signed in Paris in 1959. A revised Convention of June 1966, which came into force in December 1966, provided for the application of a common external tariff and for harmonization of the customs legislation and regulations of member countries. The members of the Union are: Dahomey, Ivory Coast, Mali, Mauritania, Niger, Senegal, and Upper Volta. The Organization of the Union is composed of a Council of Ministers of Finance, a Board of Experts, and a General Secretariat. The headquarters are located in Abidjan, Ivory Coast.

In May 1970, seven West African nations signed a protocol to replace the West African Economic Customs Union with the West African Economic Community. While the seven nations that signed the protocol: the Ivory Coast, Niger, Mali, Upper Volta, Dahomey, Senegal and Mauritania are French-speaking nations, all West African states are invited to join the new community. The new Community is specifically designed to work in the following fields: the improvement of distribution, transport and communications

---

[56] BUREAU OF ECONOMIC AFFAIRS, U.S. DEPARTMENT OF STATE MULTINATIONAL ECONOMIC ORGANIZATIONS IN AFRICA, A SUMMARY DESCRIPTION 28 (Washington 1968). Address: BP 873, Bangoi, Central African Republic.

[57] *Id.* at 31. Address: BP 28, Ouagadougou, Upper Volta.

systems, the acceleration of industrialization, and the promotion of trade exchanges in both agricultural and manufactured products.

§ 6-3.23. The Caribbean Development Bank.[58] The Bank which came into force in 1970, has been ratified by the following States: Antigua, Bahamas, Barbados, British Honduras, British Virgin Islands, Canada, Cayman Islands, Dominica, Grenada, Guyana, Jamaica, Montserrat, St. Kitts-Nevis-Anguilla, St. Lucia, St. Vincent, Trinidad and Tobago, and Turks and Caicos Islands. Article I of the Agreement Establishing the Caribbean Development Bank sets forth the purpose of the Bank as to

> [c]ontribute to the harmonious economic growth and development of the member countries in the Caribbean . . . and to promote economic cooperation and integration among them, having special regard to the needs of the less developed members of the region.

The functions of the Bank are to assist members to coordinate their development plans; to use resources more efficiently; to make their economies complementary; to expand intra-regional and international trade; to mobilize additional financial resources to aid the region's economic development; to finance projects and programs; to provide technical assistance such as pre-investment surveys and in preparing project plans; to promote public and private investment in development projects; to promote the establishment of regional and local financial institutions; and to promote the development of regional capital markets.

Membership in the Bank is open to states and territories in the Caribbean region, and non-regional states which are members of the United Nations, its specialized agencies or the International Atomic Energy Agency.

The authorized capital of the Bank was set at $50 million, divided into ten thousand shares (callable and paid-up shares) to be purchased by members of the Bank. In addition, a Special Development Fund to receive contributions and loans was created which will grant or guarantee loans of a high priority having longer maturities, longer deferred commencement of repayment and lower interest rates.

In addition to its other powers and functions, the Bank is authorized to borrow money from members or elsewhere, to buy and sell securities it has issued, guaranteed or invested in, to

---

[58] Agreement establishing the Caribbean Development Bank, with Protocol to provide for procedure for amendment of Article 36 of the Agreement, done at Kingston, Jamaica on 18 October 1969. ST/LE6/SER.D/1. Annex.

underwrite securities issued by any enterprise or entity for purposes consistent with those of the Bank; to invest or deposit unneeded funds; to borrow from Governments and international organizations.

The structure of the Bank is as follows: a Board of Governors, a Board of Directors, a President and a Vice-President. The Board of Governors, in whom all power is vested, is composed of each member of the Bank, who appoints one Governor and one alternative. Governors and alternatives serve without remuneration. The Board of Governors is permitted to delegate any power to the Board of Directors except: admission of new members, suspension of members, changing the authorized capital stock of the Bank, deciding appeals from decisions of the Board of Directors, election of directors and President, determination of their salary, determination of the Bank's resources and distribution of profits, amendment of the Agreement establishing the Bank, termination of the Bank, and distribution of its assets. The Board of Governors meets at least once annually with a majority constituting a quorum.

The Board of Directors, responsible for the general operations of the Bank, is composed of seven members. Five members must represent regional members, and two, non-regional members. It is specified in the Agreement that the Directors shall be "persons of high competence in economic and financial matters and shall be selected with due regard to the principle of equitable geographical representation." Directors hold office for a term of two years, and can be renominated for additional terms.

Voting procedures in the Bank are spelled out in Article 32. Each member of the Bank has 150 votes plus one additional vote for each share of capital stock it holds. In the Board of Governors, each Governor casts the votes of the member he represents, and all decisions will be determined by a majority of the voting power of the members at the meeting. In the Board of Directors, each director votes the number of votes of the member or members whose votes counted toward his selection.

Chapter VIII of the Agreement is devoted to the Status, Immunities, Exemptions and Privileges of the Bank. Accordingly, the Bank possesses "full juridical personality," with full capacity to contract, to acquire, and dispose of property, and to initiate legal proceedings. Specifically, the Bank is to be immune from legal process except involving its transactions; likewise all Bank property and assets are free from search, requisition, confiscation, expropriation; and is immune from taxation.

§ 6-4. The Unification of Law To Facilitate International Transactions.[59]

Those who are engaged in international trade need to know what law governs their transactions. Law differs on many points from country to country, and where two entirely contradictory laws may apply equally in a given case, it is uncertain which controls. This confusion has led in recent years to incorporating into contracts a "choice of law" clause, but these are not valid everywhere.

When the laws involved concerning a transaction conflict, the rules of private international law are applied to resolve the dispute. However, different nations have different conceptions of the rules of private international law, and thus, it is never clear exactly what rules are to be applied or what the outcome of the litigation will be. The result may depend upon the state in which litigation takes place, where the contract was entered into, or where it was substantially performed. Adding further uncertainty to this problem is the fact that a judgment obtained may not be recognized in the other, as the conditions for recognition also vary substantially.

International commercial relations cannot develop properly under such uncertain conditions. The world of trade has, therefore, long desired, worked for, and still needs, unification of international commercial law, and the rules of conflicts of laws. Notable results have been achieved through joint efforts by organized trade, the legal profession, and international institutions working on this problem. In fact, the International Chamber of Commerce has played a leading role. But, the results have been limited, and are still insufficient for today's needs, so it is clear that much remains to be

---

[59] *See generally* Bronz, *The International Trade Organization Charter,* 62 HARV. L. REV. 1089-1126 (1949); EVERYMAN'S UN 413 (1959); 1-3 INDEX TO FOREIGN LEGAL PERIODICALS (1960-1962) (for numerous articles on unification of law and uniform laws in the periodicals of many countries); J. HONNOLD, UNIFICATION OF THE LAW GOVERNING INTERNATIONAL SALES OF GOODS (Paris 1966); Nadelmann, *Uniform Legislation vs. International Conventions Revisted,* 16 AM. J. COMP. L. 34-44 (1968) (contains numerous bibliographical references); Nadelmann, *The Uniform Law of International Sale of Goods: A Conflict of Laws Imbroglio,* 17 YALE L.J. 449 (1965); Avila, *Unificación Legislativo Mercantil en América Latina,* 32 REVISTA DE DERECHO MERCANTIL 311 (1961); 2 PEASLEE, *supra* note 6, at 1205-10; Rubin, *The Judicial Review Problem in the International Trade Organization,* 62 HARV. L. REV. 78-89 (1949). For papers submitted at the World Peace Through Law Conferences, see Cobos, *Transnational Trade and Investments,* in GENEVA CONF. 306-07; Domke, *Progress in International Commercial Arbitration,* in *id.* 287-93; Goldstajn, *The New Law Merchant,* in *id.* 298-301; Roral, *The Creation of an Arbitration Center Within the Frame of the World Peace Through Law Center,* in *id.* 293-97; Langen, *International Commercial Arbitration Most Energetically Supports the Development of Supranational Law and Thus World Peace Through Law,* in *id.* 277-86; Scheffer, *Unification of Law Governing the International Sale of Goods,* in WASHINGTON CONF. 283-87; Simintiras, *Investments,* in *id.* 769-72; Zepos, *Encouraging International Investment,* in *id.* 288-90.

done to make law more uniform, thereby enabling it to become a more useful instrument for continued international economic growth and development.

Uniformity of law can be obtained through various methods. International conventions may be concluded which by themselves have the effect of making the law on the subject covered uniform among the nations party to the convention, or such conventions may simply provide that specified uniform rules shall be introduced into domestic law to become general law applicable to everybody. States may agree on a uniform or model text and then introduce the uniform text into their legislation without any international commitment. The latter method was developed especially within federal systems where law is not uniform, and has increasingly been used on the international level.

Worldwide uniformity has been achieved in special fields of the law, especially in copyright law and the law of patents. Similarly, substantial parts of transportation law such as maritime law (Brussels Conventions[60]), air law (Warsaw Convention[61]), and railroad law (Geneva Conventions[62]), have been made uniform through international agreements. Numerous countries have ratified the Geneva[63] and New York[64] conventions on the validity of arbitration clauses and the recognition of foreign arbitral awards. The law of negotiable instruments has been made uniform, or almost uniform, in the civil law world through the Geneva Conventions of 1930[65] and 1931[66] and among the common law countries through adoption of a uniform, or almost uniform, text. Differences remain, however, between the law in force in the common law countries and the Geneva uniform law.

---

[60]Convention for the unification of certain rules with respect to assistance and salvage at sea, *signed* September 23, 1910, 37 Stat. 1658, T.S. 576.

[61]Convention for the unification of certain rules relating to international transportation by air, *concluded at* Warsaw October 12, 1929, 49 Stat. 3000; T.S. 876.

[62]International Convention to facilitate the crossings of frontiers for passengers and baggage by rail, *signed at* Geneva January 10, 1952, 163 U.N.T.S. 3.

International convention to facilitate the crossing of frontiers for goods carried by rail, *signed at* Geneva January 10, 1952, 163 U.N.T.S. 27.

[63]Convention for the execution of foreign arbitral awards, *signed at* Geneva September 26, 1927, 92 L.N.T.S. 301.

[64]Convention on the recognition and enforcement of foreign arbitral awards, *done at* New York June 10, 1958, 330 U.N.T.S. 3.

[65]Convention for the settlement of certain conflicts of laws in connection with bills of exchange and promissory notes, *signed at* Geneva June 7, 1930, 143 L.N.T.S. 317.

[66]Convention for the settlement of certain conflicts of laws in connection with cheques, *signed at* Geneva March 19, 1931, 143 L.N.T.S. 407.

Dramatic results on a regional level have been achieved as well. Such uniformity has been achieved particularly among the Scandinavian countries, and private international law has, to some extent, been made uniform. The old Hague Conventions on questions of personal status[67] bind a number of European states; the Montevideo Treaties of 1889[68] and 1939[69] on private international law have been ratified by a number of Latin American States; and 15 Latin American States have ratified the convention on the Bustamante Code of Private International Law,[70] adopted in 1928 by the Sixth International Conference of American States.

Notwithstanding these achievements, much remains to be done both for the unification of private law and the unification of rules of private international law. Thus, uniformity of private international law has not yet been achieved even for Latin America. Mexico and a number of Latin American States have not ratified the Bustamante Code Convention, and some ratifications have been made with reservations practically amounting to non-ratification.

Leaving aside international organizations working in special legal field like maritime law, air law, copyright, and patents the following bodies should be noted for their work on unification of law.

§ 6-4.1. The United Nations' Unification of Laws. Following the example of the League of Nations, which sponsored the Geneva

---

[67] Special Protocol Concerning Statelessness, *done* April 12, 1930, U.N. Doc. C.27.M.16. 1931. V; Protocol relating to a Certain Case of Statelessness, *done* April 12, 1930, 179 L.N.T.S. 115, 200 L.N.T.S. 540; Convention on Certain Questions relating to a Conflict of Nationality Laws, *done* April 12, 1930, 179 L.N.T.S. 89, 196 L.N.T.S. 476, 200 L.N.T.S. 539; Protocol relating to Military Obligations in Certain Cases of Double Nationality, *done* April 12, 1930, 178 L.N.T.S. 227, 196 L.N.T.S. 476, 200 L.N.T.S. 539.

[68] The Montevideo Conventions of 1889 on private international law topics include: Patents of Inventions, *done* January 10, 1889, 18 MARTENS', NOUVEAU RECUEIL GÉNÉRAL DE TRAITES 421 (2nd ser., Gottingen 1889) (hereinafter cited as MARTENS), 37 AJIL 155 (1943); International Procedural Law, *done* January 11, 1889, 18 MARTENS 414 (1889); Copyright, *done* January 11, 1889, 90 British and Foreign State Papers 680 (1889); Patents and Trademarks, *done* January 16, 1889, 37 AJIL 152 (1943); International Penal Law, *done* January 28, 1889, 16 MARTENS 432 (1889); Application of Laws in Contracting States, *done* February 3, 1889, 18 MARTENS 456 (1889); International Civil Law, *done* February 12, 1889, 18 MARTENS 443 (1889); Collection of Commercial Information, *done* February 12, 1889, 18 MARTENS 424 (1889); Copyright, *done* February 13, 1889.

[69] The Montevideo Conventions of 1939 include: Free Professions, *done* August 4, 1939, 8 HUDSON, INTERNATIONAL LEGISLATION 418 (1931-49), 37 AJIL SUPP. 107 (1943); Intellectual Property, *done* August 4, 1939, 8 HUDSON, INTERNATIONAL LEGISLATION 412 (1939-49), 37 AJIL 103 (1943); Political Asylum and Refugees, *done* August 4, 1939, 8 HUDSON, INTERNATIONAL LEGISLATION 404 (1939-49), 37 AJIL 99 (1943).

[70] 86 L.N.T.S. 120, 254 (1928).

Conferences of 1930[71] and 1931[72] on the unification of the law of bills of exchange and of checks, the United Nations Economic and Social Council has on occasion sponsored conferences on the unification of law. Examples are the New York Conference on Enforcement Abroad of Maintenance Obligations[73] and the New York Conference on Recognition and Enforcement of Foreign Arbitral Awards.[74]

In 1966, the UN General Assembly voted unanimously to create the United Nations Commission on International Trade Law (Uncitral),[75] which began operations on January 1, 1968, with representatives who are experts in international trade law, from 29 states. Member states are elected by the Assembly for six-year terms and must include seven African states, five Asian states, four East European states, five Latin American states, and eight West European and other states, representing the world's principal economic and legal systems, both developed and undeveloped.

In 1967, the following states were elected to full membership on the Commission for six-year terms: Argentina, Australia, Belgium, Brazil, the Democratic Republic of Congo, Hungary, India, Iran, Kenya, Mexico, Rumania, Spain, Syria, Tunisia, and the United States. Elected for partial, three-year terms were: Chile, Colombia, Czechoslovakia, France, Ghana, Italy, Japan, Nigeria, Norway, Thailand, U.S.S.R., United Arab Republic, the United Kingdom, and the United Republic of Tanzania.

The resolution establishing the Commission stated that the Commission's major task is to "promote the progressive harmonization" and unification of the law of international trade by preparing a code on international trade law, by establishing new international conventions, promoting a uniform interpretation of international commercial terms, collecting and disseminating information on relevant international conventions and on relevant national legislation and modern legal developments."[76]

---

[71] Convention for the settlement of certain conflicts of laws in connection with bills of exchange and promissory notes, *signed at* Geneva June 7, 1930, 143 L.N.T.S. 317.

[72] Convention for the settlement of certain conflicts of laws in connection with cheques, *signed at* Geneva March 19, 1931, 143 L.N.T.S. 407.

[73] *Opened for signature* at New York June 20, 1956, 268 U.N.T.S. 3.

[74] *Signed at* New York June 10, 1958, 330 U.N.T.S. 3.

[75] G.A. Res. 2205, 21 U.N. GAOR Supp.   at   , U.N. Doc. A/6594 (1966), 1966 U.N.Y.B. 920.

[76] *Id.*

The third session of UNCITRAL was held in New York from April 6-30, 1970. The Commission continued its action on the four major areas of international trade law to which it had given priority, and took steps to learn the activities of other organizations working in international trade law by requesting annual reports from the Secretary-General. The Commission also considered the report of the Committee on the Uniform Law of International Sale of Goods; requested the Secretary-General to study the possibility of establishing general conditions of sales and contracts; requested the preparation of a draft convention on prescriptions; decided that a draft convention on negotiable instruments should be prepared; invited the International Chamber of Commerce to submit its revised text of the 1962 Uniform Customs and Practice for Documentary Credits Convention; decided to send questionnaires to Governments and banking and trade institutions, not members of the ICC, regarding performance, tender and repayment guaranties, and the law of securities; continued the Working Group on International Shipping Legislation and the Special Rapporteur on international commercial arbitration; and decided to establish a *Yearbook* of the Commission's activities. The fourth session of UNCITRAL is scheduled for 29 March - 23 April 1971.

Since its inception, the Commission has been central in creating a unified, international banking practice, and in preparing a draft convention which would facilitate cargo unloadings by the use of a uniform, internationally-acceptable form of documentation, and recommended the creation of a new form of internationally-acceptable negotiable instrument. Other problems of international commercial law dealt with by the Commission include the international sale of goods, international payments, international commercial arbitration, the Hague Conventions of 1964,[77] the Hague Convention of Applicable Law of 1955,[78] the Convention providing a uniform Law for Bills of Exchange and Promissory Notes of 1930,[79] the Convention for the Settlement of Certain Conflicts of Laws in connection with Bills of Exchange and Promissory Notes of 1930,[80] the Convention providing a Uniform Law of Cheques

---

[77] For *Convention on the Law Applicable to the International Sale of Goods,* see Scheffer, *Unification of Law Governing the International Sale of Goods,* in WASHINGTON CONF. 287. For text of the convention and further information, write H. E. Scheffer, General Counsellor, Ministry of Justice, Plein 2b The Hague, Netherlands.

[78] For *Uniform Law on the International Sale of Goods,* see Scheffer, *Unification of Law Governing the International Sale of Goods,* in WASHINGTON CONF. 287. For text of the convention and further information apply to H. E. Scheffer, General Counsellor, Ministry of Justice, Plein 2b The Hague, Netherlands.

[79] *Done at* Geneva June 7, 1930, 143 L.N.T.S. 257. Registered No. 3314.

[80] *Done at* Geneva June 7, 1930, 143 L.N.T.S. 257. Registered No. 3313.

of 1931,[81] the Convention for the Settlement of Certain Conflicts of Laws in connection with Cheques of 1931,[82] time limits (prescriptions), general conditions of sale, standard contracts, negotiable instruments, banker's commercial credits, guarantees and securities.

The Commission meets annually in Geneva and New York on alternative years, and in its second session (March 3-31, 1969). established working committees to deal with these topics.

§ 6-4.2. The Organization of American States.[83] In the Western Hemisphere, the Inter-American Council of Jurists, legal organ of the Organization of American States, has among its statutory assignments the promotion of uniformity of law. Among the results of the work of the Council and its permanent committee, the Inter-American Juridical Committee, is the draft of a Uniform Law on Inter-American Commercial Arbitration, recommended to the American Republics for introduction into their legislation in accordance with their constitutional processes.

§ 6-4.3. The International Institute for the Unification of Private Law.[84] Located in Rome, the Institute is a permanent international body supported by some 40 governments from Europe, Asia, and Latin America. The Institute works on unification of private law, with the exclusion of private international law (traditionally handled by the Hague Conference on Private International Law,[85] referred to in Chapter 5). The principal endeavor of the Institute has been the production of a uniform law on international sales, a draft of which was considered at an international conference held in 1952. A revised draft has been sent to the participating governments for their comments. The Institute has been working on numerous other topics, primarily in the field of contracts. Its activities are reported in French and English in the yearbook of the Institute, *Unification of Law*. The Institute has sponsored international conferences of organizations engaged in work on unification of law. The proceedings of these conferences have appeared in the yearbook of the Institute.

§ 6-4.4. Regional Bodies on Unification of Law. Regional associations and countries which have been interested in the unification of law include: the Organization of American States, the Scandi-

---

[81]*Done at* Geneva March 19, 1931, 143 L.N.T.S. 355.

[82]*Done at* Geneva March 19, 1931, 143 L.N.T.S. 407.

[83]*See* discussion in Chapter 3 of this volume.

[84]2 PEASLEE, *supra* note 6, at 1205-1210.

[85]*See* ANNUAIRE O.I. 162-68; 1 PEASLEE, *supra* note 6, at 745-50.

navian countries, the Council of Europe, Benelux, the European Economic Community, the Arab League, and others. Summary reports of work done by these groups appear in the *Yearbook of the International Institute for the Unification of Private Law.*

§ 6-4.5. **National Bodies on Unification of Law.** In nations with a federal system, special organizations have been set up to work on internal unification of law. In the United States, this work is *primarily* in the hands of the National Conference of Commissioners on Uniform State Laws. Numerous uniform laws have been produced by the Conference, several of them enacted in all states of the Union. The most ambitious work of the Conference is the Uniform Commercial Code, produced in 1952, so far enacted in several states. In Canada, the work is in the hands of the Conference of Commissioners on Uniformity of Legislation in Canada. In Russia, the Academy on Law and the States prepares and recommends uniform laws for the various Russian Republics.

§ 6-4.6. **Non-Official Organizations Working on Unification of Law.** Numerous non-official international organizations have long worked on unification of law. Among them are: the International Chamber of Commerce, the Institute of International Law founded in 1873, which works both on public and private international law; the International Law Association, founded in 1873, which holds conferences every other year, also working in both fields; and the World Peace Through Law Center also working in both fields. In a number of instances, drafts originally prepared by these non-official bodies have been taken over and acted upon by official bodies.

CHAPTER 7

Intellectual Property

§ 7-1. Introduction

As a legal classification, intellectual property[1] includes industrial property and copyright in literary and artistic work. Industriaı

---

[1] *See generally* Barton, *Limitations on Territory, Field of Use, Quantity and Price in Know-How Agreements with Foreign Companies*, 28 U. PITT. L.REV. 195-206 (1966); Bodenhausen, *Problemes Actuels du Droit International de la Propriété Industrielle, Literaire et Artistique*, 74 RECUEIL DES COURS 379-464 (1949); Boguslavsky, *International Protection of the Right to Inventions* (in Russian), in 1964-1965 SOVIET Y.B. INT'L L. 230-51 (1966); BUSINESS INTERNATIONAL, ESTABLISHING A WORLDWIDE PATENT AND TRADEMARK POLICY (New York 1965); H. DURHAM, WORLD PATENT LEGISLATION (Leyden 1967); Haertel, *Crisis of National Patent Systems: Necessity for International Solutions*, NATIONAL ASSOCIATION OF MANUFACTURERS 5-13 (1965); Haight, *International Protection of Rights in Technology*, in SYMPOSIUM ON STRUCTURES AND SAFEGUARDS OF PRIVATE INVESTORS ABROAD . . . 173-204 (1966); Kobayashi, *On Japanese Patent Literature*, 7 IDEA 250-52 (1963); Krasznay, *Results of the Cooperation Among the Countries of the COMECON in re Inventions*, 5 INDUSTRIAL PROPERTY 92-94 (1966); Lightman, *The USSR Trademark System and East-West Trade*, 10 IDEA 11-31 (1966); *id.* at 455-75; 12 *id.* at 791-817 (1968); Otani, *Introduction to the Japanese Patent System*, 7 *id.* at 13-22 (1963); Sarnoff, *A World Patent System*, CASE & COM. 16-23 (1966); Shipman, *International Patent Planning*, 45 HARV. BUS. REV. 56-72 (1967).

IDEA, the Journal of the Patent, Trademark, and Copyright Research Institute of the George Washington University, carries articles, reviews and annotations of value in the field; it also has published the discussions of 11 annual conferences of the Institute.

(Continued)

property includes inventions, industrial designs and trademarks, and applied knowledge. The protection and scope of the rights involved are determined by the national laws of the respective countries in which they are asserted. Industrial property protection rules are called patent laws in some nations. Extraterritorial rights are provided by various treaties among different states.

The significance of an effective international industrial property system and the harmonization of industrial property laws of nations lies in the fact that the systems and the laws implementing these are important means of promoting economic development and creating an international investment climate favorable to trade and the achievement of worldwide prosperity, both of which are basic to the maintenance of peace. By inducing ingenuity and investment in the less industrialized nations, patent protection can help them become more industrialized and raise their standard of living.

§ 7-2. The Paris Convention [2]

The historical landmark treaty in the field of industrial property is the multilateral agreement of 1883, the Paris Convention for the

---

For papers submitted to the conferences held by the WPTLC, see *The Challenge of the Field of Industrial Property Law*, in WORLD PEACE THROUGH LAW: THE ATHENS CONFERENCE 255-61 (1965) [hereinafter cited as ATHENS CONF.]; Davar, *Introductory Remarks*, in WORLD PEACE THROUGH LAW: THE WASHINGTON CONFERENCE 471-74 (1967) [hereinafter cited as WASHINGTON CONF.]; Davar, *Patents, Transfer of Technology and Know-how*, in WORLD PEACE THROUGH LAW: THE GENEVA CONFERENCE 250-54 (1969) [hereinafter cited as GENEVA CONF.]; Ekani, *Industrial and Intellectual Property*, in *id.* at 241-45; Faller, *Industrial and Intellectual Property*, in *id.* at 245-47; Harris, *Introductory Comments*, in WASHINGTON CONF. 269-71; Harris, *Remarks by the Chairman*, in GENEVA CONF. 234-37; King, Sr., *Industrial and Intellectual Property*, in BANGKOK CONF.; Ladas, *Industrial Property and Economic Development*, in ATHENS CONF. 366-78; Ladas, *Model Patent Law for Developing Countries*, in WASHINGTON CONF. 474-80; Ladas, *Intellectual and Industrial Property*, in BANGKOK CONF.; Ho Lee, *Assignment, License of Patents and Trademarks in the Developing Countries*, in *id.*; Medina, *Current Movements to Harmonize the Industrial Property Law of Latin-American Countries*, in WASHINGTON CONF. 480-87; Müller-Börner, *The Establishment of International Patents, Trademarks and Copyrights*, in BANGKOK CONF.; Oppenhof, *European Activities Toward Harmonization of Industrial Property Rights To Promote Economic Development and a Favorable Investment Climate*, in *id.* at 488-92; Pollzien, *Problems Connected with Licensing Abroad*, in GENEVA CONF. 248-49; Pretnar, *Industrial and Intellectual Property*, in *id.* at 254-55; Robbins, *International Harmonization of National Patent Systems*, in WASHINGTON CONF. 492-97; Talerngsri, *Industrial Property and Economic Development of Developing Countries*, in BANGKOK CONF.; United International Bureau for the Protection of Intellectual Property, *Note on Intellectual and Industrial Property*, in *id.*; Woodley, *Industrial and Intellectual Property Patents and the Transfer of Technology*, in GENEVA CONF. 238-41.

[2] Becher, *The Paris Convention for the Protection of Industrial Property* (in German), 15 ST. & R. 1480-93 (1966). For text, see 38 Stat. 1845 & 5579.

Protection of Industrial Property. The states which are parties to this Convention constitute the Union for the International Protection of Industrial Property. This Paris Convention has been revised several times to meet changing needs; the latest revision being that which took place in Stockholm in 1967.

From an original membership of 13 states, the Convention has been adhered to by at least 80 states in various stages of development, and of various ideologies. Much compatible legislation in the several member countries has resulted from the obligation of each signatory to adopt industrial property legislation which gives to nationals of the adhering nations the same rights it gives its own nationals, and thus conforms to the provisions of the Convention. Yet, each state remains free to adopt legislation that will best meet its domestic needs and conditions.

The most important provisions of the Paris Convention are the principle of "national treatment" and the principle of "unionist treatment." According to the principle of national treatment, no distinction is made between the treatment of domestic citizens and that of foreign nationals in this branch of law. By the principle of unionist treatment, persons entitled to the benefits of the Convention enjoy certain specified rights and advantages regardless of the national treatment to which they are entitled. One of these advantages is the very important "right of priority" for the filing of foreign applications for patents, trademarks and other protection. By virtue of this, a person entitled to the benefits of the Convention has a period of 6 or 12 months (depending on the nature of the protection sought) within which he may file an application for an invention or registration of a mark, whereby he is accorded priority rights as of the date of his first filed application in an adhering country. The applicant has time to decide which states other than the first he wishes to apply in. Many countries require that the owner of a patent manufacture the patented product, use his patented process, or make the invention available under license. This provision (commonly referred to as "compulsory licensing," "actual working," or "nominal working") is intended to protect both the inventor and the public. The Convention requires adherents to prohibit acts of unfair competition and specifies categories of acts which are considered to be unfair competition.

Adherence to the Convention has important advantages. The patentee usually has special know-how and technical information which he can (and usually does) contribute to the industry. The patent system is a means by which the establishment of local enterprises advances the industrialization of underdeveloped countries, for example, enabling small firms to compete on more equitable terms with large ones; a necessary protection since so many small firms are engaged in this dynamic area of commerce.

The Convention also requires adherents to render effective protection to marks and trade symbols which distinguish and identify products or services, and to protect trade names whether registered or not. Members of the Convention have the opportunity of seeking new provisions to cover their particular needs.

The Paris Convention provides that member states may conclude special agreements within the framework of the Convention on particular aspects of industrial property. Accordingly, the following agreements have been concluded: the Madrid Agreement of April 14, 1891, for the Prevention of False or Misleading Indications of Source (which was revised in 1911, 1925, 1934, and 1958); the Madrid Agreement of April 14, 1891, concerning the International Registration of Trademarks[3] (which was revised in 1900, 1911, 1925, and 1957); the Hague Agreement of November 6, 1925, concerning the International Deposit of Industrial Designs[4] (which was revised in 1934 and 1960, with an Additional Act signed in 1961); and the Nice Agreement of June 15, 1957, concerning the International Classification of Goods and Services to which Marks are Applied.[5] Two other agreements are: A Lisbon Agreement of October 31, 1958, for the Protection of Appellations of Origin and their International Registration;[6] and a Paris Convention of December 2, 1961, for the Protection of New Varieties of Plants.[7]

§ 7-3. The Berne Convention[8]

In 1886, the Berne Convention for the Protection of Literary and Artistic Works was signed by 10 states; the Berne Union today has

---

[3] Ladas, *Proposal for a New Agreement for International Registration of Trademarks,* 57 T.M. RPTR. 433 (1967); Offner, *The Madrid Agreement and Trends in International Trademark Protection,* 56 *id.* at 368-90 (1966).

[4] 47 Stat. 1789; TS 834; 74 LNTS 289.

[5] BIRPI, *Manual of Industrial Property Conventions* Supp. 1-3 (1964); J.O. 4391 (1960).

[6] *Opened for signature* October 31, 1958, 13 UST 1; TIAS 4931.

[7] Cmd. 1947 (Great Britain Parliament Papers by command); Misc. 1963:2.

[8] Mott, *The Relationship Between the Berne Convention and the Universal Copyright Convention,* 11 IDEA 306-32 (1967).

(Continued)

58 member states. The Berne Convention was revised in 1908, 1928, and 1948.

The three basic principles of this Berne Convention are: the principle of "national treatment," by which authors enjoy the same rights as nationals in any of the states which are members of the Union; the principle of "automatic protection," by which no formalities are required for the enjoyment of these rights; and the principle of "independence of protection," by which protection of the enjoyment of these rights is independent of the existence of their protection in the state of origin.

Another Convention which provides international copyright protection is the International Convention for the Protection of performers, Producers of Phonograms and Broadcasting Organizations, signed in 1961. The Secretariat is supplied jointly by the United International Bureaux for the Protection of Intellectual Property, UNESCO, and the ILO.

§ 7-4. The Universal Copyright Convention[9]

This Convention was entered into by 36 nations in 1952, under the auspices of UNESCO, stemming primarily from the knowledge that existing international copyright agreements, notably the Berne Union, held little hope for the creation of a universal copyright system. It became effective in 1955, and as of late 1969, 58 states had become members.

The Convention, while somewhat similar to the Berne Union, differs in many respects. As does the Union, it also provides "national treatment," but provides protection for only 25 years after first publication, while the Berne Union provides protection for 50 years post mortem. In addition, the Convention also permits an associated state with works first published in its territory, or by its nationals regardless of the place of publication, to condition the granting of protection on the applicant's compliance with such formalities as deposition, registration, entry, notarial attestation, payment of fees, manufacture or publication in its own territory. Further, the Con-

---

Opened for signature September 9, 1886. French text – *Actes de la 3e Conférence Internationale pour la Protection des oeuvres litteraires et artistique réunie à Berne du au 9 Septembre*, 1 LE DROIT D'AUTEUR 4 (Berne 1888). English text in the Second Schedule to the Order in Council of the United Kingdom dated June 24, 1912, issued under the Copyright Act, 1911 (1 and 2 Geo. 5, c. 46).

[9]*Done* at Geneva September 6, 1952, 6 UST 2731; T.I.A.S. 3324; 216 U.N.T.S. 132.

vention states that the copyright symbol, "C" surrounded by a circle, is sufficient for the first and subsequent publications, and that the Convention cannot be used by states which have left the Union to govern their relations with states that are still members.

§ 7-5. The United International Bureaux for the Protection of Intellectual Property (BIRPI)[10]

The Industrial Property Union, created at the Paris Convention of 1883, and the Union for the Protection of Literary and Artistic Works, created by the Berne Convention of 1886, originally maintained separate offices. Since these two Unions have much in common in organization, structure, administration and permanent organs, they were united in 1893 under a single director and shared a common building. By utilizing the same basic administrative services, they cut down expenses and obtained various other advantages. The administration of the Conventions was performed by the Secretariats under the auspices of the Swiss Government. An Interunion Coordinating Committee composed of 22 member states was established in 1962. A few years prior to 1967, a transitional system, by committee or council, was operated for the administration of the Paris, Berne, Madrid, Nice and Lisbon Unions. BIRPI's financial sources have been primarily from the contributions of states and, to a lesser extent, from fees paid by applicants for the international registration of trademarks and industrial designs.

BIRPI accumulates and disseminates information on industrial property and on copyrights (i.e., "intellectual property"). Its specialized library contains a rich store of information in the field. It publishes two monthly reviews in English and French: *Industrial Property (La Propriete Industrielle)* and *Copyright (Le Droit d'Auteur)*. BIRPI constantly seeks the improvement of the protection of intellectual property through seminars, fellowship grants, and the drafting of model laws for possible use by developing countries. It also prepares drafts and recommendations for revision of existing conventions in the field.

---

[10] *The World Intellectual Property Organization and the Administrative Reorganization of BIRPI*, 12 IDEA 673-89 (1968); UNITED INTERNATIONAL BUREAU FOR THE PROTECTION OF INTELLECTUAL PROPERTY, 1 MANUAL OF INDUSTRIAL PROPERTY CONVENTIONS (looseleaf). The Headquarters of BIRPI are located at 32 Chemin des Colombettes Place des Nations, Case Postale 18, 1211 Geneva 20.

§ 7-6. The Stockholm Convention[11]

On July 14, 1967, 43 states signed the Convention Establishing the World Intellectual Property Organization (WIPO). This Convention was the result of careful study at the five-week Stockholm Conference on drafts and proposals by BIRPI, by government and inter-governmental representatives, and by numerous non-governmental organizations including the International Association for the Protection of Industrial Property (AIPI), and by the International Chamber of Commerce.

The principal objectives and structure of the new organization are essentially the same as those of BIRPI, and, in 1970, BIRPI was merged with WIPO, with Professor G. H. Bodenhausen as Director-General. It seeks to promote worldwide protection of intellectual property and to maintain cooperation among the Unions while retaining for each Union its own independence. The organization of WIPO includes a General Assembly, which is its "supreme organ"; a Director-General, appointed by the General Assembly; a Coordination Committee, which serves as the executive organ of the General Assembly; and Conferences, to be held every three years to serve as a forum for the exchange of views on problems in the field. It is an "open-ended" treaty in that it may be adhered to by countries in addition to those who signed the Stockholm Treaty, if they qualify under the terms of the treaty. The administrative changes embodied in the Treaty do not affect the substantive provisions of the Paris Convention. The Paris Convention, itself, and the principles of "national treatment" and of the "right of priority" remain and will be implemented in the future as in the past.

§ 7-7. The International Patent Institute

Established at the Hague in 1947, this Institute is available to examine patent applications by those national patent offices which desire such services and to make searches and give opinions to individuals on the novelty of inventions. Its research and other facilities are thus very useful both to governments and to patentees who otherwise would have to bear the expense of establishing regional or local offices and would, in certain areas, find it difficult to obtain the needed expertise for efficient operations or service. The Institute examines all of France's patent applications, some of the Netherland's patent applications, and some of the Swiss patent applications.

---

[11] Goldsmith, *WIPO: A Noble Idea Whose Time Has Come,* 12 IDEA 691-701 (1968).

§ 7-8. The Work of the United Nations

The extent and focus of UN interest in patents as a means of aiding underdeveloped countries is shown in a Report of the Secretary General on *The Role of Patents in the Transfer of Technology to Developing Countries,* submitted in 1964.[12]   The Report discusses national patent legislation, government regulation of the exercise of the patent grant, and the effects of patents on the economies of underdeveloped countries, but it emphasizes the international patent system and the extension of patent protection to foreign investors.   A valuable Annex presents a "Synoptic Table of Major Provisions of Patent Legislation in 34 Countries,"[13] giving information of the following items: official title and date of current patent laws and regulations, patentable subject matter; examination by patent office, duration of patent, adherence to international patent conventions, treatment of foreign nationals, requirements for working of patents and sanctions for non-working, and other cases in which patents are subject to public use.

§ 7-9. Patent Cooperation Treaty[14]

The draft of this Patent Cooperation Treaty was released by BIRPI in May 1967.   A meeting to discuss this draft and its accompanying documents was held in Geneva in December 1968, and on June 19, 1970, a Diplomatic Conference released it in its final form. As of July 7, 1970, 21 states had signed it.

The three principal questions covered by the Treaty are filing one single application which may be used as a basis for seeking patent protection in adhering countries; preliminary search of all relevant art; and, under certain conditions, a patentability opinion or certification for use by adhering nations. Important advantages of the Treaty are that it reduces multiple national searching; enables an applicant to defer substantial expenditures for multiple filings, translations and prosecutions until he has had an opportunity to evaluate his invention as to patentability and commercial possibilities; and provides a searching and examining facility for countries which find it economically impossible to establish or maintain their own searching and examining operations.   The Treaty will thus eliminate much duplication of work on the part of the public and

---

[12] UN-New York, 1964 E/3861/Rev. 1 (Sales No.: 65.II.B.1).

[13] *Id.,* Annex Dat 62-93.

[14] Ladas, *BIRPI Plan for a Patent Cooperation Treaty,* 11 IDEA 179-98 (1967); O'Brien, *A Realistic Appraisal of the Draft Patent Cooperation Treaty, id.* at 159-78; Robbins, *The Patent Cooperation Treaty—The 1968 BIRPI Draft Compared with a Simple New Alternative Proposal,* 12 *id.* at 860-87 (1968). For text, see 9 ILM 978-1025 (Sept. 1970).

the governments, and reduce the cost of processing and maintaining patents based on a plurality of applications on the same invention in several countries.

§ 7-10. Recent European Developments

Enthusiasm for the harmonization of industrial property rights in European countries has kept pace with the efforts toward regional economic integration since World War II as a result of the realization by governments and by people that such harmonization and integration are basic prerequisites for economic development. The first steps toward harmonization, made by the Council of Europe, were two agreements relating to formalities: á 1953 Convention of Uniform Formalities Required by Patent Applications[15] and a 1954 Convention on the International Classification of Patents for Invention.[16]

The Scandinavian Patent and Trademark laws were the first examples of uniform substantive law in the field.[17] Although four national laws embody many modern trademark developments, only one law will apply for a national registration in each of the four countries. The Scandinavian countries have inserted in their recent uniform Patent Laws[18] a tentative arrangement which has been predicted to go into force January 1, 1972. This would enable a person to file an application in any of the four Scandinavian countries as a Scandinavian application which would be valid in all four countries. Almost complete substantive and procedural law uniformity would thus be achieved.

The Benelux Convention of 1962[19] relating to trademarks was the first transnational trademark law providing for registration with a supranational trademark office. The Convention, providing that the Benelux trademark takes the place of national trademarks, was ratified by the Netherlands in 1963, Belgium in 1968, and Luxembourg in 1969, to go into effect on January 1, 1971.

In 1959, the European Economic Community created a coordinating committee which drafted a European patent law.[20] This

---

[15] *Signed* December 11, 1953, European Treaty Series, No. 16, 218 UNTS 17.

[16] *Signed* December 19, 1954, European Treaty Series, No. 18, 218 UNTS 51.

[17] Müller-Börner, *The Establishment of International Patents, Trademarks and Copyright,* in BANGKOK CONF.

[18] A. Mazel, U.S. Patent Office *Employee Bulletin* No. 155 (October 1968).

[19] REVUE INTERNATIONALE DE LA PROPRIÉTÉ INDUSTRIELLE ET ARTISTIQUE 31 (French, March 1962); 52 REVUE DE DROIT INTELLECTUAL 156 (French).

[20] Comité de Coordination en Matière de Propriété Industrielle Institutee par les Etats Membres et la Commission de la Communauté Economique Européenne - Avant Projets de

(Continued)

draft law does not aim to replace the patent laws of EEC countries although this goal may be achieved in the future. It does, however, provide for eventual necessary harmonization. Independent authorities and courts would be provided for putting into force and interpreting such a new law. The Coordinating Committee failed to resolve two questions which became political issues. The first was whether third parties (nationals of countries outside EEC) should be granted access to, or rights under, the European patent system, and the second was whether the European patent should be a "Common Market" patent only, or a European patent. The EEC Coordinating Committee also drafted a trademark law which would create a uniform law of marks, establish the right to use the mark, and grant the right to defend the mark against others.[21]   This draft was not published, among other things, because of the influence of political considerations and differences in juridical concepts.

In 1970, the EEC released a Draft Convention for a European System for the Grant of Patents and a Draft Convention Relating to a European Patent for the Common Market.[22]   Under these draft conventions, a European Patent Office composed of examining sections and divisions, and boards of appeal with an enlarged board to rule on points of law, would be created with administrative and financial powers, and under the supervision of the Administrative Council. According to the procedures outlined for the granting of a European patent, an application would first be filed at the European Patent Office or at a contracting state, followed by an examination as to correctness of form, and meeting the requirements of the Convention, and a report on the state of the art obtained from the International Patent Institute at The Hague. The application would then be published to permit any interested party to present his views on the patentability of the invention. Opposition to any patent can be made within one year of the date of publication, and the European Patent Office, after hearing both parties, will decide whether to reject the opposition, or to require the amendment of the patent. Revocation proceedings may be applied for by any interested party and the Office, after hearing the comments of the proprietor, will decide whether to accept or reject the application for revocation. In addition, the Common Market Convention provides for actions for infringement which can be initiated in the courts

---

Convention Relatif a un Droit Européen des Brerets Elabourés par 6 Group au Travail Brerets, Service des Publications des Communautés Européenes (1962).

[21] 7 EUR. Y.B. 182 (1960). *See also* Froshmaier, *EEC Trademark Laws* 6 P.T.C.J. 479 (Washington, D.C., Winter 1962-3).

[22] 2 CCH Common Market Reports ¶ 5503 at 4615 (1970).

having jurisdiction under national law or under international conventions. If revocation proceedings have already been begun in the European Patent Office, national courts must stay any infringement proceedings before them until the Patent Office has delivered its proceedings before them until the Patent Office has delivered its decision. The Court of Justice of the European Communities is empowered to give a preliminary ruling in infringement cases only if interpretation of the convention or its implementing provisions is involved.

§ 7-11. Latin-American Developments[23]

The harmonization of industrial property laws in Latin American countries has been the object of activity by inter-governmental, private and public international organizations such as BIRPI, the United Nations, the Organization of American States, and the Secretariat of the General Treaties for Centro-American Economic Integration, and the Inter-American Association for Industrial Property (ASIPI).

Several Inter-American conventions on industrial property have been enacted. Examples include the Convention of Montevideo of 1889[24] which provided for reciprocal national treatment and the right of priority of application; the Buenos Aires Pan American Patent Convention of 1910;[25] the Pan American Trademark Convention of Buenos Aires and of Washington of 1929;[26] the Convention of American Republics signed in Caracas in 1911;[27] and the 1968 Central American Agreement for the Protection of Trademarks and Commercial Names.[28]

Recommendations for improving existing patent and trademark protection have been numerous. They have centered on the need for revisions of national legislation, adherence to the Paris Convention, consultation among the Latin-American states on patent and

---

[23] Harris, *Industrializing Latin America: A New Frontier for Industrial Property Transactions,* 6 IDEA 1-19 (1962); Harris, *Latin Americans View Their Own Industrial Property Systems,* 9 *id.* at 25-34 (1965).

[24] Recommendation, *Treaties for the Protection of Patents and Trademarks,* INT'L CONFERENCES 1889-1928 at 14.

[25] 38 Stat. 1811; TS 595; 155 L.N.T.S. 179.

[26] 46 Stat 2907; TS 833; 124 L.N.T.S. 357.

[27] COPYRIGHT PROTECTION IN THE AMERICAS 202 (E); UNESCO, 3 LOIS ET TRAITÉS SUR LE DROIT D'AUTEUR (France 1962).

[28] For text, see LA GACETA DIARIO OFFICIAL, 3609-15, 3625-33, 3641-50, 3657-62, 3675-78 (Nicaragua, November 25-29, 1968).

trademark matters, participation of these countries and by the Inter-American Association for the Protection of Industrial Property (ASIPI) in carrying out the program of BIRPI, simplification of formalities in patent and trademark matters, development of Latin American agreements on patent policy regarding space problems, and creation of a national association for the protection of industrial property where it did not exist.

The Inter-American Association for Industrial Property (ASIPI), formed in 1965, aims to harmonize the laws in the Latin American Countries and, to this end, has held various conferences, the latest of which was in Lima, Peru in 1969. In the meantime, Argentina, Peru, and Uruguay have adhered to the Paris Convention, joining five other American Republics that have been party to such Convention for many years (i.e., Brazil, Cuba, the Dominican Republic, Haiti, and Mexico). Colombia, Chile, and Venezuela are in the process of obtaining parliamentary approval for adherence.

§ 7-12. Recent African Developments.[29]

The African and Malagasy Organization for Economic Cooperation established an Industrial Property Office in Yaounde, Cameroon, by an Agreement signed in 1962. By the centralization of administrative procedure in a Central Office, this Agreement provides for uniform national legislation and a system of single filing. The Central Office registers the filing of applications for patents, designs, and trademarks under legislation which is effective in each of the 13 member African states formerly under French jurisdiction (Cameroon, Central African Republic, Chad, Congo-Brazzaville, Dahomey, Gabon, Ivory Coast, Malagasy Republic, Mauritania, Niger, Senegal, Togo and Upper Volta). A parallel movement is developing in East Africa where common industrial property laws may be adopted in in the near future by Kenya, Tanzania, and Uganda, with a common Patent Office having branches in each of the three states.

§ 7-13. Some Current Weaknesses and Needs

In spite of the many admirable efforts to improve the patent system nationally and internationally, many problems remain. Doctrines accepted by some countries are not recognized by others. Patents held valid in some countries are not held valid in others. Patent prosecution and infringement and validity trials are frequently

---

[29] *African and Malagasy Industrial Property Office (OAMPI),* 5 INDUST'L PROP. 206-12, 220-21 (1966).

expensive and lengthy. Patent offices in many countries have ever-increasing backlogs of unexamined cases. Examination of identical applications in several countries produces much unnecessary duplication. Delays and expenses are incurred by multiple applications for the same invention in different countries at different times.

Some countries lack systems and institutions to stimulate private activity in the field of industrial property; many lack even the necessary background to understand the technical arrangements that are required for the development of foreign private investment and foreign inventiveness. Basic legal and administrative procedures for encouraging and protecting inventions and industrial property rights are also lacking. Indeed, some juridical obstacles such as anti-trust laws inhibit the technical development which might otherwise come about.

The owner of a patent who is negotiating with a party in another country about the use of his patent faces several difficulties. A legal definition of the term "license agreement" may be lacking. The fact that an international licensing agreement involves more than one system of law creates problems. Civil law codes have general provisions relating to licensing contracts. Considerable uncertainty results from the application of different provisions and from the lack of precision in determining the extent to which these provisions will be applied by analogy. A party from a common law country may encounter difficulties, either at the time of negotiation or at the time of performance, in reaching an agreement with a party from a civil law country.

Criticisms help to point out weakness. It is natural in a complex field like that of intellectual property for rapidly changing conditions to produce new needs. It is encouraging that there are so many international agreements in this field, and that so many capable and persevering experts are toiling continuously to solve new problems as they arise. The Director-General of WIPO, Professor G.H. Bodenhausen, has contributed enormous leadership in this field. The outlook for the future, therefore, is very promising and, with time and diligence, the system which has promoted the progress of intellectual enterprises will provide greater benefits, under the rule of law.

CHAPTER 8

Human Rights

§ 8-1. Introduction[1]

Human rights define man's place in society and thus are practically related to all his activities, accompanying him and his family

---

[1] *See generally* C. DUNSHEE DE ABRANCHES, PROTEÇÀO INTERNACIONAL DAS DIREITOS HUMANOS (Rio de Janeiro 1964); ALLIENCE ISRAELITE, LES DROITS DE L'HOMME ET L'EDUCATION (Paris 1961); Amachrae, *Fundamental Rights in Nigeria*, 11 HOW. L.J. 463 (1965); Anand, *The Crises of the Right to the Freedom of Religion*, in BANGKOK CONF.; Bascunan, *Human Rights Proposal*, in WASH. CONF. 625-26; Berman, *Human Rights in the Soviet Union*, 11 HOW. L.J. 325-33 (1965); Bilder, *The International Promotion of Human Rights: A Current Assessment*, 58 AJIL 728-33 (1964); S. BRUNAUER, HUMAN RIGHTS IN HUNGARY AS AFFECTED BY COMMUNISM (Washington 1953); Cass, *Toward a World Law of Human Rights*, in BANGKOK CONF.; Castberg, *Natural Law and Human Rights*, 1 HUMAN RIGHTS J. 14-39 (1968); Collier, *Human Rights in Sierra Leone*, 11 HOW. L.J. 500-08 (1965); 5TH SUMMER CONFERENCE ON INTERNATIONAL LAW, CORNELL UNIVERSITY, INTERNATIONAL LAW AND HUMAN RIGHTS (Ithaca, N.Y. 1964); M. CRANSTON, HUMAN RIGHTS TODAY (London 1962); DeNova, *Human Rights and the Protection of Minorities*, 11 HOW. L.J. 275-91 (1965); P. DROST, HUMAN RIGHTS AS LEGAL RIGHTS . . . (Leyden 1951); G. EZEJIOFOR, PROTECTION OF HUMAN RIGHTS UNDER THE LAW (London 1964);

(Continued)

391

throughout life. When human rights are protected, society is freed from despotic and dictatorial oppression. When they are neglected, national and international peace and order are unworkable. The guarantee of human rights is a fundamental part of man's great

---

Ferguson, *The Nature and Dimensions of Human Rights in the United States*, 11 HOW. L.J. 452-63 (1965); M. GANJI, INTERNATIONAL PROTECTION OF HUMAN RIGHTS (Geneva 1962); Gardner, *Human Rights: Some Next Steps*, 49 DEP'T STATE BULL. 320-28 (1963); George, *Human Rights in India*, 11 HOW. L.J. 291-300 (1965); Glaser, *Les Droits de l'Homme à la Lumière du Droit International Positif*, in MÉLANGES OFFERTS À HENRI ROLIN 104-24 (1964); Golsong, *A Critique: Law and Human Rights*, 2 Wd JUST. 348-56 (1961); Golsong, *Implementation of International Protection of Human Rights*, 110 RECUEIL DES COURS 7-151 (1963); Golsong, *La Protection Internationale des Droits de l'Homme*, 34 Y.B.A.A.&A. 129-40 (1964); BRITISH INFORMATION SERVICES, HUMAN RIGHTS IN THE UNITED KINGDOM (New York 1958); Griffin, *The Universal Declaration of Human Rights as 'Lex Sata' and 'Lex Ferenda,' with particular Reference to the Right to a Single Nationality*, in WASHINGTON CONF. 688-94; H. GURADZ, DER STAND DER MENSCHENRECHTE IM VÖLKERRECHT (Göttingen 1956); Gyandoh, *The Constitutional Protection of Human Rights in Developing Countries*, in BANGKOK CONF.; Hambro, *Human Rights and States' Rights*, 56 A.B.A.J. 360-63 (1970); E. HAMBURGER, DROITS DE L'HOMME ET RELATIONS INTERNATIONALES (Leyden 1958); Hamburger, *Droits de l'Homme, et Relations Internationales*, in 97 RECUEIL DES COURS 293-427 (1959); HAMMARSKJÖLD FORUMS, INTERNATIONAL PROTECTION OF HUMAN RIGHTS (New York 1968) (bibliography at 71); Higgins, *Technical Assistance for Human Rights: A New Approach to an Old Problem*, 19 WORLD TODAY 174-80 (1963); Higgins, *Technical Assistance for Human Rights: The Programme in Action*, in *id.* at 219-24; Jakovljevic, *Some Questions on the International Protection of Human Rights*, in GENEVA CONF. 414-21 (1969); Jakovljevic, *The Problem of the Protection of Human Rights and International Law*, ANNUAIRE 162-71 (1963); C. JENKS, HUMAN RIGHTS AND INTERNATIONAL LABOUR STANDARDS (London 1960); JENKS, THE INTERNATIONAL PROTECTION OF TRADE UNION FREEDOM (New York 1957); JENKS, LAW, FREEDOM, AND WELFARE (New York 1963); JOURNAL OF THE INTERNATIONAL COMMISSION OF JURISTS (contains numerous Human Rights national studies); INTER-AMERICAN INSTITUTE OF INTERNATIONAL LEGAL STUDIES, INTER-AMERICAN SYSTEM 68 (Dobbs Ferry, N.Y. 1966); Juvigny, *The Legal Protection of Human Rights at the International Level*, 18 INT'L SOC. SCI. J. 55-68 (1966); Khan, *Remarks by the Chairman*, in WASH. CONF. 401-03; Khan, *Human Rights*, in BANGKOK CONF.; Kutner, *World Habeas Corpus*, in BANGKOK CONF.; Khan, *World Habeas Corpus and the Rule of Law*, in *id.*; Khan, *World Habeas Corpus, Human Rights and World Community*, in 18 DEPAUL L.REV. 3-37 (1969); A. KIADO, SOCIALIST CONCEPT OF HUMAN RIGHTS (Budapest 1966); L. KUTNER, WORLD HABEAS CORPUS (New York 1962); Kutner, *World Habeas Corpus: A Legal Ligament for Political Diversity*, in WASH. CONF. 362-74; Kutner, *World Habeas Corpus, Human Rights and the World Community*, in GENEVA CONF. 430-38; L. LACHANCE, LE DROIT ET LES DROITS DE L'HOMME (Paris 1959); Lauterpacht, *Some Concepts of Human Rights*, 11 HOW. L.J. 264-75 (1965); H. LAUTERPACHT, AN INTERNATIONAL BILL OF THE RIGHTS OF MAN (New York 1945); LAUTERPACHT, INTERNATIONAL LAW AND HUMAN RIGHTS (New York 1950); Lauterpacht, *The International Protection of Human Rights*, 70 RECUEIL DES COURS 1-108 (1947); Lee, *Human Rights and World Order*, in GENEVA CONF. 422-26; Lerner, *The Crime of Incitement to Group Hatred*, in WASH. CONF. 705-11; Luini del Russo, *Dimensions and Relevance of Human Rights Under the Rule of Law*, in *id.* at 327-42; Luino Del Russo, *The Human Person and Fundamental Freedoms in Europe*, 11 HOW. L. J. 420-29 (1965); R. MacIVER, GREAT EXPRESSIONS OF HUMAN RIGHTS (New York 1950); McDougal & Befr, *Human Rights in the United Nations*, 58 AJIL 603-41 (1964); McWhinney, *The New Canadian Bill of Rights*, 10 AM. J. COMP. L. 87-98 (1961); P. MODINOS, INTRO-

(Continued)

objective to build a world of peace and order with justice in which violence is controlled and the freedom of the individual is protected by all needed safeguards.

DUCTION TO THE STUDY OF HUMAN RIGHTS (Strasbourg 1963); C. MORRISSON, THE DEVELOPING EUROPEAN LAW OF HUMAN RIGHTS (Leyden 1967); M. MOSKOWITZ, HUMAN RIGHTS AND WORLD ORDER (New York 1958); M. MOSKOWITZ, THE POLITICS AND DYNAMICS OF HUMAN RIGHTS (New York 1968); Mousheng, *The Human Rights Program*, in ANNUAL REVIEW OF UNITED NATIONS AFFAIRS, 1961-1962, at 102-36 (1963); Nathanson, *Human Rights in Japan Through the Looking Glass of Supreme Court Opinions*, 11 HOW. L.J. 316-25 (1965); Nawaz, *The Concept of Human Rights in Islamic Law, id.* at 325-33; Obuchi, *On Fundamental Human Rights*, 44 OSAKA L. REV. 1 (1963); ONTARIO HUMAN RIGHTS COMMISSION, HUMAN RIGHTS AND RACE RELATIONS, A BIBLIOGRAPHY (Toronto 1964); Pahlavi, *Remarks by the Honorary Chairman*, in GENEVA CONF. 398-401; Perez, *Medidas Internacionales de Protennión de los Derechos Humanos*, 2 ANN. URU. DER. INT'L 275-316 (1963); Perovic, *Man, Rights and Law*, in BANGKOK CONF.; Peselj, *Recent Codification of Human Rights in Socialist Constitutions*, 11 HOW. L.J. 342-56 (1965); Rabbath, *La Théorie des Droits de l'Homme dans le Droit Musulman*, 11 REV. INT'L DR. COMP. 672-96 (1959); Rabinowicz, *Human Rights in Israel*, 11 HOW. L.J. 300-16 (1965); Rendon, *La Protección de los Derechos Humanos en el Plano Universal*, 24 REV. JUR. PERU 1000-12 (1966); Rivero, *Le Système Français de Protection des Droits de l'Homme*, 1 J. INT'L & COMP. L. 70-78 (1968); Robertson, *World Paper on Human Rights*, in GENEVA CONF. 404-18; A. ROBERTSON, HUMAN RIGHTS IN NATIONAL AND INTERNATIONAL LAW (New York 1968); A. ROBERTSON, HUMAN RIGHTS IN EUROPE . . . (New York 1963); Roullet, *Comments on Human Rights*, In GENEVA CONF. 438-39; D. SANDIFER, THE RELATIONSHIP BETWEEN THE RESPECT FOR HUMAN RIGHTS AND THE EFFECTIVE EXERCISE OF REPRESENTATIVE DEMOCRACY (Washington 1962); D. SANDIFER & L. SCHEMAN, THE FOUNDATIONS OF FREEDOM: THE INTER-RELATIONSHIP BETWEEN DEMOCRACY AND HUMAN RIGHTS (New York 1965); E. SCHWELB, HUMAN RIGHTS AND THE INTERNATIONAL COMMUNITY (Dobbs Ferry, N.Y. 1964); G. A. SELEVANOFF, HISTORICAL REVIEW OF THE RIGHTS OF THE INDIVIDUAL IN MODERN INTERNATIONAL LAW (Ann Arbor 1965); Sharma, *The Promotion of International Protection of Human Rights: Problems and Prospects*, 7 INT'L STUD. 262-78 (1965); J. SOLIS RUIZ, LOS DERECHOS DEL HOMBRE EN LA NUEVA EUROPA (Rome 1960); J. SODER, DIREITOS DO HOMEN (São Paulo 1960); Sørensen, *Volkerrechtlicher Schutz der Menschenrechte*, INSTITUT FÜR INTERNATIONALES RECHT 22-34 (Kiel Universität Hamburg 1965); Symposium on the International Law of Human Rights, 11 How. L.J. (1965); Tiwari, *Forms of International Organization Action for the Protection of Human Rights*, 1 INDIAN Y.B. INT'L AFF. 28-58 (1964); UNITED NATIONS, YEARBOOK ON HUMAN RIGHTS (1946) describes constitutional, legislative, and judicial developments in the field of human rights in state and other political units and contains texts of international agreements on human rights or extracts from them); Van der Ven, *The Right To Work as a Human Right*, 11 HOW. L.J. 347-413 (1965); Vasak, *Regionalization of the International Protection of Human Rights and Fundamental Freedoms*, in WASH. CONF. 356-62; Vasak, *L'Application des Droits de l'Homme et des Libertés Fondamentales par les Juridictions Nationales*, DR. COMM. & DR. NAT'L 335-51 (1965); Vasak, *National, Regional and Universal Institutions for the Promotion and Protection of Human Rights*, 1 HUMAN RIGHTS J. 165-80 (1968); Virally, *L'Acces des Particuliers à Une Instance Internationale; La Protection des Droits de l'Homme dans le Cadre Européen*, 20 MÉMOIRES PUBLIÉS PAR LA FACULTÉ DE DROIT DE GENÈVE (1964); Weiss, *The Office of the United Nations High Commissioner for Refugees and Human Rights*, 1 J. INT'L & COMP. L. 243-55 (1968); William, *Address*, 11 HOW. L.J. 379-86 (1965); Q. WRIGHT, HUMAN RIGHTS AND THE WORLD ORDER (New York 1943); Baquerizo, *Respect for Fundamental Human Rights as a Necessary Basis for Peace*, in WASH. CONF. 618-24.

To establish a climate in which the protection of human rights can be assured, intensive efforts must be made to provide man with adequate food, clothing, health, education, and other elements of a decent life in which he will have the opportunity to maintain a meaningful existence. In an impoverished society in which men are ignorant and diseased, personal freedom and human dignity are almost impossible. Competent, dedicated, and independent public officials must be found to care for the needs and interests of citizens and to safeguard their rights.

Increasing protection for human rights is a major—if not the major—common interest of mankind. And, nationally and internationally, the protection of these rights by law has grown enormously. This chapter chronicles the past, and indicates the ideas, principles, agencies and machinery out of which mankind's common interest can grow into a worldwide reality.

§ 8-2. Human Rights Activity to 1945[2]

Human rights have roots that go far back into history. Concern for human rights has been traced to the Code of Hammurabi of the 21st century B.C., to the philosphers of Greece and the equity of Rome, and to the Judaeo-Christian belief in the equality and brotherhood of man.

In England, the Magna Charta limited the absolute power of kings and made possible the redress of injuries by independent tribunals. The Habeas Corpus Acts of 1640 and 1679 established the law of personal liberty. The Bill of Rights of 1689 further limited the power of the Crown and protected important rights of the citizen. The Act of Settlement of 1701 established the independence of the judiciary. Certain treaties of the 17th and 18th centuries provided guarantees for freedom of religion.

At the end of the 18th century, a valuable inter-penetration of English, French, and American ideas developed in the field of human rights. The ideas of the French philosophers and encyclopedists, such as Rousseau and Diderot, as well as the British tradition of political liberty and rule of law inspired the American Declaration of Independence of 1776, the American Constitution of 1789, and its Bill of Rights in 1791. These American documents

---

[2]*See* Rimanque, *Human Rights, Legal Implications in an Historical and Philosophic Context,* 7 WD. JUST. 170-93 (1965); A. ROBERTSON, HUMAN RIGHTS IN PERSPECTIVE: AN HISTORICAL INTRODUCTION (Strasbourg 1965); SECRETARIAT, UNITED NATIONS, UNITED NATIONS WORK FOR HUMAN RIGHTS (New York 1962); J. VERZIJL, HUMAN RIGHTS IN HISTORICAL PERSPECTIVE: DOCUMENTS (Haarlem 1958).

in turn influenced the French Declaration of the Rights of Man and of the Citizen (1789). But, unfortunately, the years following these great pronouncements, except for the outlawing of slavery, showed few achievements in the protection of individual rights, and slavery, itself, while outlawed, was not completely abolished. Even the League of Nations Covenant was silent on the protection of fundamental personal freedoms, although it recognized the need for international control in limited areas of human rights, especially the protection of minorities. The International Labour Organization made important progress toward recognizing the individual as a subject of the protection of law, and united representatives of employers and workers with those of governments in drafting treaties which secured economic and social rights for individuals.

§ 8-3. Human Rights Activities of the United Nations[3]

The United Nations, prompted by a deep desire to prevent a recurrence of the atrocities perpetrated upon individuals in World War II, declared, in the *Charter*,[4] a ". . . faith in fundamental human rights, in the dignity and worth of the human person, in the equal rights of men and women . . ." (Preamble) and "universal respect for, and observance of, human rights and fundamental freedoms for all without distinction as to race, sex, language, or religion." (Art. 55)

---

[3] *See generally* Buergenthal, *The United Nations and the Development of Rules Relating to Human Rights,* in ASIL PROC. 132-36 (1965); R. CHAKRAVARTI, HUMAN RIGHTS AND THE UNITED NATIONS (Calcutta 1968); Guyomar, *Nations Unies et Organisations Regionales dans la Protection des Droits de l'Homme,* REV. GÉN. DR. INT'L P. 687-707 (1964); Henkin, *The United Nations and Human Rights,* 18 INT'L ORG. 504-17 (1965); Humphrey, *The United Nations and Human Rights,* 11 HOW. L.J. 373-79 (1965); C. MALIK, HUMAN RIGHTS IN THE UNITED NATIONS (New York 1952); Nanda, *The United Nations and Regional Arrangements To Implement Human Rights,* in BANGKOK CONF.; Quintano Ripollés, *La Protección de los Derechos Humanos en lo Universal y lo Regional. O.N.U. y Consejo de Europa,* 14 REV. ESPA. DER. INT'L 537-52 (1961); Schreiber, *The United Nations and Human Rights,* in GENEVA CONF. 427-29 (1969); Schwelb, *The United Nations and Human Rights,* 11 HOW. L.J. 356-73 (1965); *The United Nations Seminar on the Role of the Police in the Protection of Human Rights,* 34 CURRENT NOTES 42-46 (1963); UNITED NATIONS, YEARBOOK ON HUMAN RIGHTS (1946) (describes constitutional, legislative, and judicial developments in the field of human rights in states and other political units and contains texts of international agreements on human rights or extracts from them); UNITED NATIONS, DEPARTMENT OF PUBLIC INFORMATION, TEACHING HUMAN RIGHTS (New York 1963).

[4] N. ROBINSON, HUMAN RIGHTS AND FUNDAMENTAL FREEDOMS IN THE CHARTER OF THE UNITED NATIONS (New York 1945); LEGISLATIVE REFERENCE SERVICE, HUMAN RIGHTS, DOMESTIC JURISDICTION, AND THE UNITED NATIONS CHARTER (Washington 1953).

§ 8-3.1. **The Universal Declaration of Human Rights** [5]   The UN
Charter announced that one of its principal objects was to promote
universal respect for human rights, but did not define these rights
or provide for their legal protection.   Toward this end, a Human
Rights Commission was established.   In 1948, this Commission
submitted a draft Universal Declaration of Human Rights which
was adopted on December 10, 1948.   Basically, the Declaration is
an impressive statement of those fundamental rights and freedoms
considered "a common standard of achievement for all peoples
and nations."   It was not conceived, however, as a binding legal
instrument creating in each state a legal obligation of compliance.
Nonetheless, its influence has been very significant: its language
and spirit have affected the substantive law of various countries
and have led to the incorporation of human rights provisions in
the national constitutions of some states and reference to the
Declaration in the constitutions of other states.   The broad recognition of the Declaration points toward its acceptance as a part of
customary international law.

§ 8-3.2. **Human Rights Covenants and Conventions.** [6]   With
the adoption of the Universal Declaration of Human Rights in

---

[5] R. BALDWIN, HUMAN RIGHTS, WORLD DECLARATION AND AMERICAN PRAC-
TICE (New York 1950); Barclay, *La Declaration Universelle des Droits de l'Homme, La
Charte de l'O.N.U. et la Religion*, REV. DR. INT'L 23-31 (Sottile 1964); Cassin, *La Declaration Universelle et la Mise en Oeuvre des Droits de l'Homme*, 79 RECUEIL DES COURS
237-96 (1951); Gardner, *Fifteenth Anniversary of Universal Declaration of Human Rights*,
50 DEP'T STATE BULL. 19-24 (1964); C. GARCIA BAUER, LOS DERECHOS HUMAN-
OS—PREOCUPACIÓN UNIVERSAL (Guatemala 1960); Kunz, *The United Nations Dec-
laration of Human Rights*, 43 AJIL 316-23 (1949); Mirkine-Guetzévitch, *Quelques Prob-
lèmes de la Mise en Oeuvre de la Déclaration Universelle des Droits de l'Homme*, 83
RECUEIL DES COURS 255-376 (1953); Padilla, *Universal Declaration of Human Rights:
Expression of Past Achievements and Future Aspirations*, 37 PHIL. L.J. 739-47 (1962);
A. ROBERTSON, *supra* note 2; N. ROBINSON, THE UNIVERSAL DECLARATION OF
HUMAN RIGHTS (New York 1950); E. SCHWELB, HUMAN RIGHTS AND THE INTER-
NATIONAL COMMUNITY: THE ROOTS AND GROWTH OF THE UNIVERSAL DEC-
LARATION OF HUMAN RIGHTS, 1948-1963 (Chicago 1964); SECRETARIAT, UNITED
NATIONS, THE UNIVERSAL DECLARATION OF HUMAN RIGHTS: A STANDARD
OF ACHIEVEMENT (New York 1963).

[6] *See generally* BRITISH INSTITUTE OF INTERNATIONAL AND COMPARATIVE
LAW, THE EUROPEAN CONVENTION ON HUMAN RIGHTS (Ser. 5, No. 11 1965);
Carey, *Implementing Human Rights Conventions: The Soviet View*, 53 KY. L.J. 115-34
(1964); *International Convention on the Elimination of All Forms of Racial Discrimination*, text in 60 AJIL 650-61 (1966); Hassan, *The International Covenants on Human
Rights: Problems of Interpretation*, in BANGKOK CONF.; MacBride, *Le Droit de l'Homme
et les Convention Humanitaires*, 16 ANN. DR. INT'L MED. (1967); Morier, *The Declaration of the Rights of the Child*, 3 INT'L REV. R.C. 227-33 (1963); Schwelb, *International
Conventions on Human Rights*, 9 INT'L COMP. L.Q. 654-75 (1960); Schwelb, *The International Convention on the Elimination of Racial Discrimination*, 12 INT'L COMP. L.Q.
996-1068 (1966); Starr, *International Protection of Human Rights and the United Nations*

(Continued)

1948,[7] drafted by Rene Cassin, former President of the European Court of Human Rights, it was decided that a covenant to implement this Declaration should be drafted. In 1952, the General Assembly decided that there should be two separate covenants and requested the Human Rights Commission to draft an International Covenant on Economic, Social and Cultural Rights and an International Covenant on Civil and Political Rights. In 1954, the Commission submitted its two drafts to the General Assembly, and they were adopted by the United Nations in 1966.[8] As of December 31, 1969, each had been signed by 44 nations, and ratified by six: 35 ratifications are required before they will enter into force. Both covenants recognize the right of peoples to self-determination and prohibit all forms of discrimination in the enjoyment of human rights.

A state ratifying the Covenant on Economic, Social and Cultural Rights recognizes everyone's right to work, to fair wages, to social security, to adequate standards of living and freedom from hunger, and to health and education. The state acknowledges its responsibility to promote better living conditions for its people and to ensure the rights of everyone to form and join trade unions. To implement this Covenant, ECOSOC, the Specialized Agencies, and the Commission on Human Rights will comment on periodic reports submitted by the parties, and ECOSOC may then report and make recommendations to the General Assembly.

A state ratifying the Covenant on Civil and Political Rights undertakes to protect its people by law against cruel, inhumane or degrading treatment. The state further recognizes the right of every individual to life, liberty, security and privacy; the right of freedom of thought, conscience and religion; the right of peaceful assembly and association; the right of freedom to consent to marriage; and the obligation to protect children. It prohibits slavery, guarantees the right to a fair trial and to the cultural, religious, and linguistic heritage of minorities, and protects persons against arbitrary arrest or detention. To implement this Covenant, a Human Rights Com-

---

Covenants, 1967 WIS. L. REV. 863-90 (1967); J. SIMSARIAN, ECONOMIC, SOCIAL AND CULTURAL PROVISIONS IN THE HUMAN RIGHTS COVENANT (Washington 1951); UN Office of Public Information, Newsletter, International Year for Human Rights Annex 1–Status of International Conventions on Human Rights as of 1 December 1967 at 44; UNESCO, HUMAN RIGHTS COVENANTS AND INTERPRETATIONS (London 1950).

[7]G.A. Res. 217A (III), U.N. Doc. A/810 at 71-7 (1948).

[8]*International Covenant on Economic, Social and Cultural Rights* and the *International Covenant on Civil and Political Rights,* G.A. Res. 2200, 21 U.N. GAOR Supp. 16 at 49, U.N. Doc. A 16316 (1966).

mittee will be established. This Committee will comment, to both the state concerned and ECOSOC, on reports which states submit.

An optional procedure deals with international complaints, covering negotiations between the states concerned, the good offices of the Human Rights Committee and the appointment of an *ad hoc* Conciliation Committee.

An optional protocol to this Covenant provides for the right of the individual to petition the Human Rights Committee to examine his claim that a state party to the Covenant has violated rights established in the Covenant. The Committee will consider the claim in private session, forward its observations to the state and to the individual concerned, and include a summary of its activities in its annual report to the General Assembly.

Another important development toward the establishment of a worldwide legal framework to protect human rights is the adoption by the UN General Assembly on December 21, 1965, of the Convention on the Elimination of All Forms of Racial Discrimination.[9] As of December 31, 1969, 72 states had signed, and 37 ratified this Convention. The Convention provides that the contracting parties will declare all dissemination of ideas based on racial superiority or hatred and all incitement to racial discrimination to be offenses punishable by law. The Convention further provides for the creation of a Committee of 18 experts to make suggestions and recommendations to the General Assembly based on reports submitted by states party to the Convention. The Committee will communicate to the party concerned any allegation of violation of the Convention by that party, and if the latter does not submit to the Committee for clarification of the matter and if the states fail to adjust the matter satisfactorily between themselves, either state may refer it again to the Committee, whose chairman must then appoint an *ad hoc* Conciliation Commission. The Convention also provides procedures dealing with petitions for redress of grievances.

Other major human rights covenants and conventions passed by the UN General Assembly include the Convention on the Prevention and Punishment of the Crime of Genocide,[10] with as of December 31, 1969, 43 signatures, and 74 ratifications, acceptances, accessions or successions; the Protocol Amending the Slavery Convention signed at Geneva on September 25, 1926,[11] with 29 signatures and

---

[9] G.A. Res. 2106, 20 U.N. GAOR Supp. 14 at 49, U.N. Doc. A/6014 (1966).

[10] *Opened for signature* December 9, 1948, 78 U.N.T.S. 277.

[11] *Opened for signature,* December 7, 1953, 182 U.N.T.S. 51.

50 ratifications, acceptances, accessions or successions; the Supplementary Convention on the Abolition of Slavery, the Slave Trade, and Institutions and Practices Similar to Slavery,[12] with 39 signatures and 75 ratifications, acceptances, accessions or successions; the Convention on the Nationality of Married Women,[13] with 26 signatures and 42 ratifications, acceptances, accessions or successions; the Convention on the Reduction of Statelessness,[14] with 5 signatures and 2 ratifications, acceptances, accessions or successions; the Convention Relating to the Status of Stateless Persons,[15] with 22 signatures and 22 ratifications, acceptances, accessions or successions; the Convention Relating to the Status of Refugees,[16] with 20 signatures, and 58 ratifications, acceptances, accessions or successions; the Protocol Relating to the Status of Refugees,[17] with 37 ratifications, acceptances, accessions or successions; the Convention on the Political Rights of Women,[18] with 46 signatures and 65 ratifications, acceptances, accessions or successions; the Convention on Consent to Marriage, Minimum Age for Marriages, and Registration of Marriages,[19] with 19 signatures and 22 ratifications, acceptances, accessions or successions; and the Convention on the Non-Applicability of Statutory Limitations of War Crimes and Crimes Against Humanity,[20] with 11 signatures and 8 ratifications, acceptances, accessions or successions.

§ 8-3.3. **The International Labour Organization.** The International Labour Organization, founded in 1919, has as its central aim the attainment of conditions in which all human beings, irrespective of race, creed, or sex, have a right to live and develop in conditions of freedom, dignity, economic security, and equal opportunity. The ILO formulates and implements international labor standards by conventions and recommendations, engages in research, carries on educational activities and promotes human rights by technical international cooperation. To date it has adopted 130 Conventions and 134 Recommendations creating standards for the entire field of social policy. These Conventions form an international labor code in which the ultimate aim is to secure rights recognized by

---

[12] *Opened for signature* September 7, 1956, 266 U.N.T.S. 3.

[13] *Opened for signature* February 20, 1957, 309 U.N.T.S. 65.

[14] G.A. Res. 896, 9 U.N. GAOR Supp. 21 at 49, U.N. Doc. A/2890 (1961).

[15] *Opened for signature* September 28, 1954, 360 U.N.T.S. 117.

[16] *Opened for signature* July 28, 1951, 189 U.N.T.S. 137.

[17] *Opened for signature* January 31, 1967, 606 U.N.T.S.

[18] *Opened for signature* March 31, 1953, 193 U.N.T.S. 135.

[19] *Opened for signature* December 10, 1962, 521 U.N.T.S. 231.

[20] G.A. Res. 2391, 23 U.N. GAOR Supp. 18 at 40, U.N. Doc. A/7218 (1968).

the Universal Declaration of Human Rights and the International Covenants on Human Rights, but ILO's Conventions were in existence many years prior to the adoption of the Declaration and the Covenants. See § 3-2.3 for a list of these conventions.

As of December 31, 1969, The Forced Labour Convention (No. 29)[21] had been ratified by 105 states; the Abolition of Forced Labour Convention (No. 105),[22] by 88 states; the Freedom of Association and Protection of the Rights to Organize Convention (No. 87),[23] by 77 states; the Right to Organize and Collective Bargaining Convention (No. 98),[24] by 90 states; the Equal Remuneration Convention (No. 100),[25] by 69 states; Discrimination (Employment and Occupation) Convention (No. 111),[26] by 71 states; and the Employment Policy Convention (No. 122),[27] by 29 states. In 1969 (2-11 December), the ILO conducted a Regional Seminar on Equality of Opportunity in Employment in Manila, with 15 participants who held conferences with representatives of Governments, employers' and workers' groups. ILO conducts many similar Seminars and Conferences in its wide ranging and dynamic programs. Programs which are of great benefit to all mankind, as they help elevate the standard of living of the peoples of many nations.

§ 8-3.4. **The UN Food and Agriculture Organization.** The right to adequate nourishment is the most elementary aspect of man's right to life. The provision of adequate food is essential to collective security and international peace. Accordingly, the FAO aims to assure man's freedom from hunger and want. Between 1951 and 1966, it carried out more than 4,000 technical assistance projects, costing $140 million. By 1967, it had undertaken 308 Special Funds projects leading to development investment involving billions of dollars. The FAO World Food Program supports programs of economic and social development and relieves emergency situations. Its Freedom from Hunger Campaign aims to win the war on hunger by massive public support. It has developed an Indicative World Plan for Agricultural Development in an attempt to measure future world needs of food, trade, and development; has held a world

---

[21] *Opened for signature* June 28, 1930, 39 U.N.T.S. 55.

[22] *Opened for signature* June 25, 1957, 320 U.N.T.S. 291-301.

[23] *Opened for signature* July 9, 1948, 68 U.N.T.S. 17

[24] *Opened for signature* July 1, 1949, 96 U.N.T.S. 257.

[25] *Opened for signature* June 29, 1951, 165 U.N.T.S. 303.

[26] *Opened for signature* June 25, 1958, 362 U.N.T.S. 31.

[27] Convention (No. 122) Concerning Employment Policy. For text see INTERNATIONAL LABOUR ORGANIZATION, ILO CONVENTIONS AND RECOMMENDATIONS 1097 (1966).

conference to involve the world's youth directly in the struggle against hunger; and has taken steps to provide just and equitable conditions for the farmer, including reforms in land tenure.

§ 8-3.5. The UN Educational, Scientific and Cultural Organization. This organization aims, according to its constitution, to "contribute to peace and security by promoting collaboration among the nations through education, science and culture in order to further universal respect for justice, for the rule of law and for the human rights and fundamental freedoms . . . ."[28]

UNESCO's activities help to create the moral, intellectual and cultural pre-conditions of human rights. One of its basic aims has been to define human rights and to make them known and understood by people throughout the world. It has been especially active in promoting the rights to education, culture, and freedom of information, all enumerated in the Universal Declaration of Human Rights. It has worked for the improvement and extension of education throughout the world, for the equality of educational opportunity for all people, and for the promotion of understanding and respect for human rights. It has assisted states in the development of their own cultures and encouraged mutual appreciation of other cultures. It has campaigned against discrimination in the field of education, by its Convention against Discrimination in Education,[29] ratified by or accepted by 53 states which precludes "any distinction, exclusion, limitation or preference which, being based on race, color, sex, language, religion, political or other opinion, national or social origin, or economic condition of birth, has the purpose or effect of nullifying or impairing equality of treatment in education."

On May 27, 1970, the United Nations Economic and Social Council voted to adopt new procedures which would permit greater latitude to individuals who allege the violation of Human Rights. Formerly, the filing of such complaints was restricted to State Governmental representatives, but, under the new rules, non-governmental international organizations are now permitted to file such complaints on behalf of individuals.

§ 8-3.6. The World Health Organization. The Preamble to the WHO Constitution that "the enjoyment of the highest attainable standard of health is one of the fundamental rights of every human

---

[28] Constitution of the United Nations Educational, Scientific and Cultural Organization, *done* November 16, 1945, 61 Stat. 2495, T.I.A.S. 1580, 4 U.N.T.S. 275.

[29] *Done* December 14, 1960, 429 U.N.T.S. 93-121.

being without distinction of race, religion, political belief, economic and social conditions."[30] Without health, which includes physical, mental and social well-being, other rights have little significance. WHO has emphasized in its programs the development of rural health services, improvement of sanitation and health education, and the integration of specialized programs into general health services. It has assisted governments in evaluating the type of occupational health program that is needed to train nationals and to assist in undertaking various control measures. The importance of this work and the vastness of the challenge is evidenced by the alarming fact that over two-thirds of the world's population is still suffering from malnutrition.

§ 8-3.7. **The United Nations Children's Fund.** This Fund aims, among other things, to implement the provisions of the Declaration of the Rights of the Child adopted by the United Nations on November 20, 1959. That Declaration states that the child shall enjoy protection that will enable him to develop in a healthy and normal manner in freedom and dignity, that he is entitled to receive free and compulsory education, and that he shall be protected from practices fostering discrimination. UNICEF maintains that good health is a basic human right. Accordingly, it has assisted in establishing and operating maternal and child health services and, through nutrition education, attempts to improve the diet of millions in the developing countries. UNICEF helps to protect children against leprosy, malaria and other diseases and to provide teachers and equipment for various types of schools.

§ 8-3.8. **Other UN Agencies Engaged in Human Rights.** Other UN agencies active in the field of human rights include: the Office of the United Nations High Commissioner for Refugees, which enables refugees to be self-supporting, restoring their sense of dignity and relieving refugee movement tensions; the United Nations Relief and Works Agency for Palestine Refugees in the Near East, which has fed and kept in basic health a refugee population which in 1967 numbered about 1.3 million people; and the United Nations Development Programme, which supports development projects to help low-income countries realize the productive potential of their people and their natural resources. The Development Program is described in more detail in the Chapter herein on economic development, § 6-3.1.

---

[30] Constitution of the World Health Organization, *opened for signature* July 22, 1946, 62 Stat. 2679, T.I.A.S. 1808, 14 U.N.T.S. 185.

§ 8-3.9. **A UN High Commissioner for Human Rights.**[31] Experts have recommended the appointment of a UN High Commissioner for Human Rights who would review governmental reports on human rights and report to the Economic and Social Council and to the General Assembly on violations. Like the ombudsman who performs similar functions within a particular state, the High Commissioner would serve as a protector of human rights throughout the world. The Economic and Social Council, on the recommendation of the Commission on Human Rights, has recommended to the General Assembly the adoption of a resolution to establish the Office of a High-Commissioner for Human Rights within the UN framework. The Secretary-General has been asked to request the views of UN members and report to the General Assembly on the advisability of establishing this new office.

§ 8-4. **The European Convention on Human Rights**[32]

On November 4, 1950, the representative of 15 European countries signed the European Convention for the Protection of Human

---

[31] Blix, *The Ombudsman,* 11 HOW. L.J. 386-96 (1965); *International Protection of Human Rights: The Proposal for a U.N. High Commissioner,* 5 COLUM. J. TRANSNAT'L L. 150-58 (1966).

[32] For a comprehensive bibliography on the European Convention on Human Rights, see CENTRE OF INTERNATIONAL STUDIES, UNIVERSITY OF STRASBOURG, BIBLIOGRAPHY RELATING TO THE EUROPEAN CONVENTION ON HUMAN RIGHTS (Strasbourg 1967).

See also Beddard, *The Status of the European Convention of Human Rights in Domestic Law,* 16 INT'L & COMP. L.Q. 206-16 (1967); British Institute of International and Comparative Law, *The European Convention on Human Rights,* INT'L AND COMPARATIVE LAW QUARTERLY, SUPP. NO. 11 (1965); Buergenthal, *The Effect of the European Convention on Human Rights on the Internal Law of Member States,* in BR. INST. INT'L & COMP. L. 79-106 (1965); Colloquen, *La Protection Internationale des Droits de l'Homme dans le Cadre Européen, Université de Strasbourg (Paris 1961); Human Rights in National and International Law,* PROCEEDINGS OF THE COLLOQUY HELD IN VIENNA IN 1965 (Manchester 1967); Comte, *The Application of the European Convention of Human Rights in Municipal Law,* 4 J. INT'L COM. JUR. 94-133 (1962); COUNCIL OF EUROPE, EUROPEAN CONVENTION ON HUMAN RIGHTS (Strasbourg 1963); COUNCIL OF EUROPE, EUROPEAN CONVENTION ON HUMAN RIGHTS: COLLECTED TEXTS (Strasbourg 1963); Golsong, *The Control Machinery of the European Convention on Human Rights,* in BRITISH INSTITUTE OF INTERNATIONAL AND COMPARATIVE LAW 38-69 (1965); EUROPEAN COMMISSION ON HUMAN RIGHTS, DOCUMENTS AND DECISIONS (The Hague 1955-1957); Fawcett, *Some Aspects of the Practice of the Commission of Human Rights,* 11 INT'L & COMP. L. SUPP. 70 (1965); Gerbino, *Considerazioni sugli Effeti della Sentenza della Corte Europea dei Diritto dell' Uomo,* 3 REV. EUR. 14-24 (1963); Golsong, *The European Convention on Human Rights Before Domestic Courts,* 38 BR. Y.B. INT'L L. 445-56 (1964); Greenberg & Shalit, *New Horizons for Human Rights: The European Convention, Court, and Commission of Human Rights,* 63 COLUM. L. REV. 1384-1412 (1963); G. WEIL, THE EUROPEAN CONVENTION ON HUMAN RIGHTS (Leyden 1963); McNulty, *The European Convention on Human Rights: Its Sanctions and Practice,* in BRITISH INSTITUTE OF INTERNATIONAL AND COMPARATIVE LAW 75-78 (1965); Modinos, *Effects and Repercussions of the European*

(Continued)

Rights and Fundamental Freedoms. On March 20, 1952, they adopted a Protocol to this Convention which assures the protection of three additional rights. The adoption of this Convention fulfilled one of the major objectives outlined in the Statute of the Council of Europe signed in London on May 5, 1959. Article 3 of the Statute reads as follows:

> Every member of the Council of Europe must accept the principles of the rule of law and the enjoyment by all persons within its jurisdiction of human rights and fundamental freedoms and collaborate sincerely and effectively in the realization of the aims of the Council as specified in Chapter One.[33]

Sixteen nations are now parties to the Convention: Austria, Belgium, Cyprus, Denmark, the Federal Republic of Germany, Greece, Iceland, Ireland, Italy, Luxembourg, Malta, the Netherlands, Norway, Sweden, Turkey and the United Kingdom. France and Switzerland have not yet ratified the Convention. Eleven states have already recognized the right of individual petition. On September 12, 1967, the Government of the United Kingdom extended the application

Convention on Human Rights, 11 INT'L & COMP. L.Q. 1097-1108 (1962); Modinos, *La Convention Européenne des Droits de l'Homme,* 1 EUR. Y.B. 141-70 (1955); Modinos, *Coexistence de la Convention Européenne des Droits de l'Homme et du Paete des Droits Civils et Politiques des Nations Unies,* 1 HUMAN RIGHTS J. 40-69 (1968); K. PARTSCH, DIE RECHTE UND FREIHEITEN DER EUROPÄISCHEN MENSCHENRECHTSKONVENTION (Berlin 1966); Robertson, *The European Convention on Human Rights: Recent Developments,* 29 BR. Y.B. INT'L L. 432-53 (1952); Robertson, *The Political Background and Historical Development of the European Convention on Human Rights,* in BR. INST. INT'L & COMP. L. 24-37 (1965); Robertson, CONSTITUTIONAL DEVELOPMENTS IN THE COUNCIL OF EUROPE: EFFECTS OF THE EUROPEAN CONVENTION ON HUMAN RIGHTS IN INTERNAL LAW AND IN OTHER CONTINENTS (Brussels 1964); Schindler, *The European Convention on Human Rights in Practice,* 2 WASH. U. L.Q. 152-65 (1962); Schwelb, *On the Operation of the European Convention of Human Rights,* 18 INT'L ORG. 558-85 (1964); Shawcross, *United Kingdom Practice on the European Convention of Human Rights,* REV. BEL. DR. INT'L 297-305 (1965); Sperduti, *La Convenzione Europea dei Diritto dell'Uome et il suo Sistema di Garanzie,* REV. DIRITTO INT'L 161-75 (1963); Vasak, *The European Convention on Human Rights Beyond the Frontiers of Europe,* 12 INT'L & COMP. L.Q. 1206-31 (1963); Vasak, LA CONVENTION EUROPÉENNE DES DROITS DE L'HOMME (Paris 1964); Vasak, *De la Convention Européenne à la Convention Africaine des Droits de l'Homme,* 16 REV. JUR. POL. d'O -M. 59-76 (1962); Verdross, *The Status of the European Convention for the Protection of Human Rights and Fundamental Freedoms in the Hierarchy of Rules of Law,* 5 INDIAN J. INT'L L. 455-63 (1965); Waldock, *Human Rights in Contemporary International Law and the Significance of the European Convention,* 11 INT'L & COMP. L. SUPP. 1 (1965); Waldock, *The European Convention for the Protection of Human Rights and Fundamental Freedoms,* 34 BR. Y.B. INT'L L. 356-63 (1958); Weil, *The Evolution of the European Convention on Human Rights,* 57 AJIL 804-27 (1963); WEIL, THE EUROPEAN CONVENTION ON HUMAN RIGHTS: BACKGROUND DEVELOPMENT AND PROSPECTS (Leiden 1963); YEARBOOK OF THE EUROPEAN CONVENTION ON HUMAN RIGHTS, 1958-1959 (annually since 1960).

[33] Statute of the Council of Europe, *done* May 5, 1949, as amended CMD. 9527-1955 and CMD. 2748-1965.

of the Convention, including the right of individual petition, to a number of overseas territories and dependencies.

Some of the rights covered in the various provisions of the Convention guarantee to all persons in the contracting states the right to life, liberty, and security of the person; freedom from torture, slavery, and servitude; freedom from arbitrary arrest, detention, or exile; the right to a fair trial; freedom from arbitrary interference in private and family life, home and correspondence; freedom of thought, conscience, and religion; freedom of opinion and expression; freedom of assembly and association; freedom to join trade unions; and the right to marry and found a family. (Articles 2-12).

Many of these provisions were based upon the Universal Declaration of Human Rights; in the European Convention, they are defined in greater detail. Also, the European Convention imposes legal obligations on its signatories, whereas the Universal Declaration does not so do.

Perhaps the most significant contribution of the European Convention is the creation of two important institutions to ensure the observance of the engagements undertaken by them; the European Commission of Human Rights and the European Court of Human Rights. Experience under the Commission and the Court is reported *supra* pages 244-46.

Since its creation, the Commission has received approximately 300 applications each year. As of 1966, it had received a total of 3,001 applications, and of those filed in 1966, over half were from the Federal Republic of Germany; 47 per cent were in custody; and only eight percent had legal representation. The great majority of total applications received by the Commission have been held inadmissible either under relevant principles of international law, or under its rules of admission. In 1966, only five out of 303 were held admissible. Among the more renowned cases the Commission has dealt with have been the Belgian linguistics problem, the Neimeister and Wemhof cases, and those dealing with the Greek question, which ultimately resulted in the voluntary withdrawal of Greece from the European Convention on Human Rights, the Commission on Human Rights, and the Council of Europe in 1969.

§ 8-5. Human Rights in the Inter-American System [34]

The American states have provided a relatively fertile soil for the recognition of human rights and fundamental freedoms. Human rights have been guaranteed for United States citizens by the Declaration of Independence in 1776 and its Bill of Rights in 1791. Influenced by the Universal Declaration of Human Rights, many other American countries have included broad guarantees of human rights in their constitutions. Fundamental individual human rights were also proclaimed in the OAS Bogotá Charter,[35] the 1948 American Declaration of the Rights and Duties of Man,[36] and the American International Charter of Social Guarantees.[37] Judicial protection of human rights has been promoted by the work of the Central American Court of Justice (1908-1918), by proposed OAS Council studies on the protection of human rights and on the advisability of establishing an Inter-American Court of Human Rights, and by the discussion at the third Judicial Conference of the Americas held in San Juan, Puerto Rico, June 19-21, 1968, of the responsibility of the judiciary and of the lawyer in the protection of human rights.

To implement the pronouncements of these various acts, declarations and resolutions, the Council of the Organization of American States created in 1959, an Inter-American Commission of Human Rights, the objective of which is to gather information on human rights problems, carry out studies, serve as an advisory body on

---

[34] *See generally* Camargo, *The Protection of Human Rights in America*, in WASH. CONF. 349-56; CAMARGO, LA PROTECCIÓN JURÍDICA DE LOS DERECHIOS HUMANOS Y DE LA DEMOCRACIA EN AMÉRICA (Mexico 1960); Dunshee de Abranches, *Special Protection of Human Rights in the Dominican Republic*, in WASH. CONF. 343-49; *Inter-American Draft Convention on Human Rights*, 4 J. INT'L COM. 160-84 (1962); CODIFICATION DIVISION, PAN AMERICAN UNION, HUMAN RIGHTS IN THE AMERICAN STATES (Washington 1960); Sandifer, *Human Rights in the Inter-American System*, 11 HOW. L.J. 508-26 (1965); Scheman, *The Inter-American Commission on Human Rights*, 59 AJIL 335-43 (1965); Thomas & Thomas, *The Inter-American Commission on Human Rights*, 19 S.W. L.J. 282-309 (1965); *Statute of the Inter-American Commission of Human Rights*, J. INT'L & COMP. L. 144-59 (1968); VASAK, LA COMMISSION INTERAMERICANE DES DROITS DE L'HOMME (Paris 1968); Vasak, *Des Droits de l'Homme: La Commission Interamericane*, 1 HUMAN RIGHTS J. 109-12 (1968); Vasak, *La Protection Internationale de Droits de l'Homme sur le Continent Americain*, OST. Z. OF. R. 113-22 (1967).

[35] Charter of the Organization of American States, *done* April 30, 1948, 2 U.S.T. 2394, T.I.A.S. 2361, 119 U.N.T.S. 3.

[36] American Declaration of the Rights and Duties of Man. Resolution XXX, Final Act, Ninth International Conference of American States, Bogotá, Colombia, March 30-May 2, 1948, TCAS 2nd Supp. 263 (1948). *See* 43 AJIL SUPP. 133 (1948) for text.

[37] Inter-American Charter of Social Guarantees, Resolution XXIX, Final Act, Ninth International Conference of American States, Bogotá, Colombia, March 30-May 2, 1948, TCAS 2nd Supp. 254 (1948).

human rights, make recommendations to OAS member governments, and make people in the American states more aware of human rights and the need for their protection. From 1960 to 1965, the Commission handled more than 2,000 complaints or communications alleging the violation of human rights. It has also made valuable studies and reports.

The activities of the Commission in the crisis of the Dominican Republic is an impressive example of the international protection of human rights. The presence of the Commission in the Dominican Republic was requested by the "Government of National Reconstruction" and by the "Constitutional Government" which agreed to respect and enforce observance of the human rights Declaration of Bogota and to extend to the Commission all facilities needed for fulfillment of its mission. On the basis of these agreements, the Commission examined 1,105 complaints and communications regarding violations, requested the two governments to prevent or put an end to violations, visited various installations to inform itself of the conditions of political prisoners, succeeded in some cases in improving the conditions of prisoners and the freeing of others held on mere suspicion, obtained the cooperation of Boards of Investigation and Review, addressed reports on the treatment of prisoners to the competent authorities, and handled various cases presented to it. By the Institutional Act and the Act of Reconciliation, which ended the civil war in the Dominican Republic, the Provisional Government obligated itself to respect and enforce respect for human rights and fundamental freedoms enunciated in the American Declaration of Rights and Duties of Man and in the Universal Declaration of Human Rights and to cooperate with the Commission in order to obtain compliance with human rights provisions.

In Cuba, repeated and serious violations of fundamental human rights were reported to the Commission, which requested relevant information from the Cuban Government. Since this information was not provided, the Commission published a report which contained a summary of the complaints of the most flagrant alleged violations of human rights. Further denunciations led the Commission to request the consent of appropriate Cuban authorities to authorize it to visit the territory of Cuba to observe the situation at first hand. This request and subsequent requests received no answer. The Commission accordingly took the testimony of persons who had served prison terms in Cuba, and in May 1963, published a report on their findings. The Commission continued to transmit denunciations of serious crimes to Cuban authorities and made repeated requests for authorization to visit the territory to observe the situation at first hand. In April 1967, the Commission published another report on the Cuban situation, since it had received no replies to its requests.

A similar situation developed in the Commission's investigations in Haiti. When the Haitian Government failed to provide adequate information for the Commission, a request was made to visit the territory to determine the validity of the complaints on the scene. When this request was denied, the Commission published a report on the Haitian situation in 1963, and a later report in 1967.

The Commission has received allegations of human rights violations in Paraguay, Guatemala, Nicaragua, Ecuador, El Salvador and Honduras. The government of Paraguay authorized the Commission to visit its territory and such a visit led to the publication of a classified report. Failure of the government of Guatemala to furnish information to the Commission led to the publication of the notes sent, including the texts of charges and complaints. In Nicaragua, the denial of election rights was the subject of complaints. The Nicaraguan government offered information concerning the complaints but refused to authorize the Commission to visit the country as requested. It stated that violations would be taken to the proper courts and that the Commission would be informed when court decisions were handed down. When the Commission informed the Government of Ecuador of reports of violations of human rights, that Government not only sent the information requested, but also extended an invitation to the Commission to visit the country and study the situation at first hand, but due to other circumstances, the Commission was unable to do so. The Commission also received complaints alleging the violation of human rights in Honduras, and transmitted these to the Honduran authorities requesting information concerning the allegations. The Government of Honduras sent the information and invited the Commission to send representatives to investigate the reports. The Commission authorized the Chairman to prepare the investigation committee. In 1969, the Governments of El Salvador and Honduras complained to the Commission that their nationals in the other country were being discriminated against, and that their human rights were being violated solely because of their nationality. The Commission visited both countries, and following its investigations, recommended that both Governments cease such activities, indemnify citizens who had been injured, and institute measures to prevent newspaper and radio propaganda that would tend to arouse the commission of further human rights' violations.

In November 1969, at the meeting of the Inter-American Specialized Conference on Human Rights, the American Convention on

Human Rights[38] was signed by 12 nations: Chile, Colombia, Costa Rica, Ecuador, El Salvador, Guatemala, Honduras, Nicaragua, Panama, Paraguay, Uruguay and Venezuela. As of June 1970, there had been one ratification—Costa Rica—and before the Convention can enter into force, 11 states must ratify it.

§ 8-6. Human Rights in Africa and Asia

Much needs to be accomplished to promote the full realization of human rights goals in Africa and in Asia. The drafting of an African Convention of Human Rights and the creation of an Inter-African Commission on Human Rights have been widely discussed but have not yet become the subject of official proposals. Although the idea of an Asian Convention of Human Rights has been suggested, no official action has been taken, and it seems improbable that such a convention could be implemented in the near future, even if adopted.

§ 8-7. Human Rights in Islam and Muslim States[39]

Islam regards the dignity of man as foremost. The *Qu'ran* refers to "justice" 22 times and warns against persecution 299 times, denounces aggression eight times, and warns against human violations 20 times.[40]

> Islamic Law is purely individualistic, insofar as the right of every single member of the community to share public responsibility with the Calif is recognized. Any individual has the right to correct the Calif and to attack his decisions if he commits an error. Moreover, positive Islamic Law on the whole is a system of subject rights and personal privileges for all individuals as demonstrated by the text dealing with the principle of "original freedom" and the unviolability of life, liberty, property and honor.
>
> The individual is regarded in Islam as the most important unit of the Cosmos. Born free with a right to choose, he is offered Islam: The Right Path.[41]

The maintenance of freedom, therefore, cannot be temporary, or for that matter discriminatory, for anyone outside of Islam must be given the prerogative of free choice to become a Muslim and embrace the Faith.

---

[38] *Opened for signature* November 22, 1969, O.A.S. Official Records OEA/SER. K/XVI/ 1.1. Document 65, Rev. 1, Corr. 2 as of January 7, 1970. For text see 9 I.L.M. 673 (1970).

[39] The special assistance of Professor M. Cherif Bassiouni is gratefully acknowledged in the preparation of this section.

[40] MOUSSA, ISLAM AND HUMANITY'S NEED OF IT 236 (Cairo 1966).

[41] Abdel-Wahab, *Meaning and Structure of Law in Islam*, 16 VAND. L.REV. 116 (1962).

Classic Islamic Law distinguishes between *Zimmi,* non-Muslims residing under the protective covenant of the Islamic state, because they are the people of the Book and recipient of divine revelations, and *non-Zimmi,* who are not people of the Book and have no protective covenant with the state but who also live in the Islamic state. The relationship of Muslim, *Zimmi* and *non-Zimmi* falls within the purview of internal law, while relations and human rights with people who are not living within the Islamic territory are covered by the *Siyyar* or external laws or Law of Nations.[42]

Intrastate human rights are said to be unequal as between Muslims and non-Muslims, because of the political structure of the state. The state is under the sovereignty of God, its laws depend for their validity on the *Shariah,* and the Book is the primary source of law. Muslim citizens as a whole constitute the *Ummah,* or Islamic nation; and, therefore, non-Muslims are not politically a part thereof. But in no way does this affect equality before the law or equal justice. All who live under the protective covenant of the *Shariah* are entitled to all privileges and immunities without distinction as to race, religion or national origin. The only real difference is one of authority, administration and jurisdiction. This concept of separate political administration, yet with equal justice for all, is likened to the Roman concept of jurisdiction in the *jus civile.* The analogy is misleading, because the distinction in Islam is not as to the rights of the people but as to the administration of the political and legislative process of the state. Non-Muslims are not outside the "jurisdiction" as meant by the *jus civile, orbis Romanus* simply because Muslims are not *princeps orbis terrarum* (lords of the population of the globe).[43] Neither for that matter are the protective covenants between Muslims and non-Muslims a *pax Romana,* because the *Zimmi* is equal before the law in every aspect thereof.[44] The distinction remains one of political administration and not of human rights.[45]

Translated in terms of the modern socio-political context, the Muslims constituting the majority govern and legislate but cannot affect matters specifically left to the minorities by the *Qu'ranic* mandate or by covenant. Islam foresaw the possibility of the major-

---

[42] Bassiouni, *Islam: Concept, Law and World Habeas Corpus,* 2 RUT. CAM. L.J. 160 (1970) (foreword by Mr. Justice M. Zafrulla Khan).

[43] *See* Ion, *Roman Law and Mohammedan Jurisprudence,* 6 MICH. L.REV. 44 (1908).

[44] M. HAMIDULLAH, MUSLIM CONDUCT OF STATE 150 (4th ed. 1961).

[45] *See, e.g.,* Constitution of Pakistan art. 10a, which requires that the President be a Muslim.

ity repressing the minority and specified certain rights for the non-Muslim minorities which cannot be tampered with even by the ruling majority.[46]

Freedom of religious practice, personal status matters, citizenship and protection of life, liberty and property are only but some examples of specific guarantees that have to be afforded to the minorities who live under the protective covenant of the Islamic state. One author points out that: "Whereas the Muslims are endowed with full legal capacity non-Muslims are considered not to possess the same capacity: the levy of *Jizya* is a case in point. Traditional Islamic practice indicates a definite preferential treatment and higher status for the Muslim religion in the Muslim state governed by the Islamic majority; however, this does not allow the imposition of any undue restriction on non-Muslims or interference with their religious freedom and practices. In that respect, Islamic Law is not completely restrictive.[47] On the contrary, it considers itself as most benevolent and forward-looking in comparison to other legal systems in that it guarantees the rights of minorities even if they conflict with the rights of the majority.[48]

The concept of *Jizya,* which is a tax levied on non-Muslims, has often been cited as the main discriminatory feature in Islamic human rights. The nature of this tax is not well understood, since the tax is not discriminatory, but different from similar taxes levied upon Muslims,—unless the mere fact that the tax is different constitutes inherent discrimination. Traditionally, the *Jizya* constituted a 10 percent tax on income of non-Muslims, while other taxes including the duty of the *Zakat* were imposed only upon Muslims. Furthermore, non-Muslims were not required to serve in the military or any public service duty as Muslims did.[49]

It is often said that the enjoyment of life, liberty and property is an absolute right for Muslims, subject only to the limitations of the rights of the community as a whole for the maintenance of a scheme of ordered liberty which, by its very nature, requires certain self-imposed restrictions, but that the same right to life, liberty and property is qualified for non-Muslims. While this correctly reflects

---

[46] Ahmad, *Islamic Civilization and Human Rights,* 12 REV. EGYPT. DR. INT'L 1 (1956).

[47] S. RAMADAN, ISLAMIC LAW, ITS SCOPE AND EQUITY 110-12 (1961), in which the author discusses preferential treatment to Christianity in some Constitutions.

[48] M. HAMIDULLAH, *supra* note 37 at 132, in which the author states: "The ethical basis of Islam repudiates any distinction as to justice between Muslims and non-Muslims."

[49] K. CRAGG, THE CALL OF THE MINARET 339 (1964).

medieval practices in the context of the relationship of Islam and Christendom, it is theoretically incorrect insofar as the ideal Islamic state is concerned in its relationship with other treaty states or minorities living under its protection.[50]

In modern times, the emphasis in Muslim states has been on equality, and this is demonstrated by the following constitutional provisions. The Egyptian Constitution of 1958 and provisional Constitution of the United Arab Republic, Art. 7: "All citizens are equal before the law. They are equal in their rights and obligations, without distinction of race, origin, language, religion or creed." Also, Principle 2 of the law-making principles of the Constitution of Pakistan of 1962 declares that "all citizens should be equal before the law, be entitled to equal protection of the law and be treated alike in all respects." Under that Constitution only a Muslim can be a President (see Article 9 of the Constitution). Also Article 8, Paragraph 1, of the Malayan Constitution of 1957 states: "All persons are equal before the law and entitled to equal protection of the law." Paragraph 2: "Except as expressly authorized by this constitution, there shall be no discrimination against citizens on the grounds of only religion, race, descent or the place of birth in any law or in the appointment to any office or any employment under a public authority or in the administration of any law relating to the acquisition, holding or disposition of property or the establishing or carrying on of any trade, business or profession, vocation or employment."[51]

The fundamental rights of a citizen regardless of his faith in the Islamic state, says Maududi, must be as follows:

    (a) Protection of life, honour and property;

    (b) Freedom of thought, expression, belief and worship;

    (c) Freedom of movement throughout the country;

    (d) Freedom of assembly and association;

    (e) Freedom of adopting any profession or occupation and the right to own, acquire and dispose of property; and

    (f) Equality of opportunity in all walks of life, and equal right of benefiting from all public institutions.[52]

---

[50] *See* Ahmad, *supra* note 39, at 16-21.

[51] *See also* Groves, *Fundamental Liberties of Malaya—A Comparative Study,* 5 HOW. L.J. 190 (1957).

[52] *Islamic Law and Constitution* 393 (Lahore 3d ed. 1967). *See also* Schacht, *Islamic Law in Contemporary States,* 8 AM. J. COMP. L. 133 (1959).

§ 8-8. The International Year for Human Rights, 1968[53]

The United Nations declared the Year 1968 as the International Year for Human Rights to commemorate the 20th anniversary of the Universal Declaration of Human Rights. In preparation for the Year's activities, the General Assembly took steps to hasten the conclusion of two international conventions on human rights: the Draft Convention on Freedom of Information[54] and the Draft Convention on the Elimination of All Forms of Intolerance and of Discrimination Based on Religion and Belief.[55] It also hastened consideration of draft declarations concerning the Rights of Territorial Asylum,[56] which was adopted by the General Assembly on December 14, 1967, and on the Elimination of All Forms of Religious Intolerance.[57] On November 7, 1967, it adopted the Draft Declaration on the Elimination of Discrimination against Women.[58]

On March 21, 1968, a special meeting was called to celebrate the International Day for the Elimination of Racial Discrimination, a subject to which UNESCO and the Human Rights Commission had devoted considerable attention and on which they had made important recommendations. The speakers at this meeting addressed their remarks to the problem of *apartheid.*

The International Conference on Human Rights, held in Teheran, Iran, from April 22 to May 13, 1968, was a major event of the International Year for Human Rights. Its purpose was to review progress in the field of human rights since the adoption of the Universal Declaration of Human Rights in 1948; to review the effectiveness of UN methods in that field, emphasizing the elimination of racial discrimination; and to determine the measures to be taken following the celebrations of the International Year for Human Rights. Representatives from 84 countries and the Holy See, from UN bodies and Specialized Agencies, and from regional inter-governmental organ-

---

[53] *See* the May 1968 Issue of the *UN Monthly Chronicle* for the Message of the UN Secretary General for the International Year for Human Rights and for the text of the *Proclamation of Teheran.* *See also* UN OFFICE OF PUBLIC INFORMATION. NEWSLETTERS. INTERNATIONAL YEAR FOR HUMAN RIGHTS, 1968; U.S. CONGRESS HOUSE COMMITTEE ON FOREIGN AFFAIRS, U.S. OBSERVANCE OF INTERNATIONAL HUMAN RIGHTS YEAR 1968 (Washington 1966).

[54] 17 U.N. GAOR, Annexes, Agenda Item No. 29, at 7, U.N. Doc. A/AC. 4217 (1962).

[55] 24 U.N. Secretary-General U.N. Doc. A/7497 (1969).

[56] G.A. Res. 2312, 22 U.N. GAOR Supp.   at   , U.N. Doc. A/6912 (1967).

[57] Draft International Convention on the Elimination of All Forms of Religious Intolerance. Report of the 17th session of the Sub-Commission on Prevention of Discrimination and Protection of Minorities. 1963 U.N. Y.B. 340. U.N. Doc. E/CN.4/882 (1963).

[58] Declaration on the Elimination of Discrimination Against Women, G.A. Res. 2263, 22 U.N. GAOR, Supp.   at   , U.N. Doc. A/6880 (1967).

izations participated. The Conference was chaired by Princess Ashraf Pahlavi, opened by the Shah of Iran, and addressed by the UN Secretary-General. The Conference adopted "The Proclamation of Teheran" which appealed for intensified efforts to guarantee a life of freedom and dignity for all human beings. The Conference also adopted resolutions on a wide range of subjects, and broke new ground by including the right to decide the number and spacing of children and the right of privacy against new technical devices, such as hidden microphones, wiretapping, and computerized data. These two new subjects had not even been conceived when the Universal Declaration was drafted.

Members of the UN throughout the world gave a lively response to a UN request to recognize this Human Rights Year by appropriate celebration. Actions by different states included: the study, review, signing and ratification of human rights conventions; the appointment of national and local committees to organize and carry out programs to observe the International Year for Human Rights; the wide distribution of copies of human rights conventions; distribution of newsletters and other publications with human rights information for use in schools and by organizations, clubs and other groups, giving of proclamations and addresses by heads of states and cabinet members; holding of seminars, conferences and symposia an human rights; publication of special issues of learned journals on the subject; and planning of parades, pageants and other public celebrations.

Members of the United Nations commemorated the Universal Declaration of Human Rights by a wide variety of activities. In the United States, for example, the President proclaimed Human Rights Year on October 11, 1967, and on January 30, 1968, established the President's Commission for the Observance of Human Rights Year 1968, with a chairman, a vice-chairman, the heads of seven Government agencies, and 11 distinguished citizens. The Commission was charged with the task of increasing the understanding of all the world's people of the principles of human rights, laid down in the Universal Declaration, and in the Constitution and laws of the United States. Accordingly, the Commission created special committees and consulted government agencies and civic organizations. It published, and distributed widely, various posters and pamphlets. It held conferences covering various aspects of human rights. In its final report, it offered recommendations to the President for continuing action in the human rights field, including the ratification of pending human rights conventions. Inter-governmental organizations were also active in observing the International Year for Human Rights.[59]

UN Specialized Agencies and other bodies in the UN family have formulated and carried forward careful plans for human rights celebrations. On a regional basis, the Council of Europe took advantage of the opportunity to commemorate not only the 20th anniversary of the Universal Declaration of Human Rights, but also the 15th anniversary of the entry into force of the European Convention of Human Rights. A special sitting of the Consultative Assembly on September 26, 1968, emphasized the importance of the implementation in Europe of the Universal Declaration of Human Rights and other UN texts. A model lesson about the European Convention was prepared for use in schools. Copies of great human rights documents were exhibited at the Strasbourg headquarters of the Council of Europe throughout most of the year. And, members of the Human Rights staff of the Council made numerous addresses to universities, non-governmental organizations and other groups on various aspects of human rights.

Commemorative celebrations of the 1968 International Year for Human Rights were carried out by the Food and Agriculture Organization, the International Telecommunication Union, the UN Educational, Scientific and Cultural Organization, the Universal Postal Union, the World Health Organization, the United Nations Childrens Fund and many other agencies, emphasizing their special human rights interests and contributing their special talents to the protection of these rights.

Many non-governmental organizations in consultative status with the Economic and Social Council, sparked by *Ad Hoc* Committees in New York and Geneva made elaborate preparations for participation in the International Year for Human Rights. Their activities included general and special conferences on the International Year for Human Rights or some aspect of the Universal Declaration of Human Rights; the printing or distribution of UN Human Rights instruments or commentaries on them; and efforts to secure support for the ratification of Human Rights Conventions. The World Peace Through Law Center included the subject of human rights as one of the 12 panel session topics of its World Conference in

---

[59] For an account of the activities of the Organization of American States in connection with International Human Rights Year, including its Report to the Teheran Conference and its representation there, see *The Solemn Meeting of the Council, Human Rights Course in Mexico,* "The 19th Session of the Commission and the Draft Convention," the first volume of the *Yearbook,* and other information, see in particular: A/ Conf. 32/ L 10 of January 22, 1968 and further progress reports.

Geneva, July 9-14, 1967. It designated September 16, 1968, as World Law Day and celebrated this day by a conference in Geneva emphasizing human rights and the law.[60]

Among the distinguished speakers at this conference was the President of the European Court of Human Rights, Rene Cassin, who won the Nobel Peace Prize in 1968, for his outstanding contributions in the field of human rights. The Center also gave a $1,000 prize for the best essay on "What international law regime would best enhance and protect human rights."

Clearly, human rights are today a subject of international and universal concern. The review in this Chapter of the activities of organizations and the growing body of law establish that the ever-growing concern is resulting in more and more concrete action to ensure better protection and implementation of human rights worldwide.

---

[60] Lawyers and High Court Judges from thirty-five countries attended this two-day conference. The World Peace Through Law Center's Pamphlet No. 12 reports the proceedings of this Conference, including messages from the UN Secretary General and from the UN High Commissioner for Refugees. There were also addresses by numerous distinguished lawyers and judges.

CHAPTER 9
The Laws of War

§ 9-1. Origin and Development of the Laws of War[1]

The historic function of the laws of war has been to impose limitations upon international violence in the common interest of

---

[1] See J. BRIERLY, THE LAWS OF NATIONS (6 ed. New York 1963); I. BROWNLIE, INTERNATIONAL LAW AND THE USE OF FORCE BY STATES (Oxford 1963);

(Continued)

the community of states. No one doubts that it would be far better to abolish war and hostilities than merely to regulate them. The laws of war are based upon the assumption that regulation to prevent wanton and irrational destruction is necessary to promote basic humanitarian objectives. In this sense the laws of war may be described as a basic standard of human rights applicable even in war or hostilities.

Although resort to force and war has decreased as the world activities of men and nations have become more governed by law, wars still occur. This is true even though this volume has been prepared in the hope of so increasing the knowledge of the value of resort to international law that nations will hopefully eliminate their resort to force and settle their disputes peacefully. This hope has existed throughout the history of mankind. To end such an alternative as resort to war requires the existence of a credible world legal system accepted by men and nations, as war cannot be eliminated while leaving nothing to replace it. If this volume moves the world toward this goal by proving that law can indeed be a credible replacement for war, all the years of effort put forth in this work will have been justified.

International legal principles of war, relating directly to belligerent conduct during war, have slowly emerged from the practices and customs of states, from treaties and from other agreements,

CARNEGIE ENDOWMENT FOR INTERNATIONAL PEACE, THE CONTROL OF CHEMICAL AND BIOLOGICAL WEAPONS (New York 1971); CARNEGIE ENDOWMENT FOR INTERNATIONAL PEACE, THE LAW OF ARMED CONFLICTS; E. CASTREN, THE PRESENT LAW OF WAR AND NEUTRALITY (Helsinki 1954); Dunbar, *The Legal Regulation of Modern Warfare,* 40 GROTIUS SOC. TR. 83 (1955); F. GROB, THE RELATIVITY OF WAR AND PEACE: A STUDY IN LAW, HISTORY AND POLITICS (New Haven 1949); Herczegh, *The Prohibition of the Threat and Use of Force in Contemporary International Law,* in QUESTIONS OF INTERNATIONAL LAW 70 (Budapest 1964); Higgins, *The Legal Limits of the Use of Force by Sovereign States: United Nations Practice,* 37 BR. Y.B. INT'L L. 269 (1961); M. HUDSON, CASES AND MATERIALS ON INTERNATIONAL LAW (3rd ed. St. Paul 1957); R. KOTZSCH, THE CONCEPT OF WAR IN CONTEMPORARY HISTORY AND INTERNATIONAL LAW (Geneva 1956); Kunz, *The Laws of War,* 50 AJIL 313 (1956); Lauterpacht, *The Limits of the Operation of the Laws of War,* 30 BR. Y.B. INT'L L. 206 (1953); M. McDOUGAL & F. FELICIANO, LAW AND MINIMUM WORLD PUBLIC ORDER: THE LEGAL REGULATION OF INTERNATIONAL COERCION (New Haven 1961); A. McNAIR, LEGAL EFFECTS OF WAR (4th ed. Cambridge 1967); *The Legal Meaning of War and the Relation of War to Reprisals,* 11 GROTIUS SOC. TR. 29 (1926); A. NOBLECOURT, PROTECTION OF CULTURAL PROPERTY IN THE EVENT OF ARMED ATTACK (1958); O'Brien, *Biological/Chemical Warfare and the International Law of War,* 51 GEO. L.J. 1-63 (1962); J. SALONGA & P. YAP, PUBLIC INTERNATIONAL LAW 324-83 (1958); G. SCHWARZENBERGER, A MANUAL OF INTERNATIONAL LAW 181 (5th ed. 1967); Skubiszewski, *Use of Force by States, Collective Security and Neutrality* 739-855, in MANUAL OF PUBLIC INTERNATIONAL LAW (M. Sorenson ed. 1968); Q. WRIGHT, A STUDY OF WAR (Chicago 1942); Wright, *When Does War Exist?,* 26 AJIL 362 (1932).

and all states are considered bound by them. Inherent in these general legal principles of warfare is the moral standard of all civilized nations: the absolute necessity of protecting and preserving human life, including human values and institutions adhered to by all nations, in the face of military necessity.[2] This standard compels all nations to act in such a manner that, despite the necessities of war, there will be a minimal destruction of human values.

In contrast to this present standard of morality, the conduct of war prior to the 1300's, and up to the 17th century was marked by a maximum destruction of human values, and can be characterized as extremely savage and cruel. In reaction to this destruction, the concept of humanized war gained ground when propounded by Grotius in the 16th century. According to this theory, barbarous savagery during armed conflicts should be tempered largely for the self-interest of states. Victors should kill their beaten enemy only when absolutely necessary to save themselves from death or injury; conquered property should not be destroyed except for military necessity; hostages should not be killed if they have not acted against their captors; and conquered peoples should be given some liberties.[3]

Codification of these practices into a body of international legal principles was accomplished in the Declaration of Paris of 1856. In 1899, the Hague Conference promulgated 13 Conventions and resolutions setting forth the international laws of war. In the 20th century, several conventions dealing with the laws of war were adopted:

    1) The Protocol of 1925 outlawing the use of asphyxiating, poisonous and other gases, and poisonous weapons;[4]

    2) The Geneva Conventions of 1929 stating the humane treatment of sick and wounded military personnel required during hostilities,[5] and treatment of prisoners of war;[6]

    3) The Geneva Conventions of 1949: the Convention for the Amelioration of the Condition of the Wounded and Sick in Armed Forces of the Field,[7] the Convention for the Amelioration of the

---

[2] G. SCHWARZENBERGER, *supra* note 1, at 197-200; M. McDOUGAL, *supra* note 1, at 72-76.

[3] J. SALONGA, *supra* note 1, at 328.

[4] COMMAND PAPER 3604 (United Kingdom 1930).

[5] 47 Stat. 2074, T.S. 847, 2 Bevans 965, 118 L.N.T.S. 303.

[6] 47 Stat. 2021, T.S. 846, 2 Bevans 932, 118 L.N.T.S. 343.

[7] 6 U.S.T. 3114, T.I.A.S. No. 3362, 75 U.N.T.S. 31.

Condition of the Wounded, Sick and Shipwrecked Members of Armed Forces at Sea,[8] the Convention Relative to the Treatment of Prisoners of War,[9] and the Convention Relative to the Protection of Civilian Persons in Time of War.[10]

§ 9-2. Definition of War

The most common descriptions of war have focused on the nature of war as essentially the existence of armed hostilities between two belligerents.[11] For example, a dictionary definition describes war as "a state of usually open and declared armed hostile conflict between states or nations, or a state of hostility, conflict or antagonism, or a struggle between opposing forces or for a particular end."[12] On the other hand, others have focused on the nature of war as essentially a complex of relations between belligerents. Professor McDougal describes war as.

> [T]he process of coercion across state boundaries . . . in terms of certain participants applying to each other coercion of alternately accelerating and decelerating intensity, for a whole spectrum of objectives, by methods which include the employment of all available instruments of policy, and under all the continually changing conditions of a world arena. In the course of this seamless process of action and reaction, and as an integral part of it, participants also continuously assert against each other many varying claims respecting the lawfulness or unlawfulness of the various coercive practices employed by and against them, invoking in support of their respective claims both world prescriptions and world public opinion.[13]

Still other writers have stressed the nature of war as a state or condition with ensuing legal relations. According to Moore:

> Much confusion may be avoided by bearing in mind the fact that by the term war is meant not the mere employment of force, but the existence of the legal condition of things in which rights are or may be prosecuted by force. Thus if two nations declare war one against the other, war exists, though no force whatever may as yet have been employed. On the other hand, force may be employed by one nation against another, as in the

---

[8] 6 U.S.T. 3217, T.I.A.S. No. 3363, 75 U.N.T.S. 85.

[9] 6 U.S.T. 3316, T.I.A.S. No. 3364, 75 U.N.T.S. 135.

[10] 6 U.S.T. 3516, T.I.A.S. No. 3365, 75 U.N.T.S. 287.

[11] Eagleton, *The Attempt To Define War,* 291 INT'L CONC. 237 (1933); Ronan, *English and American Courts and the Definition of War,* 31 AJIL 642 (1937).

[12] WEBSTER'S SEVENTH NEW COLLEGIATE DICTIONARY 1003 (Merriam Co., Springfield, Mass. 1967).

case of reprisals, and yet no state of war may arise. In such a case there may be said to be an act of war, but no state of war.[14]

The UN Charter in Article 2(3) prohibits war:

> All Members shall settle their international disputes by peaceful means in such a manner that international peace and security, and justice are not endangered.

The Charter, also, in Article 2(4), implicit within its prohibition of war defines it as follows:

> All Members shall refrain in their international relations from the threat or use of force against the territorial integrity or political independence of any state, or in any other manner inconsistent with the Purposes of the United Nations.

§ 9-3. Basic Principles of the Laws of War

The principles of military necessity and humanity are generally referred to as the basic principles of the laws of war. They are considered basic because of their all-pervasive character—in that they inhere in all the laws of war, are fundamental to a proper understanding of the laws of war and regulate the use of coercion. The principle of military necessity is generally expressed in broad and comprehensive terms, often justifying great and unreasonable amounts and types of force. Oppenheim's formulation is typical:

> [T]he principle that a belligerent is justified in applying any amount and any kind of force which is necessary for the realization of the purpose of war—namely, the overpowering of the opponent.[15]

Applying such a formulation to actual coercive situations would result in removing the application of the laws of war altogether. The *Laws of Naval Warfare* formulate the principle of military necessity in such a way that the laws of war retain their validity:

> The principle of military necessity permits a belligerent to apply only that degree and kind of regulated force, not otherwise prohibited by the laws of war, required for the partial or complete submission of the enemy with the least possible expenditure of time, life and physical resources.[16]

Military necessity means that only that destruction necessary, relevant and proportionate to the prompt achievement of lawful

---

[13] M. McDOUGAL, *supra* note 1, at 11.

[14] 7 MOORE, DIGEST OF INTERNATIONAL LAW 153 (1906).

[15] 2 H. LAUTERPACHT, OPPENHEIM'S INTERNATIONAL LAW 227 (7th ed. 1961).

[16] U.S. DEP'T OF THE NAVY, LAW OF NAVAL WARFARE § 220(a) (N.W.I.P. 10-2 1955). The assistance of Professor William T. Mallison, Jr. is appreciated in the preparation of this and the next section.

military objectives is legal. Not only must such destruction be necessary and relevant to the attainment of military objectives, but it must also be proportionately and reasonably related to the military importance of the object of attack. As applied in past coercive situations, the irrelevance and disproportionality of the destruction must not be great.[17]

The principle of humanity, the second basic principle of the laws of war, is formulated as follows in the *Laws of Naval Warfare*:

> The principle of humanity prohibits the employment of any kind or degree of force not necessary for the purpose of the war, i.e., for the partial or complete submission of the enemy with the least possible expenditure of time, life and physical resources.[18]

While appearing to be an imprecise doctrine, the principle of humanity, together with the principle of military necessity, acts to protect important interests of the world community concerned with the least possible destruction of human and material values.[19] Both principles make wanton and unreasonable destruction illegal. While it is not difficult to apply these basic principles in clear-cut factual situations, it may be necessary to employ other and more specific legal principles in solving more difficult and complex factual situations. In any analysis, it is important to define those human and material values, or interests that should be protected. In *United States v. List* the following interests were considered:

> Military necessity has been invoked by the defendants as justifying the killing of innocent members of the population and the destruction of villages and towns in the occupied territory. Military necessity permits a belligerent, subject to the laws of war, to apply any amount and kind of force to compel the complete submission of the enemy with the least possible expenditure of time, life and money. In general, it sanctions measures by an occupant necessary to protect the safety of his forces and to facilitate the success of his operations. It permits the destruction of life of armed enemies and other persons whose destruction is incidentally unavoidable by the armed conflicts of the war; it allows the capturing of armed enemies and others of peculiar danger, but it does not permit the killing of innocent inhabitants for purposes of revenge or the satisfaction of a lust to kill. The destruction of property to be lawful must be imperatively demanded by the necessities of war. Destruction as an end in itself is a viola-

---

[17] Compare the textual formulations with those appearing in McDOUGAL & FELICIANO, *supra* note 1, at 524-28 and in O'Brien, *Legitimate Military Necessity in Nuclear War,* 2 WORLD POLITY 48-57 (1960).

[18] U.S. DEP'T OF THE NAVY, *supra* note 16, at § 220(b).

[19] *See* McDOUGAL & FELICIANO, *supra* note 1, at 522-23.

tion of international law. There must be some reasonable connection between the destruction of property and the overcoming of the enemy forces. It is lawful to destroy railways, lines of communications or any other property that might be utilized by the enemy. Private homes and churches may even be destroyed if necessary for military operations. It does not admit the wanton devastation of a district or the willful infliction of suffering upon its inhabitants for the sake of suffering alone.[20]

Although stated in terms of military necessity, this analysis is entirely consistent with the principle of humanity. And, while the two principles may appear to be contradictory, applying one as if the other did not exist would result in an unbalanced decision. It is essential to apply each principle in the light of the other if the common interests of states are to be honored. From this perspective, each principle may be usefully conceived as merely an element of a larger composite principle which comprises both military necessity and humanity.[21] At the very least, the complementary character of the two traditional principles should be recognized and stressed in order to promote and to protect those values and interests considered crucial.

§ 9-4. Situations Where the Laws of War Are Applicable

It is evident that the laws of war apply in a duly declared war with states as the participants in which all of the participants recognize its character as "war." Other less obvious situations where these laws apply, however, also exist.

One such situation where the laws of war apply is in the case of aggression. No doubt Germany's aggressive conduct in World War II violated its obligations under the Kellogg-Brand Pact[22] which had renounced the use of war as an instrument of national policy. If it therefore follows that every single military act of Germany was illegal, it would also be assumed that, if the United States and the United Kingdom are states legally employing coercion in response to aggression, all of their military acts of war would be considered lawful even though they were substantially the same as those employed by Germany.

---

[20] 11 U.S. GOVERNMENT, TRIALS OF WAR CRIMINALS BEFORE THE NUREMBERG MILITARY TRIBUNALS 1253-54 (1946-1949).

[21] *Compare* McDOUGAL & FELICIANO, *supra* note 1, at 530, who state that there is an "overriding conception of minimum unnecessary destruction [of values]."

[22] *Signed* August 27, 1928, 46 Stat. 2343, T.S. 796, 94 L.N.T.S. 57.

The applicability of the laws of war to situations of an illegal resort to coercion, was raised in the *Trial of List*[23] at the International Military Tribunal in Nuremberg at the end of World War II. The prosecution contended that, given the unlawful nature of Germany's wars against Greece and Yugoslovia, Germany could not possess legal rights as a belligerent occupant, and that the presence of her troops in those countries was therefore illegal. In rejecting this contention, the Court stated:

> For the purposes of this discussion, we accept the statement as true that the wars waged against Yugoslavia and Greece were in direct violation of the Kellogg-Briand Pact and were therefore criminal in character. But it does not follow that every act by the German occupation forces against person or property is a crime or that any and every act undertaken by the population of the occupied country against the German occupation forces thereby became legitimate defense.[24]

The soundness of this position seems evident. Unless the laws of war apply to situations of an unlawful use of force and aggression, an aggressor state might evade responsibility by being the aggressor. And, it follows that if an aggressor state is not subject to the laws of war, a defending state could also claim that it was not subject to the laws of war. If this were the case, no state would be bound by the laws of war, and the human and material values protected by the laws of war would be destroyed. If the humanitarian objectives of the laws of war are to be achieved, these laws must be applied and followed in aggressive situations.[25]

The laws of war also apply to armed conflicts not of an international character. Such conflicts include rebellions by dissident groups against established regimes, struggles for independence from colonial rule, and factional civil wars arising after independence. Since their character is local, that is, within the territorial confines of a nation-state, they are not considered to be international conflicts, and it would seem to follow that the international laws, rules or customs of war, including the 1949 Geneva Red Cross Conventions, would not apply to the conduct of hostilities between the opponents. As long as the conflict remains internal, and strictly local in nature, any intervention by third states favoring the revolutionaries would constitute an illegal interference in the domestic affairs of the sovereign

---

[23] 11 U.S. GOVERNMENT, *supra* note 20.

[24] *Id.* at 59.

[25] *See* Lauterpacht, *Rules of Warfare in an Unlawful War,* in LAW AND POLITICS IN THE WORLD COMMUNITY 89, 91-99 (Lipsky ed. 1953).

state. Underscoring the non-applicability of the 1949 Geneva Conventions to internal conflicts are the necessary considerations that not all nations have ratified these Conventions, and, in fact, many nations did not exist when these humanitarian conventions were promulgated. And, in recent years, it has been clearly proven that not all disputants consider themselves bound by such internationally-accepted customs.

Despite the primarily local nature of internal conflicts, it has been suggested that these international conventions and laws of war are nonetheless binding on the particular disputants. When during the course of hostilities, it becomes apparent that the hostilities are of a prolonged nature, and that the insurgents control a large part of the country effectively, international custom has generally considered such a situation as war. States, after having determined that war exists between the opponents, sometimes recognize both opponents as active belligerents, and accord them the international rights, and impose upon them the international obligations as belligerents under the Laws of Neutrality that govern the conduct of hostilities. If the sovereign state recognized the insurgents as belligerents, it, then, must also apply the laws of war to them, and is entitled to exercise all the rights of a belligerent in its own territory, and on international waters.

Even though hostilities between the sovereign state, and the rebels remain strictly local, both opponents, nevertheless, have the option of conducting hostilities in accordance with the international laws and customs of war. In the Korean conflict, the 1956 conflict between Egypt and France, Israel and the United Kingdom, and in the Vietnam conflict, for example, both sides claim they have followed the international laws of war. And, some states follow the practice of applying the humanitarian principles of the 1949 Geneva Red Cross Conventions[26] in all conflicts, regardless of their purely local character, without considering the belligerent or insurgent status of the participants.

Underscoring the basic applicability of the international laws and customs of war to purely internal conflicts, is the fact that the very basic principle of humanitarianism, a major force in the development of the international rules of war, calling for the preservation and sanctity of human life, as a principle of natural law,

---

[26] Convention for the Amelioration of the Condition of the Wounded and Sick in Armed Forces in the Field, August 12, 1949, 6 U.S.T. 3114, T.I.A.S. 3362, 75 U.N.T.S. 31; Convention for the Amelioration of the Condition of the Wounded, Sick, and Shipwrecked Members of Armed Forces at Sea, August 12, 1949, 6 U.S.T. 3217, T.I.A.S. 3363, 75 U.N.T.S. 85.

transcends both nation-states, and individuals, and is, therefore, universally applicable and binding. The universal nature of this principle of humanitarianism is well illustrated in the Hague and Geneva Conventions and in the Charter of the International Military Tribunal established at Nuremberg at the end of World War II. The Preamble of the Hague Convention respecting the laws and customs of war on land states that:

> Until a more complete code of the laws of war has been issued, the high contracting parties deem it expedient to declare that, in cases not covered by the rules adopted by them, the inhabitants remain under the protection and the rule of the principles of the law of nations, as they result from the usages established among civilized peoples, from the laws of humanity, and from the dictates of public conscience.[27]

The Charter of the International Military Tribunal, in its section on Crimes Against Humanity, affirmed the existence of fundamental human rights superior to the law of the State, and protected by international criminal sanction even if violated in pursuance of the law of the State.[28]   Furthermore, Article 3 of the 1949 Geneva Red Cross Conventions states that:

> . . . in the case of armed conflicts *not of an international character* occurring in the territory of one of the High Contracting Parties, each Party to the Conflict shall be bound to apply, as a minimum, provisions which require *inter alia* the humane treatment of persons taking no active part in the hostilities including members of the armed forces who have laid down their arms, and also of wounded, sick and detained persons. Also prohibited is 'violence to life and person, in particular murder of all kinds, mutilation, cruel treatment and torture and the taking of hostages.[29]

§ 9-5. Legality of War

Until the 20th century, all forms of coercion were legal under relevant principles of international law, and individual states were in no way restricted in the use of force, or in determining what justified resort to force as an instrument of national policy.

Although Grotius and other medieval writers gave vitality to the distinction, which dated from ancient Roman writers,[30] between a

---

[27] October 18, 1907, 36 Stat. 2277, T.S. 539, 1 Bevans 631.

[28] 2 L. OPPENHEIM, *supra* note 15 at 579.

[29] Convention for the Amelioration of the Condition of the Wounded and Sick in Armed Forces in the Field, August 12, 1949, 6 U.S.T. 3114, T.I.A.S. 3362, 75 U.N.T.S. 31; Convention for the Amelioration of the Condition of the Wounded, Sick, and Shipwrecked Members of Armed Forces at Sea, August 12, 1949, 6 U.S.T. 3217, T.I.A.S. 3363, 75 U.N.T.S. 85.

[30] 3 GROTIUS, LAWS OF WAR AND PEACE, CLASSICS OF INTERNATIONAL LAW 722-82 (Kelsey trans. 1925).

just and an unjust war by making the use of force legally permissible only for a good cause,[31] most states refused to accept this distinction, or its rationale until the 20th century when severe limitations were placed on a state's right to resort to coercion with the signing of the Covenant of the League of Nations, the Kellogg-Briand Pact[32] and the United Nations Charter. Under the Covenant, while coercive measures were not outlawed, member states could not use force until they had submitted the dispute to arbitration, or Council inquiry, and then they had to wait for three months after the award or decision had been rendered before resorting to force. It was forbidden to use force against a League Member who followed the terms of the award or decision, but the failure of the Council to act, or to provide a unanimous report on the situation permitted disputing states to use force as they chose.[33]

The Kellogg-Briand Pact,[34] signed in 1928, went further in outlawing war, and establishing permissible uses of coercion, than did the League Covenant. War was prohibited both as a means of settling international controversies, and as an instrument of national policy. Permissible uses of force comprised the use of coercion in self-defense, as a means of enforcing international, as distinct from purely national, obligations, between Parties and non-Parties to the Pact, and against a Party who violated the terms of the Pact.

The UN Charter has added new dimensions to the prohibitions against the use of force by totally outlawing not only recourse to war, but also the threat or use of force.[35] Coercive measures are only legally permissible in cases of collective self-defense, individual self-defense when the Security Council has failed to take the necessary steps to maintain international peace or security,[36] or upon the Security Council's recommendation to apply coercion against an aggressor.[37] Moreover, the amount of coercion to be applied relates to "such action as may be necessary to maintain

---

[31] 1 GROTIUS, *supra* note 7, at 51-90; 2 GROTIUS, *supra* note 7, at 169-85, 546-66. *See also* Coste, *A Critical Analysis of the Notion of a Just War,* 9 WORLD JUSTICE 291-309 (1968); O'Brien, *Just War and Just Revolution,* 9 WD. JUST. 333-57 (1968).

[32] August 27, 1928, 46 Stat. 2343, T.S. 796, 2 Bevans 732, 94 L.N.T.S. 57.

[33] LEAGUE OF NATIONS COVENANT, art. 10-16.

[34] August 27, 1928, 46 Stat. 2343, T.S. 796, 2 Bevans 732, 94 L.N.T.S.

[35] U.N. CHARTER art. 1-2. *See also* Nawaz, *The Doctrine of the Outlawry of War,* 13 INDIAN Y.B. INT'L AFF. 80 (1964).

[36] U.N. CHARTER art. 51.

[37] *Id.* at art. 42.

or restore international peace and security."[38]   In this context, the United Nations is however compelled to apply coercive measures in a "manner consistent with the purposes and ideals of the Organization" by obeying the laws of war which "represent a general international attempt to humanize armed conflict."[39]

§ 9-6. The Principle of Self-Defense

The principle of self-defense contained in Article 51 of the United Nations Charter, was set forth in the *Caroline and McLeod Incidents* (1838-42),[40] in the reports of the Military Tribunals of Nuremberg and Tokyo,[41] and in the *Corfu Channel* Case.[42] According to these cases, and customary international law, a state may resort to self-defense against states or individuals in response to the illegal and aggressive acts committed by them. For the resort to self-defense to be legally permissible, however, it must be justified by the principles of necessity and proportionality. According to the principle of necessity, before self-defense measures are taken, the need for them must be "instant, overwhelming, leaving no choice of means, and no moment for deliberation."[43] According to the principle of proportionality, measures of self-defense must be reasonably adapted to the nature of the illegal, aggressive act, its threat or imminence, and must be "reasonably necessary in a particular instance for achieving the lawful purpose of self-defense."[44]   Forcible measures of self-defense that either apply a higher degree of force than is reasonably necessary to achieve the purpose of self-defense, or are not called for in light of all the facts and circumstances, would therefore be illegal under relevant international law principles.   Under these principles of necessity and proportionality, the United States put forth the legality under international law of its quarantine of Cuba in the face of Soviet missiles in Cuba which threatened its security.[45]

---

[38] *Id.*

[39] Taubenfield, *International Armed Forces and the Rules of War,* 45 AJIL 676-77 (1951).

[40] J. MOORE, DIGEST OF INTERNATIONAL LAW 409 (Washington 1906).

[41] *See generally* INTERNATIONAL MILITARY TRIBUNAL. TRIAL OF THE MAJOR WAR CRIMINALS BEFORE THE INTERNATIONAL MILITARY TRIBUNAL, NUREMBERG (Nuremberg 1947-49); International Military Tribunal for the Far East; Transcript of Proceedings, 7 January and 1 October 1947 (unpublished 1947); U.S. DEP'T OF STATE, TRIAL OF WAR CRIMINALS, No. 2420 (1945); U.S. DEP'T OF STATE, TRIAL OF JAPANESE WAR CRIMINALS, No. 2613 (1946).

[42] [1949] I.C.J. 419.

[43] 29 BR. & FOR. ST. PAP. 1129, 1138, *supra* note 1, at 217.

[44] M. McDOUGAL, *supra* note 1, at 243.

[45] Maken, *Defensive Quarantine and the Law,* 57 AJIL 515-45 (1963).

While it is left to the discretion of states to determine the necessity of resorting to self-defense, and the proportionality of the response, these international standards must nevertheless be compiled with.   Claims of self-defense will be reviewed by the world community, as in the case of the War Crimes Trials of Nuremberg and Tokyo, wherein the Court referred to the standards, set forth in the Caroline decision, in rejecting the pleas of self-defense offered by the defendants.[46]

The principle of Collective Self-defense, or Collective Security, as contained in Article 51 and Chapter Seven of the U.N. Charter, permits the resort to collective self-defense in response to aggressive acts, either as a result of Security Council deliberations and instructions, since it is authorized to take forcible measures in the event of situations threatening international peace and security, or as a result of collective, group initiative in response to acts of aggression.   Collective security is fundamentally premised on the principle that states abandon the claim of neutrality when an armed attack occurs against a member of the collective group.[47] In addition to the collective security arrangements set forth in the Charter, similar arrangements existed among the ancient Greek city-states, the Perpetual League (1291), the Swiss Forest Communities, the Union of Utrecht (1579), the Confederation of the United States (1777), the Germanic Confederation (1820) and the League of Nations (1919).[48]

Collective measures of self-defense against non-UN members are also permissible.   Such measures against a Nation that has signed the Pact of Paris (Kellogg-Briand), are justified since the Pact so stipulates.[49]   Measures of self-defense against a Nation not a signatory of the Pact are also permissible on the ground that such measures do not contravene customary international law which permits the use of force for self defense.[50]

§ 9-7. The Principle of Self-Help[51]

This principle, embodying the use of force short of war to settle international disputes is composed of retorsion, reprisals,

---

[46] Article 8 of the Charter of the 1945 International Military Tribunal; 2 H. LAUTERPACHT, OPPENHEIM'S INTERNATIONAL LAW 570 (7th ed. 1961).

[47] G. SCHWARZENBERGER, *supra* note 1, at 188.

[48] *Id.* at 187.

[49] August 27, 1928, 46 Stat. 2343, T.S. 796, 2 Bevans 732, 94 L.N.T.S. 57.

[50] G. SCHWARZENBERGER, *supra* note 1, at 188.

[51] *Id.* at 184-85.

the severance of diplomatic relations, embargo, boycott, non-intercourse, pacific blockade, and collective measures under the UN Charter, and has been traditionally subject to the requirements of international law. Such measures short of actual, armed hostilities, and confrontations between states, while traditionally part of customary international law, have been limited in the 20th century. Hague Convention II of 1907 prohibits the use of reprisals to recover contract debts, and Article 2 of the UN Charter, calling on Member Nations to settle international disputes by peaceful means, to ensure the maintenance of international peace and security, specifically prohibits the use, or threat to use force to solve such disputes. Moreover, Article 37 compels nations, members of the UN, to refer such disputes to the Security Council if their solution cannot be effected peacefully.

Retorsion in response to the unfriendly, but legal acts of one nation, contemplates action of a similar nature: unfriendly, but legal according to international law. States usually retort in cases involving the unfair treatment of their nationals, or in cases involving the imposition of discriminatory and excessive import duties on their goods. Retorsion usually takes the form of applying measures similar to those complained of; in these cases, of enacting similarly discriminatory import duties, and in treating nationals of the offending nation unfairly.[52]

Reprisals, on the other hand, contemplate action of a more serious nature in response to an international tort, after the offending state has refused to repair the damage resulting from its tortious act. Reprisals under international law are legal acts since they constitute a direct response to the previous illegal act of the offending state. And, while reprisals traditionally were generally limited to action against the property of the offender, they have now been expanded to include such acts as, "military occupation, display of force, naval bombardment, seizure of ships at sea or the property of nationals of the delinquent state, freezing of assets of its citizens, embargo, boycott, and pacific blockade."[53]

Reprisals must also conform to the requirements of proportionality. According to this doctrine, the reprisal taken in response to the previous tortious act of the offender, must be of no greater force or violence than that which is reasonably necessary to achieve the ultimate objective—redress of the wrong.[54] Moreover, before

[52] *Id.*

[53] J. SALONGA, *supra* note 1, at 319.

[54] *Id. See also* Naulilaa Case, German-Portuguese Arbitral Tribunal, Annual Digest and Reports of Public International Law Cases 1927-1928, Case No. 360.

the commencement of reprisals, the state so responding is obligated to attempt to achieve its objective peacefully and to have failed in the attempt, and to make certain that the act complained of was illegal according to international law.[55]

Embargo, as a form of reprisals, consists of several actions taken by the injured nation.[56] Among other things, it consists of holding vessels belonging to the offending nation in its ports, of seizing the offender's vessels on the high seas (hostile embargo), and of preventing its vessels, and resources from reaching the offending nation (civil or pacific embargo).[57] An embargo can also be collective in the sense that several nations impose an embargo on a particular nation, preventing the delivery of certain materials and products.[58] An example of the collective embargo was Resolution 500 of the UN General Assembly,[59] which called on Members of the UN to withhold arms' and war material shipments to nations controlled or areas influenced by the Communist Chinese and North Koreans.

The boycott is another form of reprisals.[60] As in the case of embargo, this reprisal can be instituted either individually or collectively, and generally consists of ceasing all trade and business relations with the state which has acted wrongfully. The most recent boycott was that of some African and other nations against the Union of South Africa and Rhodesia for the alleged policies of racial discrimination practiced by these states.

Still another form of reprisal is the pacific blockade, termed pacific since no state of war exists. Generally, the nation resorting to this reprisal stops all ships of the offending nation from leaving or entering its ports in order to force the offending nation to accede to its demands. Such a blockade usually is directed at the flag vessels of the offending state only: those belonging to third nations are immune unless they violate conditions imposed by the blockading nation. A recent example of this form of reprisal was the blockade by the United States of Cuba occasioned by the presence of Russian missiles. The United States claimed that such reprisals

---

[55] J. SALONGA, *supra* note 1, at 318.

[56] J. BRIERLY, THE LAW OF NATIONS: AN INTRODUCTION TO THE INTERNATIONAL LAW OF PEACE 399-400 (6th ed. New York 1963).

[57] *Id.*

[58] J. SALONGA, *supra* note 1, at 319.

[59] Additional Measures Employed To Meet the Aggression in Korea, (Item 76), Resolution of 18 May 1951 (Adopted on Report of the First Committee).

[60] P. JESSUP, A MODERN LAW OF NATIONS: AN INTRODUCTION 181-82 (New York 1948).

were necessary in the face of the imminent danger and threat to its national security resulting from the presence of such missiles.[61]

§ 9-8. The Concept of Aggression

The meaning of aggression must be clarified in order to give meaning to self-defense, one of the permissible uses of coercion, but attempts to define aggression have not resulted in uniformity. Certain nations, notably Russia, have proposed draft resolutions to the United Nations of an all-inclusive character, ranging from certain acts of a non-forceful nature to the direct use of force.[62] Other states have concluded that aggression must not be limited to "armed" aggression, but must be broad enough to include certain aggressive acts, usually further defined as acts impinging on a state's freedom and independence. The Draft Convention of the Offences Against the Peace and Security of Mankind,[63] and the Draft Convention on the Definition of Aggression,[64] list aggressive acts not involving armed hostilities as: interference in the political affairs of another state, actions intending to foment civil strife in another country, and makes preparation to commit these acts a conspiracy, likewise contrary to international law and punishable as such.

Other writers have advocated that acts of an ideological, economic, social or other nature, can, under certain conditions and circumstances, constitute acts of aggression under present international law.[65]   Using international financial means to damage a nation's

---

[61] Maken, *supra* note 45.

[62] UN Doc. A/AC. 77/L.4 (1956), and Special Committee on the Question of Defining Aggression, Report 12 U.N. GAOR Supp. 16 A/3574 (1956).

[63] Draft Code of Offenses Against the Peace and Security of Mankind, International Law Commission, 6 U.N. GAOR Supp. 9, U.N. Doc. A/1858 (1951).

[64] U.N. Doc. No. A/AC. 77/L.4 (1956); also in Report of the 1956 Special Committee on the Question of Defining Aggression, 12 U.N. GAOR Supp. 16, at 30; U.N. Doc. A/3574 (1957). *See also* The London Conventions for the Definition of Aggression of 1933, 147 L.N.T.S. 67, 77 (1933); the Draft Act prepared by the 1933 Geneva Disarmament Conference, Committee on Security Questions, Conference for the Reduction and Limitation of Armaments (1933), *Politis Report,* 2 CONF. DOCS. 679-90 (1935).

[65] M. McDOUGAL, *supra* note 1, at 29-30. *See also* E. ARONEAU, DEFINITION DE L'AGRESSION (Paris 1968); Harvard Research in International Law, *Rights and Duties of States in Cases of Aggression,* 33 AJIL Supp. 819 (1939); Jessup, *The Crime of Aggression and the Future of International Law,* 62 POL. SCI. Q. 1 (1947); Mudge, *Starvation as a Means of Warfare,* 4 INT'L LAW. 228 (1969); B. MURTY, PROPAGANDA AND WORLD PUBLIC ORDER: THE LEGAL REGULATION OF THE IDEOLOGICAL INSTRUMENT OF COERCION (New Haven 1968); C. POMPE, AGGRESSIVE WAR: AN INTERNATIONAL CRIME (1953); J. STONE, AGGRESSION AND WORLD ORDER: A CRITIQUE OF UNITED NATIONS' THEORIES OF AGGRESSION (London 1958); Wright, *The*

(Continued)

currency and its economic stability, or urging citizens to revolt against their leaders, both violate the spirit and letter of international law.[66]

§ 9-9. Sanctions of the Laws of War

International rules governing the conduct of hostilities between belligerents are enforced by various means or sanctions taken against a state violating those laws. These sanctions consist of reprisals, punishment by military or judicial tribunals, protests by neutral powers and compensation.

The sanction of reprisals consists of the retaliation during the conduct of hostilities of one belligerent against the violator of the rules of war in a like or similar manner in order to urge or force him to cease his offensive conduct. This sanction has been more harsh than anticipated, however, it is absolutely prohibited to take reprisals against prisoners of war.[67] Reprisals were discussed *supra* § 9-7.

Punishment for war crimes consists of trials upon the capture of the individuals concerned, either by national military courts or internationally-constituted military tribunals, of conduct that violates relevant principles of international law, the national law of the defendant, or the law of world peace and humanity.[68] The most recent examples of this sanction were the military tribunals established in Germany and Japan at the conclusion of World War II. In

Concept of Aggression in International Law, 29 AJIL 373 (1935); Wright, *The Prevention of Aggression,* 50 AJIL 514 (1956); Zourek, *Le Definition de l'Agression et le Droit International: Developpements Recents de la Question,* 92 RECUEIL DES COURS 755 (1957).

[66] M. McDOUGAL, LAW AND MINIMUM WORLD PUBLIC ORDER 30 (1961).

[67] J. SALONGA, *supra* note 1, at 331; 2 OPPENHEIM, INTERNATIONAL LAW 561 (7th ed. H. Lauterpacht 1952).

[68] *See* J. APPLEMAN, MILITARY TRIBUNALS AND INTERNATIONAL CRIMES, (1954); Baxter, *The Municipal and International Law Bases of Jurisdiction over War Crimes,* 28 BR. Y.B. INT'L L. 390 (1951); Brand, *The War Crimes Trials and the Laws of War,* 26 BR. Y.B. INT'L L. 54 (1949); Y. DINSTEIN, THE DEFENSE OF OBEDIENCE TO SUPERIOR ORDERS IN INTERNATIONAL LAW (1965); Dunbar, *Military Necessity in War Crimes Trials,* 29 BR. Y.B. INT'L L. (1952); Glaser, *Culpability in International Criminal Law,* 99 RECUEIL DES COURS 473 (1960); M. LACHS, WAR CRIMES: AN ATTEMPT TO DEFINE THE ISSUES (London 1948); Lauterpacht, *The Law of Nations and the Punishment of War Crimes,* 21 BR. Y.B. INT'L L. 58 (1944); Mannes, *The Legal Nature and Punishment of Criminal Acts of Violence Contrary to the Laws of War,* 37 AJIL 407 (1943); Neumann, *Neutral States and the Extradition of War Criminals,* 45 AJIL 495 (1951); Schwarzenberger, *International Responsibility in Time of War,* 14 INDIAN Y.B. INT'L AFF. 3 (1965); Schwelb, *Crimes Against Humanity,* 23 BR. Y.B. INT'L L. 178 (1946).

fact, the Charter of the Nuremberg Tribunal claimed jurisdiction to try the following:

1) *Crimes Against Peace:* namely, planning, preparing, or waging of a war of aggression, or a war in violation of international treaties, agreements or assurances, or participation in a common plan or conspiracy for the accomplishment of any of the foregoing;

2) *War Crimes:* namely, violations of the laws or customs of war. Such violations shall include, but not be limited to, murder, ill treatment or deportation to slave labour or for any other purpose of civilian population of occupied territory, murder or ill treatment of prisoners of war or persons on the high seas, killing of hostages, plunder of public or private property, wanton destruction of cities, towns, or villages or devastation not justified by military necessity;

3) *Crimes Against Humanity:* namely, murder, extermination, enslavement, deportation, and other inhumane acts committed against any civilian population, before or during the war, or persecutions on political, racial, or religious grounds in execution of or in connection with any crime within the jurisdiction of the Tribunal, whether or not in violation of the domestic law of the country where perpetrated.[69]

These principles were later embodied in the United Nations Draft Code of Offences Against the Peace and Security of Mankind.[70] In 1948, the UN General Assembly passed the Genocide Convention[71] which makes genocide a crime against international law. Such criminal conduct consists of the following acts committed either during times of peace or war, with intent to destroy, in whole or in part, a national, ethnic, racial or religious group:

a) Killing members of the group;

b) Causing serious bodily or mental harm to members of the group;

c) Deliberately inflicting on the group conditions of life calculated to bring about its physical destruction in whole or in part;

d) Imposing measures to prevent births within the group;

e) Forcibly transferring children of the group to another group.[72]

---

[69] INTERNATIONAL MILITARY TRIBUNAL CHARTER, art. 6.

[70] Draft Code of Offenses Against the Peace and Security of Mankind, *supra* note 63.

[71] Convention on the Prevention and Punishment of the Crime of Genocide, *opened for signature* January 12, 1951, 78 U.N.T.S. 277.

[72] *Id.*

Protests by belligerents against the criminal conduct of an oppos-ing belligerent constitute another sanction.[73]   These protests gen-erally submitted to the other belligerent through neutral channels, are also lodged through flags of truce.   States prefer to complain through neutrals because it is anticipated that neutrals, on learning of such illegitimate activities, will then use their good offices to persuade the guilty party to desist from continuing its criminal activity.

Compensation at the end of the war is the final sanction imposed by the victor nation on states for their criminal violation of the inter-national rules of war.   Victorious states in the past demanded indem-nification for all losses and damage caused by the enemy during the period of hostilities.   This recently has been limited to indemni-fication only for property unlawfully confiscated by the enemy.[74]

§ 9-10. Legal Effects of a State of War

At the outbreak of hostilities among belligerents, their legal relations alter significantly.   It is important to note that frequently different legal effects of war exist for different purposes.   For example, the Korean War was a war for the purpose of applying the laws of war, but it was not necessarily a war for other pur-poses such as the applicability of a "war clause" in an insurance contract.   When the inquiry before a lawyer concerns whether or not a war exists, this is not usually a unified question where a single answer can be given for all purposes.   It is typically necessary to ask whether a war exists for some particular purpose and to endeavor to formulate a legal answer in terms of the purpose which is the subject of the inquiry.   Internationally-accepted legal practices have evolved: the effects of war on diplomatic relations, on enemy persons and property located within the territory and jurisdiction of the opposing belligerent, on trade and other forms of economic intercourse, and on contracts between the states or their nationals entered into prior to the outbreak of armed conflict.

§ 9-10.1. The 1949 Geneva Conventions.

The four Geneva Con-ventions of 1949 cover the protection of the following classes of persons: personnel in land warfare (including aviators); personnel in naval warfare (including aviators); prisoners of war; and civilian persons.   The four Conventions were drafted in the light of the terrible events of the Second World War, and the overriding humani-

---

[73] J. SALONGA, *supra* note 1, at 334.
[74] *Id.*

tarian objective, reflected in each Convention, was to prevent a recurrence of the abuses carried out by the Nazis in Europe and the Japanese militarists in Asia. These Conventions are law-making Conventions which impose a much higher standard of conduct than that which existed in the applicable international law during the Second World War. The obligations imposed upon belligerent states are not dependent upon mutuality and reciprocity in observance. These Conventions impose unilateral and unconditional obligations upon belligerents for the benefit of the various categories of protected persons. Without attempting to suggest all of the law-making features of these Conventions, a few may be mentioned. The taking of hostages is prohibited without any qualifications or conditions. The employment of reprisals against any protected persons is absolutely prohibited, thereby eliminating the controversies as to the character and degrees of reprisals which are permitted against such persons. It should be mentioned that the Civilian's Convention imposes a much higher standard upon military occupants than that which obtained during the Second World War.

Each of the four Geneva Conventions of 1949 contains a common article concerning the requirement of education as to the content of each Convention. This common article reads:

> The High Contracting Parties undertake, in time of peace as in time of war, to disseminate the text of the present Convention as widely as possible in their respective countries, and, in particular, to include the study thereof in their programmes of military and, if possible, civil instruction, so that the principles thereof may become known to the entire population, in particular to the armed forces, the medical personnel and the chaplains.[75]

Each government, therefore, has an obligation to conduct educational activities concerning the substance of each of the four Conventions. The International Committee of the Red Cross at Geneva has published five lessons which may be obtained upon request by individuals or governments. It is important to recognize that programs of study concerning the Conventions should be undertaken in every state which is a party to them even though there is no expectation that that state will be involved in war or hostilities. The most practical time to undertake dissemination of the Conventions is in time of peace. In addition, the Conventions are now so widely accepted that they are regarded as reflecting existing customary international law as well as conventional law.

---

[75] Armed Forces at Sea Convention, *supra* note 7 at art. 47; Armed Forces at Sea Convention, *supra* note 8 at art. 48; Prisoners of War Convention, *supra* note 9 at art. 127; Civilians' Convention, *supra* note 10, at art. 144 (with slight variation in wording).

There is no doubt but that the law of neutrality has been modified by the United Nations Charter for the member states of that Organization. Such states which are not participating in war of hostilities are no longer entitled to invoke the full scope of the law of neutrality on their behalf. In particular, their status as neutrals has been modified by their Charter obligations to assist the United Nations in repelling aggression and to extend every aid to the victims of aggression.

§ 9-10.2. **Effect of War on Diplomatic and Consular Relations.** All diplomatic and consular relations and affairs between states are immediately broken when war is declared. According to international law, diplomatic and consular personnel and their dependents are given the right to exit from the belligerent nation freely and expeditiously. They are not to be interned, interfered with, or otherwise maltreated.[76] Property incidental to diplomatic relations, including buildings and files, are usually placed under the jurisdiction and safekeeping of third, or neutral nations.[77]

§ 9-10.3. **Effect of War on Enemy Persons.** Enemy persons are so designated by either residence or nationality. Treated as enemies are nationals of neutral states if they take part in the hostilities, business corporations if incorporated under enemy jurisdiction, doing business with the enemy, take orders or instructions from enemy states or nationals, or controlled by enemy aliens. For some countries, notably the United States, enemy controlling interest occurs if 25 percent of the corporation's stock is owned by enemy nationals.[78]

Enemy persons in the belligerent's territory when war broke out (Convention of 1949 as relative to the Protection of Civilian Persons in Time of War) have the right to leave, provided that such departure is consistent with the belligerent's interests.[79] Enemy aliens who chose not to leave, or who are detained, or who demand to be detained, have the right to humane treatment without discrimination solely because they are enemies.[80] Further, they have the rights of medical treatment and hospitalization; of religious freedom; to be detained away from combat zones and not to be

---

[76] J. SALONGA, *supra* note 1, at 336.

[77] *See* Vienna Convention on Diplomatic Relations, April 24, 1964, 500 U.N.T.S. 95.

[78] 2 OPPENHEIM, *supra* note 15, at 277.

[79] Geneva Convention Relative to the Protection of Civilian Persons in Time of War, Aug. 12, 1949, 6 U.S.T. 3516, T.I.A.S. 3365, 75 U.N.T.S. 287. *See also* A. McNAIR, *supra* note 1, at 40-81.

[80] *Id.*

compelled to engage in military operations; if made to work, to be given the same working conditions as nationals; if unemployed, the right to gainful employment, or to support; not to be transferred to other countries where their lives may be jeopardized, or who have not signed the Convention; not to be interned unless absolutely necessary; adequate food and clothing; communication with the outside world; to have births and deaths accurately recorded; to have inquiries made into deaths from other than natural causes; and to release when the war ends, or when the reasons for being interned no longer apply.[81] Most states now permit enemy persons to sue or be sued in their courts during war, but in nations where they do not have this right, any actions they have that arose prior to the outbreak of war are automatically suspended until war ends, and it has been argued that Statutes of Limitations are similarly suspended.[82]

§ 9-10.4. **Effect of War on Enemy Property.** Property belonging to enemy aliens is deemed to be enemy property and subject to confiscation by the belligerent in whose territory it is located,[83] with certain exceptions stated below. Previously, states made no distinction between enemy public or private property subjecting all enemy property to seizure, but modern practices hold that while enemy public property can still be confiscated, enemy private property is merely to be taken into custody; its status to be determined when hostilities end.[84]

To classify property as enemy property, states use the owner's residence or nationality. All property discovered on enemy vessels is treated as enemy property except the personal property of the ship's crew. All vessels flying enemy flags are treated as enemy property, regardless of the owner's residence or nationality. Neutral ships will be considered enemy property if they contribute directly to the conduct of war for the enemy or if they forcibly resist legitimate visit and capture. Private enemy property on neutral vessels generally cannot be confiscated. As stated in the Hague Convention XI of 1907, enemy coastal fishing vessels, local trading ships, and religious, scientific, or philanthropic vessels, and

---

[81] *Id.*

[82] J. SALONGA, *supra* note 1, at 338-40. *See also* Garner, *Treatment of Enemy Aliens: Right of Access to the Courts,* 13 AJIL 22 (1919).

[83] 2 OPPENHEIM, *supra* note 15, at 278-79; J. STONE, *supra* note 49, at 435.

[84] J. SALONGA, *supra* note 1, at 319.

enemy ships in the belligerent's ports or taken at sea when war is declared cannot be confiscated.[85]

§ 9-10.5. **Effect of War on Trade.** Prior to World War I, there was no generally accepted rule of international law that prohibited trade and other forms of economic intercourse between belligerents and their nationals during war. At the time of World War II, however, the Trading with the Enemy Acts passed by various nations, expressly prohibited trade that could be beneficial either to the opposing belligerent or its nationals.[86]

§ 9-10.6. **Effect of War on Contracts.** The effect of war on contracts generally has been the subject of national, rather than international law, yet the practices of most states in this area have been to terminate existing contracts between belligerents and their nationals upon the declaration of war that tend to aid, or communicate with the enemy or its nationals in any way.[87]

§ 9-11. Land Warfare

Practices and customs accepted by nations during periods of armed conflict constitute international rules of warfare binding on all nations. International law as applied to land warfare governs much of the activity that a state can legally engage in during wartime, specifically distinguishing between combatants and civilians; outlining the permissible methods of conducting land warfare; regulating the destruction and seizure of enemy property; the treatment of the wounded, sick and dead, prisoners of war and the occupation of enemy territory.[88]

§ 9-11.1. **Distinction Between Combatants and Civilians.** Such a distinction did not exist until the 17th century as belligerents considered war a total armed confrontation involving the killing of both active combatants and enemy civilians.[89] This practice slowly changed, because states, including belligerents, felt obliged to take measures to protect civilians who did not contribute to military operations.

---

[85] Convention Relative to Certain Restrictions with Regard to the Exercise of Capture in Naval War, *done* at the Hague, October 18, 1907, 36 Stat. 2396, T.S. 544, 1 Bevans 711.

[86] J. SALONGA, *supra* note 1, at 342.

[87] Treaty of Versailles, June 28, 1918, art. 299, para. a, 1919 FOR. REL. (Paris Peace Conference, XIII) 55, 740, 743; Treaty of Peace with Italy, 1947, art. 81, T.I.A.S. 1648, 49 U.N.T.S. 3. *See also* Hall, *The Effect of War on Contracts,* 18 COL. L.REV. 325 (1918); G. WEBBER, EFFECT OF WAR ON CONTRACTS (2d ed. 1946).

[88] G. SCHWARZENBERGER, *supra* note 1, at 202-3; M. GREENSPAN, THE MODERN LAW OF LAND WARFARE (Berkeley 1959).

[89] J. SALONGA, *supra* note 1, at 343.

However, civilians are not always protected from all the effects of military operations. Aerial and naval bombardment of land installations, seiges and blockades all cause human suffering, and this unfortunate dilemma stems from the doctrine of military necessity which holds that "a belligerent is always justified in resorting to all measures which are indispensable to bring about the complete submission of the enemy as soon as possible, by means of regulated violence not forbidden by conventional or customary rules of law."[90]

§ 9-11.2. **Violence Against Enemy Combatants.** Violence directed against enemy combatants or enemy military personnel belonging to a belligerent's army, navy or air force and actively engaged in combat, and persons part of these military forces but not actively engaged in combat is regulated by international law.[91] Active military combatants are subject to be killed by the enemy as long as they resist. Non-active combatants, in contrast, who accompany military forces, or who act in a civilian capacity, are entitled to be treated as prisoners of war provided they are legally entitled to be with the armed forces.[92] Para-military or irregular forces are also to be treated as prisoners of war if they are commanded by a person responsible for his subordinates; they wear a fixed, distinctive sign recognizable at a distance; they carry arms openly; and they conduct their operations in accordance with the laws and customs of war.[93] Irregular combatants who do not conform to these conditions are not classified as legal members of a belligerent's forces, and are therefore not protected by international law as prisoners of war.[94] They are placed in the enemy's discretion, but they must be treated with humanity, and have the right to a fair and regular trial.[95]

§ 9-11.3. **Permissible Methods of Land Violence.** The moral standard inherent in all international rules of war: the minimal destruction of human values in order to achieve the purposes of

---

[90] *Id.*

[91] Geneva Convention Relative to the Treatment of Prisoners of War, Aug. 12, 1949, 6 U.S.T. 3316, TIAS 3364, 75 U.N.T.S. 287. *See also* Baxter, *So-Called "Unprivileged Belligerents," Spies, Guerrillas and Saboteurs,* 28 BR. Y.B. INT'L L. 323 (1951); Ford, *Resistance Movements in Occupied Territory,* 3 NED. T. 355 (1956); Trainin, *Questions of Guerrilla Warfare in the Law of War,* 40 AJIL 534 (1946).

[92] Geneva Convention Relative to the Treatment of Prisoners of War, Aug. 12, 1949, 6 U.S.T. 3316, TIAS 3364, 75 U.N.T.S. 135.

[93] *Id.*

[94] *Id.*

[95] *Id.*

war has limited the permissible methods of land violence. This principle provides that civilians must be spared as much as possible from destruction not called for by military necessity. The use of poison to contaminate food and water supplies, poisonous gases, biological and bacteriological weapons, explosive bullets, dum-dum bullets and the use of other weapons to cause mass and unnecessary human suffering are clearly prohibited by international law.[96] This would implicitly prohibit the use of nuclear weapons. Ruses and stratagems that take unfair advantage of the enemy's good faith and fair dealing, such as the misuse of flags of truce or the Red Cross emblem, or pretending surrender to the enemy, or hiring assassins to kill enemy officers are likewise prohibited since they are calculated to entrap the enemy by inducing him to lower his defenses.[97] Attacking and bombarding undefended cities, towns, villages, or buildings are also proscribed. If it is militarily necessary to attack defended towns, the attacker must first warn the victim, and not destroy churches, cultural and scientific centers, charitable buildings, historic monuments, hospitals or other buildings used to treat the wounded and sick unless they are being used for military purposes.[98] The victim must demark these buildings by clearly recognizable and appropriate signs.[99]

§ 9-11.4. Seizure and Destruction of Enemy Property. Since the 19th century, the seizure of and destruction of enemy property not related to military operations have been prohibited.[100] Enemy belligerents can seize all enemy public property during wartime as part of the spoils of war, but they cannot seize enemy private property. Property legally seized during military operations becomes the property of the captor, but property illegally seized cannot be retained by the captor: it must be returned to the legitimate owners at war's end.[101]

---

[96] Conventions with Respect to Customs on War and Land, with annex and regulations [hereinafter cited as HAGUE REGULATIONS], Declaration (IV, 3) Concerning Expanding Bullets, July 29, 1899, T.S. 403, 1 Bevans 247.

[97] Convention Respecting the Law and Customs on War and Land, with annex of regulations, Jan. 26, 1910, 36 Stat. 2277, TS 539, 1 Bevans 631.

[98] *Id.*

[99] *Id.*

[100] HAGUE REGULATIONS, art. 25, para. 9. *See also* Borchard, *Enemy Private Property,* 18 AJIL 523 (1924); Chadwick, *Foreign Investments in Time of War,* 20 L. Q. REV. 167 (1904); Drucker, *Restitution in International Law,* 15 ICLQ 263 (1966); Turlington, *Enemy Property,* L. & CONTEMP. PROB. 1 (1945); Turlington, *Treatment of Enemy Private Property,* 22 AJIL 270 (1928).

[101] HAGUE REGULATIONS, art. 25, para. g.

§ 9-11.5. Treatment of the Wounded, the Sick and the Dead. Since the 1864 Geneva Convention for the Relief of the Wounded and Sick of Armies in the Field, the treatment of the wounded, sick and dead has been a subject of international law. According to present international law,[102] belligerents must search for, collect and protect all wounded and sick enemy military personnel by treating them humanely without regard to sex, race, religion, political opinions or any other criteria; by giving them medical attention, treatment and care; and by not exposing them to contagious or infectious conditions.[103] Dead belligerents must be protected from theft, maltreatment and spoliation. Belligerents are also required to keep proper records of all wounded, sick and dead.

Both military and volunteer medical units and centers together with their personnel must at all times be absolutely protected and respected by enemy belligerents, unless they have engaged in warlike activities. If they are captured, the captor must allow them to carry on their normal medical duties, but they can be detained only so long as is necessary for them to finish their duties when they are to be repatriated. Military personnel who collect, transport or treat the wounded, such as nurses' aids, orderlies, or stretcher-bearers, are to be treated as prisoners of war, but if they are captured while performing medical duties, they are to be treated as all other medical personnel.

§ 9-11.6. Prisoners of War. The 1949 Geneva Convention relative to the Treatment of Prisoners of War[104] guarantees prisoners of war a minimum standard care and treatment. Persons entitled to be treated as prisoners of war include members of regular armed forces, militias, volunteer corps, organized resistance movements; authorized civilian members of military aircraft crews; war correspondents; members of the crews of merchant vessels, and civilian aircraft; members of the armed forces of an occupied country; and persons who have been received by neutral powers in their territory who they are required to intern under international law.

---

[102] Geneva Convention for the Amelioration of the Condition of the Wounded and Sick in Armed Forces in the Field, Aug. 12, 1949, 6 U.S.T. 3114, T.I.A.S. 3362, 75 U.N.T.S. 31.

[103] *Id.*

[104] Aug. 12, 1949, 6 U.S.T. 3316, TIAS 3364, 75 U.N.T.S. 135. *See also* Baxter, *Asylum to Prisoners of War*, 30 BR. Y.B. INT'L L. (1953); Charmaty & Wit, *Repatriation of Prisoners of War and the 1949 Convention,* 62 YALE L.J. (1953); Levie, *The Employment of Prisoners of War*, 57 AJIL 318 (1963); Levie, *Penal Sanctions for Maltreatment of Prisoners of War*, 56 AJIL 433 (1963).

Prisoners of war must be treated humanely with full civil rights, and are entitled to free medical treatment and care without discrimination based on race, nationality, religious beliefs, or political opinions. Moreover, prisoners of war cannot be forced to divulge information by physical or mental torture, or by any other means of coercion; and are entitled to give only their name, rank, date of birth and army, regimental or personal serial number. Prisoners of war are entitled to retain their non-military personal belongings, and are to be interned only on land, in clean and healthy surroundings outside the zone of military operations. Internment camps are to be clearly recognizable from the air, and their location made known to the enemy. They cannot be used to shelter military operations or installations.

Prisoners are to be housed with members of their own armed forces, or with their consent, on the basis of nationality, language and custom. They can work only in or on the camp, in agriculture, certain industries, the transporting and handling of non-military supplies, commercial business, arts and crafts, domestic service and non-military public utilities. Each prisoner has the right immediately upon capture or arrival in an internment camp to write to his family and the Central Prisoners of War Agency (set up in a neutral country), to send and receive letters and cards, to receive parcels of food, clothing, medical supplies, and religious, educational or recreational articles, and to execute legal documents such as powers of attorney and wills.

Each belligerent is required to notify the Information Bureau established in its territory at the beginning of the war, of the capture, the place and circumstances of captivity, and the state of health or death of every prisoner of war. The Central Prisoner of War Agency will collect information concerning prisoners of war and transmit it to the prisoner's home country.

Representatives and delegates of neutral states designated as Protecting Powers are permitted to visit all internment camps and to interview all prisoners. They are also empowered to use their influence to act on behalf of prisoners who are maltreated.

Seriously ill or wounded prisoners are entitled to repatriation either to their home countries or to a neutral state during hostilities, provided that any person thus repatriated does not serve on military duty for the duration of the war. Those prisoners who are incurably ill or wounded, or not expected to recover within one year, or whose mental or physical condition appears to be grave and permanently diminished, must be repatriated directly to their home countries. All prisoners are to be repatriated immediately after the end of the war except those against whom criminal proceedings have been undertaken, or who have been convicted of criminal offenses.

§ 9-11.7. **Individual Responsibility for Mistreating Prisoners of War.** One of the most controversial issues in modern international law, individual responsibility for mistreating prisoners of war, involves two main questions: (1) Does international law apply to individuals as well as to states?; (2) For what acts may an individual be held criminally responsible under international law?

That international law applies to individuals and that individuals can be held responsible for war crimes and crimes against humanity was stated by the International Military Court at Nuremberg. It declared: "Crimes against international law are committed by men, not by abstract entities, and only by punishing individuals who commit such crimes can the provisions of international law be enforced."[105]

The Law of Nations may be primarily a law between states, but states themselves operate by virtue of the will of individuals, and the individual is thus the ultimate source of authority. In a broad sense, therefore, international law has always applied to individuals, and many authors have given strong arguments for the recognition of the international legal position of the individual in modern international law.[106] In spite of the opinion of the Permanent Court of International Justice in the case of *Danzig* (Jurisdiction of the Courts)[107] that international law may in most of its spheres be applicable to states as its subjects, nevertheless, nothing inherent in the character of international law excludes its application to individuals.

Now, for what acts may an individual be held criminally responsible under international law? The essence of a crime in national law is that it injures not only the party to whom it is directed, but the community as a whole. An international crime, therefore, is an act which injures not only the state or individual against whom it is directed, but the whole international community. According to Oppenheim, ". . . war crimes are such hostile or other acts of soldiers or other individuals as may be punished by the enemy on capture of the offenders. They include acts contrary to International

---

[105] 22 I.M.T. 565-66 (1949).

[106] AMER. POL. SCI. REV. 217 (1943); Aufricht, *Personality in International Law,* in MODERN LAW OF NATIONS (P. Jessup ed. 1946).

[107] [1928] P.C.I.J., ser. B., No. 15.

Law perpetrated in violation of the law of the criminal's own State, such as killing or plunder for satisfying private lusts and gain, as well as criminal acts contrary to the laws of war committed by order and on behalf of the enemy State."[108] Article 38 of the Statute of the International Court of Justice provides the standards for determining whether an act is a war crime, and hence an international crime. If the act is a war crime, an individual can be held responsible for it under international law. It would be a great injustice if individuals were not held criminally responsible for their act or acts which cause grave harm to humanity or to the international community.[109] The Geneva Convention relative to the Treatment of Prisoners of War,[110] acceded to by the vast majority of states, imposes certain obligations on the belligerent who detains them. Breaches of these international obligations should, therefore, be international crimes, subjecting the violator to international sanctions, penalties, trial and punishment.

On the other hand, it has been argued that international law does not apply to individuals, but only to states, and that only national law applies to individuals. It is a general principle of the Law of Nations that duties and responsibilities are placed on states and nations, and not on individuals. The breach of an international duty gives rise to the collective responsibility of the delinquent state. A person cannot be punished for an act which he committed in pursuance of government or superior orders. A subordinate must always obey orders absolutely. Furthermore, obedience to military orders, not obviously unlawful, is the duty of every member of the armed forces, and no one, in a condition of war discipline, can be expected to weigh scrupulously the legal merits of orders received; that the rules of warfare are often controversial; and that an act otherwise amounting to a war crime may have been executed in obedience to orders conceived as a measure of reprisals.[111]

Nevertheless, an individual can be held responsible for an act under national or international law, if it has been branded a crime in a statute, convention or law.[112] "Superior orders" must certainly be taken into consideration in the defense of an individual standing trial for international crimes, but under no circumstances

---

108 2 L. OPPENHEIM, *supra* note 15, at 566-67.

109 2 L. OPPENHEIM, *supra* note 15, at 569.

110 Aug. 12, 1949, 6 U.S.T. 3316, TIAS 3364, 75 U.N.T.S. 135. There have been 122 ratifications and accessions as of Jan. 31, 1969.

111 L. OPPENHEIM, *supra* note 15, at 569.

112 H. LAUTERPACHT, 2 OPPENHEIM'S INTERNATIONAL LAW 567 (7th ed. 1961).

is it to be regarded as an absolute justification for criminal acts, even if the accused had to act under penalty of death.[113] In fact, military laws of many civilized nations contain express provisions to the effect that a subordinate may obey only lawful orders, such as Amendment 34 of the British Manual of Military Law. Article 8 of the International Military Tribunal Charter for the Nuremberg Trials provided: "The fact that the defendant acted pursuant to orders of his government or of a superior shall not free him from responsibility but may be considered in mitigation of punishment if the Tribunal determines that justice so requires." So, the plea of superior orders cannot be considered an absolute defense. It has been alleged that some Allied nationals in World War II committed certain war crimes, but it is no defense for an individual to claim that a war crime for which he is being tried was also committed by opposing belligerents.[114]

It seems that none of the arguments against individual responsibility for war crimes constitute sufficient legal basis for denying individual responsibility for international crimes. It may be concluded, therefore, that if an act is adjudged a crime according to international custom, international conventions, applicable national law, or the general principles of justice, then an individual may be held responsible for it under international law.[115]

§ 9-12. The Belligerent Occupation of Enemy Territory[116]

Since the 18th century, the belligerent occupation of enemy territory has been recognized as distinct from the conquest of enemy

---

[113] R. WOETZEL, THE NUREMBERG TRIALS IN INTERNATIONAL LAW 118 (1960).

[114] A. LEE, INTERNATIONAL LAW, CASES AND OTHER MATERIALS 542 (2nd ed. 1960).

[115] R. WOETZEL, supra note 113, at 121.

[116] See generally Baxter, The Duty of Obedience to the Belligerent Occupant, 27 BR. Y.B. INT'L L. 235 (1950); Baxter, Passage of Ships Through International Waterways in Time of War, 31 BR. Y.B. INT'L L. 187 (1954); M. DOMKE, THE CONTROL OF ALIEN PROPERTY (New York 1947); M. DOMKE, TRADING WITH THE ENEMY IN WORLD WAR II (New York 1943); Downey, Jr., Captured Enemy Property: Booty of War and Seized Enemy Property, 44 AJIL 488 (1950); Enemy Property, a symposium, 11 L. & CONTEMP. PROB. (1945); E. FEILCHENFELD, THE INTERNATIONAL ECONOMIC LAW OF BELLIGERENT OCCUPATION (Washington 1942); Fitzmaurice, Some Aspects of the Modern Contraband Control and the Law of Prize, 22 BR. Y.B. INT'L L. 73 (1945); Fraleigh, The Validity of Acts of Enemy Occupation Authorities Affecting Property Rights, 35 CORN. L.Q. 89 (1949-50); D. GRABER, THE DEVELOPMENT OF THE LAW OF BELLIGERENT OCCUPATION, 1863-1914 (1948); Gutteredge, The Rights and Obligations of an Occupying Power, 64 Y.B.W.A. (1952); Mann, Enemy Property and the Paris Peace Treaties, 64 L.Q. REV. (1948); Morgenstern, The Validity of the Acts of the Belligerent Occupant, 28 BR. Y.B. INT'L L. 291 (1951); Rubin, The Inviolability of Enemy Private Property, 11 L. & CONTEMP. PROB. 166 (1945); SCHIGALL, THE

(Continued)

territory and has been given the status of a legal regime and government. Accordingly, the occupant possesses full authority over the territory and its people, subject, however, to certain limitations that ensure a minimal destruction of human values. Present international law principles relative to the occupation of enemy territory, as enunciated in the 1949 Geneva Convention relative to the Treatment of Civilian Persons in Time of War,[117] primarily consist of the occupant's duties, consistent with the doctrine of military necessity, to continue the orderly administration of government; to treat the territory, its people and resources, as his own subjects, without compelling them to swear allegiance to him or to contribute to military operations; to maintain public order and safety by preserving and continuing the laws and institutions in force at the time of occupation as much as possible; by applying general rules of criminal conduct; by protecting the inhabitants and treating them humanely and with respect; by not forcibly transporting them outside the enemy territory; and by requisitioning only those goods and services solely for the occupying army, proportionate to the country's resources, and only upon the authority of the local commander. According to the Convention, requisitions of food, medical supplies and hospitals needed by the civilian population are forbidden. The occupant is permitted to collect such taxes and contributions to be used solely for purposes of administering the territory, which, however, must be assessed according to the rules in operation at the time of occupation, and only levied on the written order of the Commander-in-Chief. The appropriation and use or conversion of enemy property by the belligerent is generally limited to military property and installations which he can legitimately destroy if necessary, all state-owned monies and securities, transportation and communication facilities, and arms and ammunition supplies. Public and private property of a non-military nature can only be administered by the occupant. All religious, charitable, cultural, historic, scientific and city-owned property and buildings are absolutely immune from seizure, destruction or wilful damage. The occupant is also authorized to issue currency, provided, however,

---

ENEMY PROPERTY ISSUE, No. 246 (Public Affairs Pam. 1957); Schwarzenberger, *The Protection of Private Property in the Law of Belligerent Occupation,* 12 INDIAN Y.B. INT'L AFF. 56 (1963); Skubiszewski, *Currency in Occupied Territory and the Law of War,* 9 JAHRBUCH FUR INTERNATIONALES RECHT 161 (1959-60); Smith, *Booty of War,* 23 BR. Y.B. INT'L L. 227 (1946); Smith, *Civilians in Occupied Territory,* 4 I.C.L.Q. 140 (1955); G. VON GLAHN, THE OCCUPATION OF ENEMY TERRITORY, A COMMENTARY ON THE LAW AND PRACTICE OF BELLIGERENT OCCUPATION (Minneapolis 1957).

[117] Aug. 12, 1949, 6 U.S.T. 3516, T.I.A.S. 3365, 75 U.N.T.S. 287.

that it is done solely to promote economic order, and not to further the interests of the occupant.

§ 9-13. Naval Warfare[118]

Naval warfare between two belligerents is restricted to the high seas, and belligerents' territorial waters, lakes and rivers and the international air space as well as that of the belligerents. The territorial waters of neutral powers are immune from such conflict. International rules governing warfare on the seas, generally complementary to the rules governing land warfare, give belligerents the right to capture and convert all enemy armed vessels, and to attack all enemy public naval vessels without warning. Belligerents must warn enemy merchant vessels before attack, except where the merchant vessel is participating in naval operations as by sailing in convoys or supporting submarines; cease firing when a surrendering vessel brings down its flag; and not attack hospital, religious, scientific or philanthropic vessels, nor coastal fishing ships, local trading boats, as long as they are not participating in hostilities.

During World War II, special problems arose concerning the belligerent character of defensively-armed enemy merchant ships. No universally accepted rules define their character and states follow different practices. Some consider that such ships do not change their status merely by being defensively armed, and if capture is resisted, then the crews of such ships are to be treated as legitimate members of the enemy's armed forces, as prisoners of war. Other nations feel that armed resistance by the crew of such ships contravenes the accepted rules of warfare, and they are to be treated as war criminals

Technological advances brought about in the 20th century, the submarine and water mines, necessitated new international rules to govern their use. Accordingly, the 1907 Hague Convention No. VIII,[119] and the 1930 London Naval Treaty,[120] incorporated the uses of such weapons into the body of international law by declaring that mines must be anchored, and cannot be placed near the coast of a belligerent solely to destroy commercial shipping, tor-

---

[118] *See* Bailey, *The Sinking of the Lusitania,* 41 AM. HIST. REV. 54 (1935); Borchard, *Armed Merchantmen,* 34 AJIL 107 (1940); C. COLOMBOS, THE PRESENT LAW OF THE SEA § § 538-57, 887 (1962); The Lusitania, 251 F. 715 (U.S. Dist. N.Y. 1918); H. SMITH, LAW AND CUSTOMS OF THE SEA 78-89 (1959); R. TUCKER, THE LAW OF WAR AND NEUTRALITY AT SEA (1957), ch. 4.

[119] Convention Relative to the Laying of Automatic Submarine Contact Mines, Oct. 18, 1907, 36 Stat. 2332, T.S. 541, 1 Bevans 669.

[120] Treaty for the Limitation and Reduction of Naval Armament, April 22, 1930, 46 Stat. 2858, T.S. 830, 2 Bevans 1055, 112 L.N.T.S. 65.

pedoes must be rendered harmless if they miss their target, and submarines, before destroying a resisting enemy merchant ship, must place the ship's crew and papers in safety. Violations of this latter rule were tried by the Nuremberg International Military Tribunal in 1946.

The Hague Convention No. VIII[121] restricts naval bombardment to defended towns, ports, villages or dwellings, to legitimate military targets, and installations (even if located in undefended towns and ports) and undefended towns or ports which resist legal requisition orders. The Convention further calls for nations during naval bombardment, consistent with military necessity, not to destroy churches, museums, historical monuments and hospitals as long as they are not engaged in military operations, and to warn the victim of the attack.

International law as embodied in the 1949 Geneva Convention for the Amelioration of the Condition of the Wounded, the Sick and Shipwrecked Members of Armed Forces at Sea,[122] obliges states to protect such persons, by searching for and collecting them after naval battles, providing them with medical treatment and care, removing them from combat areas, and keeping adequate records of them. Such persons if taken aboard neutral ships no longer can take part in military operations. States must refrain from attacking hospital ships, belonging either to the enemy or to international organizations, and such ships, if captured in an enemy port, must be permitted to leave. If such ships engage in military operations, or impede the military operations of the enemy, their protection is abrogated, and enemy ships have the right to search such vessels to ensure their compliance. Hospitals ships must be clearly designated such as outlined in the Convention.

§ 9-14. Air Warfare[123]

Air warfare, although not specifically regulated by international agreements, follows practices commonly accepted by states to the extent that air warfare cannot be directed exclusively and delib-

---

[121] Convention Relative to the Laying of Automatic Submarine Contact Mines, Oct. 18, 1907, 36 Stat. 2332, T.S. 541, 1 Bevans 669.

[122] Aug. 12, 1949, 6 U.S.T. 3217, T.I.A.S. 3363, 75 U.N.T.S. 85.

[123] *See* I J. GARNER, INTERNATIONAL LAW AND THE WORLD WAR (1920), ch. 19; Jennings, *Open Towns,* 22 BR. Y.B. INT'L L. 258 (1945); D. JOHNSON, RIGHTS IN AIR SPACE (1965); Phillips, *Air Warfare and Law,* 21 GEO. WASH L.REV. 311 (1953); Schwarzenberger, *The Law of Air-Warfare and the Trend Towards Total War,* 1 U. MALAYA L.REV. 120 (1959); J. SPAIGHT, AIR POWER AND WAR RIGHTS (3rd ed. London 1947).

erately against the civilian population. However, its use can be regulated as an extension of other international agreements since these also apply to all forms of warfare. For example, the 1949 Geneva Conventions, prohibiting belligerents from attacking hospitals and other non-military buildings provided that they are so used, would likewise apply to aerial warfare. Moreover, international laws prohibiting the use of gases, poisons, biological and bacteriological weapons would similarly prohibit their use in air operations. And, the 1907 Hague Convention IV,[124] in outlawing the "attack or bombardment by whatever means, of towns, villages, dwellings, or buildings which are undefended," also interdicts the use of aerial warfare in similar operations.

In 1923, the Hague Draft Rules on Aerial Warfare[125] attempted to restrict aerial warfare to purely military objectives such as armed forces, military establishments or depots, factories and industrial centers manufacturing military supplies and military transportation and communication services and facilities. These rules, however, were never adopted.

§ 9-15. Termination of Hostilities[126]

Hostilities can end in a variety of ways, such as the defeat of one party, mutual acceptance, and by the signing of peace treaties. Hostilities can be suspended by concluding an armistice, cease-fire or truce.

Armistices, cease-fires and truces, in the usual usage of the terms, simple denote a temporary suspension or halt in the conduct of armed hostilities for whatever purposes. Generally, such agreements take place to enable both sides to remove the wounded, sick or dead from combat areas. In some cases, where it was not possible for both sides to conclude a peace treaty, these "temporary" agreements have simply been accepted as peace treaties, and may be local or general. If an armistice is seriously broken by one party, the other party can resume hostilities immediately. A cease-fire is an unconditional halt in operations, and a truce is coupled with several conditions.

A typical method of terminating war involves the defeat and capitulation of one party as evidenced in a unilateral declaration by

---

[124] Convention respecting the Laws and Customs of War on Land, with annex of regulations, Oct. 18, 1907, 36 Stat. 2277, T.S. 539, 1 Bevans 631.

[125] *Commission of Jurists To Consider and Report Upon the Revision of the Rules of Warfare, General Report,* 32 AJIL SUPP. (1938).

[126] C. PHILLIPSON, TERMINATION OF WAR AND TREATIES OF PEACE (1916).

the defeated nation, usually signifying surrender. This latter means that "if the defeated side complies with the orders given by the victor, but keeping within the limits imposed by the standards of civilization, hostilities will not be resumed."[127]

§ 9-16. Laws of Neutrality[128]

Neutrality, still an instrument of national policy for many states, notably Switzerland, has been practiced by states for centuries, essentially meaning that a nation will not take sides during an armed conflict or favor either belligerent in any way. The modern concept of neutrality imposes a system of reciprocal rights and duties on both neutrals and belligerents. According to Schwarzenberger, the basic rights and duties of states under the doctrine of neutrality are:

> (1) A neutral State must abstain from taking sides in the war and from assisting either belligerent. (2) A neutral State has the right and duty to prevent its territory from being used by either belligerent as a base for hostile operations. (3) A neutral State must acquiesce in certain restrictions which belligerents are entitled to impose on peaceful intercourse between its citizens and their enemies, in particular, limitations of the freedom of the seas.[129]

Specifically, these rights, relative to the conduct of military operations on land, consist of the duty of neutrals not to permit, and the correlative duty of belligerents not to engage in, the movement

---

[127] G. SCHWARZENBERGER, *supra* note 1, at 216.

[128] G. SCHWARZENBERGER, *supra* note 1, at 217-36; J. SALONGA, *supra* note 1, at 385-403. *See also* G. BOWLES, THE DECLARATION OF PARIS OF 1856 (1900); Brownlie, *Volunteers and the Law of War and Neutrality*, 5 I.C.L.Q. 570 (1956); Carter, *The Dutch as Neutrals in the Seven Years' War*, 12 I.C.L.Q. 818 (1963); E. CASTREN, THE PRESENT LAW OF WAR AND NEUTRALITY, ch. 3 (Helsinki 1954); *Contraband of War*, U.S. NAVAL WAR COLLEGE, 44 INTERNATIONAL LAW STUDIES 1944-1945 (1946); R. DIVINE, THE ILLUSION OF NEUTRALITY (1962); Freman, *Non-Belligerent's Right To Compensation for Internment of Foreign Military Personnel*, 53 AJIL 638 (1959); Garner, *The Outlook for the Law of War and Neutrality*, 22 GROTIUS SOC. TR. 1 (1936); Garner, *The Sale and Exportation of Arms and Munitions of War to Belligerents*, 10 AJIL 749 (1916); P. JESSUP, F. DEAK, W. PHILLIPS & REEDE, NEUTRALITY, ITS HISTORY, ECONOMICS AND LAW (New York 1935-36); Komarnicki, *The Place of Neutrality in the Modern System of International Law*, 80 RECUEIL DES COURS 399 (1952); Malkin, *The Inner History of the Declaration of Paris*, 8 BR. Y.B. INT'L L. 1 (1927); M. McDOUGAL, *supra* note 1, at 384-520; Morganthau, *The Problem of Neutrality in Europe*, 7 U. KAN. CITY L.REV. 1091 (1939); La Pradelle, *The Evolution of Neutrality* (Bourquin ed. 1936), in COLLECTIVE SECURITY 405-06; Rowson, *Contraband Lits*, 24 BR. Y.B. INT'L L. 186 (1947); G. SCHWARZENBERGER, *supra* note 1, at 8; J. SALONGA, *supra* note 1, at ch. 20; Warren, *What Are the Rights of Neutrals Now, Practice?*, 27 ASIL PROC. 128 (1953); Wright, *Destruction of Neutral Property on Enemy Vessels*, 11 AJIL 358 (1917); Wright, *Neutrality and Neutral Rights Following the Pact of Paris for the Renunciation of War*, 24 ASIL PROC. 79 (1930).

[129] G. SCHWARZENBERGER, *supra* note 1, at 219.

of belligerent troops or military supplies across neutral territory, the construction of communication or information installations or facilities, and the use of neutral territory as a base on which to organize military operations, or to enlist people into its armed forces. Neutrals can offer asylum to members of belligerent forces, if such forces are disarmed and interned. While neutrals do not have to allow wounded or sick belligerent military personnel passage through its territory, it must accept and intern such personnel of either side, if turned over to them by a belligerent. Neutrals are not obliged to prohibit commercial trading with belligerents, and have the right to resist by force such activities of a belligerent that contravene its neutral status, without losing that status.

Neutral persons located in the territory of a belligerent are not entitled to greater protection than belligerent nationals, and property, similarly located, is subject to requisition by the belligerent, provided due compensation is made. Neutrals and their property located in territory occupied by a belligerent are to be treated basically the same as enemy nationals; are protected by the 1949 Geneva Conventions; and have the right to leave the territory if their departure is not adverse to the military interests of the belligerent. Neutrals and their property located in enemy territory are generally held to assume the character of the local enemy population.

Rights and duties are also imposed upon nations regarding the conduct of naval warfare, as neutrality also applies to the territorial waters and seas of neutral states. Belligerents are prohibited from using neutral territorial seas either to conduct naval operations, or as bases for such activities, but belligerents have the right of passage through neutral territorial waters, and the right to enter neutral ports for a maximum of 24 hours, to obtain emergency supplies, or to make urgent repairs necessary to make the vessel seaworthy, but not to increase its fighting capacity. Neutrals are obliged not to give naval supplies to belligerents, to arm ships located in its jurisdiction, and to prevent ships armed in its jurisdiction from leaving its territory. While private trading between belligerent and neutral nationals is permitted, the practices of belligerents have shown the tendency in modern warfare to use all economic powers to stop trading which would benefit the enemy in any way. Belligerents have the right to visit and search neutral vessels outside neutral waters to determine if such vessels are transporting contraband, or performing other unneutral services. Neutral ships engaged in the conduct of naval operations or engaged in trading for the enemy who is unable to do so; or in breaking a naval blockade of enemy ports, are to be treated as any belligerent vessel, and can be seized and converted to belligerent ownership. All contraband, goods whose transport is prohibited by belligerents since it consists of goods necessary to the conduct of hostilities, or that would prolong hostilities, belonging to neutrals is subject to seizure, and belligerents have great latitude in determining what goods are to be so classified. Contraband, even if shipped to a neutral port, from whose territory it will be transshipped to a belligerent, is still subject to seizure, under the doctrine of Continuous Voyage. [130]

The same rules also apply to aerial warfare. Neutrals are obliged to prevent the use of their air space by belligerents, and to intern both the crews and any military aircraft that land within its territory.

---

[130] H. BRIGGS, THE DOCTRINE OF CONTINUOUS VOYAGE (1926); G. SCHWARZ-BERGER, *supra* note 1, at 232-33.

CHAPTER 10

The Impact of Computer Information, Storage
and Retrieval on International Law

§ 10-1. Present Availability of Legal Information.[1]

No profession has a greater need for accurate, complete, and up-to-date information than the legal profession. The lawyer needs

---

[1] The sources in the field of computers and the law are of two types: (i) legal publications interested in the advances in the practice of law which computers will yield and (ii) computer science publications attentive to the interest in the computer of the legal profession, and concerned about the legal implications of computer technology.

Professor Michael Duggan of the University of New Hampshire has compiled a bibliography on *Law, Logic and the Computer,* listing over 1000 articles on the subject. An especially interesting feature of this bibliography is the large number of entries from the Soviet Union and Eastern Europe.

Roy N. Freed has prepared a casebook, COMPUTERS AND THE LAW: MATERIALS AND CASES (Boston University School of Law 19   ) for use by his classes in Computer Law at the Boston University School of Law. That the casebook consists of current periodical articles in a looseleaf binder is testament to the dynamic nature of the subject.

Robert P. Bigelow of Boston, Massachusetts, had edited an introductory handbook, COMPUTERS AND THE LAW (2nd ed. 1969) under the sponsorship of the American Bar Association Section on Law and Technology.

Law-oriented periodicals on the subject include: JURIMETRICS JOURNAL (formerly MODERN USES OF LOGIC IN LAW), the quarterly of the American Bar Association Section on Law and Technology; LAW AND COMPUTER TECHNOLOGY, the monthly journal of the World Peace Through Law Center Section on Law and Computer Technology.

General periodicals which address themselves to the subject of computers and the law include: COMPUTERS AND AUTOMATION; COMPUTERS AND THE HUMANITIES; DATA-PROCESSING YEARBOOK; INTERNATIONAL COMPUTER PROGRAMS QUARTERLY; and the JOURNAL OF LIBRARY AUTOMATION.

information in all areas of his work in preparing cases for trial, in advising clients, and in his work as the legal officer of governmental, or international organizations.

In the days of Coke (1552-1634), there were some 5,000 printed cases, and only twice that number 150 years later. Today there are some three million reported cases and the number of reported decisions in the United States alone is increasing at an estimated rate of 15,000 a month. Lawyers have to search not only cases but also statutes, rules, court orders, regulations, and international treaties, all of which are increasing at an incredible rate. And, the number of law journal articles has also become staggering.

Yet, hidden away in this overwhelming mass of materials is invaluable information contained in the great libraries of the world, which would add enormously to the competence of the lawyer and to the administration of justice.[2] In the United States, the Law Library of the Library of Congress, has over one million volumes, the Harvard Law Library over one million, and a few dozen university and state capitol libraries have over 100,000. Europe has a dozen or so law libraries with over 100,000 volumes;[3] the Japanese Ministry of Justice and the Canadian Supreme Court Libraries contain over 100,000, but few other law libraries of that size exist. In Latin America, most law libraries contain less than 10,000 volumes, and most law libraries in Africa and the Middle East contain only a few hundred volumes.

The problem of a general lack of availability of these legal sources goes beyond poorly-supplied law libraries. Most larger libraries are located some distance from the offices of most practitioners, making their widespread use impractical; and law libraries generally do not permit the circulation of their volumes. Law libraries in many countries of the world lack skilled librarians to assure the efficient cataloguing and arrangement of their acquisitions. Smaller libraries often lack the most recent and, in many cases, the most valuable legal sources: law cases, statutes, regulations and other useful legal materials in many countries appear, if at all, only in official gazettes or journals and their search is made doubly onerous by the general lack or inadequacy of indexes.

---

[2] These include the law libraries of the University of Paris, the Russian Academy of Sciences, the Italian Ministry of Justice, Coimbra University in Portugal, Comenius University in Czechoslovakia, Oxford and Cambridge Universities and the Inner Templs in England, Berlin's Kammergericht, and the Palais des Nations in Geneva.

[3] AMERICAN ASSOCIATION OF LAW LIBRARIES, DIRECTORY OF LAW LIBRARIES (Chicago 1968).

The following is a summary of the problem as it exists in various areas of the world:

> Visit the office of the average United States lawyer in a large or small town and you will find he practices with little more than his state code, and his state supreme court decisions, plus a few services on specialized volumes on taxes or some other subject. In Europe a lawyer has his nation's latest (usually out-of-date) code and a few books interpreting its provisions. In Asia the practising lawyer usually has a more out-of-date code plus some newspaper and magazine commentary on court decisions carefully filed away. In Africa a lawyer will rarely have a printed code, as few exist. The African lawyer's law library generally consists of some ancient law books from either France or England, depending on which formerly ruled his nation.[4]

§ 10-2. The Importance and Feasibility of Computerized Legal Information Retrieval

Thus it is that the computer, as an augmenter of printed legal volumes, can make the law more available, more usable, throughout the world.

Lawyers need accurate legal information obtained as rapidly as possible. To search for this information is often time-consuming, frustrating and expensive. In large law firms, highly qualified and highly paid legal experts should not be used merely to search for legal information, but should be able to devote their skills to applying that information to the case at hand. In every firm, the time of the lawyer should be conserved as far as possible for analysis and decision-making, especially since legal problems today are becoming more and more complex while the need for sound, rapid answers to legal questions is becoming ever more important.

What then is the outlook for help from the computer in the search for legal information? Experts in the field do not hesitate to express enthusiasm for its potential, in spite of the difficulties encountered in the present transitional state of its development.[5] The rapid expansion of the computer industry is evidence that the extended and pervasive use of the computer in the field of law is not a mere dream but a very practical undertaking, and the ever-increasing use of the computer in many different fields of activity

---

[4] Address by Charles S. Rhyne, Clearwater, Florida Bar Association, May 1, 1967.

[5] For a discussion of the difficulties in applying computers to legal information retrieval, see Tapper, *World Co-operation in the Mechanization of Legal Information Retrieval: Work Paper on Research and Legal Information by Computer,* in GENEVA CONF. 205-16. GENEVA WORLD CONF. 205-16.

indicates that, although still in its infancy,[6] the computer is "here to stay." Its future in the legal field will depend on the vision and energy of lawyers to make the maximum use of it.

W.L.S. Trivett, a Canadian lawyer, declared that ". . . computer technology is today having a revolutionary impact on our society."[7] D.T. Moody, an American lawyer, is convinced that the computer will make ". . . a tremendous impact upon the law in the very near future . . . the speed of the computer will make the bulk of the law relatively insignificant . . . With the removal of the human element from actual researching and considering the thoroughness of computer, the quality of the lawyer's service and the quantity may increase [and] the possibility of ill-founded decision would decrease."[8]   General David Sarnoff points out that "the tide of knowledge is overwhelming the human capability for dealing with it. So man must turn to the machine if he hopes to contain the tide and channel it to beneficial ends."[9]   He feels that, "(b)y the end of the century, for the equivalent of a few dollars each month, the individual will have a vast complex of computer services at his command. . . . The computer will bring to the attorney all the pertinent laws, decisions, and precedents on any case that concerns him."[10]   It has been predicted that "(t)he computer will soon achieve such universal use in law research as to revolutionize law. . . . (t)he computer will revolutionize the whole field of law by making more law available to more lawyers and government officials in more nations and in more international organizations."[11]

§ 10-3. The Status of Computerized Legal Information Retrieval.

In 1966, the World Peace through Law Center conducted a survey of activities in the United States applying computer technology to legal information retrieval.[12]   In 1967, this survey was expanded to include European activity in the field.[13]

---

[6] The first electronic digital computer was produced in 1949; the first computer widely used for business information processing was unveiled in 1953.

[7] Trivett, *The Computer Impact on Law, Business and Finance,* 9 CAN. B.J. 206-14 (1966).

[8] Moody, *Legal Research: Computer Retrieval of Statutory Law and Decisional Law,* 19 VAND. L.REV. 905-18 (1966).

[9] Sarnoff, *No Life Untouched,* SATURDAY REVIEW, July 23, 1966, at 21-22.

[10] Plowden-Wardlaw, *The Lawyer's Center for Electronic Legal Research,* GENEVA CONF. 220-21.

[11] Rhyne, *The Computer Will Speed a Law-Full World,* 53 A.B.A.J. 420-24 (1967).

[12] WPTLC, LAW RESEARCH BY COMPUTER, No. 4 (1966).

[13] WPTLC, PROPOSAL FOR THE COMPUTERIZATION OF LAW INTERNATIONALLY, No. 9 (1967).

At the time of this writing, some 40 developmental projects are being conducted in the United States, and an equal number of research projects have been undertaken in other nations. In addition, 10 operational services offer computerized searches on both statutory and case law materials to practicing lawyers.

Countries leading in this field are: Australia,[14] Canada,[15] France,[16] Germany,[17] Great Britain,[18] Israel,[19] Italy,[20] Japan,[21] the Soviet Union,[22] Sweden,[23] and the United States.

§ 10-4. International Activities Applying Computer Technology to Law

A World Peace through Law Center Committee was appointed in 1966 to study ways in which the Center could use the computer to retrieve law on a worldwide basis. At a meeting held in Geneva in March, 1967, the Center's Committee of European Experts on Computerization of Law discussed current activity in the field and what role the Center might play. At the Center's third World Conference in Geneva in July 1967, one of 12 working Sessions was devoted to considering the international aspects of Research and Legal Information by Computer.[24] One of the highlights of the conference was the first World Exhibit on Computers and the Law, at which more than 30 displays showed computer processes and legal information retrieval projects.[25]

---

[14] See *New South Wales Bar Association Report on Modern Techniques of Legal Research,* 1 L. & COMP. TECH. 10 (1968).

[15] See Skelly, *Computerization of Canadian Statute Law,* 1 L. & COMP. TECH. 10-14 (1968).

[16] See David, *Plan de Recherche Concernant la Documentation Juridique,* 1 L. & COMP. TECH. 11-13 (1968).

[17] See Hammerbacher, *Der Computer Und das Recht,* 1 L. & COMP. TECH. 14 (1968). 12 1968).

[18] See Tapper, *Legal Information and Computers: Great Britain,* 1 L. & COMP. TECH. 18-19 (1968).

[19] See Fraenkel, *Seventeen Centuries on Tape,* 1 L. & COMP. TECH. 8-9 (1968).

[20] See Losano, *L'Information Juridique En Italie,* 1 L. & COMP. TECH. 15-17 (1968).

[21] See *Diet Library Computerization,* 2 L. & COMP. TECH. 27 (1969).

[22] See Kerimov & Andreyev, *Cybernetics Applied to Legal Problems,* 2 SOV. REV. 49 (1961).

[23] See Seipel, *Legal Use of Computers: Sweden,* 2 L. & COMP. TECH. 7-15 (1969).

[24] The following international experts presented papers at this Working Session: Colin Tapper (England), *World Cooperation in the Mechanization of Legal Information Retrieval;* Angelo Gallizia and Enrico Maretti (Italy), *Some Comments on Information Problems in Law,* Thomas C. Plowden-Wardlaw (United States), *The Lawyer's Center for Electronic Legal Research;* and Jerzy Wroblewski (Poland), *The Use of Modern Legal Research. See* GENEVA CONF. 205-34.

[25] See *WPTLC Holds Highly Successful Geneva Conference,* 1 L. & COMP. TECH. 3 (1968).

The Plenary Session of the Geneva World Conference approved a proposal calling for the establishment of a computer "data bank" in Geneva to store legal information for retrieval by Center members, governments, international organizations, and others.[26] This system would record the laws and treaties of all nations and by storing them electronic impulses would make an important contribution to the availability of legal information throughout the world.

The Center's Section on Law and Computer Technology, established in 1967, has developed a number of committees in specialized areas of the law and computer field. Its members contribute to the dissemination of computer information and to programs of future activities. The Section is aided in its work by the 14-member Committee of European Experts on Computerization of Law.

During the Bangkok World Conference on World Peace Through Law, in September, 1969, the Section on Law and Computer Technology sponsored a Seminar on Law, the Computer and Government.[27]

§ 10-5. The Impact of Automation on National Law

Automation has had a tremendous impact on such various branches of the law within national states as patents and copyrights, tax law, criminal law and justice, corporation law, commercial law, constitutional law, domestic relations, estate planning, evidence and municipal law. It has done this first, by making national law more readily available to lawyers, government officials and other persons, and second, by influencing substantive changes in the character of the law itself primarily because it is being used more in business and industry, and because it has become a pervasive part of the existence of every individual.

§ 10-5.1. Patent and Copyright Law.[28] The United States Patent
Office has made microfilm copies of over three million U.S. patents

---

[26] GENEVA CONF. 699-705.

[27] The following topics were discussed at the Bangkok World Conference Seminar on Law, the Computer and Government: (1) World Peace Through Law Center Project for Computerization of Law Internationally; (2) Computers and the Legislative Process; (3) Computers and Patents; (4) Computers and Municipal Problems; (5) Communications and Computers; (6) Presently Operating Computerized Legal Research Services (7) Copyright and Computers; (8) Administration of Justice; and (9) National Government Information Systems.

[28] Benjamin, *Computers and Copyrights,* 152 SCIENCE 181-84 (1966); Cunningham, *Information Retrieval and the Copyright Law,* 14 B. COPY. SOC. 22 (1966); Kurtz, *Patents and Data Processing,* DATA PROCESSING MAGAZINE Nov. 1964, at 9; Stitelman, *International Cooperation in Automated Patent Searching,* 1 L. & COMP. TECH. 15-19 (1968).

in order to store and to retrieve them rapidly from examiner search files.

The patent offices of the world have been overwhelmed with applications. Many of these applications are filed in more than one country, and this involves a separate examination in each of the countries maintaining an examination system. To facilitate the filing and examination of applications, the United International Bureaux for the Protection of Industrial Property has developed a "Plan for a Patent Cooperation Treaty." Another source of international cooperation in the patent area is the work of the International Committee on Information Retrieval of Examining Patent Offices, which is composed of 20 national patent offices and several international organizations. This Committee has established a "Research Associates Program," consisting of one specialist from each of the following countries: Germany, Japan, the Netherlands, Sweden, and the United Kingdom. These specialists have made valuable technological contributions in the field and by their common efforts have shared their knowledge and avoided duplication of research. Under the direction of the World Intellectual Property Organization, a World Patent Index has been put forth that would provide such basic information as the name of the inventor, name of company, title of patent and countries in which a patent had been issued in one central, retrieval place. The World Patent Index would be able to determine how many applications had been granted to one company, to one applicant, how many patent licenses on the same invention had been granted in different countries. Begun in 1965, the plan is in the stages of discussion and planning.

The United States Patent Office has been confronted with the controversial question of whether it should allow patents on computer programs. A case, still in the appellate process at the time of this writing, will become a landmark in this area. The effect of the application of Charles D. Prater and James Wei[29] for a patent on a computerized spectrographic analysis procedure has been predicted as follows:

> A basic running through the voluminous briefs submitted in the Prater and Wei case is whether a computer program, when fed into a computer, converts it into a new and 'unobvious' machine. If the answer is 'yes', then programs are patentable under existing law; otherwise, they are not.[30]

---

[29] Patent Appeal No. 7987 before the United States Court of Customs and Patent Appeals.

[30] DATAMATION, April 1969, at 174.

In the field of copyrights it has been argued that "[t]he public interest demands that progress in information retrieval methods and systems must not be impeded by copyright restrictions on the mere storage of materials in systems intended for scientific and educational use."[31] On the contrary, it has been maintained that the public interest will be ill-served if copyrighted works are not "protected at the point of input, because the lack of such protection will surely destroy incentives for the creation of educational publication for public use."[32] If no copies are made of the full text incorporated in the data processing system and the machine readable version is used only for purposes of analysis and searching, it has been argued that "the copyright owner is not harmed and there is no violation of 'fair use'"[33] Since the principle purpose of the copyright monopoly, it has been maintained, is to benefit the public by encouraging literary productions, courts "should not expand fair use to include unauthorized duplication of portions of copyrighted works by a legal information retrieval system . . . any copying by the system should be held to constitute an infringement."[34]

There has been no court activity, comparable to that in the patent area, toward a clarification of the copyright status of computer programs.[35] As in the patent area, it is necessary to define the activities and capabilities of the computer in terms of the law of copyright in order to determine the degree of protection afforded computer-oriented "writings". This, to date, has not been satisfactorily done.

§ 10-5.2. **Tax Law.** The United States Internal Revenue Service has enhanced its efficiency by increasing the use of computers in the field of tax law.[36] Such record keeping problems as the coordination of pending legal matters, the collection of legal statistics, and the making available of relevant precedents is now done on a nationwide scale by computer and computer-produced tools. An important substantive advantage of the tremendous "remembering"

---

[31] *See* 1 VALP. UNIV. L.REV. 358 (1967).

[32] *Id.*

[33] *Id.*

[34] *Id.*

[35] For some valuable discussion of the problem of copyright protection for computer programs, see the PROCEEDINGS OF THE LAW OF SOFTWARE CONFERENCE (1968), sponsored by the George Washington University Computers-In-Law Institute; PROCEEDINGS OF THE AMERICAN UNIVERSITY SYMPOSIUM ON AUTOMATED INFORMATION SYSTEMS AND COPYRIGHT LAW (1968).

[36] *See* Cohen & Uretz, *RIRA: Storage and Retrieval of Tax Law Data,* 1 L. & COMP. TECH. 2-6 (1968).

power of the computer is that it aids IRS in avoiding inconsistency between positions taken in matters of legislation and regulations and positions taken in individual litigation.

The economic value of the system is significant: "Computer operations added $134 million to Federal tax collections last year (1968), bringing the total additional revenues from this source since 1962 to $300 million."[37]

§ 10-5.3. Criminal Law, Police and Criminal Justice.[38] As the original applications for computers were in the area of record keeping, law enforcement agencies concentrated on using computers to maintain their tremendous records demands in the field of criminal law.

The United States Department of Justice operates a National Crime Information Center, "which provides state and local agencies with instant ('real time') identification data for solution of automobile property thefts and the apprehension of felons."[39]

In the administration of justice, the tremendous calculating speed of the computer has made possible the mathematical simulation of criminal court document and case flows.[40] This technique allows analysts to obtain quick answers to "what if" questions about possible reallocation of court resources. The impetus for this application of mathematical and computer techniques to court functions has been the tremendous backlog of cases developing in American trial courts. The results of this research should be both significant and of lasting value.[41]

Sweden has also undertaken research along these lines,[42] in the areas of both police and criminal information and court processing and the administration of justice.

---

[37] Internal Revenue Service News Release, January 29, 1969.

[38] *See* Sheppard, *Electronic Computers in Criminal Justice,* 8 CAN. B.J. 384-94 (1965).

[39] Crumlish, *Notes on U.S. Government Information Systems,* 1 L. & COMP. TECH. 15-21 (1968).

[40] *See* Navarro & Taylor, *Simulation of the District of Columbia Trial Court System for Processing Felonies,* 2 L. & COMP. TECH. 16-23 (1969), and a special study of the use of computers and the courts with special emphasis on record-keeping, docket and personnel matters by the World Association of Judges and the World Peace Through Law Center, *Use of Computers and Other Automated Processes by the Courts,* Pamphlet Series, Number 8 (Geneva, 1965).

[41] *See* a special study of the use of computers and the courts with special emphasis on record-keeping, docket and personnel matters by the World Association of Judges and the World Peace Through Law Center, *Use of Computers and Other Automated Processes by the Courts,* Pamphlet Series, No. 8 (Geneva 1965).

[42] *See* Seipel, *supra* note 23.

§ 10-5.4. Other Branches of National Law.

In France, the Paris Bar Association has placed the law of corporations on computer, thus offering legal information retrieval of practical interest to corporate executives and counsel.[43] Plans are being formulated to computerize the law of the European Economic Community nations individually, and to link this "data base" to one of international scope (see § 10-6 of this volume). Similar work is being undertaken in the United States at the Georgia Institute of Technology.[44] The sponsor of this project, the School of Industrial Management, is striving for the substantive advantage of making commercial law more accessible and available.

Since World War II, many newly independent nations have endeavored to create constitutional systems different from those that existed prior to independence. In some cases, their political leaders have had only slight familiarity with basic constitutional principles; in other cases, they had some familiarity with the system in operation before independence had been gained, but wanted a "new" constitution to represent the new order. This sometimes led to the adoption either of new constitutions in haste, or of the constitutions of other countries *in toto,* regardless of how well it had served, that often failed to meet the expectations of the people or of the nation's leaders. What was really needed was a facility to examine the specific provisions of many constitutions in order to select those best adapted to local needs. Unfortunately, an up-to-date printed set of the world's constitutions is not readily available; and, even if it were, it would be an enormous task to select all of the provisions on any one subject.[45] The late Charles J. Zinn, Law Revision Counsel of the United States House of Representatives, maintained that the answer is to call upon computer techniques to produce this information, and suggested a list of constitutional topics as the basis of a dictionary to facilitate the formulation of queries in connection with a "key-word" retrieval system;[46] he also compiled a list of written national constitutions and basic laws of the countries of the world, as of May 1, 1967.

---

[43] *See* Lussan, Le Tarnec & Pettiti, *Les Activities du Centre d'Informatique du Barreau de Paris,* 1 L. & COMP. TECH. 2-3 (1968).

[44] *See* Kleiner, *The Computer Impact on Searching Commercial Law,* 5 A. BUS. L.J. 75 (1967).

[45] *See* A. PEASLEE, CONSTITUTIONS OF NATIONS (rev. 3rd ed., The Hague 1965) in four volumes for a compilation of the constitutions of all nations.

[46] *See* Zinn, *Automatic Retrieval of Constitutional Information,* 1 L. & COMP. TECH. 8-10 (1968).

In the field of domestic relations, mathematical modeling techniques have been applied to the determination of alimony to persons legally entitled under Czechoslovak law.[47] The court supplies information concerning previous alimony settlements. To this is added the total of the special needs such as the sickness of the person maintained, the fact that she has her own income, the maintenance capacity of the maintainer, and minimum living expenses. The method aims to provide an objective and just determination of alimony duties, arrived at accurately and rapidly through the use of computers.

Estate planning is proving to be a field especially suitable for computer use. It is an area in which classification is by fact pattern, and the facts are relatively easily obtained. Estate planning by computer has been offered as a practical business operation for some time by a New York firm[48] and the lawyer supplies the relevant facts of a case, and the computer performs the many complicated calculations involved. The merits of the computer in this field have been described as follows:

> A computer system is fast, reliable and relatively inexpensive. It extends the scope of the practitioner's proficiency, and flags problems and opportunities formerly buried beyond his recollection in the closed pages of a mute library. Hours, often days of routine research, arithmetic calculations, verification, tabulation and other mechanical steps can be done by the computer in seconds.[49]

The computer has enormous potential in producing valuable evidence. One author[50] gives a dramatic example of a case in which a lawyer was able through the use of the computer to examine 6.25 million health charts which gave him the information he needed to protect his client and win his case. The computer took 25 minutes to make the search, and it would perhaps require a computer to calculate how long it would have taken the lawyer to check these records manually. Of course, various problems dealing with the impact of the rules of evidence used in any proceeding, have to be solved, but experts feel that the law of evidence will absorb the impact of the computer without undue shock.

---

47 *See* Vrecion, *An Automated Method for Determination of Alimony to Legally Entitled Persons,* 1 L. & COMP. TECH. 7-9 (1968).

48 Paffendorft, *Estate Planning with the Aid of a Computer,* 1 L. & COMP. TECH. 5-7 (1968).

49 *Id.* at 6.

50 Mermin, *Cases, Law and Justice: An Introductory Lecture,* WIS. L. REV. 43 (1967). (1967).

In *Transport Indemnity v. Seib,*[51] an American state appellate court held that a computer tape, as the only embodiment of business records, was nonetheless sufficient as a source of evidence.

In the field of municipal law, the computer is being used to produce up-to-date city codes.[52] Under a grant from Ford Foundation, the National Institute of Municipal Law Officers (NIMLO), an organization of American city attorneys, places the general ordinances of a city on computer tape and uses the computer to generate a variety of indexes and tables impractical to produce by manual means. This capability enhances the usefulness of municipal law as a solution to our present "urban crisis." Once "captured" on tape, the entire city code, or any part of it, is available for retrieval. NIMLO plans to establish a nation-wide municipal law information network for American city attorneys to increase the use, and the quality of municipal law.

§ 10-6. The Impact of Automation on International Law

In the field of international law, the problem of the availability of sources is even more acute than in the field of national law. As lawyers in an interdependent world are becoming increasingly involved in questions of international law practice, they therefore have an increasing need for readily available documentation on international law sources for their work in drafting, advocacy, counseling, and research.

The principal sources of international law include international agreements, court decisions, and customs. The most comprehensive treaty collections are the League of Nations Treaty Series and the United Nations Treaty Series, although they contain by no means all of the treaties entered into by states. Some states publish collections of their treaties. Many others publish their treaties only in their official gazettes, which, if indexed at all, provide only an inadequate guide to their contents, making it extremely difficult to find a particular treaty. Some states maintain no treaty publications at all. Language barriers create another problem of source material availability.

Court decisions, both international and national, constitute a second source of international law. The International Court of Justice, the Court of Justice of the European Communities, and the European Court of Human Rights publish their decisions. There

---

[51] 178 Neb. 253, 132 N.W.2d 831 (1965).

[52] *See NIMLO Completes Phoenix Code Codification - Computerization Project,* 10 MUN. ATT. 2 (1969).

are also some collections of arbitral decisions, although there is no complete, up-to-date collection, with an index to speed the work of the searcher. National court decisions on international law are much more difficult to obtain. In some countries, they are not even published. In countries in which they are published, they are often not indexed. Lauterpacht's *International Law Reports* and *International Legal Materials*, published by the American Society of International Law, cover many decisions from many countries but make no claim of complete coverage. International organization documents are even less readily available. Most organizations do not distribute their documents widely; and few libraries have anything approaching complete coverage. National legislation on international law subjects requires a search of the laws of each particular country; and here again publication, indexing, and language problems often present serious difficulties.

For customary international law material there is no systematic publication of Foreign Office sources in most countries, and such as are published often appear many years after the events covered. For only a few countries is there help from digests such as those edited by Moore, Hackworth and Whiteman in the United States, and that by Parry in England.

Although the need for making international law documentation available is both obvious and pressing, the computer has moved very slowly into this field.[53]   Peter H. Rohn, of the Political Science Department of the University of Washington in Seattle, is engaged in a project for the coding of every treaty in the United Nations Treaty Series for various items. Jan F. Triska of Stanford University has made a full text computerization of these treaties. John H. Jackson of the University of California at Berkeley has indexed several thousand GATT documents. And, a computer analysis of the Test Ban Treaty has been made. However, the international law decisions of domestic courts, the international law materials reposing in international organization documentation, national legislation on international law, and Foreign Office material on international law questions constitute a virgin field and a real challenge for the lawyer and the computer in the days ahead.

The first step in applying computer technology to the task of making international law more available is to gather together its

---

[53] *See* Edwards, Jr., *Electronic Data-Processing and International Law Documentation,* 61 AJIL 87-92 (1967); Harris, *Computers and International Law,* INT'L & COMP. L.Q. 551-53 (1966); Langevin & Owens, *Computer Analysis of the Nuclear Test Ban Treaty,* 146 SCIENCE 1186 (1964); Rohn, *The World's Treaties and the New Craftmanship in International Law,* 1 L. & COMP. TECH. 7-9 (1968).

sources. This task was begun at the Geneva World Conference on Peace Through Law in 1967 when Chief Justice of the United States Earl Warren distributed a compilation of the 300 United Nations treaties which had been submitted for ratification.[54]

When these international law documents have been collected it is proposed that the World Peace Through Law Center establish a service whereby the lawyers of the world could, by merely communicating over a teletype in their own offices, instantly obtain the collected information. Thus, only one copy of these documents need be placed in a centralized location; the computer and communications network would make each available to the lawyer, the judge, the professor or the student at his place of work for immediate problem solving. This is a laudable goal and clearly the computer has the capacity to achieve the goal. But, the enormous expense and effort of location, collection, arrangement, translation, input into the computer, indexing for retrieval and other obvious tasks yet to be performed indicate that it will be some time before the law of the world is fully computerized. In the meantime, the World Peace Through Law Center's arrangement with the International Association of Law Libraries, especially Earl Borgeson, Law Librarian of Harvard's Law School, to supply legal information upon request is serving to fill a long unmet need of jurists, professors and lawyers throughout the world. Also, the Center's volume on *Law and Judicial Systems of Nations* supplies a useful summary for use as a reference to requests for information on the laws of any particular nation.

At the Belgrade World Conference of the Legal Profession in 1971, the Center hopes to have each nation donate for an exhibit the latest copy of its laws or code. These then will be installed in the Center's World Law Library in Geneva and placed on a computer through the use of a new microfilm method. An index will be placed on the computer for speedy retrieval of any nation's laws.

---

[54] *See* GENEVA CONF. 41.

CHAPTER 11

Law for Outer Space and for Space Communications

§ 11-1. The Importance of Establishing Sound Principles for Governing Outer Space[1]

Recent, dramatic technological developments have opened up the vast area of outer space to man's exploration and use. States

---

[1] For information on Space Law, see generally AMERICAN ASSEMBLY OUTER SPACE: PROSPECTS FOR MAN AND SOCIETY (New York 1968); BRITISH INSTITUTE OF INTERNATIONAL AND COMPARATIVE LAW, A SYMPOSIUM (London 1966); Christol, *The 1966-67 Space Treaty: A Manifestation of the World Social Complex,* in WORLD PEACE THROUGH LAW: THE GENEVA CONFERENCE 151-58 (1969) [hereinafter cited as GENEVA CONF.]; Cocca, *Procedure for the Enforcement of Space Law,* in WORLD PEACE THROUGH LAW: THE ATHENS CONFERENCE 471-76 (1965)

(Continued)

have stressed the importance they attach to this exploration by spending billions of dollars, and an untold number of man-hours, to achieve both peaceful and military objectives, and the prestige that accompanies technological successes.

[hereinafter cited as ATHENS CONF.]; M. COHEN, LAW AND POLITICS IN SPACE (Montreal 1964); Collier, *Basic Problems of International Law in Outer Space,* in ATHENS CONF. 476-83; Cooper, *Backgrounds of International Public Air Law.* in Y.B. AIR AND SP. L. 3-38 (1965); COOPER, EXPLORATIONS IN AEROSPACE LAW (Montreal 1968); Coorey, *Some Legal Aspects of Use of Aircraft in* WORLD PEACE THROUGH LAW: BANGKOK CONFERENCE (1969) (to be published) [hereinafter cited as BANGKOK CONF.]; Doyle, *Communication Satellites: International Organization for Development and Control,* 55 CALIF. L.REV. 431-48 (1967); de Abranches, *International Liability Arising from the Use of Outer Space,* in WORLD PEACE THROUGH LAW CENTER: THE WASHINGTON CONFERENCE 182-83 (1967) [hereinafter cited as WASHINGTON CONF.]; Evensen, *The Stockholm Conference on the International Protection of Intellectual Property Rights,* in GENEVA CONF. 172-76; J. FAWCETT, INTERNATIONAL LAW AND THE USES OF OUTER SPACE (Manchester 1968); Goedhuis, *Reflections on the Evolution of Space Law,* 13 T. INT'L R. 109-49 (1966); Goedhuis, *Suggestions Regarding the Interpretation and the Implementation of the United Nations' Outer Space Treaty of 19 December 1966,* in GENEVA CONF. 137-50; Goldstein, *International Cooperation in the Field of Aviation Law,* in ATHENS CONF. 483-92; Haley, *International Law of Outer Space,* in *id.* at 492-505; Haley, *Parameters of Space Law: Present and Future,* in WASHINGTON CONF. 158-63; Inostroza, *Hacia un Nuevo Orden Juridico de la Era Atomica y del Espacio, Bases y Fundamentos,* 27 REV. COL. P.R. 169-230 (1967); INSTITUTE OF AIR AND SPACE LAW, CATALOGUE OF AIR AND SPACE LAW MATERIALS (Montreal 1965); C. JENKS, SPACE LAW (London 1965); P. JESSUP & H. TAUBENFELD, CONTROLS FOR OUTER SPACE AND THE ANTARCTIC ANALOGY (New York 1959); D. JOHNSON, RIGHTS IN AIR SPACE (Dobbs Ferry, New York 1965); H. KEHRBERGER, LEGAL AND POLITICAL IMPLICATIONS OF SPACE RESEARCH (Hamburg 1965); Koutajidis, *The New Guadalajara Convention,* in ATHENS CONF. 525-34; Lachs, *Space Law,* 113 RECUEIL DES COURS 7-103 (1966); Lazar, *International Cooperation in Outer Space,* in ATHENS CONF. 543-45; N. MATTE, TRAITÉ DE DROIT AÉRIEN AÉRONAUTIQUE: EVOLUTION—PROBLÉMES SPATIAUX (Paris 1964); McMahon, *Legal Aspects of Outer Space: Recent Developments,* 41 Y.B. INT'L L. 417-31 (1968); McNAIR, THE LAW OF THE AIR (London 1964); Meyer, *Der Weltraumvertrat,* 16 Z.L.&W. 65-77 (1967); J. MORENOFF, WORLD PEACE THROUGH SPACE LAW (Charlottesville, Virginia 1967); Papacostos, *International Cooperation in the Peaceful Use of Space,* in ATHENS CONF. 545-47; Poulantzas, WORLD PEACE THROUGH THE LAW OF OUTER SPACE, in *id.* at 548-49; Pradelle, *La Charte de l'Espace et des Corps Célester,* 30 REV. GÉN. A.&S. 131-40 (1967); Reich, *International Air Transportation,* in ATHENS CONF. 550-52; Shiffer & Synders, *A Few Major Requirements of International Space Law,* in 9 COLLOQUIM ON THE LAW OF OUTER SPACE, PROCEEDINGS 189-209 (1967); L. TAPIA SALINAS, TEXTOS INTERNACIONALES SOBRE EL ESPACIO (Madrid 1966); H. TAUBENFELD, SPACE AND SOCIETY (Dobbs Ferry, New York 1964); Vaicoussis, *General Principles of Space Law; the Legal Status of Outer Space; the Legal Status of the Celestial Bodies,* in ATHENS CONF. 573-75; G. VERPLAETSE, DERECHO INTERNACIONAL AEREO Y DEL ESPACIO (Madrid 1963); Verplaetse, *Relationship Between Air Law and the Law of Outer Space,* 3 DIR. AEREO 361-67 (1964); Vlasio, *Law and Public Order in Space: A Balance Sheet,* in WASHINGTON CONF., 164-81; Vlasic, *The Growth of Space Law 1957-1965; Achievement and Issues,* Y.B. A. & S. 365-406 (1965); Zhukov, *The Moon, Politics and Law,* 9 INT'L AFF. 32-37 (1966).

For information on International Communications, see Acheson, *INTELSAT: A Means for the Orderly Development and Use of International Satellite Communications,*

(Continued)

Fortunately, both statesmen[2] and jurists[3] have emphasized the absolute necessity of establishing a body of rules and principles to govern the use of outer space. It is generally realized that law should precede, rather than follow, man into outer space, so as to prevent the calamitous use of outer space as an arena for military operations and to preserve outer space for all mankind. The goal is a new system of law, brought into being by the same diligence and ingenuity characterizing scientific advances into space. Although the task is enormous, it will be realized only if states cooperate in enacting a common, peaceful law structure for the universe.

§ 11-2. Cooperative Efforts Toward an Identification of the Legal Problems of Outer Space

Efforts to develop sound principles to be followed in governing outer space have been made by both national and international organizations, and by many distinguished jurists in their participation in national and international organizations, and in conferences, seminars, and by their books and articles.[4] The United Nations has been the focal point and the General Assembly in 1958 began an investigation of space problems by appointing a Committee on the Peaceful Uses of Outer Space[5] to make an extensive study of outer space problems and to report its recommendations. The work of the Committee has resulted in several resolutions,[6] perhaps the most important of which was Resolu-

---

in GENEVA CONF. 166-72; Boffi Boggero, *The Juridical Regime of the Artificial Satellite,* in WASHINGTON CONF. 257-58; Brittenham, *International Communications,* in *id.* at 238-41; Jaffe, *Communications Satellites,* in ATHENS CONF. 505-20; Johnson, *Satellite Communications,* in WASHINGTON CONF., 230-38; Kraichiti, *Comments,* in *id.* at 259-60; Loeving, *Law in the Field of Communications,* in *id.* 249-57; Loeving, *Legal-Economic Patterns of National Communications Systems Throughout the World,* in GENEVA CONF. 179-95; Marks, *Communications—The Lifeline of Civilization,* in ATHENS CONF. 534-43; Moulton, *International Telephone Services,* in WASHINGTON CONF. 241-42; Segal, *Communications Satellites—Pathways to International Understanding,* in ATHENS CONF. 552-62; Segal, *Introductory Remarks,* in WASHINGTON CONF. 226-30; Werner, *International Communications, Progress and the Challenge of the Future,* in GENEVA CONF. 159-66.

[2] *See* President Eisenhower's proposal in his farewell address to the United Nations in 1960 and Premier Khruschev's reply in ATHENS CONF. 493-94.

[3] Most of the many writers on space law could be cited in this connection. *See, e.g.,* Haley, *supra* note 1.

[4] *See* UNITED NATIONS, INTERNATIONAL SPACE BIOGRAPHY (New York 1966).

[5] The committee was appointed pursuant to 8 U.N. GAOR 1348 (1958) and was made permanent by 14 U.N. GAOR 1472 (1959).

[6] *See* 12 U.N. GAOR 1148 (1957); 13 *id.* 1348 (1958); 16 *id.* 472 (1959); 16 *id.* 1721 (1961); 18 *id.* 1962 (1963); 18 *id.* 1884 (1963); 20 *id.* 2130 (1965); 21 *id.* 2222 (1966) (to which the Space Treaty was attached); 23 *id.* 2453 (1968).

tion 1962 (XVIII) oɪ December 13, 1963, commonly known as the Declaration of Legal Principles.[7] The General Assembly also adopted by resolution a recommended Space Treaty,[8] which entered into force on October 10, 1967. These two documents comprise the basic principles which have received the widest consensus to date.

There has been considerable discussion of the binding force of these UN resolutions. When they are adopted unanimously, as was the case of General Assembly Resolution 1962 (XVIII), they certainly express the acceptance by the adopting states of rules governing their conduct. The Space Treaty gives binding force among adopting states to the principles of the Declaration of Legal Rules and adds a few additional principles.

In addition to the General Assembly and its Committee on the Peaceful Uses of Outer Space, several UN Specialized Agencies have been active in the field. Among these are the Economic, Scientific, and Cultural Organization; the International Civil Aviation Organization; the International Telecommunications Union; and the World Meteorological Organization.

Numerous national and international organizations have also made valuable studies and recommendations on outer space. These include the Committee on Space Research of the International Council of Scientific Unions, the U.S. National Aeronautics and Space Administration, the National Aeronautics and Space Council, the National Institute of Space Law, the International Astronautical Federation, the International Academy of Astronautics, the American Bar Association, and other Bar Associations, the International Council of Spatial Law, and the World Peace Through Law Center.

---

[7] For the text of this Resolution, see 6 INT'L L. MAT. 386-90 (1967).

[8] For the text of this Treaty, see J. FAWCETT, INTERNATIONAL LAW AND THE USES OF OUTER SPACE 86-91 (Manchester Univ. 1968). *See also* Adams, *The Outer Space Treaty: An Interpretation in Light of the No-sovereignty Provision,* 9 HARV. INT'L L.J. 140-57 (1968); Christol, *The 1966-67 Space Treaty: A Manifestation of the World Social Complex,* in GENEVA CONF. 151-58; Dembling & Arons, *The Evolution of the Outer Space Treaty,* 33 J. AIR L.&C. 419-56 (1967); Goedhuis, *An Evaluation of the Leading Principles of the Treaty of Outer Space of 27th January 1967,* 15 T. INT'L R. 17-41 (1968); Goedhuis, *Suggestions Regarding Regarding the Interpretation and the Implementation of the United Nations' Outer Space Treaty of 19 December 1966,* in GENEVA CONF. 137-50; Lachs, *Le Premier Traité sur l'Espace Estra-atmosphérique,* 22 COM. INT'L 268-80 (1967); Piradov & Rybakov, *The First Space Treaty,* in 3 INT'L AFF. (Moscow 1967); Vlasio, *The Space Treaty: A Preliminary Evluation,* 55 CALIF. L.REV. 507-20 (1967).

§ 11-3. The Determination of the Limits of Air Space and of Outer Space

It has been a recognized principle of customary international law since Roman times that every state possesses complete and exclusive sovereignty over the airspace above its territory. In this century, this rule has been confirmed by the Paris Convention for the Regulation of Aerial Navigation of 1919,[9] the Havana Convention of 1928,[10] and the Chicago Convention of 1944[11] creating the International Civil Aviation Organization (ICAO). The so-called "two freedoms,": of flying across the territory of a contracting state without landing; and of landing for non-traffic purposes have, however, qualified this rule. Particulars were covered in bilateral agreements, of which the Bermuda Agreement between the United States and the United Kingdom in 1946 became the model.[12]

With the exploration of outer space, many writers, frequently pointing out the need for establishing an upper limit to airspace, have proposed many solutions.[13] It has been suggested that the von Karman line, which defines all flight below 52 miles from the Earth as aeronautical, and all flight higher as astronautical, should serve as the terminal point for the exercise of national sovereignty.[14] This view has been supported by the International Aeronautical Federation, U.S. Air Force Regulations, a draft code prepared in London by lawyers and scientists, and by the scientific fact that air molecules dissociate at about that level.

A practical problem arising from exclusive state sovereignty over unlimited airspace is the fact that few states can launch and recover their spacecraft without using the airspace of another state. The use of this airspace can, of course, be obtained by agreement with the states concerned, but this could, however, lead to the proliferation of bilateral agreements which lack uniformity and create

---

[9] Convention on the Regulation of Aerial Navigation, *opened for signature* October 13, 1919, 11 L.N.T.S. 173.

[10] *Adopted* February 20, 1928, 47 Stat. 1901, 129 L.N.T.S. 223.

[11] *Done* December 7, 1944, 61 Stat. 1180, T.I.A.S. 1591, 15 U.N.T.S. 295.

[12] Air Services Agreement and Final Act of the Civil Aviation Conference. *Signed* February 11, 1946, 60 Stat. 1499, T.I.A.S. 1507, 3 U.N.T.S. 253; as amended May 27, 1966, 17 U.S.T. 683, T.I.A.S. 6019, 573 U.N.T.S. 274.

[13] *See* Ferrar, *The Establishment of a Boundary Between Airspace and Outer Space*, in BANGKOK CONF.; Galloway, *Delimitation of Airspace from Outerspace*, in BANGKOK CONF.; L. LIPSON & N. KATZENBACH, THE LAW OF OUTER SPACE 14 (Chicago 1961); Smirnoff, *The Impact of Space Law on the Classical Notion of Air Sovereignty*, in 7 COLLOQUIM ON THE LAW OF OUTER SPACE, PROCEEDINGS 326-31 (1965).

[14] Haley, *Parameters of Space Law: Present and Future*, in WASHINGTON CONF. 159-60.

other problems. A practical solution would be for states simply to allow freedom of passage of spacecraft for peaceful purposes, but, to date, there has been no agreement among states on the upper limit of territorial peace, and no indication of a relaxing of sovereignty over that space.

Another need in the clarification of the limits of outer space is the application of the term "outer space" to all celestial bodies. The UN resolutions and the Space Treaty are not entirely clear and consistent in making this application. The ambiguity should be eliminated, and the recommendation of jurists that the term should apply to all celestial bodies should be accepted.

§ 11-4. The Peaceful Shared Use of Outer Space

The first principle enunciated by the Declaration of Legal Principles[15] and by the Space Treaty[16] is that the exploration and use of outer space shall be for the benefit of all countries without discrimination. Free access must be given to all celestial bodies, and freedom of scientific investigation is authorized.[17] As a corollary to this provision, national appropriation of outer space by any means is prohibited.[18] These principles, analogous to the freedom of the seas, clarify and confirm the principle that state sovereignty extends only to the limit of airspace, and not into outer space, and should be universally accepted. The possibility of a confrontation between a state that has become a party to the Declaration of Legal Principles and the Space Treaty and an uncooperative non-signatory state, or one between two hostile non-signatory states, could create a very dangerous situation, for which guidelines are needed. However, the adoption of these provisions by the vast majority of states, including the United States and the Soviet Union, gives to their contents a persuasive if not controlling status as international law.

Free exploration and use of outer space, like other freedoms, are limited in the Declaration and Treaty by certain requirements and prohibitions. For example, states are thereby made liable for

---

[15] 18 U.N. GAOR 1962.

[16] 18 UST 2410, TIAS 6347.

[17] Declaration of Legal Principles, art. 1, 18 U.N. GAOR 1962; Space Treaty, art. 1, 18 U.S.T. 2410, T.I.A.S. 6347.

[18] Declaration of Legal Principles, art. 3, 18 U.N. GAOR 1962; Space Treaty, art. 2, 18 U.S.T. 2410, T.I.A.S. 6347. *See also* Cooper, *Who Will Own the Moon? The Need for an Answer,* 32 J. AIR L.&C. 155-66 (1966).

damage done by their spacecraft. When the spacecraft of one state must pass through the airspace of another state, the consent of the latter must be obtained. States are also prohibited from placing weapons of mass destruction and from carrying on certain military activities in outer space or on celestial bodies. They can, however, employ military personnel, and any military equipment, but only for peaceful purposes. Furthermore, they must avoid contamination of outer space, of celestial bodies or contamination of the earth by the introduction of extraterrestial matter.

§ 11-5. The Application of International Law and The UN Charter

Both the Declaration of Legal Principles and the Space Treaty provide that activities in outer space must be in accordance with international law, including the UN Charter.[19] This broad provision offers a substantial body of law to be applied in regulating the exploration and use of outer space. It has been maintained that international law applied to outer space even before the adoption of the Declaration of Legal Principles and the Space Treaty, but in any case, this provision eliminates possible ambiguity on this important point.

Some jurists have expressed concern about the possibility of extending the conflicts, ambiguities and other imperfections of our present body of international law to outer space. One way to avoid this would be by drafting carefully elaborated multilateral conventions to cover space needs as they are anticipated, just as the Declaration of Legal Principles and the Space Treaty set out broad guidelines for the most basic points now anticipated. Such codification must be based on adequate technological information and wide agreement of states.

§ 11-6. The Maintenance of Order[20]

The Maintenance of Order is perhaps the most important principle to govern outer space, since the maintenance of peace in

---

[19] Declaration of Legal Principles, art. 4, 18 U.N. GAOR 1962; Space Treaty, art. 3, 18 U.S.T. 2410, T.I.A.S. 6347. *See also* C. CHRISTOL, THE INTERNATIONAL LAW OF OUTER SPACE (Washington 1966).

[20] Bhatt, *Legal Controls of Exploration and Use of the Moon and Celestial Bodies,* 8 INDIAN J. INT'L L. 519-26 (1966); M. McDOUGAL, H. LASSWELL & I. VLASIO, THE LAW AND PUBLIC ORDER IN SPACE (Yale Univ. 1963); Meyer, *The Term "Peaceful" in the Light of the Treaty on Principles Governing the Activities of States in the Exploration and Use of Outer Space, Including the Moon and Other Celestial Bodies* (Space Treaty, done at London, Moscow and Washington, January 26, 1967), 17 Z.L.&W. 120-34 (1968); Soraghan, *Reconnaissance Satellites; Legal Characterization and Possible Utilization for Peacekeeping,* 13 McG. L.J. 458-93 (1967).

outer space is absolutely essential to avoid universal catastrophe. Article 4 of the Declaration of Legal Principles emphasizes international peace and security, cooperation and understanding. Article 4 of the Space Treaty states categorically that outer space is to be used exclusively for peaceful purposes.

Article 10 of the Space Treaty provides that the nature and conditions of observation are to be determined by the states involved. This leaves important action to be detailed in the future, whereas a better solution to the problem would be to decide on definite, detailed procedures before states become involved in hostile or crisis situations. Similarly, while Article 6 of the Declaration of Legal Principles provides for "appropriate consultations" if potentially harmful activities are observed, no provision is made to resolve the impasse created when the states involved fail, or refuse to agree on what constitutes harmful activities. Again, states should specify in advance the procedures they will follow, such as, submitting to the United Nations a complete statement of the observations made, together with an analysis of the reasons why the activities in question are considered potentially harmful to affect its peaceful solution.

Mainland China, the Soviet Union, the United Kingdom, France and the United States now possess nuclear weapons, and other states will acquire this capability within the next few years. States who are parties to the Nuclear Test Ban Treaty of August 5, 1963,[21] which marked a significant advance in international cooperation, agreed not to test nuclear weapons in the atmosphere, in outer space, or under the water. However, Mainland China and France and other states have not become parties or adopted the treaty. As a result, no universally accepted treaty prohibits completely the use of nuclear weapons in outer space. The need for such a binding prohibition based upon universal international law is evident.

In accordance with General Assembly Resolution 1721 (XVI), of December 20, 1961, the United Nations provides a registry of objects launched into outer space. This is a useful source of information necessary to determine responsibility for space activities, liability for damages caused by space vehicles, and assistance to spacecraft in trouble. Unfortunately, the kind and extent of information required is not prescribed and to date it has been inadequate. Another weakness is the tardiness with which reports on launching objects into outer space have been made. A treaty requiring

---

[21] Treaty banning nuclear weapons in the atmosphere, in outer space, and under water, *done* August 5, 1963, 14 U.S.T. 1313, T.I.A.S. 5433, 480 U.N.T.S. 43. *See* § 14.

prompt and full information would constitute a valuable elaboration of the registration provision of General Assembly Resolution 1721 (XVI).

The use of space reconnaissance is not discussed in the Space Treaty. The principle space users have acquiesced in its use, which seems to suggest the presumption that it is lawful. It has been maintained that such flights are in the interest of mankind in that they represent an efficient form of inspection of military activities, and the avoidance of inspection has always been a major obstacle to disarmament.[22] Soviet jurists for some time considered space reconnaissance illegal, but later accepted it without protest.[23]

The possibility of using force in outer space raises the further question of what acts are permissible in self-defense. Since international law, including the UN Charter, applies to outer space, the right of self-defense, including anticipatory self-defense, would therefore exist against an actual or threatened use of force, such as sending rockets into space in an attack from earth bases. The application of a legally justifiable use of force in self-defense presents many difficulties, and the tests of reasonableness and proportionality would apply.

§ 11-7. The Responsibility and Liability of States and International Organizations for Space Activities[24]

Article 5 of General Assembly Resolution 1962 (XVIII) and Article 6 of the Space Treaty make states responsible for both governmental and non-governmental space activities. Not only does the state which launches a spacecraft bear responsibility, but the state which procures a launching, or a state in whose territory the launching takes place, also bears responsibility. Activities in outer space of non-governmental entities must be authorized and supervised by appropriate state parties.

---

[22] J. FAWCETT, *supra* note 8, at 33.

[23] Brownlie, *The Maintenance of International Peace and Security in Outer Space*, 40 BR. Y.B. INT'L L. 1 (1964).

[24] *Agreement on the Rescue and Return of Astronauts and Objects Launched into Outer Space*, 17 INT'L L. MAT. 149-54 (1968); Dembling & Arongs, *The Treaty on Rescue and Return of Astronauts and Space Objects*, 9 WM & MARY L.REV. 630 (1968); C. DUNSHEE DE ABRANCHES, ESPAÇO ESTERIOR E RESPONSABILIDADE INTERNACIONAL (Rio de Janeiro 1964); Fitzgerald, *The Participation of International Organizations in the Proposed International Agreement on Liability for Damage Caused by Objects Launched into Outer Space*, 8 CAN. Y.B. INT'L L. 265-80 (1966); Lay & Poole, *Exclusive Government Liability for Space Accidents*, 53 A.B.A.J. 831-36 (1967); S. Malik, *Liability for Damage Caused by Space Activities*, 6 INDIAN J. INT'L L. 335-62 (1966).

When an international organization conducts operations in outer space, the organization and the participating states are jointly and severally liable. Questions arising from space activities of international organizations are to be resolved by the states party to the Space Treaty either with the international organization or among themselves. This broad provision, like many others now agreed to, seems sound as far as it goes, but much is left for future negotiation. For example, is the liability of members of the international organization limited in any way, and what happens if the questions arising from space activities end in disagreement which cannot be resolved?

According to Article 8 of Resolution 1962 (XVIII) and Article 7 of the Space Treaty, states are liable for damage caused by objects launched into outer space. In response to General Assembly requests for the elaboration of the rules of liability, the Committee on the Peaceful Uses of Outer Space has produced several drafts of a treaty on the subject, although none has yet been adopted. Among the points to be resolved are the following: Does the operating state have absolute liability for damage caused in airspace, or on the ground? In what circumstances is an international organization liable when conducting space operations? What principles govern the collisions in outer space of spacecraft of different states? What procedures should govern the settlement of claims for compensation resulting from damage? What is the liability of a state for importing extraterrestrial matter which contaminates the earth?

Article 9 of General Assembly Resolution 1962 (XVIII) and Article 5 of the Space Treaty deal with humanitarian principles. The parties are to render all possible assistance in returning astronauts in the event of accident, distress, or emergency landing. They are also to inform the UN Secretary-General of any phenomenon which might constitute a danger to the life or health of astronauts. The Agreement on the Rescue of Astronauts, the Return of Astronauts, and the Return of Objects Launched into Outer Space,[25] signed by 81 nations in 1968, calls on signatories to render all possible assistance and covers such points as the prompt notification of the launching states, notification that the crew of a spaceship has had an accident, the rescue of astronauts making an emergency landing, notification of the launching state of such landing and of the rescue, searches for astronauts presumed to have been lost at sea while attempting to land, the safe and prompt return to the

---

[25] *See* 17 INT'L L. MAT. 149-54 (1968) for text.

launching state of astronauts who make an emergency landing, the return of spaceships or satellites found at sea, and the reimbursement of expenses of assistance by the launching state.

§ 11-8. The Administration and Enforcement of the Law of Outer Space

While the United Nations and other international bodies and jurists have quite naturally devoted their primary attention to the basic principles briefly sketched above, the administration and enforcement of space law, which is not provided for by the Space Treaty, will be an important area of future action. International control and enforcement of established principles and the formulation of new rules and principles in the expanding law of outer space are most important and have been emphasized by many distinguished jurists. Provision must be made for the authoritative interpretation of the Space Treaty and other international agreements and for the policing of space activities. Since international law, including the UN Charter, applies to outer space, and since the United Nations has led the discussion of outer space problems and the formulation of outer space principles, it would seem logical for the United Nations to serve as the center, for the International Court of Justice to give advisory opinions as requested and adjudicate disputes, and for the UN Specialized Agencies to formulate provisions and supervise activities within their several fields.

The continued participation of jurists in the development of sound rules for outer space, shorn as far as possible of dominating political implications, is a *sine qua non* for the days ahead. If they meet their challenge, phenomenal progress in developing a sound law for outer space will be greatly assured.

§ 11-9. Space Communications.

Communication has been called the "lifeline"[26] and the "pulse-beat"[27] of civilization. Since understanding others is the basis of friendliness, and friendliness the basis of peace, communication plays a vital role in maintaining world peace.

---

[26] *See* Marks, *Communications—The Lifeline of Civilization,* in ATHENS CONF. 534.

[27] *See* Werner, *International Communications, Progress and the Challenge of the Future,* in GENEVA CONF. 159. *See also* Acheson, *supra* note 1; Brittenham, *supra* note 1; *Le Développement des Télécommunications Spatiales,* 34 J. TÉLÉ. 281-99 (1967); Loevinger, *Law in the Field of Communications,* in WASHINGTON CONF. 249-57; Marks, *Communication Satellites—A Launch Vehicle for International Understanding,* in BANGKOK CONF.

Early communication was mainly oral, and by such devices as drums, smoke signals and bugles. People living within what we consider short distances of each other, did not "know" each other and individuals generally considered all others to be foreigners, viewing them with hostility. It was not until the middle of the 15th century that printing as known by Western civilization, broadened the scope of communications, and not until the middle of the 19th century that the first rapidly transmitted modern means of communications, the telegraph, was developed.

The development of the five major areas of modern communications, the telegraph, telephone, radio, television and communication satellites, all of which are involved in the growth of space communications, has been a model of international cooperation, primarily because it has served the self-interest of all states. In 1844, the telegraph was first publicly demonstrated, and by 1849, bilateral telegraph treaties were being signed. In 1850, an Austro-German Telegraph Union was formed, and this was followed in 1855 by the creation of a West European Telegraph Union. In 1865, the first International Telegraph Convention[28] was signed, and the International Telecommunications Union was established. This Union, the oldest and largest intergovernmental agency in the world, has held many conferences in the last hundred years, and has improved mechanisms and developed useful standards and regulations for international communications. The Union has a Plenipotentiary Conference which meets about every five years; an Administrative Council which meets annually and acts on behalf of the Plenipotentiary Conference between meetings; a General Secretariat for administrative and financial services; an International Frequency Bureau; and International Telegraph and Telephone Committee; and an International Radio Consultative Committee. Such international cooperation among governments and private telecommunications entities that occurred in the development of the telegraph has served as a valuable precedent for similar cooperation among states in the development of other forms of communications, including satellites.

The extreme importance of the telephone and its wide use for a great variety of services in both war and peace needs no elaboration. Prior to 1876, when Alexander Graham Bell patented an instrument which transmitted the first complete sentence, people could talk to each other only in each other's presence, and much time, labor and effort have been expended in developing the present long distance

---

[28] 56 B.E.S.P. 295.

telephone system. Prior to 1956, and 1964, when the first transatlantic and transpacific telephone cables were respectively laid, regular service between the United States, Europe and the Pacific was made by using high frequency radio. As in the development of the telegraph, states have felt impelled to cooperate in drafting treaties that regulate various uses of telephones and to comply with these treaties even in time of war.

The development of an international law of radio communications[29] has been the result of numerous conferences and conventions, including the International Telecommunications Convention of 1865,[30] the Berlin Conferences of 1903 and 1906, the London Radio Convention of 1912,[31] the Washington Radio Convention of 1927,[32] the Madrid Convention of 1932,[33] several Latin-American conventions,[34] the Atlantic City Convention of 1947,[35] the Copenhagen Convention of 1948,[36] the Buenos Aires Convention of 1952,[37] the Stockholm Broadcasting Agreements of 1952[38] and 1961,[39] the Geneva Telecommunications Convention of 1959,[40] and the International Telecommunications Convention of 1965.[41] Among the principles and rules developed by these conventions are: the prohibition of harmful interference, the international allocation of radio frequencies, the requirement of government licensing of radio stations, the notification of frequencies to the International Frequency Registration Board in Geneva, and the development of rules prohibiting the radio transmission of propaganda across national boundaries.

---

[29] Evensen, *Radio Communications,* in WASHINGTON CONF. 243-45.

[30] 56 B.E.S.P. 295

[31] 38 Stat. 1672, 1 I.N.T.S. 136.

[32] *Done* November 25, 1927, 45 Stat. 2760, T.S. 67, 84 L.N.T.S. 97.

[33] *Done* November 9, 1932, 49 Stat. 2391, T.I.A.S. 67, 115 L.N.T.S. 5.

[34] Inter-American arrangement concerning radiocommunications, *opened for signature* December 13, 1937, 54 Stat. 2514, E.A.S. 200.

Inter-American radio communications convention, *opened for signature* December 13, 1937, 53 Stat. 1576, T.S. 938.

Regional radio convention for Central America, Panama, and the Canal Zone, *opened for signature* December 8, 1938, 54 Stat. 1675, 202 I.N.T.S. 49.

Inter-American radio agreement, *opened for signature* July 9, 1949, 3 U.S.T. 3064, 168 U.N.T.S. 143.

[35] *Opened for signature* October 2, 1947, 63 Stat. 1581, 194 U.N.T.S. 3.

[36] 14 U.N.T.S. 307.

[37] *Signed* December 22, 1952, 6 U.S.T. 1213, T.I.A.S. 3266.

[38] Stockholm Broadcasting Agreement, *done* July 28, 1952, O.I.S. 1914 (Norway).

[39] European Broadcasting Agreement, *done* June 23, 1961, EUROPEAN BROADCASTING CONFERENCE, REGIONAL AGREEMENT FOR THE EUROPEAN BROADCASTING AREA, 1 (1961).

[40] *Opened for signature* December 21, 1959, 12 U.S.T. 1761, T.I.A.S. 4892.

[41] *Done* November 12, 1965, 18 U.S.T. 575, T.I.A.S. 6267.

Although experimental television[42] transmissions occurred shortly after World War I, it was not until 1946 that a public television service supporting an entertainment program was inaugurated. After World War II, television grew very rapidly, and has been a significant factor in national politics, in international relations, and in many other fields. Its potential uses have led to increased international demands for television coverage, and this in turn has added enormously to the significance of the impact of satellite communications to the development of a feeling of community throughout the world.

The most dramatic, recent advance in modern telecommunications is the development of satellite communications. "Never in all man's history has a new technology promised so much in the way of tangible benefits to all peoples of the world at so early a period in its development."[43] A global system is being developed to make communications available to all states, and this development has presented an unparalleled challenge to international cooperation.

The era of active communications satellites was inaugurated by the U.S. SCORE satellite, which in 1958, transmitted to the world a Christmas message from President Eisenhower. This satellite was followed in 1962 by a satellite known as COURIER and by a third satellite known as TELSTAR, which transmitted live television between North America and Europe for the first time. In 1962, TELSTAR relayed television signals between the United States and England, and between the United States and France. In October, 1964, the SYNCOM satellite gave coverage by television to North American from Japan of the opening ceremonies of the Olympic Games and in 1968, the Olympics were televised from Mexico in the Atlantic and Pacific areas.

Stimulated by early successes, the U.S. Congress passed the Communications Satellite Act.[44] This Act created the Communications Satellite Corporation (COMSAT), a private entity whose principal functions are to carry on the development, launching and operations of communications satellites.[45]

---

[42] Werner, *Television,* in WASHINGTON CONF. 245-49.

[43] Concluding remarks of John A. Johnson, Chairman of the Interim Communications Satellite Committee, in a paper presented to the UN Conference on the Exploration and Peaceful Uses of Outer Space (Vienna, August 1968). *See also* the comments in papers presented at the World Peace Through Law Conference in 1963 by Jaffe, Katzenbach, Marks and Segal, in ATHENS CONF., 505-62.

[44] Communications Satellite Act, 47 U.S.C. § 701 *et seq.* (1964).

[45] Marks, *supra* note 20, at 540-42.

In 1964, negotiations were undertaken by representatives of states whose potential use of communications satellites was sufficient to make their participation in the establishment of a global system desirable from the outset. It was agreed that the space segment should be owned and financed jointly by participants from all the major areas of the world, and that ownership shares should be related to the potential use of the global system by states. On the other hand, earth segments should be owned and financed by telecommunications entities authorized by the countries in which they are located. These negotiations resulted in two important international agreements of August 1964, an "Agreement Establishing Interim Arrangements for a Global Commercial Communications Satellite System" and a "Special Agreement."[46] Within a year these Agreements had been signed by 46 countries and by 1970 they had been signed by 74 countries.[47] The Interim Agreement created the International Telecommunications Satellite Consortium (INTELSAT) and established its political and economic goals and its organizational and financial framework. It also set up the Interim Communications Satellite Committee with responsibility for developing and operating the space segment of the global system, and provided that the Communication Satellite Corporation was to serve as the manager.[48] The agreements deal only with the space portion of the system. The individual countries decide whether or not to establish earth stations. To date, many countries have established these stations.

On April 6, 1965, the world's first commercial communications satellite, Early Bird, was launched, and for the first time, an INTELSAT satellite linked North America and Western Europe in daily telegraph communication through outer space. Early Bird provided numerous services and maintained 240 two-way voice circuits across the Atlantic Ocean and increased transatlantic communication by 50 percent. On January 25, 1971, INTELSAT IV was put into orbit with a capacity of 9,000 telephone calls or 12 color television channels, or a combination of telephone, television, data and other forms of communications. It serves as the primary relay for satellite communications in the Atlantic Basin.

Communications satellites have a vast potential for the benefit of mankind. Television programs now made available by these

---

[46] J. FAWCETT, *supra* note 8, at 72-85.

[47] The states are listed on a Chart entitled *INTELESAT III Growth Potential* published by NASA.

[48] For a discussion of the institutional framework, see Johnson, *Satellite Communications: The Challenge and the Opportunity for International Cooperation,* in WASHINGTON CONF. 234-36.

satellites have enormous educational value, such as, in the medical
field, with the observation of difficult operations performed by
the world's top surgeons by doctors in any country; with the
simultaneous publication of newspapers, magazines and books;
with the fast transmission of weather maps by meteorological
satellites providing more effective forecasts for airlines; and with
improved maritime communications systems thereby helping to
save many ships that would otherwise be lost at sea. Communications satellites have also played an important role in the communications system developed for the United States' moon-landing Apollo
program.[49]

The development of law through international agreements and
regulations governing outer space and space communications is an
essential prerequisite of peace in the universe of tomorrow. In
both space law and space communications there is unlimited
potential for wider understanding among men. In all, there is an
exciting challenge for lawyers. Leonard Marks, Chairman of the
World Peace Through Law Center's Communications Committee
has been the acknowledged world leader in much of the law development in this field. To him, and other distinguished jurists who are
his co-workers is due much of the credit for the vast growth in
international communications law which is outlined above.

§ 11-10. International Organizations in Space Cooperation.

With the advances in technology and the advent of the Space
Age, numerous international organizations have been created to
engage in cooperative space activity. Among others, these include
the Committee on Space Research (COSPAR), the International
Astronautical Federation (IAF), the International Academy of Astronautics, the International Institute of Space Law, Euro-Space, European Space Research Organization (ESRO), European Launcher
Development Organization (ELDO), and the Inter-American Committee for Space Research (ICSR).

§ 11-10.1. The Committee on Space Research.

This Committee,
established in 1958, aims to deal with transnational space research
concerning rockets and rocket-propelled vehicles. Membership, open
to all national members of the International Committee of Scientific Unions that are actively engaged in space research and to those

---

[49] J. V. Charyk, *Commercial Communications Satellites* (a paper presented at the UN
Conference on the Exploration and Peaceful Uses of Outer Space, Vienna, August 1968).
See also Cocca, *Promises and Menaces Emerging from Direct Broadcasts by Satellites,* in
BANGKOK CONF.

International Scientific Unions that are members of ICSU and who desire to participate, is composed of 18 national scientific institutions and ten International Scientific Unions. COSPAR is composed of an Executive Council, a Bureau, four working groups and a full-time Executive Secretary. The Bureau consists of the president, two vice-presidents, and four additional elected members, all elected for a term of seven years. All decisions of the Executive Council must be confirmed by a two-thirds vote of the seven-member Bureau, and all decisions are normally arrived at by obtaining the consensus of all members.

COSPAR, through its sponsorship of scientific meetings and Conferences, working groups, serves as a catalyst for the generation and development of scientific goals to be achieved by experiments; and as a valuable communication link between scientific disciplines by serving as a forum for discussion of planned and projected programs and experiments by national scientific institutions with the major purpose of maintaining scientific cooperation in fields closely related to space research and to provide a meeting place for scientific institutions.

Other activities include the advance notice of the planned launching of the U.S. Solar Radiation (III) satellite, encouraging bilateral and regional negotiations with countries, scientific conferences at which scientific papers and business sessions are carried on concurrently, the issuance of an information bulletin designed to serve as an authoritative and timely medium for news of interest to space scientists, the transmission of orbital elements' information, and other technical subjects.

§ 11-10.2. **International Astronautical Federation (IAF).** Established in 1951, the Federation aims to foster the development of astronautics for peaceful purposes, to encourage the widespread dissemination of technical information, to stimulate public interest in space flight through the major media of mass communications, and to encourage astronautical research by international and national agencies by encouraging cooperation among its member societies, among universities and research institutions, by sponsoring conferences and by cooperating with other related organizations.

The IAF is composed of a General Assembly which acts as the governing body, and in which one delegate from each voting society is represented, and of voting, non-voting and institutional members. Voting members consist of one member from any one nation, while non-voting members are composed of representatives from additional organizations from the same nations. Institutional members who are also non-voting members consist of representatives from universities, and scientific or technical institutes.

§ 11-10.3.3. International Academy of Astronautics. The International Academy of Astronautics was established under the auspices of the International Astronautical Federation in 1960, with Dr. Theodore von Karman as director. Four committees were established: publications, award and fellowship, lunar international laboratory, and a joint commission of the Academy and the IAF International Institute of Space Law to consider technical aspects of space law.

The principal functions of the Academy are to: (1) provide advice to the President of the IAF upon request, (2) conduct meetings and studies and reports, (3) publish *Astronautica Acta,* (4) award medals and prizes to encourage progress in the field, and (5) execute such other tasks deemed desirable for advancing astronautics.

§ 11-10.4. International Institute of Space Law. Established under the auspices of the IAF in 1957, and composed of physicists and lawyers, the Institute aims to define aerospace and the various regions of aerospace jurisdiction, to foster the social, scientific aspects of astronautics by holding meetings and conferences, to make studies and reports and publication thereof and to make awards.

The initial membership of the Institute includes most of the members of the permanent legal committee and additional members chosen by the *ad hoc* organizing committee. Additional members can be elected by the Executive Committee of the Institute and all are elected for life upon their acceptance.

§ 11-10.5. Euro-Space. Established in 1961, Euro-Space is a convention of European industries specializing in space research and development. Its members include concerns from France, the United Kingdom, Italy, the German Federal Republic, Belgium, the Netherlands and Sweden. The inaugural meeting attended by 55 scientists from 30 private concerns in the aircraft, electronics, and chemical fields, established working groups to study long-range communications for civil purposes, navigation, satellites for civil purposes, and anti-satellite systems for military purposes.

European interest in consolidating space efforts stemmed from a realization that such research was beyond the financial resources available to one state, and that consolidation could achieve greater results.

§ 11-10.6. **European Space Research Organization (ESRO).** Established in 1960 as the result of several conferences, ESRO is purely designed to conduct scientific research into outer space and the upper atmosphere by the use of artificial satellites space probes, and vertical sounding rockets. ESRO is composed of a Council which consists of representatives of Member States, and its decisions are carried out by a Director-General and staff in Paris headquarters. It is also composed of three sections, or Establishments: (1) Space Technology Center (ESTEC), with an associated research law (ESLAB) in Delft, Netherlands, (2) Data Analysis Center (ESDAC) in Darmstadt, Federal Republic of Germany, and (3) Sounding Rocket Range (ESRANGE) in Kiruna, Sweden.

§ 11-10.7. **European Launcher Development Organization (ELDO).** This organization, established in 1962, is primarily concerned with launching rockets and related research and in the industrial and commercial application of space satellites, especially in the field of communications. Membership in ELDO was to be the same as in ESRO, with headquarters in Europe but only seven nations have joined. The organization has a Technical Planning Staff, and a Secretariat with a Secretary-General, a Technical Director, an Administrative Director and a Director of Initial Programme.

§ 11-10.8. **Proposed Inter-American Committee for Space Research (ICSR).** Proposed in 1960, this Committee has not yet entered into force. The Committee will be designed to promote the formation of local committees composed of natural and social scientists and engineers connected with space science and technology; to send all available information to the local committees and encourage them to support the establishment of National Commissions or obtain government support for increased space research; to hold frequent local meetings; to publish periodic bilingual publications with abstracts of papers; and to promote the study of space science and programs in research centers and universities.

CHAPTER 12

Legal Education, Research and the Development of International Law

§ 12-1. Legal Education[1]

If international law is to grow and become as important as it should be in world affairs, trained users of that law are needed to

---

[1] *See generally* D. ALSPAUGH, A BIBLIOGRAPHY OF MATERIALS ON LEGAL EDUCATION (New York 1965); Cardenas, *Legal Education and Investigation,* in WORLD PEACE THROUGH LAW: THE GENEVA CONFERENCE 456-58 (1969) [hereinafter cited as GENEVA CONF.]; Esen, *Le Role des Ecoles de Droit dans le Pays en Voie de Developpement,* in WORLD PEACE THROUGH LAW: THE BANGKOK CONFERENCE (to be published) [hereinafter cited as BANGKOK CONF.]; Gormley, *European Organizations: Individual Research Opportunities,* 7 FOR. EX. BULL. 11-15 (1965); Oben, *Legal Education in the Role of a Lawyer in a Changing World,* 16 U. ST. TOM. L.REV. 118-22 (1965); O'Regan, *The Role of Law Schools in Developing Societies,* in BANGKOK CONF.; Phillips, *The Role of the Law Schools in the Developing Nations,* in BANGKOK CONF.; Redden, *The Role of the Law School in Developing Nations,* in BANGKOK CONF. Rigaux, *Education and Research in the Field of International Law,* in BANGKOK CONF.; Rye, *What Is Meant by "Legal Education in the Developing Countries,"* in BANGKOK

(Continued)

persuade their nations to accept international law more and more. Thus, for the first time, a section on legal education is included in a book on substantive law to indicate by its status that progress in legal education is essential to the growth of international law which the world community requires.

This book is aimed at acquainting lawyers and laymen with the broad outlines of international law, and with the growing number of international agencies engaged in creating law rules effective in the world community. This chapter on legal education will aid non-lawyers in increasing their knowledge of the role legal education must play in expanding international law so as to enlist their most necessary support for legal education. This volume also provides the non-expert with sufficient citations of in-depth substantive studies, lawbooks and articles, so that he may secure the full knowledge he or his clients require from those sources.

It is believed that teachers of international law are, and that they will continue to be, a major influence in the rapid growth of international law. This makes imperative a major focus upon legal education and research in any program to expand transnational law. The impact of science and technology and the rapid surge of economic growth have also resulted in expanding legal needs for well-trained lawyers. In the highly-developed nations, the need for adequate legal education has been obvious and the capacity to fill this need relatively great. These countries have many law schools with highly-trained, full-time faculties, with teaching aids and fairly complete law libraries. In contrast, many other nations are only in the initial stages of the struggle to provide legal training; and still other nations have no law schools at all.

This chapter will emphasize the problems confronting developing nations in formulating legal education and legal research systems that will enable them to participate fully in a world in which relations among other nations and their nationals are

---

CONF.; Ryu, *Work Paper on Research, Legal Education and Training,* in GENEVA CONF. 443-55; Seidler, *The Teaching of Law and Its Relation to Political Sciences and Economics,* in INTERNATIONAL CONGRESS OF COMPARATIVE LAW, 7TH UPPSALA, 1966, at 282-87 (1966); Wook Shinn, *The Role of Law Schools in Developing Countries,* in BANGKOK CONF.; Sinco, *Legal Education and Research,* in WORLD PEACE THROUGH LAW: THE ATHENS CONFERENCE 649-57 (1965) [hereinafter cited as ATHENS CONF.]; Stavropoulos, *Legal Education and Research,* in *id.* at 657-59; J. STONE, LEGAL EDUCATION AND RESPONSIBILITY (Columbus, Ohio 1959); Tarumi, *Legal Education and Research,* in ATHENS CONF. 659-60; Van Tanouan, *Research, Legal Education and Training,* in GENEVA CONF. 473-74. For general information on international cooperation in legal education, see ATHENS CONF. 628-44. Casebooks and sources of legal materials in the international field are cited below p. 493.

increasingly governed by law. It will give a few examples of pioneer activities in specific countries[2] and point out a few of the contributions of governments, foundations, and private organizations to provide trained people to meet the challenge in the field of international law.

---

[2] For articles on legal education in the following 21 countries, see for Brazil, Boaventura, *A Reforma do Ensino Jurídico o a Colaboração das Instituicoes,* 34 R. FAC. DIR. (U. BAHIA 1959-1961); for Ceylon: Nadaraja, *Problems of Law School Development in Ceylon,* 10 FAR EAST. L.REV. 467-73 (1963); for the Congo: Crabb, *Viewing Africa from Teaching Anglo-American Law at a Congolese University,* 19 J. LEGAL ED. 437-42 (1966); for Ecuador: Garcia Ortiz, *Misión de las Facultades de Derecho,* 12 BOL. INST. DER COMP. 77-89 (1963); for Ethiopia: HAILE SELASSIE I. UNIVERSITY ANNUAL REPORTS OF THE DEAN FOR THE YEARS 1964-1967; for France: Scott, *The Teaching of International Law in France,* in Section of International Law, Proceedings, 1962 at 312-24 (ABA 1963); for Germany: Jacob-Steinorth, *The Teaching of International Law in the German Federal Republic,* in *id.,* at 325-28; for Guatemala: MESA REDONDA CENTROAMERICANA DE EDUCATIÓN JURÍDICA, 1961 (Guatemala 1964); for India: Von Mehren, *Law and Legal Education in India: Some Observations,* 78 HARV. L.REV. 1180-89 (1965); for Italy, M. CAPPELLETTI, J. MERRYMAN & J. PERILLO, ITALIAN LEGAL SYSTEM 86-90 (Stanford 1967); for Japan: Oda, *Teaching and Research of International Law in Japan,* in JAPANESE ANNUAL OF INTERNATIONAL LAW 85-100 (1965); for Korea: J. MURPHY, LEGAL EDUCATION IN A DEVELOPING NATION: THE KOREA EXPERIENCE (Seoul 1965); for Malaya: Sheridan, *Legal Education in Malay,* 10 FAR EAST. L.REV. 282-87 (1963); for New Zealand: Derham, *Legal Education,* 2 N.Z.U. L.REV. 130-44 (1966); for Nigeria: Milner, *Legal Education and Training in Nigeria,* 17 J. LEGAL ED. 285-306 (1964-1965); for Puerto Rico: O'Connell, *Continuing Legal Education for the Judiciary,* 25 REV. COL. P.R. 457-70 (1965); for Scotland: de Funiak, *Legal Education and the Legal Profession in Scotland,* 38 TUL. L.REV. 361-71 (1964); for Spain: Castan Vasquez, *Tendencias Actuales sobre algunos Problemas de la Enseñaza del Derecho,* 13 REV. FAC. DER. U. MADRID 149-62 (1962); for Thailand: Kraivixian, *Legal Education in Thailand,* 10 FAR EAST. L.REV. 497-507 (1963); for the United Kingdom: Wilson, *A Survey of Legal Education in the United Kingdom,* 9 J. SOC. PUB. T. L. 1-144 (1966); for the United States: CORNELL UNIVERSITY, CONFERENCE OF LAW TEACHERS, TEACHING OF INTERNATIONAL LAW AND RELATED COURSES IN AMERICAN LAW SCHOOLS (Washington 1964); R. EDWARDS, INTERNATIONAL LEGAL STUDIES: A SURVEY OF TEACHING IN AMERICAN LAW SCHOOLS (1963-1964) (Washington 1965); A. MARNO, LEGAL EDUCATION IN THE UNITED STATES (San Francisco 1953); for the U.S.S.R.: J. B. MAZARD, LEGAL EDUCATION IN THE SOVIET UNION (Madison, Wisconsin 1938).

For articles on areas larger than countries, see Cowen, *African Legal Studies: A Survey of the Field and the Role of the United States,* in AFRICAN LAW: NEW LAW FOR NEW NATIONS 9-40 (K. N. Baade & R. O. Everett eds. New York 1963); Egbert, *Report on Legal Education and Research in International Law in Countries Throughout the World,* in WASH. CONF. 596-98; Gower, *Legal Education: Problems of Legal Training in Commonwealth Africa,* in PROCEEDINGS OF THE THIRD COMMONWEALTH AND EMPIRE LAW CONFERENCE (Toronto 1905); INTER-AMERICAN INSTITUTE OF INTERNATIONAL LEGAL STUDIES, MATERIAL DE REFERENCIA SOBRE LA ENSEÑANZA DEL DERECHO INTERNACIONAL Y MATERIAS AFINES EN LATINOAMERICA (Washington 1964); Johnston, *American Participation in African Legal Education,* 16 J. LEGAL ED. 312-16 (1963); Paul, *The Development of Legal Education in Developing African Countries,* in GENEVA CONF. 458-72 (1969); Ryu, *Legal Education in the Far East,* in WASHINGTON CONF. 752-61; Stern, *Many Paths to Heaven: A Comparison of Legal Education in Latin America and the United States,* 41 WASH. L.REV. 511-16 (1966); Twining, *Legal Education Within East Africa,* 12 INT'L & COMP. L.Q. SUPP. 115-51 (1966).

At the beginning of the 20th century, most lawyers engaged in the general practice of law had little interest or a little knowledge of international law. During this century, however, the tendency and need for international law to become "lawyers' law"[3] have increased. This has been evidenced by the expanded teaching programs of international law in law schools and the increase in the number of international law casebooks. Much, of course, remains to be done in expanding and improving international law teaching programs.[4]

Before World War I, only a very few American law schools offered courses in international law. By 1928, for example, 22 members of the American Association of Law Schools offered courses in international law; by 1937, 30 members were offering courses; and by 1953, 55 law schools in the Association were teaching the subject, although in many of these schools, international law courses were given only in alternate years or by departments outside the law school.[5] A "Survey of Courses Offered in Law Schools of the United States in International Law and Related Subjects" was prepared by the American Bar Association Special Committee on World Peace Through Law in February 1960. Of the 123 schools which furnished requested information, 75 were offering courses in international law or related subjects or both. A large number of these schools have just added such courses to their curriculum. Several large schools, with the benefit of Ford and Rockefeller Foundation grants, have established special programs with extended curricula, exchange of students and professors, and research activities. The principal reason why international law is not offered in smaller schools seems to be inadequate funds, though lack of student interest is a contributing factor. Since 1914, Conferences of Teachers of International Law have been held under the auspices

---

[3] R. J. Jennings in THE PROGRESS OF INTERNATIONAL LAW (New York 1960), states that Sir Henry Maine (writing at the end of the 19th century) spoke of international law as a "mere literary instrument," but that now it is "recognizably lawyers' law."

[4] For useful data and comments on this subject, see Bishop, *International Law in American Law Schools Today*, 47 AJIL 686-97 (1953); H. CAMINOS, LA ENSEÑANZA UNIVERSITARIA DEL DERECHO INTERNACIONAL PÚBLICO EN LOS ESTADOS UNIDOS (Buenos Aires 1958); Franklin, *The Teaching of International Law in Law Schools*, 46 AJIL 140-43 (1952); Hudson, *Twelve Casebooks of International Law*, 32 AJIL 447-56 (1938); Jessup, *The Teaching of International Law in Law Schools*, ASIL PROC. 66-74 (1947); Kunz, *A Plea for More Study of International Law in American Schools*, 40 AJIL 624-29 (1946); McNair, *The Need for Wider Teaching of International Law*, 29 GROTIUS SOCIETY TRANSACTIONS 85-98 (1944).

[5] R. EDWARDS, A SURVEY OF TEACHING IN AMERICAN LAW SCHOOLS, 1963-1964 (ASIL, Washington 1965).

of the American Society of International Law, and their proceedings have been published by the Carnegie Endowment for International Peace. In the introduction to the first of these conferences in 1914, Elihu Root, emphasized the need for a popular understanding of international law. At the Third Conference in 1928, Judge Manley O. Hudson sketched the history of the teaching of the subject in the United States, and listed the four casebooks then available,[6] pleading that more be written. The response to his plea yielded five casebooks within the next 10 years.[7]

Since World War II new editions of international law casebooks have been written by E. D. Dickinson, *Cases on International Law* (1950); C. G. Fenwick, *Cases on International Law* (1951); M. O. Hudson, *Cases on International Law* (1951); H. W. Briggs, *Law of Nations: Cases, Documents and Notes* (1952); L. C. Green, *International Law through the Cases* (1959); W. Jaeger and W. V. O'Brien, *Cases, Text Notes, and Other Materials* (1959); W. W. Bishop, *International Law, Cases and Materials* (1962); and L. B. Orfield and E. D. Re, *Cases and Materials on International Law* (1965). Also in the 1950's, Louis Sohn of Harvard Law School published two casebooks containing extensive bibliographical notes on World Law (1950) and on United Nations Law (1956).

Some useful current information on the teaching of international law in the law schools of four continents was supplied by Francis Deak in a report to the American Society of International Law at its annual meeting in April 1962.[8] On the debit side, Deak found there is a real shortage of full-time international law professors in Asia, Africa and South America, owing in large part to law salaries and the lack of other incentives such as tenure and pensions. There was also a general lack of research and teaching tools, such as efficiently-organized and well-equipped libraries. On the credit side, international law is considered an important subject, in many English, Japanese and European law schools and is often required. In these schools, the general tools for its study are adequate to excellent, and considerable interest in international law studies in the law schools of all four continents seem to exist. In addition, many universities not having full-time international law professors, do have dedicated part-time teachers.

---

[6] Those by F. Snow (1893), J. Scott (1902; 2d 3d. 1922), E. Stowell & H. F. Munro (2 vols. 1916), and L. Evans (1917; 2d ed. 1922).

[7] Those by E. Dickinson (1929), M. Hudson (1929), C. Fenwick (1935), J. Scott & W. Jaeger (1937), and H. Briggs (1938).

[8] ASIL PROC. 54-63 (1962). See Ch. 12 on the importance of legal education in developing international law, *infra*.

§ 12-2. Some Problems of Legal Education in Developing Countries

Many serious obstacles impede the establishment of a sound, vital and contributing process of legal education in developing countries. Such problems concern the absolutely essential interest and continuing support of heads of national and local governments; the need for local well-trained and dedicated legal scholars who, as a result, must be selected from abroad, creating language or cultural problems; the necessary financial support from the government, foundations or other sources for books, publications and other supplies; the shortage of classrooms and the need of repairing existing ones, depending on the anticipated number of students and local resources; the availability of such course materials as court reports, code commentaries, material on local law and legal institutions which, if not available, must be prepared by faculty research; the preparation of students in the least amount of time possible, whose financial, housing and educational backgrounds may pose serious difficulties; and a curriculum well-suited to the capacity and needs of students, and responsive to the nation's legal needs.

The type and quality of lawyers sought in developing countries is particularly crucial, and largely dependent on the country's specific needs, and to some extent, on the students' backgrounds. For example, developing nations may require the creation of an entire legal system including Ministers of Justice, Attorneys General, Solicitors General, legal advisors and staffs, and well-rounded and well-trained lawyers able to understand the country's political, economic and social needs, and able to uphold the rights of citizens and guide them in their contacts with both public and private law. And, while basic training must, of course, prepare students for competent participation in litigation, attention must also be given to the training of magistrates and minor and customary court judges since their decisions are frequently known to the people, and the quality of justice in the country judged by the quality of these decisions. Mr. Justice Minoque of the Supreme Court of Papua and New Guinea, and Chairman of the *World Peace Through Law Center Committee on Legal Education* has indicated his conviction that:

> [I]ntensive training is necessary and a course of at least one year's duration seems . . . to be the absolute minimum. Such a course ought to cover criminal law, procedure and evidence and customary law including its method of ascertainment, the area of its applicability and the ways in which conflict of laws problems where differing customs of different areas are in question can be resolved. It should embrace, too, a grounding in the basic freedoms—freedom from arrest without trial, freedom of speech,

religion and association—and the relevance of these freedoms to the exercise of jurisdiction . . . .[9]

At the same time, he thinks that longer and broader courses should be developed and mentions that such plans are presently being considered by some countries.

Apart from courses in traditional international law, the subject usually studied by law students, attention must also be given to the legal aspects of international banking, business, and investment; to international organizations and agencies for cooperation; to the international aspects of various forms of constitutional structures (for example, international voting rights in various federal or quasi-federal associations); to the ramifications of the European Common Market; and to the emergence of comparable organizations in Africa, Asia and the Americas. It is also essential that legal studies focus on questions concerning the minimum legal requirements for an effective and functioning common market, especially the minimum "uniformity" or "harmonization" that may be required of national legal systems comprising such a market.

The notion of state sovereignty, which has so often created problems in developing a world of peace and justice among the older nations, is also a source of perplexity among the developing nations. While political leaders are interested in plans for the closer association of states on a regional basis—plans which hold out much promise for future economic development and military defense, they are still reluctant to surrender any part of their newly-won sovereignty to a supranational organization. It is, however, possible that the desired economic and military objectives may be achieved without resorting to federalism of the classical kind, that is, without any effective loss of sovereignty by the associating states, a contention put forward by M. Gabriel d'Arboussier, of Senegal at the Symposium on Federalism in the New Nations held at Chicago in 1962.

Since lawyers and statesmen of emerging nations are increasingly being called upon to decide legal problems having basic and far-reaching social and economic consequences, they cannot afford to make these decisions without a liberal education, including, in particular, knowledge of how other people with similar problems managed to solve them. They will fail in the exacting tasks which lie before them unless their education is conceived in truly fundamental and philosophical terms. Nowhere is this more imperative

---

[9] Letter to Edward J. Smith, Jr., Director of Programs, WPTL Center, dated 1969, for the Bangkok Conference.

than in the law schools of the new nations. The general opinion of African legal education is that "first things should come first" and that the first need in Africa is basic legal training of a kind which qualifies the lawyer for general practice.

However, elementary legal training of a more or less technical kind is not incompatible with the current provision of something more ambitious. The concurrent establishment of research institutes attached to the new African law schools would surely not weaken them. On the contrary, it would enhance their capacity to discharge essential teaching duties.[10]

Another serious problem is the fact that the more complex legal concepts developed in legal literature do not have their equivalents in the local language. Dean James Paul, from his experience as Dean of the Ethiopian Law School, feels that one of the urgent tasks confronting legal education and research is to develop the national language in such a way that sophisticated imported legal concepts can be absorbed and made meaningful to the public at large. Obviously, unless the mass of people understand the principles of law which are applied to them, the law itself will neither be understood nor respected.

With regard to teaching methods, two points must be made. First, rote-learning must be replaced by the case and problems method, since it is necessary to train students to think and analyze, rather than simply to memorize. Because foreign casebooks are generally unavailable, the problem method may be better with an appropriate interspersing of cases. Second, attention must be given to legal writing practice, in order to help students develop the ability to write concisely and analytically.

Books are always a lawyer's basic tools, and the law library, an important source of learning for the student, is essential in his training. The library should contain the most useful publications, the best local material and enough foreign material to make the study of comparative law possible. The library, also, should be operated by a trained law librarian, consistent as much as possible with available financial resources.

The language barrier is one of the most serious obstacles facing legal education in developing countries. Countries which acceded to national independence are often reluctant to educate their future leaders in a European language, and in an international law which they consider primarily a Western product with little or no

---

[10] Paul, *Annual Reports of the Dean* (University of Ethiopia 1964-1965).

non-Western influences. (One of the objectives of this volume has been to bring cross-cultural and cross-ideological thoughts into the framework of modern international law by stating the historical and current contributions of Asian, African, and Latin American experience in international law. This material is found *supra* in § 1-5.7 - 1-5.10.) Moreover, translations and original writings from European languages into local languages have not been able to keep pace with the demand for them. Aside from this, the language problem is primarily one of communication and understanding. The metaphors used by many languages reflect purely local cultures, and are frequently misunderstood when translated. Moreover, the narrow precision of the English and French vocabulary used in international law tends to be specific and direct. This is not always the case of other languages when used in international law, and the resultant translation of the "traditional" vocabulary of international law is likely to create misconceptions which ultimately may be reflected in the meaning and application of international law by states and even to some extent, to discredit it, further adding to the difficulty of making international law relevant and significant to the legal systems of developing nations. But as stated, recognition of the contributions of developing nations to international law development is a unique feature of this volume throughout its consideration of all subjects and agencies of currently effective international law.

§ 12-3. An African Experience[11]

Prior to the early 1960's, Ethiopia had no law school, and Emperor Hailie Selassie I determined that this gap should be filled. With the help of a Ford Foundation grant, a University of Pennsylvania law Professor, James Paul, undertook this assignment, serving as the Dean of the Law School of Ethiopia for four years. His annual reports described the goals, problems and accomplishments.

Dean Paul found that few Ethiopians had legal training and that the demands upon those who did were therefore very great. Wide gaps existed between Ethiopian law written in books and the supply of professionally trained lawyers to implement it. Sources of Ethiopian law were diverse as they included local law, civil law, and common law, making French, English, and Amharic essential background languages, and making it necessary to have a faculty combining language ability, background in several systems of law, ability

---

[11]*Id.;* Committee on Legal Education for Students in Africa, Report, Cmd. No. 1255 (1961). (This pamphlet concerns problems of providing legal education for African students in England.)

to work with others as a team, and imagination and initiative in dealing with student problems.

The cumulative effect of these problems and deficiencies meant that the student's legal training was generally inadequate. Students faced the diverse languages and legal sources; were accustomed to rote-learning and required considerable training in arguing cases and writing papers on legal problems. Some lacked the funds necessary for food and shelter.

In addition, other problems equally grave, had prevented the establishment of a sound legal educational process. The lack of a suitable law building meant that one had to be found, or built and furnished; a curriculum to meet the unique needs of the law school and of the country had to be developed, and course materials had to be prepared and made available. To alleviate these problems, a law library was provided by a special grant; foreign legal scholars were invited to lecture at the law school and to offer suggestions for improvements; the law school faculty wrote monographs on practical issues of local law; a law journal was published; and the students, catching the enthusiasm of the faculty, organized a self-help hostel for needy students, adopted and administered an honor system, and in some cases assisted the faculty in research. Much was crammed into four years of effort, showing what can be done in promoting legal education in a developing African country.

In citing an African experience, it should be stressed that there are many other kinds of African experiences, so that it is impossible to describe a "typical" experience, although many African countries have had to face problems similar to those briefly sketched above. A much different experience would be that of South Africa, for example, which had established a law school as early as 1873, and which now offers a four year law course leading to the degree of Bachelor of Laws, and advanced students may acquire the degrees of Master of Laws and Doctor of Laws in this sophisticated legal education system patterned on the Roman-Dutch law of the Netherlands.

§ 12-4. A Latin American Experience[12]

In Latin America, it can be said that a traditional system of legal education is followed. Law faculties in Latin America are, for the most, part composed of part-time professors whose principal sources of income are obtained from private practice or government service. Teaching is typically by lecture and the subject matter tradi-

---

[12] Information for this Section obtained from the Inter-American Bar Foundation by the courtesy of Charles Norberg.

tional, concentrating on code rules, with little or no attention given to economic, social, development problems, with few discussions of legal issues, and with little study of court decisions. Most students are from well-to-do families since the high costs of education eliminate others, and many are part-time.

A few Latin American law schools have broken away from his traditional pattern. The University of Chile, for example, has expanded its full-time faculty, increased the number of full-time students and the length of their course and adopted the case and problem method of teaching. The University of Costa Rica is also adopting the case and problem method in some courses and is emphasizing legal reasoning rather than mere code memorization.

In recent years, the Inter-American Bar Foundation, the Inter-American Development Bank, the Agency for International Development, the United States Department of State, and United States foundations have initiated, supported or otherwise participated in various programs aiming to improve Latin American legal education. The Inter-American Bar Foundation has sponsored or co-sponsored several Latin-American legal workshops. At one of these, sponsored by the Southwestern Legal Foundation at Southern Methodist University in Dallas, Texas, selected Latin-American students took a short, intensive course in United States law and observed U.S. teaching methods. In another, two top-ranking law students from each of Brazil's law schools met for a week in Curitiba, Parana, for lectures and discussions. In Montevideo, Uruguay, lawyers from various Latin American countries and a few United States law professors participated in a week-long workshop dealing with the legal aspects of Latin American integration. Subsequently, an Institute of Law Development was established by the joint efforts of the Guanabara State University in Brazil, the United States Agency for International Development, and the Ford Foundation. Its faculty is composed of professors from several Brazilian universities and two United States professors. Young law teachers, practicing lawyers, and government officials who already have law degrees will attend part-time for one year while continuing their professional work. The Institute hopes to clarify Brazilian legislation and provide useful teaching materials for Brazilian law schools.

§ 12.5   A Korean Experience[13]

Many of the already cited problems of legal education in the developing countries have been encountered in Korea: problems involved

---

[13] *See* Kim, *The Role of the Law Schools in Developing Nations: The Graduate School of Law in Korea*, in BANGKOK CONF.; Murphy, *supra* note 2.

in building a full-time faculty; in developing a curriculum geared to the current needs of the country; in modernizing teaching methods; in supplying course materials in view of the dearth of basic published material; and in finding teachers competent in the languages used in teaching and study. In dealing with these problems, the legal profession has been fortunate in having the leadership of a distinguished Korean, Dr. Paul Ryu, as Professor and Dean of Seoul National University's Graduate School of Law and as President of the University. Dr. Ryu has played a significant role in the movement to improve legal education in Korea. In addition, the observations and reports of such great foreign legal scholars as Dean Russell Niles of New York University School of Law, Professor Jay Wesley Murphy of the University of Alabama, and Professor Myres S. McDougal of Yale have made valuable and useful contributions to Korean legal education.

The Seoul Graduate School of Law was established in 1961 to provide a truly professional law school, since Korean Law schools, in general, are "institutions of intermediate preparatory level" which train students for many professions. Among its programs some deserve special mention. The first is the publication and annotation of Supreme Court decisions, with the assistance of outstanding law students and financial support of the Asia Foundation.

The second is a scholarship program supported by United States government funds which enables a few ranking graduates to study abroad each year. Candidates for this assignment are very carefully screened. They must first pass the bar examination, an accomplishment which fewer than one percent of the applicants attain. Participants must then spend two years in training in the Seoul Graduate School of Law in special studies. A few of the top-ranking students from among these are sent to selected American universities.

The third program is an Internship Program which provides field training in the District Court and in the District Prosecutor's Office, followed by work in the office of a practicing lawyer in Seoul. Students also write a research report in their chosen field. Various pamphlets and booklets have been prepared to enable students to obtain the greatest benefit from this practical experience.

§ 12-6. An Indian Experience.

While legal education in India has existed for several centuries, modern Indian legal education and training has been severely criticized.[14] This recent criticism has stressed that legal education in

---

[14] P. TRIPATHI, LEGAL EDUCATION IN INDIA: BACKGROUND AND PROSPECTS, 1 LAWASIA 77-81 (1970).

India has primarily centered on rules and regulations, rather than on underlying principles, and that the teaching standards have been poor.

According to Professor P. K. Tripathi, Dean of the Law school at Delhi University:

> The typical Indian law college is a part-time institution where classes are held either before 10 a.m. in the mornings or, more commonly, after 5 p.m. in the evenings, so as to enable the student to engage in gainful employment or business during the better part of the day. Tired after the day's work, the student is not in a position to give his best to legal education, and hardly does he find any time for a follow-up or for supplementary reading to support the class-room instruction. The teachers, mostly part-time practising lawyers drawn on cheap salaries from the less busy and obscurer ranks of legal practitioners, have neither the will nor, generally, the competence to teach. The classes are poorly attended, although, thanks to the age-old and universally tolerated phenomenon of proxying, the attendance registers would tell a very different and optimistic story.

> The teacher lectures to the class on the various topics in the assigned subject. The lectures are of a very elementary standard. Many teachers dictate 'notes' to the class instead of lecturing. The examination consists of writing five or six short essays for every subject on topics given in a question paper. The examiner for a subject is a person other than the teacher who taught the class. This is supposed to ensure impartiality and objectivity in setting the question paper as well as in evaluating the answer books. The fact is that questions are repeated every second or third year and it is not at all difficult for a student or a teacher to anticipate them for the examination.[15]

Delhi University School of Law has in recent years attempted to change this traditional picture of Indian legal education and training. In 1963, the school established a special Committee to help reorganize the law school and improve its quality. Measures taken with the help of a Ford Foundation grant include introduction of a three year, six term, LLB course, with five courses each term, each with an examination. Eighteen of these 30 courses are compulsory, the rest elective. Teachers prepare the case materials to be considered during the year, which are given to the students at no charge, and examine the test papers of their students. In addition, distinguished American law teachers are invited to teach in the school, and Indian professors are sent to foreign law schools to study teach-

---

[15] *Id.,* at 78-79.

ing methods and techniques. In the future, scholarship funds will be made available to attract a higher caliber of law student on a competitive basis.

§ 12-7. Exchange of Law Teachers and Law Students[16]

The International exchange of law teachers and law students has contributed immensely to the teaching of law in many countries. The principal activities in this field before World War II were carried on by individuals, universities, bar associations and non-governmental organizations. The United States Government entered the education exchange field actively in 1946, with the passage of the Fulbright Act, which made foreign currency derived from the sale of surplus war properties available to send teachers and students abroad and to bring foreign teachers and students to the United States for educational purposes.

Foundations have played an important role in legal education especially in developing countries. The SAILER (Staffing of African Institutions of Legal Research) Program sends law professors to teach in newly independent states. In 1966, 21 law professors were serving for at least one academic year. African legal institutions have also been a principal interest of the Carnegie Foundation. In the Far East, the Asia Foundation has made important contributions to legal education.

Many individuals, universities, and bar associations have made generous contributions to legal education abroad. The Association of American Law Schools has a committee on Exchange of Teachers and has provided many schools in developing countries with qualified instructors.

---

[16] *See generally* COMMITTEE ON EXCHANGE OF PERSONS, CONFERENCE BOARD OF ASSOCIATED RESEARCH COUNCILS, DIRECTORY OF VISITING SCHOLARS IN THE UNITED STATES, 1967-1968 (Washington 1967); Espinosa, *The Exchange of Law Teachers and Students Under the United States Government's Education Exchange Program,* 9 J. LEGAL ED. 66 (1956); DEPARTMENT OF STATE, THE BUREAU OF EDUCATIONAL AND CULTURAL AFFAIRS, INTERNATIONAL EXCHANGE, 1967 (Washington 1967); PAN AMERICAN UNION, FELLOWSHIP AND PROFESSORSHIP PROGRAM OF THE OAS (Washington 1962); Young, *Education Exchange in the Legal Profession,* 11 J. LEGAL ED. 207-12 (1958).

Official U.S. Publications and daily issues of the Congressional Record and the Federal Register have been sent to over 100 countries by the Smithsonian International Exchange Service. *See* SMITHSONIAN INTERNATIONAL EXCHANGE SERVICE, 1966 ANNUAL REPORT (Washington 1967).

§ 12.8. Training in the United States of Persons From Developing Countries and Contributions of United States Law Professors

Several universities and educational centers in the United States provide legal education for individuals from foreign nations. Harvard Law School has had 20 to 30 graduate students each year from more than a dozen foreign countries. Yale, Columbia, Georgetown, George Washington, the University of Michigan Law Schools, among others, have also had a number of graduate students from abroad. Some of these students have been civil servants, but others have been law teachers who returned to their countries with enriched experience to continue their teaching. Some law schools, such as Southern Methodist University and New York University, have had special programs for law teachers from Latin American countries.

The deans and professors of law schools, both in their work at their law schools and in their travels to universities all over the world, have made substantial contributions through their contacts with lawyers and law professors of other countries. For example, Dean Erwin Griswold of Harvard Law School, has visited law schools in Africa, Australia, Canada, Japan, Korea, Malaysia, New Zealand, and other countries. Robert G. Storey, formerly Dean of Southern Methodist University Law School, has visited many universities in Latin American countries, in Korea, and throughout the world. Dean William Harvey of Indiana University taught in Ghana and helped reorganize its legal education system. The contributions of Professor Paul of the University of Pennsylvania (in Ethiopia) and of Professor McDougal of Yale University, of Professor Murphy of the University of Alabama, and of Dean Niles of New York University Law School have been emphasized above. Many other professors of American law schools have lectured or given law courses in various African states under the SAILER program and the programs of the International Legal Center in New York City. Similar programs have been undertaken in Latin America under the sponsorship of the Inter-American Bar Foundation and the United States Department of State. However, much further assistance from the United States is needed; clear policies in rendering this assistance formulated; and ways found to recruit experienced law teachers who are willing to undertake difficult, prolonged assignments in developing countries. This help is needed not only in the countries which lack law schools but also in many Middle Eastern and Southeast Asian nations, where legal education is a sterile operation, quite inadequate to meet today's pressing needs.

§ 12-9. Law Libraries and Exchange of Publications[17]

Many foundations, government agencies, organizations and bar association committees have assisted overseas law libraries, the training of librarians, and the employment of library experts. It is hoped that in the future, these programs will include even more significant contributions.

The International Association of Law Libraries encourages bibliographic work on an international cooperative basis, organizes seminars on law librarianship and legal research, and facilities the exchange of useful personnel. The International Relations Office of the American Library Association assembles and disseminates information on library and book activities throughout the world. The American Association of Law Librarians through its Committee on Foreign Law, establishes contacts with foreign law librarians and, when possible, makes arrangements for them to attend professional meetings, and promote international law librarianship.

The United States Information Agency presents law books to law libraries throughout the world. It also facilitates the presentation of gifts by others, as for example, in the publishers' Donated Books Program which makes available sets of books for distribution by the Agency. The Agency for International Development has occasionally helped law libraries as a part of its program for the development of legal institutions. And, by agreements with over 100 other governments, the United States Library of Congress exchanges official publications used by law students in many countries.

§ 12-10. Education in International Law[18]

Education in international law has been a neglected discipline in the law school curricula of most countries. It has had a low

---

[17] *See* AMERICAN LIBRARY ASSOCIATION, *Who Is Doing What in International Book and Library Programs?* in PROCEEDINGS OF A CONFERENCE SPONSORED BY THE INTERNATIONAL RELATIONS OFFICE (Washington 1967); Norberg, *Law Libraries,* in WASHINGTON CONF. 732-33.

The International Legal Center in New York City has taken over the activities of SAILER. Its principal purposes as announced in one of its news releases are: "to give systematic and continued attention to the role of law in the development of modern nations; to provide an international vehicle for the developmental assistance and exchange of information on the basis of the best available knowledge and experience; and to help in the creation and mobilization of greater competence and resources of personnel here and abroad in the solution of legal problems in the international field."

[18] *See generally* Deak, *Observations on International Law in Underdeveloped Countries,* in ASIL PROC. 54-63 (1962); Garcia-Arias, *The Teaching of International Law: A Con-*
(Continued)

priority in most African, Asian, and Western Hemisphere countries. Where it has been taught in these countries, the teaching for the most part has mainly been limited to traditional aspects, and opportunities for advanced study and research in the field have been rare. Most of the teaching has been done by part-time teachers who lacked the time to concentrate on the mass of expanding international law literature. With rare exceptions, law schools in these countries have lacked the basic books and documents for adequate education in the field often because foreign exchange made their purchase difficult or impossible. These facts are set forth above in various sections of this chapter.

Several factors, however are encouraging a wider teaching of international law, and the most important of these is increased interest. Demand for visiting international law professors is growing in developing countries; and the exchange of professors and students is injecting new interest, knowledge and teaching methods. International law is a required subject for the law degree in England, Japan and some developing countries and has become an important subject in the law curriculum of many Western countries. With the significant expanding structure of international law and increasing interdependence of states, its importance in the law curriculum in all law schools will increase even more in the future.

§ 12-11. Legal Research

Until fairly recently, legal research has been carried out largely by legal scholars. This is quite natural since inquiry into various legal aspects is the essence of a professor's authority, prestige, and advancement. Part-time teachers generally do not have time for much research, and the heavy teaching program of full-time teachers in small law schools eliminates their opportunity for extensive research. Much of the legal research is therefore accomplished in large research centers, located for the most part in highly developed industrial countries where funds, research assistance, and published sources of research are available. For example, the research in law now underway in Russia is indeed impressive. International organizations have also undertaken significant recent research.

---

tribution to World Peace, in ATHENS CONF. 632-35; Parry, *Creative Research and Education in International Law,* in WASHINGTON CONF. 503-14; Wade, *Research and Education in International Law,* in *id.,* at 520-25.

§ 12-11.1. **Legal Research by Law Schools and Research Centers.**[19] In 1965, the Research Director of the World Peace Through Law Center sent questionnaires to the 138 law schools approved by the American Bar Association, requesting information on legal research projects recently completed, in progress, and anticipated. Replies from 91 of these law schools reported 427 research projects on the following subjects: Arbitration, Comparative and Foreign Law, Disarmament, Human Rights, Industrial and Intellectual Property, International Communications, International Courts, International Judicial Cooperation, International Law Structure, International Law in Domestic Courts, International Organizations, Legal Education, Space Law, Transnational Trade and Investment, and United States Foreign Policy. The largest number of projects (153) was in the field of Comparative and Foreign Law. There were 55 projects on International Law Structure and 55 on Transnational Trade and Investment.

The Center report included a summary of the projects of the following outstanding United States legal research centers, many of which were supported by foundation funds: Columbia University School of Law, Cornell Law School, Duke University School of Law's Rule of Law Research Center, Georgetown University School of Law's Institute for International and Foreign Trade Law, Harvard Law School's Program of International Legal Studies, Loyola University School of Law (Chicago), New York University School of Law, Northwestern University School of Law's International Legal Studies, and Syracuse University's Procedural Aspects of International Law Institute. The projects enumerated are too varied for even summary here, and furthermore these research centers have undertaken many more projects since 1965. The Carnegie Endowment for International Peace supported a project for the preparation of a basic textbook of public international law for use principally in the universities of the newly independent African and Asian states.[20] This textbook, written by a group of renowned international law scholars from countries of various traditions, philosophies, cultures and ideologies, aims to present international law from an international rather than a national viewpoint as does this Volume.

The World Peace Through Law Center has also sent questionnaires to every known law school outside the United States. Of the 571

---

[19] Egbert, *Legal Research and Education in Countries Throughout the World,* in WASHINGTON CONF. 596-98.

[20] M. HUDSON, INTERNATIONAL LEGISLATION: A COLLECTION OF THE TEXTS OF MULTIPARTITE INTERNATIONAL INSTRUMENTS OF GENERAL INTEREST BEGINNING WITH THE COVENANT OF THE LEAGUE OF NATIONS (8th ed. 1931).

questionnaires sent out, 219 replies listed 534 legal research projects. The three subjects on which there was the largest number of research projects were Comparative and Foreign Law (235), International Law Structure (109), and New Countries (76), that is, countries which attained statehood since World War II.

§ 12-11.2. **UN Institute for Training and Research.**[21] One of the most significant recent developments in the field of research was the establishment of the United Nations Institute for Training and Research in 1965, as an autonomous institution within the UN framework. This new Institute is headed by an Executive Director, Chief S. O. Adebo (Nigeria); a Deputy Director, Oscar Schachter (United States), who serves as the Director of Research; and a 21-member Board of Trustees, chaired by Kenneth Younger (United Kingdom), which determines basic policies. Financial support is given by governments, international organizations, foundations, and individual donations.

UNITAR has conducted several training programs for young foreign service officers from developing countries, for officials dealing with problems of technical assistance, and for development financing specialists. In 1967, it held a seminar in English on the major problems of UN technical assistance and, in 1968, this seminar was handled in French for officials of French-speaking African countries. Regionals seminars on this subject are being held for Latin America, the Far East, East Africa, and West Africa. Advanced courses were given in New York and Geneva for foreign service officers, primarily from missions to the United Nations and to specialized agencies, and regional courses were given in Santiago, Chile, for Latin America; in Geneva, for Europe and the Middle East; in Bangkok, Thailand, for Asia; and in Addis Ababa for Africa. In September 1967, a seminar was held on the Teaching of Languages at the United Nations, and in January 1968, this was followed by a workshop in basic skills in modern language training for staff members.

Research projects by UNITAR include: relations between the United Nations and regional inter-governmental organizations; evaluation of the impact of technical aid programs; planning, program-

---

[21] UNESCO, REPORT OF UNITAR, E/L, 1177 (1967); UNESCO, *United Nations Institute for Training and Research. Report of the Executive Director,* E/4514, UNITAR /EX/12, 22 May 1968; United Nations Office of Public Information. Press Release UNITAR/61, 1 March 1968.

Numerous other research projects in the legal field are being carried on in various parts of the world. An example is the work of Professor Allot of the School of Oriental and African Studies in London in the field of customary African law. In the Australian area, a Legal Research Council has been created to coordinate research in several areas of the law.

ming and budgeting systems in relation to the economic and social activities in the United Nations; UN experience regarding plebiscites and elections; the use of public information and mass media on the United Nations and on UN problems; wider acceptance and application of multilateral treaties; common problems of planning, training and research institutes within the UN family; the status and problems of very small states and territories; a comparative study of measures against racial discrimination; migration of professionals from developing to developed countries; transfer of technology to developing countries; and new methods and techniques of training. In addition, UNITAR sponsors a Fellowships Program which trains selected candidates in international law.

In 1969, UNITAR made a tremendous contribution to the progressive development of international law and legal education. It completed studies of multinational public enterprises; organized a regional seminar in international law in Quito, Ecuador; cooperated with UNESCO in the Regional Training Program and Refresher Course in international law for Asia; and held lectures and seminars on various subjects for members of the permanent missions to the United Nations. In 1970, UNITAR will publish researches on international law specifically related to African nations, and on UN's structure and procedures, and will hold a regional seminar in international law in Africa.

§ 12-11.3.   **The UN Programme of Assistance in the Teaching, Study, Dissemination, and Wider Appreciation of International Law.** This Programme was established by the General Assembly in 1965, and its Advisory Committee consists of the following nations elected by the General Assembly: Belgium, Ecuador, France, Ghana, Hungary, Iraq, U.S.S.R., United Kingdom, United Republic of Tanzania and the United States.   The Programme's work has consisted of preparing a register of experts and scholars in international law; cooperating with other international organizations in disseminating information about international law; obtaining scholarships and fellowships from National Governments for students from developing countries for training in international law and relations; publicizing international law and the UN's legal work; providing advisory services of experts of international law to developing countries; and providing UN legal publications.

§ 12-11.4. **UNESCO and International Legal Education.** UNESCO is actively engaged in developing university teaching and research in international law, and in 1969, was allotted over $100,000 for its activities in this field.   UNESCO aided in the creation of the

Regional Training and Refresher Course for Asia held in the Philippines in 1969; was authorized to grant ten fellowships for 1969-1970; provided international legal consultants to Kenya, Uganda, the United Republic of Tanzania and Zambia, who gave advice on creating an international legal center for the four countries; sent a mission to several African countries to provide for the teaching of international law; authorized a study by the International Law Commission to held develop national associations of specialists in international law; embarked on a study of national institutions of higher education to establish international equivalences of university degrees and diplomas in international law; and promoted the exchange of legal publications among states.

§ 12-11.5. **Recommendations for Future Research Topics.** Improvement in the various branches of the expanding field of international law requires the identification of obstacles and recommendations to advance progress. There are many sources of suggestions for needed legal research. A brief statement on two of these sources will be made below. The first is a list of research topics recommended by the World Peace Through Law Center, including: Existing and Proposed International Courts, Space Law, International Law in Domestic Courts, International Judicial Cooperation, Disarmament, Industrial and Intellectual Property, Research and Education in International Law, the Expanding Structure of International Law, Peacekeeping (general principles), International Organizations, Internationally for Effective Cooperative Action. There are some 150 subjects in the Center's Work Program for building international law and international legal institutions.

A second valuable source of research suggestions and problem identification is found in *Design for Research in International Rule of Law,* by Arthur Larson, Director of the World Rule of Law Center of the Duke University School of Law. The 113 projects enumerated are listed under the following categories: Over-all Projects on the Law Structure of Peace; the body of World Law; Marshalling Existing Materials, "the General Principles of Law Recognized by Civilized Nations," and New and Current Facets of International Law Contributing to the World Law Concept; the Machinery of International Justice; Compliance with International Decisions; Acceptance of World Legal Systems; World Law and Communism; the Role of Law in International Economic Development; and Mutual Understanding Necessary to World Law.

Neither of the above lists of research topics claims to be complete nor definitive. When scholars, organizations and research centers undertake suggested items of research and when new problems appear, these and other lists of research suggestions will change and be adapted to the growing development of international law. Their great value lies in identifying problems and in urging scholars and specialists to seek solutions for them. They also serve to make the general public aware of the complexity of world problems and of the considerable efforts that are being made to resolve them by international law rules and international legal institutions.

CHAPTER 13

Encouraging the Growth of International Law: Recognition of Law's Potential for a World Peace Structure

§ 13-1. The Promise and Potential of a World Ruled by Law

This volume states International Law which now exists, cites sources for further research, and in some instances sets forth ideas for its expansion. It is hoped that this volume will help educate the peoples of the world—the legal profession and laymen—on their personal stake in building a world legal system. Internationalization of life due to economic, social and technological advances makes internationalization of law a necessity.

All peoples must be made aware that a world law system, the rule of law in the world, can and must be accomplished law by law, treaty by treaty, convention by convention, and institution by institution through acceptance by more nations of more international law.

The Peace Process is a Law Process. This Volume, by collecting information on existing international law and international agencies which are creating more and more international law by their rules and decisions, should help speed up the law-making processes, and encourage the essential growth of international law and its institutions.

Law cannot be used unless it is available. Making more international law more available is a primary purpose of this volume. It is an irrefutable fact that law cannot be used when it is unavailable and today in most nations of the world the legal profession and government officials do not have international law readily available to them. Law libraries have meager resources in most nations. Only two relatively complete law libraries exist, i.e., the United States Library of Congress and the Law Library of Harvard University Law School, both of which have over 1,000,000 volumes. Many nations only have law libraries of under 5,000 volumes and some nations have no law libraries at all. See *supra* pages 455-56.

If the future is to be a peaceful world order, it must be a world in which law is the controlling factor. And this is possible. Past supposed impossibilities, such as putting men on the moon, human organ transplants, generating life in test-tubes, have been achieved as have other such marvels as building whole new cities, transglobal instantaneous world communications via satellites, and giant corporations doing business in over a hundred nations. These have all been achieved by the application of man's knowledge, creativity and ingenuity. The same process of human endeavor can readily work to create that peaceful world ruled by law with justice. Such a world is, and has been down through the centuries, mankind's greatest goal.

The possibility of achieving this goal has been made more feasible by the tremendous growth in the international judicial system and in public, private and commercial international law since the end of World War II, as has been outlined in this volume. Entirely new judicial institutions have been established increasing the relevancy of international law primarily through necessity. The increasing interdependence of peoples and nations in order to cope with the economic development of the developing nations, and the character and span of large transnational corporations, whose assets in many cases are greater than the combined assets of many countries create new relationships in the world, which have in turn necessitated new law rules and legal institutions to govern the ramifications of the sum total of their activities. The fields of communications, transportation, even ideas, have all become internationalized to a great extent. Relations among nations no longer affect purely themselves in isolation from the rest of the world. The necessity of world peace through law and effective legal institutions is a reality that in no way can be considered either impossible, or unrealistic, and is, in fact, an objective which has now been accomplished in part through the United Nations.

Working steadily to clarify and promote this new reality, this new human achievement, has been the World Peace Through Law

Center. The Center has been instrumental in assembling the law of the world by publishing digests of both national and international law, by compiling a description of the world's judicial systems, by computerizing laws and treaties thereby making them more accessible, by assembling a directory of nearly all the world's lawyers and judges, by working in conjunction with various United Nations' agencies in the field of international law, by establishing members in 131 nations and over 100 working committees and Treaty Commissions to increase the use, acceptability and applicability of transnational law, and international institutions, and by making both lawyers and laymen more aware of the tremendous growth, and the potential of further growth, of the world judicial process and international law. Treaties, conventions and model laws for nations have been drafted and are being drafted.

But, it is not enough to rest on past achievements. It is necessary to realize that continued, and greater efforts are called for if a peaceful future for mankind is to be assured. Thus, it is essential for future efforts to concentrate on convincing the peoples of the world that the present machinery used to maintain world order and peace is archaic, inadequate and unresponsive to today's and tomorrow's needs, and that an entirely new system must be created. It is also necessary to improve the resources and work of organizations composed of lawyers and judges whose efforts are so vital in the building of world law and legal institutions; to apply fully the knowledge of computers and other electronic devices to this international law-making process; to mobilize worldwide public opinion in support of world peace through law by identifying this program as the only means of seeking a true world peace; to urge regional and international organizations, as well as states, to put into effect and ratify those treaties, laws, ideas and institutions that will further mankind's goal; to make available to all peoples of the world those scientific and technological advances and human productivity which can help create economic and social stability and order, and end the glaring disparities between the rich and poor nations.

But it is most important to realize that world peace through law will not be achieved overnight: it will require years, perhaps even decades, of continued struggle and work.

There is worldwide acceptance of international law. Leaders of Nations constantly state their belief in a rule of law for the world community.

In nearly every dispute between nations, their leaders claim international law supports their position. But they invariably refuse to allow an impartial body like the International Court of Justice to decide which leader is correct in his interpretation of international law. Decision by the archaic ritual of killing human beings remains today, as it has through the centuries, the method too many leaders of nations resort to as the forum for decision of their disputes with leaders of other nations.

Creating an atmosphere of world opinion in which leaders feel compelled not only to accept international law but also to accept such an impartial decision of a Court is imperative. One way to do this is to educate the public on the great value of international law, and international legal institutions. Public opinion fluctuates when a subject is not widely comprehended by the public at large. The mystery must be taken out of international law and its institutions so that the public will support and respect and expect reliance upon them. As public opinion becomes crystallized in this way, it will become a controlling force. Leaders of Nations vie for the support of public opinion. When there is a universal expectation and cry "go to Court, not war" then and only then will the rule of law become the major factor internationally that it should be.

§ 13-2. Messages from Heads of States Recognizing the Value of Law in the World Community

The universal recognition of the value of international law by leaders of nations should be a major factor in building that law and its agencies into a peace structure for the world. True it is that down through the pages of history such universal recognition has existed. But the difficult task of welding that recognition into a universally strong world legal system remains yet to be accomplished. Perhaps it will help in that task to set forth some selected recent expressions of support for the rule of law by leaders of nations. These messages were sent to the World Peace Through Law Conferences which have been attended by more than 10,000 members of the legal profession. These messages are strong current evidence of the high esteem in which law is held throughout the world. The inspiring words in these messages provide a vital impetus to the enormous efforts now underway to build law and its agencies into a peace structure for the world. Any person who will read these messages must feel a strong urge to help translate the great dream of world peace through law from dream into reality. That so many leaders of nations would put into their own words their tribute to the role of law augurs well for success in the current program to create a universally strong world legal system.

ARGENTINA

Buenos Aires, Argentina
June 10, 1961

To the President of the American Conference on World Peace Through Law

I cordially request that you transmit the following message to the Conference:

As an American, as a man of law and as a leader, I consider the outcome of the deliberations of the Continental American Conference on "World Peace Through the Rule of Law" to be of vital importance. At the present time in the history of Man, the desire for Peace has acquired a dimension and a resonance never reached before, as Science and Technology give to the alternative of War or Peace the spirit of a dramatic choice between progress on an unprecedented scale and the destruction of all Civilization.

At the same time, it continues to be true that the only permanent Peace is that which rests on Justice; and although Justice is more a moral inspiration than it is a material situation, it is also true that Law can claim the honor of being that which makes a human being more coherently directed to realizing Justice—to realize it daily in deeds and in his institutions. As a man molded by juridical disciplines, I cannot remain alien to any concern aimed at the fulfillment of Justice nor to any endeavor of the men of Law. On the other hand, as an Argentinian, I am proud of my country's invariable fidelity to an international juridical system, whose highest expression was attained by Luis Maria Drago; and do not forget that it was the eminent Argentine jurist, Juan Bautista Alberdi, who designed, with depth and lucidity, the outlines of a universal Peace based on Law and international cooperation.

Therefore, it is very pleasing for me to adhere to the purposes and the concerns of the Conference and to express sincere wishes of success for its deliberations, which I do not doubt will be a decisive contribution to the cause of Democracy and Human Rights.

With my most distinguished consideration,

Arturo Frondizi
President of Argentina

AUSTRALIA

Canberra, Australia
May 15, 1967

I am happy to avail myself of the opportunity to convey through you my greetings to this Conference of World Lawyers on World Peace Through Law. The Rule of Law is a goal for which we must strive with combined effort. Peace Through Law is a worthy objective, but it can be attained only if the moral principles which form the Rule of Law are understood and observed within nations and between nations. I hope that this Conference will prove a significant step towards the achievement of this objective.

I send my personal most cordial good wishes.

(Signed) Harold Holt,
Prime Minister, Australia

AUSTRIA

Vienna, Austria
September 12, 1965

The World Conference organized by the World Peace Through Law Center, to be held from September 12 to 18, 1965, which is aimed at arousing the conscience of people who respect the idea of law, deserves our attention since ever-present dangers threaten the hopes of man for peace.

The idea that confidence cannot exist between heavily-armed powers and that these powers will never lay down their arms in the absence of mutual confidence seems to us to condemn forever, as useless, all hopes of disarmament or of a limitation of armaments. In my opinion, mankind cannot ignore this dilemma which for our generation must resolutely be worked out in accordance with the symbolic leitmotiv, *"Pax orbis ex jure."* Law creates confidence.

I am convinced that the Washington World Conference on World Peace Through the Rule of Law is of great significance to the International Cooperation Year, and that it will contribute to a lessening of tension. I extend my warmest greetings to this meeting of representatives of the legal profession of 119 countries and send my best wishes for the success of your deliberations.

Our hopes for the success of the great idea that inspired this conference have already been expressed by Chateaubriand, who said that once ideas are born they become indestructible, and that although they may be hampered by chains, in the end they break through because they are immortal.

(Signed) Franz Jonas
Federal Chancellor of the
Republic of Austria

BOLIVIA

La Paz, Bolivia
September, 1965

The Government of Bolivia presents its most fervent wishes for the success of this conference. May the divine providence enlighten the delegates so that they find solutions to the problems which afflict the world and endanger world peace.

(Signed) René Barrientos Ortuno
Alfredo Ovando Candia
Presidents of the Military Junta of
Bolivia

BOTSWANIA

Gaberones, Botswania
August 20, 1969

On behalf of the Government and people of the Republic of Botswania I wish to convey a message of best wishes for the success of the Bangkok World Conference on World Peace Through Law.

The objectives of this Conference are fully supported by my country which is dedicated to the principle of peace through negotiation and, ultimately, through law.

In this age we have seen peace established through negotiation and we have also seen attempts to settle disputes by force. All the evidence supports our view that peace can never be based on violence. Force begets force and only through a universal respect for international law can a lasting peace be firmly established.

Owing to our limited resources it is not possible for my country to send representatives to Bangkok. I am grateful therefore to have this opportunity to assure the Conference that we in Botswania sincerely hope that your deliberations will achieve a measure of progress towards achieving what should be a priority objective for all the world, peace on earth through law.

(Signed) Sir Seretse Khama, K.B.E.
President of the Republic of Botswania

BURMA

Rangoon, Burma
25th August 1961

To the President of the Asian and Australasian Conference on World Peace Through Law

I have much pleasure in sending my cordial greetings to all the delegates and guests attending the Asian Conference on World Peace Through the Rule of Law.

As a firm believer myself in democracy based on the Rule of Law, I welcome the efforts made by distinguished jurists of the world to formulate a programme for the promotion of world peace through the application of the concept of the Rule of Law to relations among nations.

I, therefore, extend my sincere wishes for success in your deliberations at this Conference of Asian jurists.

Yours Sincerely
Maung Nu
Prime Minister of Burma

CAMBODIA

Phnom Penh, Cambodia
April 3, 1967

Your letter of 21st March, informing me of the next meeting of the "World

Peace Through Law Center," has just been brought to my attention. May I offer you my congratulations on the efforts you are making with a view to basing international relations on Law.

Nevertheless, I am bound to confess that current events leave me sceptical as to the future of International Law . . . Be that as it may, allow me to wish you some measure of success in your efforts to stop the present infernal rush towards a Third World War.

(Signed) Norodom Sihanouk
Chief of State, Cambodia

CAMEROON

Yaoundé, Cameroon
September, 1965

It is with deep interest that Cameroon follows the work of the Washington Conference of World Peace Through Law. The people of Cameroon and an immense majority of the peoples of the world are conscious of the permanent danger for mankind caused by proliferation and storage of nuclear weapons capable of annihilating efforts aimed at achieving a slackening of tension and strengthening of international peace.

We wish the Washington Conference every success for a durable peace and for the prosperity and happiness for the whole of mankind.

(Signed) A. Ahidjo
President of the Federal Republic
of Cameroon

CANADA

Ottawa, Canada
May 22, 1969

I am pleased and honoured to have been invited to send my best wishes of the Government of Canada for the success of the Bangkok World Conference on Peace Through Law and the World Assembly of Judges.

The achievement of world order based on the Rule of Law is a gradual process which must be encouraged and assisted by all peoples everywhere. The international community may be able to take some major steps forward— such as the establishment of the United Nations, from time to time, but the path is a long and difficult one. Important meetings such as yours can make a significant contribution in focusing universal attention on the need for progress towards the realization of this goal.

I am certain that the Fourth World Conference on World Peace Through Law will be particular interest and value since it is being held in conjunction with the Second World Assembly of Judges. I notice that Working Sessions are scheduled on such topics as Social and Economic Development, the Computer and Government, and Legal Education and Research. These types of discussions indicate a keen desire on the part of members of the two Organizations to keep abreast of the times and indeed to look ahead to future development in specialized areas of law.

I look forward to learning the results of your discussions and studying the conclusions reached. May I offer you every best wish for a successful Conference.

(Signed) P. E. Trudeau
Prime Minister of Canada

CENTRAL AFRICAN REPUBLIC

Bangui, Central African Republic
September, 1965

On the occasion of the World Conference on World Peace Through Law, I wish to express the complete support that I, and the people of the Central African Republic give to the noble aims pursued by this important body. My best wishes for success for the work of this conference.

(Signed) David Dacko
President of the Central African Republic

CEYLON

Colombo, Ceylon
14th September, 1961

To the President of the Asian and Australasian Conference on World Peace Through Law

It is with very great pleasure that I forward to you my best wishes for a successful Conference which is being held this year in Asia.

The great principles of the Rule of Law which regulate the domestic affairs of civilized and democratic countries must be extended to the relationship of sovereign States in world affairs if permanent stability and peace, which it is our heartfelt desire to obtain, is to be achieved. The work of your Conference in this direction deserves every encouragement and I hope that as a result of your deliberations, a real and positive contribution will be made to World Peace.

Sirim Bandaranaike
Prime Minister of Ceylon

CHILE

Santiago, Chile
September, 1965

As the Washington World Conference on Peace Through Law opens, I wish to extend to the organizers and participants of that historic meeting my cordial greetings and best wishes for their success.

As the head of a government, a man of law, and an inhabitant of a troubled world in search of new ways of life, I fully share the aims and purposes of the organizers of this Conference. I am completely convinced that true universal peace can be attained only through justice and respect for paramount rules of social coexistence resting on law. When social peace, based on the fundamental concept that each man should receive his due, is finally attained within nations, we shall be much nearer to achieving peace among nations. And when international relations are at last governed by justice, the great task of maintaining peace shall be accomplished, for peace will give dignity to man's existence on this earth.

Chile is a nation which in the course of its history has shown a decided interest in law. The Chilean community, since its independence more than one hundred and fifty years ago, has been governed by the rule of law, and our public and private lives have progressed accordingly. Even today, when the nation, through an overwhelming popular movement, has manifested its desire for profound changes in the social and economic structure, and has put me in charge of carrying them out, Chile has expressed the urgent desire that these changes be performed within a framework of freedom and law. Such is the deep significance of my presence at the head of the Government of Chile.

I have reason therefore to applaud and encourage the task undertaken by the Washington World Conference on Universal Peace Through Law.

> (Signed) Eduardo Frei
> President of Chile

REPUBLIC OF CHINA

> Taipei, Taiwan
> September 5, 1969

Rule of law as a principle in international relations has long been accepted by civilized countries all over the World. But its actual application still leaves much to be desired and should be an object of greater endeavor on the part of all concerned.

At this juncture of history when man, thanks to scientific and technological advances, is racing toward the celestial bodies, it becomes imperative for us to do everything possible to banish totalitarianism and violence from our political institutions and from the conduct of our international relations so as to eliminate the causes of international chaos and to ensure the attainment of a world peace based on justice and righteousness. Our only hope of ever attaining this goal lies in the development of a public awareness of the necessity to settle all international disputes by peaceful means, especially in accordance with international law.

The assembly in Bangkok in September 1969 of so many outstanding jurists from various parts of the world and their deliberations of such an important question will no doubt advance the cause of, and have a far-reaching impact on, world peace and the freedom and welfare of mankind.

We, the Chinese people, have been faithfully following the teachings of Dr. Sun Yat-sen, the founding father of our Republic, in the conduct of our international relations. We are ready to succor the weak and support the fallen. We stand for the upholding of justice and we are prepared to discharge our treaty obligations. Above all, we have pledged ourselves to help preserve the United Nations Charter. I believe our tenets of diplomacy are in perfect accord with the lofty purposes of your organization.

May I wish your Conference unqualified success.

(Signed) Chiang Kai-shek
President of the Republic of China

COLOMBIA

Bogotá, Colombia
June 3, 1961

To the President of the American Conference on World Peace Through Law

My best wishes for complete success of the Conference, and I take this opportunity to forward to you and, by your means, to all the distinguished lawyers who shall participate in it, my cordial respects.

Alberto Lleras
President of Colombia

DEMOCRATIC REPUBLIC OF THE CONGO

Kinshasha, The Congo
June 28, 1967

In the name of the Democratic Republic of the Congo and on my own personal behalf, it is with great pleasure that I send you this message on the occasion of the great conference on World Peace Through Law which is to take place in Geneva from July 9 to July 14, 1967. I express the wish that the work which you carry out will proceed in a spirit of serenity, so that all the differences and international litigations which divide the world today will be resolved peacefully and in conformity with the principles of the rule of law. The Democratic Republic of the Congo, a deeply peace-loving country, cannot but support the efforts which you are undertaking to this aim.

(Signed) J.D. Mobutu, President,
Democratic Republic of The Congo

COSTA RICA

San Jose, Costa Rica
April 20, 1967

In the name of Costa Rica, I send to the Members of the World Conference for Peace Through Law in Geneva, and the First World Assembly of Judges, a heartfelt and optimistic message by way of greeting and as a token of faith in the conquests which it will make.

Legal standards and values must certainly prevail in this age of struggles for social justice, harmony between nations, and the just fulfillment of the basic necessities of mankind. In an age in which this struggle is being waged likewise against hunger, ignorance and disease, the basic and essential quest is for Peace.

This age has produced fantastic means of controlling Nature and of producing material wealth within the scope of experimental science and technology. But now it is time to bring about in addition the long awaited miracle—Peace, as the fruit of maturity, of higher intelligence, of a conscient human sentiment. Legal standards and values, created through a desire for Justice and the Dignity of Man, should be the true objects of your blessings.

This Conference of all the nations of the world represents an ideology and a most important cause in the historical development of Humanity, at this stage of the Twentieth Century: that of Law, the main guide of the destiny of the relations between nations and social groups. May Law be the means by which countries, both large and small, resolve their differences and consecrate their bonds of unity; this should be the basic ideal of all men of our time.

From a country that has nourished its historical development on education and the command of Law, small though it may be, allow me to reiterate my best wishes to the participants in the Geneva Conference for the realization of their fine objectives and the peaceful existence of mankind. I do so with faith in those values that control the destiny of Humanity.

(Signed) J.J. Trejos Fernandes,
President of Costa Rica

CYPRUS

Nicosia, Cyprus
May 9, 1967

I am very happy to send my warm greetings to the Geneva World Conference on World Peace Through Law.

By emphasizing the importance of the Rule of Law in democratic societies and its role in world peace, these Conferences serve a most worthy purpose. The bringing together of members of a profession trained in the concepts of justice common to all men is a positive contribution to the furtherance of international understanding, without which there can be no peace in the world.

At a time when international tensions are mounting, it is encouraging to know that this gathering of distinguished jurists will seek to find ways of achieving world peace through the Rule of Law, the great guarantee of individual freedom and an essential prerequisite to progress.

May God bless the initiative of the organizers of this Conference and guide its deliberations to a successful conclusion.

(Signed) Archbishop Makarios,
President, The Republic of Cyprus

DAHOMEY

Porto Novo, Dahomey
September, 1965

The attendance of delegates to this Conference held in this Year of International Cooperation testifies to the fact that in spite of the diversity of social, political and legal systems there is common fund of legal principles for all the peoples of the world. All the peoples and all the nations must base their efforts on these universally accepted principles to build up a world of tolerance, justice and peace.

My best wishes for the deliberations of this Conference in the hope that they may contribute to the promotion, maintenance and strengthening of peace through law in a world constantly engaged in the search for the difficult but necessary unity of man.

(Signed) Sourou Miganapithy
President of the Republic of
Dahomey

DENMARK

Copenhagen, Denmark
September, 1965

The rule of law is essential to the maintenance of World Peace, and throughout centuries men of good will have worked toward the goal of letting a philosophy based on law decide actions of nations and establish institutions permitting law to be a decisive factor in the relations between countries.

In our time we have seen established such institutions as the International Court of Justice, the World Court of Arbitration, and lately also the Court of Europe. Many are the countries that have submitted their disputes to these high institutions rather than taking them right into their own hands, but it is to be hoped that many more will follow this example.

The rule of law is an integral part of my country's foreign policy and I am proud to say that Denmark has carried this policy to a practical test in submitting conflicts to decisions taken by the International Court of Justice, the Court of Europe and various arbitration courts.

The principle of law has a prominent position in the U.N. Charter and should be the guiding principle of all peace-loving countries. To me it is therefore promising that lawyers from all over the world gather in an effort to promote the rule of law in the struggle for world peace. On behalf of the

Danish Government and the Danish people I wish you success in this important task.

(Signed) Jens Otto Krag
Prime Minister of Denmark

ECUADOR

Quito, Ecuador
July 1, 1967

You lawyers and judges, who firmly believe in peace as the only positive means to attain the highest aspirations of mankind, have come together in a great assembly on a world scale. The proposal that prompts you to strive for the substitution of law for force in international relations, and a situation in which nations will have at their disposal viable legal systems and procedures that will quickly and conveniently solve their disputes in a peaceful manner, is the most wholesome solution that any legal congress has ever attempted. We are only too well acquainted with the precarious peace in which many exist. But when law and legal procedures are the only solution for international disputes, the tension of war and the primitive instinct of force will cease to destroy the peace and harmony of the world once and for all. You have also proposed to carry out a vast campaign of investigation to study the main institutions and standards of international law in order to perfect them and to present them in a form which will facilitate their application, thereby making them the basis for both the extensive and intensive use of law in international relations. For all these reasons, the national government and people of Ecuador, who have based their international relations on the theory that the legal standard is the only one valid for solving disputes between the States, and that their peaceful settlement is the only acceptable solution for modern civilizations, are deeply grateful to know that distinguished lawyers and judges have gathered together in such a great assembly. May your studies, solutions, and suggestions attain striking results. And eventually man, the eternal subject of the desire for justice, will offer you his gratitude. Best wishes.

(Signed) Otto Arosemena Gomez,
President, The Republic of Ecuador

ETHIOPIA

Addis Ababa, Ethiopia
September, 1965

The distinguished representatives of the legal profession who are assembled here today have come to this historic Conference to open, or rather to continue, a debate that is as ancient as mankind and to which, unfortunately, there is no known time-limit.

The endless search for better ways of ensuring world peace through law must proceed from the firm conviction that the protection of human rights is the only solid basis for a new and harmonious society, free from fear, bloodshed, destruction, tears, poverty and sickness, such as we all desire. It is, indeed, a fact too often observed to be worth repeating that, when the rule of law is trampled underfoot anywhere, the entire community of nations suffers. History will show that the absence of legal rules, or their violation by the authorities of any state, inevitably impairs the peaceful relations of that state with other states and, eventually, with all the states. If mankind is anxious to avoid a repetition of conflicts and massacres such as those which have been witnessed in recent times, then it must understand that there can be no true and lasting peace so long as the rights of the human person are constantly and seriously disregarded in any one part of the world. The progressive establishment of the rule of law all around the globe constitutes therefore, together with disarmament and technical assistance, one of the major forces in the task of defending peace and raising the moral level of humanity.

Yet, although the dignity of the human person is a universal concept and the rule of law is now on everyone's lips, mankind has made little progress on the way to the repression of violence and the suppression of arbitrary action both within particular social groups, including states, and in their mutual relations. The key to further progress must be found in the re-affirmation and implementation of those fundamental principles of dignity, freedom and equality so dear to the heart of all men aspiring to peace and justice. These principles must be observed by everyone so that the human race can devote to its betterment all the resources and energy that are now applied for destructive purposes. In this aim, all humanity agrees and looks forward to its accomplishment.

These principles are common to all of you, the jurists and lawyers of the old and the new nations, with their diversity of culture and political or social institutions. Also common to all of you is the desire to enforce these principles through legal prescriptions to which proper respect is given and through methods conducive to the security of man and, consequently, to that of society at large. May these principles and this desire serve as a broad foundation on which you can bring your ideas closer in accord and map out converging lines of action. And may your efforts be successful.

(Signed) Haile Selassie I
Emperor of Ethiopia

FINLAND

Helsinki, Finland
September, 1965

In the field of international law remarkable results have been obtained through world-wide cooperation in consolidating a legal basis for human activity in many important domains by international conventions. The contributions of the world's leading lawyers have materially furthered this momentous activity. It must be recognized, however, that in respect of the most important part of international law, the preservation of world peace through international conventions, the goal is still remote. However, no efforts should be spared to bring all the nations, step by step, closer to attaining their final purpose, a lasting world peace and to secure peaceful international cooperation. In this task the legal authorities, lawyers and professors of law of all nations have a demanding and responsible challenge.

I would like to convey my best wishes for success to the world's distinguished leading lawyers assembled at Washington, D.C., for the "Washington World Conference On World Peace Through Law". I am convinced that the Conference will have a significant contribution to make in furthering the creation of a legal system aiming at the safeguarding of world peace.

(Signed) Urho Kekkonen
President of The Republic of Finland

GAMBIA

Bathurst, The Gambia
June 28, 1967

On behalf of The Gambia, I wish you all success in your deliberations and discussions. Here in the Gambia we support and pledge ourselves to maintain the fundamental freedoms, the rule of law, and the establishment and maintenance of World Peace through Law.

(Signed) D.K. Jawara,
Prime Minister, The Gambia

FEDERAL REPUBLIC OF GERMANY

Bonn, Federal Republic
of Germany
June 16, 1967

May I send my best wishes to the organizers and the participants of the Geneva World Conference on "World Peace Through Law". During the last few weeks, it has again become obvious how important it is for law to acquire that priority which you desire it to have within the framework of inter-state relations and with regard to the adjudication and the settlement of international disputes. I therefore hope that you will be able to continue successfully the work which you began at the earlier conferences in Athens and in Washington.

(Signed) Heinrich Luebke,
President, Federal Republic
of Germany

GHANA

Accra, Ghana
July, 1967

It is with great pleasure that I associate myself with other world leaders in congratulating the organisers of this august assembly, aimed at finding the much-needed peace in this world through law and respect for human dignity.

You are meeting today at a critical period of our times. A period when recent events in the Middle East add to the already confused world of tension. It is, therefore, gratifying to note that World Statemen and peace-loving men like you are engaged in an unceasing effort to find a lasting solution to our problems. In this respect, your efforts give nothing but cause for hope.

This Conference undoubtedly will add to the achievements of similar Conferences in the past, and in your deliberations you may wish to be reminded that there are many problems which beset mankind. . . . There is the question of hunger, disease and ignorance—the root causes of social and political strife. In each of all of these lies the threat to peace and human existence for which lasting solutions should be found. Ghana, as a member of the United Nations, has a stake in peace and is continuing and will continue to play its role to that effect however limited. However, I wish to assure you that no effort or contribution by your organisation towards the realisation of peace in the world can be minimized.

Indeed, you have drawn up your own guide-lines which have been enshrined in the noble declarations at the Athens and Washington Conferences. Nonetheless you will also serve the cause of peace if you will also note and bear in mind the four principles adopted by the United Nations General Assembly at its 20th Session in Resolution 2131 (XX) which, in my view, should form the basis of a World Convenant for the maintenance and preservation of World Peace, namely:

(a) That States shall refrain in their international relations from threat or use of force against the territorial integirty and political independence of any state, however big or small, or in any manner inconsistent with the purposes of the U.N. Charter.

(b) That it should be the duty of every State to cooperate with one another in accordance with the U.N. Charter.

(c) That the principle of equal rights and self-determination of peoples should be respected; and

(d) That all States shall fulfil in good faith and without reservation the obligations assumed by them in accordance with the U.N. Charter.

These are noble principles indeed requiring the respect of all peaceloving nations. I have no doubt that this Conference will add to these ideals and save the world from the scourge of war.

I wish the Conference every success in its deliberations.

(Signed) Lt. General J.A. Ankrah,
OOV, MC, Chairman, National
Libration Council, Ghana

GREECE

I also wish to express our wholehearted support to all those who are working for the achievement of Peace and Justice in Freedom among all peoples. The Greek Nation is and has always been devoted to these ideals and I am happy to reaffirm our faith in them.

We believe firmly that the importance of Law in human relations, both on the national and international levels, is foremost, and I express therefore, once more, my sincerest good wishes for a fruitful session and a happy outcome of your efforts to contribute to the cause of International Peace.

> (Signed) George Papadopoulos
> President of the Council of
> Ministers of Greece

GUATEMALA

> Guatemala City,
> Guatemala
> May 2, 1967

I have the honour of addressing you . . . to clearly present to you my general endorsement, as a professional lawyer, of the movement of jurists that the Center judiciously conducts. Undoubtedly, mankind has forgotten at the present time that law was created as the only means of resolving controversies, and to serve as a balance between man's diverse interests; it is in law that the values of Justice and Juridical Security, which are struggling to obtain the common good, are molded. With this in view, as a lawyer and head of government, I am profoundly convinced that the social problems of modern times can and must be resolved through the juridical rules that would regulate the relations among men. While congratulating you for the results obtained up to now by the "World Peace Through Law" movement, it is my hope that the conference will be a success in impelling this fountain of juridical rules.

> (Signed) Julio Cesar Mendez Montenegro,
> President, Guatemala

HAITI

> Port-au-Prince, Haiti
> June 12, 1961

To the President of the American Conference on World Peace Through Law

The Delegation from the Republic of Haiti has received instructions to convey our Government's wishes for the complete success of this Conference.

We are vividly impressed with the liberal attitude of the President of Costa Rica, and with the good will of all the Delegates. We wish to congratulate the organizers of the Conference and the President of the Meeting, who carries out his duties tactfully and competently. And we take advantage of this occasion to express our agreement with the idea of an international Pan American Court of Justice with full powers of jurisdiction.

> Dr. Francois Duvalier
> President of the Republic

HONDURAS

> Tegucigalpa, Honduras
> June 11, 1961

To the President of the American Conference on World Peace Through Law

"DO NOT ENTER HITHER HE WHO DOES NOT RESPECT THE LAWS OF HIS COUNTRY"

The American Continental Conference on "World Peace Through the Rule of Law", meeting under such good auspices in San José, Costa Rica, is an event that we, who are interested in applying law as a supreme norm of the governments of our countries and as a permanent base in the relations among the States, look upon with great satisfaction.

It fills us with optimism when professional men of law meet "to discuss ideas on how the domain of law can be extended and fortified in international relations"; and with a positive hope in regard to the security of the future upon contemplating the vigorous advance of this universal movement through which "it is expected to arrive at agreements of the necessary means so that International Law can be directed to establish the legal base necessary if the nations and peoples are to have the opportunity of completely developing thier potentialities, without placing in danger the inalienable laws of mankind".

I have always believed that in Law, as a norm of life, exists an inseparable uniqueness. If systems of just governments could be established everywhere, we would have equally just international relations. The oppressive systems, of an anti-juridical nature, do not only proceed illegally against the peoples they oppress, but also constitute the focal point of confusion within a certain geographical radius. All the oppressors of the peoples have commenced their abominable careers subjugating their own subjects.

In this way, the advances of Law have to be registered simultaneously in a national sense and in an international area in order to be of value. It is useless to promulgate the wisest international laws or to approve abundant agreements of high human concepts, if they are destined from birth to clash against the closed wall of the tyrannies which still cover with shame the face of the earth. On the other hand it is conceivable that the purest norms of living-togetherness have application among the peoples and men who practice democratic principles without the foregoing declarations of authority or the signing of special agreements.

Democracy is for me an act of good will and faith. It is not the democratic laws that make the peoples free, but rather the free peoples who give themselves democratic laws. We have on hand for approval many laws heaped with optimistic intentions which are never applied because injustice and autocracy stand in the way of development.

A democracy can consider itself legitimate only when any citizen, even on the assumption that the case does not represent for him an immediate convenience, interests himself in the defense of laws. Men educated in the love of norms that they themselves promulgate through representative systems that the constitutional law places in their hands are the only ones capable of forming republics illustrious for their honor and integrity; and only those States that create upon a similar human base are in a position to weave International Law where the guarantees of the individual have due consideration.

Relative as is the perfection of international legislation, the undeniable fact is that it advances in gigantic steps and that at the present time no other support of living-togetherness between states exists. Therefore, it is obligatory to polish and trim the instruments which International Law employs and to make them serve the fundamental causes of liberty and democracy.

We Americans have the right to feel proud of the progress carried out in the relations of our States. The Inter-American System could well erect itself as an example to a world mangled by so many injustices and afflicted by so many discords. Every day we are obtaining victories of loyal and sincere cooperation, and are also gaining ground from violent or unlawful procedures. We have obtained the formation of ideals and common aspirations in the political as well as in the economic and social fields. We lack in giving life to the technical creations which will make workable those ideals and allow us to arrange in proper order our action with that of the whole free world, without damage to our regional personality.

This American Continental Conference has great tasks to fulfill in the course that it is to follow. Illustrious and capable men, citizens of America, attend this conference whose primary interest rests in making Law the fundamental steppingstone of hemispheric living-togetherness.

I also think that one of the most difficult tasks to be carried out by this Conference is that of making remiss Governments understand that they must strictly fulfill promises they have made when the promises consist of international contractual agreements. Not infrequently countries that have been signatories of international treaties and agreements have refused the fulfillment of its clauses or have given a unilateral interpretation to treaties established in good will in order to favor only their own interests. Such attitudes must be eradicated through the formation of a responsible conscience among those countries and governments which are disrespectful of international compromises and threats to civilized and peaceful living-togetherness.

The President of Honduras greets you cordially, and with regard to the invitation that he received from the president of the Conference and of the Costa Rican Bar Association, shares with you the conviction that the best way towards the conquest of World Peace is by re-establishing genuinely demo-cratic governments in all countries.

You could well inscribe in the threshhold of your conference room, Gentlemen, the following sentence: "Do not enter hither he who does not respect the laws of his country."

> Ramón Villeda Morales
> President of Honduras

ICELAND

> Reykjavik, Iceland
> September, 1965

It is a great pleasure for me to extend my warmest greetings and good wishes to the World Conference on World Peace Through Law at the same time as I should like to underline the fact that "Peace through Law" will be attained only if the main rules of law are the same for all, and peace will be worth while only if those main rules conform to the "Rule of Law."

It is my ardent wish that your Conference will meet with every possible success.

> (Signed) Bjarni Benediktsson,
> Prime Minister of Iceland

INDIA

> New Delhi, India
> March 31, 1967

The President . . . is glad to know that the Geneva World Conference on World Peace Through Law and the first World Assembly of Judges will be held in July, 1967. He sends his best wishes for the success of the Conference and the Assembly.

> (Signed) Nagendra Singh,
> Secretary to the President
> of the Republic of India

INDONESIA

> Djakarta, Indonesia
> July 7, 1967

It is with great pleasure that I forward to you my best wishes for the success of the World Conference on World Peace Through Law and The World Assembly of Judges.

It has consistently been the ideal and sincere aspiration of all the Indonesian people to protect freedom and justice, maintain world peace and contribute to the promotion of human welfare. To realize this ideal, I believe that we must protect human rights through law and establish social order through law, and further, that all international disputes should be settled in accordance with the principle of the rule of law.

I wish your conference great success.

(Signed) Dr. A.H. Nasution,
Chairman, People's Congress
of the Republic of Indonesia

IRAN

Tehran, Iran
September, 1965

On the occasion of the meeting of the International Conference on World Peace Through Law, it gives me great pleasure to send my cordial greetings and those of the people of Iran to all the honourable representatives at this Conference and to express the hope that their deliberations will be crowned with success.

This hope is a truly sincere one, and one which I am convinced is shared by all the people motivated by goodwill in the world at large, for, the matter under discussion here is a question of life and death for entire humanity.

There was a time when war was considered by the strong as an expensive but exciting pastime, and by the weak countries as an evil among other evils to be reluctantly borne from time to time. But today, war is no longer solely an unpleasant amusement arising from the sickness of the mind. At one time, as we have all read in history books it was possible for the world to witness wars lasting seven, thirty, or a hundred years, but today it may not even be feasible to imagine a war of several days. No one will know whether an historian will survive such a war to record its duration in history.

An important factor which we must bear in mind is that war is today no longer an economic necessity and it is on this ground that it has lost its raison d'etre.

In the course of several thousand years, that is, from the dawn of civilization, as a result of the limited supply of material resources and their fixed quantity, a tribe, or a country, which was deficient in this respect was forced to resort to war as a solution in order to meet its needs from the wealth of a neighbour. But today, the great industrial and scientific revolution in human society and the endless potentiality for the exploitation of natural resources, and, above all, the discovery of nuclear force as a source of energy, have completely removed this necessity. For today, it is possible to acquire from nature what was in the past obtained from others by aggression. Success in this respect now, not only rules out aggression towards one's neighbours, but, quite to the contrary, requires absolute cooperation with a neighbour leading to more favourable results in the interests of both.

Needless to say, this cooperation is only possible when it is based on law which is the guarantee of the equitable rights of all the members of a society or an association. Any form of international cooperation must be based on the moral principle for which this Conference is assembled, namely, on the rule of law.

In my Message to the first World Conference on World Peace Through Law, which met in Athens, I expressed the hope that the endeavours of the eminent lawyers participating in that assembly would be crowned with success, and today, I reiterate the same hope.

In the name of my people, I ardently wish your great World Conference success in its deliberations. The Iranian people in their culture and civilization of several millenia have always made peace and understanding the basis of their philosophy, thought, literature and art. Not a single page in the long history of this country will be found which is not based on this spirit of international understanding and cooperation.

I pray Almighty God to guide us all in order that we may benefit from the boundless energy which has been made available to us by science and the miracle of human thought, not as children playing with fire, but as grown and reasonable human beings, completely aware of their responsibility towards God and to future generations. I also pray that we may use this double-edged sword not to destroy ourselves and our fellow beings, but as an effective weapon in our combat against the true enemies of mankind, in other words, against ignorance, poverty, disease and judicial and social injustices.

(Signed) Reza Shah Pahlevi
His Imperial Majesty The
Shahanshah of Iran

IRAQ

Bagdad, Iraq
September, 1965

People everywhere seek peace; they know that future generations depend upon respect for law, for law is the hall-mark of human civilization. I know for certain that peace cannot be ensured unless a man's right is respected and a complete recognition of the right of nations to determine their future is acknowledged. Islamic law is based on a respect for justice. The Quoran, Sura 4, Verse 58, states "and if you are called to adjudicate between people, then justice should be your guide." Islam also abolished distinction between people and made them equal and did not recognize any distinction because of race, color or locality. The Quoran, Sura 49, Verse 13, states "O people we have created you into males and females, made you into nations and tribes in order that you know each other. The righteous among you are those preferred by God."

International cooperation cannot be secure unless the rule of law prevails and states follow the precepts of equitable laws. Under a law-observing international order, peace will prevail, nations and individuals shall be secure in their everyday life and civilization will prosper.

(Signed) Abdul Salam Mohamed Arif
President of the Republic of Iraq

IRELAND

Dublin, Ireland
June 23, 1969

Arbitration or the judicial determination of international disputes are the only alternatives to war between nations. An acceptable code of international law is, accordingly, one of the pillars of peace.

I send on behalf of our people our warmest good wishes for the success of your work.

(Signed) Eamon de Valera,
President, Ireland

ISRAEL

Jerusalem, Israel
September 4, 1969

From Jerusalem where the doctrine of moral law and the vision of universal peace were proclaimed to men I send in my name and that of the people of Israel thirsting for peace our ardent and deeply concerned hope for fruitful deliberations at this session of the World Conference on World Peace Through Law and the World Assembly of Judges.

(Signed) Zalman Shazar
President of Israel

ITALY

Rome, Italy
June 10, 1967

The President of the Italian Republic is pleased to learn of the forthcoming World Conference on World Peace Through Law which he wishes every success.

(Signed) Giuseppe Saragat,
President, Republic of Italy
(Per Ambassador J. Guisti del
Giardino)

JAMAICA

Kingston, Jamaica
July, 1967

I take this opportunity to send you my heartiest greetings and to wish your most distinguished Assembly every success in your deliberations.

It is my conviction that respect for the rule of law has contributed immeasurably to the maintenance of peace in individual communities. It has been the pre-requisite—the *sine qua non*—to every orderly society. I firmly believe therefore that if nations were to endeavour to make concerted efforts to extend respect for the rule of law beyond their national boundaires and to apply it in the International Arena, mankind would undoubtedly succeed in repelling the spectre of war which looms on almost every horizon.

Indeed, many of us have found it rather disconcerting that man, equipped with all the enormous resources and advanced knowledge, must still be searching for that haven of World Peace. Nevertheless, the gratifying thing is that you accept, as I have no doubt your colleagues who assemble with you in Geneva also do, that the search must go on and that the only way of ensuring man's continued inhabitation of this earth we cherish, is through World Peace.

It cannot be truly said that the search has always been in vain. From over three centuries ago, commencing with the signing of the Treaty of Westphalia in 1648, nations have been making Pacts, Declarations and Conventions; and in 1920 the first World Court—the Permanent Court of International Justice—was established. Events of this nature have undoubtedly marked progress towards the end we seek.

It is truly very sad that we do not seem to realize (or is it that we simply refuse to accept) that in our own hands we have the means of securing our continued existence and likewise the means of making it a peaceful one.

I urge you to continue the good work to which your Organization is so dedicated, and again I wish you ever success in your relentless efforts towards the achievement of World Peace Through Law.

(Signed) Hugh L. Shearer,
Prime Minister and Minister of
External Affairs, Jamaica

JAPAN

Tokyo, Japan
September, 1965

It gives me a great pleasure to extend my warmest greetings on the occasion of the opening of the Washington World Conference on World Peace Through Law, in this memorable year marking the 20th anniversary of the founding of the United Nations.

After the war, Japan has shown dedication to liberal democracy and a fervent desire for an international community based on justice and order. In pursuit of such an ideal society of nations, our country abandoned the use of force as means of settling international disputes, and has consistently extended whole-hearted support to the United Nations, making positive contribution to enhance its prestige and functions.

The current international situation has still some uncertain factors in it, leaving a wide gap between the reality and the ideal envisaged by the founders of the United Nations. At this time, it seems fitting to call upon all member nations to reaffirm the basic principles of the United Nations Charter and to renew their determination and concerted efforts for the reinforcement of the U.N.

Fortunately, we note a genuine aspiration for peace growing today on a global basis. Justified by such world-wide peace-loving sentiments, the present convocation will certainly contribute a great deal to the advancement of the cause of world peace, emphasizing the legal aspect which tends to be over-shadowed by other factors in the field of international politics, and urging that all disputes should be resolved in a peaceful manner.

I sincerely hope that this well-timed gathering of distinguished jurists from all over the world will, with their ripe wisdom and deep insight, accomplish fruitful results in the interest of a stable and orderly world community, and mark a significant milestone in the history of mankind in quest for universal legal rules.

(Signed) Eisaku Sato
Prime Minister of Japan

JORDAN

Amman, Jordan
August, 1965

It gives me great pleasure to convey my heartiest salutations and very sincere wishes for the success of your historic conference representing as it does, the leading minds of the legal profession from all corners of the earth.

A foremost achievement of humanity in its painful evolution toward the modern world has been the sanctification of the rule of law to relationships among nations.

The future of mankind is contingent upon the achievement of this goal. It is the more imperative and overriding when judged against the mortal peril of mutual annihilation which throws a dark shadow upon the whole globe.

Needless to state that pious hopes to achieve world peace through law would not, even with the best of intentions, achieve it.

It is the common task of us all to strive for its attainment through appropriate structures, functions and, above all, attitudes of mind and spirit which respect fundamental principles of justice, morality and equality before the law, in the relationships of individuals within each society, as well as in the relationships of societies in the community of nations.

The all-embracing agenda of the Conference, which covers innumerable aspects of life within the rule of law gives every promise of fulfilling the noble objectives for which your conference has been convened; and I can only state that all peoples of good will look forward with hopeful prayers to a successful outcome of your endeavors and a pledge to give every assistance for its acceptance as a regulator of orderly and sane behavior in the relationships of nations.

My blessings as well as those of the people of Jordan are with you and I pray to God that He may grant you the strength and the wisdom to carry out your lofty mission in order that, at long last, we may ensure world peace through law among all peoples of the earth.

(Signed) Hussein I.
His Majesty The King of the
Hashemite Kingdom of Jordan

KENYA

Nairobi, Kenya
September, 1965

Institutions of a free society are defended and sustained by the voluntary participation of every man and woman. Freedom of association enshrines equality between men and enables society to adopt free negotiation, arbitration, or a court of law as a means of settling disputes.

Man in an ordered society has discovered that the price of liberty is eternal vigilance, but this in no way conflicts with his innate desire for consensus and accord rather than contention and conflict. In such a society it is mandatory that the law of "might is right" should be abandoned in favor of the impartial rule of law. It is in this spirit that I send your Conference every good wish for success in its voluntary effort to foster resolution of disputes between men or between nations by peaceful means.

(Signed) Jomo Kenyatta
President of Kenya

KOREA

Seoul, Korea
June 20, 1967

I send my most heartfelt congratulations on the opening of the Geneva World Conference on World Peace Through Law and the first World Assembly of Judges.

Today the most ardent desire of mankind is to build a peaceful world in which everyone can enjoy freedom and prosperity. Despite this, it is deplorable to note that at this very moment conflicts and wars are threatening life, freedom and prosperity of mankind throughout the world.

Differing outlooks on the world and life or conflict of interests may account for this chaotic situation but more fundamentally, this is ascribable to the defiance of law, by which we should abide.

When the jural order has been firmly established and every state faithfully observes the law, any international conflict can be solved peacefully, I believe. I am also confident that world peace can be achieved and maintained through law.

Therefore, your efforts to pursue world peace through the establishment of law rules and legal institutions deserve our whole-hearted support and the people of the Republic of Korea and I are willing to lend every possible cooperation to this effect.

I earnestly hope that this meaningful gathering will set another important milestone in the path of man toward peace, freedom and prosperity.

I now extend my best wishes to each and all of you for a full measure of success of this conference.

(Signed) Park Chung Hee,
President, Republic of Korea

KUWAIT

Kuwait, Kuwait
September, 1965

It gives me great pleasure to send my greetings to the participants of the Washington World Conference on World Peace Through Law who have come from various continents of the world to discuss feasible ways and means for establishing relations between various states, nations and peoples on the basis of justice and fairness. Believing deeply in the principles of the United Nations Charter and the Convention of Human Rights and establishing her relations with other countries on the principles and foundations of international law, the State of Kuwait exerts every effort towards the promotion of the dictates of law for the realization of the cherished goal of establishing a world society living in peace and security. Two years have passed since your first Conference has convened and the world is still suffering from many tribulations, the foremost of which is perhaps the usurpation of the natural and lawful rights of others by force.

While discussing the means to support and develop international institutions working for the establishment of world peace and security, your historic Conference will, undoubtedly, achieve much by laying down the solid foundations for a peace based on justice and human rights for mankind at large.

May God guide your steps and lead all your efforts to success.

(Signed) Abdulla As-Salim As-Sabah
Emir of Kuwait

LAOS

Vientiane, Laos
August 9, 1965

On the occasion of World Law Day, I am very honored to send you this message as an indication of my profound respect and concern for world peace through law.

I send you my fraternal greetings on this day that is celebrated here in Laos as in all the other countries of the world where the Head of the State has proclaimed September 13, 1965, as World Law Day. All public officials, private authorities, members of the legal profession, all citizens and men of good will are invited to celebrate this day of holding appropriate ceremonies in the courts and tribunals, in the schools and universities, public places, in the headquarters of public and private organizations that recognize the necessity for international law.

Your task is immense since you are called upon from all corners of the world to work together for international cooperation and understanding in the interest of world peace.

You will be faced with innumerable obstacles inasmuch as you will have to draw upon different legal systems in order to establish rules acceptable to all. But I am convinced that your endeavor will be successful, because essentially the same concepts form the basis of all systems, namely the liberty and dignity of man.

In the course of your discussions you will have occasion to defend the principle of the rule of law, without which there can be no human justice and to stress the value of the supremacy of the system of legal government with its ideal of quality and justice and the independence of the judicial power, for the protection of the fundamental rights and freedom of man, should not be neglected.

I hope that you will set the best example to the men of all the countries of the world, showing that we can reach an understanding within the domain of law to build a world community whose structure will be based on international agreements founded on the rule of law.

I convey to the Conference my best wishes, and hope that the success of your meeting will contribute to the maintenance of world peace according to the rule of law.

(Signed) Souvanna Phouma
Prime Minister of Laos

LEBANON

Sin-El-Fil, Lebanon
June 30, 1967

I am happy to address, in the name of the Government and people of Lebanon, my sincere greetings to the delegates to the International Conference of World Peace Through Law, as well as my ardent wishes for the success of their work. Both by the example of fraternity which it provides at home and by its action on the international level, Lebanon has always supported the establishment of a universal order founded on justice. It is by treating the primacy of law as an inviolable rule that humanity will be able to surmount the difficulties which are still obstructing its progress towards a future of international tranquility and concord.

An assembly of jurists who come from such a large number of countries is highly qualified to proclaim the necessity of strict observance of legal rules in the interests of world peace.

May the Geneva Conference succeed in concretizing rapidly its noble aims for the greatest benefit of humanity.

(Signed) Charles Helou,
President of the Republic of Lebanon

LIBERIA

Monrovia, Liberia
June 30, 1967

The desire for a society regulated by common rules of conduct as a basis for a world community in which man and nations live as neighbours is evidenced by the will and consent of such scholars and jurists as you who, in an untiring and unrelenting effort, are championing the Divine Edict which commands man to depart from evil, and do good work, seek peace and pursue it. I therefore seize this opportunity to associate myself with your lofty objective of seeking World Peace Through the Rule of Law, whereby man will enjoy and breathe the air of transparent justice, the pursuit of happiness, fair play and the free association with other men.

In an effort to contribute toward the solution of the turbulent, confused and delicate state of our troubled world, caused in part by two world wars which have been brought upon us in the last half century, I entreat you always to employ the greatest weapon and attribute of your profession—clear reasoning.

There is no easy escape from all our troubles and there is no cheap and painless shortcut to peace and the rule of law. Moreover, we are continuing to subsist in one of the greatest watershed periods of history which may securely fix the pattern of civilization for many generations to come. We must concede the fact that PEACE cannot be won as WAR is won. Peace in the world, like good government, is a goal which we approach but never finally and perfectly attain. Peace like religion is the task of each new day: it must be worked at in little things and in big things so long as we breathe.

Our Creator prepared us for an awesome mission which is peace on earth being the end of man. Therefore I am very hopeful that your plenary as well as your committee deliberations will be characterized by the merits of each and all cases using to the fullest extent the talents with which you are endowed in finding a solution through the Rule of Law by which lasting world peace can be achieved.

In conclusion, I say that the image endowed with sanity, serenity and social strength of unshackled freedom, transparent justice and implicit conference remembering in all stages that Peace is a Divine attribute and the use of every part of the nerve center to secure it is worth the while.

(Signed) William V.S. Tubman,
President of Liberia

LIBYA

Tripoli, Libya
September, 1965

I am pleased to greet you on the occasion of your meeting in an endeavor to fulfill a cherished goal, and to apply law and justice rather than weapons in solving world disputes.

The world's attention today is focused on Washington for the world hopes to avoid wars and preserve our civilization.

The nascent countries are very hopeful that your meeting will bridge the differences and bring countries and nations closer to serve the human heritage.

In the name of Libya, the Arab African Country, I wish your conference every success in pursuit of the noble cause of peace.

(Signed) Hussein Maziq
Prime Minister of Libya

LIECHTENSTEIN

Vaduz, Liechtenstein
August 11, 1969

As the existence of mankind in our present time is dependent upon world peace, it is a great pleasure and honour for me that President Charles S. Rhyne has invited me to extend a message of greeting to the Bangkok World Conference on World Peace Through Law and the World Assembly of Judges.

Since all endeavours in man's society must submit themselves to certain rules and regulations, in order that the existence of man may be ensured, the discussion in the Conference is specially relevant for the protection of peace and a peaceful order. The individual countries have, for thousands of years, promulgated laws for their own use, so that the impulses of man's society may in this way be directed through specifically delineated channels. In our present age, in which man has placed previously unimagined capabilities at his service through the tremendous development of science and technology, the need for the establishment of a durable order of peace, on a worldwide basis, cannot be ignored and must be considered. If this should be realized, mankind will require a stable framework with which to make such a peace, and this stable framework can be provided only by those men committed to the study of law.

As a consequence, every human being in the world must heartily welcome the occasion of an international conference of scholars of law, convened to discuss this question.

(Signed) Franz Josef II
Prince of Liechtenstein

LUXEMBOURG

Luxembourg,
March 24, 1962

To the President of the European Conference on World Peace Through Law

In the name of the Government and the people of Luxembourg, may I express my good wishes for the success of the Rome Conference on World Peace Through the Rule of Law.

The aims of this Conference are closely associated with the aspirations of such nations as ours which look to the rule of law as one of the chief guarantees of their existence and are convinced of the need for peaceful settlement of international controversies so that mankind may move towards a better future.

With kindest regards,

Yours sincerely,

Pierre Werner
Prime Minister of Luxembourg

MALAYSIA

Kuala Lumpur, Malaysia
August 19, 1969

We are very happy to note that the World Conference on World Peace Through Law and World Assembly of Judges this year is held in the capital city of a country which has been one of our country's closest neighbours. We are happy to inform you that Malaysia supports the principle of world peace through law.

It has been time and time again proved that peace acquired under the rule of force is but illusory and, therefore, it requires bigger force to make it last. This has been proved to be futile.

One of the greatest difficulties in the world today is the difficulty of putting into practice the principle to which many of us subscribe. We therefore hope that, in your deliberations, you would also include the method how best this principle, which undeniably is recognized by most people, could be implemented in practice.

We wish the conference every success.

(Signed) The Yang di-Pertuan Agong
King of Malaysia

MALTA

The Palace, Malta
June 14, 1969

Throughout the ages law has been in the life of a nation both the unifying element as well as determining factor in the orderly and peaceful development of its political, social and economical conditions.

Given the readiness to accept the rule of law even when it may appear to run contrary to national interest.

Given the sum of all that is best in national systems of law and its interpretation by legal wisdom and judicial experience.

Given the widespread and harmonious application of law in all countries.

Then the law can achieve in the international field what it has already achieved within the nations—and it is the prayer of all peoples that this may be so.

A gathering of the most competent judicial and legal authorities of all the nations, such as the Conference on World Peace Through Law and the World Assembly of Judges, cannot but contribute in the highest degree to the attainment of such a result.

I take this opportunity to wish the Conference every success in the pursuit of its noble ideas.

(Signed) Maurice Dorman
Governor-General of Malta

MAURITIUS

Port Louis, Mauritius
June 30, 1969

The acceptance of the Charter of the United Nations by over a hundred states in the past few decades is an emphatic rejection of the use of force as an instrument for the attainment of World Peace, and casts a shadow over the concept of greater sovereignty resulting from greater might. The signing of the Test-Ban and Non-Proliferation Treaties is, if only in a limited measure, a bold step in the implementation of the increasing world-wide desire for peace.

The achievement and strengthening of World Peace, however, depends perhaps as much on the desire of all states to allow their relations with one another to be governed by principles of mutual respect, equity and justice as on a resolute endeavour in the ascertainment and international recognition of those principles. No doubt, much has so far been accomplished but much still remains to be done to uphold the fundamental rights of individuals and states.

It is fitting that the World Assembly of Judges should take place at the same time as the World Conference on World Peace Through Law, as it falls within the particular province of the Judiciary and of the legal profession to extend the operation of the Rule of Law from the narrow confines of states to the international arena.

I have great pleasure in sending the good wishes of the people of Mauritius and my own to the Bangkok World Conference on World Peace Through Law and wish it the increasing success which previous conferences have, on successive occasions, deservedly achieved in the past few years.

> (Signed) S. Ramgoolam
> Prime Minister and Minister for
> External Affairs of Mauritius

MEXICO

> Mexico City, Mexico
> June 22, 1967

On the occasion of the First World Assembly of Judges and the Geneva Conference of World Peace Through Law, in the name of the People and Government of Mexico, I convey to the participants in these important meetings, through your esteemed intermediaries, sincere greetings to which I add my best wishes for the success of their work whose noble purpose is to ensure the prevalence of law in international relations. This is a task which is incumbent, not only upon governments, but rather upon all men who play a role in the formation of public opinion in all nations, without whose support no public action can be effective and fruitful.

In this respect, I should like to reiterate, now that the world situation is overshadowed by such grave threats to humanity, the concepts that were recently expressed at Punta del Este, on the occasion of the meeting of American presidents, where we expressed our unshakeable faith in the eventual triumph of Law as the best means of ensuring the peaceful existence of mankind, in justice as the proper destiny of law, in peace as the bountiful fact of justice, and above all in liberty, for without liberty, law cannot exist, peace cannot shine, and we shall never conquer peace.

> (Signed) Gustavo Diaz-Ordaz
> President, United States of Mexico

MONACO

Monaco
September, 1965

The only form of true civilization shall be for all men as well as for all states a civilization where the law will be unimpeachable and will always take precedence over force.

(Signed) Rainier the III
Prince of Monaco

NEPAL

Katmandu, Nepal
September, 1965

On this significant occasion, I have much pleasure to extend my warm greetings to all the distinguished jurists participating at this Conference.

Most of the ills of modern times can be remedied if the principles of law are universally applied and voluntarily accepted by all nations of the world. All human beings are aware of the growing danger of their very existence posed by the stockpiling of, and competitive race in, nuclear armaments. Peace being a prime and deep concern of mankind, it has never been more important than today for the world community to strive for an ordered society through the rule of law. This objective can be achieved only if the disputes among nations are settled without threat of or resort to arms and in accordance with the noble principles of international law.

In conclusion, I wish every success to the Conference in the achievement of its noble aim, that is world peace through law.

(Signed) Mahendra Bir Bikram Shah Deva
King of Nepal

NETHERLANDS

The Hague, Netherlands
August 18, 1969

In the history of mankind the search for peace has always been a fundamental one. In spite of many deceptions, as in recent years, we are still hopeful that one day disputes between peoples or nations may be settled peacefully by international jurisdiction.

May the Bangkok World Conference on World Peace Through Law be successful in its endeavours to banish war and aggression in case of international conflicts.

(Signed) P. J. S. De Jonj
Minister-President of the
Netherlands

NEW ZEALAND

Wellington, New Zealand
September, 1965

At no time has it been as vital as it is today that the rule of law should take the place of force as the means of settling international disputes. No lasting peace will be possible until we have a world order based on, and regulated by law. In the struggle to achieve such an order the work of the international legal profession will continue to have an important share especially where there is a responsible and well-organized movement toward this goal. I am thereby very glad indeed to give my support to the Washington World Conference on World Peace Through Law. It is my hope and the hope of my Governmert that your deliberations will prove fruitful.

(Signed) Keith Holyoake
Prime Minister of New Zealand

NICARAGUA

Managua, D.N.
Nicaragua, G.A.
June 20, 1969

I take great pleasure in addressing myself to you on the occasion of the 4th World Conference on World Peace Through Law and the World Assembly of Judges which is to take place in Bangkok.

As Chief of State, as a military officer and as a citizen of Nicaragua I have always placed faith in the standards of law.

This fourth World Peace Conference dealing with justice, satisfies the permanent hope of all Nicaraguans for the rule of international law-setting bodies. It is a hope which corresponds to the civil rights tradition of the Nicaraguan people and which has been of constant concern to my government. Enthusiastically I join my thoughts with those who are organizing this conference. I wish to express my sincere desire that the results be truly conducive to a better understanding among nations, to an understanding among governments and to the betterment of all men on this earth.

I take this opportunity to express my solidarity with you and the goals of the conference and to extend my very best wishes to the delegations as well as the organizing committee.

(Signed) Anastasio Somoza
President of Nicaragua

NIGER

July 1, 1967

On behalf of the Government of the Republic of Niger, I wish the Geneva Conference full success in its work. I am convinced that a lasting and just peace in the world can only be built on respect for international law.

(Signed) Diori Hamani,
President, Republic of Niger

NIGERIA

Lagos, Nigeria
May 22, 1967

On this auspicious occasion of World Law Day, July 10, 1967, it gives me great pleasure to send you this message at this year's Geneva World Conference on World Peace Through Law and your first World Assembly of judges and other legal leaders from all over the world. May I recall that our country, Nigeria, had the houour of playing host in December 1961 to the first African Conference on World Peace Through Law held here in Lagos for the purpose of providing a forum for the progressive development of principles and procedures of international law for world peace. That was a very successful conference in which lawyers and judges from all over the world, including most parts of Africa, participated in order to demonstrate the importance of the role of law in a world community based upon law and order.

A good deal of progress has since been made by your organization as a whole, both of your inspiring and energetic leadership, and of the series of conferences held in various parts of the world. The Movement has now materialized into an institute by the establishment of the World Peace Through Law Center last year in Geneva. The World Charter for the Rule of Law you will have the honour to present to the Geneva World Conference in July constitutes, in my opinion, a comprehensive new proposal for the taking of practical steps towards the establishment of the Rule of Law throughout the World. Among the most important of these are:

(1) A declaration of generally recognized principles of international law for voluntary adherence by participating States;

(2) The first World Code of general principles of law recognized by nations as a basis for the establishment of a universally acceptable code of law;

(3) A plan for the exchange of data and the automation of international law to make legal information readily available to all nations of the world;

(4) A proposal for a workable and effective international court system for the peaceful resolution of disputes between nations and nationals of different nations; and

(5) Procedures for the resolution of disputes based on prior voluntary agreements by participating States under the aegis of the United

Nations. These are indeed worthwhile ideals for the securing and maintenance of international peace and security. For this reason, if not no other, your commendable efforts deserve to succeed.

On behalf of the Government and people of Nigeria, I wish your deliberations a very successful outcome.

(Signed) Yakubu Gowon,
Head of the Federal
Military Government

NORWAY

Oslo, Norway
September, 1965

On behalf of the Royal Norwegian Government I am pleased to have the opportunity of greeting the World Conference on World Peace Through Law.

The people of Norway firmly believe that international conflicts should be settled in a peaceful way through law, and that it is possible to realize this aim. We consider that this fundamental task, essential as it is to the safeguarding of human rights, requires the joint efforts of all of us. We are pleased to know that the representatives of the legal profession are meeting at the Washington World Conference on World Peace Through Law to examine these questions, and hope that your efforts will contribute to the promotion of peace.

(Signed) Einar Gerhardsen
Prime Minister of Norway

PAKISTAN

May 27, 1967

I am very happy to learn that the World Peace Through Law Center is holding its First World Assembly of Judges at Geneva from July 9 to 14, 1967, and is celebrating World Law Day on July 10.

Peace Through Rule of Law in my view is the adoption of a world legal system by which the conflict which is inherent in the nature of man and which results in the fighting of nations is resolved peacefully and a framework is made available for the peace and progress of all. To this there is no other choice, as by maintaining its present posture mankind may jeopardise its own survival.

The universal agreement in the political, social and economic fields can be obtained only in a legal way and through the evolution of a legal system which nations accept and for which they are prepared to work. Adoption of such principles would go far towards reducing the areas of armed conflict and be the foundation of peaceful existence of mankind. Only in this way can human progress be maintained. Else there will be a throwback to the rule of the jungle and with the present tension in the world the balance is to delicate.

I wish all success to this congregation of learned men and hope that they will conceive ideas which will influence the minds and hearts of men all over the world.

(Signed) Mohammad Ayub Khan,
N. Pk., H.J., Field Marshal,
President, Pakistan

PANAMA

Panama
July 10, 1967

I wish to take advantage of the opportunity which the conference on World Peace Through Law, soon to be held in Geneva, offers me to highlight a few concepts which in my opinion can contribute to guaranteeing world peace through law.

Undoubtedly, the primary duty of every citizen and of every legal practitioner is to spare no positive effort to promote world peace. This worthy objective becomes more easily attainable if our attention is directed to the truly positive aspect of maintaining peace through law, instead of concentrating on the secondary aspect of preventing war, a stand which entails passive resignation before what is considered the obstinate tendency of the human race to veer towards conflict and controversy.

If it is truly the aim of the organisers of this conference to focus attention on the use of computers in law research by suitable exhibitions of the technological advance in automation which will result in the acceleration of the administration of justice, we firmly believe that this emphasis on technological advance in the field of law, should be accompanied by equal emphasis on the moral and ethical structure on which legal principles rest. It is imperative to develop renewed confidence in the value and power of legal principles as an effective and efficient means of providing solutions for the differences which may arise among the nations of the world, for there exists no problem so insurmountable that it cannot be resolved by reconciliation and comprehension.

If this new confidence can be developed, our moral values which for so many centuries have inspired the rules of equity and the standards which put human conscience above all will be firmly rooted and thus able to guide international relations.

It is also necessary, if it is our desire to achieve stable and lasting world peace, that our plans should not be limited to establishing rights and duties, but to establishing an international, moral conscience which stems from the constructive and positive principle of excluding armed conflict as a means of resolving differences and controversies, and the adoption of solutions which will guarantee harmonious co-existence and lasting peace.

(Signed) Don Marco A. Robles,
President of the Republic of Panama

PHILIPPINES

Manila, Philippines
July, 1967

It is not enough to be born free. People must have a certain capacity of mind to remain free; and this demands moral and intellectual strength, for it is with this strength that they may fulfill their responsibilities to themselves and to an orderly society.

Freedom is meaningless without law, for untrammelled freedom deteriorates into anarchy or mob rule. To be free, therefore, is to maintain, among others, a continuing interest and a responsibility toward an orderly society under law.

This, in turn, will establish peace. In such a climate, mankind may then work to realize full human dignity within a just and orderly world. This, to me, is the simple concept of peace through law.

I am gratified therefore that the initiative has been taken to examine this need of humanity, more urgent now than ever before, through this eminent assembly. World Peace Through Law is a yearning of human beings as old as time. Let us hope that it will come in our own time.

(Signed) Ferdinando Marcos,
President, Philippines

PERU

Lima, Peru
July 2, 1967

Please accept my fervent wishes and may the results of your meeting contribute efficiently through the affirmation of the rule of law to the safeguarding of world peace and to the promotion of world cooperation as a firm basis of the relationship between the states.

(Signed) Fernando Belaunde Terry,
President, Republic of Peru

QATAR

Qatar
September, 1965

Whereas we believe in the high principles from which emanated the charter of the United Nations and which reaffirm the rights of every man to a free life; to achieve justice, brotherhood and equality; to uphold treaties and other sources of international law; to afford prosperity to all mankind and to develop progress and civilization everywhere.

We are therefore happy to congratulate the members of the world's legal profession for their efforts and objectives in consolidating world peace and security on the basis of the rule of law which affords peaceful and just settlements of all disputes.

We take action to recognize that the "World Conference on World Peace Through Law" is determined to establish an international legal system which will become a great step forward in the realization of human perfection and which will prevent all discrimination between men and nations, be it for national origin, race or religion.

We wish to the World Conference success in its endeavor of realizing these great hopes common to all mankind.

(Signed) Ahmad Ibn Aly Al Thani
Ruler of Qatar

RWANDI

Kigali, Rwandi
July 14, 1969

His Excellency the President of the Republic charges me with confirming to you that he approves and encourages an action like yours which assures to peace one of its principal foundations.

(Signed) Th. Ntawiha
Director of Social and Cultural
Affairs of the President of the
Rwandi Republic.

SAUDI ARABIA

Saudi Arabia
September, 1965

We are pleased to convey to you our greetings and those of the people and the government of the Kingdom of Saudi Arabia, as well as our sincere wishes for the success of your conference and for the realization of the noble aims motivating your meeting. Peace which is based on right and justice is the dream of humanity which will save it from annihilation, and is the desire of peoples which we must all earnestly endeavor to realize.

The Kingdom of Saudi Arabia, in which the Muslim holy places are located, and toward which more than five hundred million Muslims turn with their hearts, supports, by reason of its Islamic legal system, your objectives, and believes in the means you follow for the realization thereof. We, as Muslims and the [people] responsible for the service of the Muslim holy places, believe in peace which is based on right and justice as an essential part of our creed. The words "al-Islam" and "as-Salam" [peace] are derived, in our Arabic language, from the same root, and God Almighty has named Himself as Alam [peace] so mankind may appreciate the importance of peace.

Peace on earth will not be attained unless the grounds of right and justice have been firmly rooted in each state where citizens and non-citizens alike may enjoy them, so that all are assured of the authority of law to uphold their dignity, protect their possessions, and help them exercise their freedom.

In compliance with the Muslim Shari'ah provisions, which we strictly apply in our country, we place right and justice in such a position that no one can detract from it. All are equal before the law, and all appear before the courts as claimants or defendants without distinction or immunity to any one, even though he be the head of the state. Nor does the hatred of us by any foreign community prevent us from upholding justice in its favor, even against ourselves. The Kuran enjoins us, "Let not the hatred of a people incite you not to act fairly; act fairly, that is nearer to piety". In this connection, the Kingdom of Saudi Arabia has set a magnificent example for all the nations of the world. We implement the ruling which an arbitration court renders in favor of a foreign company and against the government with the same strictness and alacrity that we implement a ruling rendered in our favor. This we do voluntarily and willingly, because we are executing one of the injunctions of God Almighty.

The law is the source of light from which right and justice radiate; it is the foundation of the edifice of peace; it will not be affected by whims, or will it allow the interests of the strong to overwhelm the rights of the weak. We look forward to the results to come out of your conference and the effects to follow from it. We wish you success.

(Signed) Faysal
King of Saudi Arabia

SENEGAL

Dakar, Senegal
September, 1965

It is with joy and hope that the Senegal Government has learned of the Washington World Conference on World Peace through Law. The President of the Republic of Senegal sends the eminent lawyers of the entire world meeting on this occasion his most heartfelt wishes for the success of their undertaking. It is possible to speak of organized state-controlled society only when the rule of law has definitively replaced brute force and vengeance in the relations among men. The international society will be truly established only when the rule of law will reign supreme over the relations among states. Great progress has been made in that direction; and we, the Africans, who have suffered in the past from an international "order" based on force and discrimination, place our hopes and confidence in institutions such as the United Nations, which since their establishment have worked so hard to promote a more just order. But much remains to be done, and the spectacle of our world so divided by full-scale and smoldering conflicts should suffice to show the magnitude of the task that remains to be done.

It is you, magistrates, professors, practicing men of law who have come from the whole world and are united by the same ideal of the rule of law who have the task of exploring the paths which might be open to the states, by preparing specific suggestions that you consider most appropriate to facilitate the advance of an equitable and effective international legal order.

Let us not deceive ourselves; this task is difficult, it goes against prejudices, against solidly established enterprises. Your efforts will know ups and downs, progress and set-backs, but they will succeed because the fate of mankind depends upon them. It is with optimism and confidence that I send you my congratulations and best wishes.

(Signed) Leopold Sedar Senghor
President of the Republic of Senegal

SIERRA LEONE

Freetown, Sierra Leone
3rd November, 1961

To the President of the African and Middle Eastern Conference on World Peace Through Law

I have great pleasure on behalf of the Government of Sierra Leone to present my most sincere wishes for the success of the Conference for Africa and the Middle East on the subject of World Peace Through the Rule of Law.

The subject is a challenging and urgent one and perhaps is the most vital of all avenues for the attainment of world peace which is the desire of all peoples everywhere. This challenge must be met and I have every confidence will be met and a conference of this type is a bold attempt to solve this problem. It deserves the encouragement of all who appreciate the vital necessity for international differences to be solved on the principles of justice rather than by force.

May the delegates be inspired by all that is noble in their deliberations and may success in a realistic and positive way follow closely the results of this important conference.

Milton Margai,
Prime Minister of Sierra Leone

SIKKIM

Gangtok, Sikkim
July 19, 1965

The object of law is to achieve right conduct which alone ensures security, happiness and peace for all. This conforms to the teachings of The Buddha. Thus the rule of law has been the ideal in our little country for centuries of our history.

There can be no peace without law as there can be no law without peace. This is as much true of the entire family of nations as of any single nation. World peace can be attained only through one rule of law for the whole world.

The spectre of nuclear destruction haunts all the nations, big and small, and the spectre may shape into reality anytime. One rule of law for the whole world can and will save mankind from such end. The ways and means for evolving such rule are in the nature of things beyond the field of politicians and strategists who handle weapons of destruction. It is proper that experts and specialists engaged in the formulation and administration of laws of all nations, big and small, should offer their services in this task.

I look forward with much expectation to this eminent assemblage of legal and judicial luminaries at Washington. In engaging themselves in the formulation of an international legal system capable of maintaining peace for all mankind these great experts will no doubt play the role of humanists which is much greater than that of experts in jurisprudence. I convey Sikkim's best wishes for the success of the Conference.

I thank you for your kind thought in inviting me to associate with this essential venture.

> Yours truly,
> (Signed) Palden Thondup Namgyal
> Chogyal of Sikkim

SINGAPORE

> Istana, Singapore
> May 2, 1967

To the international assembly of eminent lawyers, judges and legal celebrities gathered at the 1967 Geneva World Conference on "World Peace Through Law", I convey the good wishes and support of the Government and the people of the Republic of Singapore. May your efforts to build World Peace under the Rule of Law meet with every success.

> (Signed) Inche Yusof bin Ishak,
> President, Republic of Singapore

SOMALIA

> Mogadiscio, Somalia
> May 18, 1967

It gives me deep pleasure to send the greetings of the government and people of the Somali Republic to you who are gathering at Geneva to discuss ways and means of endeavour for the attainment of world peace through law. We congratulate you and plead the readiness of our country to provide heartfelt support for your efforts to make world peace through Law and to make it permanent. You would like to know that the efforts of your conference which are directed towards world peace through law are the same goals of our country. We would like to inform you that World Law Day 1967 will be proclaimed throughout the Somali Republic on July 10, 1967 to demonstrate our adherence to the principles of the rule of law for mankind and his search for world peace. You have our warmest good wishes and we wish you success in your work which is destined to be of world importance.

(Signed) Aden Abdulla Osman,
President, Republic of Somalia

SPAIN

Madrid, Spain
March 27, 1962

To the President of the European Conference on World Peace Through Law

It is with great pleasure that I address these words to the distinguished delegates and observers of the European Conference for World Peace Through Law, held in the city of Rome, whose very name evokes the principle of the Rule of Law.

Never has law been as necessary for the benefit of mankind as in our times. In preceding centuries, men of good will have longed for peace and justice through the basic principles of Natural Law, out of their moral beliefs and being convinced that Law was the best way to stamp out all violence.

But in our days, the Rule of Law is not only a moral necessity, but the very condition for the survival of Mankind. Surrounded by the dreadful peril of a mass hecatomb of incredible magnitude and unpredictable mortality and sorrow, humanity clings to every movement directed to the enforcement of the Rule of Law as the last anchor of its salvation.

As jurists, you have the great responsibility of encouraging all efforts of this kind. You have always been the most conscious of the role of Justice in Society, as was illustrated in his time by that great father of International Law, Francisco de Vitoria, whose writings may well inspire the delegates of this Conference.

I send you with these words my best wishes and encouragement for the success of your noble efforts.

Francisco Franco
Head of the Spanish State

THE SUDAN

Khartoum, Sudan
April 30, 1967

On the occasion of your conference I convey to you that I whole-heartedly support your principles and appreciate your efforts to realize world peace through law and to focus the minds and hearts of men and women of good will upon the necessity to avoid chaos and disaster and to advance the objectives of achieving world peace. May I assure you that it is the sincere wish of myself, the members of the Supreme Council, the Government and the people of The Sudan that the World Law Day 1967 will be crowned with success and will meet with the blessings of all the nations of the world.

(Signed) Ismail el Azhari,
President, Supreme Council of State
of the Republic of The Sudan

SWAZILAND

Mbabane, Swaziland
July 18, 1969

The Kingdom of Swaziland, the youngest of the new independent States of Africa, is greatly concerned with the basic principles and ideals of the World Peace Through Law Center. It is conscious of the urgent need for organized effort to achieve the objectives of world peace, the development of international law and above all the acceptance and observance of the Rule of Law by all nations. In recognition of this need, there are entrenched in the Constitution of Swaziland provisions for the protection of fundamental rights and freedoms of the individual. My country will, accordingly, follow the reports of the proceedings of the Bangkok Conference with great interest in the confident hope that it will further advance the laudable aims of the organization.

On behalf of the people of the Kingdom of Swaziland, I offer my best wishes for the success of the deliberations of the Conference and for their fruitful outcome.

(Signed) M. J. Dlamini
Prime Minister
Kingdom of Swaziland

SWEDEN

Stockholm
July 9, 1967

On the occasion of the opening of the Geneva World Conference on World Peace Through Law I wish to convey to the conference my very best wishes for its success.

(Signed) Tage Erlander,
Prime Minister of Sweden

SWITZERLAND

Bern, Switzerland
June 24, 1967

It is a pleasant duty for me to welcome the participants to this Conference in the name of the Swiss people and the Federal Council. Switzerland, whose existence depends fundamentally on the co-operation and harmonious relations between the diverse elements which compose it, considers it of vital importance that internal and external peace are based on law and justice. This is why I greatly hope that your Conference will attain the success it deserves.

The evident importance of this meeting and its significance for many governments as well as international organizations, are proof of a constant and alert juridical awareness of peoples. The necessity for States to establish a system inspired by the well-known principles of international law, in order to assure lasting peace at the heart of the world community is now recognized by all.

If non-official groups endeavour to resolve the many problems posed by the establishment of such a system by elaborating projects such as international conventions, this is proof that States and individuals feel, in the present confusion of political, economic and cultural relations, the absence of a juridical order in many parts of the world. Organs already instituted by the world community cannot but welcome such an initiative which will enable them to come to a closer definition of the problems which they are called upon to solve as a consequence of the development of international relations.

The unhappy events in the Near East bear witness to the enormous difficulties experienced by States involved in a conflict and those interested in finding a definite solution. Therefore, we can only firmly hope that this Conference revives in the hearts of its participants the integrity of the law and makes them understand even more the necessity to respect juridical order for the greatest profit of all persons everywhere.

(Signed) Roger Bonvin,
President, Confederation of
Switzerland

TANGANYIKA

Dar Es Salaam, Tanganyika
September, 1965

Human society has developed as the rule of law has spread from the family to the village, from the village to the tribe and then to the nation. Only as just and enforceable law has been accepted in these different units of organisation has it been possible for people to live in peace and security with one another.

The present dangerous tension between nations, which so frequently breaks out into violent conflict, is an indication of the absence of law in the international field. It must be a matter of great concern to all who value peace and progress that efforts should be made to establish law in this remaining

I send good wishes to the World Conference on World Peace Through Law which is to be held in Washington in September. I hope the deliberations of this Conference will contribute to world peace and justice.

(Signed) Jules K. Nyerere
President of Tangayika

TANZANIA

Dar-es-Salaam, Tanzania
May 18, 1967

President Nyerere's support for World Peace Through Law has not changed. . . He remains a supporter of the ideals which the Center is propagating. . .

(Signed) J.K. Nyerere,
President, The United Republic
of Tanzania
Per: J.E. Wicken (Personal
Assistant to the President)

THAILAND

Bangkok, Thailand
September, 1965

On the occasion of the opening of the Washington World Conference on World Peace Through Law, I should like to convey to you, Mr. Chairman, and through you to the Distinguished Participants, the greetings and congratulations from the Government and people of Thailand. The honour which the Chairman has accorded me in providing me with such an opportunity is deeply appreciated. For all of us, this is an appropriate moment for felicitations and celebration. Indeed, this international gathering which is taking place comprises many eminent jurists, lawyers and legal scholars who will make the present Conference a memorable occasion and will add significance to the year 1965 as the International Cooperation Year proclaimed by the United Nations.

It is heartening to note that ranking members of the legal profession and learned legal scholars of the world now assembled, including those from my own country, will have occasion to explore the possibility of an effective international system for the resolution of international conflicts with the ultimate view to establishing and maintaining a world of peace and order for all mankind. That law should prevail in the relations between men and nations is a posture, a proposition and even a problem toward which we have tirelessly turned our efforts. Indeed, the one fundamental belief, the intellectual staple that aptly expresses the aspirations of right-thinking men in this modern world is certainly to be found nowhere else than in the concept of the rule of law which stands out clearly as the most potent idea of our times. And through the vicissitudes of contemporary political life, either national or international, or in time of doubt or crisis, this very concept has unfailingly provided guidance and sustenance or indeed a goal to help keep our hopes alive. No matter which direction the course of world events may take, we know it in our heart and mind that the rule of law is there where lies our ultimate destination.

With this note of earnest hopefulness and confidence in the future, I wish you, Distinguished Participants, every success in your noble and praiseworthy undertaking at this Conference.

(Signed) T. Kittikachoom
Prime Minister of Thailand

TRINIDAD AND TOBAGO

Port-of-Spain, Trinidad y Tobago
September, 1965

When in the course of human events, it becomes necessary for the people to dissolve the political bonds which have connected them with another, and to assume among the Powers of the earth, the separate and equal station to which the Laws of Nature and of Nature's God entitle them, a decent respect to the opinions of mankind requires that they should declare the causes which impelled them to the separation.

Pawns of international diplomacy, victims of war, hot and cold, regarded and treated as property whether landed or human, distorted in our economic development by those impertinent badges of slavery imposed by the colonial restrictions of the metropolitan country, the right to vote denied us or abridged on account of race, colour, creed or previous condition of servitude or indenture—the historical documents of a constitutional and legal nature which are presented below to accompany this message demonstrate our slow but sure progression from colony to nation.

Nothing in our brief association with sovereign states approximates the constitutional deprivations and legal disabilities which dominated our pre-independence history. Nothing in our brief career as an independent personality is inferior to the prescriptions imposed on us in the era of dependence. Nothing in the infancy of our independence compares with the inhumanity and indignity of man to man which sullied previous generations.

The amalgam of Europe, Africa, Asia and the Middle East which is geographically a part of the Americas, our heterogeneous society is based on respect for law, independence of the judiciary, freedom of worship, and the right of our citizens to form political parties of their own choice. No one is in jail for his political opinions. There is no discrimination in the public service. Careers are open to talent. Secondary education is free, based on competitive examination. Community development, in which the state fosters the self-help principle, disregards geographical location, racial origin and political affiliation. What we have is not much, but it is all our own.

To a people like ours born in the wars and cradled in the lawlessness of the colonial regime, the reign of peace and the rule of law, the achievement of World Peace through Law are not abstractions. The smallest of the small in physical area, the least of the apostles in economic resources, lacking the power to make war, we join those who make peace; kept for so long outside the law, our spirit, passing in compassion and determination around the whole earth, salutes the world and looks for equals in all lands, some divine rapport equalizing us with them.

Trinidad and Tobago, emerging from submerged colony into independent nationhood, represents yet another link in the long chain of mankind's repudiation of any contract in perpetuity to surrender its freedom—a freedom which has slowly been broadening from precedent to precedent in the development of humanity's dream of a world in which people of different races and colours dwell together in unity.

(Signed) Eric Williams
Prime Minister of Trinidad
and Tobago

TURKEY

Ankara, Turkey
August 23, 1965

On the occasion of the opening in Washington of the World Conference on World Peace Through Law, I am happy to extend to the distinguished delegates my sincere greetings and my best wishes for the success of the Conference.

I am sure that all the distinguished delegates participating in this important Conference realize that a just and lasting peaceful order to which all mankind aspire, can best be achieved by bringing peaceful solutions to international disputes that unfortunately keep apart the nations of the world. In the solution of these numerous disputes and problems which have political, economic and social aspects, respect for the "rule of law" must be our guiding principle. The principles of law and the procedures to be applied in the settlement of disputes are embodied in the Charter of the United Nations. Turkey firmly believes in these principles and is ready to cooperate sincerely with all other countries for their safeguard. As a matter of fact protection of democratic institutions, liberty and justice, maintenance of world peace with cooperation among nations and promotion of human welfare have always been the unchanging tenets of Turkey's policy.

I know that lawyers have to assume and are indeed assuming the greater role in the realization of this greatest ideal of mankind.

I wish wholeheartedly that your work will be crowned with success.

With my best wishes.

(Signed) Cemal Gursel
President of the Republic of Turkey

UNITED KINGDOM

London, England
September, 1965

It is my profound hope that the Conference opened today will make a substantial contribution to the peace of the world. The occasion is most timely. The Conference is being held during 1965, the year designated by the United Nations General Assembly as International Cooperation Year, and to mark the significance of this day it has been proclaimed as World Law Day by the President of the United States. May your Conference, which is so widely and so highly representative of the legal and judicial professions throughout the world, be as widely and highly successful as its membership merits.

It is almost exactly twenty years since the Charter of the United Nations declared in the name of the Peoples of the United Nations that they were determined "to save succeeding generations from the scourge of war, which twice in our life-time has brought untold sorrow to mankind." We are all aware of the vital peace-keeping role of the United Nations, but keeping the peace alone is not enough. It is also necessary, as the Charter proclaimed, "to establish conditions under which justice and respect for the obligations arising from treaties and other sources of international law can be maintained." Peace cannot exist without law and justice. Justice depends on the development of law and of fair and peaceful means for the settlement of disputes. Yours is a great and worthy task.

It is with enthusiasm that I send you this message of support and wishes for success from myself and my colleagues in the Government of the United Kingdom.

(Signed) Harold Wilson
Prime Minister of the United
Kingdom

UNITED NATIONS

New York City, N.Y.
September, 1965

It is my privilege and pleasure, as Secretary-General of the United Nations, to send my greetings and best wishes to the Washington World Conference on World Peace Through Law.

That so many distinguished members of the legal profession from so many countries have gathered together to discuss world peace through law is eloquent testimony of the continuance of one of man's oldest quests and deepest yearnings—a legal order among nations which will make force the servant, not the master, of law, and which will banish forever the scourge of war. While the aim of such an order may be clear, the day of its achievement still seems distant if we look at the differences and the tensions among nations at the present time. Since its inception, the United Nations has devoted much of its effort to laying the basis for the establishment of the rule of law. In the field of codification and progressive development of international law it has made slow, but nonetheless significant progress, with the conclusion of multilateral treaties on certain broad areas of the law, such as the law of the sea and of diplomatic and consular relations. Through such treaty law, it becomes possible to endow the law with the degree of certainty required if the rule of law is to have any reality, and it also becomes possible to associate both old and new states with the processes of law making. In the field of pacific settlement of disputes, particularly through judicial or arbitral procedures, the progress of the last twenty years has not been so spectacular. This is a field where confidence in a known body of law and in the machinery for its impartial adjudication is the vital factor. Such confidence must naturally be of slow growth among entities such as nations which have in the past relied on diplomacy and force to settle disputes. The United Nations may at its twentieth session initiate new studies of the pacific settlement of disputes which I hope will help to reveal the more promising areas for development in this field.

Your own deliberations will also help to clarify the issues as they will help to highlight for the public the importance of constant efforts if we are to make progress toward a rule of law. The United Nations and Governments are powerless to make real progress without informed and general public support—the sort of support made so evident by your presence here today.

I send you all my best wishes for a successful conclusion to your present session, which I hope will be but the beginning of contacts and discussions which will contribute much in the future towards giving an ever increasing reality to the rule of law.

> (Signed) U Thant
> Secretary-General of the United
> Nations

UNITED STATES OF AMERICA

> Washington, D.C.
> United States of
> America
> September, 1965

I need not here reaffirm my nation's continuing dedication to the rule of law. We will work to extend it to the relations between countries. For we believe that is the surest road to a fruitful and secure peace.

Therefore, we who seek a world of law must labor to understand the foundation on which law can rest. We must set to work to build it. For if the rule of law is an ideal, the establishment of that rule is the practical work of practical men. We must not let the difficulties of this task lead us into the twin dangers of cynicism or unreasoning faith.

For the fact is that if law cannot yet solve the problems of a tormented earth, it is steadily growing in importance and in necessity.

The first condition of law is justice. That law which oppresses the weak, or denies the fair claims of the poor, will prove a flimsy barrier against the rising storm of man's demand for justice.

Law must not be the prisoner of plunder or privilege.

Law is not the soothing keeper of the *status quo*. Law is an instrument in the battle for the hopes of man. And if it is not fashioned as such an instrument, then no matter how beautifully and logically framed, it will yield to violence and to terror.

So if we, the fortunate of the earth, would ask other people to submit to law, then we ourselves must assume some responsibility for people's liberty and people's well-being.

International law has been primarily concerned with relations between states. In pursuit of justice, it must now concern itself more than in the past with the welfare of people.

So I look forward to the day when the relief of hunger and misery and ignorance in all parts of the world will be fixed in legal obligation as it now is in my own country.

When our world law embodies the right of the despairing to hope, and the responsibility of the fortunate to help, then it will be strengthened a thousand-fold in the cause of peace.

If world conditions were largely satisfactory it would not be difficult to evolve a rule of law. But we do not live in a satisfactory world. It is stained with evil and injustice, by ruthless ambition and passionate conflict. Only by fighting these forces do we help build a base on which the temple of law may rest.

The second condition of law is institutions. Through them law receives meaning and force. And institutions themselves, through their own actions, help to make new law. The UN General Assembly has done this in peace-keeping.

The past twenty years have seen an abundant flowering of new internation structures. From the Common Market and NATO, to the IBRD and the Asian Development Bank, order and legal process have been imposed upon spreading segments of the affairs of countries.

Some of these institutions have played a large role in the prosperity of the West and in keeping the peace.

Others contribute to the progress of developing countries.

The United States has helped build many of these organizations. Their strength represents a victory for the cause you represent—a legal order contributing to the prosperity of each and the peace of all. My country intends to protect and strengthen those institutions, sharing the task with all who share our common purpose.

Central to the hope of world peace through law is the United Nations. Since its beginning, dozens of disputes, many laced with violence, have come before the world assembly. Some have remained unresolved. Many have found a settlement sufficient to allow mankind to move forward in peace. And in some places the United Nations was able to prevent conflict and bloodshed.

I hope we can strengthen the United Nations, not simply as a forum for debate, but as an arena for the solution of disputes.

That is why I have asked a great Justice of our Supreme Court, Arthur Goldberg, to become our Ambassador to the world body. The life of Ambassador Goldberg has been devoted to resolving disputes between those who at first believed that they could not yield one iota from their positions, and who came at last to sign a common agreement.

And my country will fully support the efforts of the Secretary-General to bring peace between the great nations of India and Pakistan.

Perhaps in the United Nations, and with the patient effort of individual countries, we can also halt the terrible arms race with threatens to engulf the earth. Perhaps we can succeed through an effective treaty preventing the spread of nuclear weapons, through extending the test ban treaty, by obtaining an agreement halting production of fissionable material for use in nuclear weapons and allocating substantial portions of this material to peaceful uses, by agreeing to reverse the arms race in strategic nuclear weapons delivery vehicles, and by working toward general and complete disarmament under effective international controls which must be the world's goal.

I think that we may be evolving a world consensus on which law can stand. The mass of mankind is slowly realizing the dangers of conflict and the futility of war. They are accepting their responsibility to relieve their own poverty, and the misery of their fellow inhabitants of earth. They are finding in knowledge and fear and pain that their common interest lies in common acceptance of their own obligations and the rights of others.

We can see this in a hundred small ways. During the past year the United States was present at 629 international conferences. In the short time since I became President the United States has participated in more such conferences than during the first 150 years of its history.

Of course, the great issues and the great dangers are not resolved. In the past twelve months there is not a single continent that has been spared violence. In the past 2000 years there has hardly been a decade without war.

If this were all, the future would look dark indeed. But there is another and a brighter thread which runs through the history of the race. It is man's drive to create and to live in harmony with his fellows. And that is what we call civilization.

Law is the great civilizing machinery. It liberates the desires to build and subdues the desire to destroy. And if war can tear us apart, law can unite us— out of fear or love or reason or all three.

World peace through world law will not come quickly. We must work, in a variety of ways, to create the vital conditions which may bring us to that day, to build the justice which forms it and the institutions which give it life, and to find the understanding acceptance which will make it work. This means we must be willing to accept small advances and limited goals. But the final objective is the largest and most elusive man has known: peace—peace which is not simply the absence of conflict or even of fear, but the framework for the fulfillment of human possibility.

How can we dare to hope for that which has always escaped mankind? Perhaps it is because our invention draws us together to the point where any war is civil war. Perhaps the vastness of our destructive power makes us shrink from conflict. And perhaps, under the horror and murder of this carnage-filled century, civilization has been slowly flowering—leading us toward victory in the endless battle between man's love for his fellow and man's desire to destroy him.

Law is the greatest human invention. All the rest give him mastery over his world. Law gives him mastery over himself.

There are those who say the rule of law is a fruitless and utopian dream. It is true, if it comes, it will come slowly. It will come through the practical and wise resolution of numberless problems. But to deny the possibility is to deny peace itself and to deny that flowering of the spirit which we must believe God meant for man.

I do not deny it. I believe in it. And so do you.

If others join us, then the time may yet come when you and your colleagues will be honored as path-finders toward the final armistice in man's war against himself.

> Presented personally by
> Lyndon B. Johnson
> President of the United States to
> Washington World Conference
> on World Peace Through Law

UNITED STATES OF AMERICA

> Washington, D.C.
> December 2, 1961

To the President of the African and Middle Eastern Conference on World Peace Through Law

It is with great pleasure that I send greetings to the distinguished delegates and observers attending the African and Middle Eastern Conference on World Peace Through Law in Lagos.

Although you represent diverse cultures and traditions and differing political and legal systems, this Conference demonstrates that we are all united in our belief in the rule of law. It provides the orderly framework within which we can establish an enduring peace and achieve the benefits of a free and civilized life.

As lawyers, you are given great responsibility for leadership of this effort. We have seen the successful operation of international law in established areas like the Law of the Sea. But the uncharted seas of arms control and the peaceful use of outer space demand the development of new rules of law. The tremendous strides in science and technology lend urgency to the need for these new rules and for legal institutions capable of harnessing the wonders we have created for the benefit—not the destruction—of mankind.

Supremacy of law within nations insures the freedom of man. Supremacy of law in the community of nations can free mankind from the dread of nuclear war. The rule of law must replace rule by force if we are to look forward to a stable world—a world which is hospitable to economic and social progress.

You have my best wishes for a successful Conference, and you have my deep respect for the courage and dedication with which you are meeting this challenge and opportunity for public service.

> John F. Kennedy
> President of the
> United States of America

> Washington, D.C.
> June 27, 1969

The people of the United States share the conviction that the only sure path to permanent peace is through a systematic development and adherence to the rule of law in the affairs of the nations.

We look forward to the attainment of a world free of force and violence, where disputes may be resolved by peaceful means. We are especially encouraged by the work of the World Peace Through Law Center and we will be watching with anticipation for the results of your Bangkok Conference.

I hope that this session may be a productive one for your members and for the community of nations you seek to serve.

> Richard Nixon
> President of the
> United States of America

UPPER VOLTA

> Ouagadougou, Upper Volta
> September, 1965

Two years after the international conference in Athens, the World bar has exerted new efforts in order to hold in Washington, from September 12 to 18, 1965, a second session of the Conference on World Peace through Law.

Many lawyers from all parts of the world will meet once more in order to compare their ideas with a view to finding concrete solutions to make peace triumph within our planet. Now, this noble purpose cannot be attempted unless the large powers as well as the small agree to subject themselves to the grandeur of justice.

The international meeting at Washington, then, will have to accomplish a delicate mission, of which we nevertheless expect positive results. Also, in the name of the people of Upper Volta, I extend to the eminent men of law who will be present at the conference my warmest wishes for the full success of their work.

(Signed) Maurice Yameogo
President of the Republic of
Upper Volta

VATICAN

Rome, Vatican City
July, 1967

It is with great interest that the Holy See watches the efforts of the World Peace Through Law Center, and it is happy to participate, in the person of its representatives, in the World Conference that this organisation is holding in Geneva from 9-14 July, of this year.

According to the principles that are constantly professed by the Holy See and forcibly expressed in many pontifical documents, particularly in the face of the evolution of human society during the last decades, men, regardless of difference of race, language, culture and development, all belong to the same great human family. They enjoy the same basic rights and are bound by the same fundamental duties. The sacred value of the human being must be recognised and respected in each and every one of them.

According to these same principles, human groups, in the form of peoples and nations, have equal rights. They are born to live in understanding and not strife. Peace, not war, is the normal state of mankina.

The first and irreplaceable basis of this peace is law. Everything must be done in order that force be used in the service of law, and not law to serve the ends of force. The settlement of disputes by war and violence must be substituted by an international legal organisation which would impose negotiation and arbitration even at the risk of incurring certain limitations on national sovereignty.

The Pontiff recently recalled that "It would be pure illusion to try to build peace on any other basis than that of justice, the recognition of human rights, and the common acceptance of the right of others in the same way as we would wish our own rights to be recognised. Agreement and peace are inseparable from justice and truth." (Consistorial Speech delivered on 26 June 1967, Osservatore Romano, 26-27 June, 1967.)

One aspect of this necessary prevalence of law and justice in human relations is the obligation to reduce and to progressively eliminate excessive economic, social and cultural disparities between peoples; this being a permanent source of tension and disagreement which endangers peace. The importance of this problem recently led Pope Paul VI to make it the subject of an Encyclical letter, in which he invited Christians and all men of good will to become aware of this "new name of peace" which nowadays, as has quite rightly been said, is the development of peoples, and to devote themselves wholeheartedly to it.

Copies of this important document will be distributed in various languages during the conference.

All those who participate in this conference will thereby be able to see to what extent their noble concern and their generous efforts to establish peace through law, coincide with those of the Catholic Church which cannot forget that Christ is the Divine Founder and was prophetically called "the Prince of Peace" (Isaiah 9:6), and that His descent upon earth whence He came to teach and to save, was greeted by the words: "Peace upon earth, goodwill to all men" (Luke 2:14).

> (Signed) A.G. Cardinal Cicognant
> Vatican City

VENEZUELA

> Caracas, Venezuela
> June 12, 1961

To the President of the American Conference on World Peace Through Law

I am sending you a message of encouragement and support to the Assembly of Jurists. In my position as a democrat and as Chief of State under a lawful government, I highly appreciate the value and the effort involved towards the achievement of national and international relations under juridical regulation. Treaties and agreements freely entered into between nations must be fulfilled in order that the achievement of the internal peace within nations and the desideratum of World Peace may be realized.

I extend my sincere wishes for the success of the deliberations of this Conference of outstanding men of law.

> Cordially yours,
>
> Rómulo Betancourt
> President of Venezuela

REPUBLIC OF VIETNAM

> Saigon, Vietnam
> July 5, 1967

The world, which is today dangerously threatened by the unleashed forces of all, is living through an extremely precarious period.

More than ever men of good will from all countries must combine their efforts in order to establish and develop a system of International Law based on viable institutions that are capable of maintaining good relations between states and private individuals.

On a world scale only international co-operation based on the application of Law and the principles of justice and equality can guarantee a longlasting peace and provide peaceful and fair solutions to possible disputes.

In this conviction I have much pleasure in offering the distinguished jurists who are participating in the World Conference on Peace Through Law my sincere regards and best wishes for their every success.

(Signed) Nguyen-Van-Thieu,
President, Republic of Vietnam

YUGOSLAVIA

Beograd, Yugoslavia
September, 1965

Threats to peace are ever more numerous as there exist forces which do not hesitate to secure their political and economic interests even at the risk of war. Very little is needed for the sources of conflict to be transformed into real war.

The activity of peace-loving forces is, therefore, of particular importance. They reject the use of force and war and demand that all disputes between peoples and states should be solved peacefully on the basis of respect for the principles of justice. This is all the more urgent at this moment when a number of disputes are threatening to lead to military conflicts and local wars. A great majority of states are endorsing, every day and to an ever greater extent, the idea of the need for peaceful coexistence, which is becoming dominant.

In such a situation prevailing in international relations, every effort undertaken with a view to mobilizing and strengthening the forces of peace is valuable and of paramount importance. Your movement of world peace through law has also a role to play in these endeavors, even more so as it rallies lawyers from more than one hundred nations and has as its basic aim the aspiration to secure peace in the world through respect for law.

(Signed) Petar Stambolic
President of the Federal Executive
Council of Yugoslavia

ZAMBIA

Lusaka, Zambia
August 13, 1969

It gives me and all of us in Zambia great pleasure to send you and all the delegates to the Conference of World Peace Through Law, our good wishes.

We in Zambia strongly support the principles of World Peace Through Law. We subscribe to your efforts in your endeavour to establish and promote these legal principles.

In the modern world of ever-growing world trade and the inevitable interdependence of world nations, the necessity of achieving peace through law at all levels of human activity cannot be underestimated. It is in the rule of law that the weak nations and the physically weak section of the world community can enjoy equal status with the mighty.

We sincerely hope that in the not too distant future your Organization will be rewarded for its efforts by various nations, acceptance of the legal principles for which you stand.

We wish the Conference every success in their deliberations.

> (Signed) Kenneth D. Kaunda
> President of Zambia

§ 13-3. Compilation of Additional Statements by World Leaders on the Importance of the Rule of Law in the World

Many leaders of nations, other than those quoted above, have expressed their support of the rule of law among nations. No attempt to make an exhaustive compilation has been made.

For example, President John F. Kennedy, in his inaugural address called for

> [a] new world of law where the strong are just, the weak secure, and peace preserved forever.

DWIGHT D. EISENHOWER, President of the United States:

Law Day—U.S.A., May 1, 1958:

> The world no longer has a choice between force and law; if civilization is to survive, it must choose the rule of law.

State of the Union Message to the Congress, January 9, 1959:

> All peoples are sorely tired of the fear, destruction and the waste of war. As never before, the world knows the human and material costs of war and seeks to replace force with a genuine rule of law among nations.

Gettysburg College Address, April 4, 1959:

> Another fact, basic to the entire problem of peace and security, is that America and her friends do not want war. They seek to substitute the rule of law for the rule of force . . . .

Message to Convention of the American Bar Association, August 1959:

> It is gratifying to note that one of the important matters which your convention will consider is the concept of world peace

through law. Peace cannot prevail until men and nations recognize that their conduct must be governed by respect for and observance of the law.

Letter to Senator Hubert Humphrey, November 17, 1959:

One of the great purposes of this administration has been to advance the rule of law in the world, through actions directly by the United States Government and in concert with the governments of other countries. It is open to us to further this great purpose both through optimum use of existing international institutions and through the adoption of changes and improvements in those institutions.

Delhi University Address, December 11, 1959:

A reliable framework of law grounded in general principles recognized by civilized nations is of crucial importance in all plans for rapid economic development around the earth . . . the time has come for mankind to make the rule of law in international affairs as normal as it is now in domestic affairs . . . the structure of such law must be patiently built stone by stone. It is better to lose a point now and then in an international tribunal and gain a world in which everyone lives at peace under the rule of law.

HARRY S. TRUMAN, President of the United States:

June 28, 1945:

When Kansas and Colorado have a quarrel over the water in the Arkansas River they don't call out the National Guard in each state and go to war over it. They bring a suit in the Supreme Court of the United States and abide by the decision. There isn't a reason in the world why we cannot do that internationally.

March 17, 1948:

The principles and purposes expressed in the Charter of the United Nations continue to represent our hope for the eventual establishment of the rule of law in international affairs.

FRANKLIN D. ROOSEVELT, President of the United States:

August 24, 1939:

The people of the United States are as one in the opposition to policies of military conquest and domination. They are as one in rejecting the thesis that any ruler, or any people, possess the right to achieve their ends or objectives through the taking of action which will plunge countless millions of people into war and which will bring distress and suffering to every nation of the world, belligerent and neutral, when such ends and objectives, so far as they are just and reasonable, can be satisfied through processes of peaceful negotiation or by resort to judicial arbitration.

CALVIN COOLIDGE, President of the United States:

1925, advocated:

. . . establishment of a tribunal for the administration of even-handed justice between nation and nation. . . . The weight of our enormous influence must be cast upon the side of a reign not of force, but of law and trial, not by battle, but by reason.

WOODROW WILSON, President of the United States:

1919:

What we seek is the reign of law based upon the consent of the governed and sustained by the organized opinion of mankind.

RICHARD M. NIXON, Vice President of the United States:

April 13, 1959:

Men face essentially similar problems of disagreement and resort to force in their personal and community lives as nations now do in the divided world. And, historically, man has found only one effective way to cope with this aspect of human nature—the rule of law.

More and more the leaders of the West have come to the conclusion that the rule of law must somehow be established to provide a way of settling disputes among nations as it does among individuals.

. . . the time has now come to take the initiative in the direction of establishment of the rule of law to replace the rule of force.

If we rule out, as we have and should, the use of force or threats of force as a means of settling differences where negotiations reach an impasse, the sole alternative is the establishment of the rule of law in international affairs.

October 5, 1959:

The rule of law is the very heart and soul of a free system. Freedom itself is meaningless outside the framework of law. Law provides the order that permits freedom to flourish. It mediates the inevitable disputes between free individuals. It defines the boundaries between liberty and license. It protects the individual in the exercise of his basic political rights. Law, in a word, makes freedom possible.

CHRISTIAN A. HERTER, Under Secretary of State:

July 15, 1957:

It seems to me quite evident that one of the basic facts of this age of thermonuclear weapons is that law itself must occupy a higher place in it than in previous ages. Until fairly recently war was both legal and a pragmatic means of settling international disputes. The Kellogg-Briand Pact, however,—some 30 years ago—outlawed war as an instrument of policy; and then came the Charter of the United Nations which forbids resort to armed force unless authorized by the United Nations or undertaken in defense against armed aggression.

And now that thermonuclear weapons dominate the scene, war has also become so annihilating, even for the victor, that it is unthinkable that it should be used except as a defensive weapon.

The rule of law must therefore in great measure supplant the rule of war as the final arbiter of international intercourse, if this intercourse is to continue at all.

Thus, if we are to hope that the rule of law can supplant the rule of force in the world, our work is clear. We must continue to develop the body of law, the institutions of social order, the habit of public acceptance and resort to law, and the social, economic and political health which are the essential bases of a law-abiding community. As the Greek philosopher Heraclitus said: 'The people must fight for their law as for their wall.' I would add that the people must create their law before they can defend it.

History records both splendid successes and tragic failures in man's effort to bring about the rule of law at the various levels of his social relationships. I believe that the further development of the rule of law among nations must come through a slow evolutionary process. It will depend in the first instance on the growth of mutual comprehension among all nations of the *need* for the peaceful machinery of law and of the horrors of the alternative machinery of war. Thereafter it will depend on the spread of confidence born of experience slowly accumulated in practical application of the machinery and technique of law.

In the final analysis, though, this development cannot go forward unless men everywhere are willing to make sacrifices of their personal and parochial prerogatives to the common welfare of the world community. It is this spirit which you as lawyers can help to foster through the respect which you enjoy in your local communities. By this service you can help build greater strength into the body of international law, and bring to posterity greater hope of peace, prosperity—and most important—survival.

JOHN FOSTER DULLES, Secretary of State:

May 1, 1958:

In international affairs it is impossible to sustain a just and lasting peace unless that peace is based upon law and order.

January 31, 1959:

We seek peace, of course, but we seek it in the only dependable way—the substitution of justice and law for force.

DEAN ACHESON, Secretary of State:

1950:

The action of the United Nations to put down the aggression which began on June 25 against the Republic of Korea was exactly the effective collective measure which was required. It marked a turning point in history, for it showed the way to an enforceable rule of law among nations.

GEORGE C. MARSHALL, Secretary of State:

September 17, 1947:

The Government of the United States believes that the surest foundation for permanent peace lies in the extension of the benefits and the restraints of the rule of law to all peoples and to all governments.

CORDELL HULL, Secretary of State:

July 16, 1937:

We advocate adjustment of problems in international relations by process of peaceful negotiation and agreement.

We advocate faithful observance of international agreements....

We believe in respect by all nations for the rights of others and performance by all nations of established obligations.

We stand for revitalizing and strengthening of international law.

April 17, 1940:

All peaceful nations have during recent years been earnestly urging that policies of force be abandoned and that peace be maintained on the basis of fundamental principles, among which are respect by every nation for the rights of other nations and nonintervention in their domestic affairs, the according of equality of fair and just treatment and the faithful observance of treaty pledge, with modification thereof when needful by orderly processes.

Is the future of the world to be determined by universal reliance upon armed force and frequent resort to aggression, with resultant autarchy, impoverishment, loss of individual independence and international anarchy? Or will practices of peace, morality, justice and order under law, resting upon sound foundations of economic well-being, security and progress, guide and govern in international relations? As modern science and invention bring nations ever closer together, the time approaches when, in the very nature of things, one or the other of these alternatives must prevail. In a smaller and smaller world it will soon no longer be possible for some nations to choose and follow the way of force and for other nations to choose and follow the way of reason. All will have to go in one direction and by one way. . . . The re-establishing of order under law in relations among nations has become imperatively necessary.

September 12, 1943:

Disputes of a legal character which present a threat to the peace of the world should be adjudicated by an International Court of Justice whose decision would be based upon application of principles of law.

ELIHU ROOT, Secretary of State:

1915:

It was during the appalling crimes of the Thirty Years War that Grotius wrote his *De Jure Belli ac Pacis* and the science of international law first took form and authority. The moral standards of the Thirty Years War have returned again to Europe with the same intolerable consequences. We may hope that there will be again a great new departure to escape destruction by subjecting the nations to the rule of law.

DOUGLAS DILLON, Under Secretary of State, addressing the American Bar Convention:

August 27, 1959:

Thanks to your initiative, lawyers in many parts of the world are now working to formulate an action program designed to help move mankind nearer to the goal of peace through law. This increasing consciousness of international problems in the legal profession is a significant contribution to efforts of the United States to strengthen the foundations of freedom throughout the world.

WILLIAM B. MACOMBER, JR., Assistant Secretary of State, commenting on Senate Concurrent Resolution 25:

May 19, 1959:

> The Department of State shares the concern reflected in this resolution and itself regards the development and strengthening of the world system of law among States as an essential element in the achievement of a just and lasting peace.

HENRY CABOT LODGE, United States Ambassador to the United Nations:

October 13, 1959:

> If all nations lay down their arms, there must be institutions to preserve international peace and security and promote the rule of law.

WILLIAM P. ROGERS, Attorney General of the United States, addressing the 1959 Convention of the American Bar Association:

August 26, 1959:

> In the long view the main hope for peace is that nations will be wise enough not to rely on sheer strength in dealing with each other but will move toward establishing systems based on considerations of law and justice in the resolution of international disputes.

HERBERT BROWNELL, Attorney General of the United States:

July, 1957:

> What we need is the development of the law of nations in our age which will first bind the countries of the world into solemn voluntary pacts governing their great interests on the world scene, in contrast to unilateral exploitations by the mighty. It has been well said that the emphasis in international life must shift from torts to contracts. And, also we must perfect a machinery for settlement of international disputes—not now and then or occasionally but on a total basis—under a tribunal or system of tribunals which will command general confidence as to the fairness of their judgments and whose procedures will be supported by a public opinion which will not tolerate a departure from them. We must establish an era where nations as well as individuals are subject to justice under law.

EARL WARREN, Chief Justice of the United States:

1954:

> . . . Let me speak of my deepest conviction. In these troublesome times, the hope for a peaceful world is of a world based on

law as distinct from a world based on authority. Authority is something that comes down from the top, something arbitrary and despotic.

Law in the true sense is something that springs from a common acceptance, from the deepest roots and the broadest base. It is a belief, a desire, a willingness to be governed by an accumulated code of experience.

The difference between the two was well expressed in the telegram sent by the British soldiers to our soldiers when we entered the late war. It read: 'We welcome you as brothers in the struggle to make sure that the world shall be ruled by the force of law, and not by the law of force.'

ROBERT H. JACKSON, Justice, United States Supreme Court:

1953:

Perhaps the decisive difference between Communist legal philosophy and that of the West is that our law puts rational restraints upon the use of coercive power by those in authority, while, as Vishinsky points out, Soviet law is only 'expressing the will of the dominant class,' to be enforced upon all by the 'compulsive force of the state.'

Thus their law, instead of controlling the prevailing authority, is merely another implement—mainly, we may believe, a propaganda implement in the hands of the authorities. . . .

We believe that the great purpose of achieving a peaceful world is best approached through a strengthening and extending of international law and international legal institutions along the lines of their development in the West."

. . . if a peaceful and stable international order is reached, it is not rash to predict that it will result from acceptance by the professions of all nations of an international rule of law as a curb on lawless power in control of great states.

WILLIAM O. DOUGLAS, Justice, United States Supreme Court:

1958:

We must search for those problems, great or small, on which international unity can be achieved and bring them into some system of international control. Perhaps atomic energy will be the next to lend itself to the 'rule of law.' These seem to me to be the dimensions of the problem. They indicate also the direction of our movement. The rate can be greatly accelerated if highminded men from all continents write in affirming that the 'rule of law' points the way to peace and justice. That is the leadership the world sorely needs.

More and more people are coming to realize that peace must be more than an interlude if we are to survive; that peace is the product of law and order; that law is essential if the force of arms is not to rule the world.

JOHN J. PARKER, Judge, Fourth Circuit Court of Appeals (1925-58):

March, 1958:

Law is not a mere collection of rules and forms and precedents. Law is the life principle of organized society—the categorical imperative which prescribes how organized society must live.

SENATOR STUART SYMINGTON:

September 18, 1959:

Every civilized nation has found that, as a way of settling domestic disputes, law is vastly preferable to force; and now we must set up machinery to settle disputes at the international level.

To this end, Symington made three suggestions:

A worldwide conference of eminent statesmen, lawyers and judges, who would explore more effective ways to use existing agencies, such as The International Court of Justice, for the purpose of deciding international disputes.

The State Department should give high priority to preparing a revision of the United Nations Charter. In the last 14 years the United Nations has won respect as a forum for peaceful debate and sensible solution of differences. It deserves additional authority, not inconsistent with national sovereignty.

There should be an increased exchange of lawyers, judges, and legal scholars of all nations, so that they can see first-hand how other legal systems operate and discover principles and values that are common to the laws of all nations.

SENATOR HUBERT HUMPHREY:

March 24, 1959:

. . . we cannot afford to leave a single stone unturned in our effort to develop the means for advancing international cooperation, understanding and peace. One of these means is through the strengthening of international law through the International Court of Justice. . . . I believe that a nation which is based on the principle of law and on the rule of law, rather than the rule of men, surely should take the lead in establishing an International Court of Justice with the power of law. . . . it would be a good time to invoke the rule of law and obedience to law and justice through law.

SENATOR JACOB JAVITS:

March 24, 1959:

There are tremendous possibilities in juridical action in settling questions of dispute which perplex the world. Interestingly enough, the Russians themselves have a considerable interest in juridical matters and in the way in which courts determine controversies. There may be possibilities in that connection, even with them, which may yet remain unexplored.

SENATOR RALPH FLANDERS:

1958:

World peace through world law is the attainable objective. There are two things necessary to its attainment. One is a background of popular determination the world over. The other is practical negotiation. The educational process needs to be far more fully developed and more strongly supported. The negotiations need an intelligence, an imagination, and a determination which have not yet been shown.

SENATOR WARREN MAGNUSON:

August 11, 1959:

I have long felt that the United States . . . should stimulate among all nations a dependence upon the rule of law in international dealings.

SENATOR JOSEPH CLARK:

June 23, 1959:

We are not going to be able to help the people of West Berlin in the long run unless we can advance the rule of law in the field of war prevention to replace the rule of terror under which we live.

It has been clear for some time that more vigorous efforts should be made by our Government, and, indeed by all the governments of the free Western world and of the uncommitted world as well, to making a start towards substituting world law for the present reliance on armed forces which endangers world peace.

SENATOR ROBERT TAFT:

September 25, 1947:

I do not see how we can hope to secure permanent peace in the world except by establishing law between nations and equal justice under law.

GOVERNOR LUTHER H. HODGES, of North Carolina:

October 6, 1959:

. . . As a people, we are realizing more and more that if our world is to survive we must have a community of nations based upon mutual respect made vital by the rule of law.

THOMAS E. DEWEY, former Governor of New York:

October 21, 1959:

Building peace is the most important job in the world today. It cannot be built by arms. It can only be built by law. The lawyers of the world are equipped to be, and must be, the architects of peace.

We do not deceive ourselves about the enormity of this task. The roots of war lie deep. Underlying the conflicts among nations are men's despairs and needs and competing demands. Yet surely the human heart contains, too, the seeds of peace; and world law, the law among nations, the law of peace, must be built up from the common desires and the universal purposes in the hearts of all the peoples of the world.

This is a job for practical idealists, for men skilled by their profession in transmuting the best human impulses into effective working rules. Yet we cannot afford, in being 'practical', to set our sights too low. There can no longer be peace just for us, or for any one nation; there will be peace for the whole world, or there will be no peace at all.

The American Bar Association's Special Committee on World Peace Through Law is 'practical idealism' at work. It is what Lincoln was talking about when he said that 'it is as a peacemaker that the lawyer has the superior opportunity of being a great man'.

POPE PIUS XII:

December 24, 1942:

A fundamental point for the pacification of human society is juridical order.

1944:

An old world lies in fragments. To see rising as quickly as possible from those ruins a new world, healthier, juridically better organized, more in harmony with the exigencies of human nature— such is the longing of its tortured people.

RICHARD CARDINAL CUSHING:

March 27, 1959:

Commenting on the American Bar Association World Peace Through Law Program:

[it] may well be the most significant of our time, for it can set the pattern of the future of the world.

October 1, 1959:

In the pursuit of an elusive peace we must direct our actions as well as our prayers in support of every movement which is designed to bring us closer to our goal. We know that 'justice through law' is not just a distant ideal but a precious reality that can be attained if men are willing to strive hard enough for it.

In our national life we pride ourselves on our American heritage which provides every man equal justice under the law and which gives recourse to our Court when sinister forces set out to deprive any citizen of these rights. We do not need to be reminded that even here our ideal is not yet perfectly realized but we know that our efforts will not cease until full justice is given to every man as his due.

On the international scene, matters are somewhat less encouraging. The ancient and obsolete law of force still rules in many parts of the world and the 'might is right' theory subjugates the weak to the strong. For reasonable men this situation is far from satisfactory. Only the voluntary acceptance of a rule of law, replacing violence and force, gives man the kind of society in which his best capacities can be developed. We are not brutes and we must not live according to the law of brutality; we are men designed 'in God's image' and we must live in a rational order of law governed by universal justice.

CATHOLIC BISHOPS OF THE UNITED STATES, Washington, D.C.:

November 27, 1959:

. . . statesmen of the world must continue their often disheartening quest for peace, reductions in armament, and the introduction of the rule of law into the society of nations.

CARLOS CASTILLO ARMAS, President of Guatemala:

November 3, 1955:

In these ten years it has been possible to safeguard peace despite the cold war and despite points of danger. It can be assured that in the next ten years that peace will be consolidated through the rule of justice for the well being of humanity.

NOBUSUKE KISHI, Prime Minister of Japan:

February 12, 1960:

Aspiring earnestly to an international peace based on justice and order, Japan, hopefully looks to the early advent of the day when the rule of law will be firmly established in the community of nations. As a first step toward that end, I believe it is incumbent on each nation that it abide faithfully by its own agreements with other nations and by the generally established rules of international law. Prospects for a lasting world peace will be made far brighter if this is done.

Another step toward the universal application of the rule of law is to make the fullest use of the International Court of Justice, which serves as the cornerstone of the structure of the law-abiding world.

We in Japan also believe that we must make the greatest possible effort to bolster the United Nations so that this international organization will be better able to perform its functions as the agency for world peace and for the maintenance of the rule of law.

JOHN GEORGE DIEFENBAKER, Prime Minister of Canada:

July 1958:

In the international sphere mankind is still far removed from the rule of law. It was the hope of mankind at San Francisco in 1945 that the nations of the world would put machinery into operation to interpret and enforce the law. An international Court of Justice was set up and an International Law Commission—to codify the laws of nations. But international justice still walked with faltering steps.

The question which still faces the international community is whether the application and development of international law in the operation of the community of nations is desirable and whether the apparent decline in the role of international law is not a cause for deep concern. For lawyers, at any rate, it is obvious that the international community, like any other community, requires the stabilizing and beneficial influence of law if it is to achieve orderly expansion.

KONRAD ADENAUER, Chancellor, Federal Republic of Germany:

August 30, 1959:

In a letter to Premier Khrushchev, with reference to West Berlin and other German questions:

Another precondition to the settlement of these questions is the observance of the generally valid rules of international law. If we strive toward a new, better phase, a phase of peaceful coexistence of the peoples, then we must painstakingly observe the commonly recognized rules of international law.

SIR WINSTON CHURCHILL:

July 13, 1957:

We have now reached the point where nations must contrive a system and practice to resolve their disputes and settle them peacefully. We have not so far succeeded in this. . . . The mere creation of international organizations does not relieve us of our individual responsibilities, at least not until an international system has been created which is truly effective.

DAG HAMMARSKJOLD, Secretary General, United Nations:

1955:

One of the most important political problems on which progress is needed is the working out of the specific applications and consequences of the new rule of law which outlaws aggressive force.

When we look at the present role of international law in world affairs it is difficult to feel that there has been the degree of progress there should have been in the past twenty-five years.

The fact remains that the International Court of Justice is still not adequately used by States.

E. N. VAN KLEFFENS, former President of the United Nations General Assembly, as Minister of State, Netherlands:

December 15, 1955:

The world wants peace, not at the cost of our most cherished principles, not the peace of the cemetery, not a bogus peace, but a true peace between free states mutually respecting each other's principles and institutions under the aegis of the United Nations Charter.

FRANK AIKEN, Irish Foreign Minister:

September, 1959, in the U.N. General Assembly, urged the nuclear powers to encourage groups of nations:

. . . to accept the rule of law, area by area, throughout the world.

HENRIK KAUFFMANN, Ambassador of Denmark to the United States:

July 5, 1957:

. . . our concepts and our methods, all our attitudes are antiquated when it comes to making use of law in international matters . . .

When it comes to fundamental principles of law we have by and large a common meeting ground and one would think that it would not be too difficult for nations to agree to seek an objective and friendly solution to some of their legal problems by applying generally recognized principles of law. This is however done only in rare instances. Few nations have up to now submitted their legal disputes to the Court of The Hague or to other impartial bodies. As matters stand today it is at any rate an extremely difficult, complicated and cumbersome procedure to invoke arbitration and one is often made to feel that it is not a nice thing to do. Usually it takes years and years, mountains of paper work, and mountains of dollars before anything happens. The procedure takes so long, that in most cases the peoples concerned are dead long before a decision is finally reached.

VISCOUNT KILMUIR, Lord Chancellor of England:

November 6, 1959:

In the world today there is a growing recognition that peace is essential to the survival of all that we value in civilization, perhaps even to the survival of the human race. How then is peace to be maintained? There is but one way: disputes between nations must be settled by peaceful means, by legal methods rather than by force of arms. In short, the ideal in world affairs must be law not war.

Thus it is vital that the utmost should be done to promote an intelligent understanding and respect for the operation of law. Happily there are now a number of movements devoted to this very task, among them the Special Committee on World Peace Through Law and the British Institute of Law. But these movements cannot succeed by their own unaided efforts. Their work must be supplemented by the determination of all right-thinking people to further the same ends. In particular a responsibility rests upon those of the legal profession who have special qualifications to give guidance on the usage of law and its value for peace.

VISCOUNT HAILSHAM, Lord President of Privy Council of England:

1958:

I see a world where freedom under law is the rule and not the exception for mankind. In that world the sums now spent on arms are devoted to education and research, to the elimination of disease, to the rescue of deserts from the sun . . . and to the enjoyment of the good things of life by the suffering millions of mankind.

CLEMENT DAVIES, Member, House of Commons:

August 4, 1959:

I am hopeful of the future. This has been the most wonderful century in the long history of man. Never before has any effort been made to settle international differences by reason. Always man has relied on force and his strength in battle.

AUDLEY MCKISACK, Chief Justice of Uganda:

September 11, 1959, referring to the work of the American Bar Association's Special Committee on World Peace Through Law:

. . . I cannot but feel that it would be presumptuous on my part to do more than declare my respectful and emphatic agreement with all those who support the Special Committee's aims.

DR. LUDWIG VICTOR HELLER, President des Obersten Gerichtshofer:

August 24, 1959, referring to the work of the Special Committee:

I believe that many international questions may be settled peacefully under the rule of law and that your work is leading up to a strengthening of world peace and therefore worthy to be supported.

KOTARO TANAKA, Chief Justice of the Supreme Court of Japan:

1958:

The realization of justice is a thing which interests not only one nation, but all the nations of the world.

MUHAMMAD MUNIR, Chief Justice of Pakistan:

February 28, 1958, in dedicating the new Pakistan Legal Center, paid tribute to the rule of law and called upon lawyers to lead toward a lawful world, saying:

The task is essentially one for lawyers because they are the technicians of democracy and specialists in man's relation to man.

A. G. LOWE, Chief Justice, Supreme Court of Fiji, Suva:

September 7, 1959, referring to the August 24, 1959, Report of the American Bar Association Special Committee on World Peace Through Law:

As I hold views in agreement with those expressed in the report I was most interested to read it and I wish every success to your Committee and to the American Bar Association in their earnest endeavours to create an awareness of the urgent necessity for helping to promote world peace by legal means.

DONG WOOK SHIN, Dean, Yonsei University, Seoul, Korea:

August 5, 1959, commenting on the American Bar Association program on World Peace Through Law:

I believe your creative and great effort to create a lawful world would be much appreciated not only by the world's lawyers but also many of the thoughtful-minded people. A world conference of lawyers or law professors and the regional international conferences of them should be held.

ROSCOE POUND, Dean Emeritus, Harvard Law School:

1923:

The facts of international life call for creative juristic activity. The facts of an international law that must govern peoples, not personal sovereigns, that must deal with large indeterminate groups, swayed in varying proportion by all the conflicting elements that enter into public opinion for the time being, not with individual men or with small continuous cohesive groups of individuals, demand a theory that shall grow out of these facts and interpret them for us in terms of effective effort toward perceived ends.

ALBERT EINSTEIN and SIGMUND FREUD:

1932:

Quotations from letters exchanged between Einstein and Freud:

Einstein to Freud:

Is there any way to deliver mankind from the menace of war?

It is common knowledge that with the advance of science the issue has come to mean a matter of life and death for civilization as we know it. . . .

Freud to Einstein:

The union of the majority must be stable and enduring . . . must be permanent and well organized; it must enact rules to meet the risk of possible revolts. . . . Must set up machinery assuring that its rules (laws) are observed . . . there is but one sure way of ending war and that is the establishment, by common consent, of a central control which shall have the last word in every conflict of interest. For this two things are needed: first the creation of a supreme court of judication (World Court); second its investment with adequate force. Unless the second requirement is fulfilled the first is unavailing . . .

HENRY R. LUCE, Editor and Publisher:

May 1, 1958:

There is a hunger and thirst for the rule of law throughout the thinking part of the world.

February 21, 1959:

More than ever, and on the broadest scale, the appropriate theme for America is Liberty Under Law—and this is our opportunity to work in the world. It is this theme, developed from its highest moral principles down to its most practical aspects, that can define the role that the United States must play in the world. And it can restore to us all an ample sense of the meaning and purpose of life in America, in the world, from day to day—and into the farthest reaches of vision and prophecy.

. . . The people of the world feel—and feel deeply—that today's sinister balance of power, this peace-by-mutual-terror in which we live, is a dead end. Literally a dead end. And what question is more urgently asked—from New York to New Delhi, from Akron to Accra—than: Is there no way out?

The rudely realistic answer is, of course: No, there is no way out. The invention of the most horrible weapons of destruction is that fateful aspect of human ingenuity which is irreversible. The secrets unlocked can never be sealed again.

But if there is no way out, there must be something else: a way forward. This must be a way that leads toward mastery and control, in the name of justice and liberty, over the new forces unleashed by science.

This is the way of the law.

ERWIN CANHAM, Editor of Christian Science Monitor and President of the United States Chamber of Commerce:

Statement made at Boston Regional Meeting of Lawyers, March 27, 1959:

I have no doubt that it is possible this will indeed turn out to be an historic meeting, playing its part, I hope, as a precursor of the mobilization of the large national efforts for the study and preparation of the terms of peaceful living under the rule of law. This job is still ahead of us. It is perhaps more urgent than any other job we face in our lives, and let's hope it will be undertaken and carried forward before it is too late.

DAVID LAWRENCE, Editor of U.S. NEWS AND WORLD REPORT:

September 23, 1959:

We are living in a state of international anarchy. We must instead build a firm foundation of law and order and be prepared, if necessary, to visit the condemnation of mankind on the guilty and to utilize all the instrumentalities of moral force to achieve respect for and obedience to a world system of law.

Leaders pass off the stage, but legal principles governing international behavior can form an enduring code that will help to preserve world peace.

WALTER S. OWEN, President, Canadian Bar Association:

August, 1959:

Perhaps the most important task of lawyers today is to help to build the international legal order on which the hopes for world survival so largely depend . . . creating a satisfactory system of world law means raising legal standards and promoting as much uniformity as possible so that international investment and commerce and the free movement of people can be carried on in an atmosphere of confidence and security.

CHAUDRI NAZIR AHMAD KHAN, Attorney General of Pakistan and President of the Pakistan Legal Centre:

February 28, 1958:

For us Muslims, the Rule of Law is like an article of faith. When we talk of the rule of law we are talking of an Islamic concept and an Islamic way of life.

ARTURO A. ALAFRIZ, President, Philippine Lawyers Association:

Commenting on the program of the American Bar Association on World Peace Through Law, 1959:

. . . the lawyers of our country are solidly behind the move, nay, the crusade for peace through law.

OFFICIALS OF THE COLEGIO DE ABOGADOS DE PUERTO RICO:

(Submitted by Antonio Bennazer, Executive Director of the Colegio)

April 7, 1959, commenting on the program of the American Bar Association Special Committee on World Peace Through Law:

. . . We believe that among the primary functions of the lawyer in modern society there is his duty to assume leadership in discussing the public issues of the day and assuring himself that the light shed by such discussion is used to the advancement of society. And furthermore, wherever the rule of man is substituted for the rule of law it is the inescapable duty of the lawyer to champion the restitution of the rule of law. This is the reason why we feel so enthusiastic about . . . plan of world peace through world law. It aims at the same purpose but in a specific, constructive, civilized way, which undoubtedly will result in the solution of mankind's greatest problem: the need of an adequate instrument to peacefully settle international disagreements. Its achievement will prove to be the greatest conquest of this century.

HLA AUNG, Burma Law Institute:

September 7, 1959:

In the present state of world affairs, it is highly desirable that the concept of the Rule of Law in international community be instilled in the minds of peoples of all nations so that they may build up a strong public opinion in their own countries. Governments should be urged to settle their differences by such peaceful methods of negotiation, arbitration and adjudication, rather than by resorting to force and war.

HSIEH KUAN-SHENG, President, Judicial Yuan, Republic of China:

September 8, 1959, commenting on the August 24, 1959 Report of the American Bar Association Special Committee on World Peace Through Law to the House of Delegates:

In principle I am in perfect agreement with the report of the Committee, especially the part concerning the extension of the jurisdiction of the International Court of Justice.

PETROS G. VALLINDAS, Director, Hellenic Institute of International and Foreign Law, Athens:

January 29, 1959, commenting on proposals for a world conference of lawyers:

The central idea of the Conference should be that World Peace Through Law presupposes first the gradual creation of the conviction between the individuals that the Rule of Law can prevail in their transnational relations, in the same manner as it does, in principle at least, prevail in their relation covered by municipal law.

DAULET RAM PREM, Editor of the Indian Law Quarterly Review:

March, 1958:

Let us join hands and cooperate in the sacred trust of bringing about equality, justice, right of self-determination and dignity of man not only in our respective countries but throughout the world.

THOMAS K. FINLETTER, former Secretary of the Air Force:

1955:

Law, some philosophies to the contrary notwithstanding, is not only that which is in the statute books and in the decisions. It is to be found also in the accepted opinions and sentiments of mankind. There is now, I think, no doubt that all men, I mean the individuals, not the governments, the free as well as the Communists, do not want war; that they as individuals have renounced it as an acceptable human institution. It remains only for the governments of the world to realize this and, by establishing the regulations and procedures which will enforce this sentiment, that is, this law, fulfill their duties to those whom it is their responsibility to serve.

HERMAN PHLEGER, Legal Adviser to the Department of State:

February 22, 1954:

. . . There is such a thing as international law. It has had a long and honorable, though chequered career. I predict that it will play an even more important part in world affairs in the future than it has in the past.

Indeed, in this rapidly shrinking world, it becomes increasingly evident that our survival may depend upon our success in substituting the rule of law for the rule of force.

Progress in this field of law, as in most, is slow—sometimes discouragingly slow. However, progress is being made, and will continue in our constant search for a body of law which will serve the ends of peace and security in the world.

JACQUES MARITAIN, Philosopher, Princeton University:

A free community cannot live if its spiritual base is not solely law.

LORD BERTRAND RUSSELL, Philosopher and Author:

I have spoken of liberty as a good, but it is not an absolute good. We all recognize the need to restrain murderers, and it is even more important to restrain murderous states. Liberty must be limited by law. . . . There is hope that law, rather than private force, may come to govern the relations of nations within the present century. If this hope is not realized we face utter disaster; If it is realized, the world will be far better than at any previous period in the history of man.

BERNARD BARUCH:

Quoting Wilson:

He [President Wilson], knew that without such a reign of law civilization itself might crash in ruins in another outburst of lawlessness. In the debate in the United States over the League of Nations, he said: 'I can predict with absolute certainty that, within another generation, there will be another world war if the nations of the world do not concert the method by which to prevent it.' How true that prophecy was we well know.

§ 13-4. World Law Day

Proclamations of WORLD LAW DAY are now being issued by heads of state as a part of that day's celebration throughout the World. The purposes of WORLD LAW DAY are to make the world's peoples aware of the importance of law to peaceful world order with justice. Sponsored by the World Peace Through Law Center, WORLD LAW DAY is becoming a major world-wide event, and as such it is serving as an important means of advancing public knowledge of the promise and potential of the rule of law internationally.

Illustrative of the Proclamations issued by heads of state are those issued by Presidents Johnson and Nixon in 1968 and 1969 respectively:

The White House

World Law Day, 1968

BY THE PRESIDENT OF THE
UNITED STATES OF AMERICA

A PROCLAMATION

The year 1968 has been designated by the United Nations as International Human Rights Year, and I have so proclaimed it for the United States.

In this country and in many other nations of the world substantial progress has been made in expanding human rights in practice, as well as in principle.

Yet even during this Human Rights Year, the world has witnessed—on several continents—a series of tragic acts that have denied human rights by aggression, terror, starvation, and other forms of coercion. The conscience of the world has been stunned by these acts. Men are beginning to understand that the rule of law and justice is imperative if nations are not to perish under a reign of force and violence.

More than ever it is essential that the minds of men in every nation be focused upon the necessity for world peace through law if mankind is to realize the hopes and aspirations enshrined in the United Nations Charter and the Universal Declaration of Human Rights.

To that end, the World Peace Through Law Center is meeting in Geneva this month. We hope and trust that the efforts of this eminent group of lawyers and judges will enhance the role of law and legal institutions—so that the means for peaceful settlement of disputes between men and nations may be achieved and accepted by all.

NOW, THEREFORE, I, LYNDON B. JOHNSON, President of the United States of America, believing that there should be set aside one day in Human Rights Year on which appropriate observance of the importance of the role of law to mankind's search for world peace and universal respect for human rights can be publicly recognized, do hereby proclaim September 16, 1968, as World

Law Day in the United States. I call upon all citizens of the United States, all public and private officials, members of the legal profession, public and private organizations, and all men of good will to arrange public ceremonies on World Law Day in courts, schools and universities, and other public places in order that we may rededicate ourselves to fulfilling man's need of international law for world peace.

IN WITNESS WHEREOF, I have hereunto set my hand this 14th day of September in the year of our Lord nineteen hundred and sixty-eight, and of the Independence of the United States of America the one hundred and ninety-third.

(signed) Lyndon B. Johnson
President of the
United States of America

World Law Day, 1969

BY THE PRESIDENT OF THE UNITED STATES OF AMERICA

A PROCLAMATION

Economic and social progress bears a direct relationship to the establishment and maintenance of orderly societies and a world community of peaceful nations. Thus, laws which advance economic and social development can bring about essential progress in securing freedom for all men in all nations.

Governments are rightfully concerned about the economic and social progress of people, but much can be done on a private and voluntary basis to supplement government plans and actions. Public programs, embodied in just laws at the local, national, and international levels, can advance the improvement of social and economic conditions in every community and country. Voluntary cooperation of private individuals and groups can help to bring about research, new proposals, and citizen participation which will provide essential public support for enactment of just and needed laws.

The concern and participation of the legal, professional, academic, commercial, and other sectors of the private community in the attack on the root problems of discontent—such as poverty, ignorance, and disease—are vital to the national and international welfare. Fundamentally, it is the human misery and unrest under these conditions which most directly affect man's ability to develop a peaceful and orderly world community. It is essential, therefore, that the public and private sectors of every community join together in cooperative endeavors to develop plans and programs to resolve basic social and economic needs within a framework of law on a local, national, and international basis.

NOW, THEREFORE, I, RICHARD NIXON, President of the United States of America, do hereby proclaim September 8, 1969, as World Law Day in the United States. I call upon public officials and private leaders, members of the legal profession, public and private organizations, and all men of goodwill to arrange public ceremonies on World Law Day in courts, schools, universities, and other public places in order that we may rededicate ourselves to the observance of international law and to the goals of social and economic progress, so essential to the preservation of world peace.

IN WITNESS WHEREOF, I have hereunto set my hand this fourteenth day of August, in the year of our Lord nineteen hundred sixty-nine, and of the Independence of the United States of America the one hundred ninety-fourth.

(Signed) Richard M. Nixon
President of the
United States of America

CHAPTER 14

Disarmament and Arms Control

§ 14-1. Introduction

In its ultimate sense, international law as set forth in this Volume
is the story of the struggle toward disarmament and arms control
to achieve mankind's most ancient dream: an international order
with justice. This record of experience proves that this area of all-
encompassing scope is functional only if a system of law providing
adequate mechanisms to settle disputes replaces the force system
which has prevailed internationally throughout the history of man.
The only concept yet conceived or employed to provide a credible
security replacement for arms is law.[1] Arms cannot be eliminated

---

[1] See LARSON, WHEN NATIONS DISAGREE (1961); HALDEMAN, THE UNITED
NATIONS AND THE RULE OF LAW (1966); SALTER, RESOLUTION OF INTER-
NATIONAL CONFLICT (1966); 73 et seq.: REGALA, WORLD PEACE THROUGH
DIPLOMACY AND LAW (1964); REGALA, NEW DIMENSIONS IN INTERNATIONAL
AFFAIRS (1967); GARDNER, BLUEPRINT FOR PEACE (1966); SALTER, THE PATH
FROM VIOLENCE TO INTERNATIONAL ORDER (1970); Sohn, Basic Problems of

(Continued)

leaving a vacuum; arms can only be eliminated if some other means of security replaces them. Law is the replacement for force which experience teaches works within nations and it is, therefore, the best proven replacement transnationally.

A law system, when adequately developed by sufficient law rules and legal institutions, can best prevent conflict, or when conflict occurs, can channel disputes into transnational agencies where they can be peacefully resolved. Thus, the peace process that civilization has developed is essentially a law process: the international conventions, agreements, rules, agencies, treaties and institutions covered in this Volume are a necessary prelude to disarmament. To achieve general disarmament, the World must create and support a legal system which is adequate to replace the force system—a legal system which provides a credible system of laws to replace the security now provided by arms.

History teaches that law systems have replaced arms systems within nations. In England, for example, the barons and lords gave up their private armies when the king's law, the king's courts and the king's army were strong enough to guarantee them personal and property security. The secure borders between the United States and Canada, for example, are the result of a series of arms control and disarmament agreements throughout the 19th century. As a result of their successful operation, the relations between the countries are easier than if a story of fortifications existed on either side to repel whatever threats to security could be perceived. Similar historical stories could be cited in many nations.[2] The basic principles and law system whereby such domestic force was replaced by law can work just as well internationally. This Volume demonstrates that the tremendous world-wide build-up of law rules, and international agencies and institutions is meeting some of the demands of the peoples who inhabit our interdependent world. The ever-growing demand and desire of the world's peoples that disputes between nations no longer be decided by the killing of human beings is bringing closer each day the formulation of a law system under which nations will go to court rather than to war. The concept of special armed forces to enforce the peace is growing also, and a constantly available peace army or "sheriff"

Disarmament, in WASH. CONF., 437-53; THOMAS, THE PREREQUISITES FOR PEACE (1959); JENKS, THE WORLD BEYOND THE CHARTER (1969). See also Declaration on Peace and Disarmament Presented to UN General Assembly by Nobel Peace Prize Laureates on September 21, 1970.

[2] See Pound, The Lawyer From Antiquity To Modern Times (1953); SALONGA & YAP, PUBLIC INTERNATIONAL LAW (1958); Jessup, A MODERN LAW OF NATIONS (1946).

group under UN control may soon be available as the pressure of public opinion revolts against war.

§ 14-2. The Hague Conferences of 1899, 1907 and Disarmament[3]

The Peace Conferences held at The Hague in 1899 and 1907, at the invitation of Emperor Nicholas II of Russia, were the first multilateral international conferences to consider disarmament. Count Mouraviev, Russia's Minister of Foreign Affairs, in a note dated January 11, 1899, stated that one of the purposes of the 1899 Conference was to arrive at an

> understanding not to increase for a fixed period the present effectives of the armed military and naval forces, and at the same time not to increase the budgets pertaining thereto; and a preliminary examination of the means by which even a reduction might be effected in future in the forces and budgets above mentioned.

The Conference was attended by representatives of 26 nations. When the subject of disarmament was raised, the German Representative objected and the subject was abandoned. Declarations were adopted on prohibiting the launching of projectiles or explosives from balloons, prohibiting use of projectiles to diffuse asphyxiating or deleterious gases, prohibiting use of bullets which expand or flatten in the human body, and outlawed free floating naval mines.

The 1907 Conference met from June 15 to October 18, and was attended by representatives of 44 nations. It waived the subject of disarmament, but addressed itself to the greatest effort yet made up to that time to codify international law carrying forward the codification in the Declaration of Paris of 1856. A Court of Arbitration and an International Prize Court were proposed in two of these Hague Conventions. See *supra* § 1-5.6.

§ 14-3. Disarmament and the Versailles Peace Treaty of 1919[4]

While destruction or reduction of the armaments of a nation defeated in war has been a usual action throughout recorded history, the Versailles Peace Treaty of 1919, ending World War I, went further, and sought to initiate a broader arms limitation program. In Part V, the Treaty imposed limits on the military, naval, and air power of Germany "in order to render possible the initiation of a general limitation of the armaments of all nations."

---

[3] BAKER, DISARMAMENT (1926); WRIGHT, THE CAUSES OF WAR AND THE CONDITIONS OF PEACE (1935).

[4] RIDDELL, THE TREATY OF VERSAILLES AND AFTER (1935); SCHMITT, FROM VERSAILLES TO MUNICH 1918-1938 (1939); MARTIN, THE TREATIES OF PEACE 1919-1923 (1924).

Inter-Allied commissions of control were created for the military, naval and air forces, and these functioned until 1925 when their work was taken over by the League of Nations. These inspection or enforcement arrangements were never very effective and gradually ceased to exist prior to the rearmament of Germany by Hitler in 1935.

§ 14-4. The League of Nations and Disarmament[5]

The League of Nations set out in 1920 to develop agreement on general disarmament. A Nongovernmental Temporary Mixed Commission by 1923 had drafted a Treaty on Mutual Assistance which, however, was not adopted by the League. A Geneva Protocol was then drafted in 1924 covering a definition of aggression, a general system for arbitration of disputes and a statement of enforcement measures to be taken against aggression. A disarmament conference was suggested, and, in 1925, the League's Council created a Preparatory Commission for the disarmament conference. This Conference met in May 1926, with Germany, the United States and Russia joining League members. Progress was slow and discussions drawn out and tedious. In December 1930, partial agreement was achieved on five subjects: budgetary limitations of armament expenditures, limitations of the period of service of armed forces personnel; creation of a Permanent Disarmament Commission; limitations on land, sea, and air forces; and the renunciation of chemical and bacteriological warfare.

The Disarmament Conference of February 2, 1932, was attended by representatives of 59 nations. The representatives disagreed on whether armaments should be reduced by numbers or by categories and on whether offensive armament should be distinguished from defensive armament. Others urged that the League of Nations should have a strong police force to help keep the peace.

In 1932, three limited agreements were arrived at that: (1) air attack against civilian populations should be absolutely prohibited and the number of aircraft and civil aviation regulated; (2) heavy artillery and tanks should be limited in size and (3) chemical warfare should be prohibited. Proposals containing specific disarmament figures for European nations along with proposals to stabilize armament at then existing levels were not adopted. On October 14, 1933, Germany left the Disarmament Conference and

---

[5] MYERS, HANDBOOK OF THE LEAGUE OF NATIONS (1935); ZIMMERN, THE LEAGUE OF NATIONS AND THE RULE OF LAW 1918-1935 (1939); WALTERS, HISTORY OF THE LEAGUE OF NATIONS (1952).

the League of Nations. From then on, nations returned to rearmament and power politics as a prelude to World War II.

§ 14-5. Washington, Geneva and London Conferences on Naval Disarmament: 1921-1930[6]

Immediately after the end of World War I, the United States sought to initiate conferences leading to naval disarmament limitation agreements. When the first of these Conferences convened on November 13, 1921, in Washington, the United States proposed a naval "holiday" to the Conference under which "for a period of not less than 10 years there should be no further construction of "capital ships." A scrapping of older ships and restrictions on replacements was considered. Abolition of submarines was discussed along with a wide range of other subjects including use of poison gas, insular possessions and tariffs. Seven treaties were drafted and signed in February 1922, covering limitations on naval armaments, noxious gases, submarines, customs tariffs and insular possessions in the Pacific Ocean.

The Geneva Conference assembled in June 1927, to consider limitations of ships not included in the Washington Treaty of 1922. Disagreements among representatives of nations in attendance over "parity" in ships led to a close of the Conference in August 1927 without agreement on any subject.

The London Naval Conference was then convened in January 1930. The result was a limited agreement by the United States, England, Japan, France and Italy on a five year "holiday" in the construction of capital ships with limitations also agreed on limiting submarines and aircraft carriers.

The details of these agreements is omitted because they were unrealistic in the light of the then international situation which ruled out general naval disarmament by other nations while Germany was rapidly rearming. In fact, in June 1935, Germany and England signed an agreement which recognized Germany's right to violate armament restrictions imposed by the Versailles Treaty.

The lesson of all the efforts on general disarmament from 1899 up to World War II is that disarmament agreements are ineffective without the existence of effective international verification, control and enforcement machinery.

---

[6] U.S. SENATE DOC. 126 (1922), contains text of treaties; see SULLIVAN, THE GREAT ADVENTURE AT WASHINGTON; THE STORY OF THE CONFERENCE (1922).

§ 14-6. The United Nations and Disarmament[7]

The obligation of states to disarm exists because it emanates from the legal order created by the United Nations Charter which excludes the right to make war. To avoid war, it is not sufficient simply to forbid wars of aggression, it is essential that there be effective control of the arms race by enforceable limitations on national arms. Arms necessary to maintain internal public order cannot be denied to nations, nor can arms to respond to international obligations to maintain order imposed by the common interests of the world community be eliminated. That disarmament is both necessary and urgent cannot be denied; modern weapons and delivery systems enable man to destroy all humankind. But again, let it be said no nation will give up arms to protect its own security unless, and until, that security is protected by other means.

The present abundance of arms and their ever-growing capacity represent, in itself, a permanent threat to peace, and the necessity of disarmament and arms limitation has, therefore, been recognized by all nations. And, since the end of World War II, international meetings and conferences have stressed with ever increasing urgency the necessity of limiting both the use and spread of nuclear weapons and delivery systems.

Technical developments with respect to missile and nuclear weapons after World War II caused the United Nations, upon its formation, to react promptly. The first resolution of the General Assembly in January 1946 established the International Atomic Energy Agency[8] with the specific task of devising proposals to eliminate atomic weapons and all the major weapons of mass destruction from national armaments. In Resolution 41,[9] the United Nations General Assembly recognized the central role of disarmament in relation to international peace and security calling for "an early general regulation of armaments." Since the adoption of these resolutions, the problem of disarmament has been dis-

---

[7] See generally Treaty Banning Nuclear Weapons Tests In the Atmosphere, In Outer Space and Under Water. Done August 15, 1963, 14 UST 1313, TIAS 5433, 480 UNTS 43; Treaty Providing for the Renunciation of War as an Instrument of National Policy. Signed August 27, 1928, 46 stat. 2343, TS 796, 2 Bevans 732, 94 LNTS 57; Statute of the International Atomic Energy Agency. Done October 26, 1956, 8 UST 1092, TIAS 3873, 276 UNTS 3, Treaty on the Limitation and Reduction of Naval Armament. Signed April 22, 1930, 46 Stat. 2858, TS 830, 2 BEVANS 1055, 112 LNTS 65.

[8] Statute of the International Atomic Energy Agency. Done October 26, 1956, * UST 1093, TIAS 3873, 276 UNTS 3.

[9] OFFICIAL RECORDS OF THE GENERAL ASSEMBLY, First Sessional Part II, First Committee, Summary Record of Meetings, Annex 9e.

cussed in the Security Council and at every session of the United Nations and its numerous subsidiary bodies. Underscoring the role of Security Council deliberations on disarmament is Article 26 of the United Nations Charter which makes the Security Council ". . . responsible for formulating . . . plans to be submitted to the Members of the United Nations for the establishment of a system for the regulation of armaments."

The Commission for Conventional Armaments was established by the Security Council in 1947. In 1952, this Commission and the International Atomic Energy Commission were merged by the General Assembly into the Disarmament Commission, a body that, unfortunately, has seldom met, and has accomplished little. Generally, the major powers have found it useful to establish conference machinery and bilateral security arrangements on an *ad hoc* basis linked to, but not an integral part of the United Nations.

Discussions through diplomatic channels, including meetings of Heads of State, such as the Geneva "summit meeting" of July 1953, and of Ministers of Foreign Affairs, starting with the Moscow meeting of December 1945, and the present Strategic Arms Limitation Talks (SALT), play an important role in disarmament negotiations. The Charter of the United Nations envisioned a multilateral system for the regulation of armaments and ultimate general disarmament. In reality, however, the major responsibility for disarmament was placed on the action of states since the framers of the United Nations Charter in 1945 felt that previous disarmament during the period of the League of Nations had been one of the causes of World War II.[10] The non-aligned countries have also exerted a growing and important influence by helping to bridge the gap between the positions of the major states.

§ 14-7. The Arms Race[11]

The evolution of the United States-Soviet Union arms race can be summarily explained. As both sides expanded their force levels, an action/reaction pattern of threat perception was established and was fed by rapid progress in the technology of nuclear weapons and advanced delivery systems. The mere availability of such sophisticated technology made it difficult for either side by itself to refrain from translating that technology into offensive or defensive stra-

---

[10] GOODRICH, HAMBRO AND SIMMONS, CHARTER OF THE UNITED NATIONS 211-12 (3rd Rev. Ed., N.Y. 1969).

[11] UNITED NATIONS, THE UNITED NATIONS AND DISARMAMENT, (1945-1965) UN Pub. 67.I.9), 3.

tegic armaments. This technology, coupled with each side weighing the other's intentions and then concluding that its level of destructive power might be insufficient has lead to the situation today where either nation has the power to destroy the other effectively, regardless of which one strikes first. This fact radically weakens the rationale for continuing the arms race; competitive accumulation of more sophisticated weapons cannot add to the basic security of either side.

A capacity for mutual destruction leads to a mutual interest in putting a stop to the strategic nuclear arms race. The complexity of the strategic situation must be considered along with the rival vital interests involved in order to overcome traditional impulses to seek protection based on military strength and substitute for those traditional impulses acceptance of a new method of security. Proving and securing acceptance of the credibility of a new method of security to replace arms is an enormous task. All the world's peoples, not just the peoples of the great powers, are faced with this precise problem. Overcoming this problem by securing acceptance of disarmament agreements is not an easy task, as the history of such agreements is a history of breach. But, as law and legal institutions grow in credibility, the world community disarmament agreements embodying law rules which are enforceable by legal institutions are becoming more and more credible. Just as the peace process is a law process, disarmament agreements are law agreements.

§ 14-8. Recent Developments

In September 1961, in bilateral discussions, the two nuclear superpowers, (the Soviet Union and the United States) embarked on a new phase in disarmament negotiations in agreeing that the goal of disarmament negotiations should be general and complete disarmament with measures to settle disputes peacefully in order to maintain international peace and security in conformity with the U.N. Charter.[12]   Prior to this general and complete disarmament, had not been posted as the goal of disarmament. In March 1962, at the Eighteen Nation Disarmament Conference the Soviet Union released a "Draft Treaty on General and Complete disarmament under Strict International Control"[13] and, in

---

[12] JOINT STATEMENT OF AGREED PRINCIPLES FOR DISARMAMENT NEGOTIATIONS (THE MCCLOY-ZORN AGREEMENT), UNITED STATES ARMS CONTROL AND DISARMAMENT AGENCY, DOCUMENTS ON DISARMAMENT, (1961) 439-42.

[13] UNITED STATES ARMS CONTROL AND DISARMAMENT AGENCY, DOCUMENTS, (1962), 103-27.

April 1962, the United States presented its "Outline of Basic Provisions of a Treaty on General and Complete Disarmament in a Peaceful World."[14] The rest of 1962 was spent in achieving agreement of superpowers on common areas, and the Disarmament Committee Committee began discussing the proposed Test Ban and Nuclear Non-Proliferation treaties.

The United States and Soviet plans are still "on the table." Some basic differences exist, the key issue being the timing and verification of reductions of nuclear delivery vehicles—the missiles, aircraft, naval vessels and land artillery used to deliver weapons to their targets. In view of basic differences on general and complete disarmament, it became obvious that the best procedure would be to devote the negotiations largely to "collateral" or partial arms control measures in achieving the ultimate goal.

In 1963, in the wake of the Cuban missile crisis, the Washington-Moscow "Hot-Line" direct communications link was established. In August 1963, the Treaty Banning Nuclear Weapons in the Atmosphere in Outer Space, and Under Water was signed in Moscow.[15] Since then, it has been ratified by most states. In 1964, draft proposals concerning a Non-Proliferation Treaty were presented. These proposals suggested that nations agree to: ". . . freeze . . . the number and characteristics of strategic nuclear offense and defensive vehicles;" so as ". . . to halt all production of fissionable materials for weapons use . . . to create" what will be "a system of observations posts to reduce the danger of war by accident, miscalculation or surprise attack . . ." and ". . . to stop the spread of nuclear weapons to nations not now controlling them."[16]

A further development in arms control was the 1967 Treaty on Principles Governing the Activities of States in the Exploration, and Use of Outer Space, Including the Moon and Other Celestial Bodies.[17] The principal purpose of the Treaty was to prevent the orbiting of objects carrying nuclear weapons or any other kinds of weapons of mass destruction around the earth, or the installation or stationing of such weapons on celestial bodies or in outer

---

[14] UNITED STATES ARMS CONTROL AND DISARMAMENT AGENCY, DOCUMENTS, 1962, 351-82.

[15] Treaty Banning Nuclear Weapon tests in the atmosphere, in outer space and under water. Done August 5, 1963, 14 UST 1313, TIAS 5433, 480 UATS 43.

[16] UNITED STATES ARMS CONTROL AND DISARMAMENT AGENCY, DOCUMENTS, 1964, 7-9, 17-21, 32-36, 44-48, 79-82, 101-5, 157-62, 169-70, 289-93, 367-73.

[17] Treaty on Principles Governing the Activities of States on the Exploration and Use of Outer Space, Including the Moon and Other Celestial Bodies. Done January 27, 1967.

space. The Treaty, patterned after the Antartica Treaty, also prohibits "[t]he establishment of military bases, installations and fortifications, the testing of any type of weapons and the conduct of military manoeuvers on celestial bodies . . . The use of military personnel for scientific research or for any other peaceful purpose shall not be prohibited. The use of any equipment or facility necessary for peaceful exploration of the moon and other celestial bodies shall also not be prohibited." Also in 1967, the Latin-American states finalized the Treaty for the Prohibition of Nuclear Weapons in Latin America, establishing the first denuclearized zone in the world and providing a model for other regions.

In 1967, the United States and the Soviet Union began negotiations to devise ways and means to limit anti-ballistic missiles (ABM) and strategic delivery systems. These talks began as a result of the potential technological development of the anti-ballistic missile which threatened a new arms race. At the same time, discussions were continuing on arriving at ways to halt the production of weapon-grade fissionable material and of nuclear delivery systems and ABMs, and perhaps even reducing the number of such weapons and vehicles.[18]

§ 14-9. The Nuclear Non-Proliferation Treaty [19]

This Treaty, submitted by the United States and the Soviet Union on March 11, 1968, signified the first time that states had concluded an international treaty containing provisions under which the nuclear states agreed to undertake to refrain from transferring weapons of mass destruction or relinquishing control of nuclear weapons, and from transmitting the information necessary for their manufacture to non-nuclear weapons states, i.e., those that had not developed, produced and tested such weapons by January 1, 1968. The Treaty also provides that states nor possessing nuclear weapons would not undertake to manufacture or otherwise acquire control of such weapons.

Underlying the significance of this Treaty is the increased threat of nuclear war and its resulting mass destruction occasioned by the nuclear arms race and the dissemination and possession of such weapons among more nations of the world. As more nations possess nuclear weapons, the likelihood of their use becomes greater. As stated in the Preamble of the Treaty, the Contracting Parties to the Treaty, desiring to eliminate the nuclear arms race,

---

[18] UN Doc. A1 6663, UNITED NATIONS, THE UNITED NATIONS AND DISARMA-MENT (1945-1955) (UN Pub. 67.I.9), 309-22.
   [19] *Id.*

"[a]ffirm[ed] the principle that the benefits of peaceful application of nuclear technology, including any technological by-products which may be derived by nuclear-weapons States from the development of nuclear explosive devices, should be available for peaceful purposes to all Parties to the Treaty . . ." and were convinced that "all Parties to this Treaty are entitled to participate in the fullest possible exchange of scientific information for, and to contribute alone or in cooperation with other States to, the further development of the application of atomic energy for peaceful purposes." Article III of the Treaty specifies that Signatory states conclude Treaties with the International Atomic Energy Agency to enact safeguards for the proper fulfillment of the terms of the Treaty. This Treaty came into force on March 3, 1970, and as of September 1970, 56 states had ratified.

During the negotiations on the Nuclear Non-Proliferation Treaty, the main objective of which is to prevent non-nuclear powers from acquiring atomic weapons, the non-nuclear nations insisted upon assurances that the nuclear powers would seriously pursue strategic arms negotiations.

The disarmament agreements previously concluded have been widely regarded as confidence building, preliminary steps which hopefully might lead to more meaningful agreements on strategic arms.[20]

§ 14-10. The Strategic Arms Limitation Talks (SALT)

In 1969, the two nuclear superpowers began the Strategic Arms Limitation Talks (SALT), with productive meetings in Vienna. Where national security interests may have operated in the past to stimulate the strategic arms race, those same national security interests today operate to stop or slow down the race.

In these talks, the two most powerful nations on earth are seeking ways to curb vertical proliferation of nuclear weapons or the unending bilateral competition in the strategic arms race. In December 1970, the third round of the SALT talks concluded in Helsinki where the United States and the Soviet Union made little visible progress, but both sides clarified their positions which is necessary in order to lay the ground work for future rounds. The next round began in March 1971, in Vienna, and both sides evidently believe that some kind of agreement is possible, although each of course is firmly committed to its national security first.

---

[20] *Id.*

§ 14-11. Proposals for an International Disarmament Commission and Inspection

In 1962, both the United States and the Soviet Union proposed that an International Disarmament Commission be created to verify international compliance with provisions relating to general and complete disarmament.[21] Other types of disarmament, for example, partial, might require different types of inspection and verification,[22] and it is even possible that some disarmament measures will not envisage any administrative organization to verify compliance. The two types of verification systems most often proposed include external verification and reciprocal verification. In the former, each party is able to inspect the compliance of the other without having to intrude on the other's territory. In the latter, however, each party must enter the territory of the other to inspect on site its compliance with disarmament provisions. The Antarctica Treaty for example, provides that all installations of one of the parties in Antarctica shall be open at all times to inspection by special observers so designated by the other parties.[23] Other verification proposals have called for mutual inspection; an international inspection team composed of national observers, or observers appointed by an alliance; or an inspection team composed of observers from an international organization, such as Euratom and the International Atomic Energy Agency; or any combination of the above. Still another proposal for an international inspection team was made by the Soviet Union in 1962, and envisaged its composition to be made of representatives of the three principal groups of states existing in the world; its personnel would be selected from among persons recommended by the Contracting Governments.[24] Yet another proposal advanced by the Soviet Union in 1961 called for the staff of any inspection team to be headed by an administrative council of three members representing the three principal groups of states, who would act as a single whole, and would agree among themselves on all steps which they would undertake in the execution of their duties.[25] The United States, on the other hand,

---

[21]UNITED STATES ARMS CONTROL AND DISARMAMENT AGENCY, DOCUMENTS ON DISARMAMENTS, (1962), Vol. I, 123-26, 362-66.

[22]See, for instance, the two Anglo-American drafts for the comprehensive Test Ban Treaty, of 18 April, 1961, and 27 August 1962. UNITED STATES ARMS CONTROL AND DISARMAMENT AGENCY, DOCUMENTS ON DISARMAMENT, 1961, 82-126; UNITED STATES ARMS CONTROL AND DISARMAMENT AGENCY, DOCUMENT ON DISARMAMENTS, (1962), Vol. II, 792-807.

[23]402 UNTS 71 (1962).

[24]*Supra,* note 14 at 125.

[25]UNITED STATES DISARMAMENT ADMINISTRATION (DEPARTMENT OF STATE). GENEVA CONFERENCE ON THE DISCONTINUANCE OF NUCLEAR WEAPON TESTS: HISTORY AND ANALYSIS OF NEGOTIATIONS (1961), 463.

has always insisted on a single Administrator to supervise the installation and operation of verification arrangements.[26] Inspection is still somewhat of a problem in nuclear test ban agreements, although the great powers have national means to verify. Most such blasts not in compliance with international disarmament provisions, can easily be detected outside the country of origin by modern scientific equipment.

§ 14-12. Chemical and Biological Weapons

In the area of control of chemical and biological weapons, the Geneva Protocol of 1925[27] has laid the basis for more extensive agreement. The Protocol for the Prohibition of the Use in War of Asphyxiating, Poisonous and Other Gases, and of the Bacteriological Methods of Warfare[28] has been formally ratified by 85 states including virtually all the major industrial and military nations except the United States, which is presently considering ratification. The United States Department of Defense has been and is disposing of existing stocks of bacteriological and toxic weapons. If the United States becomes a party to the Protocol, as is hoped, this agreement will be of much more potential effect. This is an area of qualitative disarmament that has received recent worldwide attention because of its harmful effects on human and animal organisms.

§ 14-13. Seabed Arms Control Treaty

On February 11, 1971, the Seabed Arms Control Treaty was opened for signature. This Treaty prohibits the spread of nuclear and other weapons of mass destruction and associated equipment to the seabed and ocean floor and to their subsoil areas, that cover some 70 per cent of the earth's surface. This Treaty represents a significant achievement in that it demonstrates the willingness of the Soviet Union and the United States to reach a measure of agreement on arms control. Much of the difficulties during negotiation stemmed from sensitive law of the sea issues and from graduated verification procedures that ultimately permit entry into seabed installations for purposes of inspection. Save for the prohibition against emplacement, the law of the sea has not been altered. Experience has shown that it is easier to keep nuclear weapons out of an area in which they have never been than to

---

[26] *Supra,* note 14 at 364, 366.

[27] THE CONTROL OF CHEMICAL AND BIOLOGICAL WEAPONS, CARNEGIE ENDOWMENT FOR INTERNATIONAL PEACE, 1971.

[28] See *id.* 125-26 for text.

control them once their presence has been accepted. The document was largely the work of the 26-Nation Conference of the Committee on Disarmament, in which the two superpowers serve as permanent co-chairman and have played dominant roles. The seabed will now join Antarctica, Latin America and outer space as nuclear free areas.

§ 14-14. The Future

In the larger context of going from the high hopes and desires of accomplishment in the vast area of general disarmament, or in specific areas such as strategic arms limitation talks (SALT) as to nuclear arms, it is clear that if arms are eliminated, they will have to be replaced by a whole series of legal agreements, treaties, and conventions which must become binding and enforceable international law.

Law institutionalizes foreign policy. Concrete steps to institutionalize the great ideal of general disarmament are being taken slowly, carefully but nonetheless taken into reality.

A new security system for the world community based on the mutual interests of humankind is slowly coming into existence.

We are changing our educational institutions.

We are changing our social institutions.

We are changing our economic institutions.

We are changing our governmental institutions.

We are changing our concerns to new subjects like environment.

All this means we must change and are changing our international institutions and the law rules they interpret, apply and enforce.

The resort by nations to the archaic method of killing human beings to decide their disputes has achieved such worldwide unpopularity as to demonstrate that it will, in fact, as it has in law, ultimately be a relic of the past—just as much of a relic as the once widely accepted dispute settling process between individuals of duel to the death. Education, communications, and possession of the ultimate in death-dealing weapons have brought the world's peoples to this realization. The next point must be the education of the world's peoples in what they must do to achieve their dream of a peaceful world order with justice. Public opinion fluctuates until it crystallizes, but when it crystallizes it becomes an almost uncontrollable factor in the affairs of humankind. More and more, a vast worldwide desire is growing into a demand that law replace force as the controlling factor in the fate of humanity. This Volume will hopefully aid toward that realization, as it is the first current comprehensive compilation of existing international law and existing international institutions. The material herein measures where we are and where we must go to achieve a world peaceful order with justice under the rule of law. This Volume indicates that we have progressed tremendously toward a truly credible world law system due to the enormous amount of law and the vast number of legal institutions which exist in today's world, but this material additionally demonstrates that we still have a long way to go. That success can be achieved is evident from the record herein reviewed. The great unfinished business of the world community is thus clear.

INDEX

A

Abdel-Wahub, 57n, 409n
Abmad, 411n
Abs-Shawcross Convention on Investments Abroad, 82-83
Accepted Standards of Performance, 9
Accra, Conference of (1958), 30
Accrement, A., 275n
Accretion, doctrine of, 103
Achaen League, 12
Acheson, Dean, 470n, 479n, 574
Acquinas, St. Thomas, 14
Acquired Rights, protection of, 66, 68-69
Act of Chapultepec (1945), 41
Act of State, doctrine of, 124
Adam, 139n
Adams, 472n
Adenauer, Konrad, 582-83
Adilla istihadiya, 63
Addis Ababa, Conference of (1960), 30
Adequate Standards of Living, 2
Adjudication, Application of International Law, 7
Admissibility of Hearings of Petitioners by the Committee on South West Africa, 223-24
Advisory Committee
 see also League of Nations, 60
Advisory Opinion on the Effect of Awards of the United Nations Administrative Tribunal, 64-5
Aerial Incident of 10 March 1953, 209
Aerial Incident of July 27, 1955 (U.S. of A. v. Bulgaria), 201, 213
Aerial Incident of July 27, 1955 (Israel v. Bulgaria), 201, 212-13
Aerial Incident of July 27, 1955 (United Kingdom v. Bulgaria), 201, 213-14
Aerial Incident of September 4, 1954, 201, 215
Aerial Incident of October 7, 1952, 200, 209-10
Aerial Incident of November 7, 1954, 201, 217
Aerial Navigation Convention (1919), 112

Aerial Navigation, Convention for the Regulation of (1919), 473
Aerial Warfare
 principles of, 449-50
 prohibition against attacking civilian populations, 598
Aetolian League, 12
Africa, 48
 diversity of, 25
African-Asian Legal Consultative Committee, dispute settlement, 185
African Commission on Human Rights, 409
African Convention of Human Rights, proposal for, 409
African Development Bank, 340-41
African Law, 25-31
 "Africa for the Africans," principle of, 30
 education in, 497-98
 ethnic origin, 26-27
 intra-African system of relations, 25
 peaceful coexistence, 27
 principle of nonintervention, 31
 sovereignty, 26
 territoriality, 27-28
 migration of people, 28
 trade, agreements of, 29
 treaties, 28-30
 distinction between pre-colonial and post-colonial, 28
 pacta sunt servanda, principle of, 28
 state succession, 29
 termination, 29
African and Malagasy Union, 153
African Regional Court of Justice, proposal for, 263
African Unity, Charter of, 26
Afro-Asian Conference
 see also Bandung Conference, 30
Afro-Asian Organization for Economic Cooperation, 341
Afro-Malagasy Organization for Economic Cooperation, 153
 Industrial Property Office, 388
Agarwala, 54n, 57n, 72, 72n

G

P

XYZ